MARKETING

THEORY ▪ EVIDENCE ▪ PRACTICE

MARKETING

THEORY · EVIDENCE · PRACTICE

BYRON SHARP

OXFORD
UNIVERSITY PRESS
AUSTRALIA & NEW ZEALAND

Oxford University Press is a department of the University of Oxford.

It furthers the University's objective of excellence in research, scholarship, and education by publishing worldwide. Oxford is a registered trademark of Oxford University Press in the UK and in certain other countries.

Published in Australia by
Oxford University Press
253 Normanby Road, South Melbourne, Victoria 3205, Australia

National Library of Australia Cataloguing-in-Publication data

Author:	Sharp, Byron.
Title:	Marketing: theory, evidence, practice / Byron Sharp.
ISBN:	9780195573558 (pbk.)
Notes:	Includes bibliographical references and index.
Subjects:	Marketing.
	Industrial management.
	Professions–Marketing.
Dewey Number:	658.83

Edited by Kirstie Innes-Will
Typeset by Diacritech, Channai, India and Polar Design, Melbourne, Australia
Proofread by Pete Cruttenden
Indexed by Glenda Browne
Printed by Markono Print Media Pte Ltd

CONTENTS

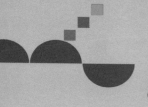

EXPANDED CONTENTS

1   What Do Marketing Executives Do? 2

Byron Sharp

2   Consumer Behaviour and Business Buyer Behaviour 32

Byron Sharp, with contribution from Svetlana Bogomolova, Marianthi Livaditis and Magda Nenycz-Thiel

3 Meaningful Marketing Metrics 78

Byron Sharp, with contribution from Svetlana Bogomolova

4 Market Research 130

Anne Sharp and Katherine Anderson

5   The Marketing Environment 182

Adrian Palmer, adapted by Larry Lockshin

6   Customer Segmentation and Targeting...218

Rachel Kennedy and Byron Sharp, with contribution from Nick Danenberg

7   Product (Goods and Services) 246

David Corkindale

8   Physical Availability, Retailing and Shopping

11 Media Decisions: Reaching Buyers with Advertising 378

Byron Sharp, Erica Riebe and Karen Nelson-Field

12 Strategic Marketing and Planning 438

Adrian Palmer, adapted by Larry Lockshin

13 Global Marketing 478

Maxwell Winchester and Tiffany Winchester

14 Social Responsibility and Ethics 512

Anita Peleg and Charles Graham

LIST OF FIGURES

LIST OF TABLES

LIST OF CASE STUDIES

LIST OF PRACTITIONER PROFILES

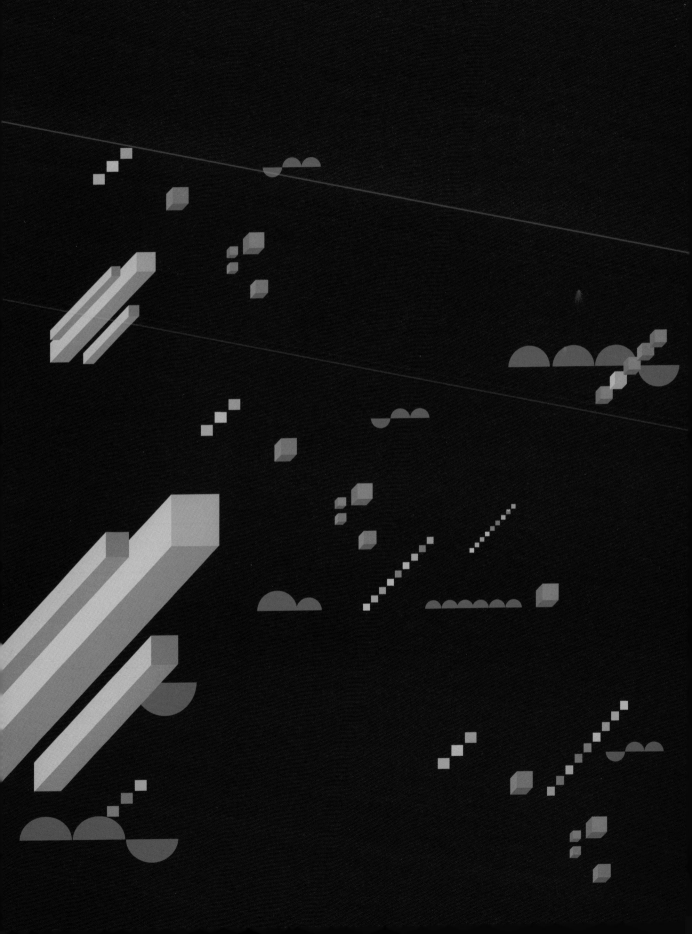

CASE MATRIX

The grid below identifies the chapters for which the case applies due to integration of ideas (x).

CASES	CHAPTER 1: WHAT DO MARKETING EXECUTIVES DO?	CHAPTER 2: CONSUMER BEHAVIOUR AND BUSINESS BUYER BEHAVIOUR	CHAPTER 3: MEANINGFUL MARKETING METRICS	CHAPTER 4: MARKET RESEARCH	CHAPTER 5: THE MARKETING ENVIRONMENT	CHAPTER 6: CUSTOMER SEGMENTATION AND TARGETING
A portable music history: Why marketing matters	X					
Starship Children's Health: Addressing customer needs	X					
Mike's Milk: Making marketing decisions	X					
Kerry Sanderson, AO— Marketing a lifetime of service to business and government	X					
The best burger: Why loyalty is limited		X				
The toothpaste case: Availability and involvement		X				
Mobile payments: Who do you trust?		X				
Leopard Controls finally shows its spots		X				
The cost of cutting back			X			
Procter & Gamble's operating shift			X			
ROI can send you broke			X			
Loyalty ladders: Why they are unnecessary and dangerous		X	X			

CHAPTER 7: PRODUCT (GOODS AND SERVICES)	CHAPTER 8: PHYSICAL AVAIL-ABILITY, RETAILING AND SHOPPING	CHAPTER 9: PRICING AND DIS-COUNTING	CHAPTER 10: ADVERTISING	CHAPTER 11: MEDIA DECISIONS: REACHING BUYERS WITH ADVERTISING	CHAPTER 12: STRATEGIC MARKETING AND PLANNING	CHAPTER 13: GLOBAL MARKETING	CHAPTER 14: SOCIAL RESPONSIBILITY AND ETHICS
X					X		
X	X				X		
					X		X
	X						
X					X		
			X				
				X			

CASES	CHAPTER 1: WHAT DO MARKETING EXECUTIVES DO?	CHAPTER 2: CONSUMER BEHAVIOUR AND BUSINESS BUYER BEHAVIOUR	CHAPTER 3: MEANINGFUL MARKETING METRICS	CHAPTER 4: MARKET RESEARCH	CHAPTER 5: THE MARKETING ENVIRONMENT	CHAPTER 6: CUSTOMER SEGMENTA-TION AND TARGETING
Advertising tracking			X			
Was there really an attitude there?			X			
Cereal sales: What caused what?			X			
Toothpaste marketing alarm		X	X	X		X
National Pharmacies				X		
Starbucks Coffee Company				X		
Defining your research				X		X
Choosing appropriate methodology				X		
Tapping into social media chatter				X		
iSnack 2.0				X		
Sealing the deal on the Stelvin screwcap					X	
Banning live exports					X	
McDonald's recognises new family values					X	X
The internet's unforeseen consequences					X	
Vaccination: Social good or social evil?					X	
The burger battle: Hungry Jack's/Burger King versus McDonald's						X

CHAPTER 7: PRODUCT (GOODS AND SERVICES)	CHAPTER 8: PHYSICAL AVAIL-ABILITY, RETAILING AND SHOPPING	CHAPTER 9: PRICING AND DIS-COUNTING	CHAPTER 10: ADVERTISING	CHAPTER 11: MEDIA DECISIONS: REACHING BUYERS WITH ADVERTISING	CHAPTER 12: STRATEGIC MARKETING AND PLANNING	CHAPTER 13: GLOBAL MARKETING	CHAPTER 14: SOCIAL RESPONSIBILITY AND ETHICS
			X	X			
X	X		X				
	X						
				X			
X							
X							
							X

CASES	CHAPTER 1: WHAT DO MARKETING EXECUTIVES DO?	CHAPTER 2: CONSUMER BEHAVIOUR AND BUSINESS BUYER BEHAVIOUR	CHAPTER 3: MEANINGFUL MARKETING METRICS	CHAPTER 4: MARKET RESEARCH	CHAPTER 5: THE MARKETING ENVIRONMENT	CHAPTER 6: CUSTOMER SEGMENTATION AND TARGETING
Toothpaste: Sophisticated mass marketing is alive and well						X
From the Model T to the Mini						X
The Ford Model T and the myth of mass marketing						X
Salmon campaign strategy: Is there something fishy going on?						X
My World My Way: Analysing the segmentation strategy						X
Disney's flop: John Carter						
Hilti: From goods to service provision						X
Foster's low-carb beer						
Shouldice Hospital: A model hospital						
Marketing the Eco-Shack						
Consolidation of the retail dollar not universal						
Sainsbury's and the power of physical availability						
Changing nature of retail in China					X	
Zara—Just getting started						

CHAPTER 7: PRODUCT (GOODS AND SERVICES)	CHAPTER 8: PHYSICAL AVAIL-ABILITY, RETAILING AND SHOPPING	CHAPTER 9: PRICING AND DIS-COUNTING	CHAPTER 10: ADVERTISING	CHAPTER 11: MEDIA DECISIONS: REACHING BUYERS WITH ADVERTISING	CHAPTER 12: STRATEGIC MARKETING AND PLANNING	CHAPTER 13: GLOBAL MARKETING	CHAPTER 14: SOCIAL RESPONSIBILITY AND ETHICS
X	X						
						X	
X							
X					X		
X					X		
X							
X		X		X	X		X
	X				X	X	
	X						
	X						
X	X						

CASES	CHAPTER 1: WHAT DO MARKETING EXECUTIVES DO?	CHAPTER 2: CONSUMER BEHAVIOUR AND BUSINESS BUYER BEHAVIOUR	CHAPTER 3: MEANINGFUL MARKETING METRICS	CHAPTER 4: MARKET RESEARCH	CHAPTER 5: THE MARKETING ENVIRONMENT	CHAPTER 6: CUSTOMER SEGMENTATION AND TARGETING
Iliad undercuts its rivals						
Santa Lucia Wholefoods: Product development decisions			X			
Game makers give it away—and increase their profits						
Kindle Fire: $199 looks like a bargain						
The tyre case: Analysing your situation to make good pricing decisions						X
The 'Legend' campaign						
Meat & Livestock Australia—We love our lamb						X
Interactive marketing goes high-tech: QR coding						
Can marketing actually make people's lives better?						
'Holiday at home': Managing a media campaign						
Pepsi's 'Refresh Project': A social media pioneer						
FarmFoods Direct: Planning for reach						
The Country Lodge learns to use online advertising effectively						

CHAPTER 7: PRODUCT (GOODS AND SERVICES)	CHAPTER 8: PHYSICAL AVAIL-ABILITY, RETAILING AND SHOPPING	CHAPTER 9: PRICING AND DIS-COUNTING	CHAPTER 10: ADVERTISING	CHAPTER 11: MEDIA DECISIONS: REACHING BUYERS WITH ADVERTISING	CHAPTER 12: STRATEGIC MARKETING AND PLANNING	CHAPTER 13: GLOBAL MARKETING	CHAPTER 14: SOCIAL RESPONSIBILITY AND ETHICS
		X					
	X	X					
		X			X		
		X			X		
		X					
			X				
X			X	X			
			X	X			
			X	X			X
			X	X	X		
				X			X
				X	X		
				X			

CASES	CHAPTER 1: WHAT DO MARKETING EXECUTIVES DO?	CHAPTER 2: CONSUMER BEHAVIOUR AND BUSINESS BUYER BEHAVIOUR	CHAPTER 3: MEANINGFUL MARKETING METRICS	CHAPTER 4: MARKET RESEARCH	CHAPTER 5: THE MARKETING ENVIRONMENT	CHAPTER 6: CUSTOMER SEGMENTATION AND TARGETING
The Turkey Farmers Association: Complexities of communication and the media						
Kondoot: A new social network site						
Virgin Australia						X
Marketing the unmanageable?						
Should companies build Chinese walls?						
Marketing a contemporary art museum: The White Rabbit Gallery						X
Foster's Lager: The taste of Australia that Australians don't drink!						
SABMiller: Glocalisation					X	
Starbucks and McDonald's: Two different strategies for coffee drinkers in Australia					X	X
What are they willing to pay? Exploiting locals until the grey market opens						
Range Rover is a posh brand and practical for farmers … or is it?						X
Facebook aims to double its global user base						

CHAPTER 7: PRODUCT (GOODS AND SERVICES)	CHAPTER 8: PHYSICAL AVAILABILITY, RETAILING AND SHOPPING	CHAPTER 9: PRICING AND DISCOUNTING	CHAPTER 10: ADVERTISING	CHAPTER 11: MEDIA DECISIONS: REACHING BUYERS WITH ADVERTISING	CHAPTER 12: STRATEGIC MARKETING AND PLANNING	CHAPTER 13: GLOBAL MARKETING	CHAPTER 14: SOCIAL RESPONSIBILITY AND ETHICS
				X	X		
				X	X		
X					X		
					X		
					X		X
					X		
X						X	
X				X		X	
X				X		X	
						X	X
X						X	
				X		X	

CASES	CHAPTER 1: WHAT DO MARKETING EXECUTIVES DO?	CHAPTER 2: CONSUMER BEHAVIOUR AND BUSINESS BUYER BEHAVIOUR	CHAPTER 3: MEANINGFUL MARKETING METRICS	CHAPTER 4: MARKET RESEARCH	CHAPTER 5: THE MARKETING ENVIRONMENT	CHAPTER 6: CUSTOMER SEGMENTATION AND TARGETING
Anti-competitive practices: Can marketers get away with them?					X	
Dilmah Ceylon Tea: Market development in Australia				X		X
Marketing encouraging recycling in a 'throw away' society						
Going green? The Conservative Party in the United Kingdom					X	
Diageo plc: Stakeholder analysis					X	
A little local difficulty with ethical sourcing						
Greenwashing					X	
Advertising to children in Sweden						
Sprout Design and the Reee Chair						
Plan A at Marks & Spencer					X	
Asbestos: A toxic trade					X	

CHAPTER 7: PRODUCT (GOODS AND SERVICES)	CHAPTER 8: PHYSICAL AVAIL-ABILITY, RETAILING AND SHOPPING	CHAPTER 9: PRICING AND DIS-COUNTING	CHAPTER 10: ADVERTISING	CHAPTER 11: MEDIA DECISIONS: REACHING BUYERS WITH ADVERTISING	CHAPTER 12: STRATEGIC MARKETING AND PLANNING	CHAPTER 13: GLOBAL MARKETING	CHAPTER 14: SOCIAL RESPONSIBILITY AND ETHICS
						X	X
X					X	X	
							X
					X		X
							X
							X
							X
				X			X
							X
							X
							X

PREFACE

This book was written in the belief that students want to know what marketing people do, and what questions managers have to tackle in their day-to-day jobs. Students want to learn what is known about marketing and what isn't—and how businesses cope in spite of these knowledge gaps. In addition to the case studies throughout, this book contains practitioner profiles that senior marketing executives have written. They describe their jobs, what they do and how they got where they are today.

Many textbooks are heavy on conceptual theory, emphasising ideas such as 'the product life cycle', and very light on evidence, and they neglect areas that are important to working managers. Senior marketing executives of corporations such as Coca-Cola, Unilever, Procter & Gamble and ANZ Bank, who sit on the Advisory Board of the Ehrenberg-Bass Institute, asked for this book to be written. They asked for a book that presented a more realistic view of the marketing world. They asked for an evidence-based introduction to marketing.

They said this book was needed because few managers ever refer to their old university textbooks, since these books just aren't relevant to their working life. Marketing textbooks don't help managers to predict what would happen if they changed the price of their product, or to set an advertising budget. We wrote this new book to provide scientific evidence, along with enlivening case studies, evidence-based theory and practical guidelines.

This textbook covers most of the same areas of marketing covered in other textbooks. Its difference is that the material provided is based on actual evidence and practice. The members of our Advisory Boards and our corporate sponsors use this evidence-based marketing approach every day in their marketing jobs.

There is a whole chapter on *meaningful marketing metrics*, to teach readers about the metrics that marketers use to assess their performance and brand health. Importantly, it teaches the skills that are needed to interpret such metrics correctly, and to avoid being misled. There is a huge industry that exists to sell marketers services, from customer relationship management software to media space and brand equity research. This textbook will help students become intelligent buyers.

Unlike most other introductory textbooks, this book includes a substantial chapter on media decisions because buying media space for advertising consumes a large part of most marketing budgets. Also, the digital revolution is making media decision making more complex than ever. Today, marketers need an understanding of all the new ways of advertising, but equally importantly, they need an evidence-informed sense of perspective. They need to be able to astutely evaluate their many options.

This textbook aims to create better informed and more sceptical, questioning managers—who can use this knowledge to develop more effective marketing programs.

Professor Byron Sharp
Ehrenberg-Bass Institute

GUIDED TOUR

How to use this book

Marketing: Theory, Evidence, Practice is enriched with a range of features designed to help support and reinforce your learning. This guided tour shows you how to best utilise your textbook and obook and get the most out of your study.

Learning Objectives

A bulleted list of learning objectives is provided to outline the main concepts and ideas that you will encounter in each chapter. Learning objectives are then reinforced in pink margin notes at critical points throughout the text. These serve as helpful signposts for learning and revision.

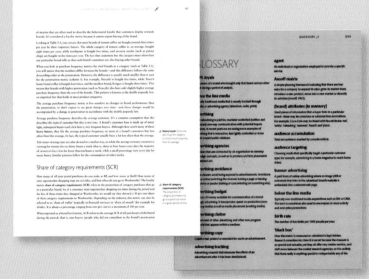

Key Terms and Glossary

Key terms are highlighted where they first appear in the text, and the definition appears in the margin notes. The definitions are also collated in a complete glossary at the back of the book for easy reference.

Industry Insights

Industry insights highlight the application of marketing in business. They are included to provide informed and up-to-date perspectives on the industry.

Critical Reflections

These pinpoint significant topics and encourage a questioning and reflective approach to the issues raised.

Case Studies

Each chapter begins with a short case about a contemporary topic to introduce the subject through a concrete example. Case examples are then provided throughout the chapter to apply the theory being discussed to real-life situations. A major case study is also included at the end of every chapter, picking up salient points from the chapter.

Business-to-Business Marketing

The application of marketing from business to business is included to reinforce this important aspect of marketing.

Summary

A short summary of key points is included at the end of every chapter to reinforce comprehension of the learning objectives and the central themes of the chapter.

Revision Questions

Carefully designed review questions have been provided at the end of every chapter. These can be used to check understanding of the key topics before moving on to the next chapter, or for group discussion and revision.

Further Reading and Weblinks

Further Reading and Weblinks at the end of each chapter are included to help broaden understanding of the topics covered and extend learning.

Practitioner Profiles

Profiles of marketing executives are included to give real insight into what marketing people do, and what questions managers have to tackle in their day-to-day jobs.

<u>o</u>book

Your **<u>o</u>book** is a truly integrated e-text with extra content and resources built in to complement your textbook. This <u>o</u>book includes

- hotlinked learning objectives—click on the learning objective to be taken to the relevant content within the chapter
- interviews with marketing professionals
- instant access to video examples that relate to the case studies and industry insights within the text
- audio chapter summaries that can be used for revision purposes
- embedded weblinks
- 'live' chapter revision questions and answers to test knowledge
- integrated dictionary and note-taking features.

Your free **<u>o</u>book** activation code is located on the back cover flap.

To access your **<u>o</u>book** go to **www.oxforddigital.com.au**.

Oxford Business Hub

To get the most from your study, explore the Oxford Business Hub: <www.oup.com.au/obh>.

The OBH includes a rich selection of resources, including

- annotated weblinks: a list of websites that will expand a student's understanding of particular topics or concepts
- further reading lists: a list of further reading resources that will expand a student's understanding of particular topics or concepts
- flashcard glossary: an interactive glossary based on the key terms of the textbook
- revision podcasts
- additional learning resources.

OXFORD
BUSINESS
HUB

oup.com.au/obh

ABOUT THE AUTHORS

Professor Byron Sharp

Professor Byron Sharp is the Director of the Ehrenberg-Bass Institute and is recognised globally as a leading expert on buyer behaviour and the interpretation of marketing metrics. He is a well-known commentator on marketing issues and research practices and 'makes a habit of challenging conventional business ideas' (Marketing Research News, UK). His research on loyalty and loyalty strategies has been recognised and funded by the Australian Research Council and major corporations around the world.

His book *How Brands Grow ... What Marketers Don't Know* has received international acclaim: 'All marketers need to move beyond the psycho-babble and read this book ... or be left hopelessly behind' (Joseph Tripodi, The Coca-Cola Company).

Katherine Anderson

Katherine Anderson is a Senior Research Associate at the Ehrenberg-Bass Institute.

Katherine's core research interests are consumer behaviour and innovative new research methodologies including online brand communities, snap forecasts and virtual reality simulations. Her research has been published in the *International Journal of Market Research* and the *Australasian Journal of Market & Social Research*.

Katherine is a member of the Australian Market and Social Research Society and an active market researcher. She has designed research for retailers, wineries, state and local government departments, financial services and global consumer goods companies.

Dr Dag Bennett

Dr Dag Bennett is Deputy Director of the Ehrenberg Centre at London South Bank University. He has fifteen years of commercial experience in the UK and the US, in brand management and marketing research. He has particular interests in habitual behaviour, developing markets and short-term purchase-to-purchase analysis techniques. His teaching includes International Pricing and Finance, and Market-Driven Marketing.

Dr Svetlana Bogomolova

Dr Svetlana Bogomolova is a Senior Research Associate at the Ehrenberg-Bass Institute for Marketing Science, University of South Australia. Svetlana's area of expertise is consumer decision-making at the point of purchase and the influence of contextual factors on shopper choices. She has published in a wide range of marketing journals, including *Journal of Business Research, European Journal of Marketing, Journal of Marketing Management, Industrial Marketing Management* and *International Journal of Marketing Research*. She teaches marketing research and brand management at undergraduate and postgraduate levels. Prior to joining academia, Svetlana worked in the marketing research industry.

Dr David Corkindale

Dr David Corkindale is a Professor of Marketing Management at the University of South Australia in the Graduate School of Business and is a member of the Ehrenberg-Bass Institute. A scientist by original training, he initially worked in the UK for a pharmaceutical company and then in the steel industry before discovering marketing and working in research for the advertising agencies JWT and BBDO in London for some years. He holds a PhD in Marketing and a Masters in Operations Research and was on the faculty of the Cranfield School of Management and the faculty of Commerce at UBC in Vancouver, Canada, for a number of years. He has written four books on marketing management and numerous papers in learned journals on the role of marketing in commercialising new technologies and, more recently, on patterns of consumer behaviour online.

Dr Nick Danenberg

Dr Nick Danenberg is the Research & Strategy Development Manager at specialist online marketing agency, e-Channel Search. Nick's focus is directed towards turning findings from analytical research into actionable, strategic insights for e-Channel, its customers and partners. Nick is a specialist in quantitative analysis, using data visualisation and data mining techniques to drive business intelligence. Prior to joining e-Channel, Nick was a Senior Research Fellow in the Ehrenberg-Bass Institute. His research into advertising effectiveness, buyer behaviour, and customer loyalty and defection has been funded by numerous national and international corporations and government agencies. Nick holds a PhD and a Masters degree in marketing from the University of South Australia.

Charles Graham

Charles Graham is a senior lecturer in marketing at London South Bank University. His research interests include social marketing, competitive intelligence and the strategic aspects of consumer behaviour, and he has conducted projects for a number of well-known social enterprises. Charles has presented his research at international conferences and published in *Journal of Marketing Management*, *Journal of Strategic Marketing*, and in *Market Leader*.

Nicole Hartnett

Nicole Hartnett is a Senior Research Associate at the Ehrenberg-Bass Institute. Nicole's research interests are centred around advertising effectiveness, to develop our understanding of the creative execution tactics that can be linked to sales success. She has conducted research with various industries, from confectionery to consumer retailers, financial services and local government.

Associate Professor Rachel Kennedy

Associate Professor Rachel Kennedy is the Director of the Mars Marketing Laboratory at the Ehrenberg-Bass Institute. For nearly two decades, Rachel has been researching advertising, drawing on empirical knowledge about buyer behaviour to better understand advertising and how to research it.

Rachel is committed to producing and disseminating scientific knowledge about marketing. She regularly speaks at major marketing conferences, has a range of publications in key marketing journals and is on the editorial advisory boards for the *Journal of Advertising Research*, the *International Journal of Market Research* and the *International Journal of Advertising*.

Marianthi Livaditis

Marianthi Livaditis is a Research Associate at the Ehrenberg-Bass Institute undertaking a Masters by Research (Business). Her research area is understanding consumer brand loyalty as a natural tendency to have bias behavioural preferences in choice situations. Marianthi currently tutors various marketing courses at the University of South Australia, and also holds Honours in Anthropology.

Professor Larry Lockshin

Dr Larry Lockshin is Professor of Wine Marketing and Head of the School of Marketing at the University of South Australia. Professor Lockshin has published over 100 academic articles and over 200 trade articles on consumer choice behaviour, packaging and wine marketing.

His research interests are consumer choice behaviour, packaging and wine marketing. He is currently working on modelling of consumer choice based on simulated shopping experiments and large panel data sets, packaging and retail influences on choice.

Dr Karen Nelson-Field

Dr Karen Nelson-Field is a Postdoctoral Research Fellow and Senior Research Associate with the Ehrenberg-Bass Institute for Marketing Science at the University of South Australia. Karen's earlier research interests included traditional media strategy, with a particular focus on the impact of media fragmentation on audience targeting. Her current research is in the social media space, in particular whether existing empirical generalisations in advertising, buyer behaviour and media hold in the social media context, and how this impacts on the ability of social media to assist brand growth. Her findings have been presented internationally including at the European Communications Symposium (Barcelona), London Business School, ESOMAR World Media 3 (Berlin), Advertising Research Foundation (New York) and the prestigious Wharton Business School (Pennsylvania). Her industry experience includes senior marketing roles in FMCG, media, tourism and major retail over sixteen years.

Dr Magda Nenycz-Thiel

Dr Magda Nenycz-Thiel is a Senior Lecturer and Senior Research Associate at the Ehrenberg-Bass Institute for Marketing Science at the University of South Australia. Magda's specific areas of expertise are brand equity and buying behaviour of private label brands. She has published her research in international journals such as *Journal of Business Research*, *Journal of Advertising Research* and *Journal of Product and Brand Management*. Magda's research findings in the private label area form a seminar for corporate sponsors in the Ehrenberg-Bass Institute, and are presented and distributed to marketers in companies around the world. Magda's current research areas also include online buying behaviour, and the validity and reliability of brand usage metrics.

Professor Adrian Palmer

Adrian Palmer is Professor of Marketing at Swansea University, Wales, UK. His first career was in tourism marketing and management. Since joining academia, he has researched and published extensively on the subject of services marketing and the efforts of service organisations to create memorable experiences. His book *Principles of Services Marketing*, now in its sixth edition, is widely used throughout the world to provide a grounding in the challenges and opportunities of marketing services. Recent research has focused on experiential aspects of consumption, with articles published recently in *Journal of Marketing Management*, *European Journal of Marketing*, and *Journal of Services Marketing*, among others.

Anita Peleg

Anita Peleg is currently a Senior Lecturer in Marketing at London South Bank University. Prior to academic life she worked in tourism marketing, public relations and market research in Israel, the US and the UK. Her specialist teaching areas are Public Relations, Marketing Research, Research Methods and Marketing Ethics, with an emphasis on experiential learning. Her research interests focus on marketing education, and she has presented and published papers on graduate employability, skills development, marketing ethics and moral education at seminars and conferences in the UK, including PRHE, Pedagogical Research in Higher Education Conferences and PRIME (Pedagogical Research in Maximising Education) publications. In 2012, Anita was awarded a National Teaching Fellowship for excellence in teaching and learning by the Higher Education Academy, UK.

Dr Erica Riebe

Dr Erica Riebe is a Senior Research Associate at the Ehrenberg-Bass Institute with extensive market research experience across a wide range of markets including government departments, financial services, insurance services, retail and rural services. Erica's research focuses on the following areas: determining effective and efficient media placement strategies, measuring the impact of changes in the media environment on audiences, predicting the uptake of new products using probabilistic scales, and determining the impact of customer loss and gain on the likely growth or decline of a brand.

John Scriven

John Scriven's research interests focus on the process of scientific research into grounded principles of marketing; the effect of marketing inputs, particularly price and advertising; and the nature of brand loyalty and competition. He has published on the effects of price changes, advertising and patterns of consumer behaviour. His teaching has a particular focus on the development of numeracy. Prior to becoming an academic, he had over twenty years commercial experience in a series of marketing, market research and marketing planning positions with three multinational corporations: United Biscuits, RJR/Nabisco and Pepsico.

Dr Anne Sharp

Dr Anne Sharp is a Senior Lecturer and Research Fellow at the Ehrenberg-Bass Institute for Marketing Science, University of South Australia. She heads the Sustainable Marketing research of the Institute and has a particular interest in evaluating marketing interventions that encourage behaviour change for improved environmental outcomes. Anne's work has been published in a range of top marketing journals such as the *European Journal of Marketing* and the *International Journal of Research in Marketing*.

She is a full member of the Market Research Society of Australia and teaches Market Research at both undergraduate and postgraduate level.

Dr Herb Sorensen

Dr Herb Sorensen is a pre-eminent authority on observing and measuring shoppers' behaviours. Beginning in the early 1970s, he built and grew one of the first in-store shopper research agencies. His 'In-Store Research Company' grew at an annualised 30% from 1989 to 2009. In 2001, he invented the global shopper tracking methodology PathTracker, publishing a dozen patents since. In the past few years his publications have focused on the store as media, dissecting the purchase process as a correlation between the footpath and the eye-path, with special attention to the final seconds of the purchase. Herb is Scientific Advisor to the TNS Global Retail & Shopper Practice, and Adjunct Senior Research Fellow for the Ehrenberg-Bass Institute for Marketing Science at the University of South Australia. Dr. Sorensen's unique perspective is the subject of his book, *Inside the Mind of the Shopper,* and he shared the AMA EXPLOR award for 'the most innovative use of technology that advances marketing research' with colleagues at the Wharton School. He has been quoted in *The Wall Street Journal, Forbes, Business Week* and *MSNBC*. Herb is on the Brain Trust panel of retailwire and writes a regular blog on shopper insights at www.shopperscientist.com.

Dr Maxwell Winchester

Dr Maxwell K. Winchester is a Senior Lecturer in Marketing at Victoria University. He is also currently the Deputy Director of Learning and Teaching in the School of International Business at Victoria University. Maxwell teaches Masters-level units in Consumer Behaviour, Marketing Communications and Marketing Management, and holds a PhD in Marketing from the esteemed Ehrenberg-Bass Institute for Marketing Science. Maxwell has consulting experience as a marketing researcher in Australia, Asia, North America and Europe. His clients have included Astra Motor Company, Cartier Asia, BHP, Pernod Riccard and a number of government agencies. He has also held a senior management position in one of Australia's largest companies and held political seats in the UK. In addition to his industry experience, Maxwell has many years of academic teaching experience globally, having held permanent faculty positions in Australia, Canada and the UK. In addition to these he has been a visiting professor in China, Singapore, Malaysia, France, Germany, Kuwait and Austria. His research interests include reflective learning and reflective practice, qualitative and quantitative research methods, empirical generalisationalist research methods and behaviourist consumer behaviour theories. He has published articles on student evaluations of teaching and reflective practice, as well as negative brand beliefs, luxury and premium brands, and wine marketing.

Tiffany Winchester

Tiffany M. Winchester is a lecturer in Marketing and a PhD scholar in the Graduate School of Business at Deakin University in Australia, where she teaches research design and analysis, and marketing management. Prior to moving to Australia, she was a Senior Lecturer in International Business at Harper Adams University College in the UK. She has also been a visiting professor at Fachhochschule Bingen—University of Applied Sciences in Germany, the Beijing Agricultural College in China, and Ecole Supérieure de Commerce de Dijon in France. Her research interests include reflective learning and reflective practice, student evaluations of teaching, and the application of marketing theory to political voting behaviour. She has published in educational journals and presented at conferences in Australia and overseas.

Project Manager
Elké Seretis

Elké Seretis is Manager of Business Development and Marketing at the Ehrenberg-Bass Institute, at the University of South Australia.

Elké coordinated a team of over thirty authors, and facilitated the execution and delivery of this book.

Elké is a corporate marketing professional with over twenty years of industry experience. She has worked in marketing research and advertising and has expertise in multi-country communication, development of integrated marketing campaigns, marketing strategy formation and brand growth. For the last twelve years, Elké has worked at the Institute, leading the marketing and business department.

She is married to Jim Seretis and has two lovely children, Isabelle and Luke.

ABOUT THE CASE STUDY AUTHORS AND CONTRIBUTORS

Dr Rodney Arambewela is a Senior Lecturer in Marketing at Deakin University, and contributed a case study.

Dr Gregory J Brush is an Assistant Professor in Marketing at the University of Western Australia, and contributed a case study.

Dr Armando Maria Corsi is a Research Associate at the Ehrenberg-Bass Institute, University of South Australia, and contributed a case study.

Vivien Chanana is a Lecturer in Marketing at the University of South Australia, and has worked on a number of definitions.

Associate Professor John Dawes is the Operations Director at the Ehrenberg-Bass Institute, University of South Australia. John contributed a piece on brand personality.

Dr Margaret Faulkner is a Senior Research Associate at the Ehrenberg-Bass Institute, University of South Australia, and contributed a chapter introduction.

Dr David R Fortin is Associate Professor in Marketing for the Department of Management at The University of Canterbury, New Zealand.

Elizabeth Gunner is a freelance marketer who has been working with the Ehrenberg-Bass Institute for the last five years, and worked on case studies, definitions, and questions and answers.

Dr Stephen Holden is Associate Professor in Marketing at Bond University, and contributed a case study.

Linda Hollebeek is a Senior Lecturer, Waikato Management School, Department of Marketing, University of Waikato, and wrote the tutorial discussion questions and activities, and the Testbank.

Steve Klomp is a Lecturer, Murdoch Business School, Murdoch University, and contributed two case studies.

Dr Kim Lehman is a Lecturer at the University of Tasmania, and contributed a case study.

Dr Nicholas McClaren is a Lecturer at Deakin University, and contributed a case study.

Kellie Newstead is a Research Associate at the Ehrenberg-Bass Institute, University of South Australia, and contributed case studies, definitions and chapter questions.

Cathy Nguyen is a Research Associate at the Ehrenberg-Bass Institute, University of South Australia, and contributed end-of-chapter review questions and answers.

Haydn Northover is a Research Associate at the Ehrenberg-Bass Institute, University of South Australia, and contributed two case studies to the textbook.

Monica Orlovic is a Research Associate at the Ehrenberg-Bass Institute, University of South Australia, and contributed definitions and a case study.

Bill Page is a Research Associate at the Ehrenberg-Bass Institute, University of South Australia, and contributed a case study and definitions.

Olivia Poropat is a Research Assistant at the Ehrenberg-Bass Institute, University of South Australia, and assisted with chapter definitions.

Dr Peter Reeves is a Lecturer at Salford Business School, University of Salford, and contributed a case study.

John Robinson is a Research Assistant with the Ehrenberg-Bass Institute, and has been largely responsible, with Arry Tanusondjaja, for the referencing of the textbook.

Arry Tanusondjaja is a Research Associate and the Research Assistant Manager at the Ehrenberg-Bass Institute, and ensured that all referencing queries were addressed in a timely manner.

Douglas Thompson is an Architectural Designer with the Permit Shop (NZ) Limited, and contributed a case study.

Professor Mark Uncles is Deputy Dean (Faculty) in the Australian School of Business at the University of New South Wales, and contributed a case study.

Dr Ekant Veer is a Senior Lecturer of Marketing at the University of Canterbury, New Zealand, and contributed a case study.

Dr John Wilkinson is Associate Head of School, School of Marketing at University of South Australia, and contributed the business-to-business marketing sections.

Ella Ward is a Research Assistant at the Ehrenberg-Bass Institute, University of South Australia, and assisted with referencing and proofreading.

Dr Steffen Zorn is a Lecturer at Curtin University in Perth, and contributed a case study.

ACKNOWLEDGMENTS

It takes a small army of writers and supporters to produce a new book like this one, so there are many people who deserve thanks. First and foremost, Elké Seretis, who assembled and managed this amazing team, and Karen Hildebrandt, who commissioned this project. Without the foresight and hard work of these two the writing would not have even started, let alone ever finished.

Thank you to everyone who directly contributed to this book, to those who reviewed chapters, and to the many researchers around the world who generated the knowledge that underpins this book.

Thank you to the marketing corporations, and their insightful managers, that provided encouragement and support for this textbook, especially the board members of the Ehrenberg-Bass Institute, who initially requested that such a book be written.

Thank you to the University of South Australia for supporting this new initiative.

Finally, thank you to my wife, Anne, and daughter Lilith for their support of this lengthy project.

Professor Byron Sharp

Schweppes Australia, p. 341; **Shutterstock**/Raisa Kanareva, p. vi (coffee) /A. L. Spangler, p. v (seating) /Aleph Studio, p. 154 /Alexander Chaikin, p. 110 /Alexander Raths, p. 254 /Alexander Raths, p. 531 /Ambrophoto, p. 342 right / AmpFotoStudio, p. 21 /Asianet-Pakistan, pp. 214–5 /Atiketta Sangasaeng, pp. 130–1 (5th tissue) /B Brown, p. 329 / Blazej Lyjak, p. vi (recycling)/Bogdan Vasilescu, p. 249 /Brent Hofacker, pp. 130–1 (6th tissue) /Cameramannz, pp. 130–1 (4th tissue) /Cienpies Design, p. 164 /Dario Sabljak, p. vi (beer) /Denis Babenko, p. 31 /Denisenko, p. 245 /Diana Rich, pp. 130–1 (1st tissue)/Dmitry Naumov, p. 212 /Dongliu, p. 483 left /E.G.Pors, p. 29 /Ed Phillips, p. 427 /Edyta Pawlowska, p. 437 /Gary Blakeley, p. v (sign) /Gordon Bell, p. 342 centre / Hasloo Group Production Studio, p. 109 / Hung Chung Chih, p. 458 /Ilja Mašík, p. vi (aeroplane) /Ivelin Radkov, p. 89 /James Weston, p. 556 /Jami Garrison, pp. 130–1 (3rd tissue) /Jenn Huls, p. 311 /Jerry Horbert, p. 534 /Jorge Salcedo, p. 360 /Jose Ignacio Soto, p. 468 / Kwest, p. 77 /Kzenon, p. 299 /Loren Rodgers, pp. 26–7 /Luiz Rocha, pp. 554–5 /Mama_mia, p. 150 /Mangostock, p. 456 /Maridav, p. 243 /Maxim Blinkov, p. 327 /Monkey Business Images, pp. 70–1, 72, 200, 386 / NAN728, p. 85 / Niki Crucillo, pp. 130–1 (11th tissue), 130–1 (10th tissue) /Pan Xunbin, pp. 126–7 /Pcruciatti, p. 291 /PhotoHouse, p. 11 /S.Borisov, p. 491 /Sandra van der Steen, p. v (rabbit) /Sergey Karpov, p. 374 /SerrNovik, p. 113 /Shots Studio, p. vi (boys) /Sonya Etchison, p. 16 /Steve Collender, pp. 130–1 (7th tissue) /Stokkete, p. 277 /Suradech Sribuanoy, pp. 130–1 (2nd tissue) /Suradech Sribuanoy, p. v (tissues) /Suwan Reunintr, p. 506 /Thomas Klee, p. v (corkscrew) /Tirawut, p. 130–1 (9th tissue) /Tish1, p. 139 /Tom Freeze, pp. 124–5 /Valerie Potapova, p. 55 /Vartanov Anatoly, p. 285 /Veniamin Kraskov, p. 406 /Violetkaipa, p. 136 /Warren Price Photography, pp. 130–1 (8th tissue) /WDG Photo, p. 511 /Winui, p. 170 /Yuri Arcurs, pp. 202, 357; **Sprout Design & Makers Co**, p. 542; **The Kobal Collection**/Columbia/Danjaq/ Eon, p. 358 bottom /Eon/Danjaq/Sony, p. 408 /Milennium Films, p. 421; **White Rabbit Gallery**, Sydney, pp. 472–5; **Wieden + Kennedy**, pp. 335–6; **Wikimedia Commons**/Public Domain, p. 252 bottom.

Text: Australian Bureau of Statistics, 'Household Income, Expenditure and Wealth', 1301.0 - *Year Book Australia*, 2012, 24/5/12, Graph 9.1; MarketingSherpa, LLC for 'PPC Campaign: Marketer learns from unsuccessful campaign to deliver 75% increase in sales' by David Kirkpatrick, *www.marketingsherpa.com*, 07-Apr-2011; Oxford University Press UK for *INTRODUCTION TO MARKETING: THEORY & PRACTICE 2E* by Adrian Palmer (2009), adaptation of pp. 40–74 chapter 2: 'The Marketing Environment' & pp. 465–498, chapter 12: 'Managing the Marketing Effort', by permission of Oxford University Press.

01

WHAT DO MARKETING
EXECUTIVES DO?

BYRON SHARP

◢ Introduction case

A portable music history: Why marketing matters

In 1979 Sony launched the 'Walkman', a small portable music device that played audio cassettes, allowing people to listen to music while out and about. In addition to being portable, it offered very high-quality (for the time) stereo sound at a low price. The Walkman advertising stressed its Japanese origin, when Japan was well known for small, well-priced, high-quality technology products. The advertising also featured teenagers in active outdoor settings and portrayed the product as culturally hip. The Walkman was very successful. There were many competitors but none had built a brand (Walkman) the way Sony had. Later on, CD and (the less popular) mini-disc versions of the Walkman were added to the range, and in 1999 Sony even launched leading-edge (and expensive) flash-memory-based Walkman products.

In 2000 Apple hit what it called a 'speedbump' in sales growth, when it failed to include writable CD drives in its computers. Apple thought that DVD drives would be more attractive to buyers but failed to take account of the rising popularity of music sharing via the internet. This event made Apple realise that digital music stored and shared via computer software was the future. That year they bought SoundJam software for managing digital music, which they further developed and launched as free software called iTunes for Macintosh computers in 2001. Months later they launched the iPod onto a market where there were several other digital music players, including Sony Walkman products and the MP3 player pioneer Rio. The original iPod was a (minor) sales success, considering that it was an expensive, high-performance product that could only connect

While success or failure depends a great deal on luck, marketing strategy has a huge influence on a brand's success or decline. There is much marketing knowledge that (if used wisely) can help to grow brands. The Apple iPod would have failed if it was a technologically faulty product, but without Apple's superb marketing, it never could have enjoyed the success that it has.

to the very latest Macintosh computers. Three years later, Apple had gained many new points of distribution, and with the launch of the first flash-memory-based iPod, sales rocketed upwards. iTunes for Windows was released, making the product attractive to the wider market. Sony unsuccessfully attempted to emulate the iPod's success with new Walkman models that offered higher sound quality than the iPod of the time. What had changed in this market, and how did a late entrant like Apple come to dominate?

Unlike Sony and other competitors, Apple made transferring digital music from a computer to their product, the iPod, simple (with its iTunes software). And it was also easy to transfer CD content to computer and then to an iPod. Apple's launch advertising didn't talk about geeky technology like MP3 encoding formats; it simply said 'a thousand songs in your pocket'. But Apple made sure they did support the MP3 codec that was at the time popular with (illegal) file sharing over the internet, while Sony refused to offer this format. Later Apple would make it simple to buy legal music from its iTunes store.

Apple's branding was brilliantly clear; iPod 'silhouette' billboards and the white earbuds became instantly recognisable. Apple spent heavily on advertising, increasing the brand's exposure each quarter (three months), as the market grew.

Its pricing was always very competitive and, as soon as technology allowed, Apple added cheaper, smaller versions to its iPod range, driving sales even higher. However, ultimately they expected mobile phones to take over these

features, so to prevent the iPod from being out-competed by a phone they worked to bundle the iPod's features into what became the iPhone.

While success or failure depends a great deal on luck, marketing strategy has a huge influence on a brand's success or decline. There is much marketing knowledge that (if used wisely) can help to grow brands. The Apple iPod would have failed if it was a technologically faulty product, but without Apple's superb marketing, it never could have enjoyed the success that it has.

INTRODUCTION

Marketing offers many exciting, rewarding careers. It is a growing profession that is short of qualified people. In 2012, AdNews reported an extreme shortage of senior marketing professionals in Australia (Blight, 2012). Marketing jobs are interesting; they require creativity, as well as insight and analytical ability.

Marketing scientists investigate how buyers buy and how marketing works. Evidence-based marketing uses discoveries from marketing science to inform marketing decision making, just as medical doctors base their advice on medical science. Marketers make decisions about what products to offer and to whom, what prices to charge, and how to advertise. Like doctors, marketers use metrics to assess the health of their brands and the impact of their marketing actions. Their job is to maintain and build the market-based assets of physical and mental availability that underpin their brand's sales today and into the future.

Marketers also play an important part in ensuring that the company culture is customer focused. However, the customer isn't always completely right, and sometimes marketing seeks to shape customer demands (for example towards healthier food options) to deliver sustainable customer value and profits.

LEARNING OBJECTIVES

After reading this chapter you should:

- have an initial appreciation of the many options and decisions marketers face each day
- understand what marketing is, and its importance
- understand what marketing professionals do
- understand how marketing science is beginning to transform marketing theory and practice
- understand the concept of sustainable marketing and the dilemmas that marketers face in balancing short-term and long-term objectives.

CHAPTER OUTLINE

Introduction

Marketing may be well paid and exciting ... but someone has to do it

The rise of marketing

Two types of marketing professional

Marketing science

Marketing metrics and market-based assets

Customer needs and wants

Sustainable marketing

Conclusion

marketing strategy: The way marketing activities are put together to achieve the organisation's aims for the brand. Marketing strategy is usually developed by the marketing leaders in consultation with key stakeholders.

retailers: The physical and online stores where the consumer can buy the end product; for example, supermarkets.

consumers: The people or companies who use the service or product.

market research: The gathering of factual information (often through observations and surveys) about the market—including what buyers think and do, particularly their watching (of advertising), buying and consuming.

brand: A distinctive and individual name or logo that is given to a product (or group of products) that distinguishes the products of one company from the products sold by their competitors.

◢ **LEARNING OBJECTIVE**
Have an initial appreciation of the many options and decisions marketers face each day

market: The total number of potential buyers for a product or service.

agent: An individual or organisation employed to provide a specific service.

KEY TERMS

advertising agencies

agent

brand

business model

business-to-business (B2B) marketing

campaign

centrally planned economy

consumers

distribution

evidence-based marketing

market

market-based assets

market economy

market research

market share

marketing interventions

marketing metrics

marketing mix

marketing science

marketing strategy

mental availability

new media

non-profit organisations

offerings

physical availability

production department

retail partner

retailers

sales

sustainable

sustainable marketing

trade

MARKETING MAY BE WELL PAID AND EXCITING ... BUT SOMEONE HAS TO DO IT

Many marketing jobs are well paid because they require a combination of skills and knowledge that not everyone has. As a marketing executive you will have to understand people and how they behave. You'll also have to gain skills for analysing market and financial data. Being a great marketer requires sound judgment as well as creativity; you'll need to analyse things quickly and estimate the probable consequences of your decisions. Importantly, marketers have to be good communicators, able to explain the **marketing strategy** to staff, **retailers** and **consumers**.

Marketers use **market research** to help understand customer desires and market opportunities so that the organisation can adapt to stay competitive. Marketers ceaselessly promote the organisation's services and products, so that customers maintain their awareness of the **brand**.

Each day, marketers make and review an enormous range of decisions, which together affect whether the firm will thrive or fail. Such decisions include:

- Should we offer a particular product or service?
- Which **market** should we target?
- What price should we charge? What different prices should we offer to different customers? At different locations? At different times of the year?
- Should we advertise on television? On which networks? When? How often? What should the advertisement say?
- Who should be our **agent** or **retail partner** in delivering the product or service? In which locations? To which consumers?

On any given day as a marketing professional you might encounter opportunities to have your product or service endorsed by a celebrity, to have a special in-store display, or to be featured in a magazine—each of these opportunities costs money and has implications for your other marketing activities; you will have to weigh these considerations and make these decisions, sometimes very quickly.

Today marketing professionals don't just work in **advertising agencies** and global brand companies such as Kraft or Vodafone. Many universities, hospitals, charities, churches and government departments have large marketing departments. **Non-profit organisations** usually have to compete for customers or donors, so marketing insights and practices are bringing new efficiencies to their operations.

The marketing world is changing dramatically as **new media** emerge, and new ways of advertising and delivering products and services are developed. Markets are becoming more openly competitive, more global and more complex. Consumers are becoming wealthier and better educated, with better access to information, so they have higher expectations. Therefore better educated marketing professionals are required.

This means that a marketing career is usually interesting: intellectually challenging as well as financially rewarding. A marketing qualification opens up opportunities to work for all sorts of organisations around the world.

●●● **TABLE 1.1** A SAMPLE OF CURRENT MARKETING JOB TITLES

BEGINNER / GRADUATE POSITIONS	INTERMEDIATE / MANAGERIAL POSITIONS	SENIOR AND DIRECTORIAL ROLES
Advertising Coordinator	Added Value Innovation Brand Manager	Advertising Planning Director
Brand Assistant	Associate Brand Manager	Chief Marketing Officer
Communication Coordinator	Brand Asset & Marketing Properties Manager	Corporate Planning Director
Junior Brand Manager	Brand Manager	Director, Advertising Research
Marketing Assistant	Business Development Manager	Director, Global Analytics
Marketing Coordinator	Campaign Evaluation Manager	Director, Global Pricing
Marketing Officer	Category Development Manager	Director, Global Shopper Insights
Sales Representative	Communications Planner	Director, Portfolio Growth
	Consumer Insight Manager	Director, Media Planning
	Category Leadership Manager	Director, Sales Research & Strategy
	Consumer Insights & Planning Manager	Director, Worldwide Agency Operations
	Consumer Promotions Manager	Export Director
	Consumer Strategy Manager	General Manager, Marketing
	Corporate Affairs Manager	Global Director, Marketing College
	Developing Markets Analyst	International Marketing Director
		(Continued)

retail partner: A retailer that has an agreement to stock a company's products.

advertising agencies: Providers that are contracted by an organisation to develop campaign concepts, as well as to produce and find placements for finished ads.

non-profit organisations: Businesses (such as charities) that do not operate with the key purpose of making a profit.

new media: New platforms for communicating with consumers that are typically digital and often linked to the internet; for example social media sites, podcasts and e-books.

●●● **TABLE 1.1** A SAMPLE OF CURRENT MARKETING JOB TITLES (*CONTINUED*)

BEGINNER / GRADUATE POSITIONS	INTERMEDIATE / MANAGERIAL POSITIONS	SENIOR AND DIRECTORIAL ROLES
	International Marketing Manager	Marketing Capability Director
	Franchise Manager	Marketing Director
	General Manager, Distribution	Market Research Director
	Marketing Analyst	Media Director
	Marketing Finance Manager	Public Policy Director
	Marketing Manager	Regional Brand Director
	Marketing & Public Relations Manager	Regional Brand Leader
	Market Research Manager	Sales Director
	Marketing Training Manager	Senior Brand Manager
	Portfolio Development Manager	Senior Category Insights Manager
	Pricing Analyst	Senior Market Analyst
	Regional Innovation Manager	Vice-President, Client Services
	Relationship Marketing Manager	Vice President, Product Development
	Sales Manager	
	Senior Sales Analyst	
	Technical Marketing Manager	
	Trade Promotions Manager	
	Trend Research Manager	

THE RISE OF MARKETING

The modern economy depends on **trade**. Marketing professionals are the people that oversee that trading. They also plan and research it, and compete against one another to deliver **offerings** to the market. As a result, products and services get produced that consumers *actually want to buy*, at a price they can pay.

Marketing is trading—buying and selling. If everyone, or every family, had to look after their own needs entirely by themselves there would be no trading, and no businesses. Now this might sound romantic—growing your own vegetables, living a simple life—but if everyone had to do this, the world would be a backward, miserable place. Who among us knows how to make ourselves a mobile phone? Or even how to make a decent cup of coffee (which involves growing, harvesting and roasting the beans, plus building an espresso machine)? Most likely we'd be hungry and cold,

---

◢ **trade:** Exchanging one thing for another; buying and selling goods and services.

◢ **offerings:** The different products (and associated benefits) that a company sells. A product offering includes many other features than just the physical product (for example packaging, service, customer support, design, special features and so on).

◢ **LEARNING OBJECTIVE**
Understand what marketing is, and its importance

living in a primitive hut, and hoping like crazy that none of us gets a toothache or anything that requires medical expertise.

The marketing revolution began about 10,000 years ago when human beings made the transition from being hunter-gatherers to farmers. The surplus crops had to be stored and counted (which led to the development of accountancy) and guarded (soldiers, police, security services), and these crops could be traded for other desirable goods and services (marketing). Trade created value, and made everyone wealthier. Trade meant that people's jobs became ever more specialised: in addition to farmers, we developed doctors, politicians, scientists, engineers and many others. It's worth remembering that our technological advances are all due to a **market economy** that allowed some people to specialise as thinkers and researchers.

market economy:
An economy in which consumer demand guides production and prices, and there is competition between privately owned businesses.

Specialisation—where one person makes shoes, while another grows grapes, and another provides legal services—creates a need for marketing, and in turn the gains from marketing allow for ever more efficient specialisation. The modern marketing economy supports very diverse specialisation: artists, brain surgeons, movie stars and even marketing scientists and marketing students.

The gains from specialisation and trading have been astonishing. When the marketing revolution was starting some 10,000 years ago there were only five to ten million people on the entire planet. They were all living (short lives) in conditions that we would today describe as miserable poverty. Today billions of people are supported by food production and marketing systems that provide amazing nutrition and variety. Consider that during the Roman Empire Italian cuisine featured no tomatoes, Thai cuisine had no coriander or chilli, and the French didn't even have any french fries! Trade (marketing) has made the world a far more interesting, and tasty, place.

TWO TYPES OF MARKETING PROFESSIONAL

LEARNING OBJECTIVE
Understand what marketing professionals do

There are two sorts of marketing professional. One is a 'doer', someone who spends most of their time doing things to promote and sell their company's brands. They act as specialised members of the **production department**, only instead of making products they make things such as brochures, web pages, promotional material and price lists. They commission designers, advertising and media agencies. They organise promotion events and in-store promotions. They collate and report sales figures and market research findings. There are marketing people who largely do the same things year after year.

production department:
The area of a business concerned with manufacturing the product.

The other, usually more senior, sort of marketing person makes informed marketing decisions and budget allocations. They design marketplace experiments and market research, they analyse data, and they are constantly learning which marketing strategies work better than others in which situations.

This book is mostly for these decision makers, or people aiming for senior marketing management. This textbook includes some deep knowledge and marketing discoveries that every marketing decision maker should know. Like professionals in other fields such as medicine, engineering

◢ **evidence-based marketing:** Marketing activities in which decisions are based on reliable, generalised knowledge about how the world works, how buyers buy and how market interventions work.

◢ **LEARNING OBJECTIVE**
Understand how marketing science is beginning to transform marketing theory and practice

◢ **marketing science:**
The study of marketing, which seeks to develop scientific laws and patterns that repeat under known conditions.

and architecture, marketers' decisions need to be informed by reliable knowledge about the way the world works. Such knowledge includes how advertising works, how price works and how consumers behave. This is what is called **evidence-based marketing**.

MARKETING SCIENCE

The first recorded university marketing course was only taught in 1902 (Bartels, 1951). For most of last century it was a discipline based on folk stories and mythology rather than any scientific study of the marketing world. Today marketing thought and practice is increasingly being informed by science.

Science is the formal study of the real (that is, empirical) world. Scientific laws allow us to understand and predict how the world behaves. **Marketing science** is the study of marketing—both buying and selling. It seeks to develop the generalised knowledge and scientific laws that inform evidence-based marketing.

Science itself is only a few hundred years old, and in that time has had a dramatic effect on every discipline that it has touched. For instance, for several thousand years medical knowledge consisted of elaborate theories that were passed down from doctor to doctor. Practically no systematic research was done and if results clashed with theory these findings tended to be dismissed or forgotten (rather than rejecting or modifying the incorrect theory). For example, the discovery that if doctors washed their hands far fewer women died from fever after giving birth was rejected and ignored because it didn't fit with theory (see Sharp & Wind, 2009). Similarly, it was discovered that fruit consumption prevented scurvy, but this discovery was then rejected or forgotten, over and over (Bown, 2005). For nearly two thousand years the dominant theory in Western medicine was that illness was caused by an imbalance in four 'humours' in the body (blood, phlegm, black bile and yellow bile) and procedures such as bleeding were widely practised to address such imbalances; such practices killed many people. Only comparatively recently were the effects of bleeding tested, and doctors discovered that it was far better to put blood back into patients than remove it. The first proven efficacious drug, aspirin, was mass marketed only as recently as last century (Jeffreys, 2005). The most junior intern today is a better doctor than the most brilliant, best educated, most renowned medieval doctor—science has transformed medicine from superstition and guesswork into a practice that works, and it gets better each year.

Marketing science is starting to affect the marketing profession in a similar way, sweeping away many myths and misplaced theories. But it is early days; most marketing professionals are unaware of even the most major discoveries of marketing science. They hold conflicting views that are based on guesses, rumour or fashion. Some marketers are scared of science, for much the same reasons as many medieval doctors rejected science: they don't understand it, or fear it will undermine their authority. Some marketers believe that nothing is predictable in marketing, but if this really were the case then it would be impossible for them, or anyone, to do their job. It turns out that there are regularities in marketing, just as there are in the rest of the physical and social worlds. We'll describe these discoveries in this textbook and discuss how they can be used to guide and predict the outcome of marketing actions.

Marketing science is sometimes called an 'applied discipline', the notion being that there are some pure disciplines (note the connotations of nobility and superiority) and then there are the applied disciplines. This mistaken idea is that marketing is really just a branch of psychology or economics. Using this logic, biology is just applied chemistry, and for that matter chemistry is just applied physics—which of course is nonsense: each of these disciplines have different focuses of inquiry. Similarly, marketing is not just applied psychology, nor is it applied economics, nor some mixture of the two (that is, behavioural economics).

Another argument is that marketing is an applied discipline because marketing knowledge is *used* by people (marketers). But all scientific knowledge is used—engineers, architects and many others apply physical science—so by this argument physics is an applied discipline.

Marketing science studies buying and selling. It has a pure focus that no other discipline can lay claim to. There are some other disciplines that apply such pure knowledge. The study of wine marketing, for instance, uses marketing knowledge and marketing's focus of inquiry but in a specific application area; there are many others ... financial services marketing, food marketing, tourism marketing and so on.

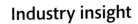

Industry insight

In 2008 the world's third-largest optometry retail chain, the UK-based Specsavers, aimed to enter the Australian consumer market and become a major player. At the time, the Luxottica Group, which has five brands (OPSM, Laubman & Pank, Sunglass Hut, Bright Eyes and Budget Eyewear) had the dominant share of optometry services—that is, supplying glasses and eyewear—with OPSM having a 35 per cent market share. Much of the rest of the market was served by small, locally based chains and sole practitioners. The market was worth around $1.5 billion in annual retail sales and was expected to grow by 2 per cent a year. The Luxottica Group had approximately 1000 stores in Australia and had tended to serve the upper end of the market, as its brands included Prada, Gucci, Bulgari, Persol and Ray-Ban. In the three years before Specsavers entered the market, the Luxottica Group had grown by 21 per cent. However,

Specsavers: Establishing a major brand in Australia

by David Corkindale

the global financial crisis that began in 2008 saw customers start to change their buying habits and switch to more affordable brands.

Specsavers' value proposition, the basis for winning customers in the market, is embodied in its name. It claims to offer glasses at a lesser price than its competitors, with offers in 2009 of two pairs of spectacles for the price of one starting from $179—and if you paid an additional $20, you could get two pairs of designer eyewear for $199. 'We have given Australian shoppers choice and what we brought into Australia is clear pricing—the price we advertise is the price you will pay at the cash counter. What you see is what you get,' Doug Perkins, one of the founders of Specsavers, said (Ooi, 2010).

For Specsavers, the provision of products in Australia was already in place, as it had entered Australia as a wholesaler in 2006. In order to become a major player in the provision of optometry services and products for consumers, it had to become widely available to them both physically, in convenient locations, and mentally. Its brand name needed to become associated with attributes such as trust and also very readily come to mind when people thought about purchasing glasses.

Specsavers set about putting in place a retail chain of conveniently located shops throughout Australia. The store roll-out was one of the fastest ever in Australian retailing history, with 100 stores rolled out in 100 days, and 150 stores operating by the end of 2008. This was partly achieved through buying out the small chains and sole practitioners who already had established their presence in the main shopping malls and shopping strips in cities and towns. To quickly establish a wide network of outlets, the company also relied on entrepreneurs to take up Specsavers franchises. By October 2010, Specsavers had 240 retail outlets in place.

In February 2008, Specsavers appointed a public relations (PR) company ahead of a planned mass media advertising campaign in August of that year. A market research company was commissioned to conduct research with small groups of people around the country into where they purchased glasses, why they went to certain optometrists, how much they spent and their perceptions about price (whether they felt that they were paying too much). Additional discussion topics included whether those interviewed had ever worn spectacles even though they didn't need to and who Australia's favourite spectacle-wearing celebrity was. Further research was conducted by another market research company to find out Australians' opinions about wearing glasses and whether these had changed, compared with fifty years ago.

The PR company sent stories about the arrival of Specsavers, and the claimed benefits to the Australian community through the news media. The research that had been undertaken gave the company data and publicity angles to gain the interest of the media in the impending launch of Specsavers and its main media advertising campaign. Subsequently, articles appeared in the media about Specsavers, their value proposition and their track record overseas. This started to build awareness in the community of the brand and its positive credentials.

In planning the launch, the market was seen as being all spectacle and contact lens wearers—young and old, rich and poor—with a slight skew towards the forty-plus age group, because people are more likely to need to wear some form of spectacles when they are forty years or over. It was recognised, however, that in promoting certain fashion-oriented products there would need to be a younger, more female skew. For the launch, it was decided to have a state-by-state roll-out program, including a media event in each state. The launch roll-out would start in Victoria and coincide with when the first stores opened in each state. The launch used Dame Mary Perkins, an award-winning businesswoman and co-founder of Specsavers (Butler, 2012), as a spokesperson. This provided an interesting media 'hook' and a person of interest for television interviews.

The state-by-state roll-out was designed as the best way to introduce Specsavers to the media, offering them their own state-based photo and interview opportunities and so gain local media coverage. Underlying the launch program were two key embodiments of the Specsavers brand's value proposition: professionalism and affordable fashion.

Specsavers identified that the most important messages to disseminate through the media were those surrounding issues of 'value for money', 'trustworthiness', 'successful concept', 'professionalism' and 'fashionableness'. The PR program of activities had the objective of growing Specsavers' brand recognition. In the first year of operation, this— together with the media advertising that commenced in August—drove consumer awareness to 30 per cent of the population. The company is reported to be spending $20 million a year on media advertising. Specsavers' advertising is also unashamedly focused on price: the Specsavers' traditional offer is two sets of frames for the price of one. Doug Perkins claimed late in 2009 that Specsavers had managed to push optical prices in Australia down by as much as 30 to 40 per cent, although competitors have refuted this. Whatever the actual figure, Specsavers' aggressive media advertising and PR allowed it to grab pricing leadership in the minds of consumers very quickly.

By the end of 2010, Specsavers had achieved a market share of 18.5 per cent and a reputed annual turnover of $340 million, beyond its initial target of $200 million.

MARKETING METRICS AND MARKET-BASED ASSETS

Every day, senior marketing executives have to interpret **marketing metrics**. In the same way that doctors make decisions based on metrics such as blood pressure, weight gain/loss and temperature, marketing managers use metrics to determine the health of their brands and to assess how their marketing decisions are affecting this health. In reading this textbook, you will learn how to correctly interpret such metrics and make better marketing decisions.

Marketers intervene in the marketplace, by changing what is commonly called the '**marketing mix**':

- the product or service
- pricing
- advertising and communication
- **distribution**.

The marketing mix is often called 'the 4Ps': product, price, promotion and place. In each of these aspects there is a huge range of options and many decisions that have to be made. Marketers can, and do, make a great many changes to their marketing mixes. For example, one consumer products company calculated that its marketers make 13,000 changes to packaging each year in the United States and Europe alone; that's 250 packaging changes each week, at a cost of more than US$50 million in design and printing costs. This can be activity for activity's sake (to keep staff busy), it can be misguided strategy that confuses consumers and causes losses in **sales** and **market share**, or it can maintain or improve the competitiveness of a company's brands. Capable marketers

marketing metrics: Measures used to evaluate marketing actions and brand performance, and to inform marketing decisions.

marketing mix: Set of manageable elements in a brand's marketing plan, adjusted to implement the marketing strategy: product, price, promotion and place.

distribution: Making goods and services physically available to buyers. This can involve selecting retailers to sell the product and supplying them with the goods.

sales: Total revenue or number of products sold during a given time frame.

market share: The total category sales that are devoted to a particular brand. It can be measured in terms of units sold, volume or dollars.

use marketing metrics to assess whether actions need to be taken, and to evaluate the impact of their actions, so that they are more likely to make the right changes.

The most commonly used marketing metric is sales, usually expressed in dollars of revenue, or units sold. More sophisticated marketers will also use a market share metric, because sales can still rise in a growing market when the brand is actually losing competitiveness.

While these measures are important, they need to be interpreted in context. Company profits can be inflated by cutting necessary expenditure (like advertising), and in a similar way sales and market share can be 'bought' with activities that deliver sales today at the expense of sales in the future. As Tim Ambler from London Business School points out, a farmer whose crops depend on irrigation from a river that flows through the farm should be intensely interested in what is happening upstream. Marketers need metrics that give insight into the likelihood of *future* sales— how risky are today's cash-flows, and how likely are they to keep flowing? **Sustainable marketing** is inherently concerned with the long term, and hence with risk—we'll discuss this in more detail at the end of this chapter.

Examples of marketing metrics commonly used by marketing managers are:

- sales (in units or dollars)
- profit contribution per sale
- market share (in units or dollars)
- percentage of sales sold on price discount
- percentage of repeat sales
- percentage of satisfied customers
- number of customers
- brand awareness (percentage)
- average number of purchases per customer
- total advertising spend
- number of customers exposed to advertising
- average number of advertisement exposures
- number of distribution outlets
- sales per outlet.

Marketing interventions, such as a new advertising campaign, don't just deliver sales today; they also contribute to the maintenance and building of **market-based assets** that determine the likelihood of future sales. The two principal market-based assets are **mental availability** and **physical availability**. Together they determine how easy a brand is to buy and for how many people. Coca-Cola has tremendous market-based assets. First, the brand is known by practically everyone: they know what Coke is, what it tastes like, what the cans and bottles look like, where to buy it and roughly how much it costs. Most importantly, billions of people sometimes notice or think about Coca-Cola—this is great mental availability. Second, Coca-Cola is physically available in nearly every supermarket and convenience store, there are vending machines in likely (and some unlikely) places that run twenty-four hours a day, and cafés and restaurants sell it too; this is great physical availability. The Coca-Cola Company has been working for decades to build these assets and continues to do so. Coca-Cola's sales today depend more on these two assets than on the current

sustainable marketing:
Marketing that involves an ongoing analysis of long-term risks in order to ensue that the business model and customer demand is sustainable.

marketing interventions:
The different actions that marketers carry out in order to meet strategic goals and grow their brand; for example advertising campaigns.

market-based assets:
The mental and physical availability that makes a brand easier to buy for more people, in more situations.

mental availability: The likelihood of a brand being noticed and/or thought of in buying situations.

physical availability:
How often the product or service is literally available in a buying situation.

level of advertising, or what price (or discount) it decides to charge today. Coca-Cola's sales are very likely next year to be at least as good as this year's sales, and they look secure for a very long time, because these market-based assets can't erode overnight.

Market-based assets constitute much of the value of any successful company. For example, the Google corporation in 2012 is worth around US$200 billion, yet it only owns net assets (such as computers, furniture, cars and cash) worth around US$30 billion, so the bulk of its value lies in its intangible assets. Some of these assets are special knowledge, patents and systems; the rest are market-based assets. The Google name, and the web domain <www.google.com>, are worth far more than any of the buildings that Google owns. When people think of searching online, they think of Google, and it's this mental availability that allows Google to sell search advertising that generates billions in revenue.

Marketers are the chief custodians of market-based assets. Their actions should maintain and hopefully expand mental and physical availability for their brands. They should have good measures (metrics) of these assets. They should know which actions are more or less likely to build these assets. Unfortunately, many marketers neither understand nor measure these assets, so they are not managing them. Without proper measurement systems in place, marketers can often unknowingly do things that damage these assets while they chase temporary sales or profits.

CRITICAL REFLECTION

1 Coca-Cola spends almost US$3 billion dollars on advertising across the globe for its brands. Considering the strength of the market-based assets of their main brands, do you think this level of spend is justified? Why or why not?

2 What do you think would happen to Coca-Cola's market share if they completely stopped all advertising for one month? Would the market-based assets continue to support the brand? What about after one year? And after ten years?

3 Coca-Cola has the advantage of being a very big and well-known brand—with a very big budget. What about small companies and new or unknown brands? How can they grow their market and build their mental and physical availability?

CUSTOMER NEEDS AND WANTS

One of the key roles of marketing people is to help the organisation understand customer needs (things that are essential or very important) and how these translate into wants. Market research, observing and surveying customers, is therefore a very important responsibility of the marketing department.

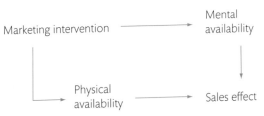

●●● **FIGURE 1.1** THE EFFECT OF THE MARKETING MIX ON SALES IS MODERATED BY MENTAL AND PHYSICAL AVAILABILITY

Marketers also have a responsibility to encourage a company culture that is responsive to customer demand. Professionals have a tendency to become absorbed in the technicalities of their profession and forget about customers. Finance managers think about money and easily forget that it comes from customers buying the firm's services and products. Engineers think about the technical details of their products and easily forget that customers may not value or understand these features. We've all encountered service people in stores, cafés and banks who act as if we, the customers, are nothing but a nuisance getting in the way of them doing their job. But customers are the only reason that any firm exists, and if they decide they don't need the firm any more then it fails. Even very well-meaning service providers such as hospitals, local governments and schools often get wrapped up in their own internal issues and fail to consider what the people they are trying to help really need or want.

Case study

Starship Children's Health: Addressing customer needs

Starship Hospital, run by Starship Children's Health, in Auckland, New Zealand, is specially for children. The entire building is shaped like a spaceship—hence the name. But the attention to the needs of their special customers goes much further than this. Every ward has an allocation of toys, and every child has a personal play coordinator to check that they are happy. When children interact with doctors, there are child advocates on hand whose primary job it is to think from the child's perspective and say things that the child may be unable or scared to say—like 'please put the drip into my broken arm so that I will still have one arm free to play with toys'. This is explicit recognition of the fact that doctors, who are trained to think of the physical medical requirements of the patient, may have difficulty also thinking of the customer needs of the child.

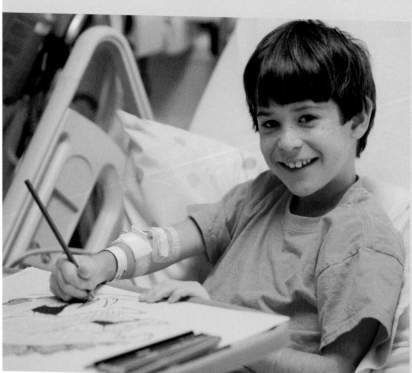

Questions

1 Why do you think that Starship Hospital has employed extra people especially for the job of monitoring the children's needs? Do you think this could be managed by the doctors, nurses or parents of the children instead?

2 What are the key benefits for the hospital in employing child advocates and play coordinators?

3   A large children's hospital in Australia is suffering from bad press. Local news stations are reporting that the doctors at the hospital are insensitive to the children's needs. Imagine that you are in charge of marketing at this hospital. What would you do?

4   Think of a scenario in a general hospital (not one specific to children) where it would be very important for individual customer needs to be considered.

Without maintaining an up-to-date appreciation of what customers might want, a firm risks missing market opportunities and being replaced by competitors who can serve customers better. In the early 2000s, McDonald's was floundering, sales growth had stalled, and people were eating better quality food and coffee. Starbucks had ridden the coffee trend in the United States, opening hundreds of stores, right under the nose of McDonald's. Subway was another outstanding success, simply selling fresh sandwiches and salads. McDonald's market research told them that group decisions to eat at McDonald's were often being vetoed by one or two people in the group, particularly women, who were health- or weight-conscious; that is, Mum was often saying no. While McDonald's had been working hard to further streamline their operations and reduce costs in order to be competitive, they had lost sight of their customers. Led by Australian-born CEO Charlie Bell, they eventually reacted with menu changes to introduce salads, then sandwich wraps, then coffee with McCafé. They even worked with nutritionists to reduce salt, sugar and fat in their products. They began more upbeat advertising, starting with the 'I'm Lovin' It' **campaign** featuring Justin Timberlake. Fortunately, McDonald's had considerable mental and physical availability, so once they rejuvenated their marketing mix to match current customer demands their sales growth rebounded. Each change was an outstanding success, and gave them the confidence to embark on serious upgrades to their stores and to open for longer hours (in many cases twenty-four hours a day), further improving their physical availability.

▲ **campaign:** A planned series of advertisements that appear in one or more media over a specific time period. The advertisements often share an idea or theme.

◢ **LEARNING OBJECTIVE**
Understand the concept of sustainable marketing and the dilemmas that marketers face in balancing short-term and long-term objectives

SUSTAINABLE MARKETING

It's often said that 'the customer is always right', and there is a great deal of truth in this statement. Firms have to understand customer tastes, perceptions and needs. However, it is a mistake to think that marketing is always about giving people what they want. The brewery that gives away free beer is terribly customer-oriented, and will have many satisfied customers—but not for long because the brewery will go broke. Customers may want things now that in the long run will hurt them or the planet. Sometimes it is better to embark on the difficult task of teaching customers to buy something different rather than simply give them what they want today. The concept of sustainable marketing acknowledges these complex issues. The aim of sustainable marketing is to provide long-term customer satisfaction. To do that, a firm must ensure both that their **business model** is financially sustainable and that customer demand is **sustainable**. That must include considering the effect of the production, marketing and consumption on society and the environment.

◢ **business model:** The way a business competes and makes money; for example Google's business model is to provide free search services to consumers and then sell search advertising to businesses.

◢ **sustainable:** Able to be maintained perpetually.

The global financial crisis that began in 2008 was sparked by unsustainable marketing practices. Financial institutions, predominantly in the United States, sold home loans to people who had very little capacity to pay back the loans within the loan periods. The slightest downturn in these people's circumstances or rise in interest rates would result in them being unable to meet their interest payments. These consumers used the loans to build and buy large houses far beyond their means, and in doing so pushed up US house prices to crazy levels. When people started defaulting on their home loan payments, the house price bubble burst; house prices plummeted, leaving some banks owed billions of dollars that had been secured against houses that were worth very little. The banking system reacted in fear, interest rates rose and banks were unwilling to lend money to any business they weren't incredibly sure about. This stifled business growth and led to job lay-offs, meaning that even more people could not meet their loan payments. A terrible spiral down into economic recession was all started by unsustainable marketing.

Many products have undesirable side effects. Cars, for instance, are an extremely popular product. They give us freedom and opportunity and save us much work; consequently, we are willing to spend large amounts of money to buy them—we really like our cars. But the World Health Organization estimates that car crashes kill around 1.2 million people a year and injure as many as 50 million people. That's worse than many major wars. Particularly disturbing is the fact that many of those killed are not car drivers but pedestrians and cyclists—a car is a dangerous weapon. These statistics oblige car marketers to work on ways to make their products less dangerous for their customers. This includes:

- researching and developing new safety features
- telling (advertising to) consumers about the importance of safety features, so that when buying they look for and are willing to pay for these features
- working with government authorities on driver education campaigns
- lobbying and supporting governments to improve road signage, reduce speed limits and add pedestrian crossings and bike lanes.

There is a clear moral duty to make car driving safer, and it also makes obvious business sense not to kill future customers—and to make your product safer so that you avoid being punished with legislation and taxes, or replaced with safer alternatives. In the past, the ethical principle (and business sense) of sustainable marketing has not been embraced by companies as well as it is today. In the 1960s, US car manufacturers were accused by consumer advocate Ralph Nader of marketing some particularly dangerous cars. *The New York Times* reported that General Motors reacted by hiring private detectives to tap Nader's phone and investigate him, looking for ways to discredit him (Nader subsequently successfully sued the company for invasion of privacy). In 1966 the US government legislated to require car companies to install safety features such as seatbelts.

The failure of the US car industry to invest in safety gave them temporarily higher profits, but it helped European (for example Volkswagen) and Japanese (for example Honda and Toyota) firms enter and succeed in the US market.

▼ CRITICAL REFLECTION

1　Do you think the car industry is doing enough today? If you were a car marketer how would you react to proposals to lower speed limits?

2　Can you think of other products that have some adverse side effects? Are the marketers of these products practising sustainable marketing? Are they thinking long term or just giving consumers what they demand today?

Some firms market to other organisations (businesses, governments or not-for-profit organisations) rather than individuals or households. This is called **business-to-business marketing**. For example, Alcoa markets to manufacturers that use aluminium as a raw material for their own products (such as aluminium beverage cans, engine components and window frames). Bosch provides automotive parts and accessories to various car manufacturers throughout the world. In Australia, Elders Limited acts as a sales agent for many grain, meat and wool producers, and also provides various agricultural products and services (such as farm equipment, fertilisers and agronomic advice) to agricultural producers.

Marketing executives in such firms need to understand not just the needs of their customers (such as a car manufacturer or an Australian wheat producer), but also developments within the markets served by their customers. For example, marketing executives at Bosch should identify and understand consumer preferences for luxury cars, rather than just the needs of BMW with respect to automotive parts and accessories, when identifying how best to promote their products and services to that firm.

Since the largest of organisational customers spend millions or even billions of dollars annually on some products, business-to-business marketing executives in some firms in effect treat each of their largest customers as a virtual market, developing a customised marketing mix for each 'mega-customer'. For such a customer, the product or service would be customised (such as a Bosch automotive components being designed for a specific BMW car model); pricing would be negotiated based on individual customer- and product-related factors; and distribution arrangements would be based on customer requirements (such as just-in-time delivery to factories in various countries, with quantities based on planned manufacturing levels at each location, which in turn are based on forecast sales of the relevant car model in different geographic markets). In addition, Bosch might establish a global team of marketing and logistics executives to coordinate communication and other customer-related activities to service BMW. Naturally, Bosch would expect BMW to commit contractually to purchasing the components for the life of the car model.

Application to business-to-business marketing

CONCLUSION

Economic theorists used to be unsure of whether there would be any difference in performance between a market economy and a **centrally planned economy**. Last century, a number of countries, such as China and the USSR, experimented with running their countries with a reduced number of markets; they allowed little or no advertising, and in many cases a single brand (for example one brand of car or one brand of chocolate) was produced in government-overseen factories. It was hoped that by reducing the costs of marketing there might be efficiency gains. These economic experiments produced dramatic findings: market economies produce vastly more output, more variety of products and services, more innovation and more satisfied consumers. Today countries such as China and Russia are market economies; advertising and brand competition are back, their economies are growing again, and there have also been dramatic improvements in the life expectancy of their citizens.

◢ **business-to-business (B2B) marketing:** Marketing products or services to other businesses rather than to consumers.

◢ **centrally planned economy:** An economy that is controlled by the government. Instead of fluctuating with demand, prices are set by the government, which also determines what will be produced, who will produce it and how much they will be paid.

Modern markets aren't perfect but they are very important and necessary. Marketing professionals play a crucial role in making sure the system works, that firms produce the products and services that customers really want. Marketing is a necessary and important business function. More than any other part of the business, marketing is responsible for understanding customers—their needs and wants now and in the future. It's an exciting profession to be a part of.

'Business has only two functions—marketing and innovation.'

—Professor Peter Drucker, management theorist

●●● **FIGURE 1.2** THE RED OCTOBER FACTORY IN MOSCOW

Russians love chocolate and today Russians eat as as much of it as people in other North European countries (which have among the highest per capita consumption in the world), but back in the Soviet era, when Russia was not a market economy, Red October was the only chocolate brand in Russia and chocolate was a very rare treat.

Case study

Mike's Milk: Making marketing decisions

By Elizabeth Gunner

Mike's Milk has been operating for twenty years. Over this time they have grown from a small dairy selling only at local farmers markets to a huge business that stocks supermarket shelves all over Australia. As the company grew, they needed more employees—a board of directors, accountants, business managers, payroll officers and marketing staff—to manage the business. The new director of marketing spent the first month of the job sitting at his desk writing a marketing plan and projecting future market share. At the end of the month, he gave a presentation to the board of directors and suggested two key changes to improve future revenue: a name change to something 'with less of a small-town feel' and a package redesign to something 'more eye-catching'. He suggested that these changes be implemented as soon as possible and that they do lots of advertising just before and shortly after the launch. After the meeting the board discussed the suggestions. They were split down the middle: half thought that the existing package and brand name were out of date and that for growth they needed a change, but the other half felt that the growth so far had come as a result of the name 'Mike's Milk', so why should they change it?

Questions

1   What do you think that the company should do? Why?

2   If the board decided to implement the changes, how do you think the mental and physical availability of Mike's Milk would be affected?

3   If you had been appointed as marketing director for Mike's Milk, what indicators would you have used to make recommendations for the brand?

4   What do you think would happen to the market share of Cadbury chocolate if they changed their name and got rid of their well-known purple package?

5   Think of a scenario where a company would benefit from changing the brand name and package.

01

SUMMARY

- The role of the marketer is to understand consumer behaviour and recognise market opportunities so that the organisation can adapt and stay competitive.

- Market research is one of the most important tools of marketing, helping us to understand buyer behaviour.

- Marketers should practise evidence-based marketing and inform decisions with scientific knowledge about the way the world works, how advertising works, how price works and how consumers behave.

- Marketers measure metrics to track the performance of their brand and aid decision making. If marketers do not understand how to measure metrics or analyse them in context, they risk making decisions that will damage their brand.

- Marketers are in charge of protecting a brand's market-based assets. Marketers aim to maintain and hopefully expand the mental and physical availiability of their brands.

- Sustainable marketing focuses on long-term customer satisfaction and a financially sustainable business model.

- Although marketing science is sweeping away many myths and misplaced theories, it is still in its early days and many marketing professionals are unaware of even the most major discoveries of marketing science.

REVISION QUESTIONS

1 A person goes into a pharmacy and tells the shop assistant that they have cut their knee. They ask for a bandage to deal with it. The assistant goes to the shelf where bandages are displayed and gives a well-known brand to the customer, who then pays for it and departs. Does this episode display good marketing practice? Give your reasons, using points made in this chapter.

2 Managers use marketing activities to help increase demand for what their organisation can provide. Think of at least one situation where demand or use of something might be desired to be reduced in the community, and think of a marketing activity that could be used to reduce this demand.

3 Think of other activities, beyond those cited in the chapter as the 'marketing mix', that managers in an organisation could use to stimulate a response from a marketplace. List any that start with the letter 'P' and try to find at least five.

4 Lifeline is a social service started by the Uniting Church in Australia that, among other things, offers a free help and counselling service over the phone for people who have a personal crisis in their life. List some of the needs and wants of:

a   individual donors who give money to support Lifeline

b   volunteers who give their time to Lifeline.

5   When you use Google to search for an item, on the results page there are little advertisements that are listed down the right-hand side of the page, as well as along the top and the bottom. When a person clicks on an advertisement, it is called a 'click through', and these are counted over time for all the advertisements that appear on that page. For everyone who searches for the item, the percentage that clicks on each advertisement is calculated and called the click-through rate (CTR).

For all advertisements for a search item that appear in position 1 in the list, the average click-through rate is 8 per cent, for those in position 2 it is 4 per cent, position 3 is 2 per cent and for position 5 it is 1.5 per cent. Draw a simple graph of this, with CTRs on the y-axis (the vertical one, and start it from zero at the bottom) and the position of an advert on the x-axis (horizontal).

If a marketing manager was planning to have a Google search advertisement and believed it would gain position 7, what would be your estimate of the CTRs it would receive?

6   In this chapter, it says in relation to marketing metrics: 'More sophisticated marketers will also use a market share metric, because sales can still rise in a growing market when the brand is actually losing competitiveness.' Explain this statement by explaining why having increased sales in a total market that is also increasing could mean you are not being as successful as you should be. It will help if you use a specific example of a product, such as a soft drink, in its overall market.

7   Some organisations do not feel that they need to think about marketing and/or employ any marketing people. What would be the circumstances, do you think, that might encourage them to think this way? Would there still be value in them paying attention to marketing management?

8   Important market-based assets are mental and physical availability. Give examples of what these might be for services such as:

a   an accountant

b   a person who has just graduated and is a freelance graphic designer

c   a well-established political party.

9   The research department of a national bakery company, that had sixty large bakeries around the country to supply supermarkets, developed an ingredient that would keep bread products tasting fresh even when they were three weeks old. The company was not doing well financially and thought it should try to cut costs to help with this situation. The company closed over half the bakeries and saved a lot of money in production costs by making all its bread products in those bakeries that were left and delivering larger batches of bread to its supermarket customers around the country once every three weeks, rather than weekly. What do you think might have happened to demand for its bread over the months that followed this decision, and why?

FURTHER READING

Ellis, N (2011) *Business-to-Business Marketing: Relationships, Networks & Strategies*, Oxford University Press, Oxford.

Seddon, G (1970) *Swan River Landscapes*, University of Western Australia Press, Perth.

WEBLINKS

Marketing:
   http://en.wikipedia.org/wiki/Marketing

Starship Children's Health:
   www.starship.org.nz

▲ **Major case study**

Kerry Sanderson, AO– Marketing a lifetime of service to business and government

By Steve Klomp, Murdoch Business School, Murdoch University, Western Australia

Kerry Sanderson, AO, is one of the most successful public sector career professionals Western Australia has produced. Through more than forty years of service she has built up a reputation of excellence and expertise that has made her sought after in the boardrooms of the private sector and seen as a respected voice, influencing the shaping of Australia's future.

This quietly spoken woman doesn't fit the image of the corporate high flyer. Very much a team player, her management style centres on influencing team thinking and structuring long-term planning. Not for her the dictatorial leadership and rash decision making that were the hallmark of so many failed business and government leaders in Western Australia in the 1980s!

Kerry Sanderson rose to prominence in late 1991 when she took over the role of CEO of Fremantle Ports. This was not her first big role—she had spent seventeen years in the Department of Treasury and four more at the Department of Transport—but it was certainly a high-profile appointment.

At the time, many in business and government circles argued that Kerry had been handed a poisoned chalice. Fremantle Ports had suffered a financial loss of more than $70 million in the previous year, container handling efficiency was nearly as low as staff morale, and few believed the unionised workforce could be dealt with successfully. Staff were resigned to a bleak future for the port of Fremantle, and the people of Western Australia cringed with embarrassment over the port's reputation.

However, the appointment proved to be a masterstroke by the then Minister for Transport, Pam Beggs. It signalled change was going to happen and that management were committed to finding solutions to long-standing problems using a more cooperative approach.

Kerry Sanderson graduated with a science degree (mathematics) from the University of Western Australia and later completed an economics degree. The widowed mother of two adult sons, she is very family oriented and has a great sense of tradition and community obligation. Her loyalty to her friends and work colleagues is well known, yet at the same time she is apolitical and self-deprecating.

Her lifetime of work saw her nominated for an Order of Australia for services to shipping, transport and governance. While it is her highest accolade, it is hardly the only award she has received. Kerry was the Telstra WA Business Woman of the Year in 1996, and in 2005 was the inaugural inductee to the Lloyd's List Maritime Hall of Fame—no mean feat for a woman in a traditionally man's world. She was also awarded an honorary doctorate from the University of Western Australia in 2005.

This quietly spoken woman doesn't fit the image of the corporate high flyer. Very much a team player, her management style centres on influencing team thinking and structuring long-term planning.

Today, Fremantle Ports has world-standard efficiency in terms of crane rates, taking into account the level of capital investment and the scale of operations.

Here is what she has to say about her time at Fremantle Ports:

It became obvious to me very early that Fremantle was a unique place. It had a very dedicated but very frustrated workforce, and union movement that were very keen to see the place succeed. It was inefficient, yes, but there were structural and process reasons for that I was determined to fix.

I knew my financial experience and workplace reform experience was going to be useful, but I also knew that reform was going to come through teamwork and a commitment to staff. I wanted to see our staff commit to the long term, and that meant that I had to commit to them long term. In my time there we achieved massive change in thinking, in processes and in a team approach to problem solving. However, even that wasn't enough in itself. We had to also use a total quality framework analysis (later the Australian Business Excellence Framework) to work out where our inefficiencies lay and set new processes in place.

Fremantle Ports actually had two small and spatially separated container terminals—an inherently inefficient situation. We consolidated both terminals into one continuous berth line and increased their size. These physical changes, along with significant waterfront reform, saw an almost immediate improvement in efficiency. Fremantle's container handling rates went from twelve to more than twenty per hour. Later, Fremantle Ports bought the bulk handling business in the outer harbour from BHP (now BHP Billiton).

The enterprise has never looked back. In 2007 we achieved a Gold Award under the internationally recognised Australian Business Excellence Framework. Fremantle Ports also received the Excellence Award for the highest awarded company nationally, and a Gold Award in the People category. This involved demonstrating increasing performance across all areas including data use and processes, continuous improvement and the monitoring of results.

Today, Fremantle Ports has world-standard efficiency in terms of crane rates, taking into account the level of capital investment and the scale of operations.

Kerry Sanderson is passionate about the future of Western Australia, particularly Perth. She sits on a steering committee for the Committee for Perth, which puts out discussion papers on what kind of city Perth should be and how to get there.

We are happy to contribute to the thinking on the future of the City. By 2050 there will be 3.5 million people living here. We have to plan for that so that our environment, our amenity and our prosperity are not compromised. It is exciting, but we need to plan. The rest of Australia doesn't seem to have woken up to Perth and its potential. We already have more listed companies per capita than both Melbourne and Sydney. For example, Wesfarmers, Woodside, iiNet, Shell and Rio Tinto all have their headquarters or their regional headquarters here, just to name a few.

On the other hand, we also have an underdeveloped public transport system and we have concerns with our carbon footprint, urban sprawl and water use.

Kerry has an articulate vision of how these issues could be tackled:

I support development around transport hubs, with shopping centres entertainment and residential areas around train lines. I love railways! They are perhaps the most efficient form of public transport, but we have only 173 kilometres of train track in Perth, whereas Sydney has around 1500 kilometres.

Buses are important too, which is why I very much supported the decision to make buses in the central city free of charge. I also think we need to look more at alternative forms of work, such as telecommuting.

Perth and Western Australia could also have the scientific research sector as the second plank in our economic base: we already have world-class oil and gas research here, agricultural research, physics, radio astronomy, bio-medical, bio-technology and others. Our research base is strong but there is room for a lot more. We also need more focus on innovation and education.

Perth needs to embrace multiculturalism more. In many ways we are better in this area than the rest of Australia, but not as good as, for example, the UK. Multiculturalism is wonderful if you embrace it; tough if you oppose it.

A member of a number of boards for organisations such as Downer EDI Limited, Atlas Iron Limited and St John of God Health Care, Kerry shows no signs of slowing down. She also has very strong views on the role of business in the community:

Business should work with government to achieve community objectives. Corporate social responsibility should not simply be a marketing exercise; it should be a commitment to the long-term prosperity of the community by organisations that profit from that community.

Corporate social responsibility should also be a commitment to the environment. It makes good business sense anyway: companies can't continue to take resources from the environment without helping it to be self-sustaining.

Organisations with which I am associated all look to contributing to the community. For example, St John of God Health Care, which has hospitals in Perth and in country Western Australia, in the eastern states of Australia and also in New Zealand, contributes 2 per cent of its profit to the community, with a strong emphasis in the field of the health of Indigenous families.

Similar to Fremantle Ports, St John of God Health Care is also committed to its staff in the long term. Staff who remain with an organisation longer build up expertise, knowledge and loyalty that is too valuable to ignore, and they are much more likely to identify with the vision of the organisation than short-term or contract employees.

Kerry Sanderson left Fremantle Ports to take up the position of Agent-General for Western Australia in London for three years, leaving the UK only after surrendering her fight with the cold English winters. She was originally appointed by Labor Premier Alan Carpenter, but took up the appointment with the endorsement of Colin Barnett's Liberal government in 2008, which demonstrates the respect with which she is held on both sides of the political divide.

Kerry defines success in the following way:

Money and career are important, but other things measure success a lot better. My friend, the late George Seddon, is an example. He was a professor of landscaping, architecture and many other fields. He left us *Swan River Landscapes* (1970) and got the public comfortable saving water by using native plants in our gardens. He was a great success, but not in the conventional sense.

My grandmother is another example. She was a huge support to our family. I remember her determination and willingness to help us all.

Success is all about the example you set, supporting others and the influence you can have on people.

Kerry has the following advice for up-and-coming young professionals:

Do what you love to do, work with people who have the same values as you, be determined and committed to the long-term goal, aim high, and take a team approach to everything. At the same time, balance your life with family, fun, learning and community.

Case study based on interview with Kerry Sanderson on 3 March 2012.

Do what you love to do, work with people who have the same values as you, be determined and committed to the long-term goal, aim high, and take a team approach to everything. At the same time, balance your life with family, fun, learning and community.

Questions

1   What is marketing and what do marketing professionals do? Is Kerry Sanderson a marketing professional?

2   Why is Kerry Sanderson in demand for positions on the boards of major companies and organisations?

3   Consider the relationship between ethics and marketing. Why are these two concepts not at odds with each other?

4   Define the term 'sustainable marketing'. Choose a company you know and discuss how that company applies the principle of sustainable marketing.

5   What is marketing science? Consider the stakeholders at Fremantle Ports and consider what marketing metrics might be gathered to satisfy the information and product needs of three stakeholders.

6   Marketers face many options and decisions every day. What dilemmas did Kerry Sanderson face in balancing the short-term and long-term objectives of Fremantle Ports?

Practitioner profile

Bruce McColl, Global Chief Marketing Officer, Mars, Incorporated

It all started with a sales job that I landed in a pharmaceutical company after completing an economics degree at Monash University. This eventually led to a brand management position within the same company. Five years later, I 'landed on Mars' and have never left. My experience with Mars has moved me from Australia to New Zealand and to Russia (see case study on page 45) and Western Europe, in various senior operational roles and across different brands. I became Global Chief Marketing Officer after nineteen years of working as a marketing professional. I'd worked in all the key product divisions of the company, so I was well networked on a global level and I had seen and learnt from countless marketing successes—and failures too.

Mars is the perfect company for me to grow as a marketer because it encourages knowledge development—even now I'm constantly learning and discovering. One of the great things about my role as Global CMO is the opportunity to share my experiences with other marketers, particularly through Mars University, a unique internal training program designed to develop a strong base of talented marketing associates. I work closely with marketers across the organisation to develop knowledge so the team shares a common understanding about the science of marketing. It's essential to ensure that Mars' global brand strategies are executed and that all marketers can contribute independently to the organisation's growth. My advice for young marketers is to find an organisation that will support your development.

I also believe it is critical that you share similar values with the organisation: ideally, a company that encourages you to put those values into practice. I feel strongly that all companies have a responsibility to have a positive effect on society and the planet, so it was important for me to work for an organisation that embraced those ideals. Today, part of my role is finding innovative ideas to involve our brands in social change (like the Pedigree Adoption Program). Those ideals are a big part of the reason I've been with Mars for all these years. Finding the right fit for you can make difference between a job for now and a lifetime career.

02

CONSUMER BEHAVIOUR AND BUSINESS BUYER BEHAVIOUR

BYRON SHARP, WITH CONTRIBUTION FROM SVETLANA BOGOMOLOVA, MARIANTHI LIVADITIS AND MAGDA NENYCZ-THIEL

◢ Introduction case

The best burger: Why loyalty is limited

By Elizabeth Gunner

No marketer should expect *all* their customers to be like Don—yet plenty of marketers (and textbooks) maintain that one of the most important roles of a marketer is to get existing customers to buy more, to love the brand and to be 100 per cent loyal, or close to it.

Imagine that you are the marketing manager for McDonald's. Which of the following consumers is a better customer for you?

Don: I eat McDonald's every day. I have never tried another hamburger, and I never will.

William: I don't eat junk food very often, but every now and again I grab a burger. When I do I usually get Hungry Jack's because it's just around the corner—but sometimes I go to McDonald's.

Don obviously wins. Clearly he's a lot more profitable, and because he loves the brand, he's perhaps spreading some positive word-of-mouth. But now take off your marketing hat and read the responses again. Don is definitely a bit unusual—who eats the same thing every day? No marketer should expect *all* their customers to be like Don—yet plenty of marketers (and textbooks) maintain that one of the most important roles of a marketer is to get existing customers to buy more, to love the brand and to be 100 per cent loyal, or close to it; that is, they want people to be more like Don. After all, the more people buy your brand and the less they buy your competitors' the better, right? But what about all those people like William out there? Common sense (not to mention decades of marketing research) says that there are a *lot* of them. But they're never going to become heavy buyers, they are never going to *love* the brand, and they won't become 100 per cent loyal. So should we ignore them? Most customers are like William; hardly anyone is like Don.

INTRODUCTION

Marketers spend a lot of effort, time and money developing strategies to grow their brands, launching new products, and producing advertisements, price promotions and public relations (PR) campaigns.

Marketers sometimes feel that all this time and money should translate into loving, caring, loyal buyers who feel a special connection with the brands they purchase. But the reality is that most of the time people are too busy getting on with the rest of life's decisions to care deeply about brands. People don't have time to agonise over a brand of deodorant, so they make a quick choice—often based on convenience or habit. Sometimes they forget about brands, even ones that they've tried and liked. And they're fickle—what they think about your brand one day will probably be different the next.

So what's the point? Why do marketers bother?

In this chapter, you will learn about loyalty, attitudes, memory and motivations—and the importance of mental as well as physical availability. Marketers do have an important role to play, and marketing is a useful tool—but it's not possible to make good marketing decisions without first understanding buyer behaviour.

///

LEARNING OBJECTIVES

After reading this chapter you should:

- understand why consumer behaviour is an essential aspect of marketing
- understand how buyers buy brands, and how much they research brand choice decisions
- understand how memory and mental availability affect consumer attitudes and loyalty
- begin to understand the differences between target marketing and mass marketing
- understand what marketers should expect from their customers in terms of attitudes and behaviours.

///

CHAPTER OUTLINE

Introduction

Knowledge is power

Most buying is repeat-buying

High-involvement decisions

Natural loyalty

Loyal switchers

Prosaic, not passionate, loyalty

The importance of memory

Why do consumers forget about us?

Emotional rational buyers

Consumer motivations

Heterogeneous consumers

Do our buyers like us?

Conclusion

///

KEY TERMS

100% loyals	empirical	product variation
(brand) attributes (in memory)	heuristics	repeat-purchasing (or repeat-buying)
'black box'	light buyer	
brand performance metrics	loyalty (in a behavioural sense)	repertoire
category	mass marketing	satisfice
choice situation	memory structures	share of mind
demographic groups	panel data	target marketing
differentiation	polygamous (or divided) loyalty	target segment (or target group)
double jeopardy law		

KNOWLEDGE IS POWER

LEARNING OBJECTIVE
Understand why consumer behaviour is an essential aspect of marketing

When you work in marketing, you will be looked to as having a better understanding of the firm's clients than anyone else in the organisation. This doesn't mean that you have to have a deep understanding of the psychology of each of your many different customers—that would be impossible (having deep understanding of the psychology of even a few customers is most unlikely)—but you'll be gradually improving your understanding of how different factors affect their buying behaviour. Meanwhile, many of the daily marketing decisions you make will be based on knowing:

- who buys?
- where?
- when?
- how much?

You will find it essential to keep track of this descriptive data for current and potential buyers: what they buy, what they watch and how consumption of your brand fits into their lives. But data is meaningless until it is interpreted, and the best-educated marketers interpret these data in light of known, law-like patterns. These patterns help them know what to look for and to spot unusual happenings. For instance, there are patterns in buying metrics that apply to industrial purchases (such as concrete and aviation fuel), brand purchases in shops, and choice of store itself. In this chapter, we don't describe these law-like patterns in detail, but instead discuss what they tell us about buying behaviour and brand attitudes.

The more traditional marketers base their views of buyer behaviour on their intuition and introspection. They prefer to learn about the buying behaviour of others by observing their own behaviour, attitudes and opinions. This is often very misleading because marketing executives are very different from their customers—they are usually better educated and better paid, but most importantly the brand means so much more to them than to consumers, because it pays their salaries! So marketers are likely to have a different view of the world (and the brand) than their buyers. That's why market research is so important—you simply can't rely on your intuition or asking your colleagues.

Fortunately, marketers are well served by a professional market research industry that consists of giants such as Nielsen and Kantar, who provide many different services in many countries, as well as numerous local specialised market research agencies. The core business of these market researchers is to conduct surveys that record the behaviours of consumers (for example watching, shopping, buying and consuming) and/or consumers' perceptions and opinions. Marketers should then interpret this information in light of what is known about the fundamentals of buying behaviour (and human psychology). In this chapter we introduce some of these fundamentals.

LEARNING OBJECTIVE
Understand how buyers buy brands, and how much they research brand choice decisions

category: A grouping of all brands that are selling the same product or providing the same service; for example, Fanta belongs to the soft drink product category.

repertoire: The different brands that a customer buys within a product category. Consumers are rarely 100 per cent loyal, but instead purchase from their own particular repertoire of brands.

loyalty (in a behavioural sense): Restricting buying to a personal repertoire of brands, which is relatively stable over time. This means buying some brands much more often than others.

MOST BUYING IS REPEAT-BUYING

A normal-sized supermarket contains about 40,000 different products, which makes even simple grocery shopping sound daunting. Similarly, in any city there are hundreds of financial institutions to choose from, thousands of accountancy practices, thousands of hairdressers, and so on. Each night, when people just want to relax and watch a bit of television, they are confronted with a choice of many, if not hundreds, of different television channels. So how does the poor consumer handle so much choice? How do they manage to do it every day, and do it so quickly?

Fortunately, most of the buying that we do is repeat behaviour, something that we have done before. For most purchases we make, we have bought from that **category** before. In fact, we have probably bought that particular brand before; almost certainly, we've bought from that store before, or one very like it. So we are pretty experienced consumers—although this doesn't mean we are experts, partly because there are so many categories, so many brands and so many shops. Also, few of us want to be experts: we just want to be knowledgable enough that we don't waste too much money or time making really poor choices. Most of the time, we feel we do pretty well without having to put too much effort in.

Many marketing textbooks tend to gloss over these facts about habitual buying, overemphasising rational decision making and thinking. Well-researched buying decisions do sometimes occur, but rarely. For the majority of brand buying and store choice, habit and convenience drives our behaviour. Consumers form a stable **repertoire** of brands or stores and repeatedly buy from them. In this chapter, we will describe this repertoire buying or, simply put, **loyalty** to a limited number of brands and consider what marketers must do to encourage loyalty to their brand, and how to disrupt, or at least nudge, consumers away from their loyalties to rival brands.

HIGH-INVOLVEMENT DECISIONS

Some buying decisions have greater consequences than others, which encourages us to be more thoughtful about them. Mostly this occurs when:

- a consumer buys from a category for the first time (for example a new mother buys nappies)
- a consumer has an intense interest in the category (for example their hobby is learning about wine)
- a poor decision would have substantial consequences (for example buying a bottle of wine as a gift for their boss or a valuable client).

But while a few wine consumers might be highly involved in their decisions, most won't be (or only on special occasions). So it's more sensible to distinguish categories where many or most consumers are highly involved. Decisions that are commonly seen as being highly involving are those for expensive products, such as cars, or ones with large financial consequences, such as home loans. Similarly, industrial purchases are often high-involvement; they can involve teams of people, often expert buyers, making detailed assessments of the options.

Surprisingly, **empirical** research shows that even in these, potentially high-involvement categories, buyers do far less careful research than might be expected. Substantial evaluation appears to be more the exception rather than the rule (notice how many purchases in categories like insurance are straight-out renewals, with no evaluation of alternatives). Hence, even though some individual buyers may feel more involved (and stressed by the purchase), together their actual brand-buying behaviours show the same repeat-buying patterns as in low-involvement buying.

For example, **repeat-purchasing** levels for car brands are quite high: near to 50 per cent repeat levels (with some variation between countries). In other words, almost half the time new car buyers buy the same brand as they bought last time (Ehrenberg & Bound, 1999). This level of repeat-buying seems incredible considering that in modern market economies there are typically sixty or so brands to choose from. Also, usually a number of years pass between purchases, models have changed, as have buyer's life circumstances and needs. The odds of someone choosing the same car brand again appear to be very slim. If buying were random, there would be less than one chance in fifty of a person purchasing the same brand again. But buying is not random; there is clear loyalty.

The 50 per cent retention rate for car brands occurs because buyers consider only around two brands on average, one of which is usually the brand they bought last time (that is, the brand they drive now) (Lambert-Pandraud, Laurent & Lapersonne, 2005). About a fifth of buyers consider only a single brand, which is almost always the one they bought last time (Lapersonne, Laurent & Le Goff, 1995). So this 'high-involvement' purchase decision doesn't seem to lead to many buyers evaluating any more than a few brands. Very similar limited search behaviour has been recorded for retail banking services and insurance, either for new purchases or repeats (Dawes, Mundt & Sharp, 2009) with even higher rates of repeat purchase.

empirical: Based on direct observation and data gathered from the real world, rather than theories, logic or preconceived models.

repeat-purchasing (or repeat-buying): When a consumer purchases the same category, or the same brand twice in a row (two consecutive purchase occasions).

The internet might have radically changed consumer behaviour by facilitating information search and consideration of competitive brands; however, research has found very limited online search behaviour. For example, Johnson and colleagues (2004) investigated the extent of web-based information searches. Using **panel data** from over 10,000 internet households, they found that on average households visit only 1.2 book sites, 1.3 CD sites and 1.8 travel sites during a typical active month in each category.

There are times when consumers spend more time on evaluation and active search (hence the value of online 'search advertising'—see Chapter 11); however, in the main they make heavy use of their memories, and are happy to buy based on existing habits. To paraphrase Roberts and Nedungadi (1995: 5): there are many brands consumers would consider if only they had thought of them.

> ◢ **panel data:** Repeat-purchasing (or repeat-viewing) data collected over time from a panel of respondents so patterns of buying over time can be seen at the individual or household level.

NATURAL LOYALTY

The !Kung San of the Kalahari Desert in southern Africa believe that babies must be taught to sit, that it does not come naturally. They prop piles of dirt around babies to push them into a sitting position. Other cultures find this amusing; similarly, many cultures find it equally amusing when Westerners talk to babies, often in 'baby talk', in the belief that babies can somehow understand such sentences and must be spoken to in order to stimulate their own speaking. Harvard professor and cognitive scientist Stephen Pinker (1994) points out that learning language, like learning to sit, comes naturally—we have a natural disposition (presumably underpinned by genetics).

Consumer loyalty may also be a natural phenomenon. Consumers' loyalty to brands has traditionally been portrayed as an outcome of marketing strategy. The traditional thinking is that it is something that must be earned (or bought) and will erode if a brand slips in its **differentiation**, value and/or service quality. However, more recently we have come to realise that this is an exaggeration; this belief does not give due attention to the fact that loyalty comes easily to consumers. The first clue that loyalty is a strong natural tendency is that loyalty is very prevalent. Consumers seldom ever buy randomly, but instead show biased purchasing, favouring some brands over others. From soap purchasing to soap opera viewing, consumers show biased non-random repeat-purchasing: in other words, they each have their own personal loyalties.

> ◢ **differentiation:** Being perceived by most or many buyers as meaningfully different from other rival brands in the category.

Loyalty is everywhere

We observe loyal behaviour in all categories, including service purchasing and corporate buying. Buyers restrict their purchases to a personal repertoire of brands—people buy far fewer different brands than they could. Ten purchases from the category usually means far fewer than ten different brands are bought—buyers keep returning to 'favourites'. And this set can be very small. (Note: We use the term 'favourites' with some caution, as it implies that buyers have strong attitudinal preferences, which usually isn't the case. All we mean by this term is that consumers have brands that they each buy more often—that is, repeat-purchasing is biased towards these brands.)

Here's another surprising example of how loyal we are. Television channel choice is somewhere where loyalty is rather unexpected; most of us think we watch television for the programs, and, aside from the genre-specific channels (for example the weather channel), we have only a vague idea of what channel offers which of our favourite programs. Also, there are no real switching costs: we can defect from one channel to another at the push of a button. In spite of all of this, television channel choice reveals the same pattern as other categories—people substantially restrict their repertoires and show loyalty.

Figure 2.1 was compiled by Ehrenberg-Bass Institute researcher Virginia Beal, based on Nielsen data on US households' television viewing. It shows the number of television channels each household has access to in their subscription and how many they actual watch each week. The key point is how quickly the line flattens: when a household has access to forty channels, they watch about a dozen or so each week; households with access to eighty channels watch a few more than a dozen each week; and households with access to 200 channels still only watch a few more than a dozen each week.

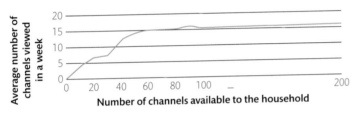

●●● **FIGURE 2.1** NUMBER OF CHANNELS VIEWED PER WEEK

What Figure 2.1 shows is that viewers keep returning to their favourite channels. There is obvious loyalty. Most viewers watch enough television to watch many more channels than they do, but they prefer to restrict their personal viewing repertoire. This figure would look almost identical if it concerned brand buying in any product category: that is, it instead showed the number of purchases made by an individual and how many different brands they had bought. Loyalty is everywhere, it seems.

Brand loyalty is part of every market, even in so-called 'commodity' categories (such as rice or flour). It is a sensible buyer strategy, since this tendency to be loyal is useful to human beings in balancing risk and saving the precious commodity of time.

Loyalty without differentiation

It's common to think that brand differentiation is essential for loyalty, that consumers can not behaviourally show loyalty unless there are meaningful differences between brands. This is the notion that loyalty occurs because each consumer finds the brand that suits their needs best and so then buys this rather than the other options. This all sounds very sensible, but it turns out to be an exaggeration, and one that ignores the natural tendency for consumers to be loyal.

●●● **FIGURE 2.2** TOILET ROLL ORIENTATION

The *over* orientation and the *under* orientation

Source: http://en.wikipedia.org/wiki/Toilet_paper_orientation

Similar examples of behavioural loyalties have been noted, and studied, for choice of seat in lecture theatres, computer terminals in computer labs, even toilet roll orientation. There is a Facebook page dedicated to those who say they must always have the television volume on an even number. Another page exists for people who use all the same coloured pegs when hanging out washing. Consumers commonly cite 'habit' as the reason for such loyalties (or that 'it makes life easier'), but it is also common for these behavioural loyalties to subsequently lead to attitudinal preferences. For instance, talkback radio stations find no shortage of people to take sides in debates about which way is the correct or best orientation for toilet paper rolls.

The natural tendency towards brand loyalty is revealed in experiments that show how rapidly consumers form loyalties—even when choosing between identical products. In one experiment, each day, for twelve days, loaves of bread from the same commercial oven were offered on a tray for choice by forty-two different households (Tucker, 1964). The loaves were wrapped identically and each day one was labelled 'L', another 'M', another 'P', another 'H', and so on. The position of the 'brands' on the tray was rotated. In spite of the loaves being identical, many of the respondents quickly adopted loyalties, with each household favouring a particular brand. Some also favoured positions on the tray (for example tending to choose the brand that happened to be on the left or right of the tray). This landmark study concluded that 'it is clear that such loyalties are more than trivial, even though they are based on what may seem trivial distinctions' (Tucker, 1964: 35).

McConnell (1968) replicated and extended this experiment, but this time with bottles of (identical) beer. Again the experiment showed that consumers quickly formed their own personal loyalties, some households favouring brand M, others favouring brand L, and so on.

Table 2.1 shows the probability of a household purchasing the same beer brand as they last time on each of the experiment's 'purchase occasions' from the second to the twenty-fourth. As can be seen, on the first few repeat purchases there was a near perfect (1.00) probability that a household would choose a different brand than they had on the previous trial; in other words they were switching brands. But this rapidly changed: within a few purchases there was only around a 50 per cent chance a household would switch from the brand they bought last, and this dropped even further with subsequent purchases.

●●● **TABLE 2.1** INDEX OF SEARCH BEHAVIOUR

BRAND M	PAIRS OF ADJACENT CALLS													
	1–2	2–3	3–4	...	7–8	...	10–11	...	13–14	...	16–17	...	19–20	...	21–22	22–23	23–24
Index of search behaviour	1.00	.89	.58	...	.42	...	.19	...	.38	...	.19	...	.25	...	.09	.24	.12

Index of search behaviour for brand M—the proportion of buyers of Brand M at one call who bought another brand at the following call.

Source: Charlton & Ehrenberg, 1973: 304

Charlton and Ehrenberg (1973) re-analysed McConnell's data and confirmed that the loyalty patterns that emerged in the experiment matched those found in real-world repeat-buying. So consumers quickly developed loyalties that were like real-world behaviour, where there was no product feature or packaging differentiation, no advertising, and no differences in physical availability. Loyalty, it seems, needs little prompting: it comes naturally.

The pattern of individual loyalty underpins regularities in **brand performance metrics** in many, if not all, markets (Ehrenberg, Uncles & Goodhardt, 2004). This is evidenced by the empirical **double jeopardy law**, which shows that brands with large and small market shares differ substantially in how many people buy them, but differ far less in terms of how loyal their buyers are to them (Ehrenberg & Goodhardt, 2002). Ultimately, then, every brand gets its share of loyal customers, seldom more or less than others. Therefore, it is logical to conclude that consumer loyalty is more to do with consumers themselves than with specific features of the brand.

LOYAL SWITCHERS

Natural loyalty is rarely exclusive. Buyers usually buy more than one brand from each category, and the more purchases an individual makes from a category, the more brands they buy. **Polygamous (or divided) loyalty** is quite the norm.

So any brand should expect that most of their buyers will not give them exclusive, 100 per cent loyalty. Table 2.2 lists the proportion of a brand's buyers in a particular year who were exclusively loyal to that brand. The average for this selection of brands is 11 per cent of their buyer base. Notice that the categories that are purchased less frequently have higher levels of **100% loyals**. Analgesics are bought only five times a year on average, and because this is a skewed average more than half of all households bought from the category only once. These once-only buyers, by definition, have to appear among the 100% loyals: if you only buy once then you can buy only one

brand performance metrics: The different statistics that marketers measure and use to track the performance of their brand. These include market share, penetration, repeat-buying rate and other metrics (described in Chapter 3).

◢ **double jeopardy law:** A marketing law that states the relationship between size and loyalty metrics: brands with less market share have far fewer buyers, and these buyers are slightly less loyal (i.e. small brands suffer twice).

◢ **polygamous (or divided) loyalty:** The propensity for buyers to be loyal to several brands within a category (to shop within a repertoire).

◢ **100% loyals:** Consumers of a brand who bought only that brand and no other brand during a period of analysis.

brand. As time goes by, these buyers make more purchases and the proportion who are 100 per cent loyal drops dramatically. This can be seen in categories such as breakfast cereals and yoghurts, which are bought more frequently and so show much lower levels of 100 per cent brand loyalty.

●●● **TABLE 2.2** 100% LOYALS ARE THE MINORITY

	ANNUAL CATEGORY PURCHASE RATE (AVERAGE):	BRAND SIZE (MARKET SHARE) (%)	100% LOYALS AMONG BRAND BUYERS (%)
Analgesics	5.1		
Nurofen		8	28
Boots		3	26
Panadol		2	29
Deodorants	5.6		
Lynx		17	21
Dove		7	17
Nivea		2	10
Ready to eat breakfast cereals	21.5		
Kellogg's		29	7
Cereal Partners		17	2
Weetabix		9	2
Yoghurts	29.7		
Muller		24	7
Muller Light		14	4
Ski		4	2
Danone		3	2
Average		**11**	**11**

Source: Kantar Worldpanel

So consumers are loyal but are they are also switchers! They are each loyal to a personal repertoire of brands: that is, they buy some brands far more often than others. But they are happy to switch around between the brands within their repertoire. They are 'loyal switchers'.

There are other product categories where consumers 'subscribe' solely or mostly to one brand, usually for long periods, until they defect to another (Sharp, Wright & Goodhardt, 2002). For example, consumers usually have only one mobile phone network, and one mortgage provider, at a time. However, if we widen our market definition—say from mortgages to financial services—then we see repertoires again: where a firm or a consumer will use several banks, insurance companies and superannuation funds. In many cases, they could use a single brand to provide all these services (credit card, mortgage, personal loan, car insurance, house insurance, superannuation fund, and so on), but few buyers do that. Typically they have a repertoire where one brand dominates, and then a number of other brands account for the rest of their buying; for example, one main financial institution and a few others. Much the same pattern is seen for supermarket shopping; we typically have one store where we do most of our shopping (often the closest one to our home) and then a number of other stores we occasionally visit. This pattern is referred to as 'high first-store loyalty' (East et al., 1995).

PROSAIC, NOT PASSIONATE, LOYALTY

Why do buyers have such a strong tendency to be loyal? And why is this loyalty polygamous? These two important questions reveal a good deal about buying behaviour.

Essentially the answer is that consumers adopt brand loyalty as a strategy to simplify their lives. It's neither because they have decided that a particular brand is the perfect one for them, better than all the others, nor that they feel a great emotional bond to it. That's why they are loyal but polygamously so.

Consumers do not care a great deal about most of the many hundreds of brands that they buy. They are busy living their lives, which are filled with many more important decisions than whether to choose Gucci or Prada, Nike or Adidas, Sony or Mitsubishi, Danone or Yoplait—in most cases they are happy with either. The big decision (and it often isn't very big) is whether or not to buy from the product category—for example, 'Do I really need a new dress today?' In comparison, brand choice is quite trivial. But it is still a decision that has to be made, and faced with so many available brands consumers use loyalty to reduce their thinking, time, effort and risk, usually without even realising they are doing it. As Bruce McColl, Global Chief Marketing Officer of Mars, Incorporated (see profile page 30) says:

> Most of us go through life finding it hard enough to have good relationships with the real people in our life, let alone all the brands we buy.

When a marketing executive looks at their customer base and their buying, they see that most of their customers buy very infrequently. The brand is a small part of those customers' lives because they buy it so rarely. Buying rates follow a known statistical distribution, the negative binomial distribution (NBD), which is typically very skewed, so there are a few heavy buyers of the brand and many, many light (occasional) buyers. So, most buyers buy the brand at less than the average rate, and even 'fast-moving consumer goods' (FMCG) brands are only seldom bought by most of their customers. For example, if a household that buys Kellogg's Special K buys more than once a year then they are one of the brand's heavier buyers—in fact, well more than half their consumers buy it only once or twice a year (or even less frequently).

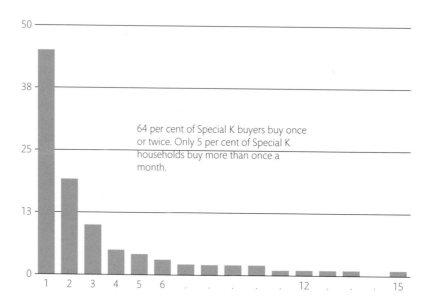

64 per cent of Special K buyers buy once or twice. Only 5 per cent of Special K households buy more than once a month.

●●● **FIGURE 2.3** PERCENTAGE OF KELLOGG'S SPECIAL K BUYERS BUYING X TIMES PER ANNUM

Source: TNS SuperPanel, UK, July 2007

These are quite normal figures, even for large brands. There are two reasons why most of a brand's customers are light:

1   First, product categories have a lot of **light buyers** (see Figure 2.4). There are many categories that everyone buys but still most people don't buy very often. For example, most people travel on planes but only once every few years (or even decades), while a few people travel very often. Some people eat rice most nights, while many others eat it a few times a year at most. Category purchasing rates follow a skewed distribution quite like the one shown above for the individual brand Special K.

2   Second, each time people buy from the category they distribute their purchases out among several brands—polygamous loyalty. So, even heavy category buyers buy individual brands infrequently.

So, we marketers have to accept that our brand is a small part of the lives of most of our customers. This is the marketing world we live in; rather than seeking to change this, we need to learn how to operate best in this world. It reminds us that marketing is a constant battle for attention, and that we must work to prevent our customers from forgetting us.

light buyer: Someone who buys the category or brand less frequently than the average.

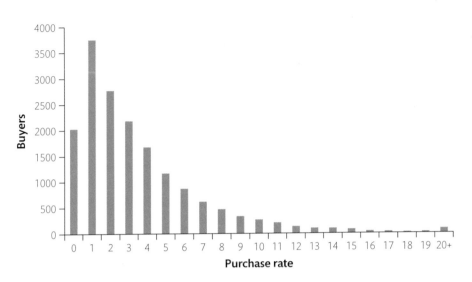

●●● **FIGURE 2.4** SKEWED DISTRIBUTION OF BREAKFAST CEREAL CATEGORY BUYING

Source: Kantar WorldPanel UK (2009) data

Industry insight

Mars and the Russian rouble crisis

In August 1998, Russia defaulted on its foreign loans, and the rouble (the Russian currency) crashed. Banks closed, people lost their savings and credit dried up. Consumer goods manufacturers operating in Russia were faced with a big problem. Small stores, suddenly in a weak financial position, were very worried about having money tied up in products sitting on shelves and were hesitant to reorder any new stock. As orders came to a halt, supermarket shelves became bare and distributors started going out of business. Many of the large foreign-owned companies, under pressure from shareholders, quickly scaled back or abandoned operations in Russia.

The Mars, Incorporated marketing team for Russia had to make a quick decision about the future of their operations. They had already suffered financial losses, sales revenue was dropping steadily and the economic situation was not likely to improve quickly. Despite this, Mars decided to take a long-term perspective and invest in finding a solution to regain a foothold in the Russian market. The key problem was availability; with empty shelves and no new orders to fill them, it was impossible for customers to buy Mars products.

The Mars team came up with the idea of providing products on consignment to their customers (distributors). It was a simple concept, but a huge financial risk in a very unstable economic climate. Although they had no orders, Mars produced millions of dollars worth of products, which they gave to their distributors, who passed the products on to thousands of small Russian retailers. The arrangement allowed small retailers to fill their shelves with Mars products without paying a cent (until the product was sold and they reordered). The effect was immediate—the products were back on the shelves, consumers were buying the products, and distributers were back in business.

Because retailers no longer had to pre-pay, Mars products were risk-free to put on shelves. Not only had Mars managed to resume distribution to the existing retail outlets, but also more and more retailers wanted to stock Mars products, and in just a few years the Russian team had significantly increased product availability to over 500,000 distribution points across the country.

With the physical availability problem solved, Mars could resume other marketing activities such as advertising. With many organisations suffering financial losses, or withdrawing from the market, the cost of buying media space had dropped significantly in Russia. The Mars team could now take advantage of the reduced advertising costs. In order to get the most from a limited budget, they focused their spend on running a few advertisements more often rather than investing in developing new ads. They also scaled back on product development and packaging changes, which not only reduced operating costs but also strengthened brand equity, as brands became more recognisable and easy to find.

When the Russian economy finally bounced back, Mars had secured a strong market presence and an excellent distribution network. The region is now one of the most financially valuable for Mars globally.

Several elements of Mars' structure and operational policy played a big support role for the team during the Russian crisis. Mars is a privately owned organisation with a decentralised structure that encourages local organisational freedom. Instead of pressure from shareholders or management in another country, decisions are made at a local level. This meant that the Russian marketing team could make their own assessment and decisions and then act immediately. Their decision was informed by Mars' five principles for operational freedom, which include mutuality—the belief that everyone should benefit from the business that Mars conducts. Because they decided to try to stick through the Russian crisis, they not only saved their own business but also kept distributors in business and put products back on the shelves for Russian consumers. The experience provided a valuable and dramatic learning experience for those involved, many of whom now hold very senior corporate roles within Mars globally.

THE IMPORTANCE OF MEMORY

◢ LEARNING OBJECTIVE
Understand how memory and mental availability affect consumer attitudes and loyalty

So, why do some brands loom larger in our repertoires (that is, we buy them more often) than other brands? The main answer is that some are more *physically available* to us (like the supermarket that is closest to our home) and more *mentally available* to us. Our buying relies heavily on our memory. Some brands have managed to embed themselves better in our memories; they have a richer more relevant web of associations, so they are easier to recall, recognise and even notice. This makes their advertising and packaging more effective (it may also make their stores or branches, if they have them, more effective), which in turn enhances their mental and physical availability advantage over other brands. This is one of the key reasons why loyalty can be very long-lasting.

We don't buy most brands in any category, but rather we keep going back to just a few. The reason that we don't buy most of these other brands is not usually because we reject them, but mainly that we don't notice and/or think of them. Memory is very important. It is a major determinant of what brands we buy, and which we do not buy. Advertising also works via memory (see Chapter 10).

Some **choice situations** depend heavily on recall, in that we have to bring products or brands to mind along with information on their features and suitability for our needs at that moment. This recall determines which shops we go to, what we type into a search engine and so on. A brand that is not recalled has no chance of being purchased, no matter how good it is. So, in most cases this recall level becomes the dominant factor affecting a brand's sales.

In other situations, brands are visually present on a shelf, on screen or on a price list or menu. Here, noticing and recognition matter, as well as recall. Recognition, of course, depends on memory, but noticing does too—buying is often 'goal-directed behaviour', which means that people are looking for something (for instance, a type of cat food, perhaps one with chicken in it): we use our memories to help see.

We tend to think of memory like a computer hard drive or a library that we occasionally have to delve into ('hmm, let me think'), but memory is integral to all brain activity. When we listen to a song, our brain is interpreting it with memories—if the music stops suddenly we can sing or hum the next part, which shows that we are anticipating almost every note. Without instantaneous retrieval from memory you couldn't be reading this text now—your memories tell you what words mean. So our memories affect what we do, and don't, see.

Everyone knows that retrieval from memory is imperfect and inconsistent (we even temporarily forget the names of our best friends sometimes—and the PIN numbers of our credit cards!). Our modern understanding of memory tells us that an individual person's awareness of a brand is best thought of as probabilistic, not absolute; in the right circumstances the brand is easy to notice, easy to recognise and easy to recall, but this varies a great deal depending on the circumstances, including the time and mood. It depends on tiny random things, such as what you happened to be thinking about the second before.

A simple model of memory is that it consists of 'nodes' that hold information—this is known as the associative network theory of memory (Anderson, 1973). If two pieces of information are associated (for example Coca-Cola and 'red') links are said to exist between these nodes. Buyers have a network of information (also referred to as **attributes**) linked to the brand name. So, for example, McDonald's is associated with hamburgers, yellow arches, fast food and so on. These links are developed and refreshed through experiences such as buying and using the brand, or being exposed to marketing activities such as advertising or other people's experiences via word of mouth or observation.

choice situation: The moment when and place where a consumer makes a purchase decision. Examples include selecting a type and brand of milk in the supermarket aisle, deciding on a charity to donate money to, or ordering a drink at a bar.

(brand) attributes (in memory): Small pieces of information that a buyer links to a particular brand—these may be conscious or subconscious associations.

The more extensive and fresher the network of memory associations, the greater the brand's probability of being noticed or thought of in the variety of buying situations experienced by buyers. So building mental availability is about developing these different links to increase the scope of the network in memory—the brand's **share of mind**. A cue like 'a summer drink at the beach' will bring Coke to mind for many Australians, whereas a cue like 'sitting down for a drink at a coffee shop' is far less likely to bring it to mind. Yet, for Coca-Cola, the opportunity to sell Coke at coffee shops probably now today far outstrips the amount of bottles they can hope to sell at the beach. You can see the obvious marketing challenge (and opportunity) for Coca-Cola.

share of mind: The quantity and quality of memory links that connect information to a particular brand in the consumer's mind.

How to build and refresh memories

An important part of marketing is working out how to design advertising that will be easy for consumers to process so that brand memories are refreshed and (sometimes) new memories are built. Using existing memory associations is one way to facilitate memory encoding and storage. Effective advertising often taps into existing **memory structures** consumers have concerning the product category. This is one of the (good) reasons why much advertising in a category shares many similarities—have a look at a fashion magazine such as *Vogue* and compare the clothing or perfume advertisements. You will see that each different brand makes use of many of the same category-relevant cues. In fact, many ads use exactly the same format.

memory structures: Categories and interrelations within memory that help information recall.

Linking verbal information with visual cues (thus engaging both verbal and visual systems) can also help to encode information more thoroughly. This is the reason why brands have characters (such as 'Snap', 'Crackle' and 'Pop' for Kellogg's Rice Bubble, known as Rice Krispies in the United States and United Kingdom—both brand names use the same distinctive characters), logos (such as the Nike 'swoosh') and slogans (for instance, 'Aussie/ Kiwi kids are Weet-Bix kids').

A verbal mention of the brand of insect spray Mortein, along with the distinctive red and white logo, provides two links in memory. Louie the Fly, a cartoon character who has been killed in every Mortein advertisement for decades, adds another visual element to the memories devoted to the brand. The humour of the ads and the likeable nature of the Louie character encourages viewing and adds a positive emotional charge to the brand information, which also aids the encoding of such memories.

●●● **FIGURE 2.5** LOUIE THE FLY

Making the information relevant to the person or current situation is another way in which marketers can influence the level of encoding. Have you ever seen an ad for a car in a car racing show? Or a celebrity from a television show in an advertisement during the commercial break for that show? These are examples of advertising created and placed strategically in the matching context of the program. The encoding of those ads may be deeper, because their information matches the context of what viewers are watching at the time, making it more relevant to them (Tulving & Thomson, 1973). Research in this area is ongoing.

WHY DO CONSUMERS FORGET ABOUT US?

Our marketing and our brand is ignored and forgotten by most people most days. Our brand's mental availability will never be as high as we would like it to be. This is the reality for all marketers, as marketing is an ongoing battle for attention, with constant striving for improvement in our marketing communications.

Even the mental availability we have already built erodes. The main reason is competitive memory interference—consumer's lives, and the advertising of competitors, get in the way and make it harder for consumers to retrieve memories of our brand. Try to sing a song while you are listening to another one you know—it is very difficult, if not impossible. This is a simple illustration of competitive memory interference, and how competitor advertising interferes with memory recall.

The filing system of long-term memory is quite like a messy desktop, where pieces of paper that are needed more often tend to find themselves near the top of the pile because they are frequently being needed and placed on top, whereas items that aren't needed so often find themselves gradually sinking to the bottom, and becoming harder and harder to find. When a brand stops advertising, it starts sinking in memory. So there is an ongoing marketing task to maintain mental availability, especially if competitors advertise. This, and the fact that they have so many (light) buyers, is why most large consumer brands are also large advertisers. It is possible to build a brand with very little advertising, but very hard to maintain a large brand without it. This is discussed more in Chapter 10.

EMOTIONAL RATIONAL BUYERS

By now you should have a very human picture of the typical buyer. These are real 'flesh and blood' people who have busy lives. They have limited information and limited time in which to consider their options, and their actual ability to weigh options is limited by their fragile memories (the soft-wiring of the brain) and also their intelligence. This picture is true even for industrial buying teams made up of experts who are paid to do thorough jobs evaluating options. Fortunately, humans have evolved a number of ways of dealing with these limitations while still making pretty good decisions. For all our limitations, we are pretty good at shopping and buying useful things within the small amount of time that we wish to devote to these tasks.

In recent years, psychology, aided by advances in neuroscience, has made worthy progress in understanding how humans use emotion in conjunction with conscious rational thinking to arrive at decisions and drive behaviour. It's often thought that emotions get in the way of sound decision making, clouding judgments—certainly, any parent observing their tired emotional children will support this model of the world. But what is usually forgotten is that everyday decision making depends enormously on emotion. It's as if we know of the limits of thinking ability and information so we deliberately factor hunches and feelings substantially into our decision making. Imagine you bought yourself a lottery ticket for $10 during the week, then just before the lottery draw someone asks to buy the ticket from you for $20. Do you take the offer? How do you feel? Most people don't want to sell their ticket—yet $20 is a good price, twice what you paid, and you can always buy another ticket in another lottery. But selling feels wrong. The fact that someone is offering $20 makes you feel it must be worth more. Maybe it's special; maybe this person knows something. But all this specific thinking comes later; the emotional feeling came immediately and probably led you to decide 'no' well before you had come up with a reason why you shouldn't sell. In this case, it seems like emotions are getting in the way of sound decision making, but that feeling (that if someone else wants something then it must have some value) is often very sound, that little emotional alarm bell is useful—if for no other reason than that it helps us make fast decisions.

How quick come the reasons for approving what we like!

Jane Austen, *Persuasion*, 1817, chapter 2

Decision making, even for trivial decisions, is rarely like figuring out a maths equation or a logical puzzle. To make real-world decisions, we have to also decide which information to pay attention to, we have to make judgments about the reliability of each bit of information we have, and very often we have to factor in undependable predictions about the future. Even deciding what to cook for dinner tonight requires estimating how we (and maybe others) are going to feel when we eat it in several hours time—will lasagne or ravioli make us happier? What sort of mood will we and they be in, come dinnertime? Described like this, it all looks terribly tricky—and on top of this we also have to decide how much thought and time to put into this decision. Yet, most of us handle such complexity and unknowns, usually (although not always) with ease and little stress, and we seldom spend long on it. We couldn't do this without our emotions: they play vital roles in directing our attention, deciding how long to spend on a decision, and whether or not to engage any conscious, deliberate problem solving. Emotions guide the ongoing decision of what to pay attention to and how much conscious processing to devote to the item of primary attention. We rarely opt for answers that don't feel right, and will assemble rational arguments to back up what we feel, which shows just how integral our emotions are to our decision making.

Non-conscious thinking

Much of our thinking is non-conscious. Consider the vast number of decisions that have to be made each day, such as which shoe to put on first, how much coffee to drink at breakfast, how fast to drive and so on. Many times these decisions are made without conscious thought, but somehow they *are* made. An awful lot is going on in our brain, guiding our behaviour, below our level of consciousness. Have you ever arrived at your destination having driven in a car and yet not been able to remember the last ten minutes of the driving because you were thinking of something else? Do you recall making a decision to start daydreaming during a lecture? Very unlikely. Perhaps you can instead recall telling yourself not to daydream, yet still it happened. Just who is in charge of your brain? Well, it turns out that the conscious thinking that you are aware of, that you can 'observe', is just a small part of your actual thinking. We know our own selves far less well than we imagine.

Evolutionary psychologists and biologists tell us that our brains evolved to help keep us alive and to have children, thereby passing on genes for the sorts of brains that were useful (at keeping us alive and having children). If while climbing a mountain a rock above you falls towards your head, you duck, your heart rate jumps, oxygen intake increases and adrenaline pumps into your bloodstream—your brain has given all these and many other orders and triggered bodily changes and behaviour before you even know it. Conscious thinking is slow; it's used (sometimes) for learning, for researching, for figuring things out and for planning. Meanwhile, our brains can trigger an awful lot of behaviour without having to do much conscious thinking.

This is how people can enter a supermarket without having exactly in mind what to buy for dinner and leave ten minutes later with dinner ingredients, having done very little thinking and evaluation, in spite of the fact that the supermarket contained 40,000 items and potentially billions of different dinner ingredient combinations. We are good at engaging our conscious brains only when absolutely necessary, and good at doing a lot of behaviour 'on autopilot'.

This has considerable implications for market research. Asking buyers directly why they did something, like why they bought that particular brand last week, is naïve, because very often they do not know why. Being asked a question can make them develop a rationalisation or theory of why they did what they did. So the market research will elicit an answer, and it may even be one that consumers believe, but it may be incorrect.

This is why people can flick through a fashion magazine's first twenty pages of advertising in very little time at all, feeling very little cognitive effort. It also explains how advertising can affect people without the advertising containing lots of information, or even any new information, and without consumers devoting much conscious information processing to the advertising. This is discussed in Chapter 10.

Heuristics

Economists used to work with the model of buyers being rational, in the sense of trying to maximise their utility (benefit). This has been much criticised as being unrealistic, with critics arguing that consumers are happy to **satisfice** rather than seek what is best. However, these critics miss the point: all models are simplifications. They are never, strictly speaking, true—the point is that they are nonetheless useful in describing the world. In this case, the model of rational buyers works reasonably well: demand goes down when prices go up, higher quality items get higher prices, brands that improve their quality improve their sales, faulty products seldom last in the marketplace. There is no doubt that buyers, in aggregate, are able to behave pretty rationally in their best interests,

satisfice: To satisfy and suffice: a term coined by Nobel Prize–winning economist Herbert A Simon (1957).

even though no human is perfectly rational and our rational thinking is always limited by us having incomplete information.

However, increasingly economists have been documenting irrational, but regular, behaviour; for example, a dollar is worth a dollar—everyone knows this and yet people will expend considerable effort to save $2 off the price of a book (or a tank of petrol) and yet consider a $2 saving on a washing machine as irrelevant. In 2002, the Nobel Prize in Economic Sciences was awarded to a psychologist (not an economist), Daniel Kahneman, for his work with Amos Tversky on prospect theory. Prospect theory is partially based on the empirical observation that consumers are more sensitive to losses than gains—something which is not strictly speaking rational, but in many situations useful. It seems that people can be irrational but in consistently, and hence predictable, ways. This allows public policy makers and marketers to anticipate these irrational behaviours.

The root of these behavioural patterns is people's use of **heuristics** to simplify decision making. Heuristics are short-cuts, simple rules hard-coded by evolutionary processes or learnt from experience. Rules of thumb, hunches, intuitive judgments, educated guesses, trial and error approaches and common sense are all examples of heuristics. Examples of heuristics when answering multiple choice tests include:

- 'always choose the first one that feels right'
- 'when you don't know, choose C'.

Examples of heuristics used when shopping include:

- 'choose the brand you recognise'
- 'choose a/the market leader'
- 'choose the most expensive' (if wishing to ensure good quality)
- 'choose the cheapest' (if wishing to save money)
- 'choose the middle-priced' (if seeking best value for money).

One of the most basic heuristics is to assume that products with higher prices are often higher quality. Now if we did this all the time, like robots, we could be exploited by unscrupulous marketers who simply put high prices on poor products. But consumers aren't idiots: they use this heuristic judiciously, but fairly often, because it is very often correct.

Much of the psychology research on heuristics has been to expose biases in human thinking (see the box of common biases on page 53) with the implication that a lack of conscious logical thinking leads to poor decisions. Certainly sometimes it does, but research also shows that heuristics can often lead to better decisions and more accurate predictions than more complex procedures based on more information (Gigerenzer & Todd, 1999). This seems surprising: we have an in-built cognitive bias that tells us that decisions that are more thought out should always beat faster decisions based on less data. If we really believed this, we should spend a lot more time thinking about things, but we don't, because the utility to be gained from all that extra thought is often very little, especially when it comes to the usually trivial task of choosing between brands or providers. The waiter asks you what you would like to drink. Your friend just ordered a Coke. Now, if you really put your brain into gear, you might be able to think of something to drink that you would enjoy better than a Coke, but not much better. And your friend's order has already established that the place sells Coke and hasn't run out. And you know your friend is hardly going to disapprove of an order that is the same as his. Using the choice heuristic 'I'll have what he's having' saves time and mental effort, and works pretty well in delivering enjoyment with low risk.

heuristics: Experience-based mental tools that people use to simplify decision making.

Some common biases

Social proof—This is when people look to the behaviour of others as a guide to their decision. Choosing a brand because it has the greatest market share is an example, as is choosing a restaurant because it has a queue. It seems safer to eat at the popular restaurant.

Anchoring—This is where people focus on one attribute, or a piece of information, and thus neglect to consider some other factors. The anchoring and adjustment heuristic shows up when people have very little information and so latch on to any clue they have, even if it is not particularly relevant. For example, if a question is framed differently it elicits different answers. When Americans are asked to estimate the percentage of African nations that are members of the United Nations, if the question 'is it more or less than 10 per cent?' is included in the phrasing, the average response is '25 per cent', whereas if the question is phrased as 'is it more or less than 65 per cent?' the average response is '45 per cent'. If respondents are asked the population of Canada and told that the population of Australia is 20 million, they give lower estimates than if they are told that the population of Australia is 40 million. This example may, for some people, also be due to the *similarity heuristic*, where people know that Australia and Canada are similar in some ways (for example both are members of the British Commonwealth) and so they assume they are also similar in population (even though there is no logical basis for this assumption).

Availability bias—This is when people estimate the frequency of an event (that is, how often it happens) or the proportion in the population, based on how easily an example can be brought to mind. People find it easier to think of words that start with the letter 'R' (for instance, 'reading', 'red', 'right') than words that have 'R' as their third letter ('strict', 'care', 'person'). So, because of the availability bias they estimate that there are more words that start with 'R' than words that have 'R' as their third letter (which is incorrect). This mental availability can be influenced by media coverage, movies and books, and by a person's own particular (limited) life experiences. For example, when asked to estimate the probability of causes of death, people overestimate dramatic events they have seen in movies and/ or events that are regularly reported in the media. They typically estimate that more people die from homicide than suicide, when it reality it is the other way round. They vastly overestimate the chances of dying from shark attacks and airline crashes, and underestimate the chances of dying from common causes such as influenza or being hit by a car while crossing the road.

A related bias is the propensity to favour something if it is familiar (this is known as the *familiarity heuristic*). Also similar is the propensity to favour things that are beautiful, symmetrical and/or easy to process (*processing fluency bias*); for example brand names that are easy to pronounce.

Marketers can use knowledge of these heuristics to frame offers. For example, leading market share brands often signal that they are leading brands, thus encouraging buyers to rely on social proof. New movies invite consumers to make similarity judgments ('brought to you by the producers of *Kung-Fu Panda*'). Food manufacturers highlight single features such as 'contains no added salt', hoping to convey a more general impression of nutritional soundness. Packaging designers test their designs for processing fluency, not only to help consumers read what is on the pack but also to benefit from processing fluency bias.

Consumers use heuristics because overall they work pretty well. But it is not difficult to see how they can lead us astray. This raises an ethical issue for marketers: when is framing an offer in light of known heuristics helping consumers out, and when is it leading them astray?

CONSUMER MOTIVATIONS

1   Can you think about moments when a claim on a pack made you think that something was more healthy than it really was? For example, 'light' chocolate bars have less fat but more sugar than the regular ones, and the same is often true with yoghurts.

2   The law forces retailers to include the price per 100g on the pack. What misleading price framing techniques can this prevent?

3   Why do you think retailers like to have at least three options priced differently in a category and two top ones are usually priced very close to each other? What are they trying to achieve?

As marketers, we are deeply interested in questions that consumers might find rather trivial. For example, we want to know why consumers buy particular brands, or more specifically: 'Why did you buy that brand of shampoo four times last year and that one only twice and that one only once?' This makes it difficult to gain a reliable answer by simply asking consumers—they don't really know, or simply can't accurately recall. Besides, each of our consumers may have different idiosyncratic reasons.

It is important, though, to remember that the ultimate reason why consumers buy a brand is because it is a route to the benefits provided by the product or service category overall. People buy Fords, Toyotas and Renaults because they have a need for transportation: personal, convenient, relatively safe, comfortable, affordable transportation.

In the award-winning book *Simply Better* (2004), Patrick Barwise and Sean Meehan remind marketers that consumers care most about the basic benefits of a product or service category. Brands that slip behind their competitors in providing these benefits suffer badly.

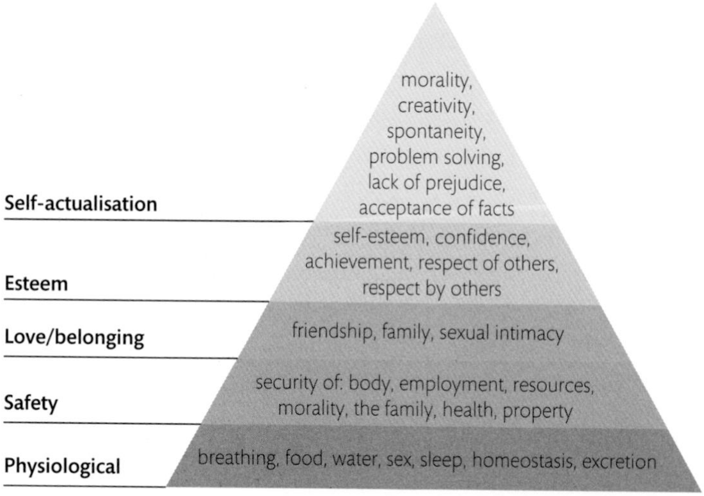

An extremely important part of marketing is understanding consumers' needs, and therefore the benefits they seek. Product and service features have to be developed to meet these needs. Sometimes features have to be translated and explained to consumers. It's important to remember that buyers are seeking benefits, not features. Marketers have to point out clearly how their product's features deliver benefits.

Abraham Maslow developed a hierarchy of motivations (Figure 2.6). Maslow was trying to explain why people are driven by particular motivations at particular times: hence, the hierarchy—his idea being that people's behaviour would not be driven by high-level motivations until the lower ones were fulfilled. This makes some basic sense: if you are dying of thirst you are (probably, but not definitely) less worried about recognition from your peers. However, human behaviour turns out to be hideously complex and

●●● **FIGURE 2.6** MASLOW'S HIERARCHY OF MOTIVATIONS

Source: Maslow, A (1954) *Motivation and Personality,* Harper & Row, New York.

situation-dependent, meaning that the predictive and explanatory value of the hierarchy is very low. People living on incomes of only a dollar or two a day will still spend some of that meagre income on things like entertainment. Maslow's hierarchy is nevertheless an excellent reminder of the many basic needs that human beings have. How they are translated into particular desires or wants varies among different cultures, countries and **demographic groups,** and even situations—but the basic motivations are the same.

> **demographic groups:**
> Groups used by marketers as a way of dividing the population into useful segments; for example based on gender, race, income and/or location.

Case study

The toothpaste case: Availability and involvement

By Elizabeth Gunner

Philip has been working in the marketing department for Shine-Brite, a market-leading toothpaste manufacturer, for thirty years. He has managed package redesigns, launched new product lines with different colours and tastes, and he pioneered a particularly successful advertising tactic. Philip spent a long time agonising over the new campaign, but finally settled on a strategic direction. Advertisements were run in print media, as well as on radio and television, asking customers to really think about their toothpaste choice. Teeth are important for talking, eating and (most importantly) for smiling. Brushing is what protects teeth and keeps them healthy—so choosing the right toothpaste is a big decision.

Meanwhile, out in the suburbs, Doug has stopped in at his local convenience store. He remembers he's out of toothpaste and walks down the personal hygiene aisle. He scans the shelves for the familiar Shine-Brite package (normally he uses Shine-Brite) but can't find it, so he grabs a packet of Macleans instead and heads off to buy some lunch.

Questions

1 Define mental and physical availability and discuss them in relation to the toothpaste brands mentioned in this case study.

2 Which is more important for a brand's long-term health—mental availability or physical availability?

3 One of the other brands on the shelf was Aquafresh. Doug didn't even consider buying Aquafresh. Why do you think this was the case? How could Aquafresh improve the likelihood of Doug buying their product next time he is in this situation?

4 What advice would you give to Philip to improve his marketing strategy?

5 What does this scenario tell us about customer involvement and the decision-making process? How many purchase decisions can you remember making this week where you carefully considered more than four brands?

HETEROGENEOUS CONSUMERS

◢ **LEARNING OBJECTIVE**
Begin to understand the differences between target marketing and mass marketing

◢ **mass marketing:**
A strategy where the marketer focuses on the entire market rather than a specific segment of consumers.

◢ **product variation:** When one company offers more choice to the consumer by selling different variations of the same product; for example, Coca-Cola, Diet Coke, Coke Zero, Vanilla Coke, etc—or even different brands (Fanta, Sprite).

◢ **target marketing:**
A strategy that identifies a target segment and focuses marketing communications on speaking directly to this group.

◢ **target segment (or target group):** A group of potential buyers within a market that share some common attributes and that are seen as desirable and valuable as customers.

Consumers are different from one another. They have different ages, genders, cultural backgrounds and levels of education. Even two people who are very similar (in age, education, income and so on) can have very different brand repertoires, and buy from the same category at different rates. Next time you are in a supermarket queue, have a look at the trolleys of the person in front of you and the person behind you. The odds are that their basket of items looks nothing like yours. In fact, they are buying a whole bunch of brands that you seldom if ever buy—they are buying 'odd' stuff! What this shows is that you have your repertoire and they have theirs, and the overlap is pretty small. A typical shopper buys only a few hundred brands in an entire year out of the thousands in the store (Sorensen, 2009), so statistically the chance that your repertoire has a substantial overlap with the person in front of you in the queue is pretty low. Similarly, odds are that your best friends bank at different banks than you, go to different hairdressers and different doctors, and holiday in different places.

Similar people have different repertoires, different preferences and loyalties. Different brands have built different degrees of mental availability in each of their individual brains. These memory structures started to be built a long time ago, and it has happened slowly, with a great deal of serendipity coming into play. Few of us can recall where all the brand memories we have came from, nor why some are fresher than others—there are quite simply a million little reasons, a million past events (like seeing a billboard advertisement, hearing a friend mention the brand, or watching a product placement in a movie, perhaps without realising).

On top of these differences in the memories (and behaviours) of similar people, there are also demographic and biological differences between people that can give them different needs and wants, and affect their buying behaviour. Simple things like the size of your car or your fridge can determine how often you shop, what size packages you buy, even what brands you select. How many people live in your house, or how many employees you have (for industrial buyers) will affect some of your buying behaviours. Most of the important differences are obvious: for instance, women's clothing is largely bought by women not men, children's television networks have more young viewers and stores receive more of their custom from people who live or work nearby. But these differences and the effect on buying behaviour can still be complicated, because there are many differences between people, especially in their lifestyles.

Mass marketing is often caricatured as treating all customers as if they are the same, but there is hardly a large brand on the planet that does not provide **product variation**. Variants often have different pricing, different advertising and so on. Mass marketers react to the heterogeneity in the market—they place stores in the north to reach northerners and stores in the south to reach southerners. Coca-Cola advertises in English in Australia and Spanish in Spain (and on Spanish-speaking television channels in California). This is sophisticated modern mass marketing.

There is a type of dumb **target marketing** though. This is when marketers ignore the heterogeneity among their customers and talk about a homogeneous **target segment** instead. It's popular for market researchers to present a profile of the target consumer almost as if there were just one sort of buyer of the brand (for example 'they shop at JB Hi-Fi and their favourite television program is

True Blood'). Sometimes they go so far as to give this target consumer a name (for example 'Emily') as if all buyers were the same person. This sort of profiling is dangerous: it underplays the real heterogeneity within the market and can lead to marketing plans that fail to reach many of the brand's current and potential buyers.

Segmentation studies are used by marketers to understand the heterogeneity in their market. Such studies look for useful ways to group people, because not all heterogeneity matters. For example, people have different hair colours. Now, this may be useful to know if you are marketing hair dye, but not if you are selling earth-moving equipment, or practically anything else for that matter. The segmentation study should be looking for differences between consumers that affect how they respond to marketing.

Very often the practical bases for segmentation are obvious and need no sophisticated research. For example, children watch different media from adults and react to different stimuli (they really like toys and cartoon characters), so if your buyers include a lot of children then you'll probably need some different media to reach them and different advertising content to catch their attention. If your buyers speak different languages, then your website, brochures and other advertising need to accommodate these different languages. The most obvious difference between buyers is physical location—if you offer house-painting services in Brisbane, you are unlikely to win many clients in Perth. Marketers need to make their brand physically available to potential buyers, so very often this will mean taking into account that different people live and work in different places.

Other often important differences between buyers include their cultural background, income, age and lifestyle—that is, what other things do they do? What media do they watch? When do they work? When do they shop? What size household do they live in? And so on. For business-to-business markets, other important differences include what industry the customer is in, how large their business is (turnover, number of employees) and where they do business (internationally or locally). How such major differences affect buying behaviour, needs and preferences in your product or service category is usually not difficult to establish using market research. Then marketing decisions can be made about how to react to these differences between buyers in your marketplace.

DO OUR BUYERS LIKE US?

▲ **LEARNING OBJECTIVE**
Understand what marketers should expect from their customers in terms of attitudes and behaviours

> I do not like broccoli. And I haven't liked it since I was a little kid and my mother made me eat it. And I'm President of the United States and I'm not going to eat any more broccoli.
>
> George Bush, US President, 1989–93

Another difference between consumers is that we each have different likes and dislikes. The memories stored in our heads of these likes and dislikes are called attitudes—positive or negative evaluations or feelings. These include opinions about brands, which can be a general brand attitude, such as liking Diesel but not FCUK, or more specific attitudes about specific features; for example, I might think that David Jones offers the better service but that Myer has better prices.

Marketers often overestimate the importance of brand attitudes in changing buying behaviour, and further overestimate their ability to change attitudes with advertising.

//

Post-war perceptions

Imagine that you are a political leader in Germany at the end of the Second World War, seeking to rebuild your country's economy. Your task is to determine which industries have the most potential. You identify the German car industry as a likely candidate; Germany has many fine engineers and factories such as those of Mercedes-Benz, Volkswagon and BMW. But sales will very much depend on selling to European and US consumers, who very recently were at war with Germany. What is their attitude towards German brands? To find out, you commission a survey of British and French consumers. The attitudinal message comes back loud and clear. In effect, consumers say: 'We will never buy a German car ... never!'

Likewise, US citizens in the late 1940s would have baulked at the idea of buying Japanese radios or televisions. Market research agencies are bound to have reported that Japanese brands would never be successful in the US, especially those with brand names that sounded particularly Japanese, such as Sony, Seiko, Casio, Mitsubishi and Yamaha.

But as it turned out, people's strongly negative attitudes did not stop them buying German and Japanese brands.

Marketing's attitude problem

When marketers face challenges such as how to make people recycle more or use less energy, they very often translate the problem into an attitude issue, such as 'how do we get people to care more about the environment?' Similarly, when faced with the very traditional marketing challenge of how to grow sales, marketers translate the issue into something like 'how do we get people to love our brand more?' or at least 'how do we get more people to think better of our brand?' Marketers do this because they operate according to a very deeply held assumption that attitudes determine behaviour—and that attitudes can be changed by advertising.

Consequently, marketers too often reach for strategies that feature persuasion-oriented communication, trying to tell people why this brand is better, or why they should hold a good opinion of the brand. Such strategies include:

- telling people the product has a particular superior feature
- making people care more about the brand
- making people feel good about the brand
- creating more advocates (who will tell others how good our brand is).

Marketers also spend much of their market research budgets asking people their opinion of their brand. These used to be known as 'usage and attitude' surveys. Today they are more likely to be called 'brand equity trackers'—ongoing surveys that contain large batteries of evaluative perception questions, such as 'which brand(s) do you think are:

- best for people like me?
- good value?

- trendy?
- for discerning buyers?
- caring?'

Many of these tracking services also feature proprietary '**black box**' attitudinal measures of things such as brand equity, loyalty, commitment and emotional connection to the brand. Each agency claims that their special attitude metric can be used to predict when a brand will soon gain or lose market share before the trend starts. No one has ever proved this, but some marketers fall for the claims and subscribe to the services.

'black box': How the metric is measured or calculated is kept hidden.

This is a symptom of marketing's 'attitude problem'. Marketers are quick to say that if you build a better mousetrap the world will not beat a path to your door—they know that good products don't just sell themselves. Yet they invest much effort and hope in packaging changes, launches of new flavours and many other small improvements. Marketers can easily overestimate the importance of these small differences because they are justifiably proud of their company and their brands. It's easy to fall into the trap of thinking that customers care much more than they actually do— thinking that consumers know and care about the work that went into shaping their dog biscuit to look fresher, redesigning their 'easy to open' lid ... or that consumers will care a great deal if they are told about these changes.

Marketing's attitude problem means that marketers very easily fall into the trap of seeing their job as trying to change buyers' attitudes. They can be so conditioned to believe that behaviours will follow attitudes that they forget their direct goal of changing behaviours. It is also easy to underestimate the importance of the ongoing battle for consumers' attention.

Why behaviours don't follow attitudes

Most of us would like to be nicer to our colleagues and family. We would like to eat more healthily, exercise more, spend more time with our loved ones, be more conscientious. Yet, we find it rather difficult to bring our actual behaviour in line with our more saintly attitudes. One major reason is that we simply keep forgetting our attitudes, or rather we fail to remember them at the right times. Another is that we have conflicting intentions: we like feeling lean and strong, but we also like chocolate cake; we want to buy brands that are good for the environment, but we also want to save money, save time, buy what tastes good, what looks nice, what the kids will like and so on.

Even though we do try to act in line with our beliefs and attitudes, we are also strongly affected by the environmental context and what pops into our head at the right moment. On holiday we will behave differently, when in a rush we will behave differently, when with different friends we will behave differently—it's very hard to use attitude to predict what we will do without taking these many other influences into account. This is why in psychology over the past few decades researchers have increasingly downplayed attitudes and placed much more emphasis on the many other forces shaping behaviour (Foxall, 1997).

Some marketing books dismiss real-world buying patterns, such as polygamous loyalty, as merely the messy real world deflecting consumers from their true intentions. The (silly) idea behind such thinking is that consumers would really like to be 100 per cent loyal (to the best brand for them), but things like stock-outs and price specials make them buy some other brands. But this interpretation doesn't fit the facts, because when we measure attitudes and intentions we see that consumers' opinions and plans reflect their prosaic uncommitted loyalty (Sharp, 2010). Consumers can hold an attitude about rival choices, such as thinking that Twix bars are a nice sweet treat, while also holding that opinion about Kit Kats (see Romaniuk & Gaillard, 2007 for evidence)— sometimes we notice one brand, sometimes the other. And when it comes to brand choice we often simply don't care that much. Most of us have made important decisions—even decisions that will substantially financially affect us, such as which credit card to use or which insurance policy to buy—without much evaluation (Dawes, Mundt & Sharp, 2009). We've also let advertising talking about the various product features go straight over our heads; we did not have time to listen or didn't care. We keep doing this partly because experience has taught us that it doesn't matter that much. Some bank marketers seem to think that if they can convince the population that their bank is a little more customer-oriented, they will win massive market share. Interestingly, credit unions (which have low market share) have convinced many people they are a bit more friendly, yet most people haven't moved to bank with them. Your bank may actually be friendlier than mine but it's unlikely to be by much and it really doesn't worry me.

Case study

Mobile payments: Who do you trust?

In 2011, advertising agency Ogilvy & Mather released data from a market research survey that asked consumers which brands they trusted to handle mobile payments. Patel (2011b) summarised the finding as 'consumers trust the same brands that handle their payments today', implying bad news for new potential entrants such as Google and Apple.

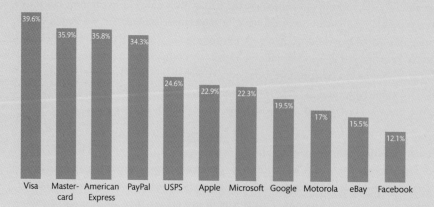

Questions

1   What do you think about this summary? Could you have predicted these survey results? Why or how?

2   Do you think these attitudes would change once people started using or saw others using a Google or Apple mobile payment system?

Even if we wanted our behaviour to be based on our attitudes, our ability to use our attitudes to guide our behaviour depends on memory. Our recall of brand attitudes is highly variable: one time we recall something nice about one brand, and next time we recall another brand.

What this means for the practical marketer is that they should spend very little time worrying about consumers' attitudes, and instead spend more time thinking about how to make the brand easier for consumers to notice, to think about and to buy—mental and physical availability.

Here are three facts about brand attitudes that show how little influence attitudes have in changing buying behaviour.

1 Brand attitudes reflect past buying behaviour

By the late 1960s, research evidence was clear: attitudes were not strong causes of behaviour. Instead, the evidence showed that behaviour was a better predictor of attitude (Foxall, 2002). Forty years later, surprisingly few marketing textbooks have caught up, and much academic and market research is still predicated on the belief that there is a simple relationship where attitudes cause intentions, which in turn cause behaviour. But the evidence shows a picture that is more often around the other way—brand attitudes largely reflect buying behaviour, and changes in behaviour mostly precede changes in attitude.

So, in market research attitude surveys we see a clear pattern where brands that have more users in the survey score higher on evaluative questions (such as 'do you like this brand?')—and brands with fewer users score lower on the attitude metric. So larger market share brands tend to score higher. This is largely driven by familiarity. If people don't use a brand, they are more likely to know nothing or little about it, and they are less likely to say they like it. But even when the scores are compiled only for those who know of the brand, the brands with more users still score a little higher. For example, among viewers of a particular television program, the more often a viewer watches it, the more favourably they will rate it in a survey (Barwise & Ehrenberg, 1987).

The more attitudinal (evaluative rather than descriptive and/or factual) in nature a question is, the more precisely we can predict a brand's score on that question—simply by knowing how many past users the brand has in the survey and how often they have used the brand.

So, brand attitudes largely reflect existing loyalties. If someone uses a brand, they are much more likely to say nice things about it than someone who does not use it. And the more often that they buy the brand the more favourably they tend to rate it.

2 Intentions reflect past buying behaviour

Early follow-up surveys after the US Census showed that households who said they intended to buy a new car were, unsurprisingly, more likely to actually buy one than households that said they did not intend to buy (40 per cent, compared to 7 per cent). However, since most (90 per cent or more) of households fell into the non-intenders group, this is where most car sales came from (Theil & Kosobud, 1968). This is quite counterintuitive for a car marketer—to realise that most of next year's sales will come from households who when interviewed say they are not planning on buying a car next year. Clearly it is easy to be deflected from one's intentions (in both directions—note that 60 per cent of people who said they would buy next year didn't).

For many repeatedly purchased categories (such as groceries, shoes, television programs, petrol or lunch) we don't really form plans in our head—at least, not long before actual purchase. So, when we are asked about our intentions, we instead largely report an estimate of our future behaviour, which we, quite reasonably, base on our past behaviour. Again, this means that brands that have more users will score higher on intentions: the more people who have bought them in the recent past, the more people who will say they intend buying them in the near future.

The strong influence of past behaviour on intentions produces the counterintuitive result that intentions are unexpectedly low for growing brands, and unexpectedly high for dying brands. If there are two brands that have currently equal market share, but one is a new, growing brand and the other is an old, declining brand, then intention surveys will record a higher score for the dying brand than the growing one. This is because the dying brand has more past users who know the brand and are therefore more likely to mention it in an intention survey (such as 'which brands of chocolate bar do you intend buying in the next three months?'), while the growing brand has fewer past users, so it isn't mentioned as much. In the future, the growing brand's sales will exceed the dying one, so common sense would suggest that the growing brand should have more people intending to buy it in the future, but what actually happens is that when people are asked their intentions they base their reply on what they have been doing (or the effect that this has had on their memories). What's actually happening in the marketplace is that the growing brand is rolling out physical availability and building mental availability (for example through advertising and publicity), so more people than thought they would actually end up buying it in the future, while the opposite story holds for the declining brand.

3 Brand attitudes are probabilistic

Attitudes have long been thought to be difficult to change and therefore strongly held. This view seemed to be supported by the *stability* of brand scores in attitude surveys—brands pretty much get the same score on this month's survey as they got last month. For example, if 28 per cent of people say they like Zim and only 4 per cent of people say they like Zappo, then on the next survey Zim won't just dominate again, it will score around 28 per cent and Zappo will again score around 4 per cent.

However, in 1994 an academic research team (that included the famous Andrew Ehrenberg) looked at something that previously had been largely ignored. Instead of asking different people in each survey, they re-interviewed the same people as in the previous survey. They did this because they were interested in how many people changed their answer from one survey to the other. Surprisingly, they found that, on average, only around half the time did people give the same attitudinal response they gave previously. This was a shocking finding. Were people really changing their opinions all the time?

So while 28 per cent of people might say they like Zim on each survey, only about half of the people who endorsed Zim on the first survey do it again on the second survey. Zim still scores 28 per cent, because every person who said they liked it on the first survey but not on the second is replaced by someone who didn't say they liked Zim on the first survey but now does on the second survey.

Previously, marketers interpreted attitude survey data like this: if 28 per cent of people ticked the 'like' box (or upper end of a liking scale question) for Zim, that means that there are consumers who like Zim (around 28 per cent of the population) and consumers who don't (the remaining 78 per cent of the population). But now we know that the correct interpretation is that much more than 28 per cent of consumers like Zim, but only sometimes—attitudes are probabilistic.

This discovery has been replicated and extended many times since, with several PhDs written on the topic. We now know that individuals' attitudinal responses over time follow very similar patterns to their buying behaviour. Consumers buy brands in a polygamous manner, not buying the same brand each time but selecting from a personal repertoire—and this is how they give attitudinal responses too. Sometimes they say Omo washes whiter, sometimes they say Surf does. If they buy Omo more often than Surf, they say Omo more often, and they rarely express attitudes about brands not in their buying repertoire.

Consumers' responses vary, in a probabilistic way. This is similar to how the result of a coin toss varies (either heads or tails) but each coin tossed has a probability of 50 per cent of landing on either side; there is lots of variation from toss to toss, but an overall pattern (50/50). The probabilistic behaviour in market research surveys is probably largely due to the fact that consumers' responses depend on their memories, which aren't perfect, and so which particular brand comes to mind in any instance varies. Professor Frank Bass once speculated that the human brand might have an inherently probabilistic aspect to it (1974); decades later, this discovery supports his view. This doesn't mean that consumers are doing complex calculations in their heads; it just means that which brand comes to mind and which one they choose to tick on the survey is due to many highly variable causes, some inside the brain (such as particular synapses firing in the brain at just the right time) and others out in the environment (such as seeing a brand's pack in the rubbish bin shortly before doing the survey).

This also strongly suggests that brand attitudes, while enduring, are typically not strongly held. In the same way that we are rarely 100 per cent behaviourally loyal to one brand, neither are we 100 per cent attitudinally loyal—sometimes we say one brand is best and sometimes another, because we like them both, but not in a particularly passionate way.

There are some broad differences between organisational and consumer buying behaviour, and between the needs and wants of organisational and household customers.

Generally, for non-trivial purchasing decisions, organisational buyers tend to place greater emphasis on matching logistic and technical requirements with product and supplier capabilities, and are thought to be less influenced by emotional factors. For major purchasing decisions that might require supply over long periods, risk avoidance often is an important factor. For example, consider a car manufacturer evaluating several supply proposals relating to a major component for a braking or steering system. Due to concerns about risk, the car manufacturer is likely to reject a proposal from a potential supplier lacking experience or solid financial backing, even if the price is most attractive.

Due to the complexity and financial or strategic importance of some supply arrangements, it is quite normal for several people from different departments within the customer organisation to be involved in major purchasing decisions. In some cases, various meetings are held by members of the 'buying centre', with salespeople and technical specialists from

Application to business-to-business marketing

a potential supplier organisation, to ensure that customer requirements and supplier capabilities are fully understood before a purchasing decision is made. Similarly, negotiations might be conducted during several meetings—perhaps over several weeks or even longer periods of time (even years)—involving senior purchasing and sales teams, before supply contracts are agreed upon and signed. These costly processes are justified (and required) when projects are of strategic importance or high value, such as the construction of a new factory or high-rise building complex, or a billion-dollar contract for the purchase of coal by a power station over the next decade.

Of course, personal factors do have influence in many organisational purchasing situations. Indeed, many business-to-business salespeople would be aware of organisational buyers who have been influenced by personal issues, including whether or not they personally like or dislike the salesperson!

As mentioned earlier in this chapter, important differences between customers within organisational markets include the industry in which the organisation operates, the size of the organisation (number of employees, turnover) and where the organisation operates (internationally or locally, for example). Similar to demographic differences among consumers, these organisational differences can result in differences in the buying behaviour of organisational customers. For example, government departments and not-for-profit organisations often use formal tendering methods for their purchases, partly to ensure a perception of financial integrity among the public and other stakeholder groups; while business firms might do so only for major capital equipment purchases. In a large firm, a major purchasing decision is usually made by several executives, while in a small family-owned firm such a decision is often made by just the owner.

Customer needs and wants also can be influenced by organisational factors. First, very large organisations would tend to require much greater quantities of products and services than small organisations in the same sector. For example, General Motors, which sold nine million vehicles worldwide in 2011 (General Motors, 2012), represents a much larger sales opportunity for potential suppliers such as Bosch or Bridgestone than Ferrari, with annual sales of only 6400 vehicles (Ferrari, 2012). The New South Wales government would have a much higher expenditure on office cleaning services than the much smaller Tasmanian government. Such differences in scale make some potential customers much more attractive than others. However, this also depends on the capabilities and size of the potential supplier. For example, a small but highly specialised automotive components manufacturer in Italy might be able to match the demanding specifications of Ferrari, but would lack the capacity or investment capital to consider pursuing opportunities at large automotive firms such as General Motors or Toyota.

Second, purchasing decisions can also be influenced by the business and marketing strategies of organisations. For example, as a leading international hotel chain, Marriott International mainly targets business and personal travellers with large expense accounts or high incomes, while a typical budget hotel mainly targets travellers on restricted budgets. Consistent with its target markets and high prices, Marriott International would ensure that furniture and furnishings purchased for its hotels are luxurious, stylish and of a high standard, with cost being a secondary issue. On the other hand, the budget hotel would place emphasis on cost rather than luxury when making purchasing decisions, consistent with its budget pricing strategy (and image). In effect, there often is broad consistency between an organisation's business and marketing strategies and its purchasing strategies.

The differences between organisational customers and household consumers have major implications for the importance of the sales function and how it operates. The fundamental principles of marketing, as taught in this book, broadly apply in both consumer and business markets. However, as in consumer markets, there are large differences within organisational markets regarding both buying behaviour and customer needs, which marketers need to take account of.

CONCLUSION

Buying behaviour, whether it is in an industrial setting, buying online or shopping in a store, follows certain fundamental patterns. Buyers are usually buying from categories that they know quite well, and they know a few brands in the category far better than any others. They loyally repeat-buy these brands and switch around between them. It seems that for brand buying we bring our attitudes into alignment with our behaviour more often than we seek to bring our behaviour in line with our attitudes. It is often more difficult to change behaviour to match a newly changed attitude. So attitudes have a weak impact on changing behaviour. But they also have a reinforcing effect on existing behaviour. For example, buying a brand reinforces the attitude (reminds us that we like the brand), which in turn reinforces repeat-buying behaviour. Much marketing is concerned with reinforcing, not changing, attitudes: encouraging consumers to keep on loyally buying our brand.

Attitudes and intentions can sometimes be an influence for behaviour change, but they tend to be weak influences, also needing changes in situation to bring about behaviour change. So, when marketers want to change behaviour—for example get more people to start buying their brand— they need to focus more on the situational and environmental drivers of behaviour. They need to build mental and physical availability for their brand to make it easier for these people to buy. Advertising is used to keep reminding people that the brand exists and how it might fit into their lives. Other parts of the marketing mix are used to make the brand easy to notice, buy and use.

●●● **TABLE 2.3** THE NEW CONSUMER BEHAVIOUR MODEL

Past world view	Attitude drives behaviour	Brand loyals	Brand switchers	Deeply committed buyers	Involvement	Rational, involved viewers
New world view	Behaviour drives attitude	Loyal switchers	Loyal switchers	Uncaring, cognitive misers	Heuristics	Emotional, distracted viewers

Marketers should be on the look out for barriers to the behaviour that they want to bring about. The industry insight 'Mars and the Russian rouble crisis' (page 45) gives an excellent example of how a company removed a barrier for their customers (retailers) and turned a problem into an opportunity. There will be different barriers for different customers; for some the brand will be too far away, for others it is one that they rarely think of, and for others it is missing a feature.

Marketing decisions depend on knowledge about consumers, how they buy the category and how they come into contact with the brand and its advertising; that is:

- who buys?
- where?
- when?
- how much?

This is information that you, as a marketing professional, will never stop analysing in order to keep up your understanding of your market.

02

SUMMARY

- Buyers rarely do lots of careful research before buying. In general, they make heavy use of their memories and simplify purchase decisions using existing habits and convenience.

- All consumers are naturally loyal, but this loyalty is rarely exclusive. Most consumers form a personal repertoire of brands and restrict their purchases to the brands within that repertoire.

- Consumers are more likely to buy brands that are more mentally and physically available to them at the time of the purchase decision.

- Memory is an important part of decision making—the greater mental availability a brand has, the more likely it will be purchased. Advertising plays an important role in refreshing and sometimes forming these brand memories.

- Customers can hold the same attitudes about rival brands. Although they are more likely to say nice things about the brands they use, an individual customer's attitudes are highly unpredictable for any particular point of time or situation.

- Information about buyers and potential buyers (who buys, how much, when and where) is useful for marketers when interpreted in light of what we know of buyer behaviour (and human psychology).

REVISION QUESTIONS

1 The managers of a supermarket held a discussion with a group of their regular customers to ask them what they did not like about their store. One customer said she did not like their fish and did not buy it. When asked why, she said it was 'packaged' on a little tray wrapped in cling-film and in a cooled display cabinet: 'I only buy fresh fish.' Other customers agreed with her. The managers were later assured by their fish buyer that the fish was bought off fishing boats every morning and was of the highest quality. It was sold wrapped for customers' convenience.

   What might be the reasons the customers believed the fish was not fresh?

   To overcome the problem, should the supermarket put up signs in the fish display to 'educate consumers' and say that the fish is fresh? Why or why not?

   If the supermarket then created an area where whole fish were displayed on ice and customers could buy pieces of fish cut from these, should the price per gram be the same as that for the packaged fish? Why or why not?

   How would you explain such findings to your boss? How would you suggest that it could be determined whether these results were good or bad?

2 When buying a new car, what proportion of buyers only considers one brand? When looking to buy a book online, how many sites do consumers visit? When a household has access to forty television channels, how many do they usually watch in a week?

In your own words, explain the reason for this typical behaviour.

How would you explain such findings to your boss? How would you suggest that it could be determined whether these results were good or bad?

3   Imagine that you are responsible for managing a brand and your boss says that you must increase sales of it over the next three years. She believes that one of the following strategies is the best. Which one would you tell her is the best, and why?

a   increase the loyalty of its customers

b   increase the frequency of consumption of the customers

c   increase the customer base

d   a lot of (a) and a little of (c)

e   a lot of (c) and a little of (a)

f   none of the above

How would you explain such findings to your boss? How would you suggest that it could be determined whether these results were good or bad?

4   You are managing a brand and a market research study reveals the following:

a   68 per cent of the people who bought your brand in the first three months of the year did not buy it in the second three months

b   32 per cent of your customers bought a competitor's brand during the second three months.

How would you explain such findings to your boss? How would you suggest that it could be determined whether these results were good or bad?

5   Why do you think that British and US consumers bought German and Japanese brands in the years that followed the Second World War?

6   Explain why it is important for brands to have logos and slogans to assist them to be preferred by consumers in buying situations.

7   McDonald's offer wine and beer in their restaurants in France but not in Australia; in Malaysia, no burgers are offered with bacon in them. Are McDonald's practising mass marketing or target marketing? Explain your answer.

FURTHER READING

Kahneman, D (2011) *Thinking Fast and Slow*, Farrar, Straus and Giroux, New York.

Salt, B (2006) *The Big Picture*, Hardie Grant Books, Melbourne.

Sharp, B (2010) *How Brands Grow*, Oxford University Press, South Melbourne.

WEBLINKS

Bacnet (building, automation and control networks):
www.bacnet.org

Distech Controls:
www.distech-controls.com

Green Building Council of Australia (GBCA):
www.gbca.org.au

NABERS:
www.nabers.com.au

LonMark International:
www.lonmark.org

New South Wales Office of Environment and Heritage:
www.environment.nsw.gov.au

◢ **Major case study**

Leopard Controls finally shows its spots

By Steve Klomp, Murdoch Business School, Perth

Introduction

DCE Electrical have been in business for more than twenty years and in that time have always punched above their weight in terms of contracts won and the level of quality achieved. Beginning life as a humble, one-man electrical contracting firm with a focus on client service, DCE Electrical soon got the attention of major telecommunications and contract management companies and began providing installation, upgrade and maintenance services all over Western Australia, particularly in Perth and the south-west of the state. The company gradually took on larger and larger contracts and more and more staff, and became known for its expertise in air-conditioning, electrical distribution and power generation. In the late 1990s, the firm decided to also compete in the field of building management systems (BMS), an area growing in importance as the world turned its attention to environmental protection. Leopard Controls was born.

Building management systems

Building management systems do exactly as the name implies: they control, monitor and manage building systems such as air-conditioning, lighting, power, access and security. A BMS can manage an entire building or even a group of buildings to ensure their correct operation and efficiency. These systems are completely automated and the design algorithm is written to ensure the greatest level of operating efficiency possible. This equates to lower running costs for building owners and tenants, much higher reliability and, of course, a much lower impact on the environment in terms of energy use.

Today, building management systems use sophisticated, microprocessor-based controllers and interface with their human managers via computer graphical programs. They are linked to the internet and it is not unusual for a BMS to be able to send an alarm to a maintenance team across town or even in another state. They can even be reprogrammed from another country and are frequently designed to report energy use or air-conditioning running times directly onto remote databases. Very clever!

The modern, multi-storey building is an expensive structure. It often houses multiple tenants and is required to comply with government regulation throughout its life. These three factors make a BMS an essential part of the design. They also make it a significant part of the cost.

As a rule of thumb, building services represent 10 per cent of the overall cost of a new building and a BMS is around 10 per cent of the cost of the building services. Put another way, if a new building will cost $100 million to build, the owners will expect to pay $1 million for the building management system—a significant sum.

Perhaps even more important, however, is the maintenance and upgrade costs of a BMS. A building is not a static environment. Tenants come and go, buildings are upgraded and redecorated, and the building services are continually being serviced and maintained. This means that the BMS will require maintenance

DCE Electrical have been in business for more than twenty years and in that time have always punched above their weight in terms of contracts won and the level of quality achieved.

and upgrade services on an ongoing basis and this work can be so lucrative some BMS provider companies have been known to take a substantial loss on the initial installation in order to secure the more profitable ongoing work.

●●● LINDSAY GITTOS AND LINDSAY DICK (MANAGING DIRECTORS OF DCE ELECTRICAL AND ITS OFFSHOOT, LEOPARD CONTROLS) AND TONY TIMPSON (MANAGER, LEOPARD CONTROLS)

Energy rating systems for buildings

Building owners are increasingly using BMSs in order to achieve high environmental protection ratings. These ratings demonstrate the 'green' credentials of the organisation and are often used in occupation cost analyses by tenants. Protection ratings come from initiatives such as NABERS and Green Star.

According to its website (www.nabers.com.au), NABERS is a performance-based rating system for existing buildings that measures the operational impact of building on the environment and compares that performance with that of other buildings. NABERS is an acronym for the National Australian Built Environment Rating System—a national initiative managed by the New South Wales Office of Environment and Heritage.

Another energy, water and gas use rating system—Green Star—is run by the Green Building Council of Australia (GBCA). It is a national, not-for-profit organisation committed to the adoption of green building practices by Australian builders.

Background to the industry

The Australian building management system industry is dominated by three major players: Honeywell, TAC (formerly CSI) and Siemens. As well as dominating the Australian scene, these three organisations are very large, global companies. Honeywell is currently the clear leader in the BMS field, based on number of current installations. There are also many smaller players in the BMS marketplace.

'We then tell them we can do the work, we are very experienced, we have the resources and we are client oriented. We say that they will get a good price and a high quality installation—and most of our clients sign up then and there.'

The industry is profitable enough to continually attract new players. However, existing competitors are keen to protect their share of the marketplace. They seek to erect barriers to entry wherever possible. One such barrier is the use of proprietary software and proprietary product types.

Proprietary product simply means that, even when installed in a building, the ownership of the software (and occasionally, the firmware) remains with the original supplier. It also means that software cannot be shared, at least not easily. Proprietary product suppliers also frequently enter contracts that ensure that they are the only future supplier of new product, maintenance or repair work.

Further to that, proprietary software developers very often oppose the so-called 'open source programming'. If communications is not 'open source' then products from different manufacturers will not 'talk' to each other.

The effect of this barrier to entry is to completely shut new competitors out of the market place. They are only able to supply their products for new buildings—and securing this sort of work as a new industry entrant is very difficult indeed.

It also means that owners of existing buildings, short of completely removing a system and starting again, lose the option to change suppliers once a system is installed. Pricing is difficult to control and poor service difficult to counter. Even choosing potentially cheaper options for maintenance and upgrade work is an onerous task.

On the other hand, the arrangement probably improves the reliability of a BMS system because performance can be guaranteed and servicing tends to be done by the same personnel from the same company.

Leopard Controls looks for a competitive edge

Back in the 1990s, Leopard Controls was a small player in industry terms. It was always going to be difficult for the firm to gain a foothold in the marketplace. However, Managing Director Lindsay Gittos believed his firm could be successful by offering clients something they had never previously had—choice.

Leopard Controls decided to offer non-proprietary products that used newly developed open source software. There would be no 'lock in' contracts and no monopolising of the work. The company would offer design and installation, maintenance and upgrade services based on competitive price and good service alone. If the client was not happy with the service, reliability and price offered by Leopard Controls they were free to go back into the marketplace at any time and choose another product, another supplier, or both.

Any new products would happily work with the original system and so would any upgrades built on to the original platform. If the client decided to begin using another firm, Leopard Controls even agreed to offer parts and expertise for the original system to that competitor—at fair market prices.

They were taking a big risk—but the company believed they had always offered good pricing and good service and they saw no reason why they shouldn't continue to be judged on that basis, and that basis alone.

Clients agreed—and began knocking on the door. Leopard Controls secured work all over town, and began to grow very quickly.

●●● RAY COWIE, WORKSHOP MANAGER, LEOPARD CONTROLS

The search for a BMS

Leopard Controls needed to be able to offer a building management system, but didn't have the in-house expertise to design and manufacture one themselves. They searched the world for a system that was not only reasonably priced and of sufficient quality, but also 'open' in programming terms.

Technically, 'open source programming' really refers to seven layers of interconnection between devices. These layers include the physical layer (how the plugs fit together), the electrical isolation layer and the radio frequency layer, all the way through to the communications protocol each device must use. The protocol is the language, the 'talk' between devices, but all layers are equally important if interconnection is going to be possible. Experts therefore often refer to 'open system interconnect' (OSI). The most common OSI standards used in the building management system world are LON and Bacnet. These OSI systems often use Tridium, which is 'front end' software that can combine both platforms and many other proprietary systems.

The company finally settled on using the Canadian firm Distech, which manufacturers both Lon and Bacnet-based equipment. LON and Bacnet have been around since the 1990s. LON communications protocol software can be downloaded free by anyone with an internet connection. Originally known as Lontalk, LON now has more than ninety million devices using this protocol installed around the world. Leopard Controls buys 'off the shelf' equipment that can be programmed and installed by anyone with knowledge of BMSs and the electrical industry. The Distech equipment or equivalent can be sourced from dozens of suppliers around the world.

Managing Director Lindsay Gittos talks about why a client should use his company, Leopard Controls:

> Basically the reason is the same reason a homeowner chooses a particular electrician to fix a light in his home. Every electrician drives a van, wears safety boots and a uniform, has a mobile phone and an advertisement in the phone book—but only a few of them give the sort of service the clients want.
>
> We give our clients the service they want. If a building operator wants to upgrade their building, we say that we use 'open protocol' based products which are available everywhere and can be designed and installed by many service agents. Then we give them a list of these agents!
>
> Most of our clients are quite surprised at this point! We then tell them we can do the work, we are very experienced, we have the resources and we are client oriented. We say that they will get a good price and a high quality installation—and most of our clients sign up then and there.

The challenge from the big end of town

In the building industry, contracts can come from 'top-down selling' or from 'bottom-up selling'. Top-down selling happens when a supplier contacts the top management of an organisation and 'sells' their products. Top management very often does not have any knowledge of the products themselves, but they sign major contracts based on product reputation and marketing. Top-down marketing is expensive and out of reach of smaller companies but does reap very large rewards.

Bottom-up selling basically means selling to companies for whom you already work. For smaller businesses, bottom-up selling can mean the opportunity to gain vital cash flow, and it is a great way to build reputation and experience in an industry, which makes it a favoured method for new industry players like Leopard Controls. However, as it involves targeting people who do not make major purchase decisions, this sales method does not build a client base quickly and is not generally the way to secure major contracts.

Conversely, top-down selling involves researching and then targeting the major decision makers in larger organisations. This method is time-consuming and expensive—but is much more profitable in the long term. Top-down selling is used by established industry players with considerable experience and reputation.

In 2011, Leopard Controls got the chance to tender on the BMS for the Perth International Airport redevelopment. They faced stiff opposition from a very large, well-credentialled, US-based multinational company. To give you some idea of the size of this company, it has 130,000 employees worldwide and turns over in excess of US$35 billion per year. This major industry player was also expert at top-down sales—but Leopard had been supplying BMS services to the site since 2005.

In the end, it all came down to a choice between the big multinational and the small local company; the closed system versus the open system. The stakes were very high, with massive construction expected on site up until 2018, the prestige of such a marquee site to be used in future marketing and the promise from ongoing maintenance work.

●●● LINDSAY GITTOS, MANAGING DIRECTOR OF DCE ELECTRICAL

Lindsay Gittos describes the presentation to the tendering board:

> We had forty-five minutes. Twenty minutes was spent spruiking our company, products and past achievements with the remaining time spent on a technical question and answer session. Only two

companies were invited to do this—Leopard Controls and the multinational firm. We knew the multinational had been busy top-down selling on this project for over eighteen months. They had focused on top company management and the engineers and consultants working on the project. But we also knew that the airport tendering team had consulted with their staff on the ground, the people who were involved with the day-to-day operation of the BMS system. These were the same people we had been impressing for the last six years.

Three of our management team attended—Lindsay Gittos, Tony Timpson (General Manager of Leopard Controls) and Lindsay Dick (co-Director of the Company). We all had experience at handling ourselves in the board room but this was a new level. Leopard Controls were first. We thought our performance was strong but it was a little disconcerting to see our opposition as we walked out of the presentation—all six laden with briefcases, laptops, documents and product!

We had been over and over our pricing for stage one construction and it was tight. This contract was very important to the development of our company, it was more than just ongoing work for us; it represented everything we have been working towards for over ten years. We knew it would come down to a comparison between price and service. Had we done enough?

We won!

Regarding the future of Leopard Controls, Gittos says:

Today we have built a lot of BMS systems and we have contracts for a lot of maintenance work. Leopard Controls has outfitted office blocks in the CBD, major shopping centres, telecommunications buildings and of course Perth Airport is ongoing.

We now have the complete skill set 'in house' and the cash flow to be a very serious industry player. We are one of very few companies expert in the application of Bacnet, LON and Tridium, all open systems. We have employed a full time OH&S and QA manager who will create the processes so the company can become Quality Assured [AS/NZS ISO9001:2008], which we see as essential to the future of the company. We are now considering how to expand from here.

When asked what their biggest need at the moment is, Gittos responds:

The company has done very well over the last twenty years, mainly through lots of hard work. We have also been lucky, and while I believe luck is actually preparation meeting opportunity, I have

to admit that at times we have been very lucky indeed! We need to become more professional in our approach to strategic planning and in identifying opportunities.

We need research done on the market and our clients, on how to advertise ourselves. We need to consider other markets, both around Australia and around the world. Leopard Controls also needs to look at breaking into other industries. For example, the mining industry in Western Australia offers a lot of opportunities— but we are not sure how to go about getting this work.

We expect to remain Perth-based so that we can have economies of scale in areas such as payroll, HRM and engineering, but want to be able to do installation and maintenance work anywhere. We also want to be a company using triple-bottom line reporting within two years.

We want to look at the level of profitability in everything we do, our decision-making process and we want to know what is important at different points on the life cycle of our products.

We also need to identify our real competitors, particularly in other attractive markets, and work out how to counter their competitive advantage.

Basically, we need to hire a professional marketer!

This case study is based on a personal interview with Mr Lindsay Gittos, Managing Director, DCE Electrical, February 2012, Perth

Questions

1   What could a marketing professional do for a company like Leopard Controls?

2   Make a list of the short-term and long-term objectives of the company and consider how these two sets of objectives might clash. How can Leopard Controls make their marketing efforts sustainable?

3   In some ways the Leopard Controls approach to gaining market share could be considered naïve. It may be good for the clients, but is not necessarily good for the business itself. Growth can be slow and erratic because price and service quality perception can fall victim to the mood state of the client. Profitability is also dependent on a high activity level. What are the advantages and disadvantages of this approach to business?

4   What metrics would you use to evaluate this business on an ongoing basis? How you would use these metrics to make operational and strategic decisions?

Practitioner profile
Emma Fletcher, Senior Marketing Manager, South Australian Tourism Commission

When I finished high school, I was accepted into a medical radiation (nuclear medicine) course. After a year and a half, I decided it wasn't for me, so I took some time off to travel overseas. It was while I was away that I realised that I was more interested in a business-focused career, and when I came home I enrolled in a bachelor of management, majoring in marketing.

Looking back, I definitely made the right choice. Marketing is such a dynamic field—there are so many different types of marketing positions in so many different industries. I know that in a specialist field such as nuclear medicine I would never have been able to enjoy that same level of flexibility.

I started my career as a market research analyst, moved to a brand management role in the banking and finance sector, and now I am working in the tourism industry. Each marketing job I've had has been different, so I've developed a wide range of practical skills and a useful knowledge base. That range of experience is what helped me to win my current position. All the skills and experience from my previous jobs help me in my current role and will continue to be useful in the future.

As Senior Marketing Manager, a big part of my role is marketing planning. This includes planning for one-off projects, as well as long-term strategic planning for our brands and sub-brands. Important parts of planning are analysis and insights: seeing where we are in relation to competitors, tracking and monitoring our brands and campaigns to see what worked well and what didn't work. Collecting information and analysing and tracking data can be expensive and time-consuming, but without it you can't make good marketing decisions. Marketers need to invest this time to make sure everything else we do isn't wasted and that we don't miss out on opportunities for growth.

Like most managers, my schedule is busy, and I have a lot of competing responsibilities, but at the end of the day everything I do is a step towards the main goal: promoting South Australia. And that is what I love the most about my job. I get to showcase the things that are great about South Australia, and get more people to enjoy and experience my state.

03

MEANINGFUL MARKETING METRICS

BYRON SHARP, WITH CONTRIBUTION
FROM SVETLANA BOGOMOLOVA

◢ **Introduction case**

The cost of cutting back

In October 2006, the US chocolate and candy bar maker the Hershey Company was facing a lot of questions from Wall Street financial analysts. They suggested a link between the chocolate giant's recent decrease in advertising spending and its lower than expected sales. But *AdAge* reported that Hershey's management were adamant that they were right to spend less on consumer advertising, based on their work in statistically modelling the causes of sales. 'Our marketing mix modelling still reinforces that trade spending has the highest return on investment ... efforts closer to the point of consumption and the point of sale tend to have the higher returns,' said Hershey CEO and President Rick Lenny (Thompson, 2006).

In the following year, *Forbes* magazine reported that Hershey would earn less that year than previously forecast and Hershey announced plans to close its last two factories in Canada and cut jobs in a Pennsylvania chocolate factory (Gutierrez, 2007).

In 2009, under the management of new CEO David J West, Hershey was able to announce that

Two years later, *The Wall Street Journal* reported that Hershey was delighting the stock market and its share price had climbed 47 per cent in a year. Since 2008, it had tripled the annual advertising budget and sales were up 10 per cent.

two of their major brands, Reese's and Kisses, were both regaining market share. 'I'm pleased with the progress we continue to make,' said West, 'market-share performance is tracking nicely with core brands responding to the marketing investments we have made' (Bryson-York, 2009). Advertising spend had been increased by 40 per cent.

Two years later, *The Wall Street Journal* reported that Hershey was delighting the stock market and its share price had climbed 47 per cent in a year. Since 2008, it had tripled the annual advertising budget and sales were up 10 per cent.

It is said that history often repeats itself, and Deborah Cadbury's book *Chocolate Wars* reports that thirty years earlier, in the 1970s, when Hershey were the leading US chocolate manufacturer, management were looking for cost savings and their first move was to slash the advertising budget. 'The Mars sales team, inspired by Forest Mars, went on a crusade to promote Mars produce into every possible store at Hershey's expense. Mars was fast overtaking its rival.' (Cadbury, 2010: 275)

INTRODUCTION

Just as doctors need measures to assess the health of their patients, marketing managers need measures to assess the health of their brands and to judge the effects of their marketing campaigns. Sales revenue and contribution to profit are vital metrics but they aren't enough. They can show a decline or an increase, but more metrics are needed to help explain why this happened. A thorough metrics system includes: financial metrics, buying behaviour metrics, memory metrics, customer profile metrics and marketing activity metrics. In order to interpret any metric correctly, marketers need to be aware of benchmarks and expected patterns (in other words: is the score high, low or as it should be?).

LEARNING OBJECTIVES

After reading this chapter you should:

- be able to explain what marketing metrics are and give examples
- understand how metrics are used in practice
- have a clear understanding of the difference between behavioural and memory metrics
- be able to give examples of the most commonly used benchmarks in marketing metrics
- understand the concept of correlation, and tests for inferring causality
- be able to describe some common mistakes in interpreting metrics.

CHAPTER OUTLINE

Introduction

Why marketers need metrics

A system of marketing metrics

Financial metrics

Behavioural metrics

Memory metrics

Customer profile metrics

Marketing activity metrics

Physical availability metrics

Looks can be deceiving

Conclusion

KEY TERMS

brand equity

brand image

customer relationship
    management (CRM) systems

customer-based metrics

customer lifetime value (CLV)

customer satisfaction

customer value

heavy buyer

market penetration

net promoter score

profit contribution

purchase frequency

random sampling variation

share of category requirements
    (SCR)

share of voice (SoV)

word-of-mouth (WOM)

WHY MARKETERS NEED METRICS

▲ **LEARNING OBJECTIVE**
Be able to explain what
marketing metrics are
and give examples

If you aren't measuring something, even in a rough way, then you can't be managing it. Chefs look at, smell and taste their food—usually as they cook, not only afterwards. They do so in order to assess if their actions are making the food hotter, sweeter, saltier, tastier and so on. Similarly, marketing managers need measurement to assess and guide their marketing actions. Marketing metrics let managers know how the brand and business is performing; and marketing metrics can provide diagnostic information on how to improve things. Without a comprehensive set of meaningful metrics, a marketing director simply cannot tell if they are doing a good job or not.

Contrary to popular belief, you don't have to be a maths geek to be good at interpreting quantitative data. In this chapter, we'll show how a sound understanding of what metrics mean, plus some simple rules of data presentation, can give a marketer real advantages: the ability to see meaning in data where others can't, and the ability to present persuasive data-driven arguments.

Are metrics meaningful?

Increasing amounts of money and management attention are being spent on marketing metrics. Marketers are demanding metrics for management purposes, and for reporting performance to company boards, shareholders and outside groups. For example, companies now report metrics on their environmental record. Research agencies, media companies and consultants are pumping out new metrics. Yet many of these metrics are misleading or unhelpful.

Marketing academic John Bound once described his long career as a market research manager in large corporations (before joining academia) as excelling in wasting his company's money—with a note that he was sure that people do every bit as good a job today as he did then. Most market research is done technically very well, but it often fails to produce useful meaningful marketing metrics. The wrong things can be measured, in the wrong ways, and things may be misinterpreted.

There is no point in tracking and regularly reporting metrics that do not change, or do so very slowly. A good (and well-funded) medical practice will measure the weight and blood pressure of patients each time they visit. But, sensibly, they will measure the height of adult patients only rarely. Many marketing metrics such as **customer satisfaction** and **brand image** are measured and

▲ **customer satisfaction:**
The measurement of
how many consumers
are satisfied with the
company's product/
service, thought to
capture how well an
organisation meets
or exceeds customer
expectation.

▲ **brand image:** The
perception of the brand in
the minds of consumers.

▲ **random sampling variation:** The error in survey results because a random sample can only ever be approximately representative of a larger population.

reported far too regularly. Fortunately for market researchers, **random sampling variation** makes the figures wobble around a bit from survey to survey, providing the illusion of change. Much management time is then wasted coming up with erroneous explanations for movements that are simply random sampling variation. It keeps a lot of market researchers in business.

Figure 3.1 shows evaluation of service performance scores across five major Australian brands over a ten-year period. Apart from a small dip around 1998 for all banks, performance seems to be around 7 to 8 out of 10. Much of that variability is likely to be accounted for by random sampling variation. Note that exactly the same data presented using a truncated scale (the graph on the right) creates the illusion of dramatic changes, changes that would require marketers to provide an explanation.

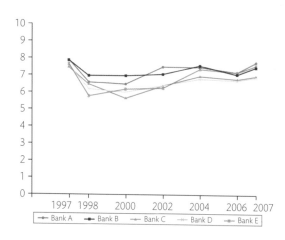 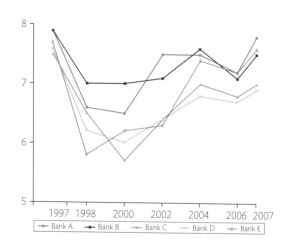

●●● **FIGURE 3.1** EVALUATION OF SERVICE PERFORMANCE OF MAJOR BANKS, 1997–2007

Source: Real, disguised banking survey data from Ehrenberg-Bass Institute

▲ **market penetration:** The extent to which a product is recognised and bought by customers in a particular market.

▲ **brand equity:** The financial value of a brand's market-based assets (mental and physical availability). Also sometimes used to refer to a consumer's subjective assessment of how much better or preferred the brand is. Under this latter (not very useful) definition, higher quality, higher priced brands have higher equity.

Table 3.1 shows brand satisfaction with personal computers has not changed much over the past ten years. Even the differences between brands' scores (which we explain later in this chapter) are consistent over time.

Similarly, there is little point in tracking and regularly reporting metrics that are already perfectly predictable from other metrics. Medical practitioners will not test male patients who complain of sickness in the morning for pregnancy—from the fact that they are male it is perfectly predictable that they are not pregnant. Many marketing metrics are predictable from market share or from how many customers the brand has (**market penetration**). The scores on these metrics are always higher for larger market share brands. Much market research, in effect, consists of asking respondents in numerous different ways (different questions) how often they buy the brand (see 'Marketing's attitude problem' on page 58).

Finally, there is little point in tracking and reporting metrics when you do not know what they mean, how they relate to other metrics and marketing actions or what level they should be. Many special proprietary metrics sold by market research agencies fall into this category. Just because a measure is given a name that sounds important (such as '**brand equity**' or 'brand health') doesn't mean it necessarily is.

●●● **TABLE 3.1** BRAND SATISFACTION WITH PERSONAL COMPUTERS, 1995–2008

	BASE LINE	95	96	97	98	99	00	01	02	03	04	05	06	07	08	PREVIOUS YEAR % CHANGE	FIRST YEAR % CHANGE
PERSONAL COMPUTERS	78	75	73	70	71	72	74	71	71	72	74	74	77	75	74	–1.3	–5.1
APPLE	77	75	76	70	69	72	75	73	73	77	81	81	83	79	85	7.6	10.4
DELL	NM	NM	NM	72	74	76	80	78	76	78	79	74	78	74	75	1.4	4.2
HP	78	80	77	75	72	74	74	73	71	70	71	73	75	76	73	–3.9	–6.4
GATEWAY	NM	NM	NM	NM	76	76	78	73	72	69	74	72	73	75	72	–4.0	–5.3
ALL OTHERS	NM	70	73	72	69	69	68	67	70	69	71	74	77	75	72	–4.0	2.9
COMPAQ	78	77	74	67	72	71	71	69	68	68	69	67	72	73	70	–4.1	–10.3
IBM	78	78	74	71	74	73	75	71	NM	NM	NM	NM	NM	NM	NM	N/A	N/A
NEC	NM	NM	71	66	67	NM	NM	NM	NM	NM	NM	NM	NM	NM	NM	N/A	N/A

Source: American Consumer Satisfaction Index (2008) *Second Quarter 2008—Manufacturing/Durable Goods & E-Business*, retrieved 3 August from <www.marketingcharts.com/interactive/google-apple-defy-declining-customer-satisfaction-trends-5749/acsi-index-computer-industry-scores-q2-2008jpg>

Imagine if your doctor measured your blood pressure and when you asked why and what it meant she replied 'no idea … we were taught how to measure blood pressure at medical school, so I do it for all my patients—always have'!

Let's continue with this medical example for a moment. When a doctor measures a patient's blood pressure as, say, 140 over 90, they have a piece of data that is meaningless in its own right—is this high, low or just right? And why does this matter? If the doctor takes the patient's blood pressure a second time on another day, using a different sphygmomanometer, and the reading is still 140 over 90 then the doctor is somewhat reassured about the reliability of their equipment and the credibility of the result. This is important, but the doctor still has nothing more than a meaningless (but reliable) piece of data.

To turn this data into information, the doctor needs scientific knowledge, such as how blood pressure scores relate to one another, how they vary between healthy and unhealthy individuals, and how blood pressure varies with age, gender and medication. Given such knowledge, the doctor may then declare that 140 over 90 is high (not low or just right) and they know what this means for health.

Marketing professionals also need scientific knowledge in order to make their marketing metrics meaningful and to improve the quality of their management. Marketing research managers need such knowledge to avoid wasting money on pointless market research.

This chapter recommends a range of metrics based on logic and many decades of serious research. We explain what the metrics mean, to the best of current knowledge. Based on this understanding, we advise against some metrics and recommend when to collect each metric, so that money is not wasted collecting some metrics too often.

Some market research agencies may dislike this book when it recommends against spending money on market research to collect particular metrics. But overall this book promotes the increased use of metrics, which is good news for the market research community.

Some experienced marketers will find it confronting to hear that their favourite metric does not mean what they thought it meant (that is, that they are being misled), or perhaps that it is not useful at all. However, this chapter is a guide for marketers: it should provide much greater understanding of marketing metrics, and thereby provide the tools to improve accountability, to justify marketing budgets and to improve marketing effectiveness.

Finally, for those grappling to construct a decent system of marketing metrics, this chapter provides a serious practical guide, and one based on volumes of independent empirical evidence rather than the desire to sell a particular consulting service, software or market research product.

◢ **LEARNING OBJECTIVE**
Understand how metrics are used in practice

◢ **customer-based metrics:** Metrics that measure things such as customer satisfaction, awareness and perceptions of the brand. They can be quantitative and/or qualitative.

A SYSTEM OF MARKETING METRICS

In this textbook, our focus is largely on **customer-based metrics**. The marketing department is usually responsible for collecting these metrics, and is supposed to have specialist knowledge about how to interpret them. It is against these metrics that so much of marketing's performance is evaluated.

Without these marketing metrics, marketers are 'flying blind', spending shareholders' money without a proper understanding of what needs to be spent and where—and with little ability to evaluate the effect of their expenditure. These vital marketing metrics describe:

- brands' activities in the market; for example new product launches, price increases, changes in pack size, and so on
- how the market is reacting to these changes; for example how buyers are buying, at what prices, and so on
- how the brand's market-based assets are holding up.

There are other metrics that are of interest to marketers, such as metrics on the degree of staff turnover in the marketing and sales departments, salary rates, and metrics relating to staff knowledge and competencies. These are not the focus of this textbook.

Why measure market-based assets?

Marketing interventions by the brand and its competitors affect buyer behaviour, and thereby sales and other financial performance metrics. But any marketing effect is moderated by the brand's existing market-based assets—intangible assets that have accumulated due to years of trading activity and marketing effort. For example, advertising works harder for brands with widespread physical and mental availability, because for brands with patchy availability some of the advertising simply falls on fallow ground: if a bank doesn't have many branches in the West, then much of its advertising to Westerners is wasted.

These market-based assets need to be measured in order to understand and correctly evaluate the longer-term effects of marketing activity. These metrics are also needed to evaluate brand performance, because some marketing activity may potentially erode these assets, and so erode future sales, while still generating acceptable sales and/or profits today. For example, marketing activity that skews to heavier, more regular buyers of the brand will generally be more efficient; it's cheaper and easier to reach these buyers, partly simply because they are a smaller group, but also because they are more receptive (they notice the advertising). However, such a strategy can temporarily maintain profits while market-based assets, sales and market share begin eroding.

Similarly, a brand can post a good **profit contribution** by simply underspending on marketing (see 'The cost of cutting back' on page 79). Cuts in marketing expenditure go straight to the bottom line, which mean this is an easy path by which to boost profits or simply maintain profit levels in the face of superior competition. This is why board members and external financial analysts look to revenue and market share as important metrics to have alongside profit—to give the profit result context and meaning. Similarly, they want to see how much has been spent on marketing, and so activity metrics such as spend and **share of voice (SoV)** are therefore important. However, managers might rightly claim that their reduced marketing expenditure reflects gains in efficiency ('we are spending less but on better marketing'). In order to evaluate this claim, senior management need metrics on revenue and market share, but they also need metrics that report the state of the brand's market-based assets. When put together, these metrics can tell a comprehensive story about brand performance and marketing efficiency.

> **profit contribution:** The piece of your sales that contributes to your profit; the sales price received minus the expenses or variable costs.

> **share of voice (SoV):** A measure of the total number of mentions that a company gets in its target media relative to its main competitor. It is a measure of awareness and image in the media rather than in the minds of the target audience.

Case study
Procter & Gamble's operating shift

In 2012, Procter & Gamble's Chief Executive, Bob McDonald, promised to deliver US$1 billion in savings by 2016, as part of a company-wide cost reduction of US$10 billion. Most of these cost savings would come from reducing marketing staff numbers. P&G's internal surveys have shown that marketing staff find the company too bureaucratic, and so cutting layers of management may improve things.

But not all the savings will come from reducing staff. So, how much marketing expenditure will be cut?

'Similar to R&D, we are not looking to make dramatic cuts in the support of our brands,' said McDonald (quoted in Farey-Jones, 2012). 'In fact, we want to increase reach, increase frequency and increase the effectiveness of our advertising impressions with consumers.'

However, McDonald did imply that some substantial reduction in marketing spend would occur, but justified it by saying efficiency would increase: 'Even delivering a modest level of efficiency each year can amount to nearly a billion dollars of savings versus simply letting these costs grow at the same rate as sales.' This efficiency gain, he said, would come largely from using new digital and social media.

To cut costs without sacrificing impact, McDonald (quoted in Farey-Jones, 2012) said P&G is using technology to shift spending from more traditional vehicles like television to digital and mobile advertising and more efficiently target consumers, 'allowing us to build one-on-one personal relationships with every consumer'. He also expects to use more multi-brand efforts to spread spending more efficiently among brands. He cited the kickoff of P&G's Summer Olympics program in January, which he said delivered more than 2.5 billion impressions in traditional and social media the first month alone and produced a bigger overall impact than the brands could have had by spending individually.

AdAge reported that overall, the cost-cutting program P&G outlined was two to three times deeper than financial analysts had been expecting (Neff, 2012).

Questions

1   There is little doubt that P&G will implement its cost cuts, but will it be able to offset the reduction in marketing spend by achieving greater efficiency of its spend?

2   How will management and investors be able to tell if P&G has increased efficiency, or whether it has simply reduced the marketing support for its brands, which will eventually later show in reduced sales?

We now discuss various important and useful marketing metrics in the following categories:

1   Financial metrics

2   Behavioural metrics

3   Memory metrics

4   Customer profile metrics

5   Marketing activity metrics

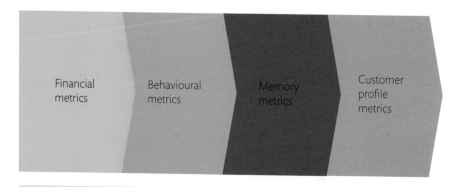

Source: Adapted from B Shaw (1998) *Improving Marketing Effectiveness*, Profile Books, London, p. 108

FINANCIAL METRICS

Financial metrics include things such as sales revenue, profit and cash-flow impact. None of this is rocket science and it is taught in any basic business or accounting course. So, in this textbook we concentrate mainly on the customer-based metrics. However, there are some important aspects about some popular financial metrics that are not always well understood by marketers—these are explained below.

Profit and profit contribution

$$Profit = Sales\ Revenue - Costs$$

Profit is easily calculated for a single discrete business: it is the money left over (for owners) after all expenses are paid. However, calculating profit for parts of the business (for example for business units, brands or products) is more tricky. A decision has to be made regarding how much of some costs that span many parts of the business (costs such as the CEO's salary) should be allocated to each individual part of the business. How this is done will affect the reported profit of that part. For example, if an unfair amount of central costs (often called overheads) are allocated to a particular activity or brand, then it may look unprofitable. Or if too little overheads are allocated to a product, it will look artificially profitable. Management accountants worry a good deal about getting these cost allocations right, and individual managers argue a good deal about them—every brand manager wants less cost allocated to their brand; every sales manager wants less cost allocated to their region.

One way to side-step these arguments is to look at profit contribution instead. Here, only direct costs are allocated to the brand or activity. These are the costs that are purely associated with producing and marketing that particular brand. What's left over (sales revenue minus direct costs) is the brand's contribution to the firm's central costs (and its profit). Determining which costs are directly caused by the brand or activity can also be tricky: the important thing is to allocate costs as similarly as possible to each activity or brand so that fair comparisons can be made.

Profit margin

Profit margin is a metric that is used regularly to compare particular products. A simple way of thinking about profit margin is that it says how much the firm earns from these sales after deducting the direct costs of manufacturing the product or providing the service. It can be summed up as 'what's in this for us'. Technically speaking, profit margin refers to how much contribution to fixed costs (and profits) a firm earns from its sales revenue, expressed as a percentage of that sales revenue. So, a profit margin of 20 per cent means that 80 per cent of sales revenue disappears in 'production' costs and 20 per cent remains to contribute to fixed costs and potential company profit.

Changes in profit margins are often seen as an indicator of the firm's or brand's competitiveness, with eroding margins suggesting that a brand is losing competitiveness. For this reason, firms will explain to investors if there are other reasons for changes in profit margins. For example, technology companies often warn investors that profit margins will lower for a while when they bring out new technology (such as bringing out iPad 4 after iPad 3), but then, gradually, as production costs reduce, profit margins will move upwards. For fashion retailers it is the reverse: they earn high margins on a new season's clothes, then towards the end of the season they discount remaining stock, and so profit margins fall.

Because profit margins are typically calculated without including sales and advertising costs, they don't really tell us how profitable something is, but they do give insight into how much can, and should, be spent on marketing the product. However, to do so it is important to convert the percentage into dollars: a high profit margin on a product that sells very little is worth little, while a low margin on a very high-selling item may be worth a great deal. Ferrari probably make higher profit margins than Toyota on each car they sell, but Toyota makes more profit (indeed Toyota's profits are several times greater than Ferrari's entire sales revenue).

Profit margins also give us some idea of how much we can discount a brand. If its margin is very small, there is very little room for discounting without going beyond the point of negative profit margin (where the brand actually loses more money the more it sells).

Return on investment (ROI)

The notion of return on investment (ROI) is very popular in marketing, although the term is used very loosely; it is often used simply to mean accountability or to refer to any financial metric.

ROI refers to the percentage return on some marketing activity. In other words, all the returns from the campaign less the costs (the 'investment') of the campaign, divided by the costs of the campaign.

$$ROI = \frac{Returns - Investment}{Investment}$$

So, if $100,000 was invested in extra advertising, and it yielded $1,110,000 in extra sales, which delivered $110,000 in profit contribution ($1,000,000 went in costs of delivering the services or products), the equation would be:

$$\frac{\$110,000 - \$100,000}{\$100,000}$$

which becomes:

$$\frac{\$10,000}{\$100,000}$$

which is a 10 per cent return, or a $1.10 return for every $1 'invested'.

It sounds logical to compare the performance of campaigns in terms of their returns, but there are problems with ROI. Dangerous problems.

First, most marketing activity pays off for the company not by producing easily measured extra sales, but rather by maintaining existing market share. And many marketing campaigns are ongoing, so it isn't possible to quarantine discrete investments and once-off returns. For the same reasons, no one tries to calculate the ROI of the human resources department or the senior management group.

Second, ROI is a percentage (or a ratio) of the initial investment, not a dollar figure. A small campaign with a high ROI can be worth far less in dollars than a large campaign with a low ROI. So, it is quite possible to post ever-increasing ROI on marketing campaigns but deliver less profit. Shareholders care about overall dollar profits, not the ROI percentage on individual campaigns. Use of ROI to compare marketing options typically leads to smaller campaigns. Indeed, any firm can gain infinite return (!) on its advertising investment by simply ceasing advertising. ROI also encourages campaigns that produce immediate, obvious returns (such as price discounts) and campaigns that target existing, heavier buyers (who were more likely to buy anyway).

Case study
ROI can send you broke

John believes that marketing should be financially accountable. 'Marketing might be an art,' he likes to say, 'but it is a commercial art.' He works as marketing director for a large consumer goods company that sells many brands throughout Asia. Several hundred people work in his marketing department and over the past five years he has trained them all on the use of return on investment (ROI) to evaluate their marketing activities. Everybody knows that John expects a high ROI on each and every thing they spend money on.

Today, John has just returned from yet another disappointing meeting with the Chief Financial Officer. He feels under pressure because the CFO again berated him for disappointing sales revenue and profitability growth. John had hoped that shifting the marketing department's emphasis onto ROI would have earned him the respect of the CFO as well as earning the company healthy profits. He can't understand what has gone wrong. Marketing department projects and expenditures are showing higher ROIs than they ever have before. But a number of the company's brands, including the largest, are losing market share and profitability is declining.

It's not uncommon for marketing professionals to be criticised by their peers, especially those in the finance department, for a lack of appreciation of commercial realities. It's certainly true that some marketers get too wound up in the artistic side of marketing and neglect the need to make sales and satisfy customers. But today in modern marketing departments there is a far greater emphasis on commercial matters and on justifying marketing expenditures.

This emphasis on accountability is good. We need to prune waste, and identify good practices. We need to be able to judge our marketing interventions. To do this, many marketers today say they pay great attention to ROI. Unfortunately, many of those who say this don't really know what ROI means. Marketing Professor Tim Ambler of London Business School, a former managing director and qualified accountant, writes:

> ROI is not so much understood as waved about as a totem to ward off evil spirits, namely those trying to cut advertising expenditure: 'We are using ROI to establish the budget, so leave us alone.' Look behind these claims and you are unlikely to find much substance.

Also, many marketers don't understand how inappropriate this metric can be as a judge of marketing investments.

ROI is a simple equation that results in a percentage. Take the contribution to profits that is returned from the marketing 'investment' and divide it by the cost of the investment: ROI (%) = profit contribution/marketing costs.

So, if we conducted a direct marketing campaign that cost $80,000 then our investment is $80,000. If that direct marketing campaign sold one million extra products on which we earn twenty cents in profit margin for each unit sold, we have a return of $200,000.

$$\frac{200,000}{80,000} = 2.5 \text{ (or 250\%)}$$

This looks like a fantastic return, and the ROI technique looks very useful. But there are serious problems.

The first is that ROI takes attention away from the actual return, in dollars. It's the size of the actual return that matters to shareholders. Marketing expenditure is only a part of a company's total expenditure, and often only a small part. What matters is how effective it is, not how efficient it is. An ROI of $1.50 (150 per cent) on a million dollar campaign is $500,000, while an amazing $5 (500 per cent) ROI on a $10,000 campaign is still only $40,000.

Concentrating on ROI tends to encourage smaller campaigns, as these are more likely to generate higher ROI, even if dollar returns are small. It can also encourage cutting marketing expenditure; indeed, it's possible to deliver infinite return on advertising expenditure by slashing advertising to zero.

ROI tends to encourage campaigns that target existing customers, and heavier customers. These show higher ROI largely because many of the sales aren't really extra sales but sales that would have happened anyway, or sales that have merely be brought forward in time. The danger is that ignoring light buyers of the brand prevents growth, and encourages erosion of market share.

It's good to be careful with costs and for marketing activities to be evaluated in quantitative terms—but ROI is not a sensible marketing metric.

Customer value and customer lifetime value

▲ **customer value:** The profits a firm earns by having a particular customer during a particular time period (such as last year).

▲ **customer lifetime value (CLV):** An estimate of the profitability of a customer to a firm over their lifetime as a customer.

Customer value refers to the profits the firm earned by having a particular customer (for instance, last year), while **customer lifetime value** (**CLV**) is an estimate of the future profitability of the customer over their lifetime as a customer; that is, until they are no longer a customer.

As discussed earlier, profitability is simple to correctly calculate for a single firm but is a much more problematic concept to apply to units or activities within a firm. This is especially true when applied to customers, for the following reasons:

- It can be difficult to even estimate how much a particular customer is currently buying from the firm. Customers often have multiple relationships with the firm, and their buying may be recorded in separate databases without the company realising that they are the same customer. This is particularly true for large firms, and in business-to-business (B2B) settings for large customers where different divisions may each open different trading accounts.
- Customers vary in their behaviour over time due to random influences (having visitors, taking holidays, unseen expenses and so on), so it can be hard to correctly classify a customer.

- Over the longer term, customers change, as their lifestyles change with age and changes in circumstance. So, a very profitable customer may become less profitable—for example, perhaps they start using another provider for some of their requirements—or a low-value customer may in the future be very valuable. Therefore, a classification based on what they purchased last year may undervalue or overvalue the real value of the customer.

- Customer profitability is not the same as potential profitability if the firm finds ways of serving them differently or if they change their buying behaviour. Often a firm knows only what the customer is buying from them and does not know what they are buying from other providers—so what appears to be a small customer may actually potentially be a very large one.

- Allocating costs to individual customers, or even customer groups, can be a very subjective exercise, and these cost allocations have a big effect on the calculation of customer value.

Customer lifetime value calculations are even more problematic. They have all the above problems but also require predicting how much a customer or customer group will buy in the future, and what the costs of servicing them will be. Furthermore, CLV requires an estimation of how long the customer will remain a customer. This can be difficult to estimate, especially when many customers who have defected actually return some time later. CLV calculations usually depend on a number of uncertain assumptions and patchy data.

The point of trying to calculate customer value or customer lifetime value is said to be to decide which customers are most worth acquiring and which customers are worth spending most money and effort on retaining. However, in practice the most profitable customer tends to be the very next customer that the firm acquires, whoever they are, because typically fixed costs do not increase. As long as the purchases the customer makes exceed the direct costs of supplying them, they make healthy contributions to the firm's profit. Similarly, customers who don't appear to be very profitable still make a contribution, and if they were lost (some consultants talk of firing unprofitable customers) then company profits would actually decline.

In practice, customer value estimates often have little more accuracy or practical value than simple classifications (Donkers, Verhoef & De Jong, 2007) such as heavy versus light customers. In B2B markets it can be particularly useful simply to note, for example, the size of the firm you are selling to. A firm with thousands of employees and billions of dollars in sales revenue usually offers more potential return and less risk than a customer with only a few employees and small revenues. Similarly, in consumer markets wealthier households and households with more people often offer greater potential.

A more fruitful exercise than calculating customer profitability is to identify particular behaviours that are costly or beneficial to your firm, and encourage or discourage these, and/or change pricing to change the financial attractiveness of these behaviours. For example, in recent years banks have increased fees for transactions that occur within branches. This was because they identified these behaviours as particularly costly for banks—much more costly than if customers undertook their transactions online. The increased fees made branch transactions more profitable for banks and encouraged more people to use online banking, which also saved banks money.

 CRITICAL REFLECTION

Should banks try to recover the full costs of branch transactions, or are there marketing benefits of having customers come into branches?

Learn to stop worrying and love your CFO

Marketers complain that chief financial officers (CFOs), and consequently CEOs, don't give marketing its due respect. A commonly proffered solution is for marketers to learn to 'speak the language' of the CFO, to prove the return on marketing investments. This has led some marketers towards abstract management accounting terms that depend on equations and heroic assumptions based on scant data or econometrics (with its own dubious subjective assumptions). We do not recommend this path. It is hardly likely to endear you to the CFO: they expect marketers to be experts in their domain, not play at being amateur financial wizards. Marketers simply need to know how to convert appropriate marketing metrics into dollars, which is usually much easier than many marketers realise—and is best done with the involvement of the finance department.

LEARNING OBJECTIVE

Have a clear understanding of the difference between behavioural and memory metrics

BEHAVIOURAL METRICS

The first thing you'll want to know when you take charge of a brand is how much it sells, and to whom. Buyer behaviour metrics are based on what buyers actually do; for example how many people buy a product or a brand, what they buy (which particular brands), how many items they buy (just one, or bulk purchase), when they buy the product (every week, every month), what other brands they buy, at what price, from which retailer, and so on.

●●● **TABLE 3.2** MOST COMMON SOURCES OF BEHAVIOURAL INFORMATION

SOURCE	DESCRIPTION
Panel data	Consumers are recruited to record their purchases using dairies or electronic scanners; for example scanning barcodes of all the products they bought as soon as they return from a supermarket. This data allows for very detailed information about all purchases the household made. In the future, portable devices are likely to be used to gather panel data on shopping and media viewing. Media (advertising) viewing data is largely already collected by hardware or software: for example software monitors website visits.
Scanned data	Consumers use loyalty cards, such as Flybuys cards or frequent flyer cards, and the system automatically records their purchases at the checkout in store. This data is limited to retailers who participate in such loyalty or electronic tracking schemes, so purchases made elsewhere are missing.
Surveys	Buyers are asked in an interview which brands, when and how much they bought. For example: 'Which brands of soft drink did you buy last time? Which one before that?' The downside of this source of data is that consumers are not very good at noticing their own behaviour. Moreover, consumer memories of specific details are not very reliable, so they easily forget such (unimportant for them) details. This could result in missing or inaccurate information about their purchases.

Some behavioural metrics that are used daily by marketers and marketing analysts include sales, market share, market penetration, purchase frequency, share of category requirements (SCR), solely (100%) loyal customers, defection rate, and customer complaints and recommendations. These are discussed in more detail below.

Sales

This metric is relatively obvious, but it is worth mentioning that it can be expressed in a number of different ways, such as:

- revenue dollars
- units sold
- weight or volume sold
- number of purchase occasions.

So, when talking about sales, it's worth being clear on what exactly you mean. For example, many respectable business publications and news agencies (including *Businessweek*, *Forbes*, the *Wall Street Journal* and Reuters) reported that sales of Amazon's Kindle Fire suffered a sales collapse in early 2012. Reports ran along the lines of: 'Amazon, which stormed into the market in the fourth quarter of 2011 to grab second place with 16.8 per cent of the market selling of 4.8 million units, saw its share decline significantly in the first quarter to just over 4 per cent, selling just 750,000 units.' But these 'sales figures' were not based on consumers actually *buying* the Kindle Fire: they were *shipments* from Amazon to other retailers. Of course, Amazon shipped many tablets for the final quarter of 2011, the holiday (shopping) season, but not all of these sold to consumers, leaving leftover inventory that depressed shipments in the first quarter of 2012. So Kindle's sales did not crash in 2012, because they were not as healthy as people had thought in 2011, which explains why the 4.8 million units shipped to stores in the last quarter of 2011 had little effect on Apple's sales of 11 million iPads.

Market share

The metric **market share** refers to how much of the total sales in a product category go to a particular brand; that is, what is its share of the market? Again, it can be expressed in volume or value—high-priced brands will have higher value share than volume share.

Market share can be expressed as:

$$\frac{\text{Sales of the brand}}{\text{Sales of the product category}} \text{ as a percentage}$$

Why should managers care about a brand's market share? Why not simply look at sales revenue? The reason is that it helps assess performance relative to the growth of the entire category. A brand that experienced a 10 per cent increase in sales over last year looks to be performing very well, but not if category sales grew by 30 per cent. In this case, rival brands are doing better, and this shows up in the brand losing market share and perhaps competitiveness (for example perhaps it is too expensive). So, market share allows for performance to be gauged independently of category growth or decline, which provides another way to judge marketing performance.

Because this metric is relative to other brands, it is independent of the time period used to calculate the metric. A brand's market share for a week is the same as it is for a month or year (unless its sales actually increase or decrease relative to competitors during the period). A brand with a stable 7 per cent market share has 7 per cent whether a month's or a year's worth of sales data was used to calculate the metric. Many other metrics, such as penetration and purchase frequency, refer to a specific length of time. So, for example, a stable brand that has 9 per cent penetration in a month will have higher penetration (say 56 per cent) in a year.

Market share can also be presented as a rank; that is, which brand has the highest market share (is ranked number one), which has the second-highest, the third-highest, the fourth-highest and so on.

///

Warning: Market share is a widely used metric, which seems very sensible; however, it has a dark side. Research has shown that firms that chase market share as a primary objective earn lower profits and are more likely to go broke (Green & Armstrong, 2005). Firms aim to grow, because this potentially will deliver more profits and less risk (of profit variation). In other words, it is a means to an end, not an end in itself. But it seems that if they are obsessed with beating their rivals, they will be willing to sacrifice profits in order to win market share. This is not a good strategy. It was made popular some decades ago when a consulting company (The Boston Consulting Group) popularised the concept of an experience curve combining with other economies of scale; this suggested that it was worthwhile 'buying' market share with reduced profitability today, because unit costs would drop dramatically as the brand grew, delivering great returns in the future when the brand had much larger market share. Empirical evidence does not support their claim. Firms that focus on making profits make more money than firms that focus on beating their competitors, so market share should be considered as part of a sensible strategy to earn more profits, and not as a single end goal.

Market penetration

Market penetration describes the size of a brand's customer base in a given period of time; that is, how many customers bought the brand in that period. Penetration is usually calculated as a percentage of the total number of customers who bought from the product category in that particular time period. This is sometimes referred to as relative penetration, whereas absolute penetration is the percentage of all panellists, or all shoppers, who bought the brand. Because absolute penetration includes those that did not buy from the category, it is always lower than relative penetration. Relative penetration scores can look artificially high if a narrow definition of the product category is used (for example 'our brand Just Juice has very high penetration of the multi-pack, 250 ml, boxed, reconstituted fruit juice market but much lower penetration in the fruit juice market or among all supermarket shoppers').

A brand's penetration score depends on the time period—the longer the time period, the more people had the opportunity to buy the brand. This means that metrics from different lengths of time should not be compared. Some marketers do not understand that the penetration metric is time-dependent. You will sometimes hear a manager say 'my brand has reached its limit for penetration; it's extremely high', particularly if they have a large brand and are used to seeing metrics based on an entire year. This is nonsense. No brand has reached its penetration limit unless it is a complete monopoly (has 100 per cent market share). A brand that has high annual penetration has much lower weekly penetration. In an infinite time period, every brand might conceivably have a penetration score of 100 per cent.

A very high penetration score can also mean that the analyst is defining the category very narrowly. For example, Coca-Cola might have high annual penetration among all people who bought cola in a given year, but will have much lower penetration among all those that bought carbonated soft drinks, and even lower still among all those that bought all soft drinks (including water and fruit juices). Narrow product category definitions can give a very distorted view of the world, and are not recommended.

It is important to note that a period that is twice as long as another will mean a brand's penetration score is higher, but not double. A brand that has 10 per cent penetration in a month will have less than 30 per cent penetration in a quarter (three months). This is because of repeat-buying: while a brand's sales may be the same each month, many of these purchases will be from people who bought the previous month and now repeat-purchase. These customers have already been counted in the penetration score, so are not counted again.

It is worth nothing that the sum of all brands' penetrations will usually be much more than 100 per cent (as is evident in Table 3.3, where the penetrations add up to 222 per cent). Why is that? The reason is that the same customer could have bought more than one brand in the time period. For example, if Sandy Jones, a mother with three teenage children living at home, buys a jar of instant coffee about once a month, in a year she has an opportunity to buy as many as twelve different brands. In the calculation of brand penetration for each of those brands, Sandy will be double- or even triple-counted in the overall category. That's why the total of all the brands' penetration scores would be more than 100 per cent.

The table is sorted by penetration in descending order, starting from the highest penetration at the top, and going down to the lowest. You might notice that the famous brands (the ones that you probably know well, such as Nescafé) have higher penetrations than smaller, less well-known brands (such as Red Mountain or Asda Rich Roast). Therefore, penetration is indicative of how big or small the brand's market share is.

Note that penetration could also be calculated for the entire category. For example, 80 per cent is the penetration of the instant coffee category. This means that 80 per cent of the shopper population have bought at least one tub of instant coffee (of any brand) in the specified period. Interestingly, annual category penetration of a toothpaste is only slightly higher (86 per cent) than that of coffee: not everyone, it seems, brushes their teeth with (supermarket) toothpaste.

●●● **TABLE 3.3** EXAMPLE OF PENETRATION, PURCHASE FREQUENCY AND OTHER METRICS FOR THE INSTANT COFFEE CATEGORY

BRANDS	MARKET SHARE	PENETRATION	PURCHASE FREQUENCY	SCR	100% LOYALS
Nescafé		51	5	46	10
Kenco		40	3	33	5
Nescafé Gold Blend		23	3	30	3
Douwe Egberts		21	2	21	2
Tesco		9	4	31	1
Carte Noire		8	3	22	1
Tesco Gold		8	3	29	1
Maxwell House		7	3	17	0
Morrisons		6	3	25	1
Sainsbury's		6	3	25	1
Nescafé Café Menu		6	3	16	0
Aldi		6	3	25	0
Lidl		5	3	25	0
Asda Great Value		5	3	22	0
Sainsbury's Full Roast		4	4	32	1
Tesco Classic Gold		4	3	25	0
Red Mountain		4	2	17	0
Options		3	2	14	0
Asda Rich Roast		3	4	28	0
Kruger		3	3	18	0
Average			3	25	1

Source: TNS data UK 2010

Purchase frequency

purchase frequency:
How *often* the customers who bought the brand during the period (its penetration) bought it (on average) during that same period.

Penetration is usually reported alongside average **purchase frequency** because together these two metrics make up a brand's sales.

$$\text{Penetration} \times \text{Purchase frequency} = \text{Total sales}$$

Purchase frequency refers to how *often* the customers who bought the brand during the period (its penetration) bought it (on average) during that same period. This metric is the first of a number of metrics that are often used to describe the behavioural loyalty that customers display towards brands. It's considered a loyalty metric because it counts repeat-buying of the brand.

Looking at Table 3.3, you can see that most brands of instant coffee are bought around three times per year by their respective buyers. The whole category of instant coffee is, on average, bought eight times per year, while toothpaste is bought five times, and savoury snacks (such as potato chips) are bought twelve times per year. The fact that customers buy the category more often than any particular brand tells us that each brand's customers are also buying other brands.

When you look at purchase frequency metrics for rival brands in a category (such as Table 3.3), you will notice that the numbers differ between the brands—and this difference follows the same descending order as the penetration. However, the difference is usually much smaller than is seen for the penetration metric (column 3). For example, Nescafé is bought five times, while Tesco's home brand coffee is bought four times, and the smallest brand, Kruger, is bought three times. This means that brands with higher penetration (such as Nescafé) also have only slightly higher average purchase frequency than the rest of the brands. This pattern is known as the double jeopardy law, an empirical law that holds in most product categories.

The average purchase frequency metric is less sensitive to changes in brand performance than the penetration, so don't expect to see great changes over time—and those changes would be accompanied by a change in penetration in accordance with the double jeopardy law.

Average purchase frequency describes the *average* customer. It's a common assumption that this describes the *typical* customer but this is *not true*. A brand's customer base is made up of many light, infrequent buyers and a few heavy, very frequent buyers. Although there aren't many of these **heavy buyers**, they lift the average purchase frequency, so most of a brand's customers buy less often than this average. In fact, the typical customer usually buys a lot less often than the average.

heavy buyer: Someone who buys the category or brand more frequently than the average.

Television viewing rates are also skewed in a similar way, so while the average in many countries is viewing for twenty-five to thirty hours a week (that is, three to four hours every day) the majority of viewers in fact view for fewer than ten hours a week, while a small percentage view every day for many hours. Similar patterns follow for the consumption of other media.

Share of category requirements (SCR)

How many of all your petrol purchases do you make at BP, and how many at Shell? How many of your supermarket shopping trips are to Coles, and how often do you go to Woolworths? The loyalty metric **share of category requirements (SCR)** refers to the proportion of category purchases that go to a particular brand. So, if a consumer went supermarket shopping ten times during the period and for five of those times they shopped at Woolworths, we would say they devoted a 50 per cent share of their category requirements to Woolworths. Depending on the industry, this metric can also be referred to as 'share of wallet' (typically in financial services) or 'share of mouth' (for example for drinks). It is always a percentage ranging from zero per cent to a maximum of 100 per cent.

share of category requirements (SCR): The proportion of category purchases that go to a particular brand in a given period of time.

When reported as a brand level metric, SCR refers to the average SCR of all purchasers of the brand during the period; that is, non-buyers (people who did not contribute to the brand's penetration score) are not included in the calculation. So if a brand had only two buyers and one gave it 40 per cent SCR and the other 80 per cent, the brand's SCR would be 60 per cent.

Continuing with the example in Table 3.3, Nescafé is the leading market share brand and it also has the highest SCR, at 46 per cent. In other words, those customers who bought Nescafé during the period on average satisfied about half (46 per cent) of their needs for instant coffee with Nescafé. Of course, some customers bought only Nescafé (100 per cent SCR), and other Nescafé buyers largely bought other brands, so the average across all these different Nescafé buyers was 46 per cent.

SCR, like other loyalty metrics, shows the double jeopardy pattern, being somewhat higher for brands with greater market share, and lower for their smaller rivals.

SCR is another time-dependent metric, so the length of time it refers to must always be reported. Over longer time periods of analysis, the average SCR reduces. This is because with more time, and therefore more purchase occasions, consumers tend to have larger repertoires—and any one brand in their repertoire gets a smaller share. However, the decline in SCR over time is not linear; doubling the time period doesn't tend to reduce the SCR by half; and with longer and longer time periods the SCR tends to level off. This is because eventually almost the full repertoire of each consumer is revealed, and allowing more time and more purchases seldom includes any new brand purchases.

Case study
Loyalty ladders: Why they are unnecessary and dangerous

Many market research houses now market a 'loyalty ladder' or 'loyalty pyramid' product. These dissect a brand's customer base into four to six groups, starting with something like 'no awareness' at the bottom and ending with something like 'passionate loyals' at the top. This classification is usually based on behaviour (or claimed behaviour) such as share of category purchases devoted to the brand in question. Some add attitudinal statements into the customer classification. Others, like the conversion model, claim to be entirely attitudinal. These differences in practice actually make little difference to the pyramid shape or scores.

The first problem with these loyalty ladders is that they are a waste of money. They are basically showing the distribution of customers with different SCRs for the brand. Marketing science has known for decades that loyal behaviours and attitudes follow a set statistical distribution (the NBD-Dirichlet), and so any brand's true loyalty ladder can be accurately predicted simply from knowing its size compared to rivals. If it has 100 per cent relative share, then all customers will be at the top of the ladder. So all these elaborate ladders do is reflect the brand's relative popularity (that is, market share) and some random sampling errors, which loom large when you have four to six groups.

| Advocate |
| Supporter |
| Client |
| Customer |
| Prospect |
| Suspect |

These ladders are attractive because intuitively marketers feel it's their job to move people along this path, up this ladder. They also provide some entertainment value ('that looks interesting')—which is fine, because that's all they are: an entertaining, expensive way of presenting, and obscuring, loyalty metrics.

Unfortunately, they aren't simply harmless entertainment showing the heterogeneity within any brand's customer base or market (from non-buyers to high loyals). They are dangerous because they obscure the fact that the ratios of non-buyers to light buyers to medium and heavy buyers are perfectly predictable (by the NBD-Dirichlet). So, they are set. If a brand gains in market share or sales, the ratios all move in a predictable way. All loyalty ladders do is *show* these ratios, but they imply that you can change the ratios through particular strategies. This is wrong: they will only change if you increase or decrease market share. So loyalty ladders are misleading and unhelpful for the following reasons:

- They imply that managers should target particular levels of the ladder. This is wrong.
- They imply that some brands are stronger or weaker—when really they are reporting brand size.
- They are a waste of money spent on market research and reporting. Most of the tiny changes and differences they report are sampling (and other) errors.
- They imply that awareness is a 'one-off battle', that once someone is aware they always notice, recognise and recall your brand—this is nonsense, and dangerous thinking.
- They imply that 100% loyals are a brand's most valuable customers, whereas far more volume comes from heavy category buyers who buy a number of brands.
- They distract marketers from the real issue, which is how to grow penetration (reach all sorts of category buyers).

Solely (100%) loyal customers

Can you think of a product category where you only ever buy one brand, never any others?

The proportion of solely loyal—that is, 100 per cent loyal—buyers, refers to the percentage of a brand's buyers who bought only that brand and no other *during the period of analysis*. So, these are the people for whom the brand had 100 per cent SCR.

This sounds like an exciting loyalty metric, and these customers sound like very interesting people: very desirable customers from a marketer's perspective—because they are completely loyal, buying no other brands. However, the reality turns out to be more down to earth. As we mentioned in Chapter 2, the vast majority of customers buy from competing brands, and therefore are not 100 per cent loyal to any single brand. So, the proportion of solely loyal customers is usually relatively small. For example, for most brands of instant coffee (see Table 3.3, last column) it is around 1 per cent of their buyers in a year.

The proportion of 100% loyals is larger in subscription markets, such as mortgages or mobile phone contracts, where customers tend to have a single provider for a lengthy period of time until they switch. However, if we think of these categories more broadly—say, banking rather than simply mortgages—these subscription categories again look like repertoire categories, where typically buyers hold repertoires of brands as they buy different services from each.

The exact proportion of 100% loyal customers that brands have depends on the length of time we look at. Over short periods of time, people haven't bought many times from the product or service category, so they haven't had the opportunity to buy many different brands. Every single buyer who has bought only once from the category during the time period is classed as 100 per cent loyal. So, in short time periods there are many more 100% loyal customers, in just the same way that average SCR for a brand is higher in shorter time periods of analysis.

Solely loyal customers tend to be light buyers of the category, because the more someone buys from the category, the more opportunities they have to buy other brands—and once they do, they would no longer be classified as solely loyal. While some marketers track this metric to try to grow the number of solely loyal customers, research shows that this loyalty metric depends on a brand's market share. Larger share brands have more 100% loyal customers. In other words, unsurprisingly, this loyalty metric also follows the double jeopardy law. This can be seen in Table 3.3, where Nescafé has the greatest proportion of solely loyal buyers.

Defection rate

Defection rate is the proportion of the total customer base (all those who used to buy the brand in the past) who have stopped buying the brand. In other words, this metric describes the proportion of customers that the brand has lost. In repertoire markets, where consumers are continuously shuffling between brands, it is much more difficult to separate real change from random wobbles in purchasing. This metric is easier to measure in industries such as finance, where a customer closing an account or being inactive is fairly obvious. Survey data simply asking if there are brands that the consumer has stopped using is also quite reliable.

At first glance, the idea of customer loss sounds like a dreadful event to most marketing managers. Every lost customer has to be replaced by acquisition of a new customer just to maintain share. Losing customers might be a signal that the brand's service quality is poor or variable. However, academic research has found that almost half of customers who have stopped buying a particular brand have done so for reasons that had nothing to do with the brand (Bogomolova, 2009). These reasons were lack of need for the whole category (when consumers no longer required the particular product—for example, no longer needing a business loan after selling the business) or other life and taste changes generally beyond the marketing manager's control. Even growing, successful brands lose customers. So, the 'zero defection' idea proposed by Reichheld and Sasser (1990) is simply not possible.

Defection rates, like other loyalty metrics, follow the double jeopardy law. So defection improves (that is, a smaller percentage of the customer base is lost each period) if the brand has higher penetration, if it has more customers (Sharp et al., 2002).

Research has shown that the thing that really distinguishes declining brands is not that they have unusually high customer defection, but rather that they have unusually low acquisition. Similarly, growing brands don't enjoy low (or non-existent) customer defection; rather, they excel at customer acquisition (Riebe et al., forthcoming).

Customer complaints and recommendations

It's likely that complaining customers represent (hopefully!) a tiny proportion of the overall customer base, but by monitoring the general level of customer complaints a firm can judge its service delivery. Also, by analysing these complaints the firm can gain diagnostic information about which aspects of its service are failing. Increasingly, firms are monitoring online complaints, not just complaints made directory to the firm. Similarly, firms are monitoring online **word-of-mouth** to measure recommendations as a sign that the firm is doing some things particularly well.

In recent years, the **net promoter score** has become quite a popular measure of claimed willingness to recommend. However, research has not supported the claims that this metric is capable of predicting a company's future performance (Sharp, 2008; Keiningham et al., 2007).

Contrary to popular belief, it does not measure actual recommendations but only claimed willingness to recommend (presumably if asked), so in effect it is an attitude measure asking if the customer is happy enough with the brand that they would recommend it. It does not measure willingness to give negative word-of-mouth (East, 2008). Recently a new measure that measures propensity to give actual (and both positive and negative) word-of-mouth has been proposed (East, Romaniuk & Lomax, 2011).

word-of-mouth (WOM): Unpaid, uncontrolled oral or written communication about a brand or business circulated by the public; it can be positive or (more rarely) negative.

net promoter score: A measure of customers' claimed willingness to recommend a company's product or services to others.

 CRITICAL REFLECTION

Reflect on the use of behavioural metrics in marketing. What questions can these metrics answer for marketing managers? What questions can't behavioural metrics answer?

MEMORY METRICS

Memory metrics usually describe what consumers think and feel about a product or a brand (as opposed to what they actually do—measured by behavioural metrics). For example, answers to questions such as 'How much do you like the brand Google?' or 'How do you feel about the brand Virgin?' or 'What words or association come to mind when you think of Rolex?' are examples of how people perceive products or brands. The accumulation of all these thoughts and feelings is sometimes referred to as consumer-based brand equity.

The primary source of such information is consumer surveys. There are other ways of finding out what is in people's heads, such as psychological experiments and memory tests, but these tend to be small-scale, expensive and difficult to generalise to populations. While data mining of online chatter or word-of-mouth can be used to evaluate consumer sentiment, it doesn't provide measures of consumer memory structures.

Memory metrics describe information that consumers have in their memories in relation to a product or a brand. The following are the memory metrics most commonly used by marketing managers:

- brand awareness
- brand image associations
- mental availability
- attitude
- customer satisfaction and service quality
- intention to buy (or consider) a brand in the future.

All memory metrics are strongly affected by past behaviour, so larger share brands with more people who have used them, and more recently, score higher. This has to be considered when interpreting memory metrics.

Brand awareness

Brand awareness reflects how many customers know the brand; that is, whether they have any brand information in their memories and how easily this brand-related information comes to mind. There are three major types of brand awareness:

- The *top-of-mind (first mentioned) unprompted awareness* metric describes the chance that a particular brand would come to mind first when customers are asked to think of a product category (without any brand information presented). For example, if you are asked to think of a soft drink brand, Coca-Cola might be the first brand to be mentioned. This is usually reported as the percentage of respondents who mentioned the brand as their first recalled.
- *Unprompted awareness* refers to the likelihood of brands to come to mind when thinking of a product category (after the first top-of-mind brand has been named). This is usually reported as the percentage of respondents who mentioned the brand among those that they recalled.
- *Prompted awareness* (sometimes referred to as recognition) describes which brands consumers recognise when they are prompted with either the brand name ('Have you heard of Dr Pepper?') or when being shown a logo or packaging for that brand.

Unsurprisingly, the first two awareness measures (unprompted or free recall) are harder for consumers, so fewer consumers will recall the target brand, while the last one could potentially easily result in 100 per cent recognition for large brands. Therefore, for a given brand, the scores for each of these awareness measures would differ in the following order: top-of-mind being the lowest score and prompted awareness being the highest.

To track changes in brand performance, marketing managers should consider which of the three brand awareness metrics would be the most appropriate for the brand of a particular size (because of the possible ceiling effects in prompted metrics for large brands and floor effects for the small brands, which might never get mentioned in the top-of-mind metric) (Romaniuk & Sharp, 2004). Managers also need to consider which is more important to them: buyers' ability to recall the brand (from a product category cue) or buyers' ability to recognise the brand

(Rossiter, Percy & Donovan, 1991). Recognition is more important for products that are usually seen before purchase (such as products sold in retail stores); recall is more important for products that are usually recalled (such as accountancy services).

These awareness measures all suffer from shortcomings. Recognition because it is too easy and doesn't necessarily measure how noticeable a brand is, especially on a crowded shelf. Recall because only a single cue, the product category name, is used. These shortcomings in both concept and measures have led to the mental availability approach, which will be discussed shortly.

Brand image associations

Other memories about brands are brand image associations or links that consumers have between the brand and various attributes and qualities. These perceptual attributes could be anything from a simple description—for example 'has a strong taste' (for Vegemite) or 'has purple packaging' (for Cadbury chocolate)—to a description of quality ('is a premium quality brand' for Lindt chocolate), a benefit that it presents ('keeps my skin moist' for Palmolive, perhaps) or identifying the type of users who need it ('for busy mums', for Huggies).

Brand image metrics consider specific association (for example which brand has the strongest association with the attribute 'provides the best value for money'). This is sometimes referred to as brand positioning. Contrary to popular belief, research does not support the idea that being uniquely associated with an image attribute leads to brand preference—it seems better to be well known than seen as the only brand with an attribute (Romaniuk, 2007).

Mental availability

Mental availability, also sometimes called brand salience (Romaniuk & Sharp, 2004), refers to the ability of buyers to notice and/or bring the brand to mind in buying situations. This behavioural tendency is underpinned by the memory structures relating to the brand: the quality and quantity of memory links to and from the brand. Quality has two aspects: the strength of the association and the relevance to buying situations.

Buyers use different cues when retrieving brands as buying options. For example, cues for something to eat in the morning may include something low in fat, something healthy and something quick. Buyers may also use more abstract cues—such as colour and the style or size of the packaging—to identify and notice specific brands. They may be totally unaware of the cues they are utilising.

By building memory links to attributes, marketers can increase:

1   the number of people who think of a particular brand
2   the number of times each person thinks of a particular brand as an option (to buy).

Linking a brand to attributes means the brand now has some probability of being bought; this is an infinitely higher chance of being bought than when the brand was not thought of at all.

Mental availability is a valuable asset, which, along with physical availability, makes up much of the financial value of a brand.

One approach to measuring these memory structures is to count the total number of brand associations from brand perception surveys, and to present the metric as a 'share of mind'; that is, the brand's share of all brand associations (Romaniuk & Sharp, 2003).

The specific cues that do, or don't, elicit the brand can also be of diagnostic value to marketers, suggesting what they need to include in their marketing communications. A brand's performance on specific cues can also be used to evaluate advertising, to see if it is refreshing and building the desired memories.

Attitude

Attitude is an evaluation of a product or a brand. Attitudes range in polarity from extremely positive (you love it), to neutral, to extremely negative (you hate it). Attitudes can be measured for products or services, brands within these categories, and brand features.

In Chapter 2 we discussed the weak causal influence of attitudes on behaviour, and the stronger effect of behaviour on attitudes. Consequently, measuring attitudes often provides little or no additional information to measuring past behaviour or claimed behaviour.

Customer satisfaction and service quality

Customer satisfaction and perceptions of the quality of service are often considered important metrics for companies that provide service to customers; for example banks, telecommunication providers, energy suppliers, internet providers, hairdressers and so on.

Broadly, these attitudinal metrics describe how satisfied customers are with the service and product overall, and with different aspects of the service delivery. There are many aspects or dimensions of service. The ones most commonly measured are:

- reliability—for example how accurate and precise the records are
- responsiveness—the timing of service delivery
- empathy—the level of interest staff show in customers
- assurance—how knowledgable and trustworthy the staff are
- tangibles—physical facilities and surroundings, such as the ambience of the bank branch, the quality and functionality of ATMs, and so on.

These five dimensions comprise a SERVQUAL instrument originally proposed by academic researchers Parasuraman, Zeithaml and Berry (1988) and widely adopted by the industry.

Customer satisfaction and service quality are often measured as an agreement with a particular statement on a scale ranging from 'strongly agree' to 'strongly disagree', with 'neither' as a mid point. For example, 'Please express you level of agreement with the statement: "I am very satisfied with the service that Commonwealth Bank provides"' is an example of an overall satisfaction question.

Service companies use these metrics as key performance indicators, along with financial metrics, such as revenue. It is quite common in service organisations (such as banks, and even universities) for bonuses of CEOs and top management to be linked to customer satisfaction ratings.

A common alternative to measuring customer evaluations of service is to directly measure service delivery. This can be done with automated measures (for example measures for how quickly service staff answer the phone) or by surveying customers who have very recently had a service encounter (asking questions such as 'Did the installers clean up before they left?' or 'Did they offer to show you how to operate the backup unit?'). 'Mystery shopping' is also a technique used to directly measure service delivery. Here, researchers pose as customers and record aspects of the service. Research has show that service delivery varies from encounter to encounter, so quite a number of service encounters need to be measured if valid results are to be gained for single stores or service centres (Dawes & Sharp, 2000).

Intention to buy

Intention to buy a product or a service is commonly used by the market research industry as an indicator of future behaviour. While the idea of being able to predict future behaviour sounds very appealing, it turns out that these metrics are not good at predicting change in behaviour. The reasons why were discussed in Chapter 2. Intentions tend to reflect past behaviour (Bird & Ehrenberg, 1966). For example, people who bought the brand in the past are quite good at estimating that they will continue doing so in the future. Estimating purchase of something for the first time is a whole new ball game. Even if a customer has a strong intention to buy an iPhone, there are a lot of different factors that could prevent him or her from doing so. For example, the brand may not be available in Australia at the time of release in the United States, the product might not be in stock when a customer urgently needs a phone, or the iPhone may be linked to only one telecommunications service provider but the customer does not or can not use that provider. All those factors could prevent the actual behaviour from happening, even though the customer had the intention to buy the iPhone (and reported so in a survey).

Intention metrics are a measure of consumer's plans. As such, they can be an appropriate measure of the effectiveness of persuasive communication, the type of advertising that aims to instil such plans.

A related, but different, type of measure asks consumers to estimate the likelihood (or probability) that they would buy something in the future. These measures are more suited to predicting future behaviour. Measures such as the Juster scale have been shown to be quite effective in certain situations (Brennan & Esslemont, 1994; Brennan, 2004; McDonald & Alpert, 2001; Wright, Sharp & Sharp, 2002). However, likelihood measures are also influenced by past behaviour and so are better at predicting behaviour that is regular, rather than changes in behaviour.

 CRITICAL REFLECTION

Reflect on attitudinal and perceptual metrics. Which three metrics would you want to track for your company if you are working for:

1   Apple iPhone?

2   Telstra?

3   Red Cross?

Justify your choice.

CUSTOMER PROFILE METRICS

Customer profile metrics describe customers, and are used to help marketers identify and reach all the different buyers in a brand's category. They include such metrics as a customer's gender, age or income. In selling to businesses, the descriptive metrics are things such as industry type, size of company, and office location. It's pretty obvious that dog food buyers are people with dogs, but who buys taco shells, or furniture polish? This isn't so obvious, and therefore calls for market research. It's very important for marketers to understand who their different buyers are, where they live, what media they consume, and how, when and where they shop.

It's dangerous to assume. The typical cosmetics buyer is a different sort of person from the typical buyer of electric tools. The audience for CNN is different from the audience for Nickelodeon. Yet, these are not completely separate groups, and you may be surprised to learn how many customers these categories share.

Extensive research has demonstrated that the demographic characteristics of customers who buy competing brands within the same product category are, in fact, very similar (Kennedy & Ehrenberg, 2000). So, the people who buy L'Oréal are largely the same sorts of people who buy Dove. This means that the profile of the category buyer provides a very useful benchmark against which to compare the brand's customer profile. For example, if half the category buyers but only 40 per cent of the brand's buyers are male that might indicate a failure of the brand's marketing to reach men. Similarly, geographic skews can often highlight physical availability shortfalls in particular areas.

MARKETING ACTIVITY METRICS

If sales unexpectedly rise or fall, it's vital to know what marketing activity the firm was undertaking at the time and just prior to the event—in order to puzzle out why the sales volume changed. It's also vital to know what competitors were doing. So, to understand the effects of marketing, it's important to measure, over time, what marketing activities the company is actually doing. For example, to record how much is being spent on advertising, in which media, for which market. Unfortunately, and somewhat surprisingly, managers often fail to systematically record their own marketing activity, let alone record the activity of competitors.

Marketing activity metrics are also necessary for the firm to keep track of its marketing investment. They answer questions such as 'Are we doing enough? In the right places?' or 'What has changed in the marketing strategy?'

A firm's media agency can provide detailed metrics describing how many people were exposed to the brand's advertising, how many times, in a particular period of time. Public relations agencies can provide information on company press releases, news articles and what coverage these are getting in the media. Market research agencies can provide metrics on the prices and price promotions of your brands and competitors. But many other metrics require the company to keep records itself, metrics such as:

- how many stores were visited by sales representatives
- when the new packaging was launched
- how much money is being spent on particular initiatives
- when competitors started and ended their sales promotion.

It's wise to collect a wide range of marketing activity metrics, and to keep collecting them over time. This provides marketing analysts with useful raw material to investigate how your markets and marketing works. It allows questions that emerge in the future to be tackled. It is very difficult, or impossible, to generate data on the past if it wasn't collected at the time.

PHYSICAL AVAILABILITY METRICS

Physical availability means making a brand as easy to notice and buy as possible, for as many consumers as possible, across as wide a range of potential buying situations as possible. This includes more than retail penetration, but also presence in store. It includes hours of availability, and ease of facilitating the purchase. Being easy to notice and buy is essential, because buyers do not have strong preferences even for the brands they are loyal to; they are happy to buy alternatives from within their personal repertoires (and they regularly do).

Physical availability allows a consumer to buy and consume a product or service, so physical availability metrics include:

- number of distribution points
- hours of opening
- geographical coverage of distribution points
- geographical coverage of delivery points
- number of display points in store
- number of shelves devoted to the brand.

> I'm surprised how often marketers of consumer goods and services will say, 'Oh well, we have practically 100% availability'. They point to their brand's presence in all the leading supermarket chains, or their national branch network or their website that can take orders 24 hours a day. None of this comes close to 100% availability. Perhaps the problem is the word 'availability'; I don't mean 'available if a consumer is motivated to seek out the product', I mean *readily* available. Like the often reported desire of Coca-Cola to be no more than 'an arm's length away from desire'. Against a standard like this, it's easy to see that every company has potential to improve the physical availability of its brands.

> B Sharp 2010, *How Brands Grow*, Oxford University Press, South Melbourne

LOOKS CAN BE DECEIVING

Many metrics depend on consumer surveys. A major misconception about market research is that you can tell what a question measures just by looking at it. For example, if the question contains the words 'service' and 'satisfaction' or 'quality', then surely it measures customers' experience of our service. This just seems like common sense. But common sense is often misleading. For example, it's common sense that the Sun moves through the sky around the Earth—it's obvious, but wrong.

Questions in market research surveys should look right, but this isn't enough. If it looks like a duck, walks like a duck, and quacks like a duck then it probably is a duck. Unfortunately, market researchers and their clients tend to go no further than checking that it looks a bit like a duck—but, as a bird watcher will tell you, there are loons, merganisers and all sorts of other water fowl that look like ducks.

Relying only on our personal subjective assessment of what a question measures is dangerous and stupid. For a start, it often leads to arguments between managers, and miscommunication, as each user of the research sees a different finding (is the lake full of ducks or loons?). If we are going to spend our company's money on market research, we should know clearly what it is we are measuring.

Case study
Advertising tracking

B&T magazine once ran an interesting article, comparing how four current Australian television commercials performed on some advertisement tracking (Sinclair, 2004). One of the questions for each (recognised) commercial was whether it 'encourages me to try/buy the brand product'. At first sight, this seems a sensible question, supposedly telling the marketer if their advertising is going to generate sales. But what does it really measure? If a consumer agrees to this statement, does it mean:

- they think the commercial is trying to encourage people to buy? That is, it is making an obvious sales pitch.
- that they find the commercial personally motivating (making them want to buy)?

Or are they just saying they are likely to buy the brand (which probably has more to do with whether or not they currently buy this brand than whether or not the commercial motivates them)?

Or is it some sort of complex mix of the above, different for different people, and different for different campaigns?

TELEVISION COMMERCIAL	ENCOURAGES ME TO TRY/BUY THE BRAND (% AGREE)
Herron ibuprofen	48
Landrover	48
Bulla ice cream	41
Coca-Cola	21

Source: Sinclair, 2004: 13

It turns out that three different commercials all scored similarly, with the Coca-Cola commercial being the odd one out. Is this simply because respondents correctly identified that the commercial doesn't make a hard sell pitch (it just shows some impressive skateboarding)? Or is it because many respondents, particularly the older ones, don't drink cola much? Or because it really wasn't thought to be motivational? Who knows? Does anyone believe that the Coca-Cola advertisement was the least sales effective, less than half as good as the other commercials?

The Herron brand ibuprofen (an analgesic) had a commercial that rated well, perhaps because it is a hard-sell advertisement, an ad directly comparing the Herron ibuprofen with Nurofen, the brand leader. This is an unusual situation because the two products are made of exactly the same ingredient. The Herron advertisement essentially says 'we are the same ingredient formulation, but Australian-made and cheaper—why would you buy Nurofen?' That's a directly persuasive message. So, perhaps the surprise isn't that it rated reasonably well; the surprise is that only 48 per cent of respondents said that this ad 'encourages me to try/buy the brand product'. What is really being measured? Is the ad not motivational? Who knows?

Without testing across many ads with different content, it isn't possible to know what this question really measures. You can't work it out simply by looking at the question.

Case study

Was there really an attitude there?

A common mistake is to assume that any question about the customer's attitude actually indicates what people think about the brand. It is assumed that people carry these attitudes around in their heads and that these mental constructs determine their purchase behaviour. It is seldom considered that there may have been no attitude there until the question was asked. Respondents are generally polite; they give answers to questions even if this means formulating an opinion for the first time. I'm sure that a great many of the billions of hamburgers that McDonald's have sold were consumed without much thought about how they tasted. The hungry teenager who has eaten many burgers previously has probably stopped thinking about their burger before it hits their stomach. People who fly regularly have usually forgotten about the flight experience within seconds of leaving the plane. It would take something rather unusual to happen on the flight for them to actually record an evaluation of the service experience. And as far as the total package goes (price, conditions, booking ease, lounge, in-flight food, entertainment and so on), it would take more effort than most people are willing to give to add these up in an overall evaluation. But they will make a (rather futile) attempt to do so if surveyed by a market researcher. So, don't make the mistake of thinking you are measuring someone's attitude; they probably didn't have one until they were asked.

This is why a respondent could easily give contradictory answers, and is perhaps part of the reason why academic research shows there is only about a 50 per cent chance that anyone gives the same answer if asked the same attitude question twice (Dall'Olmo Riley et al., 1997).

How was the flight ?	'Oh, ah, excellent.'
And the in-flight meal ?	'Oh, now that wasn't that good.' (Perhaps I was hasty saying the flight was excellent.)
And the friendliness of staff?	'Very friendly and helpful.' (Yes, it was a good flight.)
And the take-off time?	'It was late.' (Come to think of it, I should be annoyed.)
So how was the flight?	'Umm … ?!?!'

As previously discussed, any question with the words 'service' and 'satisfaction' or 'quality' is usually assumed to measure customers' evaluation of our service delivery. So it is inferred that improvements in the quality of service delivery will be reflected in this metric. And so when satisfaction scores drop, management usually seek to institute service improvement programs, presuming that this will remedy the low score. But global satisfaction questions can show weak relationships with actual service delivery. Instead, the scores move with events such as the weather, seasons, major publicity, advertising, etc. So investment in service delivery would generate little return in terms of movement in the overall service quality metric. This is not what most managers expect, nor how they interpret satisfaction metrics—if they go up, they are mistakenly sure it is due to service quality (and their actions).

Similarly, research shows that student ratings are affected by things like how attractive looking the lecturer is (this is particularly the case for male lecturers—perhaps there is much greater variation in attractiveness among male lecturers) (Hamermesh & Parker, 2005).

As you can see from the cases above, you can't judge a book by its cover … or a market research question by simply looking at the words in the question. More is needed. To work out what a question is really measuring you need to know how the measure varies in relation to other metrics and how it really reacts to changes in the marketplace. And this requires R&D and experiments. Careful work is needed to avoid reaching the wrong conclusions: for example, thermometer readings are higher at the beach than at the office, and people smile and laugh more at the beach than at the office, which could easily lead one to conclude that thermometers measure how happy the nearby people are. A bit of careful experimentation will easily test such a hypothesis—and hopefully lead one to the conclusion that thermometers actually measure ambient temperature, not happiness.

MARKETING BENCHMARKS

◢ **LEARNING OBJECTIVE**
Be able to give examples of the most commonly used benchmarks in marketing metrics

To interpret a metric score, marketers need to know what to expect. This section lists some of the most important benchmarks that marketers will observe in their metrics. These relationships between metrics have been observed in many different real empirical data sets; hence, they are described as being law-like. We know that these patterns are universally evident in most, if not all, product or service categories, including groceries, alcoholic drinks, banking, cars, store choice, even television viewing.

Deviations from these expected and well-known patterns often means that something went wrong with the measurement, analysis or interpretation. Real deviations are potentially interesting and worthy of investigation.

The brand size effect

Most people intuitively expect that brand attitude scores would vary idiosyncratically, depending on things such as the brand's image, history or quality. So attitude scores would be independent of brand size. There would be large brands that weren't particularly liked (and hence destined to decline) and many small brands that appealed highly to particular people. But research shows that brands with more users (larger market share brands) strongly tend to score higher on all memory metrics, especially attitudinal evaluations (Bird & Ehrenberg, 1966, 1970; Romaniuk, Bogomolova & Dall'Olmo Riley, 2012). This is because consumers say more about brands they use. Understandably, they know far less about brands that they do not use, and are far less likely to bring them to mind. When forced to make comments on brands that consumers don't use, or don't use so often, consumers tend to give conservative, middling ratings, so a brand with more users will score higher. All this seems obvious, now that you know. Unfortunately, many people don't know this, even some experienced market researchers (or perhaps they just keep forgetting). It's rare to see memory metrics adjusted for the number of brand users of each brand in the survey. Many surveys of memory metrics even neglect to ask respondents which brands they use. Without adjusting for brand usage, it isn't possible to correctly interpret many metrics, and major mistakes can easily be made in interpreting scores. The most obvious is that brands with high market share assume that they perform strongly on many customer-perception-based performance metrics, while small brands worry that they are doing a poor job because they don't score so well on perceptions of trust, service and so on.

There are other, less obvious mistakes that stem from the same brand usage effect; for example, let's say SuperSave Bank wanted to know how well it was doing at providing investment information to its customers. It commissioned a market research agency to survey its customers with names drawn from the bank's own customer database. Respondents were asked questions about how knowledgable and friendly the bank's staff were, as well as questions about their impressions of the bank's advertising, its website, newsletters and investment guidebooks. Customers who also banked with other banks were asked the same questions about these other banks so that SuperSave bank could compare its own scores. SuperSave was delighted in the results, which clearly showed it was doing a better job than other banks. Can you spot what was wrong in their interpretation? By drawing the sample from their own customers they have skewed the results in their favour. The sample of their customers will include respondents who do all their banking with them, but the scores for other banks all come from people who also bank at SuperSave Bank. In effect, they have surveyed other banks' less loyal customers—this would show up in any behavioural metrics, but it will also affect all the memory and attitude metrics.

Knowing a brand's penetration (how many users it has) allows estimates or predictions of a lot of other behavioural and attitudinal metrics. This way, memory metrics can be adjusted and fairly compared (Romaniuk & Sharp, 2000, explains how).

As Andrew Ehrenberg (1988) put it:

> Of the thousand and one variables which might affect buyer behaviour, it is found that 999 usually do not matter. Many aspects of buyer behaviour can be predicted simply from the penetration and the average purchase frequency of the items, and even these two variables are inter-related.

It means that if your brand is small (or few of the respondents in the survey use your brand), it should expect to score lower on memory metrics than brands of larger size.

The double jeopardy law

The double jeopardy law is probably the most famous scientific law in marketing, and it is an example of a pattern that is driven by brand size.

It says that smaller market share brands are penalised twice: not only have they fewer customers who buy them (their penetration is smaller than that of big brands), but also customers who do buy them do so less often—and in memory metrics, less popular brands are known by fewer people and those people are slightly less likely to say they like it. Marketers have observed the double jeopardy law across many product categories, ranging from supermarket goods such as butter, chocolate and soft drinks, to durable goods (for example cars or electronics) and services (banks or energy suppliers). But why does this pattern occur?

Take a closer look at the penetration column of Table 3.3. If you sum up all penetration figurers for all the brands, you notice that the total sum is more than 100 per cent. The total penetration of more than 100 per cent indicates that competing brands in fact share the same customers: that's why they are 'double counted' in the penetration figures. For example, if one week Mary bought Douwe Egberts brand coffee and in another week Aldi coffee, she would be counted as a customer of both brands.

With the knowledge that competing brands share the same customers, we can now explain the double jeopardy effect. A customer who buys a small brand also occasionally buys big brands (that's why they are big—they are bought by more people). So, on a given purchase occasion (for example in front of a supermarket shelf) this customer has a chance to buy a small or a big brand (so the chance of buying a small brand is already lower). This, however, does not happen to a big brand, because many of its customers are less likely to know and consider small brands (that's why they are small—less people know and buy them). Another way of thinking about it is that larger market share brands, because they have greater mental and physical availability, are just that bit easier for their customers to repeat-buy. Customers of smaller brands, with less physical and mental availability, find it a little more difficult to buy them so often.

With a knowledge of the double jeopardy score we know what to expect when looking at the attitude or repeat-buying metrics for brands.

Case study
Cereal sales: What caused what?

In 2013, sales of Rise-And-Shine breakfast cereal rose, much to the satisfaction of the company's marketing department. Kimberly, the General Manager, was delighted to report this result to the management board, but they then asked for an explanation—what had caused this happy event? Kimberly asked her marketing manager, who said it was probably due to the new advertisement he had launched, though he admitted that the firm's media agency were also claiming it was due to their media selection. Kimberly asked her sales manager and he claimed it was due to the sales team winning extra shelf space in some supermarkets after a rival brand changed its packaging and lost sales. Meanwhile, the innovation director said that changes in the product formulation for several brands, improving the nutritional content of the breakfast cereal, had obviously met with favourable retailer and consumer reaction. And to top it all off, the company's accountant noted that summer had been particularly good in 2010, which meant that cold breakfast cereals, which Rise-And-Shine are particularly strong in, probably sold better.

Questions

1   Who was right? Perhaps all or some of the explanations were true, or perhaps none?

Marketing managers are regularly intervening in the market, with interventions such as new advertising, changes in price, publicity events, changes to service conditions and new products. All these things cost money, so we need them to do something. So managers need to establish what the effects of these marketing interventions were, and what the effects of marketing interventions by competitors were. Similarly, when something happens in the market, such as sales going up or down, managers look for causes. Otherwise, they are 'flying blind'.

In addition, managers are regularly faced with evaluating potential services that they could buy. For instance, consultants try to sell them marketing programs such as events, publicity, loyalty cards and **customer relationship management (CRM) systems**; market research agencies try to sell them tracking services; and different media try to sell them advertising space. Each vendor makes claims about the effectiveness of their service, and these claims are often backed by research studies that purport to prove the causal effects. Managers need the necessary knowledge to be able to evaluate these causal claims.

So all managers (not just marketing managers) need to know how to establish a reasonable estimate of whether something really has caused something else. This can often be difficult: what follows is a helpful guide to determining causality.

customer relationship management (CRM) systems: Information systems for gathering and analysing information on existing clients with a view to deepening knowledge, improving relationships and growing sales to those customers.

TYPES OF CAUSALITY

In marketing, we are generally interested in changes in things like buying (for example product or brand adoption, customer retention or acquisition), or changes in sales volumes or revenues, or changes in market share. Potential causes usually include things such as advertising, pricing, product features, customer service, weather, competitor actions, economic climate, government legislation and so on.

The rule of temporal sequence

Generally, we only suspect a marketing intervention of being causal if it occurred before or simultaneously with the marketplace event or change. That said, it is a common mistake in marketing to assume something was the cause of something else just because it happened shortly before it. The marketing world is replete with case studies that purport to 'prove' that X is a good thing to do because of one example where a firm did X and then sales rose. Roman generals used to consult the pecking patterns of a chicken before deciding whether or not to go into battle, presumably because a chicken once was seen pecking in a particular way immediately prior to a particularly successful or unsuccessful battle. Such superstitious mistakes occur in marketing too. Shortly before Tesco overtook Sainsbury's, its main rival supermarket in the United Kingdom, Tesco launched a loyalty program. Many commentators then attributed Tesco's success almost entirely to this loyalty program, yet Professor Robert East's analysis showed that Tesco was on a trajectory to overtake Sainsbury's market share long before launching the loyalty program (see East, 1997).

If a marketplace event only ever occurs after a particular intervention then we would suspect that that marketing intervention was the cause of that event; for example, sales only occur when the store is open. However, more often we observe less clear-cut relationships; for example, sales of ice creams tend to be higher on warmer days, but not always. Again, we might suspect a causal relationship but now it is a *probabilistic one*: warmer days increase the probability of good sales but don't guarantee them. Such causal relationships can be harder to spot, and are certainly easier to make mistakes about.

Sometimes an intervention might be *necessary but not sufficient*. For example, it is usually impossible for a new product to gain a break-even sales volume without distribution in retailers, but distribution alone rarely generates sufficient sales.

Even if we are sure of a causal relationship, we often want to go further to quantify it. For example, we want to know how many extra sales we will enjoy for every extra thousand dollars we spend on advertising. Without careful experiments, it's very easy to get this estimate wrong.

Common mistakes

The most common mistake is to confuse correlation with causality. Correlation refers to an association between two variables. For example, television viewing is moderately correlated with age: as people get older they have a tendency to watch more television. Salaries are strongly correlated with education levels: most people with university degrees earn more than people who only graduated from high school. Correlation is a necessary condition for causality. It's something that makes us suspect causality, but it does not prove causality. For example, while we were growing up, the length of our arms was correlated with petrol prices: each year our arms got longer and each year the price of petrol increased. But the length of our arms had no causal influence of petrol prices—which is proved by the fact that our arms have now stopped growing but petrol prices continue to rise.

This is what is known as a *spurious correlation* (or coincidence), where there is no relationship between the two variables other than the fact that they both changed over time. For example, over time there has been a decrease in the numbers of pirates, accompanied by an increase in global warming. To infer that the lack of pirates causes global warming (Figure 3.2) would be a mistake

▲ **LEARNING OBJECTIVE**
Understand the concept of correlation, and tests for inferring causality

▲ **LEARNING OBJECTIVE**
Be able to describe some common mistakes in interpreting metrics

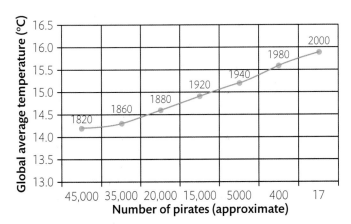

●●● **FIGURE 3.2** THE SPURIOUS CORRELATION BETWEEN PIRATE NUMBERS AND GLOBAL TEMPERATURE

of assuming causality from spurious correlation (this example comes from a famous letter: see www.venganza.org/about/open-letter).

There are other correlations that are not spurious but still do not mean that the marketing intervention causes the marketplace event. Champagne advertising spend is highest just before Christmas and New Year, which is the peak sales period for champagne, and the advertising spend is lowest in the middle of the year, when sales are also lowest. This is a strong correlation, but what is the causal relationship? Does all the champagne advertising lift champagne sales, or is it the high sales of the festive season that entices champagne brands to spend more on advertising?

In this case, the main causal relationship is probably mainly in reverse: increased category sales at Christmas and New Year cause each of the champagne brands to advertise more, as they all fight for their share of a larger than usual market. Their combined weight of advertising might also have a causal effect on total category sales, but the main reason that sales are up is that people are celebrating, not because the brands are advertising as they fight for market share.

Bigger fires tend to attract more firefighters, but this doesn't mean that firefighters cause fires to get bigger. This is another case of *reverse causality*.

Sometimes a marketing intervention and a marketplace event can be correlated because they are *both caused by a third variable*. Advertising spend tends to be higher during times of strong economic activity and lower during recessions—likewise sales are higher during these times of strong advertising spend and lower during the recessions. From this we might conclude that the level of advertising in the overall economy causes the overall level of sales, when in reality it may really be more that the economic climate affects both the spending of consumers and the advertising spending of firms.

If two things are both moving in the same direction, it can look as if one is causing the other, but it isn't clear which one. For example, over the past decade Apple's sales revenue has been rising and its scores on attitude surveys have also been rising—more people say they like the brand, feel good about it, intend to buy it and so on. Market research firms, especially those selling the results of such attitude surveys, usually interpret this as a causal relationship; that is, that improvement in

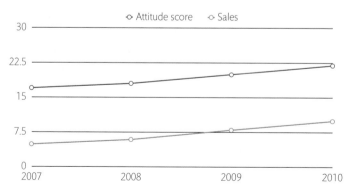

●●● FIGURE 3.3 ATTITUDES AND SALES MOVE TOGETHER—WHICH CAUSES WHICH?

the public's attitude towards Apple is resulting in increased sales. But research shows that attitude scores for any brand improve if more people buy it (Bird & Ehrenberg, 1966, 1970). So it could instead be interpreted as a causal relationship but in the other direction: increased sales each year results in improved attitude scores.

Of course, the causal relationship might be in both directions; if Apple has more buyers then it has more people likely to say something nice about it in a market research survey, and if more people feel good about Apple then they are probably more likely to buy it in future. Which relationship is stronger? Is the effect of attitudes on behaviour strong enough that the attitude scores can be used to predict whether next year's sales will rise or fall? To answer these questions we need to look for an inflection point, a point where the trend started or ended, such as when Apple's sales and attitude scores started rising. Which started rising first, the sales or the attitude? And if either stalls, which stalls first? Usually we find that the change in the trend (the inflection point) appears in sales first and then later in attitudes, which suggests that sales has a greater effect on attitude scores than attitudes have on sales.

A more correct causal interpretation in this case is that Apple began launching new products into growing categories, for which it gained a great deal of attention, at the same time it began growing its physical availability. These changes had a direct effect on consumer attitudes but an even greater indirect effect, as they drove sales, which in turn affected attitudes. So the real story is of other variables, mental and physical availability (and good, well-priced products), that drove both the two metrics we were looking at (attitudes and sales).

Beware of special secret metrics

There are many consultants who peddle to marketing managers various special metrics (that you can only buy from them) that claim to predict a brand's future. These special metrics are supposed to measure something like the brand's health, equity and/or the loyalty of its customer base. The key idea is that the 'stronger' the brand appears on these metrics then the safer it is, and the brighter its future will be, while if the brand's score on these metrics slips, managers need to take action.

Many consultants cite correlations to 'prove' the predictive capability of their metrics. A typical sales pitch goes like this: 'In the past, attitudinal measures have shown poor correlations with behaviour, but our new whizz-bang metric taps deep emotional motivations [or insert any other psycho-babble here], to deliver stunning predictive accuracy.'

Then they show correlations between brands' scores on this special metric with performance metrics like market share, changes in sales, profits or even stock prices. That last one should ring alarm bells in any thoughtful marketing manager—how come they are trying to sell me this market research product when they could be off earning a fortune on the stock market!? They will show correlations of 0.7 or above. This looks impressive, but it needn't be, as we now explain.

Correlations between any two metrics can range from r = 0 (no association) to r = 1.0 (a perfect association). Correlations can be positive if the two metrics go up and down together, or negative if one metric moves in the opposite direction to the other. For example, people wear less clothing in hotter temperatures, so if we measured the temperature and the average weight of a group of people's clothing on many different days it might show a negative correlation like that in the following table.

DAY TEMPERATURE (C°)	AVERAGE WEIGHT OF CLOTHING (KG)
10	4.5
15	3.8
20	2.9
25	2.8
30	2.0

As temperatures go up, the average amount of clothing worn by people in the group goes down: r = –0.98.

This is a very strong correlation, and it's pretty reasonable to assume a causal relationship—that heat causes people to wear lighter and less clothing.

Now, we could have calculated the correlation using data on every single individual in the survey instead of using the average weight of everyone's clothing. This would give us more data, with more variation—we all know a few people who wear lots of clothing even on hot days, and some who wear little more than jeans and a T-shirt whatever the weather. So the correlation would be expected to be lower, but overall we'd still expect a correlation (a negative one in this instance).

Attitude – Behaviour correlations

The correlation between individuals expressing a particular attitude (in a survey) and their subsequent behaviour is generally only around 0.4 (Kraus, 1995). And even this correlation score is inflated by surveys asking about very regular behaviour (for example attending church or not), rather than new behaviours or changes in behaviour.

Therefore, marketing consultants use this as a (low) benchmark. Look, they say, the correlation between my special brand score and its market share next month/year is 0.7; that's far better than anything reported in the academic literature! The implication is that it is amazingly predictive.

But there are several things very wrong with this. In actual fact, brand level correlations between attitude and sales are very good, largely because behaviour (buying) affects attitude. Brands with higher market share (more sales) have many more customers, and so they score higher on attitude surveys—because people tend to say nice things about the brands they know and/or use (and are less positive, less likely to say anything, about brands that they do not use).

These correlations will be the same if you compare each brand's attitude score to its future sales or its past sales, simply because sales and market share tend to be very stable. It's a trick—a sleight of hand—when a consultant tells you of the great correlation to future sales without telling you that the correlation to past sales is just as good or (usually) better.

Such a correlation tells us nothing about the metric's ability to predict a future *change* in a brand's sales or share. Correlations are not a good way of assessing predictive ability, or even model fit. Look below at attempts to predict tomorrow's temperature in Adelaide, Australia. Each prediction and reading is taken about a month apart, starting in summer and ending in winter. The predicted temperatures go down as winter arrives, but this is hardly impressive prediction (it's a bit like predicting that growing brands will increase sales a bit in the next period). Otherwise, the predictions are miserable; they are always wrong—sometimes too high, mostly too low. The correlation, however, is very near perfect: 0.99 to be precise.

The hopeless predictions are shown in the right-hand column:

ACTUAL TEMPERATURE (C°)	PREDICTED TEMPERATURE (C°)
39	43
32	36
24	22
21	18
17	15

$r = 0.99$

So even a super-high correlation may simply be telling you something you already know: for example that winter is cooler than summer, that Barclays Bank is a much bigger brand than Bendigo Bank, or that Coca-Cola sells many more cans than Mountain Dew.

Similarly, consultants show charts such as this:

'Look,' they say, 'improvements in our brand health/equity score correlate with rises in sales. That's proof of predictive power. It tells you if you improve your equity score then you will enjoy sales gains; that is, equity causes sales.'

But this does not show that equity causes sales. Correlation is not causality. What this most likely shows is that as the brand wins more sales—that is, has more customers—there are more people to express an attitude about the brand. So as the brand grows its equity score improves.

Again, such charts show that the special metric 'predicts' last year's sales just as well, if not better, than next year's. It's a 'rear-vision mirror'. It would be much more impressive if the metric could predict *a change* in the brand's fortunes before it happened; that is, if it could predict when brands will start moving upwards and when they will stop, and predict when brands will start moving down and when they will stop. No one seems to have ever been able to reliably do this.

Application to business-to-business marketing

Many metrics applicable to consumer marketing are also relevant to business-to-business marketing. However, due to the relatively small number of customers in most business markets and the tendency of organisations to establish medium- to long-term supply arrangements for major requirements, behavioural and other marketing metrics often can be obtained with less difficulty than within consumer markets. Frequently, the sales force can obtain sufficient information from and about major customers and prospective customers to allow the marketing organisation to develop a sound understanding of behavioural metrics.

The underlying reason for most organisational purchases—direct or indirect support of some business activity—means that purchase quantities at the product category level are based mainly on rational reasons and, therefore, that sales forecasts of many product categories can be estimated reasonably accurately. Indeed, some business-to-business sales forces develop sales forecasts based on business planning information obtained from major organisational customers. Together with the potential long-term nature of supply arrangements, this factor also means that the calculation and interpretation of customer lifetime value has greater relevance in business-to-business marketing. Given the wide range in the size of organisations, as suggested earlier in this chapter, such calculations enable prioritisation of sales force efforts (although factors other than just customer size need to be considered, such as how well the firm's offering matches customer needs relative to competitive offerings, or the likelihood of the customer organisation being affected by competition within its own markets).

Given the importance of relationship management within business-to-business marketing, it has been suggested that relationship management metrics are necessary, comprising measures of 'relationship policies and practices, trust, relationship commitment, mutual cooperation, and relationship satisfaction' (Lages, Lancastre & Lages, 2008: 690).

The existence of buying centres associated with most major purchasing decisions adds complexity to the understanding of organisational buying behaviour. For example, interpretation of metrics regarding factors such as brand salience or customer satisfaction require consideration of the level of involvement of respondents in decision-making processes or in the actual use of products.

CONCLUSION

It's impossible to be a good manager without some sort of understanding of what causes what. Now, the reality for modern managers is that they will only ever have a rather hazy knowledge of the impact of any particular marketing action on the marketplace. There are consultants who claim to be able to quantify cause and effect with pinpoint accuracy (for example through the use of statistical models); however, these claims are hugely exaggerated. Therefore, for managers it's more important to avoid making one of the big mistakes of assuming something is causal when it isn't, or missing the real cause altogether—and to try to construct an experimental design around your marketing activities so that you have a better idea than your competitors of what really causes what, what works and how much.

3

SUMMARY

- Marketers can monitor the performance of their brands using metrics.

- Metrics can describe how customers behave, and the financial implications of this behaviour. They can describe consumer memories, or what type of people they are.

- Metrics can also describe the marketing activities that we and our competitors undertake.

- Used together, all these different types of metrics give marketers some ability to sort out what is happening in the market, and what causes what.

REVISION QUESTIONS

1   Name key behavioural metrics a marketing manager should be using to assess the performance of their brand. Which ones are the most important metrics? Why?

2   Name key memory metrics a marketing manager should be using to assess the performance of their brand.

3   Discuss the difference between behavioural and memory metrics. Describe what information each type of metric represents. Why is it important to separate these two types of metrics?

4   What is a benchmark? Discuss examples of benchmarks for behavioural and memory metrics. Why are benchmarks so important for interpretation of the marketing research data?

5   Imagine that you are a brand manager for Cadbury chocolate. Outline at least two behavioural and two memory brand performance metrics that you would like to use as a brand manager. Explain (in one or two sentences) why and how each metric will be used to monitor the performance of your brand.

6   Outline what results you would expect to see in each of the metrics you outlined in question 5. Do not write a wish list of what you would like! Using your knowledge about your brand and competitors (size, etc) make realistic assumptions about what levels you can expect to see numerically (for example about 30 per cent market share and almost 100 per cent prompted brand awareness).

FURTHER READING

Ehrenberg, A S C, Uncles, M D & Goodhardt, G G (2004) 'Understanding brand performance measures: Using Dirichlet benchmarks', *Journal of Business Research*, vol. 57, no. 12, pp. 1307–25.

Keiningham, T L, Cooil, B, Andreassen, T W & Aksoy, L (2007) 'A longitudinal examination of net promoter and firm revenue growth', *Journal of Marketing*, vol. 71, pp. 39–51.

Morgan, N A & Rego, L L (2006) 'The value of different customer satisfaction and loyalty metrics in predicting business performance', *Marketing Science*, vol. 25, no. 5, pp. 426–39.

Uncles, M (2011) 'Understanding brand performance measures' in *Perspectives on Brand Management*, M Uncles (ed.), Tilde University Press, Melbourne, Australia.

WEBLINKS

Did satisfaction drive Apple's growth?:
http://byronsharp.wordpress.com/2011/09/21/satisfaction-drives-apples-growth-or-not/

Do special brand health metrics predict the future?:
http://byronsharp.wordpress.com/2010/06/20/do-brand-loyalty-commitment-engagement-metrics-work/

◢ Major case study

Toothpaste marketing alarm

Imagine you are the Marketing Insights Director of Colgate Palmolive. You recall a time earlier in your career, when Margaret, the Senior Category Manager for Colgate toothpaste, stood at your office door. She was clearly very concerned and was waving the report from the global market research supplier, which she had recently received. It showed that in the US, Procter & Gamble's Crest brand had almost double the market share of Colgate (37 per cent compared to 19 per cent). In itself this was not a surprise, as this difference had been the case for some years; the reason why Margaret was upset was the two graphs in the report (Figures 3.4 and 3.5) that showed the sales volume of each rival brand according to the recent repeat-buying behaviour of their consumers.

What was concerning Margaret was that the percentage of Colgate's sales that came from loyal

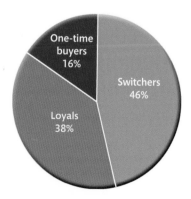

●●● **FIGURE 3.4** CREST CONSUMER BASE

Source: Spaeth & Hess, 1989

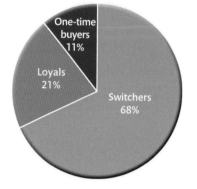

●●● **FIGURE 3.5** COLGATE CONSUMER BASE

Source: Spaeth & Hess, 1989

It seemed that Colgate's sales came much more from 'switchers'—people who bought Colgate at least once in the analysis period although most of their buying was of other brands.

customers was almost half that of Crest's sales from 'loyals', where 'loyals' were defined as people who bought the brand for the majority of their toothpaste purchasing during the analysis period used for the market research study. It seemed that Colgate's sales came much more from 'switchers'—people who bought Colgate at least once in the analysis period although most of their buying was of other brands.

Margaret needed an explanation of the apparent customer behaviour in the market. Her brand's sales seemed very reliant upon people who were not very loyal to it. Was this what the research finding meant? Why was the basis for Colgate's sales apparently so much less healthy than Crest's? Was the brand in serious trouble? She had recently developed a marketing plan that had set some ambitious growth targets for the brand's sales level over the next year.

After discussing the report, you and Margaret decided you needed more information and commissioned further market research of toothpaste buyers. This was to break down the market share of each company's brand to examine the switchers within both the Crest and Colgate customer bases. A questionnaire was devised and a survey conducted among similar people who had been surveyed for the earlier report. The first question in the survey asked about the attitudinal loyalty of purchasers of toothpaste to the major brands in the market. In the report from this second study was a diagram, shown here as Figure 3.6, which was the percentage of switchers who agreed with the statement 'This is my preferred brand'.

Figure 3.6 therefore showed that Crest's switchers were substantially more likely to say that Crest was their preferred brand than was the case for Colgate's switchers.

The survey's second question asked customers about their perceptions of the quality of toothpaste brands, and Figure 3.7 shows the quality perceptions of the switchers in each brand's customer base.

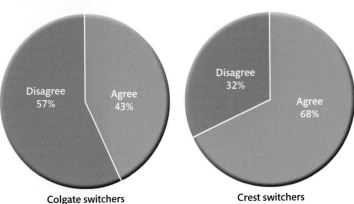

Colgate switchers   Crest switchers

●●● **FIGURE 3.6** PERCENTAGE OF BRAND USERS WHO SAID 'THIS IS MY PREFERRED BRAND'

Source: Spaeth & Hess, 1989

It could be seen that both Crest and Colgate buyers perceived both brands to be quality products—as they should, because these are both well-made products manufactured by large, experienced companies. However, it was observed that people who bought Crest, and who also often bought other brands, were slightly more likely to state that Crest was a quality brand than Colgate.

In its report on the second study to Colgate, the market research agency offered in its conclusion section some 'brand insights':

- Colgate's sales volume comes mostly from non-loyal buyers.
- Colgate is 50 per cent more dependent on switchers than Crest.
- Colgate buyers are less loyal, both behaviourally and attitudinally.
- Even Colgate buyers think Crest is a quality product.
- Crest is a quality product but it has perception problems and lacks loyalty.
- Crest seems to be attracting the wrong sort of buyer.

These insights were followed by some recommendations for action. These included that Colgate needed:

- more persuasive advertising that stressed Colgate's quality
- advertising to be conducted comparing Crest unfavourably to Colgate in features and benefits
- media schedules that achieve high frequency of exposure of the advertisements so as to shift attitudes
- further research studies to identify the profile of Colgate 'loyals' with the aim of attracting more people like them.

Margaret and you thanked the market research company for their work after they had made a presentation of their findings and recommendations, saying that you agreed with their analysis and recommendations. When discussing the findings afterwards, you and Margaret both agreed that the recommendations made sense in the light of the apparent market circumstances. You felt that others in the marketing management community would agree with them, as the insights and proposed strategy appeared reasonable, and not unusual.

A marketing consultant happened to be visiting Colgate's marketing department about another matter a week later and was shown the reports on the toothpaste market research and asked his opinion on the conclusions and proposed actions. He was aware of the

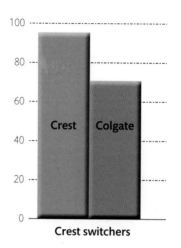

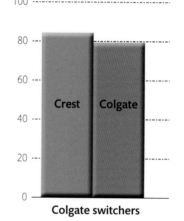

●●●FIGURE 3.7 PERCENTAGE OF BRAND BUYERS WHO SAID 'THIS IS A QUALITY PRODUCT'

Source: Spaeth & Hess, 1989

> He stressed that there was nothing in this market research that suggested that the Colgate brand had any image or perception problem.

scientific studies of buyer behaviour conducted by Andrew Ehrenberg and the need to interpret marketing metrics against known patterns in consumer behaviour.

He advised that you and Margaret were allowing yourselves to be unnecessarily alarmed by the market research findings. He said that Colgate's loyalty metrics, both attitudinal and behavioural, were normal for a brand with half the market share of Crest. Indeed, he explained that all the other research findings were essentially just a result of the fact that Colgate has half the market share of Crest in this market—and hence fewer buyers, who also would buy less often in any period of time. The metrics in the reports, he said, did not show why Colgate was half the size; they were what they were *because* of Colgate's size.

He stressed that there was nothing in this market research that suggested that the Colgate brand had any image or perception problem. The brand was not 'weak' or 'unhealthy'—it was simply smaller than Crest, which had long been the case, and had long been known by management.

This case study is derived from material in Sharp, B (2010) *How Brands Grow*, Oxford University Press, Australia & New Zealand, pp. 1–5.

Practitioner profile

Ron Bates, Project Leader, Strategic Analytics Group, Kraft Foods, Consumer Insights & Strategies, United States (New York)

My first field of study was chemical engineering—I completed bachelor's and masters degrees in it, and then went into the workforce. The first five years of my career were in research and development (R&D) for a large American manufacturing company, American Cyanamid. Because I was working in the department for materials science, I was exposed to marketing and sales of innovative materials: 'plastics' as Dustin Hoffman was advised in cult 1960s film *The Graduate*. I developed an interest in the application of quantitative methods to marketing and finance and began to pursue an MBA.

While completing my MBA, I moved out of R&D and into a product management role at NCSS, a company that marketed business planning, financial analysis and database management software. The position gave me experience in software development, marketing, sales and customer service for major corporate clients.

When I completed my MBA, I moved to a leading CPG company, General Foods, which (through a series of acquisitions) eventually became Kraft. I worked in a range of roles for General Foods/Kraft including managing marketing analytics and management information systems teams across multiple domestic businesses. After fifteen years, I joined the corporate analytics team, which is where I have spent the rest of my career at Kraft. I will retire this year, but will likely move on to yet another stage of my career.

I got to where I am today because I am intrigued by mathematics, discovering patterns in data, market structure, and new methods for analysing the impact of marketing on our businesses. I have always held the belief that 'there is nothing so practical as a good theory' (Kurt Lewin). On top of that, I had had experience in multiple business functions, including marketing, research, media effectiveness measurement and more. I also had the interpersonal skills to create

effective networks within corporate environments that demand multifunctional collaboration.

I've stayed with General Foods/Kraft all this time (nearly forty years) because it is has been a great organisation to work for. They are leaders in consumer and retailer analytics because they have deep resources, powerful staff and are driven by management that ask challenging questions on how to move the business forward.

With Kraft, I had the pleasure to work with Andrew Ehrenberg and apply the Dirichlet model to the US instant coffee market. I also arranged for Ehrenberg and, more recently, Byron Sharp's team to run lectures for our consumer insights group. It was possible at Kraft because it is a company that values training and personal development—and I know that is something that I've benefited from greatly in my career.

04

MARKET RESEARCH

ANNE SHARP AND KATHERINE ANDERSON

◢ Introduction case

National Pharmacies

National Pharmacies stores operate across metropolitan and regional South Australia, Victoria and New South Wales. A very established company, National Pharmacies has been in the market for over ninety years with the vision of 'enhancing the accessibility of quality healthcare to our communities'. It is a mutual organisation where profits made through operations are returned to their members in the form of benefits and discounts. National Pharmacies therefore have a strong interest in understanding their shoppers and in making their stores as easy as possible for customers—when you are sick, you do not want to have to search for the product or brand you need. So when it came time to update the layout of their stores they commissioned market research to understand shopper behaviour.

The researchers, together with the National Pharmacies managers, set four objectives for the research:

- understand shoppers' 'path to purchase' to the store
- identify in-store navigation patterns across their fifty-eight stores
- determine how long customers typically spent in different sections of the store
- determine the number and nature of staff interactions in-store.

To meet these objectives, National Pharmacies used two complementary research methods:

- observation in seven National Pharmacies stores to capture the actual in-store behaviour of 1000 shoppers and their interactions with staff
- in-person interviews with 300 of these shoppers as they exited the store to provide explanations for the behaviours observed in store by researchers and understand the decisions leading consumers to the store.

Many market research projects mistakenly rely on the ability of consumers to recall their shopping behaviour. Direct observations more accurately capture what consumers do in store; interviews then provide additional insight into the behaviours observed. This research provided National Pharmacies with insight into what drives store choice and how many purchasing decisions are made outside the store. This evidence supported their many out-of-store marketing efforts, including catalogues, regular television advertisements and direct mail.

The information about typical navigation patterns in store helped identify 'hot spots' (where lots of shoppers were concentrated) and 'cold spots' (where few shoppers ventured) in the new layout, and opportunities for store managers to grow sales and help customers by putting commonly purchased categories in convenient locations.

Recording interactions with staff reinforced not only the need for good customer service, but also the need for more signage to help customers navigate the new store layout. More than half of all shoppers interacted with staff, most commonly seeking guidance about the location of products or brands. This research helped National Pharmacies focus on improving the ease and convenience with which items could be found in store.

> National Pharmacies have a strong interest in understanding their shoppers and in making their stores as easy as possible for customers—when you are sick, you do not want to have to search for the product or brand you need. So when it came time to update the layout of their stores they commissioned market research to understand shopper behaviour.

INTRODUCTION

Market research informs good marketing decisions. Indeed, one of the first tasks for a new marketing manager is reviewing the existing market research to learn about the industry, the organisation's customers and the buying process.

As a marketing executive, you'll need information to do your job. You have to understand the markets you are operating in, the customers you serve (as well as the ones you don't), your suppliers, competitors and a myriad of other players and factors. You'll need analytical skills to comprehend data and to make sound decisions based on the information at hand. Many times you won't be able to answer a question or make a decision with the available information and will have to commission research. Judging the quality of the data requires specific skills and an understanding of the methods typically used to obtain market information.

This chapter provides just such knowledge: giving an overview of how market research can aid marketing decision making; introducing the approaches and methods commonly used; and explaining how to commission good research, as well as judge the trustworthiness of market research already conducted. It also outlines some principles for the analysis and presentation of results, so that what the data is saying can be easily understood and disseminated. The chapter outlines all you need to be an astute buyer and user of market research.

LEARNING OBJECTIVES

After reading this chapter you should:

- understand the role of market research in an organisation
- be able to prepare a brief to commission market research
- be able to describe various market research methods and their practical applications
- recognise the strengths and limitations of market research methods.

CHAPTER OUTLINE

Introduction

The central role of market research

Emergence of the market research industry

Jobs in market research

Commissioning research—the brief

Key stages of the research process

Secondary data and knowledge of buyer behaviour

Qualitative and quantitative data

Sampling

Research design

Understanding analysis

A well-written research report

Conclusion

//

KEY TERMS

causal research	non-probability sampling	research proposal
confidence interval	non-response rate	response rate
confidence level	open-ended questions	sample size
descriptive research	probability sampling	secondary data
exploratory research	probability theory	significance level
many sets of data (MSoD) approach	research brief	statistically significant
	research objectives	univariate analysis
multivariate analysis	research population	

THE CENTRAL ROLE OF MARKET RESEARCH

◢ **LEARNING OBJECTIVE**
Understand the role of market research in an organisation

Market research gives us a view of our market. We need it in order to understand what consumers know and think, how they behave and how a company's efforts are being received—and to identify opportunities for growth.

Market research allows us to identify marketing opportunities and problems. It is used to generate, refine and evaluate marketing actions, to monitor marketing activities and market performance and to identify the ways in which specific marketing activities can be made more effective.

Market research provides 'bread and butter' information, the basic marketing metrics that every manager needs on a daily basis: Who buys? Where? When? and How much? This descriptive data for current and potential buyers underpins decisions about distribution, pricing, advertising and promotions and also allows us to see how customers are responding to the decisions we make.

Research reduces the risk that a manager will make a poor decision. Marketing managers have heightened awareness and knowledge about the products and services they work with. This is not surprising given the hours they spend thinking and interacting with them! But this makes them very poor judges of how a 'typical' customer thinks and feels, and that is where market research can help.

Market research involves:

- specifying the information required
- designing the method for collecting information
- managing and implementing the data collection process
- analysing the results
- communicating the findings and their implications.

●●● **TABLE 4.1** DIFFERENT ROLES IN MARKET RESEARCH

PLANNING	UNDERSTANDING	EVALUATING
Which markets to enter	Customer needs and preferences	Customer satisfaction
Which products or services to offer	What customers think of existing products and services	The effectiveness of a brand's marketing mix
Which customers to target	How customers use products and services	
Potential sales of new products	How markets change over time	

There are three main groups of 'players' involved in the market research process and each has a different role:

- a client or organisation that has a particular managerial problem and wants to commission market research
- the market research agency that designs and conducts the research
- respondents—people from whom information is collected (they can be general public, potential or actual customers, or some other group of interest).

CRITICAL REFLECTION

How might the following organisations use research in their business? Think about the sort of questions these organisations may research and who they would need to involve in the research to get their questions answered.

- Commonwealth Bank of Australia
- Centrelink
- Qantas
- Woolworths
- Haigh's Chocolates
- your local city council

Think about your own personal experiences with market research. What roles have you experienced? How might the perspectives of research users (clients), participants and research analysts be different?

EMERGENCE OF THE MARKET RESEARCH INDUSTRY

While humans have long been asking questions and anecdotally noting and recording how and why people buy, the emergence of market research as a formal industry is relatively new. Fledgling market research companies started to emerge in the early 1900s. By the 1930s, most large consumer goods companies in the United Kingdom and United States were doing research, and the first published books started to appear, with *Market Research* by Paul Redmayne and Hugh Weeks being published in 1931. Market research became increasingly commercially important with the emergence of brand advertising.

Today, marketers are well served by a professional market research industry that consists of some multinational providers, such as Nielsen and Kantar, as well as many local market research agencies. The market research industry is well structured. In Australia there is an industry body called the Australian Market and Social Research Society (AMSRS). They provide a code of professional conduct, as well as accreditation procedures for research providers, and training for researchers.

The global market research industry turnover was over US$31 billion in 2010, according to figures released by the European Society for Opinion and Marketing Research (ESOMAR, 2011). Europe makes up 42 per cent of the market by spend, followed by North America (34 per cent), Asia–Pacific (16 per cent), Latin America (6 per cent) and the Middle East and Africa (2 per cent).

Marketing fact

The Nielsen Company is the world's largest market research organisation, employing around 36,000 people. It largely collects behavioural data, in over 100 countries. The company's operations are divided into two areas of focus on consumer behaviour: buying and viewing. That is, it collects metrics on buying behaviour and also on how advertising media is viewed, read or listened to.

JOBS IN MARKET RESEARCH

Market research offers the chance to work in a wide variety of areas—from consumer goods to industrial marketing, government, financial products, pharmaceuticals, charities or media. In fact, almost any area you can think of benefits from research. If you work in a market research company, you have the opportunity to work across multiple industries at the same time, potentially making every day fascinating and different. You also learn how various businesses work and interact with their customers. You gain analytical and communication skills that you can use in any walk of life.

Market research is also applied to social issues, where profit or sales is not the main measure of success for a company. In this context it is referred to as social research. Here, much the same sorts of questions need to be asked about how people think and behave. In social research you have the opportunity to help government authorities plan communications strategies to make healthier communities, save lives (for example drink driving research), build a sustainable future (for example encourage behaviour change around home energy usage) or to conduct polls that help to understand our political direction.

Over your research career, you will have the opportunity to specialise, perhaps in specific research techniques, or on types of products and services that most interest you. Good researchers with strong expertise command high incomes and employment packages. To get an idea of what marketing can mean to you, listen to young Australian researchers talk about what it means for them to be in the market and social research industry in a video produced by the AMSRS. 'Research. A Fascinating Life' can be viewed at <www.youtube.com/watch?v=uP62a3DopAs>.

Case study

Starbucks Coffee Company

Starbucks started with a single store in 1971. Today it has over 15,000 stores across fifty countries. Over the years, Starbucks has expanded its product range beyond coffee and coffee-shop products. Starbucks wants to understand:

1 what products it is known for among its consumers

2 whether the brand name 'Starbucks Coffee' is limiting its ability to enter new product categories and expand internationally into non-coffee markets.

If a name change is required, Starbucks will need to understand how current and potential customers will react.

How could this problem be researched? What sort of research is required and what respondent groups should be included in the research?

COMMISSIONING RESEARCH— THE BRIEF

Before market research can be undertaken, managers must be clear about the **research objectives** and what information is required to meet them. Research objectives describe what the research will achieve in broad terms. Examples could include:

- Determine the market potential for a new car-sharing service in suburban Sydney.
- Benchmark the level of customer satisfaction among our Melbourne customers.
- Identify how our brands are perceived in relation to our competitors.

Typically, a study has one overarching research objective and two or three smaller objectives or questions, which together provide the information required to make a decision or meet a marketing objective.

Good research objectives are linked to marketing objectives, but research and marketing objectives are different. While marketing objectives outlines what the organisation wishes to achieve—for example to increase sales or raise consumer awareness—research objectives specify what information is to be collected. Market research does not make decisions; it only provides the information to do so. Research cannot raise consumer awareness or increase market share—but it can collect information to help decide on appropriate ways to achieve such marketing objectives.

A **research brief** is a written document that formalises what you want to achieve with your research. The research brief describes why the organisation wishes to conduct research, outlines what information it aims to collect and articulates the objectives for the research. The brief also sets out the timelines to be met and the resources available. Often the brief also provides an indication of whether quantitative (more numerically based) or qualitative (more based on identification of issues) data is required and whether results should be reported back as raw data, in a presentation or as written report.

The brief does not need to outline a method for collecting the research, although it can mention approaches used successfully in the past. Recommending a particular approach to collecting data in the brief can prevent research providers from suggesting solutions that may be ideally suited. Remember, researchers are paid for their expertise in conducting market research—allow them to advise your organisation about the method.

research brief: Written by the research client, this document outlines the management problem behind the research, the research objectives and the resources available.

Research brief structure

Typically a research brief includes:

1   a brief introduction to the company and the industry

2   background to the research project (what the management problem is)

3   the research objectives and specific questions to be answered

4   the desired research outcomes (how the research will be used)

5   any methodological recommendations (not compulsory or always advisable)

6   outcomes to be delivered; for example a report or a presentation

7   budget available

8   timeline

9   the client team for the project.

The brief must be well thought out and clearly articulate what is required, as it lays the foundation for the research to follow. To get the research underway, the brief is either sent to the organisation's internal research coordinator or a few reputable market research providers or is listed for public tender. AMSRS maintains a database of accredited market researcher suppliers, as does the European Society for Opinion and Marketing Research (ESOMAR) and the American Marketing Research Association (MRA). Professional accreditation should be a key criterion when selecting a research provider. Accreditation ensures researchers are trained in market research and bound by ethical codes of conduct and industry standards. This protects the buyers of research. Other criteria useful when selecting a research provider are discussed in the box below. If a brief contains commercially sensitive information, research agencies can be asked to sign a non-disclosure agreement prior to receiving the brief.

From a researcher's perspective, the most important aspects of the brief are:

1   why the organisation requires research (the background to the issue)
2   what information is needed for the organisation to make a decision or proceed with a course of action.

Often a meeting or phone conversation is useful in clarifying these aspects of the brief. Once a researcher fully understands the purpose of the research, they can use their professional expertise to develop a research plan that will deliver the desired information. A researcher may also work with organisations to ensure problems are correctly identified or diagnosed and to help set (realistic) research objectives.

Criteria for selecting research providers

research proposal:
Written by the research provider, this document sets out how the market research agency proposes to meet the client's research objectives.

The following are useful criteria for selecting research providers:

- a good working relationship with mutual trust
- an understanding of the organisation and the research problem
- a strong level of interest in the research question(s) and willingness to make suggestions
- ability to meet the required timelines
- experience, qualifications and knowledge of staff
- industry accreditation and reputation
- presentation skills.

Researchers are more likely to be selected for their ability to develop a good working relationship (through trust and interpersonal communication) and their understanding of the organisation's issues and willingness to work with the organisation than for their technical expertise. Price is sometimes used as a basis for selecting a research provider, but, in reality, providers have similar costs, so lower prices mean less service.

CRITICAL REFLECTION

1   Why is the research briefing such a critical stage in the market research process?

2   Write a checklist of things to clarify at a briefing meeting from the perspective of a research buyer.

3   What questions would you expect a good market researcher to ask of a company issuing a research brief?

4   You are the marketing manager of a monthly magazine with national circulation. Identify three research objectives you might have. In your discussion, state why these research objectives are important and useful ones to have. You do not need to specify the research methodology, timeframe or budget, but you *do* need to discuss what respondent group(s) you would need to include in the research to meet your research objectives.

From the brief, research providers develop a **research proposal** that outlines how they would conduct the research, the methods they would employ and the costs involved. A proposal typically discusses what sort of raw data is required (for example perceptions, behaviours, and whether hard numbers are needed or issues just need to be identified) and provides a few different options for conducting the research.

Case study

Defining your research

You are a marketing manager for Bunnings Warehouse, a national company that sells tools, home renovation equipment and outdoor garden plants for domestic, rather than industrial, customers. You have commissioned market research. Bunnings believe that they have several customer groups, who they want to know more about in their research:

1 passionate gardeners

2 home 'do it yourself' renovators

3 loyal Bunnings customers

4 defected Bunnings customers.

For each group of customers, suggest three questions that you might expect to see from your research provider that attempt to define that customer group. In your discussion, include any limitations you can see with the questions.

Industry insight

Ironfish

By Bill Page

Marketing matters in places you wouldn't expect. Social marketing is the application of marketing principles to achieve social change—such as wearing seatbelts, healthy eating or wearing sunscreen. It is often used when the need for change is well accepted, but getting people to engage in the new behaviour is difficult. Traditionally, social marketing has involved the application of conventional marketing to social issues, but has developed its own vocabulary, ideas and tools (Peattie & Peattie, 2003). Social marketing is used to inform and educate, create behaviour change, lobby for beneficial laws and achieve social advocacy (Donovan, 2011).

In Cambodia, much of the population suffers from anaemia, and need to get more iron in their diet. Forty-five per cent of women in Cambodia suffer from iron deficiency, which usually just means listlessness and tiredness in Western countries, but can lead to poor brain development in babies, premature birth and uncontrolled bleeding during childbirth. Across the developing world, serious anaemia affects two billion people—it's a major problem, and doing something to help these people could improve their lives.

In wealthy countries, iron deficiency can be easily treated by eating more red meat or by taking iron supplements, but both options cost far too much for developing nations. Cast iron releases itself when used for cooking, so cast iron pots impart enough to help combat anaemia, but they are heavy and expensive, so it is difficult to convince the women of Cambodia to use them. Cost and convenience are common barriers to change.

Like all marketing, the Ironfish campaign began with market research. By consulting with 'key informants' who were willing to talk to outsiders, such as the wives of village elders, researchers were able to understand more about why iron pots aren't popular. A problem previous researchers hadn't considered was that there's no Tupperware (or equivalent) in rural Cambodia: people often leave food in the pots to eat later, and the iron makes the food taste bad.

Biomedical scientist at the University of Guelph Chris Charles and his team found an alternative: simply including a lump of iron in a cooking pot gives enough iron to combat anaemia, and it can be taken out and used again in other cooking. But the ugly shape of the lump and the strange idea isn't very appealing, despite the health benefits.

'We knew some random piece of ugly metal wouldn't work … so we had to come up with an attractive idea,' notes Charles. 'It became a challenge in social marketing.'

To determine the shape of the cast iron they would promote to the village, research again played a key role. More interviews with key informants were conducted, and three potential designs were tested in focus groups. The lumps needed to have the minimum weight and maximum surface area, to be made as cheaply as possible and to impart the greatest amount of iron into the food. The possible designs were a flat disc, a lotus flower (which holds a special place in Cambodian culture) and a lucky fish from the Mekong River, which runs through the area. The fish proved the most popular in testing.

'We designed it about 3 or 4 inches long, small enough to be stirred easily but large enough to provide up to about 75 per cent of the daily iron requirement,' said Charles. The fish are made locally for about $1.50, and last for five to ten years.

The team combined their fish with an education program designed to explain what anaemia actually is, and why they should use the fish itself. To help get the message out and remind people to use their iron fish they ran an advertising campaign involving hats, T-shirts and posters put up around the village. While the barriers of cost and convenience had been eliminated through careful design and consultation, the information and education campaign was useful in creating awareness of the problem and ensuring that villagers saw a need to use the iron fish.

Research played one final important role in the iron fish's adoption. It helped to identify that a key barrier to consistent usage was that people thought of it as a medicine, so kept it with the rest of their medicines—up high, where it was dry and safe. Of course, if it's safe, it's not doing anyone any good. This research finding lead to additional education encouraging people to keep it next to the cooking area, instead of with the medicines.

'We're now getting fantastic results; there seems to be a huge decrease in anaemia and the village women say they feel good, no dizziness, fewer headaches. The iron fish is incredibly powerful.'

The results achieved by the iron fish are far greater than anything done with expensive iron pots. The increased time spent in research and development was easily justified by the improvement in results. So, by combining medical knowledge with market research, Cambodian women no longer suffer anaemia as badly.

Charles is heading back to Cambodia to follow up with the women and check their iron levels. He expects that most of the women will still be using the fish—but as usual, we await more research to find out how successful it has been. What was the main thing these biomedical scientists learnt about the role of research in informing marketing? 'You can have the best treatment in the world, but if people won't use it, it won't matter.'

This case study is based on a personal interview with Chris Charles, 2012.

Questions

1   Market research played a critical role at different points in addressing this medical issue. Identify what these roles were and discuss their importance.

2   Can you think of a similar social problem where market research might play a useful role?

3   Can you think of a product or service that was either created or improved in response to market research?

KEY STAGES OF THE RESEARCH PROCESS

Once a research proposal has been accepted, the real work can start. The process of research can be split into six key stages.

1 identifying research objectives
2 determining the information required and the broad approach
3 research design
4 fieldwork data collection
5 data preparation and analysis
6 report or presentation to communicate results.

The marketing manager should be very involved in the first two stages, as they are shaped by why the research is needed and how it will be used by the company. Stages three to six are where the research company leads. However, the client still has an important role to play here, providing customer contact details, viewing the fieldwork in action and shaping the way in which the results are presented.

SECONDARY DATA AND KNOWLEDGE OF BUYER BEHAVIOUR

Secondary data

secondary data: Data that exists for purposes other than the project at hand.

Too many new research projects are commissioned without reviewing what research the organisation has already done, or what knowledge already exists in the public domain. **Secondary data** is data collected for some purpose other than the current research problem at hand. It may be past research projects, company records, industry reports or any other information that can be used to assist with the current research problem. At the very least, secondary data can help shape your questions, approaches and measures, may provide some comparison data for your research, or even partially answer some of your questions; freeing up research time and dollars to look at other issues.

Secondary data comes from two key sources—internal and external. Internal data may include past research projects on the same topic, sales figures, documented history of the product or brand development, and marketing intelligence information like feedback from front-line staff, consumer complaints and so on. This should be a starting point, as it is may be relatively easy to get and should cost you nothing. So, keeping track and order in internal data is important—it potentially can save a lot of time, money and effort, and save you needing to research the same thing twice.

External sources of secondary data may include statistics—for example from the Australian Bureau of Statistics (ABS)—academic and industry publications, syndicated research reports (when you can buy a particular piece of the research, such as the size and nature of the health care market in Australia) and various databases. The challenge is to fit the information you can find to your current research objectives, as they are almost never a perfect match. For example, your research objective is to estimate the likely demand for a new MP3 player, but the secondary data only describes the past sales figures for portable CD players.

Knowledge of buyer behaviour

Relatively undervalued, but equally important, is having knowledge of the patterns that can be seen in different types of data and the marketing science laws that apply across industries and time. Such 'contextual' knowledge gives a framework to both analyse and interpret your data, as well as potential explanations for the patterns you may see. It also provides a framework for how best to present data.

For example, many research reports use tables to present their findings, and these tables are typically ordered by brand alphabetically. Yet our knowledge of buyer behaviour tells us that many patterns in the data are linked to market share and that ordering tables in terms of share can highlight these to the researcher as well as the reader.

For example, we would expect to see more people associating a snack food brand with a large market share with a positive attribute than we would a smaller share brand. Take the candy bar market in New Zealand as an example. In this market Cadbury Moro is the number-one bar brand. We would expect to see Moro associated with a positive attribute such as 'a good between meal snack' by far more respondents than we would a smaller share brand such as Cadbury's Pinky Bar. This is not because Pinky is not perceived as being as good a snack, but because people tend to say things about brands they use and not much about ones they don't. While Pinky has been on the market since 1961, it is still a much smaller market share brand than Moro. If we controlled for the market share effect by just looking at the association among the Pinky Bar buyers and among the Moro Bar buyers, we would see that a very similar proportion of each of the two particular brand's users make that same positive association. Without this knowledge, it would be easy for a manager to think Pinky Bar was not perceived as favorably as Moro Bar.

Fortunately, there is a wealth of such contextual knowledge available to draw on in marketing. Much of this has been discussed in earlier chapters. It is important to choose a research provider that has such knowledge of marketing science and of how to best present data to show expected patterns. This is discussed more in 'A well-written research report' later in this chapter.

QUALITATIVE AND QUANTITATIVE DATA

◢ **LEARNING OBJECTIVE**
Be able to describe various market research methods and their practical applications

There are two broad types of data collected: qualitative and quantitative. Qualitative data provides in-depth, rich-in-detail information about the motives of respondents and their thoughts and feelings about it. It is more exploratory in nature and is typically unstructured. Collecting qualitative data

sample size: The total number of people from whom data is collected.

tends to be much more expensive per respondent, so typically **sample sizes** are small. Qualitative research, therefore, tends to be focused on identifying what issues exist, rather than estimating how much of a behaviour exists. Typically, qualitative research is conducted first to help define or measure the problem, behaviour or issue. Qualitative research may also be useful for idea generation (for example 'What changes would improve our gym facilities?'); to explain unexpected survey results ('Why did some shoppers in our store stay a long time but buy nothing?'); and to learn about how respondents think and talk about certain issues before developing a quantitative survey ('Do people use the term "mortgage" or "home loan"?').

An incorrect assertion that is often made about research with a qualitative focus is that the findings are not able to be generalised, because samples are not representative. If this were true, it would mean your research money was entirely wasted! Of course researchers do generalise their results beyond the few people they interviewed: qualitative data tends to tell us what issues exist, but nothing precise about the level of incidence of these issues. So we can generalise about what it is people think or do, we just cannot put reliable percentages against each pattern. For example, say you are interested in the choices people make when buying camping equipment. You find from some qualitative research that people own tents, swags and both tents and swags. You cannot say exactly what proportion of the entire camping population will own each or both pieces of equipment, just that each of these situations exists. To quantify the size of the tent, swag and multiple equipment camping ownership groups, quantitative data is needed, and usually from a broader, larger cross-section of campers.

Therefore, qualitative researchers should still be concerned about the representativeness of their sample, even if it is small. Unfortunately, due to the cost of recruiting qualitative samples, many researchers cut corners and end up with very biased samples of unusual, non-typical respondents.

Quantitative data provides specific numerical information from a representative, usually large, sample of respondents. Quantitative data is structured, usually as a pre-written questionnaire with checklists or response scales, so it can be analysed using statistical techniques. For example, a questionnaire may be drawn up to determine what proportion of the population has a university degree. Whereas qualitative research is about identifying what issues or behaviours exist, quantitative research is about determining the incidence or prevalence of behaviours and issues.

Many textbooks give the impression that only qualitative data can provide the in-depth understanding required for decision making. This is not true; many deep and useful things can be learnt from numbers. For example, you can learn a lot about how people use your product and what benefits you should focus on in advertising by observing who buys your product at the supermarket. Take fresh pasta sheets as an example. By recording the number of people who buy them with a pre-prepared sauce or with fresh ingredients and whether it is families or couples who are buying them, you can learn a lot about how the product is used. Whether quantitative data is required is determined by the research objectives and the information required for decision making.

Companies should not choose an approach just because 'it sounds exciting', or because it has been done in the past. No matter how innovative and exciting the research methodology is, if it does not provide the answer to your research objectives, it is useless.

Collecting qualitative data

LEARNING OBJECTIVE
Recognise the strengths
and limitations of market
research methods

There are different approaches to collecting qualitative data. This section outlines the ones you are most likely to come across in a commercial market research context. Each method has strengths and limitations.

Focus groups

Focus groups are used extensively. However, focus groups have a very high cost of interview per respondent (starting at around $300 per person) and the samples tend to be highly unrepresentative. This high cost of recruiting respondents to focus groups is one reason why they are so unrepresentative. Budget limitations mean that sample sizes are usually small—typically there are eight to ten people in a group and only a few groups for each research project.

The main reason for non-representativeness, though, is that focus groups require so much of respondents—respondents usually have to travel to a specific location at a specific time to discuss an issue or brand for more than an hour. This means that most 'normal' customers don't want to participate in a focus group, which introduces bias into the research. Focus groups tend to skew to people who are either heavy users of the category or brand being researched or who have higher than normal involvement with the issue. It is because they are interested and have a lot to say that they are prepared to make the effort to be part of the research. While it is possible to learn from these customers, it is critical to realise that the research findings may not apply to the whole market, since lighter users were excluded from the research. In most categories, light users make up most of the market, and in spite of their light buying still generate about half of a brand's sales. Ignoring these customers is a very dangerous approach!

Additionally, focus group findings are vulnerable to being unduly influenced by the group moderator (who may steer the discussion in line with their own pre-conceived ideas of the findings) or by group dynamics (one or two people being dominant).

Finally, the depth of information you get from any one person is limited, as in an hour each person only has a few minutes to state their views and experiences.

However, focus groups do have a few positives. One advantage is the ability for respondents to interact with products as they discuss them and for the researchers to observe group interactions. This can be very useful for 'disaster checking' products. For example, if everyone in five focus groups (around fifty people) responded negatively to a blue pack design, it clearly suggests that using blue is a bad idea. Another advantage is that in some cases, individuals may recall or share more in a group discussion than when they are interviewed alone. For example, if you want to understand how people choose a vet, it may be worthwhile to have dog and cat owners discuss their choices and experiences in a group. The group interaction will result in more data being generated than a one-on-one conversation.

When recruiting respondents for a focus group, it is best to recruit randomly from whatever population you are trying to research, although this can be expensive. Selecting from pre-screened lists of willing respondents or encouraging respondents to nominate acquaintances (snowball sampling) saves money, but potentially at the expense of data quality.

A note of caution: Focus groups should not be used for advertising testing. Advertising is 'consumed' quickly and alone, so having a group discussion about it for an hour not only heightens discussion to a very artificial level, but also creates an unnatural environment compared to how advertising exposure naturally occurs. Finally, people differ a great deal in their reactions to particular advertisements—which means large samples are necessary to get a true picture of market reaction.

Depth interviews

Depth interviews are commercially underrated as a means of gathering qualitative data. They involve a one-on-one semi-structured discussion in which a respondent can talk about their motivations, beliefs, attitudes, behaviour and experiences on a particular topic. Given their one-on-one rather than group nature, this method is especially suitable for sensitive or private topics such as personal finance or health. Depth interviews also allow each respondent more time to express their opinion in full. In a focus group, each respondent only gets a few minutes to express their opinion, whereas in an interview they can talk for much longer. This means depth interviews are a good choice where experts in particular fields (for example senior managers) are the target market, or where complex decisions (such as buying a car) are being researched.

Another advantage of depth interviews is that they allow the researcher to observe the respondent in their home or work environment. This may allow the researcher to directly observe things they may be discussing (for example how food is managed in the home). Also, respondents may be more willing to participate in a depth interview, as the researcher makes the effort to travel to them rather than asking the respondent to come to a central location at a set time.

A limitation of depth interviews is the time and effort they take to conduct. Only a few interviews can be completed per day by an interviewer and, if respondents are geographically dispersed, travel can make the process slow and expensive.

Like focus groups, depth interviews suffer from subjectivity of interpretation by the researcher. There is no way to know whether the interviewer accurately captures what the respondent is saying, or how much they project their own values and thoughts onto the answers given. Depth interview questions can also be very hard for the respondent to answer. For example, asking people about their 'ideal' brand produces disappointingly few answers. People are very good at thinking about products and services in a choice context ('I like this one better than that one'), but far less able to construct offerings ('This is what my ideal brand would be like'). Depth interviews, like focus groups, rely on the respondent's memory to be able to answer the questions, and this can sometimes be a real challenge for repetitive low involvement behaviours (for example 'What fuel stations have you shopped at in the last month?') and for behaviours that occur infrequently (just try thinking back to when you last purchased a new bed pillow!). This is where the next methodology can be very useful.

Observational research

The majority of research techniques rely on respondents recalling their own behaviour. Observational research is different in that it records information on consumers' actual behaviour as it happens.

This is extremely useful for companies in retail networks—such as supermarkets, department stores, pharmacies, banks and so on. Most shopper behaviour is habitual and low involvement, making it hard for respondents to recall their behaviour accurately even though it may be undertaken quite frequently (East, Wright & Vanhuele, 2008: 13). Compounding this response error is the phenomenon of telescoping. Telescoping is consumers' tendency to reduce or increase the length of time between behaviours of interest than is actually the case (Morwitz, 1997). This phenomenon frequently affects behaviours such as purchase occasions, where consumers will report having made a specific number of purchases within a monthly period, for example, but will actually also include purchases made in the month prior to that (East & Uncles, 2008; Schwarz, 1999).

Observational research can be expensive to conduct due to the amount of time involved in designing research instruments such as maps and questionnaires to record behaviours of interest, then collecting observations and coding them so they can be analysed, quantified and verified.

Research instruments must be carefully designed and tested before the research is conducted, in order to ensure behaviours are observed and recorded in a consistent manner.

Observation is the only method that can provide information such as how customers navigate through a store: what customers look at, where the shopper 'hot' and 'cold' spots are, and how many shoppers who browse a category actually buy from it.

It is useful to combine observational research with other research methods, such as exit interviews, that give shoppers an opportunity to explain the thinking (or lack thereof) behind what is observed. For example, there are many potential explanations why someone may browse for half an hour in a store and not make any purchases: the shopper may not have been able to find what they were looking for; may just have been there to browse, deliberately; or may be delaying their actual purchase to another shopping occasion.

Observational research can provide both qualitative and quantitative data. It can be used at the start of a research project to identify what behaviours occur that might need to be captured in later research stages or in a quantitative context to put timings and proportions against certain behaviours.

Other approaches

There are many other techniques for collecting qualitative data, including storytelling, projective techniques, ethnographic research, reflective journals and picture collages. You will not encounter most of these in commercial research projects. In appraising any of these approaches, keep in mind the issues raised with other approaches and maintain a focus on how the findings can be useful. Many of these lesser-used approaches produce rich visual and verbal output and this can be very useful for developing communication that will appeal to the market. It is interesting and stimulating to see these findings, but they can be quite limited in their overall contribution to understanding the market and how to manage your brand better.

Getting the most from qualitative research

Some clients are reticent to be involved in qualitative research or they question how the results were arrived at. Perhaps because the methods are so reliant on a particular interviewer or moderator, clients feel they cannot comment or ask questions as they would with a more impersonal questionnaire. However, these methods are the ones most prone to researcher influence and respondent bias. Clients have the right to see and comment on the prompt sheet—the interview or focus group questions that will be asked. You should expect to see profiles of the respondents involved in the research and how they were chosen detailed in the report. The conclusions drawn should be illustrated with direct quotes from respondents. It is also common industry practice for clients to view focus groups in a special room behind one-way glass or by remote camera. Always check the marketing skill level and experience of the researchers—this is especially important in qualitative research, where the findings are far more prone to selective interpretation by the researcher.

Collecting quantitative data

There are many methods for collecting quantitative data, each of which has benefits and limitations. The ones you are most likely to come across in a commercial market research context are outlined below. Quantitative data is collected using a structured survey or questionnaire so it can be analysed numerically. Quantitative projects usually involve samples of more than fifty, necessitating the use of a standard research instrument. Surveys are either self-administered by respondents or administered by an interviewer, depending on the methodology used.

Telephone surveys

Until as recently as 2005, telephone surveys were the most commonly used method for collecting quantitative data in developed countries such as Australia. They were the 'gold-standard' research method because 95 per cent of the population could be reached by telephone (Levy & Lemeshow, 2011) and people were generally more willing to answer research questions over the phone. Data could be obtained this way more quickly and cost-effectively than with door-to-door surveys. For these reasons, government, polling and media audience measurement research was always conducted by telephone (Crassweller, Rogers & Williams, 2008; Baim et al., 2009).

The popularity of telephone research is declining as the proportion of households covered by fixed-line phones declines and the proportion of 'mobile only' households increases. As of 2010, only 83 to 90 per cent of Australian households were estimated to be contactable via fixed-line phones (Australian Communications and Media Authority, 2010: 46), with similar figures seen for European and US populations. However, mobile phones are not usually sampled in telephone research.

response rate: The proportion (percentage) of the sample initially selected to take part in the survey that actually participates in the research.

Telephone **response rates** (the percentage of people who agree to participate in a telephone survey) are also declining. The AMSRS estimates that on average telephone surveys achieve a response rate of 27 per cent and that the rate is dropping by 2 to 3 per cent per year (Bednall, 2000). In part this is because people find unsolicited phone calls intrusive and such calls have increased greatly in the last decade. Costing $33 million, the Australian Do-Not-Call Register was established by the Australian government in response to community concern over the growth in unsolicited telemarketing calls. Market and social research is exempt, because it aims to collect information, not make sales or build databases. The research industry supports the register, as it helps make it clearer to consumers that research is different from telemarketing and serves an important purpose.

Despite these issues, telephone surveys still have some key advantages. Respondents can be selected randomly on the basis of their phone number (random digit dialling) or from the local telephone directory. This delivers greater diversity and hence representativeness in the data. Surveys can be conducted by highly trained interviewers at a central location. Most of the major research agencies maintain phone rooms of interviewers who are able to collect hundreds of survey responses in a single night. Additionally, telephone surveys allow you to reach a geographically dispersed target population, which is very hard to do face to face.

Interviewers can use computer administered telephone interviewing (CATI) software to ask survey questions and record responses straight into a database for immediate analysis and reporting. CATI computers are networked to each other, enabling samples to be controlled for representativeness and for callbacks to be made at times that are more convenient for respondents.

Collecting data by telephone is less expensive than collecting data face to face, but more expensive than mail or online surveys. A typical telephone survey with a sample of 300 will cost anywhere from A$10,000 upwards.

Internet surveys

Online panels are regularly used by marketing managers to conduct research on a global scale. For marketers, the key advantages of internet surveys are their cost-effectiveness, particularly for large samples, and the flexibility with which they can be used. Graphics and videos can be easily integrated into online surveys, enabling packaging, products and advertising to be shown. Programming can be added to online surveys to skip respondents over survey questions that are not relevant and filter them into questions which are. This improves the survey experience for respondents and shortens the survey.

Internet surveys allow qualitative as well as quantitative data to be collected, through **open-ended questions**. Consumers will often provide quite lengthy responses in text fields because they are able to complete the questions in their own time and place. Once data is entered by respondents, it is available immediately for analysis (no coding is required), allowing researchers to review responses and to add or change questions if needed.

open-ended questions: Questions in a qualitative survey that have a text field for the response, allowing consumers to type in their own answers of any length.

Data can be collected very quickly using online surveys. Typically, hundreds of responses are collected in just a few days if the survey is emailed to a large customer list or online panel. Surveys can also be posted on social networking sites such as Facebook, publicised in store or on company websites or programmed to 'pop up' on internet browsers. Response rates vary depending on which of these methods is used, but people tend to respond quickly—with online surveys sent to customer lists, 60 per cent of people who respond do so in the first forty-eight hours. Reminders can be emailed after a few days to further increase response rates.

The representativeness of online surveys is a concern, partly because not everyone is online. In Australia, at least 72 per cent of the population regularly accesses the internet (ABS, 2009b), but rates of access are lower in rural and elderly populations. The representativeness of samples from Australian online panels is discussed below.

The software used to create and distribute online surveys is easy to use and readily available. Most research agencies are able to design and manage online surveys for a fee. Once an online survey has been built, the incremental cost of including more respondents is quite low, making it an ideal method for large-scale quantitative research.

Using online panels for research

Online panels are regularly used by marketing managers to conduct consumer research. For marketers, the key advantages of online panels are:

1   Sample size—relatively large samples of consumers (500 or more) can be surveyed for a few thousand dollars. With online panel surveys, there is set-up fee for designing and managing the survey and a per-respondent fee. These fees are fixed at the start of the project, providing budgetary certainty for managers.

2   Sample characteristics—respondents can be selected for studies on the basis of the demographic and behavioural data they provided when registering for the panel. This data is often extensive, covering not just their age, location and income level but also shopping habits and preferences. Quotas can be set to ensure the final sample is representative across whatever criteria the research requires.

3   Speed—survey data can be collected very rapidly. Most large panels are capable of collecting many hundreds of survey responses in just a few days.

The key disadvantages of online panels are:

1   Incomplete coverage—only a small proportion of the population participates in online panel surveys. In Australia, a country where more than 70 per cent of the population regularly accesses the internet (ABS, 2009b), less than 5 per cent of the population probably participates in online panel surveys. Some types of people are extremely difficult to research using online panels—the elderly, highly paid executives and people with low levels of education and literacy all tend to be underrepresented on online panels.

2   Uncertainty in generalising results—not everyone has access to the internet, and people aren't usually selected randomly from the population to join online panels. This violates the fundamental principles of sampling theory, the theory which enables researchers to generalise results from a small sample to a larger population with a known degree of certainty.

3   Difficulty in verifying respondents—verifying the age, gender and socio-demographic characteristics of online panel respondents can be difficult. The impersonal nature of the internet means some people may register with false details to be eligible for more surveys.

In Australia, Nielsen operates a large online consumer panel called Homescan. The panel tracks the grocery purchasing behaviour of 10,000 Australian households on a weekly basis. Households are provided with a handheld scanner with which to record their purchases on a continuous basis. This scanner data is linked to demographic and psychographic information about the households, providing in-depth information about consumer purchase patterns and preferences. Such information is useful to managers in understanding consumer behaviour and determining the effectiveness of marketing mix changes. The sample of households is monitored closely and regularly rewarded with incentives to ensure response rates remain high and the panel remains representative of all Australian households. These are key benefits of a panel-based approach.

Mail surveys

Mail surveys were once a very popular research method, but their use has steadily declined as the coverage of the internet has grown. Collecting data by mail is a slow process, with weeks or even months between surveys being printed and returned surveys being ready for analysis. Multiple reminders often need to be sent, adding time and costs to a project.

Like online surveys, mail surveys are self-administered. Respondents are responsible for reading the survey instructions and answering the questions. Consequently, mail surveys must have very clear instructions and look appealing. However, with mail surveys it's not possible to build in data checks to force respondents to answer every question or answer questions in a certain way. Unlike for online surveys, incomplete data is a major problem for mail surveys. Furthermore, because responses are recorded on paper, coding responses, particularly open-ended responses, into a data file can be a time-consuming (and expensive) process.

Mail surveys, unless they are well done, tend to have very low response rates (less than 10 per cent of the surveys sent out are returned). It's easy for potential respondents to ignore mail surveys, throw them in the bin, lose them or simply forget to respond. Frequently, the only people who go to the effort of completing and returning a mail survey are highly involved with the research topic, heavy users or hold a very strong (polarised) opinion. This results in samples that are very biased and of limited usefulness for decision making. However, if mail surveys are personalised, reminders are sent and incentives are used to encourage people to complete them, mail response rates can be regularly over 60 per cent (Dillman 1978, 2000). So care must be taken when designing a mail survey. Photocopied surveys on poor-quality paper receive very poor response rates, as do surveys that are long, poorly formatted, or difficult to read or to complete. Unsolicited surveys addressed to 'the householder' will likely be viewed as junk mail and discarded. Personally addressing surveys ('Dear Joe') will increase the chance of a survey being opened. Sponsorship by a trusted organisation such as the Red Cross or a university tends to improve response rates, but may not be possible.

Despite their limitations, mail surveys may still be useful for:

- customers who already receive written communications from an organisation. It may be cost-effective to include a short survey with a letter or catalogue, although response rates are likely to be low.
- surveying populations with limited internet coverage, such as the elderly or remote communities. Mail surveys may reach more people than than telephone or internet surveys for these populations, although response rates will likely be lower.
- surveying consumers (or potential consumers) clustered in a geographic area such as a street or a suburb. Mail surveys combined with personal follow-ups may obtain a reasonable response rate.
- topics that require to information to be read, an opinion to be formed or information collected before responding.

In-person surveys

Sometimes the best way of collecting data is in person. Personal interviews or intercept surveys are commonly used:

- to reach people who would otherwise not participate, such as store managers, mining engineers, busy mums or people without phone lines. The physical presence of an interviewer means rates of refusal are much lower than with other methodologies, especially if the survey is short. Surveys may be collected door to door or in a central location such as a shopping mall.
- to survey groups that are defined by their behaviour immediately after the behaviour takes place. For example, supermarket shoppers can be surveyed immediately after their shopping trip or airline passengers after a flight. This reduces recall biases and makes securing a sample of the right consumers easier.
- to conduct product demonstrations or taste tests as part of the research process.

Personal surveys can be either interviewer-administered or self-administered. If the survey is self-administered then the researcher's role is to recruit respondents, provide them with the survey instrument and clarify any questions the respondent has about the survey. This increases response rates and data quality. Respondents complete the survey themselves, either on paper or with a web-enabled device such as an iPad, and then return it to the researcher. Using web-enabled devices greatly reduces data coding costs and allows for more flexible surveys. Having researchers administer the survey is easier for respondents, as they do not need to read or write, but it will make the research more expensive.

Intercept surveys—where people are approached in a public place such as a shopping mall—are not as effective as they used to be. Fieldwork agencies report that mall traffic plummeted from an average of thirty completed questionnaires per location per day in the 1970s to a mere five a day in the late 1990s (Miller & Lundy, 2002; Bock & Treiber, 2004). Agencies also report that more than 80 per cent of shoppers avoid being recruited for a mall survey by avoiding eye contact, and around one-third refuse to participate.

Biometrics

By Haydn Northover

Biometrics is the measurement of the biological reactions of the body in response to stimuli. The potential of pursuing biometric measurement is that it may help researchers avoid a reliance on self-report techniques, especially when in excess of 90 per cent of thinking is considered to take place in the subconscious.

The main tools by which this information is collected include: a functional magnetic response imager (fMRI), which measures oxygen changes in the brain; an electroencephalogram (EEG), which measures minute electrical signals emanating from the brain; and other tools that monitor heart rate, perspiration and respiration, among other symptoms. Each measure has its own strength. For instance, measuring sweat (from the fingertips) is a marker for increased arousal towards a stimulus, whereas measuring blood flow from the brain indicates which regions are involved in certain tasks; that is, which regions 'light up' when one makes a decision or sees an advertisement.

This area of research is new. As such, while a lot has been uncovered, there remains much that is still to be discovered, or even to be confirmed. Scientists that utilise fMRIs or EEGs acknowledge that the brain is so incredibly complex and the field so new, that applying the current findings into a marketing field (termed neuromarketing) is challenging at best. Much of the 'evidence' in the neuromarketing field has yet to be replicated, and as such should be treated with caution.

In short, marketers should be very sceptical of claims being made in this area—particularly if they come from people selling biometric services to marketers. Being sceptical fundamentally means asking questions of the supplier to substantiate any such claims.

Getting the most from quantitative research

Clients should work with a research provider to weigh up the relative benefits and limitations of different quantitative survey methods. The method used will depend on the specifics of the project, including who needs to be sampled and how they can be contacted, whether the presence of an interviewer is necessary and the time and resources available for the research. In some instances, combining two or more survey modes is necessary to overcome the limitations of one method and to provide options for respondents.

For quantitative research, the research instrument—the survey or questionnaire—is critical. As a client you should work with your research provider to identify what information must be collected and how information needs to be structured for management decision making.

Case study

Choosing appropriate methodology

Imagine you are the marketing manager for Target in Australia. You want to conduct research so that you better understanding your customers' in-store behaviour. After sending out a brief, you have received three proposals to conduct research:

1 The first proposal recommends a quantitative observational research methodology. It recommends observing 500 customers, over a week, in one particular store.

2 The second proposal recommends a series of focus groups with people who say they shop 'at least once a week' at a Target store.

3 The third proposal recommends a telephone survey with a cross-section of shoppers who meet the minimum criteria of saying they shop at a Target store 'more than once a month'.

Compare and contrast the information that would be obtained from using each of these methods. Discuss the nature and quality of the data or findings, and whether it can be generalised or not. Be sure to discuss any 'unique' information that might be unearthed by one methodology but not another, and why this is.

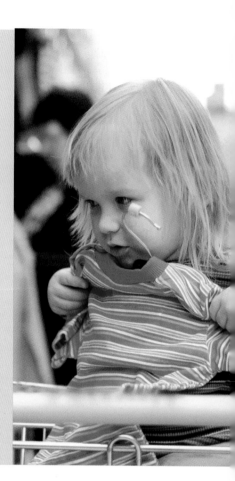

SAMPLING

A census is where everyone in a population is surveyed in the research. The Australian Census happens once every five years. The last one occurred in 2011. In contrast, most market research is conducted using samples. Generally it is too difficult, time-consuming and expensive to conduct a census, and that level of accuracy in the results is not required. A sample is selected to represent the population, in the expectation that the research can be generalised back to the whole population. Sampling is like taking a spoonful of soup from a pot to determine its flavour. To be sure of the flavour, you must stir the pot before sampling and select a 'representative' spoonful. Sampling for market research is the same: you don't need to taste the whole pot, but you do need to select a spoonful that contains all the essential elements of the soup (stock, carrots and so on). A good sampling procedure or method, like stirring the pot, helps ensure a representative sample is selected.

 CRITICAL REFLECTION

What fieldwork statistics would you, as a client, like to have reported to you for:

1 a telephone-based research project?

2 a mail-based research project?

3 a face-to-face intercept survey in a shopping mall?

To be confident in generalising the results from a sample, the sample needs to:

- represent all aspects of the population and not exclude particular types of people
- be selected randomly or in a way that ensures the sample does not bias towards particular types of people.

In market research, the **research population** refers to the group of people the research is trying to understand. Typically, this is existing or potential customers of the commissioning company.

research population:
The group of people who meet the criteria to be included in the research. Sample results from research are generalised back to this research 'parent' population.

Researching small populations

While most market research is conducted with samples, some populations are small enough that it is possible to conduct a census. For example, business-to-business enterprises that produce highly specialised goods may have fewer than 100 regular customers, making a census of all 100 customers relatively easy. Similarly, employee satisfaction research is usually conducted as a census, so every employee has the chance to participate.

Table 4.2 shows which conditions are most favourable for using a census, versus a sample.

●●● **TABLE 4.2** DETERMINING WHETHER TO USE A CENSUS OR A SAMPLE

CONDITIONS	SAMPLE	CENSUS
Population size	Large	Small
Population diversity	Small	Large
Cost of sampling errors	Low	High
Budget available	Small	Large
Time available	Short	Long

Customer samples

Most organisations maintain databases of their customers, primarily for billing and communication purposes. Samples can be selected from these databases. A database typically contains telephone numbers, postal addresses and/or email addresses. What the database contains will determine the method of research that can be used. For example, if an online retailer, such as Innerbooti, who make faux fur bootliners, scarves and vests, has a database containing the email addresses of all its customers, market research projects should be conducted by email. Hundreds or even thousands of customers could be included in the research—email surveys are very cost-effective.

Organisations with loyalty programs or store cards may have databases of hundreds or even thousands of customers. While these can be used for customer research, the samples tend to be biased towards heavier and more frequent customers and exclude light customers. This is problematic, as light and infrequent customers often make up a significant proportion of an organisation's customer base and have different opinions and purchase behaviours.

Organisations, such as Kraft, Ford and Sony, that market consumer goods, and service businesses such as restaurants do not usually maintain complete databases of customers that can be used for research. They may have databases of customers who have entered competitions or contacted the organisation (regarding warranty issues or complaints), but such databases cannot provide a complete or representative sample of customers. For such organisations, the best approach may be to sample customers at the point of purchase, using intercept interviews. For example, Kraft could sample Vegemite buyers in supermarkets, although they would need the permission of the store owners. Alternatively, large companies may be able to start with a sample of the general population and screen out people who are not customers or users of their product categories to build a representative sample. This approach would capture a broader sample of customers, including some who purchase infrequently.

Organisations may also be able to use pre-established research panels to recruit a sample of customers. Research panels are databases of consumers who have agreed to participate in market research, either in person, via the telephone, in mail surveys or, more commonly, over the internet, in return for money, points or prizes. Research panels are maintained by research suppliers all over the world.

Random sampling, research panels and in-store research can also be used to secure a sample of potential customers for an organisation. Potential customers can be an important group to research, particularly if an organisation is aiming to grow its customer base. Potential customers may encompass anyone living in a particular area or buying from a particular product category. Researching the customers of your competitors may also provide insights into new opportunities.

Sampling considerations

1 How you sample

probability sampling: Method of sampling where a set of respondents are selected from the population or database at random.

non-probability sampling: Method of sampling where a set of respondents are selected by a researcher or when respondents elect themselves to be involved.

Once the population has been defined and a database or method for selecting and contacting respondents has been identified, the next step is to determine a procedure for sampling. The sampling procedure outlines how people or groups will be selected from a larger population or a database for inclusion in the sample.

The selected sample may need to be even ten times larger than the final sample, due to non-response, a problem discussed on page 163.

Sampling procedures are either probabilistic or non-probabilistic in nature. With **probability sampling** respondents are selected from the population or database at random. Probability sampling methods produce samples that are less likely to be biased and are scientific in their properties. With **non-probability sampling** respondents are either selected by the researcher or the respondents elect themselves. This sampling method can introduce bias.

Table 4.3 outlines the main probability sampling methods.

●●● FIGURE 4.1 POTENTIAL CUSTOMERS CAN BE AN IMPORTANT GROUP TO RESEARCH

●●● TABLE 4.3 PROBABILITY SAMPLING METHODS

	SIMPLE RANDOM SAMPLING	SYSTEMATIC SAMPLING	STRATIFIED SAMPLING	CLUSTERED SAMPLING
Description	Respondents are selected randomly from the population or database, and each person (or group) has an equal chance of being selected.	Respondents are selected systematically from the population or database after the starting point is selected randomly.	The population or database is first divided into strata or groups, and respondents are then selected randomly from within each strata.	The population or database is grouped into clusters and a few clusters are selected randomly for research. A census of each cluster is conducted.
Example	Eight-digit telephone numbers are randomly generated to dial.	Every nth number in the phone book is dialled or every nth visitor to the Vegemite aisle is interviewed.	Telephone numbers are divided into high, medium and low socio-economic areas based on their location and numbers selected randomly from within each area. This is only necessary if people from different socio-economic bands respond differently.	Households are grouped according to their location, and a few suburbs or cities are selected randomly for research. Every household in the selected regions is included in the research.

Simple random sampling and stratified sampling are most commonly used for mail, in-store, telephone and online research. The key disadvantages of these approaches are that samples may not be perfectly representative of the population—more men than women (or vice versa) may be selected because of random chance. Also, people outside the target population may be selected. Some of the randomly generated telephone numbers may be fax lines or business numbers, and some visitors to the Vegemite aisle, for instance, may not buy the product.

Stratified sampling ensures the sample is representative of the population across the stratified dimensions. This is only necessary if the different strata respond differently to the research. The number of respondents selected for each strata may be proportional to the population or reflect the importance of that strata to the organisation or research objectives.

Cluster sampling is used for face-to-face research to reduce the time and cost associated with travelling to different locations to interview respondents. The population is divided into clusters and a few clusters selected for research. Cluster sampling is only advisable if respondents in different clusters will have similar attitudes and behaviours. For example, taste tests for pasta sauce in Melbourne would likely produce the same results as taste tests in Sydney.

Table 4.4 outlines the main non-probability sampling methods.

●●● **TABLE 4.4** NON-PROBABILITY SAMPLING METHODS

	CONVENIENCE SAMPLING	JUDGMENT (PURPOSIVE) SAMPLING	QUOTA SAMPLING	SNOWBALL SAMPLING	ADVERTISING
Description	Respondents who can be reached easily, quickly and inexpensively are selected. Respondents may be self-selected (volunteers) or researcher-selected.	Respondents are selected based on who the researcher thinks is interesting or appropriate for the research.	Quotas or minimum samples are set for different criteria and respondents are selected based on whether they fill the required quotas.	Respondents are asked to recommend or refer other respondents who meet the study's criteria.	Researchers advertise for respondents and select from the people who respond.
Example	Quick polls are taken of people on the street or visitors to a website. Surveys are conducted in shopping malls.	Respondents for a study of a supply chain are selected based on their expert knowledge of different stages of the supply chain.	A company sets quotas based on sales in each region to ensure the sample is representative of their customer base.	Students who are considering a particular university degree are asked to recommend other students (friends) who are considering the same degree.	Researchers advertise for mums willing to participate in focus groups at childcare centres or toy stores.

The aim of convenience sampling is to obtain a large number of responses quickly and inexpensively. However, using these responses for decision making is inadvisable. Where respondents are selected haphazardly, there is no statistical basis for projecting the results from the sample of respondents to the larger population of interest. Furthermore, there is no means of determining how accurate the results are; **confidence intervals** (see 'Probability theory and error margins', below) cannot be calculated. This is the case with all non-probability (that is, non-random) samples.

Judgment sampling is often used when researching small groups of experts and when conducting **exploratory research** to understand an issue or behaviour. If a researcher wishes to understand the scope of an issue or behaviour, they must handpick respondents with different behaviours or opinions. For example, a researcher may interview satisfied and dissatisfied customers, or new, recent and lapsed customers.

Quota sampling is used to ensure that the final sample is representative of the population on certain dimensions. Quota sampling is often necessary because certain groups, such as younger men, are more difficult to engage in research. Setting quotas for these difficult groups ensures they are still included in the final sample. Quota sampling is less rigorous (and less random) than stratified sampling. With stratified sampling, a random sample of young men, for instance, is selected and each is interviewed; with quota sampling, a convenience sample is selected and the most easily accessible young men are interviewed.

Snowball sampling is used when the respondents being targeted are quite rare and are difficult locate—for example, people who drink de-alcoholised wine or who own a horse. Asking respondents to refer friends who will fit the study's criteria can reduce costs substantially. However, the research may be biased, as the people suggested are likely to be similar in their attitudes, behaviours and/or demographics to the nominating respondent. Snowball sampling is often used when recruiting focus group participants, because finding willing respondents can be expensive.

Hard-to-find respondents may be able to be located through advertisements, either online, in magazines and newspapers, or in public places. Similarly to ads for medical trials, the research requirements and incentives on offer should be advertised, along with a phone number or website contact. Advertising tends to produce very biased research samples, as only people with lots of spare time or a keen interest in the topic (or in the incentives for participation) will respond.

Which sampling method is appropriate depends on the project's objectives, how accurate results need to be, the population and how much diversity there is within it, the lists or databases available for sampling, and the amount of time and money available. A good researcher will outline the costs and benefits of different sampling approaches and make clear how a sample will be selected. A good manager should understand the importance of sampling and understand the impact it has on results and the analyses that are possible.

Probability theory and error margins

Sample research is based on probability theory. **Probability theory** is the theory that a sample, if sufficiently large and well chosen, will likely provide results that are accurate and similar to the result you would get from the true population. It is possible to calculate how similar (or different) the real population results are likely to be from the sample results if the sample was selected randomly and the sample is larger than thirty. This is the main advantage of probability sampling.

confidence interval: The margin or numerical range of sampling error around a research result.

exploratory research: Research in order to gain an understanding of what the issues are; for example, how the presence of children under five years of age affects a parent's supermarket shopping trip.

probability theory: The theory that if a sample is sufficiently large and well chosen, it will likely provide results that are accurate and similar to the results for the true population.

A confidence interval is the margin or numerical range of sampling error around a research result. There is always some level of error or uncertainty around the results from a sample. Not everyone in the population was surveyed, which means the result for the sample you have may be a little higher or a little lower than the result obtained from either other samples or a census of the whole population you are interested in. This error is presumed to be distributed randomly and is referred to as random sampling variation.

The confidence interval surrounding a result should always be reported. Confidence intervals can be reported in two ways:

1   as a range—say the research finding from your sample is 20 per cent. There is a 95 per cent probability that the true population result would lie between 15 per cent and 25 per cent for a sample size of 300.

2   as a single figure—the population finding is somewhere in the range of 20 per cent, plus or minus 5 per cent, for a sample of 300.

The confidence interval is calculated using a formula that takes into account the:

- research results from your sample
- sample size
- level of confidence required.

confidence level:
The level of certainty that the true population result lies within the stated confidence interval.

The **confidence level** is about how much risk you want to take in your decision making. It is the certainty the researcher or marketing manager wants to have that the true population result lies within the stated confidence interval. If a researcher wants to be 99 per cent sure that the population result lies within the stated range, then the confidence interval will be fairly large—to make sure it is captured. If a researcher elects to have more risk, the range becomes smaller and the chance that the population result is outside the specified range increases.

Figure 4.2 shows a research result, derived from a sample, of 56 per cent. The 90 per cent confidence interval is shown in orange. There is a 90 in 100 chance that, if we did a census, the actual population result would lie within the range of 47.8 to 64.2 per cent. This also means there is a 10 in 100 chance it lies outside this range. If we want to lower the risk, and say only make it a 1 in 100 chance the result is outside the range (that is a confidence interval of 99 per cent), then the range increases to between 43.2 and 68.8 per cent—as shown in green.

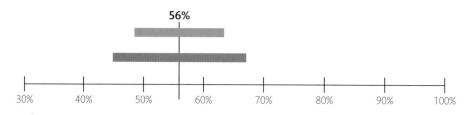

●●● **FIGURE 4.2** VISUALISING CONFIDENCE INTERVALS

In industry practice, 95 per cent is the most commonly employed confidence level. This means there is a 5 per cent risk that the population result lies outside the specified range. This is a level of risk that most marketing managers are comfortable accepting, because many decisions would be unchanged even if the 'true' population result was quite a few percentage points different from that seen in the research sample. For example, a manager researching preferences for soup flavours would likely not proceed if only 20 per cent of soup drinkers said the flavour of leek and blue cheese appealed to them. Even if 30 or 40 per cent liked the flavour, the decision to 'can' (reject) the idea would probably still be made, as the appeal is so limited.

CRITICAL REFLECTION

Identify the fundamental differences between probability and non-probability sampling methods.

2 Sample size

In research, the *sample size* is the total number of people from whom data is collected. For any research project the sample size is a major consideration, because it drives costs and determines accuracy and the sub-group analysis that is possible. Typically, market research has samples of between 300 and 600 respondents, although samples are smaller for qualitative or exploratory research. The sample may be larger for ongoing projects—or tracking projects, as they are called— where the objective is to look at changes over time.

When determining the sample size for a project, it is often necessary to make trade-offs between the level of accuracy required and the budget available. The larger the sample, the more accurate the results; that is, the more they are likely to be a true reflection of the actual population the sample represents. Statistically speaking, increasing the sample size reduces the sampling error around results and increases confidence in their accuracy. This is why researchers often recommend sampling as many respondents as you can afford. However, increasing sample size has diminishing returns. This seems counterintuitive. The larger the sample gets, the smaller the gain in accuracy from adding each additional respondent. For example, increasing the sample from 300 to 400 respondents reduces the sampling error by approximately one percentage point, whereas increasing the sample from 400 to 500 reduces the sampling error by half a percentage point (for the same proportional result, at a 95 per cent confidence level).

Importantly, the ideal sample size for a project is not determined by the size of the population. A larger parent population does not mean the sample has to be larger than for a smaller parent population. You would use the same sample size for a population whether it was 20,000 or 1 million. This is true once the parent population gets over about 2000. If the parent population is less than 2000, you would adopt a different method for calculating sample size and can get away with having a smaller sample.

The following factors influence the sample size for research:

1   the type of research—qualitative research usually involves fewer than 100 respondents because it requires in-depth engagement and aims to gain a deep understanding of an issue, without the need to put numbers against the various viewpoints. Similarly, exploratory research usually has smaller samples. **Descriptive research** usually has larger samples (300 respondents or more), because the incidence of the issues needs to be estimated.

descriptive research:
Research that establishes the incidence of an issue or behaviour, such as how many people buy a product, when they buy or what they buy; for example, how many people regularly 'tweet'.

2   the importance of the research and the level of accuracy required—if a very important or costly decision is to be made, then a larger sample is required to provide greater accuracy. Furthermore, more risk-adverse organisations, such as government agencies, typically require high levels of accuracy.

3   how the data will be used—if the data is to be used quantitatively or for analyses that require lots of sub-group analysis, a large sample is generally required.

4   the difficulty of securing targeted respondents—if securing respondents is very time-consuming or costly, this limits the sample. Similarly, the final sample may be small if refusal rates are high and only a small minority of those contacted agree to participate in the research.

5   the time frames and resources available—securing a large sample requires time, money and personnel. Small research budgets and short time frames typically result in small samples. As small samples reduce the accuracy of the data, tight time frames or small budgets may inhibit the usefulness of research conducted.

3 Representativeness

To be able to generalise the results from a sample to the greater population of interest, the sample must be representative of the population as a whole. An unrepresentative sample, no matter how large it is, will not provide reliable information for decision making.

Samples may be unrepresentative in terms of:

1   demographics—respondents may be older, more educated, skewed to females or otherwise different from the population of interest

2   responses—respondents may be more informed, involved or opinionated about the topic of interest than the population of interest.

Both types of unrepresentativeness can bias the research.

If a sample is randomly selected, sufficiently large, and most people responded, no effort need be made to ensure its representativeness. However, most samples have some element of response bias. Rarely is it possible to contact everyone who was selected, and rarely does everyone who was selected agree to participate. Participating in market research is always voluntary and many people refuse. For example, with telephone research, half of the customers selected may not be contactable during the survey period and only two-thirds of these may be willing to participate in the research. Where contact and agreement rates are low (below 40 or 50 per cent), the people who do participate are likely to be different or unrepresentative in ways that affect the research. For example, telephone research tends to underrepresent groups that are busy, such as young people, or people who are less willing to answer the phone, such as men.

Response rates are an important metric for judging the trustworthiness of research. The response rate is the proportion (percentage) of the sample initially selected that actually participates in the research. Here is an example of how response rates are calculated:

$$\text{Response rate} = \frac{\text{Total number of interviews achieved}}{\text{Total interviews + Refusals+ Non-contacts}}$$

$$33\% = \frac{335}{335 \text{ agreed} + 165 \text{ refused} + 500 \text{ not contactable}}$$

The **non-response rate** is the proportion (percentage) that was either not contactable or refused to participate.

$$\text{Non-response rate} = \frac{\text{Number of refusals} + \text{Non-contacts}}{\text{Total number of interviews} + \text{Refusals} + \text{Non-contacts}}$$

non-response rate: The proportion (percentage) of the sample initially selected to take part in the survey that was either not contactable or refused to participate.

In market research, there is usually a 30 to 40 per cent non-response rate, with peaks of 60 and 70 per cent non-response for some methodologies. Researchers should aim for response rates of over 50 per cent and use survey methods that can achieve reasonable response rates (see Gendall, 2000).

Weighting is commonly used to make unrepresentative samples appear more representative. Weighting involves statistically readjusting the sample to match the population it was collected to represent. Demographic variables such as age, gender, geographic location and income are commonly used for weighting. Yet weighting does little to improve the reliability of results and can have unexpected results. With weighting, groups that were underrepresented, such as elderly people, are up-weighted (given more weight) to make the sample appear more representative. However, the few elderly people who participated may not be representative of all elderly people. For example, someone who is ninety-one years old and participates in an internet survey is quite unusual for their age; up-weighting their response makes the sample less representative in other ways and makes the overall results even more unusual. It is far better to put effort into getting a good cross-section of respondents in the first place than trying to correct for a sample that is not representative.

In summary, sampling can have a big impact not just on results but on what you can do with them. A good researcher will talk through exactly how the sample will be selected. Managers should understand the trade-offs that are made and ensure they understand the limitations and strengths of the approach they choose.

Case study
Tapping into social media chatter

Is the monitoring of social media sites a substitute for research? Social media tools such as consumer forums, blogs, Facebook, Google+ and Twitter provide platforms for people to talk about the brands and products they use—and therefore opportunities for organisations to monitor what is being said about their brands. They also provide data. Instead of asking consumers what they think in market research surveys, organisations can listen in to what consumers are saying online.

However, there are some problems with this approach. Here are some of the issues to consider.

1 Do people really talk about brands?

People do talk about brands and products that are part of their everyday lives—Google, Apple, Coke, McDonald's and Facebook are among the most talked about brands. But people talk more about these brands in the 'real', offline world, than online. TalkTrack estimates that 76 per cent of 'branded' conversations occur face to face (Keller & Libai, 2009), so monitoring online chatter only captures a small fraction of the conversations that happen every day.

2 Who is doing the talking?

Research firm Forrester has found that a very small minority of people (6 per cent) account for the vast majority (80 per cent) of all brand impressions in social networks such as Twitter and Facebook (Keller, 2011). On Facebook, far less than 1 per cent of fans engage with the brands they befriended, and even fewer comment or say anything interesting at all about the brand in any given week (Nelson-Field & Taylor, 2012). This means that the opinions through social media monitoring come from a few disgruntled or enthusiastic chatterboxes. The sample is unusual, so the 'data' is unlikely to be representative of the opinions of all users or people.

3 What are people talking about ?

Finally, social media monitoring is unlikely to provide deep insight into what people *really* think about brands and products. Online discussions about brands are typically aimed at providing advice to other consumers, not outlining deeply held brand beliefs or describing behaviours (Mangold, Miller & Brockway, 1999). Furthermore, most comments are positive in nature, which is different from the data obtained through representative survey research. Bourque, Hobbs and Hilaire (2000) examined more than 10,000 comments made online about a brand of coffee machine and compared them to the results of a large online survey. They found that social media commenters said more positive things, not because they were nicer or more honest, but because they were simply more likely to be users of the brand than survey respondents. This demonstrates that the sample provided by social media monitoring is skewed.

Questions

1   What are the key issues with using social media monitoring as a research method? What are the issues with: coding and interpreting the data; the sample; meeting research objectives; and generating usable research outcomes?

2   Is social media monitoring suitable for determining how much people are talking about a brand or product?

3   If a brand monitors its social media mentions for a month, how large is the sample likely to be? Who is likely to be included in the sample? Will it be biased? Based on your understanding of sampling theory and techniques, is it a good sampling approach?

There are some special issues related to sampling and the use of secondary data and online panels within business markets. As already mentioned in this chapter, business markets occasionally comprise very few (but very large) customers. Due to different business strategies or other factors, those customers could have very different needs with respect to some products or services. A market research project within such a market could require a census of all customers in the population (business market) to obtain reliable information.

For some products or services targeting business markets, there are distinct market segments based on factors such as industry type. For example, requirements or specifications for production-related software could vary substantially across agricultural, manufacturing and mining industries. Sampling for a market research project aimed at identifying needs for such products within the business market would need to take account of different market segments. Information obtained about each market segment would be used in decision making about the offerings to be developed for the market. Research findings that substantial differences exist between market segments would confirm the need for different offerings to be developed for different industries.

As mentioned in Chapter 2, major organisational purchase decisions usually are made by several people, not by just one person within the purchasing department. Also, there could be various people within the customer organisation involved in some way in the use of a product or service, with no individual aware of all aspects of that use, or of the performance of a particular supplier. Consequently, market research aimed at identifying experiences or opinions of organisational customers often requires careful consideration regarding target respondents from various departments within relevant organisations, and regarding the type of information that respondents from different departments would be able to provide reliably. The research brief and, later, the research process need to take account of such considerations.

A review of secondary data is often useful as a starting point in a market research project. Internal sources of secondary data include customer information obtained by salespeople and other employees dealing directly with customers. Salespeople in some firms also collect industry- or market-related information, including customer perceptions of competitive offerings. Given the high value of many organisational customers, appropriate maintenance of internal data is particularly important to business-to-business marketers.

Online panels specifically comprising business executives are available in many countries. Typically, researchers are able to specify target respondents based on personal criteria such as occupation, seniority within a company hierarchy, and types of product or service for which the respondent has a purchasing role as a decision maker or influencer; and organisational criteria such as annual revenue, number of employees and industry type.

Application to business-to-business marketing

RESEARCH DESIGN

Most market research surveys are cross-sectional and aim to collect descriptive information about a market or customer group at a single point in time. Often they occur just once or on an ad hoc basis to answer specific questions such as 'What do customers think of our new website?' or 'What features do recreational skiers consider when choosing an Australian ski field?' The focus of analysis is to compare the responses of different groups within the sample (say, people who live in a regional versus metropolitan area) to see how they vary in attitudes and behaviour. However, studies may also be longitudinal in nature—occurring repeatedly over time. In such instances, researchers are more interested in how results change over time. Service quality and satisfaction studies fall into this category. They are typically carried out on an annual basis.

Many larger companies also have continuous tracking studies that bring in information on key marketing performance metrics on a regular basis. These tracking studies interview different respondents each week, taken from the same population, and aggregate them into a single quarterly data file and report. Such panel data is designed to help managers understand trends in metrics such as customer satisfaction, brand perceptions, advertising awareness and brand usage.

Less frequently, you come across longitudinal studies that track the same individuals over time. This is more common in social research, where researchers might be trying to understand the impact on life events or particular interventions on a group of interest. For example, we may be interested in a group of people who have been out of the paid workforce for longer than five years due to parenting responsibilities. We may wish to know how an intervention such as a consultation with a career advisor may affect them, or the effect of a life event such as their youngest child starting school. In this case, we need to track the same people to observe changes over time and to be able to link the changes to specific events. Such panels can be expensive to maintain, because people change their address or stop responding and also because it requires effort to maintain their interest in the panel.

causal research:
Research that looks at the relationship between variables and the direction of the relationship between them; for example 'What is the impact of an increase in store opening hours on store traffic?'

Another way to classify research is by its purpose. Exploratory research has the primary aim of understanding a market or situation when little is known; for example, how does the presence of children under five years of age affect a parent's supermarket shopping trip? It is most commonly associated with qualitative research approaches and with situations and companies where the client and researcher are not sure what the research will uncover. Descriptive research is where the purpose is to gain a picture or snapshot of a situation or market at a particular point in time. This type of research establishes the incidence of the issues: how many people buy, when they buy and what they buy. An example might be finding out how many people regularly 'tweet'. Such research draws upon quantitative and qualitative research and constitutes the bulk of commercial research activity. The final type of research is **causal research**. This is where the research aims to find the relationship between variables and the direction of the relationship between them; for example, 'What is the impact of an increase in store opening hours on store traffic?' Such research is typically associated with quantitative data and a longitudinal, or repeated cross-sectional, research design.

CRITICAL REFLECTION

For each of the following situations, decide whether the research should be exploratory, descriptive or causal:

- establishing the relationship between the placement of a particular advertisement within a group of advertisements and viewer recall of the ad
- investigating consumer reactions to the idea of a new bio-bin service to recycle organic kitchen waste as part of council services to a household
- identifying target market demographics for a new shopping centre
- identifying consumer understanding of the term 'organic' in the fresh vegetable category.

UNDERSTANDING ANALYSIS

The main aim of analysis is to organise and summarise the data so that patterns can be identified and insights generated.

All the previous steps in the market research process—establishing the research objectives, methodology, sample size and sampling method—and the nature of the data determine the final stages of the research process: analysis and reporting. For example, with unstructured qualitative data, only key themes and verbatim comments can be reported. Statistical analyses can only be applied to quantitative data where the sample was selected randomly, a reasonable number of respondents were sampled and the questions asked were structured. For this reason, it is important to think about what analyses are needed in a report when first designing a research project. Analysis is also guided by the knowledge the researcher has about the nature of the data, what pattern they expect and what statistical knowledge they have. Typically, different approaches to analysing the data should arrive at the same broad findings.

Complex statistical techniques are not always necessary—much can be learnt from simple descriptive statistics. Simply knowing where, when and how many products are sold is often very informative, and more complex statistics may not be necessary.

Univariate analysis

For quantitative data, analysis should start with getting a feel for the data and what it is saying. Calculating frequencies (counts) of each variable (question) is a good place to start. This provides an overview of how much variability there is in the way respondents have answered the survey. Calculating the mean, median and mode and range of the data provides information on the distribution of responses. As you can see from Figure 4.3, when the data is skewed, the mean, median and mode do

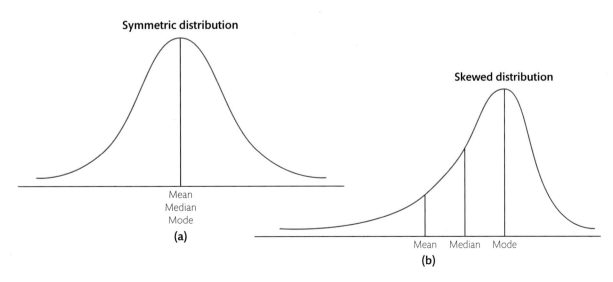

●●● **FIGURE 4.3** SYMMETRIC AND SKEWED DISTRIBUTION

not align. If the data is 'normal' they do. So assessing all three values tells you something about the spread of responses, or measure of central tendency.

This type of analysis, involving looking at each variable in turn is known as **univariate analysis**. Variables include:

- mode—the most frequently occurring value
- median—middle value when ranked in order from highest to lowest
- mean—the average, calculated by the sum of all the values divided by the number of cases
- *range*—the largest to smallest value.

univariate analysis:
Analysis that involves looking at each variable's relationship with another in turn.

Multivariate analysis

More advanced techniques can be used to look at multiple variables simultaneously and establish the relationships between them, but not necessarily the causal direction. The most common forms of such **multivariate analysis** include regression analysis factor analysis, cluster analysis and choice modelling. These techniques have the aim of data reduction—summarising, grouping or sorting the data to make patterns easier to see and to help identify the underlying relationships between variables. They require specialist skills, but a good researcher should be able to explain the analysis to the client and be explicit about the assumptions that have been made in the analysis.

multivariate analysis:
Analysis that involves looking at multiple variables simultaneously and establishing the statistical relationships between them in that set of data.

Identifying patterns in the data

Limitations of statistical significance tests

A result is called '**statistically significant**' if it is unlikely to have occurred by chance. Most research takes a sample of respondents rather than surveying the entire population. When a sample-based result is 'statistically significant', it means that something like that result should be found in the parent population and the result is not just due to having taken an unusual sample. In other words, statistical significance tests calculate the probability that relationships apparent in a sample of data are the result of chance variations that arose in selecting the sample. A very low probability indicates that the result is unlikely to be due to chance. The probability that is calculated is affected by the size of the sample and so with large samples, even small differences from what would be expected in the data will be deemed statistically significant.

statistically significant:
Unlikely to have occurred by chance.

The term 'significant' here does not necessarily mean important or meaningful, as it does in everyday speech. Nor does it mean causal, or predictable in the future. It is also not a guarantee of scientific rigour. It just indicates that the observation 'probably happened' in that population.

Moreover, significance tests do not address common research issues such as non-response bias in the sampling, and response error. Tests of significance should always be accompanied by effect-size statistics, which approximate the size and thus the practical importance of the difference.

Significant sameness and many sets of data

A **many sets of data (MSoD) approach** to analysis is a move away from significance testing and best-fit statistical techniques focused on a single study, to the identification of repeated patterns across multiple data sets. Results that repeat are far more trustworthy; they provide for predictability by telling us something about where (the conditions) the results hold. Significant sameness is about seeing in a new data set a similar pattern that has already been empirically observed in other data sets, preferably over a range of conditions, to establish the pattern's scope.

Significant sameness is said to exist when there is some degree of generalisability between two sets of data or findings. If a common pattern has already been empirically established in studying previous data sets, this provides the prior model or norm against which we have to compare any new sets of data (Bound & Ehrenberg, 1989). This approach avoids isolated and uncertain findings and protects against the uncritical acceptance and dissemination of erroneous and questionable results (Hubbard & Armstrong, 1994). Something which has held just once has hardly held at all. A finding needs to be seen in repeated observations and/or circumstances before it can be said to be generalisable. But in order to find generalisable results, one must actively look for them. This typically requires a coordinated research program across many sets of data and over time.

At present, the research industry has an overemphasis on one-off uncorroborated empirical studies. Indeed, most research in marketing still appears to be based on the strict application of statistical techniques to single data sets. This results in a measure of best-fit over that particular data set, but does not give results that can be generalised over many conditions.

An MSoD approach is also a different approach to analysis than the tests of significance and best-fit criteria that are prevalent in much current market research. Replication studies require a move away from the statistical tests that are designed for single sets of data (SSoD). There are no established methods that can be routinely applied to analyse the replications that extend over MSoD. Instead, we look for 'significant sameness', established through straightforward descriptive statistics such as averages, means and mean average deviations. The researcher looks for a single equation that can describe the relationship between the variables of interest across the MSoD (Ehrenberg, 1994). By providing a description of the relationship that holds for multiple sets of data, the relationship is more likely to be correctly described that if only one set of data was considered.

many sets of data (MSoD) approach:
Identifying commonalities and repeated patterns across multiple sets of data.

Industry insight

Changes in quantitative research

By Byron Sharp

In 1990, AARNet, Australia's forerunner to the internet, linked the nation's universities and the Commonwealth Scientific and Industrial Research Organisation (CSIRO). Then Apple released a breakthrough 40-megahertz desktop computer—described by the press of the time as 'wicked fast'; the first web browser was still a whole three years away.

In the last few decades, dramatic changes have occurred in the way that data can be collected, stored, manipulated and transmitted. Internet-based panels have replaced many telephone surveys, and increasingly there are research products based on recording what people do and say online. The next few decades will see further changes, including technological advances in statistical software, and the continued rise of pseudo-scientific data modelling techniques.

Market researchers have increasingly adopted the choice modelling approaches that have been so popular in the academic literature since the 1980s. Statisticians, on both the buyer and supplier side, enthusiastically endorsed new multivariate techniques and their associated research methodologies. This is all in spite of the almost total lack of predictive validity testing, and the fact that there have been few, if any, generalisable (that is, reusable) findings produced by such 'best fit' modelling approaches. This decade has seen a proliferation of 'black box' quantitative research approaches, often marketed with sexy brand names and wild claims of predictive ability. Data on the effectiveness, or otherwise, of these approaches has seldom found its way into the public domain, where it could be scrutinised by independent assessors. There is no doubt that market research is becoming more technologically sophisticated, but this cannot be equated with being scientific—because in the 1990s and 2000s it has meant quite the opposite.

A WELL-WRITTEN RESEARCH REPORT

A research provider's job is to make the research understandable through giving the client context, explanation and summarisation. Even the most complex of analyses should be easily understandable to the reader if the researcher has done a good job in their report writing.

While there is variation across each research project, typically market research reports have the following structure:

1   Executive summary—outlines key findings, implications and recommendations. This is the most commonly read part of the report.

2   Project background—is very similar to the content of the brief, which outlines why the research is needed and how it came about.

3   Research objectives—again links back to the client's brief, and details what the research is about.

4   Methodology—outlines who was included in the research, how they were selected, how many of them participated, the main fieldwork statistics, the type of analysis used and so on.

5   Findings—the structure of this section can vary a lot, depending on the project. It usually starts with simple descriptive information, then moves on to more complex findings.

6   Conclusion and recommendations.

7   Appendices—researcher profiles, a copy of the research instrument, such as a questionnaire or focus group prompt sheet, verbatim responses and so on.

Guidelines for writing a research report
Adapted from 'Report Writing' by Andrew Ehrenberg

These are some very simple principles that should guide report writing.

1   Give the main results and conclusion first. Everyone is busy and wants the key findings of the research up front. So, start at the end. This also gives the reader the mental framework to understand the detailed findings in the rest of the report, if they choose to read on.

2   Revise. When a reader cannot understand something, it is always the writer's fault. The process of revising will help you to make new connection between findings, identify parts that need to be clearer and improve flow.

3   Signpost. It if far easier for a reader if you signal what is coming up in the report. Use headings and sub-headings but make sure they are meaningful.

4   Keep words and sentences short.

5   Be brief. This is much harder than writing a lengthy report. Just because you have done the analyses does not mean you need to present them all.

6   Write with your reader in mind. What will they do with the report? What are they hoping to get out of it? This will help you focus on what you are saying and why you are saying it.

Presenting data

Most research reports use tables, charts and figures to convey findings. Again, there are some principles that can help to make the results clearer for the reader.

Tables should be used to tell a story about your data. This story needs to be easy for the reader to see in the numbers in your table or in your chart. For this reason, a 3D spider chart or a table with lots of numbers to two decimal places are unlikely to be the best way to convey your findings. The box below gives some simple rules for effective data presentation.

Rules for effective data presentation

1   Round to whole numbers—no decimal places. People cannot think to the level of accuracy of decimal places. Patterns and relativities between numbers are far easier to spot when presented as whole numbers.

2   Sort tables by meaningful numbers, rather than alphabetical order.

3   Use averages or medians to highlight trends.

4   Indicate totals where appropriate, especially where numbers add up to 100 per cent.

5   Use a story line—one sentence that summarises what the reader should take away from the table or graph.

CONCLUSION

Marketers need good empirical data in order to make decisions about their product offerings, pricing and promotional strategies, advertising and distribution networks. By commissioning market research, managers are able to gather data about consumer behaviours and perceptions, such as satisfaction, brand and ad awareness, category purchase drivers and salient brand associations. Well-designed quantitative and qualitative research projects can provide managers with specific, objective and trustworthy information for evidence-based decision making. Even smart managers sometimes don't think straight or have all the information they need to make a decision. As the financial and marketing implications of making a poor decision increase, so does the value of good market research.

Market research does not always involve the collection of new data: secondary sources such as sales data, census data and statistical bureau reports may also be useful. Few questions are entirely original to the world, and secondary data can therefore provide a starting point for many projects. Qualified market researchers and specialist market research agencies can assist in designing, collecting and analysing data to meet particular research objectives.

To be astute users of research, managers should understand the research process and how to assess the accuracy, reliability and generalisability of all types of data. Managers should appreciate the strengths and limitations of different research methods and understand that different sampling approaches may be necessary. At the conclusion of a project, managers have a role to play in ensuring that market research results are understood, communicated clearly and used by the organisation in decision making.

04

SUMMARY

- The market research industry in Australia is large, well-structured, has extensive codes and guidelines and a main industry body, as well as quality accreditation standards and procedures.

- Market research is one of the most important tools of marketing, helping us to understand buyer behaviour. It lowers the risk of making an incorrect marketing decision by providing an understanding of how customers view products and services. Marketing managers have heightened awareness of and involvement with their brands and categories, making them unrepresentative in their views.

- The research brief is a critical document, produced by the commissioning company, that sets out what the research objectives are and the resources the company has for the project.

- Secondary data and knowing how data behaves are essential elements to build into a research project.

- Sampling uses a small number of individuals as a basis for drawing conclusions about a whole population. The sample chosen needs to be representative of population want to draw conclusions about.

- The results of research should be clearly and simply communicated.

REVISION QUESTIONS

1   Think about your personal experiences with market research to date. What roles have you been in the most to date? What roles or aspects of market research do you not have any experience of yet?

2   Is it possible to make sound marketing decisions without market research? What advantages over 'gut-feel' decision making does research offer decision makers?

3   Discuss the aims and objectives of the AMSRS, which can be found on their website: www.AMSRS.com.au. What resources does the AMSRS provide to protect respondents, buyers of market research and providers of research services?

4   Think of some examples of how the AMSRS and their Code of Professional Behaviour can protect each of the parties involved (respondents, buyer of market research and the provider of research).

5   Outline a research design using observational research for the following situations:

    a   The Department of Transport wishes to know the level of seatbelt use in cars.

    b   McDonald's wish to know demand for drive-through versus eat-in versus take-out services for one of their metro stores.

6   Comment on the research design and sampling for the following proposed research projects:

a   A golf club is interested in determining how it is perceived in terms of image among its users. They call a random selection of users from their new members list and ask each person a series of questions.

b   A university lecturer wants to find out about how people under twenty-five years of age make educational choices. She asks each of her tutorial classes to complete a survey, offering a 1 per cent bonus grade to every student who completes the survey.

c   Jetty Surf in Melbourne is interested in why people go scuba diving and snorkelling, how often they go and what equipment and clothing they wear. They plan to send a single mailout questionnaire to 5000 households in the greater CBD of Melbourne.

7   Critique the following methodologies in terms of sampling, non-response, reliability and validity of results:

a   A supermarket is interested in determining how it is perceived in terms of image among shoppers. Cashiers drop a short questionnaire into the grocery bag of each customer prior to bagging the groceries. There is a box for returns at the front of the store.

b   To assess the extent of its trading area, a shopping mall places interviewers in the car park on a Monday and also Friday evening. After people park their cars, interviewers walk up to them and ask them for their postcode.

c   To assess the potential for a new season of *American Horror Story*, the television station invites people to ring a charge-per-minute telephone number to vote 'yes' or 'no' to whether they would like to see another season or not.

8   What questions would you expect a good market researcher to ask of a company issuing a research brief?

9   Why do we need to sample? List as many factors as possible that impact on the decision about sample size.

FURTHER READING

Brock, T & Sergeant, B (2002) 'Small sample market research', *International Journal of Market Research*, vol. 44 (quarter 2), pp. 1–10.

Charles, C V, Dewey, C E, Daniell, W E & Summerlee, A J S (2011) 'Iron-deficiency anaemia in rural Cambodia: Community trial of a novel iron supplementation technique', *The European Journal of Public Health*, vol. 21, no. 1, pp. 43–8.

Gendall, P (1998) 'A framework for questionnaire design: Lablaw revisited', *Marketing Bulletin*, vol. 9, pp. 28–39.

Gendall, P & Esselmont, D (1992) 'Market research: What it can and can't do', *Marketing Bulletin*, vol. 3, pp. 63–6.

Graeff, T & Harmon, S (2002) 'Collecting and using personal data: Consumers' awareness and concerns', *Journal of Consumer Marketing*, vol. 19, no. 4, pp. 302–18.

Hoek, J, Gendall, P & Kearns, Z (1994) 'What we say or what we do?', *New Zealand Marketing Educators Conference*, pp. 273–9.

Mahmoud, O (2003) 'Why smart managers don't think straight', *Admap*, February, issue 436.

WEBLINKS

Australian Marketing and Social Research Society (AMSRS):
www.amsrs.com.au

Cumming, G (2009) 'Dance of the *p* values:
www.youtube.com/watch?v=ez4DgdurRPg

European Society for Opinion and Marketing Research (2012) '26 questions to help research buyers of online samples':
www.esomar.org/knowledge-and-standards/research-resources/26-questions.php

Ikonfilm (2008) 'Research. A Fascinating Life':
www.youtube.com/watch?v=uP62a3DopAs

◢ Major case study

iSnack2.0

Vegemite, the yeast concentrate spread, is an Australian household breakfast staple. It is used on toast and crumpets, in sandwiches and as a cooking ingredient. It was invented in 1922. The billionth jar of Vegemite was produced in 2008. On 13 June 2009, Kraft released a new version of Vegemite, which contained Vegemite and cream cheese. A competition was run to give the product a name. The winning name was iSnack2.0, and it was announced during the AFL grand final. The winning name was chosen by marketing and communication experts to appeal to the younger market with its association with iPods and iPhones.

The reaction was immediate and strong, with industry likening the backlash to that seen when Coca-Cola changed its Coke recipe and rebranded it as New Coke. Just four days later, Kraft announced plans to abandon the name, with the Head of Corporate Affairs admitting 'the name isn't resonating with success or favour'.

A new name, 'Vegemite Cheesybite' was announced in October that year, after the company posted six new alternatives and asked the public to vote on them (see Figure 4.4).

> The winning name was chosen by marketing and communication experts to appeal to the younger market with its association with iPods and iPhones.

Which of these names is your first choice?

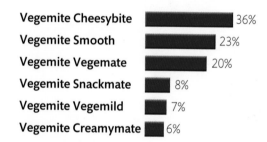

Vegemite Cheesybite	36%
Vegemite Smooth	23%
Vegemite Vegemate	20%
Vegemite Snackmate	8%
Vegemite Vegemild	7%
Vegemite Creamymate	6%

% of total sample who had a name preference (*n* = 30,357)

●●● **FIGURE 4.4** SURVEY OF POTENTIAL NAMES FOR NEW VEGEMITE AND CREAM CHEESE PRODUCT

Source: Quantum Market Research, October 2009 from 'The vote is in: VEGEMITE CHEESYBITE is the people's choice', retrieved 3 July 2012 from <www.kraft.com.au/products/media_release_vegemite_vote.aspx>

Questions

1 What lessons can be learnt from this case about how market research can help to reduce risk in decision making?

2 What research would you suggest should have been done before deciding on a name for the new product?

3 How did research play a role in the renaming of iSnack2.0? Do you think the company approached the second go at naming in the best way? Why or why not?

GERATE AFTER OPENING
SPREAD IT ST
145g NET
NEW
VEGEMITE
KRAFT
NAME ME
X
See back
for details
A deliciously different Vegemite experience
SPREAD IT STRAIGHT ON
NEW
VEGEMITE
KRAFT
iSnack
2.0

Practitioner profile
Kathryn McArthur, Consumer Insights Manager, Colgate-Palmolive (Sydney)

I didn't have a career in mind when I started tertiary education study. I enrolled in psychology and, to be honest, I wasn't sure where it would take me. I just knew that it was something I found fascinating. After I graduated, I started my first full-time job working for an insurance company. It wasn't exactly my dream career, so I continued studying psychology at the same time, completing my postgraduate qualification at night.

In the end, following my passion for psychology was the right decision, because it led me to consumer and marketing research. I was attracted to consumer insights because it combined marketing decision making with consumer psychology. It was the perfect fit for me, and I've never looked back.

My career really started in a couple of boutique research agencies. It was such a fascinating (albeit demanding) environment and certainly fast-tracked the development of my marketing knowledge. I worked on projects for radio stations, FMCG (fast-moving consumer goods) brands, pharmaceutical companies, alcohol manufacturers, the tourism industry, finance companies, fast-food retailers … the list goes on. After seven years, I had worked on more advertisements, pack designs, product development projects, brand plans and portfolio strategies than many marketers would experience in their whole career.

The agency work was great, but I wanted to experience the next step—how the research findings were applied and embedded within the organisation. It was something that I couldn't experience while I was working at the agency, so I switched to the client side.

Working at a bigger organisation like Colgate-Palmolive is the perfect balance for me. With so many brands to work with, I still get the variety that I loved in the agency, but I can also be hands on with the application of the research. As Consumer Insights Manager, it's part of my responsibility to see that our research is guiding the company to make good decisions.

When I started in this field, I didn't realise that the learning would never cease. But actually it's one of the things I love the most—being part of an industry that is flourishing with new ideas and methodologies. Not all of them are good (in fact, some are decidedly suspect), but that is part of the learning curve in the research industry.

To this day, I keep refining my thinking, keeping up to date with new disciplines that are informing marketing and research and continuing to hone my skills. You'd think after twenty-plus years I'd be a little bored or even jaded, but I've been blessed to have a genuine and enduring interest in what I do. If you looked at my bedside table at the moment you'd see a stack of books on the latest topics—neuroscience, behavioural economics and some good old-fashioned books on brand strategy and advertising.

I'm a fan of brands and consumers, and, yes, some might say a geek, but it's that curiosity that has driven my career. Having passion for your work and curiosity to know more are two of the critical traits of a great insights professional. It spurs you to dig, to experiment, to learn, to grow and to help people and brands prosper.

05

THE MARKETING ENVIRONMENT

ADRIAN PALMER, ADAPTED BY LARRY LOCKSHIN

◢ Introduction case

Sealing the deal on the Stelvin screwcap

By Armando Maria Corsi

The 1970s were a period of great change for the Australian wine industry. Advances in technology were quickly implemented along the supply chain, and new winemaking skills stimulated consumers to demand something more than the traditional products they were used to drinking. But consumers rejected non-traditional closures on bottles, retaining their preference for cork.

One of the most significant innovations of the 1970s was the introduction of a new type of closure: the Stelvin® screwcap. This closure improved the technical advantages of the standard closures used to seal wine flagons and completely removed problems of cork-taint (a specific flavour imparted by infected corks), inconsistent quality and leakage of wine, which used to characterise approximately 1 to 10 per cent of the wines sealed with a natural cork. Yet, the new closure didn't fit with consumers' perceptions of a high-quality wine. So, in 1984, after a few years of poor sales performance after adopting the Stelvin® seal, several major Australian producers reverted to corks. A decade or so later (in 2000), the Australian winemakers of the Clare Valley region decided to reintroduce Stelvin® screwcaps, but only for closing their premium Rieslings. This time, the new closures were received more positively by the media and consumers, and gradually people began to accept the new type of closure. Over the last ten years, some of the so-called 'New World' wine-producing countries (such as Australia and New Zealand,) have converted to Stelvin® screwcaps. However, the 'Old World' wine-producing countries (such as Italy, France and Spain) largely continue to seal their bottles with natural corks.

> The 1970s were a period of great change for the Australian wine industry. Advances in technology were quickly implemented along the supply chain, and new winemaking skills stimulated consumers to demand something more than the traditional products they were used to drinking. But consumers rejected non-traditional closures on bottles, retaining their preference for cork.

INTRODUCTION

In the previous chapters we have looked at what marketing professionals do, how buyers buy and the different metrics that marketing managers use to make decisions and evaluate their actions. In this chapter, we look at the marketing environment and the different elements of the micro-environment and macro-environment that affect business operations. We also focus on the importance of understanding the marketing environment and its impact on how buyers buy and what this means for developing a marketing strategy.

LEARNING OBJECTIVES

After reading this chapter you should:

- appreciate how the environment might affect marketing activities
- understand the elements of the micro-environment
- understand the elements of the macro-environment
- be able to discuss how to monitor changes in the micro- and macro-environment.

CHAPTER OUTLINE

Introduction

The marketing environment

The micro-environment

The macro-environment

Internal environment

Monitoring and responding to environmental change

Conclusion

KEY TERMS

birth rate	economic growth	marketing environment
business cycle	fertility rate	micro-environment
competitors	gross domestic product (GDP)	pressure groups
demography	intermediaries	shareholders
disintermediation	internal environment	stakeholders
ecological environment	macro-environment	SWOT analysis

THE MARKETING ENVIRONMENT

An environment is everything that surrounds and impinges (has an effect) on a system. A good system must be able to react and adapt to environmental change. An example is a central heating system, which operates in an environment where a key factor is the air temperature. If there is a drop in the air temperature, the thermostat reacts by increasing the system's output so that the correct temperature is maintained.

Sometimes a failure to react to environmental change can be fatal—for example, the human body may die if it fails to adjust to certain environmental changes such as very low temperatures. In the same way, marketing can be seen as a system that must respond to environmental change. Businesses may fail if they do not analyse their environment and adapt to external changes such as new sources of competition or changes in **stakeholders'** expectations.

Businesses operate in complicated environments where there are many factors and external influences that can impact on operations. This is also true of the **marketing environment**, which covers all the external factors that can affect buyer behaviour and reduce the ability of marketing managers to grow their brands.

Naturally, some elements in a firm's marketing environment are more direct and immediate in their effects, while others may seem further removed from operations and difficult to assess in terms of their likely impact on a company. As such, and in order to assist in analysis and understanding, we divide the marketing environment into different levels:

- The **micro-environment** covers the elements that impinge directly on a company such as customers, **competitors**, suppliers and distributors. The company has a direct relationship and direct dealings with many of these aspects (for example current customers).
- The **macro-environment** encompasses things that are beyond the immediate environment but can nevertheless affect an organisation. A business may have no direct relationships with legislators as it does with suppliers, yet legislators' actions in passing new laws may have profound effects on the markets it seeks to serve, as well as affecting its production costs. The macro-environment also covers a wide range of nebulous phenomena such as factors represented as general forces and pressures rather than institutions.
- As well as looking to the outside world, marketing managers must consider the impact of non-marketing factors within their own firm—the **internal environment**.

The elements within each of these parts of an organisation's environment are described in more detail below and illustrated schematically in Figure 5.1.

LEARNING OBJECTIVE
Appreciate how the environment might affect marketing activities

stakeholders: Everyone who will be affected by the actions of the organisation, or who will be charged with carrying out these actions. This may include suppliers, customers, employees, people who live nearby, and so on.

marketing environment: The individuals, organisations and forces external to the marketing management function of an organisation that impinge on the marketing management's ability to develop and maintain successful exchanges with customers.

micro-environment: All those other organisations and individuals that, directly or indirectly, affect the activities of the organisation.

competitors: Organisations that compete for the same consumer spending, with a directly or indirectly substitutable product.

macro-environment: The larger, wider forces that have influence over companies and economies, including political, social and economic forces.

internal environment: Components of an organisation, such as the employees, physical tools and communication methods, which affect corporate culture.

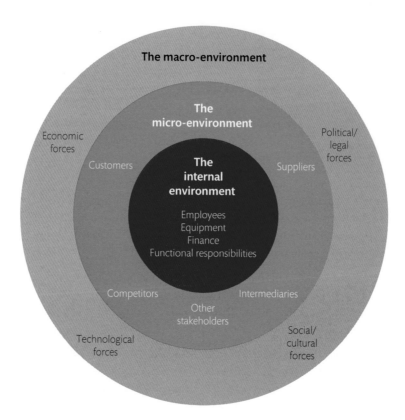

●●● FIGURE 5.1 AN ORGANISATION'S MARKETING ENVIRONMENT

◢ LEARNING OBJECTIVE
Understand the elements
of the micro-environment

◢ intermediaries:
Middlemen, such as
wholesalers, resellers or
transport agencies. They
help large companies
to deal with smaller
companies, who then
deal with consumers
individually.

THE MICRO-ENVIRONMENT

The micro-environment comprises all those other organisations and individuals that, directly or indirectly, affect the activities of the organisation. Some of the key groups within the micro-environment are customers, competitors, **intermediaries**, suppliers, government, the financial community, local communities and pressure groups, each of which we will discuss in more detail.

Customers

Customers are a crucial part of an organisation's micro-environment. An organisation and particularly marketing management should be concerned about the changing requirements of its customers and should keep in touch with these changing needs by using market research (see Chapter 4). As an example, consider the change in the menus of fast-food chains over the last twenty years; most now include healthier options or low-calorie choices, and some feature menu items made with organic meat, or with no/reduced trans-fats. Similarly many coffee chains and (more recently) chocolate manufacturers are promoting their choice to use fair-trade beans. Most of these changes are led by evolving consumer preferences.

In an ideal world, an organisation should understand its market demand so well that it is able to predict overall customer responses, rather than respond or act defensively, but it is certainly not always the case. In 2009, Cadbury had to act quickly after their decision to add palm oil to their milk-chocolate blocks led to boycotts and consumer protests in New Zealand. The negative media generated by outraged consumers eventually led the company to reverse the decision and remove the palm oil from their chocolate bars in both New Zealand and Australia.

Competitors

Most companies operate within highly competitive markets, so keeping an eye on competitors and trying to understand their likely next moves can be crucial. Think of the manoeuvring and out-manoeuvring that appears to take place between competitors in such highly competitive sectors as budget airlines and mobile phones. But who are a company's competitors? The most obvious are the direct competitors—those that offer products or services that are very similar and satisfy customers' needs in a similar way; for example Coca-Cola and Pepsi. But there are also indirect competitors, which satisfy a fundamentally similar need (such as thirst) but perhaps do so in a different form—for example energy drinks, water, coffee and juice. Indirect competitors are more difficult to identify and are easier to fail to notice, but because they provide for some of the same underlying needs marketers must consider them in their long-term plans.

CRITICAL REFLECTION

What is a competitor for a cinema? Is it another cinema? iTunes? Or some completely different form of leisure activity, which satisfies a similar underlying need for entertainment, such as a sporting event or live music?

Intermediaries

Companies cannot ignore the intermediaries such as wholesalers, retailers and agents, which may be crucial interfaces between themselves and their final consumers. Large firms usually find it difficult to deal with each one of their final consumers individually, so they choose instead to sell their products through intermediaries. Even in some business sectors, access to effective intermediaries can be crucial for marketing success. For example, food manufacturers who do not maintain shelf space in the major supermarkets find it difficult to achieve large-volume sales.

Channels of distribution comprise all those people and organisations involved in the process of transferring the physical product and the title to a product from the producer to the consumer. Sometimes products will be transferred directly from producer to final consumer—a factory selling specialised kitchen units directly to the public would fit into this category. Alternatively, the producer may sell its output through retailers; or, if these are considered too numerous for the manufacturer to handle, it could deal with a wholesaler who in turn would sell to the retailer. More than one wholesaler could be involved in the process.

Intermediaries may need reassurance about the company's capabilities as a supplier that can work with them to supply goods and services in a reliable and ethical manner. Many companies have suffered because they have failed to take adequate account of the needs of their intermediaries. For example, both The Body Shop and McDonald's have faced protests from their franchisees, which felt threatened by marketing strategies that were perceived as being against their own interests.

Because of the importance of intermediaries, their activities and the activities of competing intermediaries must be monitored as part of the micro-environment.

Suppliers

Suppliers provide an organisation with goods and services that are transformed by the organisation into value-added products for customers. For companies operating in highly competitive markets where differentiation between products is minimal, obtaining supplies at the best possible price may be vital in order to be able to pass on cost savings in the form of lower prices charged to customers. Where reliability of delivery to customers is crucial, unreliable suppliers may thwart a producer's marketing efforts.

For example, Apple has made a number of large, even multi-billion dollar, investments to assist its suppliers in Asia to build factories (for example for manufacturing display screens for iPhones and iPads), ensuring that Apple has high-quality and low-cost reliable supply, and making it difficult for competitors to match Apple's features and prices.

In business-to-business marketing, it is important to understand how suppliers, manufacturers and intermediaries work together to create value. The idea of a value chain is introduced later in this chapter. Buyers and sellers are increasingly cooperating in their dealings with each other, rather than bargaining over each transaction in a confrontational manner.

There is an argument that companies should behave in a socially responsible way to their suppliers. For instance, many people feel companies should favour local suppliers rather than possibly lower priced overseas producers. Many supermarkets proudly promote locally produced ranges of food. A company must also decide whether to divide its orders between a large number of suppliers or place the bulk of its custom with a small handful of preferred suppliers. It may also wish to consider whether it should favour new businesses, or businesses representing minority interests, when it places its orders.

Another type of supplier is one that aids the company in its activities: an advertising agency or a law firm would be an example of this type of supplier.

Changes affecting suppliers and the competition between suppliers must also be part of the monitoring activity of the micro-environment.

Government

The demands of government agencies often take precedence over the needs of a company's customers. Government has a number of roles to play in a commercial organisation's marketing environment, as outlined below:

- Government agencies, such as Fair Work Australia, regulate many activities that have a direct or indirect impact on what products a company can offer to its customers. For example, legislation requiring employers to pay a minimum wage has added to the costs of companies, leading to price rises for many labour-intensive service industries such as restaurants, and movement of some activities to low-wage countries for many manufacturing companies.

- Governments levy taxes that will most probably be incorporated into a firm's selling prices, thereby affecting the size of demand for its products. Different levels of government can levy different taxes as well as have different requirements for registration and compliance.
- Government is increasingly expecting business organisations to take over many responsibilities from the public sector; for example with regard to the payment of sickness and maternity benefits to employees.
- It is through business organisations that governments achieve many of their economic and social objectives; for example with respect to regional economic development and skills training.

Companies often go to great lengths in seeking favourable responses from government agencies. In the case of many private-sector utility providers, promotional effort is often aimed more at regulatory bodies than at final consumers. Most industry sectors maintain lobbying efforts in a nation's capital to try to influence regulation and have their say in the formation of new laws and procedures.

The financial community

The financial community is made up of the financial institutions that have supported, are currently supporting or may support the organisation in the future. **Shareholders**, both private and institutional, form an important element of this community and must be reassured that the organisation is going to achieve its stated objectives. Many market expansion plans have failed because the company did not adequately consider the needs and expectations of potential investors. Recently, many smaller companies and some larger ones in Australia were not able to renew their financing arrangements, when banks and other funding agencies refused to renew loans and financing instruments during the financial crisis of 2008–09. Companies that were unable to cut back on expenses or had not prepared other means of obtaining necessary cash suffered; and some had to close.

shareholders: In effect, the owners of a company. Ownership is split into many parts, each for sale on the share market. Shareholders have a range of rights, from a share of profits (that is, a dividend) to control over the company.

Local communities

Market-led companies often try to be seen as a 'good neighbours' in their local communities. Such companies can enhance their image through charitable contributions, sponsorship of local events and support of the local environment. This may be interpreted either as part of a firm's genuine concern for its local community or as a more cynical and pragmatic attempt to buy favour where its own interests are at stake. If a fast-food restaurant installs improved filters on its extractor fans, is it doing this genuinely to improve the lives of local residents, or merely to forestall prohibitive action taken by the local authority? Perhaps both are part of the company's objectives.

Pressure groups

Members of **pressure groups** may have never been customers of a certain company and may never be so in the future. Yet, a pressure group can detract seriously from the image of a company that its marketing department has worked hard to develop.

pressure groups: Groups that stand for a cause, sometimes known as lobby or advocacy groups.

Pressure groups can be divided into those that are permanently fighting for a general cause, and those that are set up to achieve a specific objective and are dissolved when this objective is met. Pressure groups can also be classified according to their functions; for example, sectional groups (such as trades unions and employers' associations) exist to promote the common interests of their members over a wide range of issues, while promotional groups fight for specific causes (for example, the Tarkine National Coalition was formed to lobby against development in the Tarkine wilderness of western Tasmania).

Pressure groups can influence the activities of businesses in a number of ways:

- Propaganda is used to create awareness of the group and its cause (for example through press releases to the media). Many pressure groups have effectively used social networking websites to rapidly mobilise opposition to companies that they see as operating in an antisocial way.

- The pressure group can seek to represent the views of the group directly to businesses on a one-to-one basis. (Many environmental pressure groups seek to advance their cause by 'educating' companies that may be ignorant of the pressure group's concerns.)

- Increasingly, pressure groups have resorted to direct action against companies, which can range from boycotts to physical attacks on a company's property. Organisations targeted in this way may initially put on a brave face when confronted with such activities by dismissing them as inconsequential, but often the result is to change the organisation's behaviour, especially where the prospect of large profits is uncertain.

Case study

Banning live exports

By Elizabeth Gunner

Australia's response to the 2011 'Ban Live Export' campaign led by Animals Australia and the RSPCA is a good example of how pressure groups can affect business and trade. The campaign began with an exposé aired on the ABC program *Four Corners*, showing confronting footage of animal abuse recorded by Animals Australia during their investigation of the live trade of Australian cattle to Indonesia. The program sparked a huge public response and prompted the Australian government to ban live exports to several Indonesian facilities. Stakeholders and cattle farmers reported significant loss of export earnings as a result of the government response.

Questions

1   What does this case make you think about the power of pressure groups? Do you think that the cattle farmers would have considered this outcome before the documentary was aired?

2   Can you think of examples similar to this, where a pressure group has generated a large response, but the government hasn't acted? Why do you think the Australian government acted in this instance and not others?

3   In this case a documentary was launched on free-to-air television, but there was also a website developed and a lot of word-of-mouth publicity through social media sites such as Twitter and Facebook. Do you think social media leads to more people becoming involved in political issues? Why or why not?

4   How might marketers use social media as a public relations tool?

It should not be forgotten that businesses themselves are often active members of pressure groups, which they may join as a means of influencing government legislation that will affect their industry sector. The Business Council of Australia (BCA) and the Tobacco Advisory Council (TAC) are two examples of high-profile industry-led pressure groups.

Pressure groups are increasingly crossing national boundaries, reflecting the influence of supranational institutions such as the European Union and the increasing influence of multinational business organisations. Friends of the Earth and Greenpeace are examples of multinational pressure groups.

Value chains

The concept of a value chain is introduced here to help understand the complex marketing relationships that can exist between a company and its customers, suppliers and intermediaries.

Most products bought by private consumers represent the culmination of a long process of value creation. The company selling the finished product probably bought many of its components from an outside supplier, which in turn bought raw materials from another outside supplier. This is the basis of a value chain in which basic raw materials progressively have value added to them by members of the value chain. Value adding can come in the form of adding further components, changing the form of a product or adding ancillary services to the product offer.

Consider the example shown in Table 5.1 of a value chain for instant coffee. The value of the raw beans contained in a jar of instant coffee or sold to a roaster may be no more than a few cents, but the final product may be sold for over $4. Raw coffee beans have little value to most consumers, especially if they are located in Africa, but a cup of hot coffee located near their work is worth paying for. The value chain describes how the basic has been transformed into something of greater value, with each step of the process adding some value.

●●● **TABLE 5.1** A VALUE CHAIN FOR COFFEE

VALUE CHAIN MEMBER	FUNCTIONS PERFORMED
Grower	Produces a basic agricultural product; for example coffee beans
Merchant	Adds value to the coffee beans by checking, grading and making beans available (selling) to coffee manufacturers
Coffee manufacturer	By processing the coffee beans, adding other ingredients and packaging, turns beans into jars of instant coffee or roasts, and markets whole beans; through promotion creates a brand image
Wholesaler	Buys bulk stocks of jars of coffee, or whole beans, and stores them in warehouses close to customers
Retailer	Provides a facility for customers to buy coffee at a place and a time that is convenient to them, rather than from the manufacturer
Coffee shop	Adds further value by providing a ready-made cup of coffee in pleasant surroundings

For retail products, particularly ones in coffee shops, much of the value is created in the last step of the value chain. The cost of rent, heat, lighting and staff salaries easily dwarfs the cost of the raw materials such as coffee. When you buy a cup of coffee at a coffee shop you are largely paying for these things, not the coffee or the sugar or the milk. Coffee shops could charge customers a standard fee to enter the door or sit at a table and then price the coffee very low. Such pricing would more accurately reflect their costs, but consumers don't understand or think this way about the value chain, so they wouldn't accept it.

Value can only be defined in terms of customers' perceptions, so much of the transformation process described above may be considered by some people to have no value. Some coffee drinkers may consider that processing the coffee to make it into instant granules destroys value by spoiling the full taste that can be obtained from roasted beans. For such people, the most important point in the value-creating process probably derives from the growing and selection of the coffee beans. For others, paying $4 for a skinny latte in a Gloria Jean's coffee bar may be considered good value, because they particularly like the convenience and atmosphere in which the coffee is served—and the skill of the barista.

Value chains are not limited to physical products. Services must create value chains to serve their customers as well. For example, a bank may source funds to offer mortgages from several sources—from local depositors and from off-shore wholesale money markets—with each source providing a different mix of services, such as interest rates and availability. The bank may decide to offer some or all of its different mortgage products through a range of channels: from agents or brokers to online to branch-based employees. Each of these channels may add some extra value, such as personal service or convenience.

Relationships between members of the micro-environment

In considering value chains, we can see that the marketing effectiveness for a firm can be highly dependent upon the firm's relationships with other members of its micro-environment. Very few organisations are able to produce and distribute everything they sell to customers entirely within their own resources. Certainly, few can produce their own advertising or legal services. Instead, they will most probably outsource these services, and they may also use intermediaries to sell their products. It follows that relationships between a company and these external organisations can be critical for delivering value to customers. The individuals and organisations that make up a firm's micro-environment are often described as its 'environmental set'. An example of an environmental set for a computer manufacturer is shown in Figure 5.2.

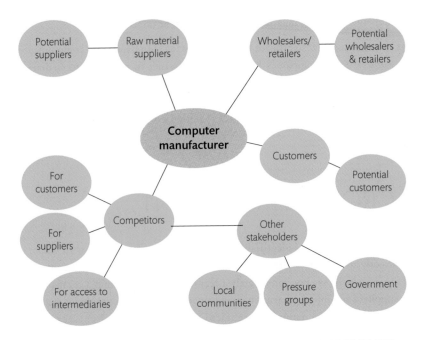

●●● **FIGURE 5.2** THE ENVIRONMENTAL SET OF A COMPUTER MANUFACTURER

Around the world in recent years there has been some significant redistribution in power, away from manufacturers to retailers. The growing strength of retailers in many sectors has given them significantly increased bargaining power in their dealings with manufacturers whose goods they sell. By building up their own strong brands, large retailers are increasingly able to exert pressure on manufacturers in terms of product specification, price and the level of promotional support to be given to them. According to market research group Kantar Worldpanel, the United Kingdom's big four grocery retailers—Tesco, Asda, Sainsbury's and Morrisons—now account for more than three-quarters (76.2 per cent) of the grocery market. In Australia, Woolworths and Coles (part of Wesfarmers) account for over 80 per cent of grocery sales; when Foodland/IGA is added, the figure is close to 90 per cent. However, while many manufacturers may be dependent on big supermarkets for further sales, this dependency is not reciprocated, with very few retailers relying on one single supplier for more than 1 per cent of their supplies.

Communication within the micro-environment

With no communication, there is no possibility for trading to take place. Although we talk today about a communications 'revolution', marketers of previous centuries have also faced the challenge of rapid developments in communication, as evidenced by the great advances in trade that took place following the developments of canals, steamships, railways and the telephone. New internet-based communications have enhanced the ability of companies to rapidly exchange information with their suppliers and intermediaries, and this has allowed for the development of increasingly efficient supply chains. Without efficient communication systems, attempts to introduce 'just-in-time' production systems and rapid customer response are likely to be impeded.

disintermediation:
Removing the middleman, bringing consumers directly in contact with the manufacturer.

The internet plays an increasingly significant role in allowing companies to communicate with their final consumers. Some companies have used the internet to cut out intermediaries altogether through a process of **disintermediation**. It was thought that the internet would remove *all* middlemen, but in reality it has allowed a new generation of 'information intermediary' (for example Expedia.com and coveraustralia.com) to create value by distributing information on travel and insurance, respectively.

LEARNING OBJECTIVE
Understand the elements of the macro-environment

THE MACRO-ENVIRONMENT

While the micro-environment comprises identifiable individuals and organisations with whom a company interacts (directly and indirectly), the macro-environment is more nebulous. It comprises general trends and forces, which may not immediately affect the relationships that a company has with its customers, suppliers and intermediaries, but sooner or later, as the environment changes, these trends and forces will alter the nature of such micro-level relationships. As an example, a change in the population structure of a country does not immediately affect the way in which a company does business with its customers, but over time it may affect the number of young or elderly people with whom it is possible to do business.

Most analyses of the macro-environment divide it into a number areas. The most common ones are:

- economic environment
- political environment
- social and cultural environment
- demographic environment
- technological environment
- ecological environment
- internal environment.

These are discussed in more detail below. It must, however, be remembered that the division of the macro-environment into these areas does not result in watertight compartments. The macro-environment is complex and interdependent.

Economic environment

Economic growth and the distribution of income are important factors for business. Few business people can afford to ignore the state of the economy, because it affects the willingness and ability of customers to buy their products. Marketers therefore keep their eyes on relevant aggregate indicators of the economy, such as **gross domestic product (GDP)**, inflation rates and savings ratios. In addition to measurable economic prosperity, the level of perceived wealth and confidence in the future can be an important determinant of demand as well. In the global financial crisis beginning in 2008, Australia's economy remained strong, mainly due to mining revenues. However, retail sales in 2011 were down because people perceived themselves to be less well off and did not purchase Christmas presents at the usual rate. If consumers' confidence is low, a high proportion of income tends to be saved. If confidence is high, consumers are more likely to borrow, so that their expenditure is greater than their income.

Figure 5.3 shows Australian relative consumer income (real gross domestic income) from 1996 to 2010. The global recession beginning in mid-2008 is evident. Reduced spending by consumers and businesses accompanied the recession, as well as lower house prices and fewer loans. Australia's

economic growth: An increase in the output of an entire economy— that is, the amount of goods or services produced—in real terms.

gross domestic product (GDP): The total value of all goods and services produced by an economy (usually a country) in a single year.

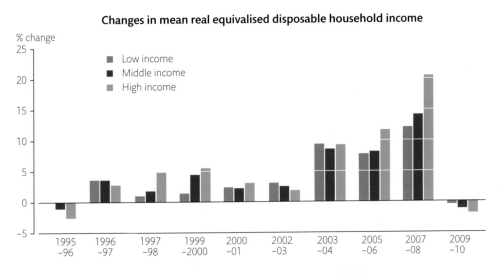

●●● FIGURE 5.3 AUSTRALIAN RELATIVE CONSUMER INCOME, 1996–2010

Source: Australian Bureau of Statistics, 2012c

overall economy recovered more quickly than the United States or the United Kingdom, although much of the GDP increase from 2009 to 2010 was due to exports of raw materials. This means that consumer spending did not increase in 2010 proportionate to the growth in GDP.

The effects of government policy objectives on the distribution of income can have profound implications for marketers. During most of the post-war years, the tendency has been for income to be redistributed from richer to less well-off groups. In Australia, higher-rate taxation and the payment of welfare benefits have been instrumental in trying to achieve this. In late 2008, the Australian government decided to give a one-off payment to all taxpayers to help them cope with the global financial crises, which caused a recession in many Western countries. Sales during that Christmas were high and retailers were generally happy. Subsequently, consumers slowed their spending and retail sales decreased during most of 2009 and only started to recover in 2010.

Multiplier and accelerator effects

Through models of national economies, firms try to understand how increases in expenditure (whether by government, households or firms) will affect their specific sector. The multiplier effect of increases in government spending (or cuts in taxation) can be compared to the effects of throwing a stone into a pond of water. The initial spending boost will have an initial impact on households and businesses directly affected by the additional spending, but through a ripple effect will also be indirectly felt by households and firms throughout the economy.

A small increase in consumer demand can lead, through an accelerator effect, to a sudden large increase in demand for plant and machinery, as manufacturers seek to increase their capacity to meet this demand. Demand for industrial capital goods therefore tends to be more cyclical than for consumer goods, so when consumer demand falls by a small amount, demand for plant and machinery falls by a correspondingly larger amount, and vice versa.

Business cycle

business cycle: The periodic fluctuation in levels of economic activity, influencing profitability, output, productivity and employment. The cycle consists of periods of boom, downturn, recession and upturn.

Companies are particularly interested in understanding the **business cycle** and in predicting how it will affect their sector. If the economy is at the bottom of an economic recession, this may be the ideal time for firms to begin investing in new production capacity, ahead of the eventual upturn in demand. Adding new production capacity during a period of recession is also likely to be much cheaper than waiting until an upturn in the economy puts upward pressure on its input prices. During periods of economic boom, firms should look ahead to the inevitable downturn that follows. A problem of excess capacity and stocks can result when a firm fails to spot the downturn at the top of the business cycle. Analysing turning points in the business cycle has therefore become crucial to marketers. Missing an upturn at the bottom of the recession can lead to missed opportunities when the recovery comes to fruition. On the other hand, reacting to a false signal can leave a firm with expensive excess stock on its hands.

It is extremely difficult to identify a turning point at the time when it is happening. In early 2006, the United Kingdom's economy appeared to be going into recession, and many companies scaled back their investment in stocks and capacity. However, the economy soon bounced back after just a short blip, and the predicted recession did not set in until 2008.

Business cycles also affect the marketing expenditures of firms. Typically, during a recession firms cut back on marketing, especially advertising; while during an upturn in the economy firms increase advertising and marketing expenditures. Some research has shown that it is easier to gain consumer attention for advertisements during a recession, due to less competition, so it may pay to increase advertising at such a time. Also, during recessions more people eat and entertain at home, so depending on your business it may be the right time to increase communications to the market. On the other hand, if you are a supplier to the restaurant or travel sector, then it is probably a good idea to cut back during economic downturns.

Market competitiveness

An analysis of the macro-economic environment will also indicate the current and expected future level of competitor activity. An oversupply of products in a market sector (whether actual or predicted) results in a downward pressure on prices and profitability. Markets are dynamic, and what may appear to be an attractive market today may soon deteriorate as the market matures.

Political environment

The political environment in its broadest sense comprises governments, politicians and the pressure groups that bring pressure to bear on politicians and governments. The political environment can be one of the less predictable elements in an organisation's marketing environment. Marketers need to monitor the changing political environment, because political change can profoundly affect a firm's marketing. Consider the following effects of change in the political environment on marketing.

- While Western countries are generally politically stable, the instability of many governments in less developed countries has led a number of companies to question the wisdom of marketing in those countries. In some cases it is difficult to gain market space due to restrictions on international companies in favour of local ones, or difficult to repatriate any profits if the currency is not traded.
- In countries with well-developed political systems, firms should understand the consequences for their business of a change in government. For example, how would a manufacturer of luxury cars react if a left-wing socialist government, pledging to impose higher taxes on expensive cars, was elected to replace a more right-wing government? Firms should not just wait for the election results, but should try to predict the likely results and plan for changes to their marketing activities.
- Governments are responsible for protecting the public interest at large, imposing further constraints on the activities of firms (for example controls on pollution, which may make a manufacturing firm uncompetitive in international markets on account of the associated increased costs).
- The macro-economic environment is very much influenced by the actions of politicians. Government is responsible for formulating policies that can influence the rate of growth in the

economy and hence the total amount of spending power. It is also a political decision as to how this spending power should be distributed between different groups of consumers and between the public and private sectors.

- Government policies can influence the dominant social and cultural values of a country, although there can be argument about which is the cause and which is the effect. For example, did the Australian government's drive for economic expansion and individual responsibility during the late 1980s change public attitudes away from good citizenship and towards those of 'greed is good', or was this a change in culture that would have occurred regardless?

- Increasingly, the political environment affecting marketers includes supranational organisations, which can directly or indirectly affect companies. These include trading blocs—such as the European Union, Association of Southeast Asian Nations (ASEAN) and North American Free Trade Agreement (NAFTA)—and the influence of worldwide intergovernmental organisations (such as the World Trade Organization) whose members seek to implement agreed policy.

▼ CRITICAL REFLECTION

Consider the following examples of contemporary cultural changes and the possible responses of marketers.

- According to Australian Bureau of Statistics (ABS), more women than men graduate in Australia from bachelor's degrees each year. In 2006, women represented 54.8 per cent of all tertiary education students (ABS, 2012b) up significantly from 29.9 per cent enrolled in 1970.

- In 2011, the labour force participation rate for women was 58 per cent (ABS, 2009c) almost double the figure from 1961, when it was at 34 per cent (ABS, 2012a).

- A report by the Future Foundation predicted that women would be the major breadwinners in a quarter of United Kingdom families by 2030 (Doughty, 2007).

Social and cultural environment

It is crucial for marketers to appreciate fully the cultural values of a society, especially where an organisation is seeking to do business in a country that is quite different from its own. Attitudes to specific products change over time and at any one time can differ between groups in society.

Even in home markets, business organisations should understand the processes of gradual cultural change and be prepared to satisfy the changing needs of consumers. For example, the increasing number of money-rich, time-poor households has been targeted by suppliers of services ranging from home shopping and domestic cleaning to personal coaching. Busy lifestyles have contributed to an increase in the number of parents seeking kindergartens for their young children. A desire by mothers to return to their career as soon as possible after the birth of their child and a decline in the geographically close extended family have led to an increase in private childcare services.

 ecological environment: Commonly referred to as 'the environment'—anything from the natural world that will have an effect on the business, be it climate change, the need to avoid polluting, or a flock of birds interfering with power transmission lines.

One of the bigger changes over the last century has been an increase in life expectancy. Australia's ageing population means that there is a growing number of elderly people that have different needs and values. Another recent change is the increasing concern about the **ecological environment**. This shift in values has led to a greater variety of 'green' consumer products.

There has been much discussion recently about the concept of cultural convergence, referring to an apparent decline in differences between cultures. It has been argued that basic human needs are universal in nature and, in principle, capable of satisfaction with universally similar solutions. Many companies have sought to develop one core product for a global market, and there is some evidence of firms achieving this (for example Coca-Cola or McDonald's). The desire of subcultures in one country to imitate the values of those in another culture has also contributed to cultural convergence.

Critics of the trend towards cultural convergence point to a growing need for cultural identity, which has been expressed, for example, in the rejection by some Muslim fundamentalist groups of the values of Western society. This poses new challenges for Western companies that seek expansion overseas. How can Coca-Cola be sure that its brand name and product offer will be the object of aspiration for the dominant groups in a country, rather than a hated symbol of an alien system of capitalism?

Demographic environment

Demography is the study of populations in terms of their size and characteristics. Among the topics of interest to demographers are the age structure of a country, the geographic distribution of its population, the balance between males and females, and the likely future size of the population and its characteristics. Changes in the size and age structure of the population are critical to many firms' marketing. Although the total population of most developed countries is stable, their composition is changing. Most developed countries are experiencing an increase in the proportion of elderly people, and companies who have monitored this trend have responded with the development of residential homes, cruise holidays and financial portfolio management services aimed at meeting this group's needs. At the other end of the age spectrum, the **birth rate** of most countries is cyclical, resulting in a cyclical pattern of demand for age-related products such as baby products, fashion clothing and family cars. Developing countries, on the other hand, typically have a much younger population with an increasing demand for fashion, mobile phones and social activities.

demography: The study of human populations in terms of size, density, location, age, sex, occupation, education and other characteristics.

birth rate: The number of live births per 1000 people per year.

Consider the following changes in the structure of the Australian population and their effects on marketers.

- Women giving birth to fewer children—the **fertility rate** dropped from 2.9 to 1.9 babies per women between 1969 and 1979. This was mostly attributed to fewer women in their twenties giving birth (although some fertility rate decline was observed for all age groups). Since 1979, the fertility rate has dropped even further and in 1999 the average number of babies per woman was 1.7 (ABS, 2006a).

- Women having babies later in life—in 1979 nearly one in four births (24 per cent) were to women that were over thirty years old. This figure increased substantially: by 1999 almost half of all births (47 per cent) were to women aged thirty and over. The percentage of women having their second birth aged over thirty was 52 per cent in 1999, up 8 per cent from 1993 (ABS, 2006a).

- More couples not having children—it was estimated in 2000 that 24 per cent of the women in their reproductive years would never have any children. This mirrors the trend in other developed countries, with recent estimates of permanent childlessness in the United States and United Kingdom at 20 per cent and 22 per cent respectively (ABS, 2006b).

- Increase in number of households—it has been projected that in 2031 there will be over 11.4 million households in Australia. This is a significant increase in the number recorded for 2006, which was 7.8 million households. While the number of households is projected to

fertility rate: The number of babies a woman would have in her lifetime were she to have the exact current average number of babies for women her age.

increase, the average number of people within the households is projected to decrease slightly, from 2.6 in 2006 to between 2.4 and 2.5 people per household in 2031 (ABS, 2011b). Thus, the number of households is projected to grow faster than the overall population.

- Increase in single person households—in 2006, there were 1.9 million single person households. That number is projected to increase significantly by 2031, to 3.2 million single person households, which will mean the proportion of households containing just one person is over one quarter of all households (28 per cent) (ABS, 2011b).

- Ethnic diversity—the ethnic composition of Australia is increasingly diverse. In 2006, it was estimated that nearly one quarter of all Australian residents (24 per cent) were born overseas. Between 2005 and 2006, 180,000 people migrated to Australia. That is 72 per cent more than in the same period ten years previously; this largely reflects changes in economic conditions and government policy (ABS, 2008).

Case study

McDonald's recognises new family values

Statistics have continued to chart the decline of the stereotypical nuclear family of two parents and 2.4 children. However, advertisers have often continued to portray this 'ideal' type of family in their advertising, despite the fact that fewer people can directly relate to it. The fast-food restaurant McDonald's recognised this trend with a UK advertising campaign that portrayed a boy arranging for a meeting between his separated

parents in a branch of McDonald's. Behind the departure from the 'happy families' norm in fast-food marketing was the realisation that the number of families in the United Kingdom with single parents has risen from 8 per cent in 1971 to nearly one quarter in 2002. McDonald's claimed that it could not credibly position itself as a family restaurant and show only pictures of mum and dad and two kids without the risk of alienating parents and children from different households. But would McDonald's incur the wrath of critics who might accuse the company of actually contributing to family breakdown? With an eye on such worries, McDonald's advertisements left the impression that the couple were going to get together again.

Questions

1 Consider some of the recent changes in the Australian population that have been detailed in this chapter. Do you think that this should change the way that advertisers portray a 'typical' family in commercials?

2 If you were a carpet supplier, would you focus your advertisements on single person households and ignore stereotypical family households?

3   Do you think that companies that still continue to feature the 'typical' family in their ads are at a disadvantage?

4   Do you think that individual parents and children would stop using a brand or service because they felt they did not identify with the family in the advertisement?

Technological environment

The pace of technological change is becoming increasingly rapid, and marketers need to understand how technological developments might affect them in four related business areas:

- New technologies can allow new goods and services to be offered to consumers; for example mobile internet and new anti-cancer drugs.

- New technology can allow existing products to be made more cheaply, thereby widening the market for such goods by enabling prices to be lowered. In this way, more efficient aircraft have allowed new markets for air travel to develop.

- New opportunities for companies to communicate with their target customers have emerged, with many companies using computer databases to target potential customers and to maintain a dialogue with established customers. The development of mobile internet services offers new possibilities for targeting buyers at times and places of high readiness to buy.

- Technological developments have allowed new methods of distributing goods and services. For example, Amazon used the internet to offer book buyers a new way of browsing and buying books; iTunes has had a major impact on retail music stores.

Case study
The internet's unforeseen consequences

The development of the internet has had profound effects on the marketing activities of some business sectors. As an example, the budget airline sector has capitalised on the ability of the internet to cut out intermediaries and reduce the airlines' costs.

However, while many observers correctly predicted that travel and financial services would rapidly embrace the internet, some other predictions have proved wide of the mark, suggesting that there is a very complex interaction between the technological, social and economic environments. Consider the following predictions, which were made in 2000 when 'dot.com' mania was at its height.

1 Predictions were made that commuting would lessen, as more people would work from home, using the internet to communicate with their work colleagues. Traffic congestion in big cities would disappear and commuter rail services would lose customers. However, in reality 24/7 access to their work email has allowed many people to choose a pleasant residential environment and to live much further away from their work, because access to the internet now allows them to work from home for two or three days a week. Overall, the travelling distances of many people in this situation have actually increased, resulting in more rather than less total commuting.

2 Conferences were predicted to disappear in favour of video conferencing. Why bother travelling to a meeting or conference when you could meet 'virtually' from the comfort of your desk, and at a lower cost? However, face-to-face conferences have continued to prosper. The technology that enables many people to work in isolation may have indirectly contributed to a desire to counter this with more face-to-face meetings with greater social content.

3 Main street shops were being written off in 2000, when online companies like lastminute.com were experiencing great success. However, the convenience of shopping in the city centre or at suburban shopping centres and the problems for internet suppliers in arranging home delivery were underestimated by advocates of internet-based shopping.

We seem to have an inherent tendency to overstate the short-term effects of technological change but understate the long-term effects on our behaviour. With the development of new technologies enabling high-speed mobile internet services, further predictions are constantly being made. Do we really want to download full-length feature films to watch on our mobile phones? Will there be more unforeseen 'killer applications', such as SMS text messaging, which was almost left out of the specification of first-generation mobile phones because no useful role for it was foreseen? Perhaps the long-term effects of the internet are more subtle, contributing to individuals' sense of connectedness with narrowly selected commercial and social groups, no matter where they may be located, while reducing the traditional sense of community that has been associated with diverse groups of people living together in close proximity.

The unforeseen consequences of the internet emphasise how difficult it can be to understand the consequences for the marketer of a changing marketing environment. These examples demonstrate the importance of understanding the linkages between different elements of the marketing environment; developments in the technological environment can be sensibly understood only in conjunction with changes in the social environment.

How Amazon changed the way we read

By Haydn Northover

The arrival of the internet bought with it a lot of hype about the end of traditional 'bricks and mortar' stores. In the early days of the internet, it was just hype and we didn't see a lot of change. But slowly the hype is becoming a reality as more and more physical stores succumb to continued pressure from online retailers.

The emergence of Amazon.com was seen as the prime signal of the demise of the traditional bookstore. What was less apparent at the time was the pressure Amazon would bring to bear on the humble book itself.

This is a story of how Amazon changed how we read, and how Amazon will continue to alter retailing, beyond book sales.

Amazon.com was launched in 1995. At the start, it only sold books, but it has since expanded to offer everything from toys to software and much more besides. Today it is considered the world's largest online retailer.

It wasn't until 2001 that the company achieved a quarterly profit, and not until 2003 that they were able to announce a profit over a full year. Yet it was part of the strategy—a conscious decision to prioritise growth over profit. As one early investor in Amazon stated, such a focus on growth instead of early profit made it 'impossible to duplicate what we had done' (quoted in Frey & Cook, 2004). This growth-focused strategy allowed Amazon to offer an increasing range of products online, but, more importantly, it also meant the company was able to invest in innovative technology and consumer electronics such as the Kindle e-book reader.

The death of high-street stores with the advent of the internet may have been exaggerated initially, but today suggestions indicate that some of those predictions are coming true. The Borders Group of bookstores collapsed, in part due to the increase in non-conventional retailers such as Walmart and Target, but also to the growing competition from online retailers, particularly Amazon. It was estimated that in 2009 Amazon sold 19 per cent of all printed books, more than either of the largest traditional booksellers in the United States, Barnes & Noble (17 per cent) or Borders (10 per cent), before it collapsed (Institute for Publishing Research, Credit Suisse estimates, quoted in Yarrow, 2010).

Investment in Lab 126 helped Amazon produce the e-book reader Kindle, which was launched in 2007. This device changed not only how we purchased books, but also how we read them. Barnes & Noble now offer their own e-reader, the Nook, yet Amazon's Kindle accounts for approximately half of all e-book reader sales (IDC, 2011). E-book sales are growing, and are approximately 14 per cent of all book sales (James L McQuivey, Forrester analyst, quoted in Miller & Bosman, 2011); Amazon sells more e-books than hardcover and softcover books combined.

Amazon placed importance on early growth and acquisition ahead of profits. This allowed them the opportunity to acquire resources that would enable future growth and take advantage of the changing market environment. The most obvious example is the development of the Kindle. While e-books still only account for a small portion of total book sales, Amazon's business model already sees them dominating total book sales, ahead of traditional bricks and mortar stores, all the while moving quickly to dominate the e-book reader categories that might very well signal the demise of paper books.

Foresight, continued investment and adherence to a plan have paved the way for Amazon to become the premier online retailer. In retailer competition, Amazon is projected to reach revenue parity with Walmart by 2024 (O'Dell, 2011).

Ecological environment

Issues affecting our natural ecology have captured the public imagination in recent years. The destruction of tropical rainforests and global warming have serious implications for our quality of life—not necessarily today, but for future generations. Marketing is often seen as being in conflict with the need to protect the natural ecology. It is very easy for critics of marketing to point to cases where greed and mismanagement have created long-lasting or permanent ecological damage. Have rainforests been destroyed partly by our greed for more hardwood furniture? More locally, is our impatience for reaching our destination quickly the reason why many natural habitats have been lost to new road developments?

A market-led company cannot ignore threats to the natural ecology, for two principal reasons:

1   There has been growing pressure on natural resources, including those that, directly or indirectly, are used in firms' production processes. This is evidenced by the extinction of species of animals and the depletion of hardwood timber resources. As a result of overuse of natural resources, many industry sectors, such as fishing, have faced severe constraints on their production possibilities.

2   The general public has become increasingly aware of ecological issues and, more importantly, some segments have shown a greater willingness and ability to spend money to alleviate the problems associated with ecologically harmful practices.

INTERNAL ENVIRONMENT

Labour-intensive service industries have long realised that recruiting, training and motivating the right staff is an important basis for delivering value to customers. In conditions of full employment, companies must sell themselves as good employers so that they can recruit the people who will ultimately deliver marketers' promises to customers. In 2011, Australian business magazine *BRW* conducted a survey in partnership with the Great Place to Work Institute to find out Australia's best companies to work for. They surveyed 55,400 employees from 207 companies to find out if they trusted their leaders, had pride in their company and liked the people they worked with. The number one spot went to Google Australia, whose 312 employees benefit from a fun culture (bean-bag filled meeting rooms and ping-pong tables), perks (a free cafeteria) and appreciation and reward for staff (who can spend 10 per cent of work time pursuing their own projects). Staff also have a sense of pride in the company and a sense of community within the workplace (Bailey, 2011).

Marketers do not operate in a vacuum within their organisations. Internally, the structure and politics of an organisation affect the manner in which it responds to environmental change. We are all familiar with lumbering giants of companies who, like supertankers, plough ahead on seemingly predetermined courses and find it difficult to change direction. During the late 1990s, such well-respected companies as Coles Myer in Australia and Marks & Spencer in the United Kingdom were accused of having internal structures and processes that were too rigid to cope with a changing external environment. Simply having a strong marketing department does not guarantee that a firm will be best able to adapt to change. The existence of a central marketing department may in fact create internal tensions that make them less effective at responding to changing consumer needs than if marketing responsibilities in their widest sense were spread throughout the organisation.

Two aspects to a marketing manager's internal environment are of importance here: the internal structure and processes of the marketing department itself (where one actually exists), and the relationship of the marketing function to other business functions. These are discussed more fully in Chapter 12.

MONITORING AND RESPONDING TO ENVIRONMENTAL CHANGE

◢ LEARNING OBJECTIVE
Be able to discuss how to monitor changes in the micro- and macro-environment

There are many examples of firms that have failed to read their marketing environment and have eventually withered and died. To avoid this fate, a firm must:

- understand what is going on in its business environment
- respond and adapt to environmental change.

As organisations become larger and national economies more complex, the task of understanding the marketing environment becomes more formidable. Information about a firm's environment becomes crucial to environmental analysis and response.

Information about the current state of the environment is used as a starting point for planning future marketing strategy, based on assumptions about how the environment will change. Information is also vital to monitor the implementation of an organisation's marketing plans and to note the cause of any deviation from plan. Information therefore has both a planning function and a control function.

Information collection, processing, transmission and storage technologies are continually improving, as witnessed by the development of scanners and other computer-based information systems. These have enabled organisations to greatly enhance the quality of the information they have about their operating environment. However, information is becoming more accessible not just to one particular organisation, but also to its competitors. Attention is therefore moving away from how information is collected to how to make use of the continually growing information.

Large organisations operating in complex and turbulent environments often use information to build models of their environment, or at least sub-components of it. Some of these can be quite general, as in the case of the models of the national economy, which many large companies have developed. From a general model of the economy, a firm can predict how a specific item of government policy (for example increasing the rate of GST on luxury goods) will impact directly and indirectly on sales of its own products.

The crucial role of information in marketing analysis and planning will be returned to in Chapter 12.

SWOT analysis

SWOT analysis:
An important part of a marketing plan, outlining the internal strengths and weaknesses, and external opportunities and threats.

SWOT is an acronym for strengths, weaknesses, opportunities and threats. A **SWOT analysis** is a useful framework for assessing an organisation and its marketing environment, summarising the main environmental issues in the form of opportunities and threats facing an organisation. These external factors are listed alongside the organisation's internal strengths and weaknesses. An opportunity in an organisation's external environment can be exploited only if it has the internal strengths to do so. If, on the other hand, the organisation is not capable of exploiting these because of internal weaknesses, then they should perhaps be left alone or the weaknesses improved. For this reason, the terms 'opportunities' and 'threats' should not be viewed as 'absolutes', but assessed in the context of an organisation's resources and the feasibility of exploiting them.

An example of a SWOT analysis is given in Figure 5.4, where an established manufacturer of ready-prepared chicken products reviews its strengths and weaknesses in terms of the opportunities and threats that it faces in its environment.

Marketing opportunities can come in many forms, and each should be assessed for its attractiveness and success probability. Attractiveness can be assessed in terms of potential market size, growth rates, profit margins, competitiveness and distribution channels. Other factors may be technological requirements, the extent of government restrictions, availability of government grants, ecological concerns and energy requirements. Measures of attractiveness must be qualified by the probability of success, which depends on the company's strengths and competitive advantage. Probability of success is likely to be influenced by, among other things, the firm's access to cash, lines of credit or capital to finance new developments, technological and production expertise, marketing skills, distribution channels and managerial competence. A simple matrix can be constructed to show the relationship between attractiveness and success probability.

An environmental threat is a challenge posed by an unfavourable trend or development in a company's environment that would lead, in the absence of action by the company, to the erosion of the company's market position. In this case the threats should be assessed according to their seriousness and the probability of occurrence. A threat matrix can then be constructed.

Strengths	Weaknesses
Established and widely recognised brand name	Only has a narrow product range
Good distribution network	Shortage of production staff
Strong financial base	
Opportunities	**Threats**
Growing demand for chicken products	Possibility of health scares
Rising income will result in increased demand for ready-prepared meals	Intense competition from supermarkets' own label products
	Tighter safety standards may increase costs

●●● **FIGURE 5.4** SWOT ANALYSIS FOR A HYPOTHETICAL ESTABLISHED MANUFACTURER OF READY-PREPARED CHICKEN MEALS

In order for an environmental analysis to have a useful input to the marketing planning process, a wide range of information and opinions needs to be summarised in a meaningful way. The information collated from a detailed environmental analysis can be simplified in the form of an environmental threat and opportunity profile (ETOP). This provides a summary of the environmental factors that are most critical to the organisation and can be useful in stimulating debate among senior management about the future of the business. An example of an ETOP is given in Table 5.2. Some analysts suggest trying to weight these factors according to their importance, and then rating them for their impact on the organisation.

●●● **TABLE 5.2** AN ENVIRONMENTAL THREAT AND OPPORTUNITY PROFILE OF A CAR MANUFACTURER

FACTOR	MAJOR OPPORTUNITY	MINOR OPPORTUNITY	NEUTRAL	MINOR THREAT	MAJOR THREAT	PROBABILITY OF OCCURRENCE
Political New transport policy sees introduction of tax on use of cars in town centres					✓	0.1
Economic Tax on petrol increases by 5 cents				✓		0.4

(Continued)

●●● **TABLE 5.2** AN ENVIRONMENTAL THREAT AND OPPORTUNITY PROFILE OF A CAR MANUFACTURER (*CONTINUED*)

FACTOR	MAJOR OPPORTUNITY	MINOR OPPORTUNITY	NEUTRAL	MINOR THREAT	MAJOR THREAT	PROBABILITY OF OCCURRENCE
Household spending falls for two quarters in succession					✓	0.2
GST on new cars reduced	✓					0.1
Market						
Overseas competitors enter market more aggressively				✓		0.3

Application to business-to-business marketing

For business-to-business marketers, special issues exist with respect to supply chains, business cycles, cross-cultural factors and technological change.

As discussed earlier in this chapter, it is important for business-to-business marketers to understand the operation of supply chains, which comprise several levels of suppliers and intermediaries working together to create value for end-customers. For reasons related to supply strategy, many organisational customers now seek cooperative relationships with their major suppliers, taking a long-term approach to their supply relationships rather than an adversarial negotiating position over each transaction or short-term supply contract. This change in business approach has implications for business-to-business marketers, such as the need to move from transaction-based to relationship-oriented selling strategies.

As we have also discussed, business cycles influence organisations as well as consumers. During economic downturns, most firms would have lower sales revenues and, therefore, would require fewer raw materials, components and related products and services during those depressed economic times. While governments often increase their expenditures during economic downturns (to bolster the economy), they often decrease their expenditures in some areas during such times. These factors clearly impact on sales in business markets generally. In particular, sales of capital equipment such as new manufacturing plant, mining equipment or commercial aircraft, for example, often suffer severe declines in response to economic downturns (and benefit from major rebounds in response to economic recoveries). Therefore, business-to-business marketers need to pay as much attention to business cycles as marketers of consumer products—and even more so in the case of capital equipment suppliers.

It is important for marketers to understand the cultural and social values of a society, especially if aiming to enter foreign markets. For business-to-business marketers, it is equally important to understand differences in business culture across those countries in which the firm plans to conduct business. For example, recognition of a strong preference among organisations in a particular country for dealing with local suppliers would enable a foreign supplier to realise the importance of using local intermediaries within that market.

Technological change also offers opportunities to business-to-business marketers,. For example, major advances in medical technology have resulted in the development of new equipment for hospitals, medical research institutions, dental surgeries and general practitioners. The internet and related technological developments have resulted in new business services such as web development—not to mention Google's massive growth in advertising revenues from corporate clients, reaching almost US$38 billion in 2011 (Google, 2012).

CONCLUSION

The marketing environment comprises the individuals, organisations and forces that impinge on the activities of marketers. Some of the effects are direct and relatively immediate (in the micro-environment), while others are essentially forces for change in the future (in the macro-environment). Marketers must also understand the internal structures and processes of their organisation, as these can affect the development and implementation of marketing plans (the internal environment).

This chapter has stressed that marketers should understand the needs not just of their customers, but also of a much broader range of stakeholders. Although social responsibility by firms can achieve long-term paybacks, there can still be doubt about what is the most responsible course of action. The issues of social responsibility and ethics will be explored in more detail later in Chapter 14.

05

SUMMARY

- Marketing takes place within a broad system of economic, social, political and technological relationships.

- Value is created through interaction with other individuals and organisations that make up the marketing environment.

- The marketing environment cannot be neatly divided into distinct areas. A good marketer seeks to understand the complex linkages between different parts of the marketing environment.

- Micro-environment influences may demand urgent attention, but macro-environment influences can have a more profound long-term effect on an organisation's marketing.

REVISION QUESTIONS

1   Explain briefly what you understand by the 'marketing environment' of a business.

2   'Suppliers and intermediaries are important stakeholders in the micro-environment of the business.' Explain the evolving role and functions of these stakeholders in today's marketing-oriented business.

3   Critically discuss the links between the internal environment of an organisation and its external marketing environment.

FURTHER READING

Ahmed, P K & Rafiq, M (2002), *Internal Marketing: Tools and Concepts for Customer Focused Management*, Butterworth Heinemann, Oxford.

Blanchard, O & Sheen, J (2009), *Macroeconomics Australian edition*, 3rd edn, Pearson Education, Harlow.

Burda, M & Wyplosz, C (2009), *Macroeconomics: A European Text*, 5th edn, Oxford University Press, Oxford.

Donaldson, B & O'Toole, T (2007), *Strategic Market Relationships: From Strategy to Implementation*, 2nd edn. John Wiley, London.

Griffiths, A & Wall, S (eds) (2011), *Applied Economics: An Introductory Course*, 12th edn, Pearson Education, London.

Hofstede, G, Hofstede, G J & Minkov, M (2010), *Cultures and Organisations: Software for the Mind*, 3rd edn, McGraw-Hill, Maidenhead.

Mattsson, L-G & Johanson, J (2006), 'Discovering Market Networks', *European Journal of Marketing*, vol. 40, nos 3–4, pp. 259–74.

Palmer, A & Hartley, B (2011), *The Business Environment*, 7th edn, McGraw-Hill, Maidenhead.

Prenkert, F & Hallén, L (2006), 'Conceptualising, Delineating and Analysing Business Networks', *European Journal of Marketing*, vol. 40, nos 3–4, pp. 384–407.

WEBLINKS

Introduction to scenario thinking and planning:
www.gbn.com/about/scenario_planning.php

Planning the marketing mix:
www.cim.co.uk/marketingplanningtool/tech/tech4.asp

Pricing:
www.themanager.org/Knowledgebase/Marketing/Pricing.htm

Super brands in Australia:
www.superbrands-brands.com

Word-of-Mouth Marketing Association:
http://womma.org/main/

The following links are relevant to the case study on pages 212–15:
Australian Vaccination Network:
www.avn.org.au

Information on vaccination:
www.vaccines.me

Pros and cons of controversial issues:
www.procon.org

◢ **Major case study**

Vaccination: Social good or social evil?

By Stephen Holden, Bond University

'Prevention is better than cure,' said the Dutch philosopher Erasmus. Today social marketers promote vaccination programs based on this notion. However, there are others, such as the Australian Vaccination Network, who campaign against vaccinations, using the same tools as those promoting vaccination. This conflict raises some interesting issues about the ethics of marketing in general, and social marketing in particular. Is social marketing a good thing? Why or why not? And do social marketers have greater rights than other types of marketers?

Early social marketing

Smallpox is an untreatable human disease that kills as many as 20 to 30 per cent of those infected, and leaves many of the survivors scarred, blinded or both. Fortunately, this 'ancient scourge' that has roamed the Earth for over 3000 years can be prevented (World Health Organization, 2012) and indeed today has been eliminated.

In Ancient India and Turkey, immunity to smallpox was induced by exposing people to smallpox blisters, often as infants. The practice was brought to Britain in 1721 by Lady Montagu, wife of the British Ambassador to Turkey. However, many were sceptical as Voltaire details in the opening of his letter 'On inoculation' (Voltaire, 1909–14):

> [Europeans consider] the English are fools and madmen. Fools, because they give their children the small-pox to prevent their catching it; and madmen, because they wantonly communicate a certain and dreadful distemper to their children, merely to prevent an uncertain evil. The English, on the other side, call the rest of the Europeans cowardly and unnatural. Cowardly, because they are afraid of putting their children to a little pain; unnatural, because they expose them to die one time or other of the small-pox.

In 1796, Edward Jenner showed that vaccinating people with cowpox, a relatively benign disease in humans, protected against smallpox.* While this proved safer than inoculation with smallpox, vaccination was doubted and publicly mocked. Nonetheless, the British government actively promoted vaccination against smallpox (by offering it free) with the *Vaccination Act* of 1840, and later introduced the *Compulsory Vaccination Act* in 1853. This counts as an early example of social marketing. While some social marketers consider their domain only covers the promotion of 'voluntary behaviour change' (Grier & Bryant, 2005), social marketing more generally accepts that this is not a defining feature, and that law and mandatory requirements are a part of their toolbox (Donovan, 2011).

* The words inoculation, vaccination and immunisation are often used today synonymously. Inoculation was the word originally used for using smallpox to immunise people against smallpox, while vaccination was the word created (by Jenner) for using cowpox to immunise people against smallpox; immunisation is the outcome of either process.

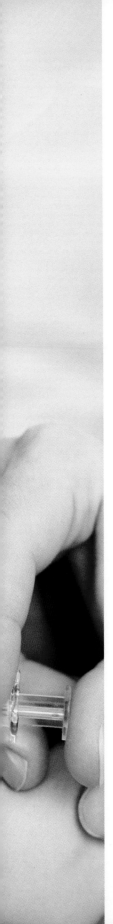

Is social marketing a good thing? Why or why not? And do social marketers have greater rights than other types of marketers?

Of course, governments (and other social welfare agencies) do not always get it right, and even if they did, people resent being told what to do. Once vaccination was made compulsory in England, the anti-vaccine movement became organised. Paul Offit, a paediatrician in Philadelphia says these anti-vaccinators 'were great at mass marketing. It was a print-oriented society. They were great pamphleteers. And by the 1890s, they had driven immunization rates down to the 20 percent range.' (Wallace, 2009). Offit claims that an outbreak of smallpox in England and Wales in 1893 led to over 1400 unnecessary deaths.

Social marketing challenge

Today, both pro-vaccinators and anti-vaccinators are both great marketers. Each use the full range of tools available to them, including and not limited to advertising, brochures, education programs, presentations, public relations, websites and social media, to promote what they believe is the appropriate individual behaviour that supports the common good.

The primary conflict between pro-vaccinators and anti-vaccinators is around beliefs about the 'common good'. Pro-vaccinators believe that vaccinations are good for preventing disease threats—and the evidence clearly suggests that they are. Offit regards anti-vaccinators as a significant social threat, as he explains in his 2011 book, *Deadly choices: How the anti-vaccine movement threatens us all*. People opting out of vaccination allow for outbreaks of diseases such as whooping cough (pertussis) and meningitis caused by *Haemophilus influenzae* type b (Hib) that had virtually disappeared in the Western world. The resulting tragedy is that unvaccinated children can contract a preventable disease, which can result in permanent brain damage or death.

Anti-vaccinators believe that the vaccinations themselves pose risks. In the eighteenth and nineteenth centuries, it was the spiritual risks that were highlighted by clergy members such as Reverend Edward Massey, who declared vaccination dangerous, sinful and diabolical (White, 1896). Today, the threat of the afterlife barely rates a mention, but the threat to health in this life is a critical issue. Anti-vaccinators claim that vaccination can pose serious health risks. One widely reported claim is that the MMR (measles, mumps and rubella) triple-vaccine has been linked to autism. While a meta-analysis (that is, an examination of multiple independent studies) finds no support for the claim that MMR causes autism (Demicheli et al., 2012), this same meta-analysis does report evidence that the vaccine has been associated with some serious, albeit infrequent adverse, events. Responding to similar findings in the early 1990s, Japan ended the use of the MMR triple vaccine in 1993 (Hope, 2001). Anti-vaccinators use such information to support their arguments that vaccine manufacturers are motivated to cheat in their studies and disguise adverse events in order to protect their products and their profits.

The pro-vaccinators argue that, on balance, it does appear that vaccinations save more people than they harm. The pro-vaccinators are therefore adopting a utilitarian stance (Bentham, 1961/1789; Mill, 1859/1991): the greatest good for the greatest number. The utilitarian view has been challenged in multiple ways, but one relevant to the discussion here is that it subordinates individual rights to group rights. As noted by the political philosopher John Rawls (1971), 'interests requiring the violation of justice have no value'.

The primary conflict between pro-vaccinators and anti-vaccinators is around beliefs about the 'common good'.

The anti-vaccinators pick up on exactly this criticism when they argue that vaccination programs deprive individuals of their freedoms and their right to choose for themselves and their children. The anti-vaccinators are adopting what is known as a libertarian stance (Nozik, 1974): that individual rights cannot be dominated by the group.

Aggregate versus individual benefits

At the heart of this issue is benefit to the group as a whole versus individual, personal choice. Governments around the world have promoted vaccination programs in the interests of public health, often offering partially or fully subsidised vaccinations. Some vaccinations (such as influenza, pneumococcal or HPV) are widely promoted and people are encouraged to take them. Other vaccinations (such as pertussis and measles) are required for entry to school, although typically with exemptions allowed for those who have religious, health or personal reasons for refusing. Meanwhile, anti-vaccinators promote a non-compliance alternative that directly competes with the typically government-sponsored marketing efforts.

Ultimately, pro-vaccinators and anti-vaccinators at an individual level differ primarily in terms of the risks that they wish to take. Those that vaccinate are not willing to risk contracting a preventable disease; those that do not vaccinate are not willing to risk an adverse reaction to the vaccination.

The marketing efforts of both pro-vaccinators and anti-vaccinators rely on the successful transmission of their respective (and conflicting) messages through society. The conflicting marketing efforts of both sides almost certainly contribute to confusion in the market.

Ironically, the marketing battle between pro-vaccinators and anti-vaccinators parallels the biological battle. Just as marketers rely on social networks in successfully transmitting their messages to the population, contagious diseases such as smallpox, measles, pertussis and influenza rely on social networks for their transmission and distribution throughout a population!

Questions

1   Research the evidence both for and against the MMR vaccine (you can use some of the sources referenced in this case study and the websites listed on page 211). What do you think? Would you use this vaccination? Would you recommend the vaccination to others? Would you vaccinate your children? Should this vaccination be promoted to others? Should it be mandatory?

2   Do all government efforts to increase vaccination count as social marketing?

3   Does a government have the right to decide for the public what is best in this situation? Do parents have a right to decide for their children what is best? Who should have the right to decide if there is a conflict between what government and parents want?

4   One of the features of social marketing is that the goal is for some social good. Does this mean that social marketing is always ethically good?

5   Is marketing ethical? What determines whether marketing is ethical or not?

Practitioner profile
Daniela Cavuoto, Commercial Marketing Campaigns Manager, ANZ, Melbourne, Australia

Marketing was always of interest to me. I wanted a business career, but I didn't want to miss out on the opportunity to be creative in my job. A career in marketing seemed like the perfect balance.

Gaining experience and working in a marketing environment helped to cement my decision. My first marketing role was as a Marketing Assistant for the Ehrenberg-Bass Institute, a university research institute. Even though it was an entry-level position, it was in a small marketing team so the job was hands-on, with lots of variety and responsibility. It was a fantastic opportunity and I developed skills and techniques that I've used throughout my career.

The biggest advantage of my first job was that it helped me develop stakeholder management skills and understand the complexities of the marketing environment. I had direct contact with clients, managed suppliers and worked with a variety of different internal stakeholders. Not only did this build my ability to communicate effectively and to understand the needs of external customers, but it also taught me about the importance of internal organisation.

Today, as a Campaigns Manager at ANZ, being flexible, organised and passionate about what you do is important. It's also essential to have an understanding of your marketing environment to ensure all activities are aligned with internal objectives. Finally, you need to make sure what you are doing is distinctive in the external competitive environment.

In my role, I manage end-to-end integrated advertising campaigns and marketing budgets, assist in strategic planning, support brand compliance and secure all the necessary approvals from internal stakeholders. Measuring return on investment is also really important. I am accountable for setting and meeting targets and delivering on agreed outcomes.

To do all this, I have to consider the external competitive environment and our organisational objectives, and ensure that all our marketing activities align with the strategic plans. This can't be done without an understanding of the overall marketing environment.

I love being involved in so many different aspects of the business and collaborating with different agencies and stakeholders. I get to manage projects and then see the direct return and sales impacts of these activities. It's really satisfying to see your hard work rewarded with great results for the company.

06
CUSTOMER SEGMENTATION AND TARGETING

RACHEL KENNEDY AND BYRON SHARP, WITH CONTRIBUTION
FROM NICK DANENBERG

◢ Introduction case

The burger battle: Hungry Jack's/Burger King versus McDonald's

The burgers may be better at one of the outlets, but which has the better marketing strategy? Both Hungry Jack's and McDonald's primarily market burgers, chicken products, fries, breakfast items, drinks and desserts in their outlets, and they look remarkably similar—but there are some fundamental differences in marketing strategy.

McDonald's serve nearly 68 million customers daily (McDonalds, 2012), which they put down to a strategic focus on menu choice, quality and value. Clearly these things are important, but McDonald's also has a strategy of consciously appealing to different kinds of audiences, across different occasions. Their McCafés, drive-throughs, playgrounds, family meals, kids meals and local variations to their menu—along with their recent promotion of healthier alternatives such as salads, wraps and fruit—all aim to appeal to different consumers.

This approach differs from that of Hungry Jack's, the exclusive Australian master franchisee of Burger King Corporation. Burger King began in a similar way to McDonald's, with its menu consisting predominantly of hamburgers, fries, soft drinks and desserts. In 1957, they added a signature item: the 'Whopper'. This quarter-pound hamburger was created as a way to differentiate Burger King from other burger outlets at the time. The Burger King speciality sandwich line was introduced in 1979. It was an attempt to target a specific demographic: 18- to 34-year-olds. It was believed that this demographic would be willing to spend more on a higher quality product.

Thus, in recent times the Burger King strategy has been one of focusing on key target segments or, in the company's lingo, courting 'super fans': 18- to 34-year-olds, who account for half of all the visits to Burger King. Their 'I am Man' campaign (available to watch on YouTube) typifies their approach. An article in *The Wall Street Journal* (Jargon, 2010) describes their strategy:

> Some Burger King franchisees and industry analysts say the company's marketing and advertising focus on super fans alienated women, children and other customers … Six years ago, after years of slumping sales, Burger King decided to focus on the group that spends the most money at its restaurants. These young men and women visit fast-food burger chains on average almost 10 times per month … Burger King tried to distinguish itself from rivals by addressing young men, in particular, like 'the cool uncle who tells you how it is,' says John Schaufelberger, Burger King's senior vice president of global product marketing and innovation.

Burger King have also been moving away from mass advertising. In 2008, they spent US$327 million on measured media in the United States, down to US$308 million in 2009 and US$301 million in 2010 (Bruell, 2010).

Clearly, even quite similar competing brands can have quite different strategies that they can put behind their efforts and resourcing.

Clearly, even quite similar competing brands can have quite different strategies that they can put their efforts and resourcing behind.

INTRODUCTION

This chapter introduces and critiques ideas that have dominated marketing strategy for decades. We distinguish between:

1   segmenting a market into groups of buyers with similar traits and targeting those different groups with different offerings

2   offering different options into a market to address heterogeneity in demand, without particularly targeting specific groups of people.

Marketing textbooks and some practitioners tend to make two mistakes concerning segmentation and targeting:

1   believing that it is wrong to aim for the entire market, and that instead the narrower the targeting the better

2   assuming that complex techniques that identify subtle (hidden) segments are the basis of more effective targeting.

In this chapter, we explore and debunk each of these misplaced assumptions.

LEARNING OBJECTIVES

After reading this chapter you should be able to:

- understand the difference between segmentation-based targeting and sophisticated mass marketing
- discuss the measurement and return on investment implications of segmentation-based targeting and mass-market approaches
- implement smart targeting.

CHAPTER OUTLINE

Introduction

Segmentation-based targeting

Who really is your target?

The logic and appeal of narrow targeting

Brand user profiles seldom differ

Targeting all the market with product variants

Segmentation does not necessarily maximise returns

Talking to everyone is possible

Database-driven targeting: A common trap

Smart targeting in practice

Conclusion

market partitions   market segmentation   positioning   targeting

SEGMENTATION-BASED TARGETING

Buyers differ from one another in their buying behaviour, and a buyer's individual behaviour varies depending on their situation or mood and changes over time. Marketers can choose to cater for some or many of these differences. How they choose to do so will depend on the capabilities of their company, and what their competitors are doing. Sometimes, differences in buyer behaviour will correspond with particular types of people or organisations (for example owners of larger cars tend to have larger families), but this happens far less often for brand choice (for example Myer shoppers are not very different people from general department store shoppers).

Market segmentation is the process of dividing up the market into distinct sub-groups (target segments) of buyers that react differently to different marketing. It is useful if these differences in behaviour relate to identifiable characteristics in people (see 'Customer profile metrics' in Chapter 3, page 106) because that allows a marketer to target particular people (segment members). For example, men and women have different body shapes, and so require different designs of most clothing. Also, there are usually cultural conventions that dictate that men and women wear different items of clothing (women have adopted trousers, but it seems unlikely that men will ever adopt bikinis). Men and women have tendencies to read different magazines and, to some extent, watch different programs. Such obvious differences mean that clothing marketers typically segment the market by gender. Children are smaller, so they are also treated as a segment. The most common way to segment a market is to do so based on geography, because people who live and/or buy in different regions need different distributions of goods/services and advertising.

Targeting is the practice of creating differences in the marketing mix to cater for these different segments, or choosing not to serve some segments. This includes developing a brand image to appeal to a particular segment (often called **positioning**).

How might a marketer choose to segment the market? There are many ways in which an entire market could be broken down—that is, segmented—into smaller sub-markets (target segments). Tables 6.1 and 6.2 outline some of the typical bases in consumer and industrial segmentation studies, respectively.

These segmentation criteria can be combined; hence, a marketer could (if they wanted to) end up targeting a grouping such as women aged twenty-five to thirty-nine who are fashion-conscious, earn more than $40,000 and regularly watch the television show *Glee*.

LEARNING OBJECTIVE
Understand the difference between segmentation-based targeting and sophisticated mass marketing

market segmentation: Analysing the differences and commonalities in buyer behaviour in order to identify target segments.

targeting: Adjusting the marketing mix to cater for different target segments or choosing not to serve some segments.

positioning: Developing a brand image to appeal to a particular target segment.

●●● **TABLE 6.1** TYPICAL BASES USED IN CONSUMER SEGMENTATION STUDIES

SEGMENTATION BASE/VARIABLE	EXAMPLES
Demographics	Age, gender, income, occupation, education, family size, geography
Psychographics	Attitudes, opinions, activities, personality, lifestyle, interests, values—combined with demographics
Behavioural	Usage rate, main brand, media used
Other	Occasion/situation, benefits sought, media habits

●●● **TABLE 6.2** TYPICAL BASES USED IN INDUSTRIAL SEGMENTATION STUDIES

SEGMENTATION BASE/VARIABLE	EXAMPLES
Demographics	Industry, location, number of employees, public or privately owned
Strategy	Distribution channels used, growth ambitions, local or export marketing

CRITICAL REFLECTION

It has been suggested that the following segments can be found across a number of categories (Haley, 1984: 35).

SEGMENT	ATTRIBUTES
Status seeker	Very much concerned with the prestige of the brands purchased
Swinger	Tries to be modern and up to date in all activities
	Brand choices reflect this orientation
Conservative	Prefers to stick to large, successful companies and popular brands
Rational	Looks for benefits such as economy, value, durability and so on
Inner-directed	Especially concerned with self-concept
	Considers themselves to have a sense of humour, and to be independent and/or honest
Hedonist	Concerned primarily with sensory benefits

1 Select some very different categories you have made purchases from; for instance, cheese, coffee, hire cars or banking. Which segment would you describe yourself as belonging to? Would that be stable over time and across all the purchases you make in each category? What about other categories?

2 Is this a useful categorisation? In what way could you use it? Do you think it makes sense to think of people as belonging to a particular segment? Can you see any gaps or problems with this approach? Consider Yankelovich's (1964: 90) observation: 'we must understand we are not dealing with different types of people, but differences in people's values. A woman who buys a refrigerator because it is the cheapest available may want to buy the most expensive towels. A man who pays extra for his beer may own a cheap watch.'

It sounds as if market segmentation can be very complicated, as Professors Timothy Bock and Mark Uncles explain:

> In empirical studies, almost every consumer behavior variable has been proposed for segmenting markets (Wind, 1978)—from social class (Martineau, 1958) to astrological sign (Mitchell & Haggett, 1997) … For managers and analysts, this array of segmentation variables can be quite daunting. The salutary tale of one healthcare company that commissioned 18 segmentation studies over a five-year period without implementing any of them serves to highlight the problem (Weinstein, 1993).

But it need not be so complicated.

Segmentation of the market needs to meet a number of criteria in order to be useful to the marketer. First, the segment characteristic must be measurable. If the marketer (or market researcher) cannot measure the presence or level of the characteristic, then the marketer will be unable to use that characteristic as a segmentation base. A first step is to know the number of members in a segment, then how to reach them. More broadly, marketers need to be able to answer the following 'who', 'how', 'where' and 'what' questions in relation to the segment:

- Who are the buyers?
- How can we reach them? (Through what media?) How are the segment customers different from others?
- Where are they located? Where do they purchase?
- What are their interests and behaviours? What do they buy and/or like?

A wide variety of approaches to market segmentation has long been discussed and practised. Texts that give a good overview of these are listed in the 'Further reading' section at the end of this chapter. Briefly, alternative approaches have included:

- the 'Q' technique of factor analysis, multi-dimensional scaling and other distance measures (Haley, 1968)
- AID (Assael, 1970)
- CHAID (Babinec, 1990)
- conjoint (Green & Krieger, 1991)
- canonical correlation analysis (Bologlu, Weaver & McCleary, 1998)
- heuristic identification of noisy variables (HINoV) (Carmone Jr., Kara & Maxwell, 1999).

It is further complicated by the fact that there are different names for the same technique.

All statistical segmentation techniques relate the behaviour or ratings of each respondent to those of every other respondent and then seek clusters of individuals with similar response patterns (Haley, 1984). Clusters are identified as groups of people who had similar responses to each other and different responses to respondents in other groupings. Whatever the statistical approach selected, the end result of analysis is a small number of segments—usually specified beforehand by the analyst (usually less than seven).

It is easy to get technical, but really there is no need. Most segmentation analyses that are of any practical value produce very obvious intuitive segments (for example geographic segments); if they do not, the segmentation is unlikely to be of practical value.

▼ CRITICAL REFLECTION

As a class, assign individuals to groups so there is as much likeness within the groups and as much difference between groups as possible. Discuss whether everyone agrees on the characteristics used (for instance physical attributes, personal attitudes, knowledge, age or intelligence), on the number of groups, and on the membership of groups. Would someone else doing the same task come up with the same solution? How could you evaluate if you have a good solution? What issues does this exercise highlight for segmentation solutions?

Importantly, the segments worthy of being targeted must be of a certain size. That is, substantial enough so that the expenditure of resources in targeting and reaching them will give the business a good chance of being profitable. It is also vital that segments are targetable. We must be able to reach members of our segment and they should respond consistently to our offers. In summary, segments need a number of fairly obvious traits in order to be useful. Marketers look for easily identifiable characteristics of buyers that relate to substantial differences in buying, such that there is likely to be value in targeting customised marketing mixes to these different segments.

Segmentation-based targeting is illustrated in Figure 6.1.

> An entire market comprises of distinct, heterogeneous needs —
> typically with groups of individuals sharing more homogenous needs.

↓

> Segments are identified in the market based on characteristics that are
> observable, measurable and stable.
> They are mutually exclusive and describe all the buyers in the category.

↓

> A target segment is selected. It must be large enough to be profitably served by a given marketing
> mix. Individuals in it must be reachable and respond in a similar way.

↓

> A brand offering must exist or be created with a targeted marketing mix
> to reach and appeal to the segment
> (with minimal wastage to those outside the segment).

●●● **FIGURE 6.1** SEGMENTATION-BASED TARGETING PROCESS

Application to business-to-business marketing

Possible characteristics or dimensions for segmentation of business markets have been identified earlier in this chapter (see Table 6.2). Within business markets, special issues exist with respect to segmentation and targeting due to: (1) large variations in size of organisation, (2) major differences in business and external factors across industries or sectors (such as agriculture, government, manufacturing, mining and service industries); and (3) major differences in business strategies of some organisations, even in the same industry.

Large variations in size result in some organisational customers spending a lot more than others on particular products or services. For example, as mentioned in Chapter 2, General Motors, with an annual production of about nine *million* vehicles worldwide, represents a much, much larger sales opportunity for potential automotive components suppliers than Ferrari, with an annual production of less than nine *thousand* vehicles. Such differences in size make some potential customers much more attractive than others. Therefore, in effect, size of customer is a major dimension of market segmentation in many business markets, with much more marketing attention being devoted to large organisations than their smaller counterparts. Of course, the attractiveness of a potential customer also depends on the capabilities of the *supplier*. A small but highly specialised automotive components manufacturer in Italy might be able to match the demanding specifications of Ferrari, but probably would lack the capacity to pursue opportunities at General Motors.

Industry- or sector-related differences result in very different needs between some organisational customers. For example, the type of product marketed by an organisation often influences its own needs as a customer. Freight services required by South Australian manufacturers are not usually critical with respect to shipment time. Reliability, geographic coverage and price might be the key criteria of such firms when deciding on which freight service providers to use for the shipment of their manufactured products. However, shipments of fresh produce, such as South Australian lobsters or strawberries, require use of freight service providers with rapid transport capabilities (as well as a record of reliability and careful handling of cargo).

Major differences in business strategies, even in the same industry, results in some organisational customers having different needs with respect to product quality (and, therefore, cost) and levels of cooperation expected from suppliers of key components. For example, consider differences in strategies regarding product quality. A manufacturer of expensive, high-quality products probably requires components to be of high quality in terms of appearance and reliability. Cost probably would be a secondary factor. Conversely, a competitor adopting a low-price strategy probably places much greater emphasis on cost of components (and less on quality and reliability). Companies such as Apple, with business strategies including promotion of their responsible corporate citizenship, often require their major suppliers to implement responsible operating practices (Apple, 2012).

Due to these differences in organisational needs or preferences, many business markets comprise diverse market segments, some segments requiring supply offerings at opposite extremes on dimensions such as cost, quality, reliability and collaborative capabilities. Suppliers need to assess whether their capabilities are adequate to serve a wide range of customer needs and, if so, how best to do that; or whether to ignore some market segments for which the firm does not have appropriate capabilities to adequately match the needs of customers comprising those segments. For example, a low-cost manufacturer might lack sophisticated research and development (R&D) capabilities (since development of those capabilities would increase overhead costs) and, therefore, probably should not attempt to compete within a market segment demanding high-quality products, product innovation and R&D collaboration.

WHO REALLY IS YOUR TARGET?

It is normal to think of a brand's target as being people who will have a high likelihood of purchasing your product. But what about those people who are influencers? They may have different profiles from those who are actual buyers or consumers. For example, for university courses, the consumers—primarily people in their late teens—are different from those who are often equally important to reach, because of the influence they have on the purchase decision: parents and teachers. Future customers may also be influencers: children increasingly influence parents' choices, but they will also become buyers themselves in the future.

Case study

Toothpaste: Sophisticated mass marketing is alive and well

The example of toothpastes is proposed by Kotler and colleagues (2007) as a shining example of target marketing. The authors claim that the brand Colgate provides numerous varieties to the market, each successfully targeting and meeting the needs of a unique segment of buyers. Along with 'normal' toothpaste, these include toothpastes for children and for those with sensitive teeth, variants such as gel toothpaste, toothpastes for tooth whitening and tartar control, and toothpaste with extra strong fluoride.

From the toothpaste packs, we may infer some of the segments to which these offerings appeal (Table 6.3).

●●○ **TABLE 6.3** COLGATE PRODUCT OFFERINGS AND RELEVANT SEGMENT

PRODUCT OFFERING	SEGMENT OF USERS
My First Colgate	Children, one to six years
Colgate Sensitive	People with sensitive teeth
Colgate Advanced Whitening	People seeking to whiten their teeth
Colgate Cavity Protection	People seeking to avoid cavities

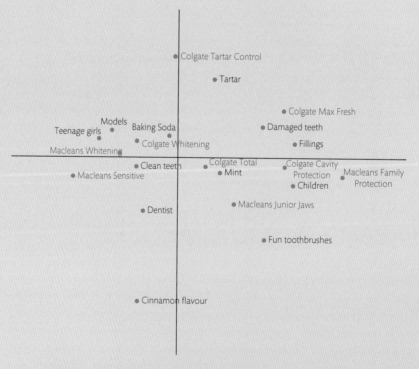

●●○ **FIGURE 6.2** HYPOTHETICAL PERCEPTUAL MAP OF TOOTHPASTES

Perceptual maps such as Figure 6.2 are read like road maps—with things that are close together being said to be similar (for example, Colgate Cavity Protection is a good fit with children), and things a long distance from each other seen as different (cinnamon flavour is not a good fit with Colgate Max Fresh or any of the brand offerings shown). Attributes in the centre of the map define the category (for example 'mint' and 'clean teeth'). Traditionally, marketers will look for gaps along relevant attributes as openings for new offerings or for attempted repositionings. This assumes that it is possible to reposition a brand and/or that having a unique positioning is a good thing. In fact, many successful profitable brands just reflect the category along core, shared attributes.

Despite this, every brand needs to stand out and be noticed. Each brand needs to have its own look and feel (through use of colours, characters, shapes and so on) that are consistently used, so it always looks like itself, avoiding confusion with competitors. That is, brands need distinct assets irrespective of whether or not they are seen as different or differentiated. This is discussed further in Chapter 10.

CRITICAL REFLECTION

1   Evaluate the toothpaste segments against the necessary criteria for segments. Consider any other brands or offerings that exist in this market as well.

2   What information does the toothpaste segmentation add that differs to the simple list of product offerings? How would this information change marketing practice?

3   Why is a 'normal' toothpaste on offer, when there are products more tailored to people's specific needs?

4   Is Colgate a target marketer, or are they still trying to sell to all toothpaste buyers?

THE LOGIC AND APPEAL OF NARROW TARGETING

Some businesses only target a defined segment and are successful in what they do. Examples include insurance companies that only target pensioners (Australian Pensioners Insurance Agency) and women's only gyms (such as Contours). Far more common are firms who target a particular geographic area (for example West Croyden Plumbing), usually from the simple necessity that they are a small firm and cannot service clients further afield.

But how targeted should a brand try to be? Is it wrong to try to sell to all category buyers?

Strangely, the current textbook view of target marketing is that trying to sell to the entire market is wrong and that modern marketers have moved beyond this. A typical story (for instance from Kotler and colleagues, 2007) is that marketing has passed through three stages.

1   *Mass marketing*—when firms mass produce, mass distribute and mass promote their single product to buyers.

2   *Product-variety marketing*—when firms produce two or more products that have different features, styles, quality, sizes and so on; for example, Coca-Cola producing several soft drinks packaged in different sizes and in different flavours, designed to offer variety to buyers rather than to appeal to different segments, because consumers have different tastes in different situations and they also seek variety and change.

3   *Target marketing*—when firms identify market segments, selects one or more of them, and develop products and marketing mixes tailored to the people in each. For example, Coca-Cola now produces soft drinks for the sugared-cola segment, the diet segment and the non-cola segment.

The unsupported argument is that the third approach works better. Certainly this sort of argument has influenced marketing practice, but real-world evidence does not support the idea that it is best, and there are problems with the logic. For instance, it is unclear in what ways the examples of 'target marketing' differ from the less sophisticated 'product-variety marketing'. Coca-Cola now markets many brands of drink, more than 400, yet 78 per cent of its volume sales come from one brand. Does Coca-Cola really use different brands to satisfy the distinct needs of particular groups of buyers, or is it really to satisfy demand for variety (that is, individuals buying different products across time)? How is offering non-cola soft drinks to the 'non-cola segment' materially different from product variety marketing?

To answer these questions, we might look at whether or not Coca-Cola's brands sell to different people from other brands. Do Fanta drinkers drink Coke and vice versa? Table 6.4 shows the proportion of various soft drinks' customer bases who also bought a Coca-Cola during the period. It demonstrates that a high proportion of each (and every) brand's buyers also bought Coca-Cola, and this proportion varies little between the different brands—it's always about 70 per cent. Indeed, several of the brands are marketed by Coca-Cola.

●●● **TABLE 6.4** BUYING OF COKE BY BUYERS OF COMPETING BRANDS

SHARING OF CUSTOMERS	
BUYERS OF	PERCENTAGE OF COMPETITIVE BRAND BUYERS WHO ALSO BOUGHT (REGULAR) COCA-COLA
Diet Coke	65
Fanta	70
Lift	67
Pepsi	72

Source: UK TNS 'Impulse Panel'

This is direct evidence that these brands do not sell to distinct segments of people. It is clear that Coca-Cola's other products are not manifestly targeting the non-cola drinkers, as most of the Fanta drinkers *also* drink Coke. This pattern of switching, the duplication of purchase law, is widespread and normal for most product categories (see Chapters 2 and 3). The implication here is that no brand should adopt narrow targeting: they all sell to all buyers of the category.

BRAND USER PROFILES SELDOM DIFFER

A number of researchers have empirically tested whether or not competing brands have different sorts of customer bases—something that would be a logical outcome of segmentation and targeting strategy.

As far back as 1959, Evans found little difference in the personality of buyers of rival car brands (Evans, 1959), and this was replicated by Westfall (1962). More recently, Ehrenberg and colleagues demonstrated that the profiles of users of competing brands seldom differ (on a whole host of different demographic and psychographic characteristics), and when they do vary, it is typically not by much (Hammond, Ehrenberg & Goodhardt, 1996; Kennedy, Ehrenberg & Long, 2000; Kennedy & Ehrenberg, 2001; Uncles, Kennedy, Nenycz-Thiel, Singh & Kwok, 2012). The consistent finding is that there is no distinctive 'Coke buyer' or 'Pepsi buyer', but rather that there are 'soft drink buyers', and their characteristics are similarly reflected in each soft drink brand's customer base.

This research was based on standard industry data (from many varied categories)—the sort that would often be used to conduct segmentation studies. The variables included extensive information on users' attitudes, lifestyles, demographics and media exposures. The results demonstrate that brand-specific segments generally do not exist—interchangeable brands usually compete in what for them is a single, unsegmented mass market. There is no support for the idea that competing brands each appeal to a unique sub-set of users that look different from the customer bases of competitors.

Exceptions do exist, and are mostly obvious; for example, local banks skew to their home markets.

TARGETING THE WHOLE MARKET WITH PRODUCT VARIANTS

Markets also regularly include sub-markets that are functionally different, such as children's versus adult's cereal brands, butters versus margarines versus health-oriented spreads, or diet versus full-fat offerings. These sub-markets are referred to as **market partitions** (Ehrenberg, Uncles & Goodhardt, 2004) and are usually weaker than expected and due mostly to functional differences, not to the brand's different image positioning. Partitions can be identified by looking at deviations from expected levels of sharing based on behavioural data—that is, deviations from the duplication of purchase law.

market partitions:
Closely competing products within an overall market; for example, children's cereal products among all cereal products.

In many cases, a brand's range will operate across the partitions for its category. For example, Kellogg's Frosted Flakes is bought more often by families with children and Kellogg's All-Bran is consumed a bit more often by adults.

Partitions, or rather the brands within them, sometimes skew to slightly different customer bases. For example, sweeter breakfast cereals tend to sell more to households with children. But these skews are often slight.

Colgate do not use different distribution channels for their tartar-control product compared to their breath-freshening variety. Their products are on the same shelf, in the same stores, put there by the same merchandisers. The prices of these products are typically within a few cents of one another, and while there might be different ads for some products (mostly there is brand-level advertising), they are typically in the same (mass) media vehicles. Television in particular is known for its wide, unsegmented reach, so any marketing mix that employs television for much of its advertising will necessarily reach a mostly unsegmented audience. The difference in the marketing mixes in this case is almost exclusively the difference that exists between the products themselves, and advertising is only to 'bring to public notice' that different products exist and are available. This seems to fit Kotler's definition of product-variety marketing: selling different items to largely the same people.

It is important to have product offerings that appeal to enough of the market to enable them to have sufficient scale to be successful. They should be promoted effectively, priced competitively and distributed as widely as possible. But typically these strategic decisions do not require a focus on segmentation or the restricted targeting of a market in order to be successfully implemented.

Sophisticated mass marketers can offer a great deal of customisation without having to identify and target different buyers. For example, a great deal of customisation occurs at the point of sale, where buyers make choices about:

- payment options
- delivery options
- packaging options
- volume of the order
- insurance options, and so on.

This sort of customisation is offered to all customers and is not based on identifying particular types of people and targeting them.

SEGMENTATION DOES NOT NECESSARILY MAXIMISE RETURNS

▲ LEARNING OBJECTIVE
Discuss the measurement and return on investment implications of segmentation-based targeting and mass-market approaches

The process of segmentation and targeting does not guarantee the maximum return from marketing expenditure. Even where it does guarantee the maximum sales response for a given segment, this need not coincide with the most effective overall spend. A neat illustration of this is given by Wright and Esslemont (1994: 15–16):

> Suppose our segments are old folks and yuppies. We might research the old folks market, and find that the optimum advertisements showed happy pensioners, sitting by their firesides, and that an extra $10,000 of advertising spending on media that exclusively targets this group would lead to [an] additional $100,000 of sales to pensioners. In the yuppy segment research might show the best advertisements to have youngsters racing their BMWs, and that an extra $10,000 of advertising spent reaching yuppies would result in the yuppies spending an extra $150,000.

Hypothetically, each of these approaches maximises the sales response within each respective segment. Wright and Esslemont (1994: 16) continue:

> The targeter would say that we should therefore target the yuppy segment, since its advertising response is 50 per cent greater than the other segment, and show advertisements with young motorists. But our success as a company depends on total sales, not sales in a particular segment. What we should have done is find out which advertisement would produce the best response from the market as a whole. It is *logically possible* that the pensioner advertisement would produce $70,000 of purchases from the yuppies, while the yuppy advertisement could irritate the pensioners so much that they buy nothing. In this case the targeter's argument is false—we do not achieve the best result by targeting the segment with the best response.

Table 6.5 demonstrates what Wright and Esslemont (1994: 16) point out—that the best result is not achieved by targeting the segment with the best response.

●●● TABLE 6.5   RESPONSE TO $10,000 OF ADVERTISING

	YUPPY RESPONSE	PENSIONER RESPONSE	MARKET RESPONSE
Yuppy mix	$150,000	$0	$150,000
Pensioner mix	$70,000	$100,000	$170,000

Source: Wright and Esslemont (1994: 16)

Here we are not suggesting that the segmentation targeting approach is *always* inferior to mass marketing—simply that segmentation is not always superior to mass marketing. There are and will always be conditions under which segmentation is not the best, most profitable course of action.

Thus, despite the pensioner marketing mix delivering a smaller response among the pensioner segment, the overall market response is higher. Wright and Esslemont then show an example where the optimal marketing mix for targeting each individual segment is quarantined from generating any response from any other segment. They also show that since the focus is on *total market response*, it is possible for a sub-optimal marketing mix at the individual segment level—say, a mass marketing campaign—to be more successful overall.

●●● TABLE 6.6   RESPONSE TO $10,000 OF ADVERTISING, WITH NO 'SPILLOVER' TO OTHER SEGMENTS FOR SEGMENT-SPECIFIC CAMPAIGNS

	YUPPY RESPONSE	PENSIONER RESPONSE	MARKET RESPONSE
Yuppy mix	$150,000	$0	$150,000
Pensioner mix	$0	$100,000	$100,000
Sub-optimal mix	$90,000	$90,000	$180,000

In Table 6.6 we can see that it is possible that a marketing mix that is sub-optimal within each segment can still give the greatest total market response and return on investments.

A vital additional practical point is that unless the media habits of the segments are very different, then reaching the specific segment without wastage will generally not be possible.

TALKING TO EVERYONE IS POSSIBLE

Earlier it was suggested that there are reasons why marketers may want to limit who they talk to. Reasons include: the expense involved in talking to everyone; difficulty in appealing to all types of buyers in a market; and that different companies vary in their abilities to serve different segments of the market.

But there is some counter-evidence to these ideas. While creating commercials for high-reach media such as television can be expensive, such mass media is cheap on a per person basis (approximately two to three cents per person). This per person cost is very cheap versus other means of contact such as direct mail or salesperson calls. It is particularly cheap when one puts in context that many marketers do not know who exactly is in the market for their product this week or month. Hence, for most serious marketers, mass marketing is more cost-effective than targeted approaches.

While it may not be difficult to appeal to all buyers in a market, there are many successful advertising agencies that do a very good job for their clients in appealing to a very broad base of users. This is the case for brands such as Apple, Sony, Nike and many more. The goal should be for brands to be as inclusive as possible (rather than being too selective, which limits the possible size of the brand). If this requires having an especially talented sort of advertising agency then that's what a marketer should look for.

Case study
From the Model T to the Mini

Henry Ford is reputed to have made the statement, 'Any customer can have a car painted any colour that he wants so long as it is black'. The Ford Model T is a fine (even if dated) example of mass marketing—one car, appealing to all potential users. Within the same category we can head to the other end of the spectrum, with the individual customisation promoted by Mini.

On the Mini website (www.mini.com.au), the 'My Mini' feature gives you the option to 'build and price your own Mini—just the way you want it'. It has been suggested that of every 200,000 Minis produced, only two are the same.

If you truly want to be unique, you can take it even further with a customised paint job (see www.miniusa.com/#/build/paintShop-m), ensuring your tailored product is a one-off:

But is this individual level tailoring at the extreme, with each car truly unique for its user? How different is the Mini from other car brands that offer buyers choices of colours, trim, wheels, air-conditioning and delivery times?

Clearly, it is not total tailoring, as all are variations on a small range of offerings (that is, at the end of the day, they all look like a Mini). For companies to be profitable, they typically need to have scale, or it is difficult to be competitive and offer customers sufficient value. Tailoring to individuals or even small groups of users comes at the price of scale. Take Takeoka Jidosha Kogei—the Japanese car company that makes its cars from scratch. While clearly this would give them scope for more tailoring, in a 2010 *Sydney Morning Herald*

article, company head Takeoka was asked whether there are plans to ramp up production from the current 100 vehicles a year. He exclaimed: 'The company cannot build that many!' (Poupee, 2010).

Great brands are all built on scale—HSBC, with its 100 million customers worldwide, is just one example of the many brands that have overcome cultural hurdles to find broad appeal.

DATABASE-DRIVEN TARGETING: A COMMON TRAP

Current practice in some industries is to use the recency, frequency and monetary value (RFM) of past behaviour to estimate each customer's future response and hence determine the priority segments to target. Industries such as banking, insurance and the like, which hold large customer databases, are prime culprits.

Here it is common to estimate the profitability for each customer in a database, in order to segment the database. However, this usually means targeting those who would have bought the brand anyway (that is, those who regularly buy the brand often, spend a lot and are currently in the market). Resulting marketing activities often include implementing costly promotional offers.

The reality is that a small, targeted campaign can only have a small effect on overall sales. But it can take up a lot of management time and resources that could have been invested elsewhere. Focusing on any segment (for example past users) can lead you to neglect other customers—especially light customers, who we know are important for growth (as discussed in Chapter 2).

Also, the logic is wrong: marketing efforts should not be concentrated on the heaviest, most profitable customers, but on the customers who will react most to the marketing attention. These usually turn out to be the lightest buyers of the brand, not its most loyal buyers.

It is easy to get a high response on a sales activity if you only approach people who are likely to buy anyway (your heavy customers), especially if you are giving them a special offer (which is reducing your margin). But this is not what brands need to do if they want to grow. All brands lose a number of customers with the passing of time (some move, die or just forget about the brand). Growing brands acquire more new customers than they lose (Riebe, forthcoming). Thus, broad reaching activity becomes a necessity for finding possible new customers as well as maintaining light and current customers.

CRITICAL REFLECTION

Below is an advertisement for a market research service sold to marketers. It shows indices concerning the cars driven by US Sheryl Crow fans. So, if 10 per cent of Americans drive Jeeps, this says that among Sheryl Crow fans 14 per cent drive Jeep. What is misleading about this advertisement? Do you agree with the conclusion that Jeep and Sheryl Crow could benefit from cross-promotion? Explain your answers.

Source: NPD release August 2011

SMART TARGETING IN PRACTICE

Unless there are compelling, data-driven reasons to do so, the default approach for marketers is that the entire market (all people or companies that buy from the category) is the target for communications and other marketing activities. The aim should be for inclusion rather than exclusion.

This doesn't mean treating all customers the same. As we have discussed, marketers usually offer much customisation, many different options. They understand that their market contains many different sorts of people, and that people vary in their moods and situations.

But sophisticated mass marketers also look for ways to standardise; to gain scale and cost efficiencies. They aim to market brands that look distinctive (more on that in Chapter 10), while making the brand and its marketing as appealing as possible to as many category users as possible.

Smart marketers take a number of steps to ensure they do not over-target. They:

1   make sure they understand and document who buys the category

2   always check real numbers instead of relying only on indices. Indices can be useful to highlight skews but they can also overinflate small differences. Focus on absolute useful numbers, rather than 'statistical' differences, to underpin strategy

3   quantify any skews (for example demographic skews) in brands and media

4   realise that adding a brand, SKU or focusing on a specific occasion is typically about selling more to the same people (many of whom are light category users)

5   know that heavy buyers are not (by themselves) the key to growth

6   use overall profit contribution rather than campaign ROI to assess marketing performance

7   look to maximise overall sales and margins, not just response from the target market.

There are times when targeting may present a good business opportunity (that is, women's only gyms). But it should not be the default (as you are limiting your market from the start). Do the maths. Check that the returns from targeting outweigh the costs and are greater than a return from a larger group with a lower propensity. Be thorough about calculating the costs, so that you correctly calculate returns including fixed costs/overheads. Think about who you are not reaching—what is the cost of them not getting the marketing activity from your brand? For example, what happens if light buyers do not get reinforcement, but see a competitor ad or offer?

▼ CRITICAL REFLECTION

It seems logical to target the heaviest, most valuable (i.e. highest customer lifetime value), most loyal customers with extra advertising or greater service, discounts and other benefits. But this is a marketing fallacy; what really matters is how customers are going to react to any marketing intervention.

1   Can you think of reasons why targeting your heaviest customers might yield little return?

2   Why is targeting like salt in cooking (i.e. a little bit can do some good, but it needs to be used with restraint)?

Case study

The Ford Model T and the myth of mass marketing

There is a great deal of variety in markets: customers vary and so do marketing mixes. The idea that once upon a time there were companies that offered only a single marketing mix is undoubtedly a myth. The most commonly cited example of mass marketing, the Ford Model T, may have only come in the colour black but there were delivery and payment options, and choice of dealers and after-sales accessories.

Between 1909 and 1927, fourteen different body styles (such as four-door touring, or two-door sedan) were offered. Separate chassis were available for independent coachbuilders. On top of this, Ford also sold other models of car than the Model T.

Thus, we see that mass marketing has always involved some product-variety marketing as well as some segmentation and targeting. This is still true today. Smart marketers are sophisticated mass marketers: they target all category buyers, working out clever, profitable ways to cater for meaningful differences in preference.

In 1914, Henry Ford chose to standardise the colour black for his product. His decision appears to have been justified, because the Model T went on to achieve a staggering 50 per cent global market share. At that time, most consumers were more concerned with price, durability and performance on the very poor roads of the time than with colour. Only later, when other cars could match the Model T's quality and price, would colour become important to them. This example shows how marketers have to make careful decisions about catering for variation in preferences and never lose sight of the real target—the market.

Case study

Salmon campaign strategy: Is there something fishy going on?

Salmon is consumed almost equally by males and females, and the underlying driver of seafood (and salmon) consumption is taste. Despite this, the 2010–11 campaign for Tasmanian Salmon used the slogan 'Beauty Food'. This concept was developed in response to insights into a particular segment, generated from focus group discussions. The target consumer was a single female aged between twenty and twenty-five. This represents less than 10 per cent of the potential market for salmon. The campaign media strategy was strongly weighted towards select women's fashion and beauty magazines.

Questions

1 Is this a good campaign approach?

2 What are the risks and/or opportunities?

3 Who should be included in research for campaign development?

4 As well as the advertising and media implications mentioned here, is such a segmentation approach likely to have other implications (for instance in terms of distribution and pricing)?

5 Choose another campaign and critique it in terms of its target audience. Is it targeting a specific or a broad audience? What works well or is risky?

CONCLUSION

An important lesson is that it is just as dangerous to focus narrowly on a particular segment of buyers as it is to chase so broad a market that the firm is not capable of competitively winning/serving. The art of marketing is to find ways of serving a broad and heterogeneous market without giving up on any segment. This requires a deep understanding of not just the differences between people but also the similarities.

06

SUMMARY

- In terms of marketing strategy, marketers have a number of key options, including:

    - segmenting a market into groups of buyers with similar traits and targeting those different groups (segments) with different offerings

    - a mass market approach, including different product options to address heterogeneity in demand, without particularly targeting specific groups of people.

- A focus on segmentation and targeting is popular, but there are some misplaced assumptions and poor costing practices in the discipline. Marketers should be cautious before deciding not to focus on the entire market.

- Targeting a defined segment can be sensible, such as a geographic region, but all segments need a number of traits in order to be useful, including easily identifiable characteristics of buyers that relate to substantial differences in buying.

- While complex techniques are commonly used to identify segments, raw numbers and total market response should underpin any decision making.

- Smart marketers ensure they do not over-target, by understanding who is buying the category, as well as understanding the importance of light buyers to brand growth.

REVISION QUESTIONS

1   What are the characteristics that segments must have to be useful?

2   List three very different car brands or models. What is the segment that each appeals to? How do the car manufacturers attempt to target the group of users? What tactics do they attempt to use to position the cars differently?

3   Think of an example where the users of a product are not the buyers themselves. What are the implications for targeting?

4   What is smart targeting? How might it apply to the sale of ladies shoes?

5   It is not uncommon to hear a business claim something like, 'We're going to target "big-hearted team players"'. Is it actually possible to focus on such a group? Is it likely to be a good business decision?

6   Think about segmentation and competitive response. Identify a market and describe it from this perspective. For instance, do different competitors appeal to different segments? Do some segments attract more competitors? What does this mean for the appeal of segmentation for increasing the return on investment from marketing spend?

7   How is a segment different from a partition? What are the implications for marketers in thinking about segments versus partitions?

8   If you could target precisely, would you want to? Identify the criteria you would have for who you would want to specifically target. Give consideration to the NBD distribution of buying rates before finalising your criteria.

FURTHER READING

Ephron, E (1993) 'The ghost of network past: TV fragmentation doesn't mean tighter targeting,' in Ephron on Media, retrieved 29 May 2012 from <www.ephrononmedia.com> (note: log-in required).

Nelson-field, K & Riebe, E (2010) 'The impact of media fragmentation on audience targeting: An empirical generalisation approach', Journal of Marketing Communications, vol. 17, no. 1, pp. 51–67.

Sharp, B, Tolo, M & Giannopoulos, A (2001) 'A differentiatied brand should appeal to a special segment of the market ... but it doesn't!' in S Chetty & B Collins (eds) Bridging Marketing Theory & Practice, Australia and New Zealand Marketing Academy, Massey University, New Zealand.

Wind, Y (1978) 'Issues and advances in segmentation research', Journal of Marketing Research, vol. 15 (August), pp. 317–37.

WEBLINKS

For advertising literature, case studies, data, agency links and more, see Warc:
   www.warc.com

Wikipedia list of links to advertising agencies:
   http://en.wikipedia.org/wiki/List_of_advertising_agencies

YouTube (Use search terms such as 'advertising', 'commercials' and 'Super Bowl'):
   www.youtube.com

Key journals/trade magazines

   www.journalofadvertisingresearch.com

   www.internationaljournalofadvertising.com

   http://journalofadvertising.org

   www.warc.com/BrowseAdmapIssues.info

Key industry bodies

Advertising Standards Bureau:
   www.adstandards.com.au

Australian Association of National Advertisers:
   www.aana.com.au

Advertising Research Federation:
   www.thearf.org

For additional training for those wanting to work in an agency in Australia, see AdSchool:
   www.adschool.org.au

◢ **Major case study**

My World My Way:
Analysing the segmentation
strategy

By Elizabeth Gunner

The board of directors for Australian travel guide company My World My Way are concerned about declining market share. Scared of losing their number one position to Lonely Planet, they've hired a marketing consultant, who begins his first day with an inspiring presentation: 'Meet Kev,' he says, gesturing towards a projected image of a male in his late teens, with scuffed shoes. 'Kev is eighteen. He has two siblings and his parents are reasonably well off. He's pretty popular and spends his weekends playing club footy and going to parties with his mates. Kev's just about to finish school, and is desperate for some independence. That's where we come in. Imagine that everywhere Kev goes, we are there saying "Hey, what about a gap year? Can't you see yourself spending six months in Asia or South America?" These guides are great for travelling on a budget. Suddenly Kev's got an idea. He starts buying guides and reading up. He asks mum and dad for a My World My Way backpack for Christmas. He 'likes' us on Facebook and he talks about us with his friends ...'

'Kev is our future,' concludes the consultant, 'we know what he likes, where he goes and how to talk with him. If we get Kev now, we've got him for life—every trip from his first to his last.'

Questions

1   The marketing consultant is suggesting a highly targeted marketing strategy. What is the difference between a target marketing strategy and a mass marketing strategy?

2   Do you think a target marketing strategy is appropriate for My World My Way? What are the advantages and disadvantages in this instance?

3   Imagine you are the Marketing Director for Lonely Planet. What would you do in reaction to My World My Way's new strategy? What are the opportunities and threats?

4   You have been hired as a consultant for My World My Way. The board hands you some survey results showing that lots of My World My Way customers are also buying other travel guides, even though they said that My World My Way is 'great value for money' and 'an informative travel resource'.

   a   What can you tell the board about these results? Should they be concerned by these findings?

   b   What marketing advice would you give?

Imagine that everywhere Kev goes, we are there saying "Hey, what about a gap year? Can't you see yourself spending six months in Asia or South America?"

Practitioner profile
Sally Roscholler, Manager—Media & Marketing Insights, The Herald & Weekly Times

Having completed a bachelor of business with honours, I undertook voluntary work in the marketing departments of Destination Melbourne and Intrepid Travel in 2002. During my time at Intrepid Travel, I met an inspiring photojournalist who asked me to work with her on a new adventure travel magazine entitled *Get lost!*. I worked across marketing, design and editorial in the first two years of the life of the magazine, which is now in its thirty-first edition. A key benefit of small organisations is cross-departmental experience—and lots of it! In my second year I was sent to Indonesia to write a story for the magazine about Lombok. Tough job, but someone has to do it!

In early 2005, I joined The Herald & Weekly Times (HWT) as a marketing assistant in the media and marketing insights department (M&MI). M&MI is responsible for analysing and communicating research insights across the business to assist with advertising and business development.

In May 2006, I was promoted to the position of marketing analyst. In this role, I worked predominately with the Victorian *Herald Sun* agency and the *mX* sales teams. Devising strategic responses to briefs in limited time was commonplace. Clients want media firsts, integrated opportunities and value adds. While adrenaline levels are high it makes for an exciting work environment. Especially when you win business!

In February 2007, I was promoted to the position of senior marketing analyst, and given responsibility for News Limited's national sales team, NewsNet (now News Australia Sales), which managed national advertisers based in Melbourne.

In July 2008, I was promoted to the position of team leader and given responsibility for the management of a team of marketing analysts. Management has been one of the most rewarding roles of my ten-year career. As team leader, I published a regular eDM (electronic direct marketing publication) titled *BiteSize* to give advertisers an update on commercial highlights and opportunities at the *Herald Sun*. I also worked on creative *Herald Sun* advertising campaigns appearing in *B&T*, *AdNews* and *Mumbrella*. In 2009, I won 'Supervisor of the Year' at the annual HWT advertising sales awards.

In July 2010, I was promoted to my current position of Manager of Media & Marketing Insights, and I now report to the Victorian Advertising Sales Director.

The current rate of change for media platforms is unprecedented. It is an extremely challenging and exciting time to be in the industry. HWT is traditionally an above-the-line media company but it is now transforming itself to embrace the new and evolving media landscape. I thoroughly enjoy working for such a progressive company and am excited about what the future holds.

07

PRODUCT
(GOODS AND SERVICES)

DAVID CORKINDALE

Disney's flop: *John Carter*

In March 2012, Disney launched a blockbuster film called *John Carter*. It cost US$300 million to make and US$100 million was spent on marketing it. In the first week, it took only US$30 million in the cinemas where it was shown, and was expected to lose Disney US$200 million (BBC News, 2012). The movie is a fantasy story based on a series of books by Edgar Rice Burroughs, the creator of Tarzan and author of *The Land that Time Forgot*, involving a veteran of the American Civil War who is somehow transported to Mars, forced to wear a loincloth and confronted with a succession of monsters. Because of the many poor reviews it received and the negative audience feedback, fewer cinemas showed it, or they showed it for less time, and some may even have reduced ticket prices by running promotions, all of which further reduced overall box office takings.

Even if more money had been spent on advertising and promoting the film, it would not have been successful in reaching the revenue targets originally set for it. In other words, having a sound product is the necessary starting point for being successful in the marketplace. The other marketing mix decisions are necessary, but not sufficient on their own to achieve success.

What other marketing lesson can we draw? The title, or the name, of the product is important. Names matter. What does the title *John Carter* tell anyone about the product or what it has to offer? Apparently the original proposed title was *John Carter of Mars* but this was ditched, as Disney marketers believed that people were not interested in Mars or, indeed, science fiction generally (*The Economist*, 2012a). Given the huge success of the sci-fi movie *Avatar*, this judgment and decision seems questionable, and it could have been tested by market research.

Another Disney film that was equally expensive to make and also received mediocre reviews, *Pirates of the Caribbean: On Stranger Tides*, which was released a year earlier, went on to make over US$1 billion. It had a title, or name, that identified the brand line it came from and, based upon this familiarity, what to expect: Johnny Depp doing ironic swashbuckling in an action movie with occasional special effects and a racy story. This is another lesson: a brand name that people are familiar with and associate with things they like is a valuable marketing asset.

This is another lesson: a brand name that people are familiar with and associate with things they like is a valuable marketing asset.

INTRODUCTION

In this chapter, we look at products in the broad sense of both physical products (goods) and core services (services) that organisations produce and offer. Banking, retailing, tourism, education, health and education are just some of the many major service industries. In today's developed economies, therefore, the majority of businesses and organisations are engaged in offering services, and consequently many of the people engaged in marketing activities in organisations are marketing services. This includes marketers in government agencies and not-for-profit organisations. However, whether you are marketing shoes, holiday insurance policies or facilities for the aged, you will draw on the same marketing principles and practices. Products (whether goods or services) are the starting point for devising the marketing mix by which marketers plan to stimulate and manage demand from the marketplace.

LEARNING OBJECTIVES

After reading this chapter you should:

- understand what a product is
- be familiar with the key elements in product strategy
- know the process of developing and marketing new products
- know how to use the product category life cycle model to understand and plan the evolution of new products
- know ways of extending the life of a product and/or finding additional customers for it
- understand why services do not need to be marketed differently from goods.

CHAPTER OUTLINE

Introduction

What comprises a product?

The marketing mix and branding strategies

Product categories

Developing and marketing new products

Product category life cycle (PLC)

Marketing services

Conclusion

Ansoff matrix

consumer products

continuous innovations

discontinuous innovations

dynamic continuous innovations

industrial products

line extension

product category life cycle (PLC)

relational market-based assets (rMBAs)

technology boom

WHAT COMPRISES A PRODUCT?

▲ **LEARNING OBJECTIVE**
Understand what a product is

One purpose of marketing is to help customers achieve their objectives in life, whatever these might be. It can be argued that fulfilling most objectives in life requires the provision of a product or service. For instance, if we want to travel from A to B, we could go on a bus and thus use a bus *service*. If we wanted to drive there, we'd have to have bought a car (a physical good), or else hire one or go in a taxi (both of which are services). Thus, we can either use a good or a service to achieve the same end. If we want our clothes washed, we could take them to a laundry *service* or we could buy a washing machine. If we go to the cinema or a concert it is the *experience* we seek: the goods, service and environment that we access while there make up the experience. The film content or the act we see is the main product we buy, but the other products and services complement it, to enhance the experience. It is therefore important to first understand what the fundamental needs or desires of consumers and clients are, in order to devise or select the nature of the good or service that will fulfil these.

Case study

Hilti: From goods to service provision

The Swiss company Hilti provides professional-standard power tools, such as electric drills, for companies in the building industries. It was finding that many of these products were being seen as commodity items by its customers, and that customers were starting to buy cheaper competitors' products. Hilti responded by offering large building contractors a service whereby the contractor did not need to purchase the power tools outright. Instead, Hilti would guarantee to supply the required set of well-maintained tools every day to a client's construction site. In this way, the building contractor would not have to buy, own and maintain the power tools, which was attractive to them. In fact, the client's need was to have access to power tools but not necessarily to own them—they make money by building things, not by owning equipment. Hilti also benefit by being able to ensure that their products are always working well and that they have a continuing income stream from companies with whom they maintain a relationship. Thus, a company that used to market equipment is now a service business, but still uses the same products.

When we fulfil a need, we are often provided with both a physical good and a service—they are part of the total offer. For instance, if we go to a restaurant we expect a degree of service and a congenial ambience, as well as the food itself. If we told friends that we went to a good restaurant last night, we would probably include consideration of the goods (food), staff manner (service) and general atmosphere in our assessment. If we buy a flight on an airline (a service), there are many physical items we expect to come with it, such as a comfortable seat and good food. So businesses seeking to fulfil a need and stimulate and manage demand for it in a market often need to market a 'package' of both physical goods and the services that go with it.

Products therefore may be physical goods, services or service products, the latter being something like insurance for a car or home contents. We can therefore think of there being core products (such as the restaurant food) or core services (the airline flight), and then complementary services or goods that make them more complete. So, in practice, a product is rarely just a single item. In the rest of this chapter, we will primarily discuss decisions about core products *and* core services, but we will just use the term 'product' to keep things clear. However, keep in mind that marketers also need to consider the complete product 'package'.

What to provide as the product, or product package, is a fundamental decision for an organisation and its marketers. It is the basic offer to the market and all other elements of the marketing mix, such as the price and availability, must complement it so as to meet the full requirements of potential customers and the marketplace.

If the good or service is not capable of meeting customers' basic needs, usually no amount of adjusting of the other elements of the marketing mix can overcome the basic deficiency. For instance, if a brand of umbrella always lets rain through, then no matter how much advertising there was of it, or how low its price, few people would buy one to protect themselves against rain.

◢ **LEARNING OBJECTIVE**
Be familiar with the key elements in product strategy

THE MARKETING MIX AND BRANDING STRATEGIES

The product together with the other mix elements can be thought of as a bundle of benefits put together to satisfy the needs and wants of consumers or customers. Purchasers choose the product they perceive will best satisfy their needs and/or solve their problems. Additionally, it needs to be made available to them in a convenient way, be priced appropriately for them and be brought to their attention.

Customer-oriented firms seek to benefit in the marketplace by trying to ensure their total offer—that is, the marketing mix and branding—is perceived well by their targeted segment(s) compared to the total offers of their competitors. Choosing what to offer and how to offer it may require careful research in order to understand the customers' needs and wants, preferences and priorities.

Brand fit

As a company provides a product into the marketplace over time, it accumulates **relational market-based assets (rMBAs)** in terms of reputation and goodwill from satisfied customers, and these are embodied in a brand. A new product that meets customer needs and has an appropriate marketing mix may still not be successful in the marketplace if it does not have rMBAs, or if the brand and its associations are not supportive or are inappropriate for the customers it is intended for. To be successful in a marketplace, a product has to not only fulfil customers needs and have an appropriate marketing mix, but also have appropriate rMBAS and appropriate branding.

relational market-based assets (rMBAs): Assets that arise from the co-mingling of the firm and its product with entities in its external environment, including distributors, retailers, end-customers, other strategic partners, community groups, and even governmental agencies.

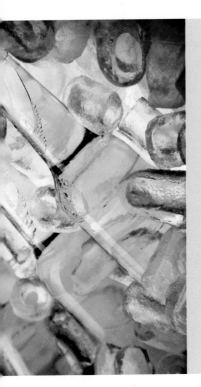

Case study
Foster's low-carb beer

In 2010, the Foster's Group introduced a new type of low-carb beer in Australia, called 'Pure Blonde'. It had lots of advertising support and was made widely available in pubs and liquor stores. A year later, one of their competitors, Lion Nathan, launched a similar product but called it 'Hahn Super Dry', using the well-known Hahn brand name, thus making it a **line extension**. Hahn Super Dry had similar levels of advertising to Pure Blonde, was distributed at a similar price and to much the same degree. Very soon, it outsold Pure Blonde by a ratio of two to one. Later, Foster's, realising their mistake, put out a very similar product to their original one, but this time called it 'Carlton Dry', capitalising on a well-established brand name. This example demonstrates the value and strength of how an appropriate brand name, and one with broader, less targeted appeal, contributes to the success of a product in the marketplace.

Features

Once the core need customers are seeking to meet or the fundamental benefit they are seeking to gain has been understood, the components and features of the product can be devised. For physical goods, these could include such aspects as size, design, style, colour, quality and packaging. The importance of each of these to potential customers varies from market to market. A plain white, simple cotton T-shirt might command a price of $5. But in a distinctive colour with a Nike 'swoosh' logo, it might command a price of $30! Some further important features of a product are considered next.

line extension: Further versions of a product in the same category put into the market using the same brand name as the original; for example, the many versions of powdered coffee bearing the Nescafé brand name.

Product name

As noted earlier, a brand results from the accumulated experiences people have of buying, using, owning and maintaining it. This may include the development of relationships with the suppliers and servicers of the product. If all these experiences are favourable and other people talk well of it, the brand will have strong positive rMBAs. So, over time the name of a product will acquire positive associations. The original meaning of the name may be irrelevant to this or never have any interpretable meaning anyway. For instance, Facebook is not about faces or books, and Amazon was originally known only as a South American river or the name of female warriors in Ancient Greek mythology. Similarly, you probably do not knowingly use your 'computer' to do any mathematical or computing work, but this is the generic term we use for such machines.

However, when naming something, it is helpful if the name meets the following criteria to aid it in the marketplace. The name should:

- describe the benefits or solutions that it provides; for example Cash Converters, ComfortBra, SolarGuard
- be short, distinctive and easy to remember; for example Express Post, EasyJet, Cool Mints
- suggest authority and trust; for example Commonwealth Bank
- be able to be used in other languages and countries without the need for local translation, or if it does require translation, then this is easy and maintains the same meanings and associations. For example, Coca-Cola does not require translation, but this has come about through longstanding use around the world. The US government passed a bill during the Second World War that US soldiers had to be provided with Coca-Cola wherever they were, so supply depots were set up in many parts of the world for this.

- be registered, so no one else can use it, and any distinctive features legally protected. For instance, the mauve colour that Cadbury chocolate uses for its wrapping is copyrighted and it can only be used by Cadbury products.

Logo

The ability to create a visual representation of a product or brand name is another factor to take into account when devising a name. A couple of examples are shown in Figure 7.1.

The arrow in the FedEx logo suggests speed and forward direction. The original name of Federal Express meets many of the criteria for a name listed above. In the US NorthWest airline logo, the compass arrow points north-west. Do you see any other symbolism? The company name also meets many of the ideal name criteria.

●●● **FIGURE 7.1** LOGOS THAT ALLOW NAMES TO BE REPRESENTED VISUALLY

Labels and packaging

Labels and packaging, along with distinctive logos on them, are yet further marketing decisions and activities that have to be undertaken by marketers. Packaging is not simply used to protect goods but also to draw attention to them on a shelf and add value. This is particularly the case for products bought as presents or for personal reward. Given what we have said earlier about the importance of the brand helping to stimulate demand for a product, its prominence on the packaging in the form of a logo is vital.

In some cases, the packaging contains information about the use or purpose of the product and/or instructions for the product's use. There are important laws that govern the packaging of certain types of products. For instance, there is a Foods Standards Code in Australia that prescribes labelling and packaging requirements for many foods. What can be described as 'Made in Australia' is regularly a contentious issue as, for instance, a food product grown in another country may be labelled as 'Made in Australia' if it has been imported from another country but has received further processing or had 'value added' in some way in an Australian factory.

Product mix and range

Another dimension of product strategy is the 'product mix'. In devising a particular product, its attendant features and the marketing mix, an organisation must take into account what else it may be providing to the marketplace. It must be careful not to offer something too similar to what it already offers, so as not to carry the costs of making and supplying two products when one is perceived as sufficient by the market.

However, it is conventional in many industries to offer a range of products that nevertheless fulfil the same basic need. For instance, car makers offer a range of cars under their manufacturer's brand name that differ broadly in size, quality and price. All cars in a manufacturer's range are usually capable of filling the basic need of providing transport from A to B. Some have special capabilities for special needs, such as off-road travel, but these are the exception. The commercial logic of providing a range of options is to allow customers to aspire to own or use something that provides emotional benefits as well as a few extra functional ones. It is well known that if three versions of a product, such as a microwave oven, are offered at three prices, most people will buy the mid-price one rather than the one at the lowest price, even though it would serve the main purpose quite adequately. They can get perceived value of having made a good choice. However, some people do like to feel that they have bought 'the best' while others are satisfied to know they bought 'the cheapest'. Here, the supplier gains value, from providing a range of products, as well as the customer. In countries with planned economies, like the old Soviet Union, the benefit to both parties was lost on bureaucrats who only allowed one version of something to be made. Making a range was seen as 'wasteful' and unnecessary.

The product mix is defined in terms of the breadth and depth of its range:

- *Breadth* positions the company as a 'generalist'; that is, one that seeks to serve many customer types and provide solutions for a wide range of problems with products that are probably adequate but not special. Bunnings Warehouse would be an example.
- *Depth* positions the company as a 'specialist'; that is, one that focuses on serving particular needs, perhaps in just one or a few industries.

Case study
Shouldice Hospital: A model hospital

The Shouldice Hospital near Toronto in Canada follows the 'depth' product strategy. It is known the world over for dealing most successfully with inguinal hernias in men. It deals with no other medical ailments, unlike most other hospitals. It is a for-profit hospital and is said to be the most profitable hospital in the world per patient, but its fees are not high. Some patients return later for a reunion with fellow patients, they liked the time they spent there so much! It is profitable, medically excellent and its patients love the experience—a difficult combination to achieve in the hospital industry.

PRODUCT CATEGORIES

consumer products:
Products bought by private people for their personal use or consumption, or for the personal use of other people such as their family members or friends.

industrial products:
Products bought for further processing and sale or for use in conducting a business.

Some products are made for purchase and use by ordinary people or householders, while others are made for use by companies. The former are called **consumer products** while the latter would be termed **industrial products**. Some products are made for both industrial and consumer use, but are made available via different marketing mixes: industrial versions may be sold in bigger amounts and through different distribution channels. For instance, cattle farmers provide lime for their animals to lick at certain times of the year and buy this in large bags, paying about $5 a kilogram; if their spouses own and keep a horse to ride domestically, they also often acquire a lime product for the animal, but this comes in a small, attractive package at a price equivalent to about $50 per kilogram.

Many consumer products start in the marketplace as industrial ones, with a later version and marketing mix being developed for consumer use. Computers were only available for industrial use for many years, before the 'personal computer' was devised after computer components became cheaper and smaller. Microwave ovens were used in commercial kitchens many years before they were made available for domestic use. The traction control equipment in family cars today and other technical features come from those first developed for Formula One racing cars.

Other kinds of products that can benefit from being professionally marketed are:

- people; for example Lady Gaga
- places; for example Australia by Tourism Australia
- events; for example the Olympic Games
- organisations; for example Cancer Council Australia.

However, all of these provide products and services which are themselves marketed, and it is usually through the success or otherwise of these that the 'parent' develops its brand positioning in the marketplace.

DEVELOPING AND MARKETING NEW PRODUCTS

What do we mean by 'new'?

There are three categories of new products: discontinuous innovations, continuous innovations and dynamic continuous innovations

Discontinuous innovations and major product innovations: products with a completely new set of attributes. Such innovations usually give rise to a new product category. For instance, the invention of an aeroplane led to a major international industry that had not existed before, while the development of mobile phones in the 1980s by companies such as Motorola and Nokia led to the still-expanding role and use of such devices.

Minor innovations, comprising small-scale alterations to existing products, are known as **continuous innovations**. An example would be the way that the main front lights on cars have changed shape from circular to 'tear drop'; another would be how different flavours or cavity prevention ingredients of toothpaste are periodically introduced to the market.

The third class of innovations is **dynamic continuous innovations**, where the technology used may be new but the product into which it is put is, to all intents and purposes as far as the user is concerned, just an improved form of what already exists. The development of LED lights for use as car headlights is an example of this type of innovation: LED is a different technology from the electric filament light bulb, but is used in just the same way by consumers—you flick a switch and the lights come on. Diesel engines in cars are another example of a dynamic continuous innovation—diesel is a different technology but the user does not have to learn anything new in order to drive a diesel car.

Major, discontinuous innovations usually require behavioural change by the potential users and this is a reason why they sometimes take a long while to be adopted. For instance, in around 1753,

LEARNING OBJECTIVE
Know the process of developing and marketing new products

discontinuous innovations: Products with a completely new set of attributes to other existing products and that require users to change or learn new behaviour; for example, digital music downloads.

continuous innovations: Products with a minor innovation to other existing products; for example, a toothpaste product introducing a new ingredient.

dynamic continuous innovations: Products that utilise a new technology in an existing product but do not require the user to change or learn new behaviour; for example, LED lights for car headlights.

James Lind, a surgeon in the British navy, discovered that eating citrus fruit prevented scurvy in sailors on long sea voyages. He published his evidence for this after conducting extensive experiments. However, the innovation was not actively used until Captain Cook adopted the practice during the three-year voyage that resulted in his discovery of Australia: on his return to the UK in 1771 he proudly reported that there had been no cases of scurvy. It took at least a further 50 years for all ship captains in the British navy to widely follow the advice.

A further reason why discontinuous innovations take a long while to be successful in a market is that they typically require new methods of delivery and service. When personal computers started to be sold, there needed to be people who could repair them out in the community when they stopped working. Otherwise many people would not have bought one for fear of breakdowns. When Edison invented the electric light globe, he also had to invent the way in which electricity could be generated in a mass way and distributed to houses, as without this no one would buy or use his product!

The distinction between continuous and discontinuous innovation is important. A continuous innovation has a combination of attributes that is similar to those of products that are already on the market. The set of competitive products, as well as the majority of the market actors involved in production and marketing of these products, remains essentially the same. The basic attributes and the use of these products are known by most potential consumers. Although the minor innovation may contain some new features that distinguish it from similar products in the market, its adoption will not require major behavioural changes on the part of its users; this is a very significant factor. The usage situations are mostly known for these products. So, valid consumer evaluations regarding their future adoption behaviour, or relatively valid expert opinions regarding the market developments, are possible prior to the introduction of a minor, continuous innovation in the market. Moreover, since the product category to which the minor innovation belongs remains essentially the same, data about the diffusion of the product category can still be extrapolated. Therefore, marketing decisions for a continuous innovation are straightforward. If a new product is a continuous one and is just the next generation of an established product, the marketing decisions can be made on the same bases as before and remain essentially the same.

Discontinuous innovations, if they are successful in the market, can bring great rewards to the suppliers of them. However, discontinuous innovations are often very difficult to market, as potential customers have no experience on which to base feedback to market researchers, who might ask about reactions to a proposed marketing mix when they are undertaking pre-launch studies. The zip fastener took many years to become widely used, as people were used to buttons and found them adequate. Only when zips were used as fashion items did they start to become widely adopted.

Acquiring new products

Companies do not always come up with new products themselves. A company can acquire new products through several methods.

First, it can copy products that have been developed elsewhere; for example new products from other regions or countries. International companies have access to intelligence from their operations in different countries. Companies can also observe what their competitors are producing or learn of impending new products through various methods of competitive intelligence.

Alternatively, a company can purchase the ability to produce or supply a new product by:

- acquiring a licence to do this from another manufacturer
- acquiring a patent that allows it to use a specific technology or process
- acquiring a company that has a new product.

Google has moved into many new markets by buying companies that have developed technologies and products in new areas. In 2012, it acquired Motorola's mobile phone operations as a way of moving into making phones as well as supplying the operating system Android for them.

Application to business-to-business marketing

As stated earlier in this chapter, one purpose of marketing is to help customers achieve their objectives. Within business-to-business marketing, this purpose translates into helping organisational customers achieve their company goals. From the viewpoint of the customer, most goods and services are not purchased for their own sake, but as a means of contributing toward successful organisational operations.

For example, as explained in the feature on Hilti, that company provides equipment that assists building contractors to perform their construction tasks in a cost-effective manner. The Hilti Fleet Management system enables a building contractor to avoid upfront equipment investment; minimise administrative workload; benefit from certainty regarding the overall monthly tool, service and repair costs; avoid costly downtime; and ensure compliance with safety standards through the regular replacement of tools (Hilti, 2012). Similarly, Elders provides various products and services that assist farmers to increase the productivity of their lands and to maximise the income from their livestock and produce.

As previously mentioned, the product, together with the other elements of the marketing mix, can be viewed as a bundle of benefits that collectively satisfies the needs and wants of customers. Appropriate enhancements can increase the value to the customer. Within organisational markets, enhancements such as highly specialised advice or collaborative product development can greatly increase the value of a supplier's offering, occasionally transforming a commodity product to a distinctive product plus service 'bundle'. In such situations, the service component can become the key reason for the particular supplier being preferred.

For some industrial products, some elements of the marketing mix have less value in organisational markets than in consumer (or household) markets. For example, colour, style, logo and labelling are often unimportant to organisational customers. Conversely, quality, reliability and credibility are often much more important considerations to organisational customers, especially if the product has a significant influence on the customer's operations (such as communication systems for a police force or advertising services for a marketing organisation).

Within business-to-business marketing, new product development often involves cooperation or collaboration between supplier and customer organisations. For example, the commencement by car manufacturers in the 1980s to reduce the weight of their vehicles led to many manufacturers of car components developing lighter products, some switching from iron or steel to aluminium as a raw material for metal components. Various firms cooperated with their major supply chain partners, including the car manufacturers, to successfully undertake such developments. Similar cooperation has occurred more recently with the development of components for hybrid vehicles.

As previously mentioned, innovative new products often are introduced to organisational markets before being adapted for consumer markets. For example, during the 1970s and 1980s, facsimile machines replaced telex machines for urgent inter-office and inter-company written communication. Only later were facsimile machines adapted for the consumer market. Similarly, mobile telephones initially were introduced for business executives and tradespersons, replacing pagers that previously were used by such people for urgent communication. Only later were consumers markets targeted by mobile telephone manufacturers and telephone service providers.

The service that accompanies a new product can influence its success. Service is discussed later in the chapter, but it is particularly important within organisational markets since the effect of inadequate performance in any aspect of service is often significant. For example, later in this chapter, six dimensions of service are briefly discussed: reliability, assurance, tangibles, empathy, responsiveness and recovery. These dimensions tend to be particularly important within organisational markets since the effect of inadequate performance in any of these areas is often significant. For example, unreliable supply delivery of a car component can cause the closure of an entire car manufacturing operation, as occurred in April 2012 when CMI Industrial went into administration due to financial difficulties and caused the temporary shutdown of Ford's Broadmeadows and Geelong plants in Victoria (Drill, 2012).

In summary, all factors relating to products are relevant within organisational markets, but the importance of some factors is quite different between consumer and organisational markets.

The new product development process

If a company decides it needs to develop new products internally, rather than acquire them through the methods mentioned above, there is a systematic process that it can follow. Ideas for new products can come from customers and an analysis of customer needs, or they can come from inside the organisation. The steps that are usually followed after ideas for new products have been gathered are:

- idea screening
- concept development and testing
- marketing strategy development
- business analysis
- product development
- test marketing
- market introduction.

We discuss idea screening in the following section. Marketing strategy development and market introduction are covered in the section below on the product category life cycle, while the other stages involve market research (covered in Chapter 4).

Idea screening

In evaluating any new product proposal, irrespective of whether it is a product or service product, a company will consider a wide variety of factors in the idea screening stage. Two main kinds of criteria to use in screening are financial criteria and market criteria.

Financial criteria include:

- the costs of entering the market
- the costs of operating in the market
- the probable margins and levels of profitability
- whether the costs of operating within the market are likely to change at all over the next few years
- the costs of market exit
- the costs of operating through intermediaries
- levels of financial risk
- whether scope exists for alliances and/or joint ventures in order to share any risk
- the costs of developing the service proposal yet further.

Market criteria include:

- the size of the market
- its growth rate and the nature and significance of any trends
- the number of competitors
- the importance of the market to each competitor
- the nature, bases and intensity of competition
- the number of customers
- customer location
- buying motives and expectations
- the frequency of purchase
- probable levels of customer loyalty
- the opportunities for enticing customers away from competitors
- the scope for cross-selling and value-added packages
- patterns of distribution
- the degree of price competition
- the scope for strong segmentation targeting and positioning
- the extent to which experience gained in other markets might be applied to the new product in its proposed markets.

PRODUCT CATEGORY LIFE CYCLE (PLC)

All product categories and markets are in a state of evolution to some degree. This is because customers are affected by the changing circumstances in which they live. For instance, the economy changes, laws change, the weather patterns change and new technology can alter many aspects of life, including jobs. The effects of these changes can be seen in the overall sales patterns of established products and services over time. It is also seen that when a successful discontinuous innovation is adopted and/or a major improvement is made to an existing product, the sales pattern over time follows a distinctive pattern of low initial sales followed by a vigorous growth period and finally a period of fairly steady sales levels, sometimes followed by a decline. This pattern of sales over time can be likened to the life of a person: birth, growth, maturity and decline. This has given rise to the concept of the **product category life cycle (PLC)**.

Different marketing decisions need to be taken during each stage of the PLC in order to adapt to the changes in both demand and supply in the market. Marketing managers should modify their strategies and tactics constantly if they are to realise the profit potential of their product in each stage of the PLC, and the expected general category life cycle can help guide them.

Table 7.1 shows an idealised PLC with the typical profit curve. The reason for the profit curve not following the sales curve is that:

- in the introduction period, costs may be greater than revenues
- when the category is strongly growing, demand may be greater than supply, so that prices can be high; strong category demand and high prices attract more suppliers to the market
- near the top of the growth phase there are a lot of suppliers, so competition will increase at the same time that growth in demand might be slowing. This causes price competition, with consequent lowering of profits.

Table 7.1 also gives the broad marketing objectives and strategies recommended for each stage of the PLC.

The PLC applies to product categories rather than individual brands. The usual depiction of the PLC is based on averages and is best not applied to individual products or brands.

The PLC has been criticised as a planning tool because of the difficulties in predicting the length of each stage, the volume of activity and the timing of the transition from one stage to another. But, despite these problems, it does give marketing managers a basis for making marketing decisions.

The conditions for a product being profitable are more favourable during the growth period. When the period of decline seems to be setting in, there are ways for possibly enabling a particular product or the whole category to rise and/or the 'life' of the category to be extended.

The typical changes in the marketing mix as the PLC evolves are also shown in Table 7.1.

●●● **TABLE 7.1** SUMMARY OF THE PHASES OF THE PRODUCT CATEGORY LIFE CYCLE AND ASSOCIATED MARKETING OBJECTIVES AND STRATEGIES

	Introduction	Growth	Maturity	Decline
CHARACTERISTICS				
1 Sales	Low sales	Rapidly increasing sales	Peak sales	Declining sales
2 Costs	High cost per customer	Average cost per customer	Low cost per customer	Low cost per customer
3 Profits	Negative	Profit growth	Lessening profit	Declining profit
4 Customer	Innovators	Early adopters	Early majority–Late majority	Laggards
5 Competitor	Few	More in number	Stable number beginning to decline	Declining numbers
OBJECTIVES				
	Create product awareness and trial	Maximise market share	Maximise profits and defend market share	Reduce expenses and milk brands
STRATEGIES				
1 Product	Offer basic product	Offer product extension service warranty	Diversify brand models	Phase out weak products
2 Price	Charge cost +	Price to penetrate market	Price to better match competition	Possibly raise price
3 Distribution	Build selective distribution	Build intensive distribution	Even more intensive	Selective phase out of unprofitable outlets
4 Advertising	Build product awareness among early adopters and dealers	Build awareness and interest in mass market	Stress on brand difference and benefits	Reduce to level to retain hardcore loyals
5 Sales promotion	Use heavy sales promotion to induce trial	Reduce sales promotion due to increased consumer demand	Increase to prompt brand switching	Reduce to minimal level

Source: Corkindale, D R, Balan, P & Rowe, C W (1996) *Marketing: Making the Future Happen*, 2nd edn, NelsonITP, South Melbourne, pp 48–9.

LEARNING OBJECTIVE
Know ways of extending the life of a product and/ or finding additional customers for it

Ansoff matrix: A simple planning framework indicating that there are four ways for a company to expand its sales: grow its market share, introduce a new product, move into a new market or diversify its activities (Ansoff, 1965).

Extending the PLC

How to try to maintain or grow sales volume when a PLC has reached the maturity stage is a common problem. One way to identify possible growth options for extending the PLC is to use the **Ansoff matrix**, shown in Figure 7.2.

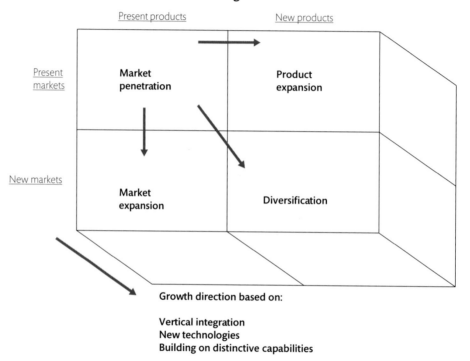

●●● **FIGURE 7.2** THE ANSOFF MATRIX

Source: adapted from Ansoff, H I (1957) 'Strategies for Diversification', *Harvard Business Review*, Sept-Oct.

In the above framework, 'market' means customers. For a firm that wishes to grow its sales volume, there are four options to pursue.

The first is *market penetration*, where the firm focuses on gaining share at the expense of its competitors. Various marketing tactics could be used to achieve this, but essentially these would be based on the marketing mix.

The next option is *product development*. The essential idea here is that the firm examines what their current customers need and are buying from other firms. They ask themselves: why can't we supply that to them? The firm aims to trade on the fact that it is known to the customer and it has in place much of the infrastructure, rMBAs and know-how to do business with them. A simple example is that for a long time McDonald's did not offer breakfasts and did not open until lunchtime. They subsequently adopted 'product development' and now offer breakfast.

The third option is *market expansion*, to find new customers for the firm's existing products or services. A simple example would be a Sydney firm moving to additionally offer its products in Victoria, with similar clients to those it had in its home state.

The last option is available theoretically, but it is usually a bad idea: it is when a firm attempts to *offer things that are new to it and to customers it is not used to dealing with.* This strategy is high risk and usually fails.

At a simpler level, there are three strategies that might be considered to help achieve PLC extension in sales. These are also ways of implementing one of the chosen options from the Ansoff framework:

- modifying the market
- modifying the marketing mix
- modifying the product.

Modifying the market

A common response to the marketing challenge of a mature product is to seek new market segments for it. These segments might be found in the general marketplace, as was the case in the expansion of personal computers and mobile phones from the business market to the domestic sector. International expansion is another market modification strategy. This was the approach that was followed by Disney with the launch of Disneyland in Paris and Hong Kong, from its home base in the United States. Technologies that are reaching the end of their life in one country may still be appropriate in less developed economies. This has the advantage of generating a longer life span for the technology and the chance of recouping the original development costs.

Modifying the marketing mix

Changes in the positioning of a product by varying its marketing mix can be used to achieve greater market penetration or to open up new segments of the market. Expanding availability can boost sales; for example, a growth strategy of The Body Shop was to try new channels of distribution with the introduction of party selling. However, such changes should be based upon sound analysis and the identification of untapped needs and segments.

Modifying the product

A further strategy for marketers seeking growth in a mature market is to consider product modification. This might involve relatively minor changes in the product's size, flavour or function, as was done, for instance, with the introduction of miniature-sized Mars Bars or the orange-flavoured Kit Kat chocolate bar. It is also what happens when a new model of a car is produced. However, such changes should not be done without a market-based reason. Other examples of product modification include the miniaturisation of products that has led to cameras in mobile phones, and the addition of power to traditional hand tools.

◢ **technology boom:**
When one technology
or capability is added to
an unrelated product or
service and creates an
added benefit through the
synergy that occurs.

Adding a new technology to an old product and consequently causing a revitalisation in its PLC is called the 'technology boom'. PC sales were stagnating in the early 1990s and then the internet came along, and with it email. PC sales then started to grow again as a new set of people realised the value of email and subsequently acquired an internet-connected personal computer.

It is sometimes difficult to draw the line between what is new product development and what is product modification. In a practical sense, it really does not matter how you categorise a strategy. The process of product modification should follow the same framework and customer research as would be followed for a new product's development. The distinction is relevant only in the sense that the costs and risk of failure will normally be less with a modified product than a completely new product.

As a result, some observers suggest that many companies have relied too heavily on line extension strategies, as opposed to investing in real new product development and have thus produced a proliferation of 'new, improved' versions that have marginal extra value to customers.

◢ LEARNING OBJECTIVE
Understand why services
do not need to be
marketed differently
from goods

MARKETING SERVICES

Marketing a service is essentially the same as marketing physical products. For both, we have to understand customer needs and buying behaviour, identify segments, formulate a marketing mix taking into account relevant rMBAS and the brand's strengths, and manage the brand through the PLC.

However, some commentators on marketing say that services have different characteristics compared to goods. They therefore imply that the marketing of services is different. The claimed differences are said to be due to the 'characteristics of services' cited below. Here, we examine them to ascertain whether they are, indeed, exclusive to services or not. A service is said to be a deed or action, so it is:

- *intangible*—many services cannot be seen, sampled or tested before purchase, making the *risk* of a purchase greater than for tangible products that can be examined and tried before buying. However, are hotels, shops and transport (such as bus services) 'intangible'?
- *perishable*—a service, such as a booking for a seat on a plane, is perishable. If the plane leaves with an empty seat it cannot be sold later, and so services can be highly perishable; they have no shelf life, which means that services cannot be stockpiled to meet fluctuations in demand. However, are finance loans and education 'perishable'? I hope not! Fruit and vegetable products are perishable, too.
- *inseparable*—customers often have to go to the provider to consume a service, because production, distribution and consumption take place simultaneously. Operational staff—those skilled professionals and technicians who provide a service, such as dentists, educators and coach drivers—must have direct contact with customers. However, you do not have to be present when your car is serviced or your lawn is cut; both are services.

- *heterogeneous*—it is a person who gives a service and who determines its quality and the quality of customer care; people are variable in their performance and this makes it difficult to ensure the consistency of the services provided. Because each service purchase is unique and involves a direct buyer–seller interaction, all services are said to be heterogeneous. However, many services, such as those of an ATM, are made and delivered by technology, just as products are, and so the quality can be assured and is not variable.

So, we can see that it is not possible to generalise that all services possess these so-called characteristic differences between a product and a service.

We can, however, divide services into 'hard' and 'soft' ones, with the latter being those that are exclusively delivered by people. A soft service, such as an intellectual service like education or consultancy, does possess the four characteristics cited above. This makes it difficult for a prospective client to assess the worth of the service and its likelihood to meet their need. In this case, they have to buy on trust and the service provider must work hard to provide clues as to their credibility. However, in the B2B world, companies commission the construction of special pieces of equipment and are also buying on trust that these will work as required when they are delivered; so, again, buying on trust is not confined to services.

How aspects of the marketing mix are operationalised may have a different *emphasis*, depending on whether what is offered is primarily a service or a good, but, in principle, the same decisions and actions have to be made. For example, we have to make pricing decisions for both. It is difficult to judge the worth of some services until we experience them, so how we may support a proposed price may be done in a somewhat different way for a service compared to a product. We may, for instance, have to offer a guarantee—although that also applies to some goods products. We may use testimonials—but that is also used for some goods products.

For soft services, the *selling* and *pricing* of them may be more difficult, but the overall marketing process is still the same.

It may be easier for competitors to replicate the marketing mix of a rival's services, particularly soft ones, than for goods products as they do not have to have expensive equipment. For example, any law firm can hire well qualified lawyers, have nice offices, charge much the same fees as others and promote themselves just like others. So, how do they compete? They compete on their reputation and experience—their rMBAs. So, we might conclude that gaining and maintaining rMBAs are more important for these types of services than for other (goods) products.

 CRITICAL REFLECTION

1 Many brands deliver a variable mix of service and product, which is one reason it is hard to know what customer satisfaction scores really measure. Rather than tracking satisfaction, how might a company measure its product quality and its service quality separately?

2 Brands are rarely successfully extended beyond the product category that they are known for. Examples of commonly cited failures include Harley-Davidson perfume and Bic underwear. Yet there are a few extraordinary exceptions; for example, the Husqvarna brand is used on sewing machines, motorcycles and chainsaws; Yamaha is used on pianos, motorcycles, outboard motors, hi-fi equipment and electric wheelchairs; and Walkers is the leading brand of potato chips (crisps) in the UK, where Walkers is also a famous brand of shortbread. Why might these rare exceptions exist?

Service quality and customer service

There is often little distinction between the marketing of products and services. Customers and consumers expect 'good service', whether it be from a restaurant (a typical service) or from the supplier of an industrial oven (a typical product). Hence, an appreciation of the delivery of service is critical to the management of marketing.

Quality service delivery has the following six key dimensions:

- reliability—performing the promised service accurately
- assurance—competence, courtesy, credibility and security
- tangibles—physical appearance of staff, buildings and equipment, for example
- empathy—communication and understanding the customer
- responsiveness—timely service
- recovery—the ability of an organisation to rectify aspects of their services (and products) that have caused dissatisfaction to customers.

The relative significance of these dimensions will vary for different organisations and depend to some extent on the nature of goods and services that are offered. For example, a bank's customers will find the provision of security to be particularly important, whereas it may be of little concern to customers of a hairdressing salon.

Collaborative products and services

In today's world, many organisations aim to satisfy customers or consumers by creating goods and services collaboratively with, and through, other organisations. The computer company Dell is a classic example: Dell gains orders from potential clients for computers and then, with its network of suppliers of various computer parts, puts together the required computer. In this way, specialist suppliers are harnessed so that a good product is created at an attractive cost. Once all manufacturers in an industry adopt this model of operation, the market becomes, in effect, one where *networks* are competing against each other for the eventual consumer, rather than there being competition between individual companies. Managing partners in such collaborative networks then becomes very important. Competition for the best supplier to a network may be as important as competition for consumers.

CONCLUSION

Customers buy and respond to the total offer made by a company that includes the product, the rest of the marketing mix, and the rMBAs and/or the brand. A major responsibility that marketing managers have is to ensure that their company's products continue to meet the needs and wants of existing and potential customers. The decisions involved in keeping the product relevant and up to date with changing customer needs out in the marketplace also involves decisions about the ancillary features of a product, such as packaging and labelling. The marketing manager also has to be alert to new needs and opportunities that may appear in the marketplace and that warrant developing new products to serve these. In this case, decisions have to be made about how to put these into the market, including choosing an appropriate name. Having done this, the marketing manager will then be involved in helping manage the product as the product category it is in evolves through its life cycle stages, including seeking ways of extending or even growing its sales when the category may be in decline. Whether it is a physical good or an intangible service, the marketing analysis and decisions involved are essentially the same, and if they are not kept right for the marketplace it is unlikely that making changes to other mix elements, such as price or promotion, will enable a deficient product to sell. For example, it is generally recognised that Kodak relied on continuing to make films for non-digital cameras for too long, which lead to its demise.

07

SUMMARY

- Most organisations are involved with the provision of services and so marketing managers are very often marketing a service.

- Many customer needs are satisfied through the provision of a service, and many products are acquired in order to be able to provide the self-provision of a service.

- Products can be categorised into those that are primarily physical goods and those that are primarily services In order to satisfy customer needs; in many markets a package comprising both is often required.

- The marketing mix must complement the product and the product strategy to help gain the desired response in a market.

- There are many other factors and decisions that have to be considered in order to make a product complete for the marketplace, including brand fit; features such as size, style, design and colour; product name; logo; and labels and packaging.

- Products can be categorised as consumer or industrial products and they often start as the latter and are then introduced as the former.

- Decisions on product mix and product range may need to be made.

- There are three types of innovations: continuous, discontinuous and dynamic continuous. Discontinuous innovations are the most difficult to introduce to a market as they require customers to learn new behaviours and new service providers to be available.

- New products can be acquired by an organisation by buying or licensing from other companies, copying those of rivals or observing overseas markets.

- Organisations develop new products internally, through an advised series of steps. New product ideas and concepts should be screened early in the process for the ability to meet financial and market criteria.

- Product categories pass through a series of life cycle stages in their market, and for each stage there are specific marketing objectives and strategies that should be aimed for.

- Ways of thinking about how to extend the life of a product include the Ansoff matrix and harnessing the technology boom.

- Fundamentally there is no difference between the marketing of services and goods.

REVISION QUESTIONS

1   Think of a situation where the core need that customers seek is provided by an *experience*. What products and service products would also need to be provided to help create the experience? What, if anything, would make the marketing of an experience more difficult than that of a service product?

2   When you buy a ready-to-eat meal in a packet in a supermarket, are you acquiring a product? Explain your answer. In a restaurant, is the meal you buy a product? Explain your answer.

3   Think of a product or brand name that meets each of the five ideal criteria for a name. Can you think of an additional desirable property that a name of a product should have?

4   Think of an example of a discontinuous innovation. What probably encouraged and enabled it to become widely adopted?

5   Research has shown that less than one third of new product ideas come directly from the customer. How does this relate to the marketing approach of developing products based on customer needs and wants? Why do you think this is the case?

6   Think of an example where the technology boom has revitalised the PLC of a product category.

7   Do you agree that marketing service products is no different from marketing goods-based products? Give your reasons.

FURTHER READING

Chakravorti, B (2004) 'The new rules for bringing innovations to market', *Harvard Business Review*, vol 82, no. 3, pp 58–67.

Christensen, C M, Anthony, S D, Berstell, G & Nitterhouse, D (2007) 'Finding the right job for your product', *MIT Sloan Management Review*, vol. 48, no. 3, Spring, pp. 38–47.

The Economist (2011) '1100100 and counting', vol. 399, no. 8737, June, pp. 67–9.

The Economist (2012b) 'The third industrial revolution', 21 April, retrieved 3 June 2012 from <www.economist.com/node/21553017>.

Moore, G A (1991) *Crossing the Chasm: Marketing and Selling High-Tech Products to Mainstream Customers*, Harper Business Essentials, New York.

Okazaki, S (2009) 'Mobile finds girls' taste: Knorr's new product development', *Journal of Interactive Advertising*, vol. 9, no. 2, pp. 48–59.

Page Moreau, C, Lehmann, D R & Markman, A B (2001) 'Entrenched knowledge structures and consumer response to new products', *Journal of Marketing Research*, vol. 38, no. 1, pp 14–29.

Pine, B J & Gilmore, J H (1998) 'Welcome to the experience economy', *Harvard Business Review*, vol. 76, no. 4, July/August, pp. 97–105.

Shaw, B (1998) *Improving Marketing Effectiveness*, Profile Books, London.

Tapscott, D & Williams, A D (2010) *Macrowikinomics: Rebooting business and the world*, Portfolio, Penguin Books, Canada.

Troye, S V & Supphellen, M (2012) 'Consumer participation in coproduction: "I made it myself" effects on consumers' sensory perceptions and evaluations of outcome and input product', *Journal of Marketing*, vol. 76, no. 2, pp. 33–46.

WEBLINKS

How to market a brand new product:
www.inc.com/guides/201106/marketing-a-brand-new-product.html

Put your customers to work:
http://discussionleader.hbsp.com/hbreditors/2008/09/letting_volunteers_build_your.html

Tontine's award winning campaign for date stamped pillows results in 20% sales increase:
www.campaignbrief.com/2011/10/version10-starthtml0000000149-42.html

The Australian Effie Awards Entry Form 2011:
www.effies.com.au/effies/attachments/535273d8-55e3-48a8-8e3f-12a025486f32.pdf

David Maister's Marketing Professional Services podcasts:
http://davidmaister.com/podcasts.archives/2/

Joseph Pine on the Experience Economy:
www.youtube.com/watch?v=pXv3cfvJ9F8

◢ **Major case study**

Marketing the Eco-Shack

By Gregory J Brush, Assistant Professor in Marketing, University of Western Australia and Douglas Thompson, Architectural Designer with the Permit Shop (NZ) Limited

Background

New Zealanders have a love affair with their houses. Saving a deposit for your first home is a common life priority. The mortgage payments and running expenses that follow consume a significant amount of household resources. However, as families evolve and grow, their living requirements also change; for example, a spare room may be needed to accommodate a study or home business, or an older child or elderly parent that has returned to the family home. With a favourable national tax system for home ownership many New Zealanders acquire additional rental properties. These are often seen as an effective retirement fund and a physical symbol of wealth and comfort. Additionally, with our love of the outdoors and a mainstay of New Zealand culture being the summer vacation to the beach, mountain, lakes or rivers, we invariably require accommodation in these often very remote areas.

Introduction

In an age of increasing climate change, there is a need to consider the sustainability and environmental impacts of our housing and accommodation choices. The greening of the built environment is a result of greater public awareness, information and understanding of how the buildings we live, work and play in affect the natural environment, our bank balances and our health. But what do we really mean when we say a product is 'green'? It is a broad term that people are instantly drawn to but can only vaguely define. It is often linked to other words such as 'sustainable', 'environmental', 'carbon footprint', 'ecological', 'carbon neutral', 'biodegradable', 'energy efficient', 'renewable', 'organic', 'recyclable', 'alternative energy', 'non-toxic', or 'eco-'anything. Supermarket shelves are filled with 'green' or 'eco' products, and we may not mind paying a little more for the eco-toilet paper to ease our environmental guilt about all the plastic packaging in the rest of our shopping. The purchase of 'eco' supermarket products can be a relatively simple choice, as

In an age of increasing climate change, there is a need to consider the sustainability and environmental impacts of our housing and accommodation choices.

the additional cash outlay is generally not large. But how green and deep are our pockets when it comes to the built environment?

Recent changes to New Zealand building regulations have identified that a lot of existing homes, generally those built prior to 2000, are under-insulated. This often leads to cold, damp environments and health problems. New building developments now have an increased insulation rating requirement. There are also subsidies for insulating existing buildings built prior to 2000, including installation of solar water heating. These are accessed through the Energy, Efficiency and Conservation Authority (EECA). Through better insulation, solar hot water, low voltage bulbs and appliances we use less power.

Local authorities are encouraging further environmental efforts. Some local authorities have low water-flow fitting regulations. Also, there is encouragement by some local authorities to install water tanks to catch run-off from the roof for non-potable water use, and reuse of grey water (laundry and shower water run-off) is also encouraged for plant watering. These measures reduce demand on our water supply, waste-water treatment and stormwater services.

The general movement by our regulatory authorities in terms of the built environment is to reduce, reuse and conserve, with a strong emphasis on design. These outcomes are achieved by various products that may or may not be 'green' in their sustainability or production. Examples include wool insulation versus polystyrene insulation, and plantation timber versus imported hardwood. There are several choices for any building element, and their selection will be based on factors such as cost, long-term return, toxicity and appearance. The 'eco'-ness of any building is subjective, but in general we could say that it is any building where the construction, materials and ongoing costs reduces, reuses and conserves the natural environment.

The process of constructing any new building, extension or renovation, 'eco' or not, is often a long, stressful process. The only thing that you can guarantee is that it will take longer and cost more than expected. Recent changes to the building regulations allow for a 'sleep out' of up to 10 square metres be placed on a section (with or without an existing house) without any council permits. This change is a key factor behind Doug and Paul's development of the Eco-Shack.

The Eco-Shack Concept

Doug has been in the building industry for over ten years, with mostly residential experience. He has recently completed his National Diploma in Architectural Technology (NDAT), which qualifies him as a draughtsman. He has also appeared on television as a builder and presenter on *Mitre 10 DIY Rescue*, and for two seasons as a judge on the popular *Mitre 10 Dream Home*. His main focus is on creating a successful design and building company with an 'eco-slant'. Paul is a qualified welder with a small pipe welding company that he is aiming to expand. They both see the potential of the Eco-Shack and have come up with two products—the standard Eco-Shack and the Urban Eco-Shack. Both owners are keen and practical, but have no marketing experience.

Eco-Shacks are basically transportable buildings, 2.4 to 3 metres wide, to varying lengths from 3.6 metres up. The width allows Eco-Shacks to be easily transported and sited by a Hiab truck (the mounted crane on the back of the truck can lift up to 10 tonnes) or helicopter. The shacks are built to NZS3604 (New Zealand timber-framed building) standards and will last a minimum of fifty years given proper maintenance. The following are the specifications of the standard 2.4 x 6 metre Eco-Shack:

- plantation pine timber framing
- above minimum standard wool insulation
- eco-ply cladding
- under floor water tank (catchment off the roof)
- photo/voltaic panels (solar power)
- wind turbine
- battery storage
- composting toilet
- battery powered water pressurised plumbing
- Califont hot water shower
- galvanised steel chassis
- drop down decks and awnings
- double glazed joinery (windows/doors)
- long run colour steel roofing
- phone/data connection
- variety of interior fit-outs.

The standard Eco-Shack is built in modular form so that the specifications can be easily modified, depending on a client's needs. The Eco-Shack developers believe their product would be excellent for low-impact off-the-grid living. It is easily transportable and sited and is ready to operate, given a bit of sunshine, wind and rain (or water truck initially). The cost of a basic unit with specs as above is in the range of NZ$35,000 to $40,000. Several other firms, including Portable Rooms and Cabin Fever, offer similar accommodation but are not geared to off-the-grid living.

The specifications for the Urban Eco-Shack are:

- 3.6 x 2.4 metre floor area with 0.9 x 2.4 metre deck
- plantation pine timber framing
- above minimum standard wool insulation
- eco-ply cladding

> The standard Eco-Shack is built in modular form so that the specifications can be easily modified, depending on a client's needs.

●●● THE ECO-SHACK
Source: Douglas Thompson

- double glazed joinery (windows/doors)
- long run colour steel roofing
- phone/data connection
- NZS3604 (New Zealand timber framed building) standards
- two power points
- wool carpet
- sensor light
- smoke alarm.

This unit fits under the 10 square metre rule, and therefore does not need a council permit. The unit price is NZ$12,500. The Urban Eco-Shack is a ready-made solution, without the hassle of builders and the requirement to attain a council permit. The Eco-Shack developers believe that there are two possibilities for this kind of unit: sell them or build and rent them out. There are currently a few companies offering the build and rent option. Portable Rooms and Cabin Fever both offer sale and hire options. While their units sell at approximately $2500 less than the proposed Urban Eco-Shack product, the owners of Eco-Shack believe their steel foundation/chassis and choice of eco-materials, above-specification products and weatherproofing are superior.

The Auckland-based owners have constructed a prototype Urban Eco-Shack and have advertised it on Trade & Exchange (www.sella.co.nz) and in *The New Zealand Herald*, with no response. Auctions on Trade Me (www.trademe.co.nz) have resulted in over 200 views and ten to fifteen watchers with a couple of questions per auction, but not one bidder. The owners feel there is potential for the Urban Eco-Shack, as well as the standard Eco-Shack, but they may not be the same market. The owners are drawn to the standard Eco-Shack with its environmental concepts, but wonder whether there is greater market potential for the Urban Eco-Shack.

Questions

1　Using the four common bases for segmenting markets, identify and describe a consumer segment in New Zealand that could be interested in the Urban Eco-Shack.

2　Identify and describe a business segment in New Zealand that could be interested in the standard Eco-Shack.

3　Discuss how you would brand and position the Eco-Shack product you selected to the segment you chose in question 1 or 2.

4　The Eco-Shack is currently priced using a cost-plus approach. Discuss the advantages and disadvantages of using a cost-oriented pricing approach.

5　Select and justify an alternative pricing approach that Doug and Paul could use to price the Eco-Shack.

Practitioner profile

Nicola Weideling, Marketing Manager, Secondary Division, Oxford University Press Australia & New Zealand

My first field of study was English literature and language, my second publishing. I hadn't really thought about marketing as a career for me, I just knew that I wanted to work with books. But then I studied marketing as part of my publishing course and I realised that marketing was what I really wanted to be involved in. So I decided to gain as much marketing work experience as I could while I was completing my course. Oxford University Press (OUP) was an obvious choice for me: it was a publisher, it was on my doorstep (literally—I lived around the corner!) and I had made some OUP marketing contacts through my position as Chair of the Oxford branch of the Society of Young Publishers, so I used these. I was lucky enough to be given work experience within the marketing departments of Oxford Paperbacks (Oxford World's Classics and Oxford History of Art), Electronic Publishing (essentially the Oxford English Dictionary on CD-ROM) and Reference Marketing (specifically foreign language dictionaries). When I graduated, I took a role within the marketing department of the English Language Teaching division at OUP.

Having worked in marketing for over fifteen years at companies including Oxford University Press, Heinemann and Pearson, I have witnessed a major shift in how companies communicate with customers. Print is no longer king; gone are the days of lengthy research and development, design and print times for a bulky print marketing catalogue. A plethora of social media and file-sharing software options now offers 'real time' delivery of marketing message to customers; this makes it a very exciting time to be in marketing.

I love working in marketing; it gives me the opportunity to work with passionate, creative, talented people, and to use different marketing media to promote beautifully designed books with interesting content to students and teachers. Oxford University Press is a great fit for me—and for the bookworm in me, as the staff discount on books isn't bad either!

08

PHYSICAL AVAILABILITY, RETAILING AND SHOPPING

BYRON SHARP AND HERB SORENSEN

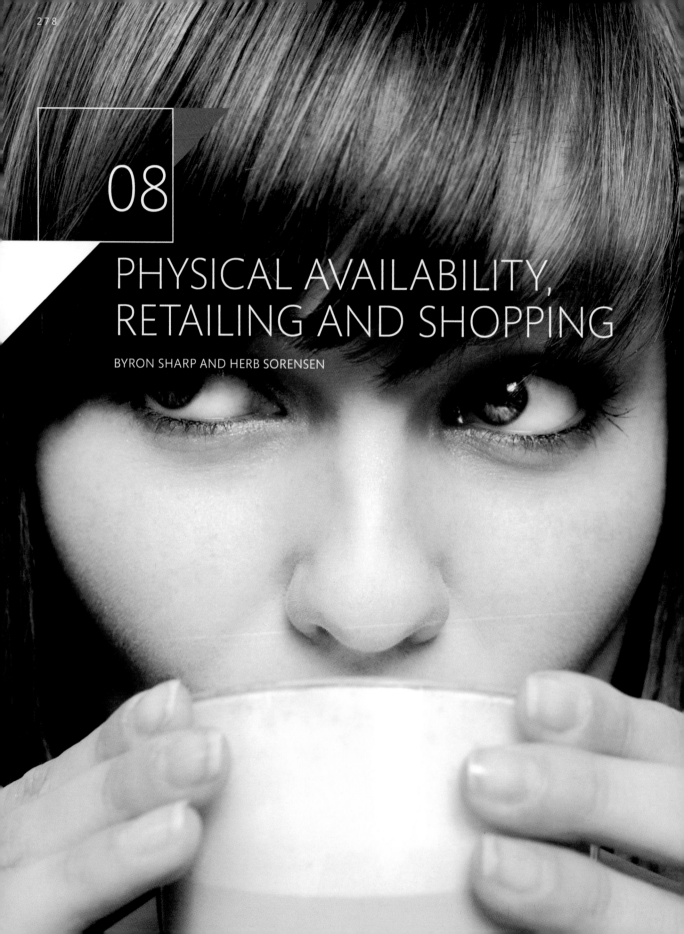

◢ Introduction case

Consolidation of the retail dollar not universal

By Haydn Northover

More and more we see the consolidation of the retail dollar, as large companies grow to become giants and smaller retailers can no longer compete. In Australia, it's particularly noticeable with supermarkets, where giants Coles (owned by Wesfarmers) and Woolworths are everywhere. In the United Kingom, it's a similar situation with Tesco and Asda. But while you can see this trend in many sectors, not all industries have been changed by the financial might of large organisations.

Consider the Australian coffee market. The US-owned global coffee-house chain Starbucks Coffee Company expanded into the Australian market in 2000. Within a short amount of time they had opened eighty-five stores. Despite following the retail mantra of success, 'location, location, location', in 2008 Starbucks began closing down stores. They had failed to gain a foothold in the Australian market, which is largely driven by small independent cafés.

Some suggest the highly standardised Starbucks' offer failed to meet the individual needs of Australia's diverse culture. Others feel that the rapid store roll-out resulted in too many underperforming stores. Apparently, a sizeable number of people just didn't like the Americanised version of coffee served by Starbucks. Starbucks' failure in Australia is likely to be due to a combination of factors. What's clear, however, was that a global standardised retail chain does not represent a guaranteed home run.

When Starbucks entered Australia, it entered an established coffee market in which independent cafés already provided high-quality products and service. Starbucks was unable to break the hold these existing cafés had on the market, and it had to scale down operations. It doesn't mean there aren't new opportunities for Starbucks. They are likely to find future success in markets—such as China—that don't enjoy an established coffee culture. But this is more likely to happen somewhere where Starbucks can shape the coffee culture itself, rather than compete against established routines.

> More and more we see the consolidation of the retail dollar, as large companies grow to become giants and smaller retailers can no longer compete.

INTRODUCTION

Retailing is a fascinating field. We can all use everyday observation to learn about how retailing works, the strategies and tactics retailers use, and how the sector is evolving. This chapter gives an overview of retailing, then explains how retailers compete—that is, gain and lose customers—against each other. The chapter proceeds to outline a number of scientific laws of shopping that have been derived from years of empirical study. Concluding the chapter is a brief section on how retailing may evolve in the future.

LEARNING OBJECTIVES

After reading this chapter you should:

- understand the importance of retailing
- appreciate the controversy about retailers placing cost pressure on suppliers
- be able to describe how retail stores share customers with each other over time
- understand and be able to explain the basic consumer repeat-buying patterns that apply to retailers
- be able to identify major recent trends in retailing; what they have meant for suppliers, retailers and consumers; and how these trends will continue in the future.

CHAPTER OUTLINE

Introduction
Retailing
How stores compete
Empirical laws of shopping
The future of retailing
Conclusion

KEY TERMS

capital investment	infrastructure	retail
chains	manufacturing	retailer advertising
cognitive effort	merchandise	stock-keeping units (SKUs)
conglomerates	negative inflation	supply chain
distinctive assets	panel scanner data	
eye-tracking studies	profit margins	

RETAILING

The famous French General Napoleon Bonaparte once dismissively referred to England as 'a nation of shopkeepers', but his description could apply equally well to Australia today, where 1.2 million people (of a total working population of around 12 million) work in **retail**. This makes retailing the single largest employer in the country; as a point of comparison, there are only 60,000 active members in the Australian military. This concentration in the retail sector tends to be present in any developed country. Walmart is the world's largest retailer (the second largest is France's Carrefour) and is also the world's largest private employer, with over two million employees. The French military today has 350,000 employees, while Carrefour alone employs almost 500,000 people—so today France too is clearly a nation of shopkeepers!

The efficiency and effectiveness of the retail sector is terribly important for any country's economic well-being. Poor countries have noticeably chaotic, inefficient retail sectors that do a rather patchy job at making goods and services available to consumers. Poor **infrastructure**, such as roads or railway systems, often hinders the movement of goods from makers to shops.

By current standards, Australia has a very well-developed retail sector. It is unusual in that it has a high degree of concentration, with two very large retail **conglomerates**: Wesfarmers (owner of Coles Supermarkets, Bunnings Warehouse, Liquorland, Target, Kmart and others) and Woolworths Limited (Woolworths, Safeway, Big W, Dan Murphy's and others). Almost 40 cents in every retail dollar spent in Australia goes to these two firms. This does not appear to have been detrimental, at least in the short term, to Australian consumers, who have received lowering real prices and increasing choice over time. However, there are concerns that these two chains have so much power that they might have undesirable effects on the **manufacturing** sector and may push smaller retailers out of the market (Washington, 2011; ABC News, 2011).

Kinds of retailers

In the twenty-first century there is a wide range of retailers, and it is important for marketers to be familiar with how they function. The following is an overview of the make-up of the retail industry:

- *department stores*, such as David Jones—here, we find product lines laid out in separate departments, such as women's and men's clothing, home furnishings, cosmetics, and so on. Companies may operate as 'shops within shops' and pay rent as a percentage of takings to the host store.
- *supermarkets*, such as Woolworths—these are large, self-service stores carrying a very wide range of consumer goods. They are typically located in suburban shopping strips or centres, or in out-of-town retail parks, although many supermarket chains have recently opened smaller city-centre sites. The supermarket chains are often the first with new customer initiatives, such as loyalty cards or in-store bakeries. Low prices based on large-scale efficiency are hard for smaller independent stores to match.

retail: Selling goods or services directly to the final consumer for their personal, non-business use.

infrastructure: The basic physical and organisational structures and facilities (such as buildings, roads and power supplies) needed for the operation of a society or enterprise.

LEARNING OBJECTIVE
Understand the importance of retailing

conglomerates: Large corporations that are made up of diverse companies operating in different fields.

manufacturing: Producing or making some thing on a large scale with the help of machinery and equipment.

- *discount sheds or 'category killers'*, such as Toys 'R' Us—these stores often stock bulky items such as furniture and electrical goods. The 'category killer' terminology results from the tendency of some very large specialist stores to put competing independent retailers out of business.
- *speciality shops*, such as Sportsgirl (clothing) or Carphone Warehouse (mobile phones)— these are typically found in central business districts of cities or prime retail sites in towns. Increasingly these stores are part of a branded chain.
- *convenience stores*, such as 7-Eleven—geographically, and also in terms of the range of products on offer, these stores fill the gap between supermarkets and 'traditional' corner shops. While independently owned convenience stores have tended to decline in number in recent years, the major supermarket operators have expanded into this area.
- *cash-and-carry warehouses*, such as Costco—these usually offer cheaper groceries and durable goods to consumers or cater to traders and small retailers.
- *market traders*—these remain significant outlets for many low-value products. Although they have generally declined in importance in recent years, some types of market, such as farmers' markets, have expanded.
- *online retailers*—some online retailers, such as Amazon, have no physical shops that interface with the public. However, most online retailing is in fact accounted for by 'bricks and mortar' retailers.

Growth of chains

chains: Multiple outlets that are commonly owned and controlled, have centralised buying and merchandising, and sell similar line of merchandising; for example, supermarket chains.

The twentieth and twenty-first centuries have seen a trend towards national **chains** of retailers and a trend towards increasing self-service. This shows that the primary purpose of retailing is to reach consumers, to bring products and services to them, not to do much in the way of active selling. These two trends continue today. Self scanning in supermarkets is becoming more common, and there are some shopping centres that feature only chain stores; indeed it is not uncommon in the USA for there to be new towns where every single restaurant is a member of a chain.

The chain store is such a powerful factor in retailing that it's worth considering an example in some more depth. Consider, for example, The Great Atlantic & Pacific Tea Company, better known as A&P. Mark Levinson (2011b) 'tells the story of a company that built the modern consumer economy by turning the antiquated retail industry into a highly efficient system for distributing food at low cost.' In 1870, A&P introduced Thea-Nectar, a branded, prepackaged product, 20 years before the practice became common to the industry.

THEA-NECTAR
IS A PURE
BLACK TEA
with the *Geeen Tea Flavor*. Warranted to suit all tastes. *For sale everywhere.* And for sale wholesale only by the **Great Atlantic & Pacific Tea Co.**, 8 Church St., New York, P.O. Box 5506. *Send for Thea-Nectar Circular.*

Over the eighty years from the introduction of Thea-Nectar, through the Great Depression and two world wars, A&P used their sharp focus on brand value to become the world's largest retailer—the first billion-dollar business in the world. As Levinson explains (2011b: 55–9):

We would rather sell 200 pounds of butter at 1 cent profit than 100 pounds at 2 cents profit. While selling food cheaply was good for consumers, it was bad for the hundreds of thousands of retailers, wholesalers, and manufacturers who needed high food prices in order to make a living.

The financial principle driving the long and shopper-friendly growth of A&P was not **profit margins**, but *overall* profits (a return for their investment). This means that A&P's profits were driven more by keeping investments low and traffic high, than by turning a profit on the sale of individual items. During the years of turbulence during which A&P grew and thrived, keeping their **capital investment** low meant they could shave margins and drive prices even lower (and demand higher) by becoming more efficient themselves, and forcing their suppliers to do the same.

Over the past forty years, Walmart has leveraged the same efficiency-focused, low-price approach as A&P, and has thereby demonstrated that consumers benefit from it—the typical household in the United States saves US$2500 per year, even if they never shop at Walmart (Barbaro, 2008). The cost savings arise because of Walmart's disruptive focus on cost, first in their own operations, but more importantly back down their **supply chain**. The efficiency improvements in the supply chain rebound to the benefit of other retailers and non-Walmart shoppers as well. As long as multiple suppliers continue to compete to get their products into Walmart stores, innovation will not suffer.

HOW STORES COMPETE

All retailers strive for a share of the shopper dollar, with competitive rivals endlessly trying to out-do each other with new stores, better locations, improved store layouts and technology, and in many cases extensive advertising of price specials. Is there any generalised knowledge about the ways in which competition between rival retailers occurs? In this section we look at some patterns in buyer behaviour and consumer cross-purchasing among competing retailers.

The repeat-purchasing patterns that occur in brand buying (as described in Chapter 2) also occur in store choice. Studies have shown these patterns to hold true for supermarket chains, department stores, petrol stations, fast-food chains and even women's fashion boutiques, in countries such as Australia, the United States, the United Kingdom, Japan and China (Keng & Ehrenberg, 1984; Uncles & Hammond, 1995; Uncles & Kwok, 2009). So, rival stores compete fairly much head-on against one another, unless they are physically located far apart. Stores, and store chains, with great mental and physical availability are visited by many more shoppers—who spend slightly more at those stores than they do at other stores with *less* mental and physical availability (another example of the double jeopardy law in action).

Table 8.1 illustrates this repeat-purchasing pattern with some data on department store shopping in Adelaide, South Australia. The stores are listed in order of market share. The double jeopardy pattern (see Chapter 3) is clear: larger market share store chains have larger customer bases (penetration) and slightly higher loyalty (both average purchase frequency

profit margin: The amount by which revenue from sales exceeds costs for a business.

capital investment: Investment in fixed assets for business or industrial use, such as machinery, equipment and so on.

LEARNING OBJECTIVE
Appreciate the controversy about retailers placing cost pressure on suppliers

supply chain: The sequence of processes that moves a product or service from its production point to the point of availability to the consumer.

LEARNING OBJECTIVE
Be able to describe how retail stores share customers with each other over time

 CRITICAL REFLECTION

How can a store—say, in a suburban shopping centre—improve its physical availability? Isn't it fixed by the location that it already has?

and average share of department store shopping trips). David Jones, which is the most upmarket department store in the group, stocking some exclusive premium brands, does not gain more loyalty than its rivals. Kmart has the largest market share, penetration and loyalty—which has a lot to do with it having more stores than its rivals.

●●● **TABLE 8.1** DEPARTMENT STORE SHOPPING IN ADELAIDE, SOUTH AUSTRALIA

DEPARTMENT STORE	PENETRATION (%)	SHOPPING FREQUENCY (NUMBER OF OCCASIONS)	SCR (%)
Kmart	48	4	34
Target	44	3	27
Myer	35	3	23
Harris Scarfe	32	2	19
David Jones	12	2	18

Source: Ehrenberg-Bass Institute survey data, cited in Sharp, B & Sharp, A (1996) 'Positioning and partitioning' in A M Martin & S R G Starr, Jr (eds) *Australia New Zealand Marketing Conference*, Department of Marketing, University of Auckland, p. 723.

So these retail chains compete largely in terms of mental and physical availability. Brands with more availability are bought by more people, and these people find the brand a little easier to repeat-purchase.

This pattern of repeat-purchasing does not mean that the functional differences between the retail chains are irrelevant. When we look at how they share customers with each other (see Table 8.2) we see that, broadly, the duplication of purchase law holds—all the brands share customers with one another, and they each share more of their customer base with the larger brands. However, it is not difficult to see deviations (marked in bold) from what the duplication of purchase law would suggest.

●●● **TABLE 8.2** DUPLICATION OF PURCHASE IN DEPARTMENT STORE SHOPPING IN ADELAIDE, SOUTH AUSTRALIA

DEPARTMENT STORE	PERCENTAGE WHO ALSO BUY FROM DEPARTMENT STORE				
	KMART	TARGET	MYER	HARRIS SCARFE	DAVID JONES
Kmart	–	28	21	18	**4**
Target	33	–	25	17	**5**
Myer	32	32	–	18	**12**
Harris Scarfe	35	27	24	–	10
David Jones	**20**	23	**42**	26	–
Average	30	28	28	20	8

Source: Ehrenberg-Bass Institute survey data, cited in Sharp, B & Sharp, A (1996) 'Positioning and partitioning' in A M Martin & S R G Starr, Jr (eds) *Australia New Zealand Marketing Conference*, Department of Marketing, University of Auckland, p. 723.

David Jones shares less of its customer base (than the law says is normal) with Kmart and Target. This could be due to the fact that David Jones is an upmarket retailer while Kmart and Target are not. However, this explanation suffers from the fact that Harris Scarfe, which is certainly not an upmarket department store, shares its customer base pretty much as expected with David Jones; indeed David Jones shares a higher than expected amount of its customers (26 per cent compared with an average of 20 per cent) with Harris Scarfe. This is all explained by the fact that, at the time these data were collected, David Jones had only a single store in Rundle Mall (in Adelaide's city centre). This meant it shared more with other store chains that also had Rundle Mall stores—Harris Scarfe in particular, with a store almost opposite David Jones. The store chains with their main stores in other shopping centres (Kmart and Target) shared fewer of their customers with David Jones. Kmart, in spite of being the market leader, actually had no Rundle Mall store but a number of stores in other shopping centres. David Jones customers therefore had reduced opportunities to also shop at Kmart (due to the lack of a Kmart Rundle Mall store), although 20 per cent still did (not too far below the average of 30 per cent). But Kmart customers had very little opportunity to shop at David Jones due to its single store, so only 4 per cent shopped there (half the average of 8 per cent).

So, we see that a chain store's location and the number of locations a chain has have a huge effect on how many shoppers a store attracts, how loyal they will be and which other stores it will compete with most closely. It's not surprising that some retailers talk of the three essentials of retailing: location, location, location!

In many car-oriented societies, a vital part of physical availability is car parking space. Westfield Group is a successful, Australian-based, international developer and operator of shopping centres. Its success in the United States depended heavily on building shopping centres that included large amounts of car parking, often underneath or on top of the shopping centre.

Case study
Sainsbury's and the power of physical availability

UK supermarket chain Sainsbury's has been doing rather well lately. Over Christmas 2011, they astounded financial analysts with their performance compared to other retailers. Like-for-like sales were up 3.5 per cent compared to the Christmas 2010 quarter, and they overtook Asda to become the second largest supermarket chain in the United Kingdom. How did they do it?

Chief Executive Justin King highlighted one crucial factor—12,000 tons of salt. No, they didn't sell it; they used it on their car parks when it snowed, ensuring that their stores were accessible to customers. 'You just have to get on with it and provide the best for customers. There is no doubt the snow had an impact, but if you lie back and become a victim to the snow, then you're not doing what we're here to do. Some [retailers] did better than others,' said King.

To consolidate their success, they opened 700,000 square feet of new stores and upgrades.

This is a clear example of the power of physical availability.

Source: Adapted from www.cityam.com/news-and-analysis/sainsbury
%ez%80%99s-sees-record-festive-sales

Industry insight

Oroton: Increasing physical availability in current and new markets

By Monica Orlovic

Australian fashion retailer Oroton is challenging the depressed retail market by reporting increased profits.

While most retailers in Australia are struggling to boost consumer spending, Oroton is defying the trend. David Jones, which is regarded as Australia's 'high end' department store, announced that its profits would drop considerably by as much as 40 per cent for the full 2011–12 financial year.

OrotonGroup stated a 4 per cent increase in net profits for the first half of the 2011–12 financial year (compared to the same time period in the previous year). Sales for this part of the year rose by 9 per cent.

OrotonGroup CEO Sally MacDonald claimed that the profit increases were achieved despite a very challenging retail environment.

What is Oroton doing to achieve such success?

The luxury retailer of handbags and accessories is focusing on growing its Asian markets and lowering costs within Australia.

'We believe the retail market in Australia is restructuring rather than in a cyclical downturn,'

MacDonald said (AAP, 2012). She announced that Oroton will continue to build its Asian prospects, as this market presents better growth opportunities.

Oroton revealed that its Asian business is growing and accounts for 10 per cent of its overall store network. OrotonGroup has opened eight new stores and closed one store across Australia and Asia so far this financial year. There are now sixty Oroton-branded stores trading in Australia and Asia, and thirty-two Ralph Lauren–branded stores in Australia (for which it holds an exclusive licence).

'We continue to roll out our directly operated Oroton stores in South-East Asia. In the last half we opened a further two stores in Malaysia (one close to the border with Singapore), and we have plans for further stores later this calendar year, with the next store opening in Kuala Lumpur in July,' MacDonald said (Stockdill, 2012).

Another factor contributing to Oroton's success is the exceptional performance of its online sales. Oroton.com saw a massive increase in sales of more than 60 per cent in comparison to the same time last year.

LEARNING OBJECTIVE
Understand and be able to explain the basic consumer repeat-buying patterns that apply to retailers

panel scanner data:
Data captured at the point of sale by scanning the barcodes of products.

EMPIRICAL LAWS OF SHOPPING

Marketing textbooks usually spend a good deal of time talking about brand choice and little time talking about the context within which these choices often occur—that is, in a shop. Until recently shopping behaviour had not been extensively studied. Researchers often interviewed shoppers, and **panel scanner data** allowed them to track what brands the shoppers bought, but little was known about the shopping trip itself. This has changed. In this section, we present nine empirical law-like patterns concerning shopping behaviours that have been observed in supermarkets, pharmacies, convenience stores, hardware stores and wine stores around the world. In describing these empirical laws and their implications we focus on grocery stores, but the laws can be applied to a wide range of store types. They concern purchase goals, mental and physical availability, limited time, many short trips, selective purchasing, top-selling items, colours and symbols, specials and set paths.

Purchase goals

The first empirical law is that *shoppers go to stores because the stores have something they want to buy*.

Implications: Shoppers do sometimes enjoy aspects of shopping, but they mainly shop because they have to in order to get the things they want. Almost everyone enters a store with a purchase goal in mind, which is very often a specific brand. Although this mental list does not preclude them from buying other things, it is the primary motivation for visiting the store. So stores are a means to an end, and few people visit them unless they want to buy something. This is good news for retailers because it means it is possible to get people to buy more: they will if they find things that they want. It also means it is possible to attract more people to the store; again, this will work if you can show them things that they want. This is why **retailer advertising** (appropriately) almost always features the products and services that retailers sell, while many service providers, such as management consultancies, banks and universities, too often forget to advertise their 'products'.

Another implication of this law is that the primary source of shopper dissatisfaction is not being able to find the product they wish to buy. Being out of stock or having a small range often reduces repeat business. A sure sign of a store in distress is a lack of stock; this in turn reduces the store's attractiveness to shoppers and its business woes become even worse (leaving the company even less money with which to buy stock).

> **retailer advertising:**
> Advertising by retailers about their products, offers and specials.

Mental and physical availability

The second empirical law is *that mental and physical availability largely determine store choice*.

Implications: Shoppers rarely go far out of their way and certainly seldom drive or walk past many rival retailers they know of in order to go to a particular store. However, they will go past stores that they do not think of. In choosing which (nearby) store to shop at, shoppers make substantial use of their memories, going where they recall they can get something, where they recall how to get there and where they can park. So retailers need to locate stores near customers and traffic flows of customers. This location imperative is something that retailers put a great deal of research into and tend to be very good at. But stores also need to advertise; they need to build memory structures. Branded chain stores are increasingly out-competing their rivals because shoppers notice and recognise them faster, due to their advertising and the fact that every store in the chain looks—is branded—the same.

Limited time

The third empirical law is that *shoppers only spend a certain amount of time in store*. They are very reluctant to increase this amount of time, but if they find that their shopping has taken less time than expected they may buy more.

Implications: In Chapter 2 we discussed how consumers were busy leading their lives. This shows in their shopping behaviour. While the amount of money that a customer spends on a particular trip can and does vary a great deal from one trip to another, the time they spend in store is less elastic. When a shopping trip is slower than expected, shoppers curtail their spending so as not to go far 'over time'—understandably, they have other things they need to do that day. When a trip is easier and faster, shoppers tend to buy more. If it is faster than expected then they have some spare time, and if it is easier to see things they want, then they are more likely to buy them. All of this usually happens unconsciously for the shopper, and the end result is that there is a relationship between shopping convenience and total store sales: the easier and hence faster that consumers find what they want, the more they buy (as illustrated in Figure 8.1).

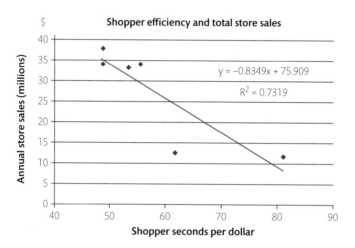

●●● FIGURE 8.1 THE FASTER SHOPPERS SPEND, THE HIGHER TOTAL STORE SALES

Source: Sorensen, H (2009) *Inside the Mind of the Shopper*, Pearson Education Inc., Upper Saddle River, NJ, Figure 1.4.

Many short trips

The fourth empirical law is that *people make many short shopping trips and fewer longer shopping trips.* The most common shopping trips (about 15 per cent of them) are to buy a single item, even in supermarkets. In fact half of all trips result in five or fewer items being bought (see Figure 8.2).

Implications: Retailers need to provide for these quick shopping trips by making it highly convenient for shoppers to find the few items that they are looking for. Even large stock-up shopping trips involve hunting for relatively few items out of the tens of thousands in a store. A huge implication of this law is that stores should be extremely careful of (and try to avoid) moving the location of items. Product categories should be as visible as possible, and the store should be full of useful navigational aids.

Apple currently holds the record for the fastest roll-out of stores to achieve US$1 billion sales per annum, and its stores continue to generate some of the very highest sales revenue per square metre. It is worth noticing that Apple stores are extremely open, with no aisles impeding shoppers' view. From almost anywhere in the store it is possible to see every product category.

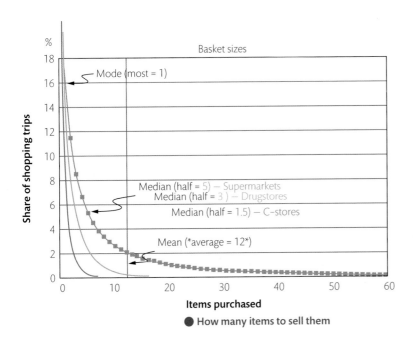

● ● ● **FIGURE 8.2** NUMBER OF ITEMS SHOPPERS BUY

The very successful Costco in the United States uses a similar strategy. 'DaveKing' (2012) writes:

> I wonder when supermarkets or other stores will mimic the Costco strategy for store layout? Costco has a regularly changing center-store which promotes 'treasure hunting' and impulse purchasing while the perimeter aisles stay relatively constant. Shoppers expect and enjoy the changing center store at Costco but they also have the comfort of knowing that the 'outer store' categories such as cereal, paper, frozen foods, etc, will be in the same place from trip to trip. Perhaps a Costco inspired store layout can generate new interest and increased sales in supermarkets that have looked pretty much the same (and lost share) over the last twenty or thirty years?

Selective purchasing

The fifth empirical law is that *a typical household buys only 300 to 400* **stock-keeping units (SKUs)** from a supermarket in an entire year.

Implications: Shoppers are clearly very selective and very loyal, repeat-purchasing the same items again and again, without a great degree of variety seeking. Given that supermarkets usually stock between 30,000 and 50,000 items, every shopping trip involves 'looking for a needle in a haystack'. The clutter and large choice of stores is one reason why consumers adopt loyalty heuristics—it speeds shopping and reduces **cognitive effort**. Because of their loyalty, shoppers usually know where to find what they are looking for. Again, the implication is that stores should avoid changing where items are located in the store.

◢ **stock-keeping units (SKUs):** Each product stocked by a store; for example, different pack sizes or flavours of a particular brand.

◢ **cognitive effort:** Mental effort, using reasoning, intuition or perception.

Top-selling items

The sixth empirical law is that *while a typical supermarket sells 30,000 to 50,000 items, the top-selling 1000 items will make up about half of the supermarket's sales.*

Implications: This is true for most if not all retailers: while they sell (almost) everything they stock, some items sell in far higher volumes than others. This means these items are in more shoppers' repertoires; for example, bananas are such an item in Australian supermarkets. This concentration effect in item popularity gives stores some ability to help shoppers to buy quickly, by ensuring that the really high-selling items are in the paths taken by most shoppers and very easy to see.

A mistaken strategy adopted by some retailers is to hide these top-selling items in faraway places within the stores. The logic is that customers will hunt for these items and along the way see other things and buy those. It turns out that any such gains are more than off-set by reduced sales of the high-selling items. One reason is that on any 'hunt' shoppers are extremely single-minded and rarely see anything other than what they are looking for. The other reason is that while these items are higher selling it doesn't mean that shoppers can't necessarily do without them (or buy them next time, or in another store). If they don't see an item easily then it often doesn't make it onto their mental list. It is extremely frustrating not to be able to find something that you want—which is bad for the store. But there is no frustration in not seeing something that you might have bought but which wasn't in your mind—this also is bad for the store. The lesson is that successful retailing is about making popular items very easy to be seen and bought by lots of people; together, these improvements will generate more sales.

Colours and symbols

eye-tracking studies: A research methodology that determines which part of an advertisement or packaging consumers look at, by tracking the pattern of their eye movements.

distinctive assets: Non-brand-name elements that are unique to the brand and can evoke the brand in the memory of many consumers (for example, characters such as Louie the Fly for Mortein).

merchandise: Goods bought and sold.

The seventh empirical law is that *shoppers read very little in store—instead they react to colours and symbols.*

Implications: Human beings are very visually oriented. Compared to our primate 'cousins', we rely far more on visual information, and contrary to popular management texts (such as Lindstrom, 2008) we make little navigational use of other senses such as smell. When in a store there is an enormous amount to read, but eye-tracking studies show that shoppers are very selective about what they read. Reading slows them down, dragging out the shopping trip. So, instead, shoppers learn to navigate using colours and symbols that allow them to find an item on a cluttered shelf quickly.

Smart marketers are doing their own **eye-tracking studies** and redesigning shelf layouts and packaging so that consumers can 'read' this information more quickly. Very often this involves making the brand's **distinctive assets** more prominent and using pictures, logos and colour to quickly guide the shopper.

Smart retailers are using colours and symbols to make the store layout easier to understand, and easier for shoppers to be able to grasp the full range of **merchandise**.

Specials

The eighth empirical law is that *shoppers have been trained to buy specials*.

Implications: Shoppers like to save money, time and mental effort when shopping. Specials, especially when they are clearly flagged, allow shoppers to save all three. While, as you will learn in Chapter 9, price promotions are seldom seen by people who do not already have the brand in their repertoire, they reduce the cognitive effort needed to pick a brand from one's repertoire by simply taking the one on special. Navigational aids can do the same thing; for example a tag that points out the best selling item.

Set paths

The ninth empirical law is that *shoppers follow pathways of open space, and that the checkout is a magnet (they speed up towards it)*. Studies recording the paths that shoppers take through stores show a strong predilection for them to move into open space and to avoid narrow aisles.

Implications: Since it is difficult to make consumers alter their path, it is better to put the products where they go and make the products easy to see.

Case study
Changing nature of retail in China
By Mark Uncles

Retailing in China is changing rapidly, as people are increasingly living in cities and becoming wealthier. The size and potential of the Chinese market is also attracting retailers from overseas. Carrefour and Auchan, both from France, have sizeable presences, as do Walmart (United States) and Tesco (United Kingdom). Strong forces of convergence are at work, making Chinese retailing less distinguishable from international norms.

First and foremost, there is growing acceptance of modern retail formats. Hypermarkets and shopping malls look fresh and inviting, and in the urban hubs of China there is no shortage of customers willing to adapt to, and accept, new formats. This has not always been easy; consumers have had to learn new ways of going about such everyday tasks as buying goods and services. For instance, notwithstanding the fact that numbers of sales assistants

(who are often on commission) are more numerous in Chinese stores than is typical in the West, modern formats tend to require consumers to be willing to serve themselves (as at supermarkets and convenience stores) or make use of user-directed technologies (as is the case with online retailing) (Liu et al., 2008).

If these trends gather momentum, the story of retailing in China could mirror the history of the decline in 'Mom & Pop' stores in the West. However, the jury is out. Even in large cities, shoppers continue to patronise small outlets and wet markets, as well as hypermarkets and supermarkets (Uncles & Kwok, 2009). Urban densities and the reliance on public transport are such that travelling long distances to shop is not practical and this favours local or neighborhood-based retailing and argues against out-of-town developments. Small-scale retailing and improvisation persist—you rarely have to travel far to find a bicycle repair shop, a family-operated fast food outlet or a neighbourhood hairdresser in a Chinese city.

LEARNING OBJECTIVE
Be able to identify major recent trends in retailing; what they have meant for suppliers, retailers and consumers; and how these trends will continue in the future

negative inflation: Falling prices, resulting in growth in sales not occurring.

THE FUTURE OF RETAILING

Retailing is continuing to change, and this change creates many marketing opportunities.

In recent decades enormous progress has been made in making supply chains more efficient and effective. By improving information flows back and forth between factories and cash registers, less money is tied up in stock sitting in warehouses. It also means stores stock fewer out-of-fashion items that don't sell. This greater efficiency has lowered costs, and hence lowered prices (in supermarkets, white goods and electronics stores many categories have **negative inflation** over the past ten years). However, the outcome of these supply chain enhancements that has most caught the eye of the public has been in the rise of fashion retailers like Spain's Zara and Japan's UNIQLO who deliver new fashions from the catwalks to the street in record time and at low prices.

Elsewhere, global delivery systems have allowed factories to be located where there is low-cost labour and tremendous scale. Chinese manufacturing combined with Walmart's scale of ordering hasn't just benefited Chinese workers and Walmart shoppers; other retailers and their customers all around the world have also benefited.

The internet has facilitated this supply chain revolution, but the internet's most visible effect has been online shopping. For goods that can be delivered digitally, the internet has the potential to completely replace physical stores. This replacement has practically already happened for music, and books and movies are following rapidly.

It was originally thought that the internet would allow manufacturers to sell directly to end-users, as in the case of computer company Dell. However, many of the largest internet retailers are the traditional 'bricks and mortar' retailers (such as Woolworths and Tesco) while the other internet giants (Amazon, iTunes and eBay) are retailers, not manufacturers.

Traditional, physical 'bricks and mortar' stores offer a key advantage: providing customers with the opportunity to inspect the goods close up before buying. This is why many consumers prefer not to buy products such as clothing and fresh fruit and vegetables online. Convenience and speed, followed by lower prices, are the main benefits that encourage people to shop online. This is why online shopping for groceries grew very slowly at first, because many early grocery websites and their deliveries weren't convenient. Shopping websites have improved greatly, and shoppers' fear of making payments online have much reduced, yet many 'bricks and mortar' stores still offer greater convenience—so long as they continue to do so, they will survive.

It's worth noting that Apple, which is an extremely successful online retailer (selling hardware, software, music, movies and books), is also opening many new Apple stores around the world.

So, predicting the future of retail is very difficult, but competition is only likely to increase, with even rural stores facing online competitors. Consequently, retailers need better qualified managers and a greater understanding of marketing. Meanwhile, everything looks good for the shopper, because whatever happens greater choice, lower prices and greater convenience seem guaranteed.

CONCLUSION

It sounds self-evident, but the retailer exists—survives—by making it easy for shoppers to buy things. Knowing some empirical laws of how shoppers buy helps the retailer to ensure that stores are easy to visit and easy to buy from. New forms of competition such as e-retailing have made retailing even more competitive than before. For traditional 'bricks and mortar' retailers to survive against each other—and against online retailing—they have to keep finding ways to offer range, convenience and value.

▼ CRITICAL REFLECTION

Retailer power is seen as a huge threat by many suppliers. Many farmers, for example, say that retailers putting prices down makes farming unsustainable. What are the pros and cons of retailer power?

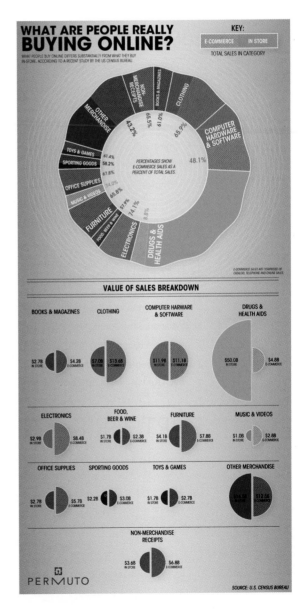

● ● ● **FIGURE 8.3** WHAT ARE PEOPLE REALLY BUYING ONLINE?

Source: Buysight, 2010

08

SUMMARY

- Advanced economies have very large retail sector, employing huge numbers of people.

- One of the most powerful concepts in retailing, indeed in business, over the past 150 years is the chain store.

- There are orderly patterns in shopper penetration and purchase frequency metrics for retailers—the double jeopardy law and the duplication of purchase law.

- There are known 'laws' of shopper behaviour just like there are laws in chemistry or physics. Everyone involved in retailing or supplying to retailers should know about these regular patterns.

- Advances in information technology have made supply chains for retailers and retailer themselves much more efficient. Retailers are now more active in strategically sourcing suppliers with huge-scale economies. This efficiency has resulted in lower prices for consumers.

REVISION QUESTIONS

1   Should a retailer try to lengthen the amount of time people spend in its stores? Why or why not?

2   What does the duplication of purchase law tell us about how a retailer can grow its market share?

3   Why do chain retailers tend to do better than independents?

4   Many people see the digital revolution as being bad for traditional retailers, but what advantages have there been for traditional retailers in the digital revolution?

FURTHER READING

Davies, C (2012) 'Tesco sales slump part of consumer revolution changing the way we shop', *The Guardian*, 12 January, retrieved 10 May 2012 from <www.guardian.co.uk/business/2012/jan/12/tesco-consumer-revolution-internet-shopping>.

Gilmore, P (2005) 'Grocery stores and supermarkets', *Encyclopedia of Chicago*, retrieved 10 May 2012 from <http://encyclopedia.chicagohistory.org/pages/554.html>.

Levinson, M (2011b) 'A history of chain stores, and their enemies: Echoes', *Bloomberg*, 26 November, retrieved 10 May 2012 from <www.bloomberg.com/news/2011-11-25/a-history-of-chain-stores-and-their-enemies-echoes.html>.

Mercer, C (2005) 'Tesco Asda price cuts pressure consumers', *William Reed Business Media SAS*, 11 April, retrieved 10 May 2012 from <www.bakeryandsnacks.com/Markets/Tesco-Asda-price-cuts-pressure-producers>.

Pilgrim, D (2008) *Real Life Guides: Retail*, 2nd edn, Trotman, United Kingdom.

Schell, O (2011) 'How Walmart is changing China', *Atlantic Magazine*, December, retrieved 10 May 2012 from < www.theatlantic. com/magazine/archive/2011/12/how-walmart-is-changing-china/8709/>.

WEBLINKS

Herb Sorensen:
www.herbsorensen.com/herbsorensenarticles.html

Oroton:
www.orotongroup.com

◢ Major case study

Zara—Just getting started

By Kellie Newstead

As the rest of the Australian retailing economy was flailing in April 2011, reporting lost consumer confidence and increasing online shopping, the Zara Sydney store was just gearing up to open its doors, on all three levels of the new Westfield 1400 m² store.

And open they did, amid shopper mayhem. Customers queued for hours and were quick to swipe items before they could make it to the shelf. Some estimates quote 80 per cent ($1.2 million) worth of stock being sold on the first day's opening in Sydney. A few months later, the Melbourne Bourke Street store opened, with hundreds of people lining to get in.

So how do they do it? Zara has a unique business model that essentially boasts good quality, on-trend merchandise and affordable prices, resulting in staggering profits. Each year, the reported 200 designers on staff put out around 20,000 items. The global distribution centre in Spain moves around 2.5 million items per week, and nothing stays in the warehouse for longer than seventy-two hours at a time.

Chief Communications Officer Jesus Echevarria is quoted as saying the strategy of the fast-fashion retailers is 'the complete opposite' to the traditional model. He says, 'it's a matter of customer feedback. We are pretty quick to react.'

Zara puts the success down to using customer feedback to design their range. However, it is the business model that incorporates speed rather than unique innovation that sets Zara apart from the rest.

It is reported that Zara uses customer feedback and a daily sales analysis from all 1830 stores to compile manufacturing plans within forty-eight hours. These plans are then communicated to 1500 factories in Asia, Spain and Brazil—the garments are then delivered to stores within three weeks. This means that Zara stores can be replenished with small-batch fashion choices twice a week.

Zara stocks many different products: apparel for men, women and kids, plus bags, accessories and shoes. While Zara has at times been criticised for copying major designers, they insist that it is the customer-driven focus that gives shape to the products that they design worldwide.

From humble beginnings in 1975, when the first Zara store opened on a street in A Coruña, Spain, Zara now operates in eighty-two countries, with online shopping also available. Retailers like Zara represent a new wave of retailing, bringing production even closer to customer demands.

Questions

1   What can competitors learn from Zara?

2   How is Zara succeeding if they don't have a unique product to offer?

3   Where can Zara go from here?

Zara has a unique business model that essentially boasts good quality, on-trend merchandise and affordable prices, resulting in staggering profits.

Practitioner profile

Neil Retallick, Chief Executive Officer, Friendly Pharmacy (Sydney)

One of my earliest jobs was working as a cosmetics buyer for Myer. It was my first introduction to marketing, and ultimately it changed my career. In a department store, the role of the buying team is to decide which brands should be put on the shelves. This involves deciding which brands you think the customers will be interested in, and then negotiating with those companies. So, as a cosmetics buyer, I met regularly with the marketing people from most of the big-name international cosmetics brands.

Essentially, all of the brand managers wanted the same thing—to sell more products. But what varied significantly was *how* they planned to do it. I wasn't surprised that each brand had a different marketing strategy—that's the nature of competition—but these were theoretical differences. It seemed that everyone had a different understanding of how consumers behave and how marketing works. Some of what they were saying sounded plausible and rational, but a lot seemed contrived and convenient—there was a large grey gulf in between. I guess I found it intriguing—and I needed to find out which was which. So, I enrolled in a marketing program.

Now, after all these years of working in retail and consumer goods marketing, I can't say that I've uncovered the whole truth. I've certainly discovered that there are a lot of myths out there, but also that there is a lot of evidenced knowledge and that using this wisely can really make an impact on your brand and businesses growth.

The best jobs that I've had have certainly been with those organisations that invest in marketing research and appreciate the huge rewards that can be extracted from it. In consumer goods marketing, where brand strength comes from sales growth, knowing what customers want is crucial. Customer analysis should drive decisions about which products you develop, what they look like and which shelf they sit on.

In my job, I oversee development of marketing plans, promotional campaigns, websites, customer magazines, packaging, new products and product ranges. I also make a lot of decisions about media channels, pricing, distribution channels, export markets, acquisitions and product launches. For every one of these activities and decisions, I have to call on my knowledge of customer behaviour and understanding of the retail process.

In my field, being successful means finding new insights into consumer behaviour and learning things that my competitors don't know, then applying that knowledge every day in my work. I am just as intrigued by marketing now as I was when I started. The wonderful thing is that this curiosity has helped me to build a great career. I also know that there's so much more to discover: that's what keeps me excited.

09

PRICING AND DISCOUNTING

DAG BENNETT AND JOHN SCRIVEN

Iliad undercuts its rivals

By Dag Bennett

In France, the mobile phone services market has long been dominated by three main suppliers: Orange, part of France Telecom; SFR, owned by Vivendi; and Bouygues. These companies compete with each other through advertising and slightly differentiated product offerings. What they rarely do, however, is challenge each other on pricing. As a result, all three were comfortably profitable in the early twenty-first century.

In 2012, that changed with the entrance of Free Mobile, a new mobile telephone services brand of Iliad, headed by Xavier Niel. On 10 January 2012, Free introduced a new mobile service plan that offered unlimited domestic and international calls, SMS and mobile data for €19.99 per month. While it was difficult to compare this price directly with the plans of other suppliers (deliberate obfuscation makes shopping more difficult) it appeared that the plan was about half the price of similar offerings at the time.

Free Mobile directly challenged the market leaders, who had built up one of the most expensive mobile markets in Europe. In 2011, mobile users in France spent an average of €392 (about US$500) compared with €181 in Germany and €167 in Portugal, according to the research firm Gartner. Free Mobile was able to offer a low price by building on its existing broadband and television service network. In order to obtain the licence to become the fourth big operator

in France, Free Mobile had to overcome fierce lobbying from France Telecom and the other operators, who were worried about Iliad's reputation for cutting prices. In fact, Xavier Niel seems to have a penchant for upsetting his complacent rivals by undercutting them whenever he can.

At the press conference that launched the service, Niel said, 'You now have the chance to teach your operator a lesson. You have two choices: you can sign up with Free, or you can call your operator and ask them to match our rates.'

In response to this assault, Orange began sending text messages to its subscribers, reassuring them that it was checking to make sure they had the appropriate calling plan for their usage. Meanwhile, there was some protection for the existing suppliers in the fact that their customers were locked into long-term contracts. Free Mobile, on the other hand, does not require a minimum subscription period.

Marketing and customer service could also be challenging for Free: while Orange, SFR and Bouygues have networks of shops across France, Free plans to operate only a handful of stores, relying mostly on internet sales. This is core to the low-price strategy that relies on the industry-leading low cost base.

> Free Mobile directly challenged the market leaders, who had built up one of the most expensive mobile markets in Europe.

INTRODUCTION

Price is one of the elements that consumers consider in making a choice. It is part of a brand's position; for example signalling quality or functionality as well as the cost of producing it.

But price can also be varied independently of the rest of the brand attributes; for example by offering a special reduced price where it can be assumed that the rest of the brand's attributes are unchanged. Price is not often the all-important factor for consumers. The cheapest brand is very rarely the biggest in any market. Most consumers spend little time considering price and have poor recall of the price they have paid for an item. Nevertheless, when price is varied, volume tends to change in line with basic economic theory (price up means volume down), but by different amounts in different circumstances.

This chapter considers what marketers need to know about pricing to make better price-related decisions: how to set a price, and what will happen when price changes relative to the competitive environment.

LEARNING OBJECTIVES

After reading this chapter you should:

- understand the role of price in the marketing mix
- be able to differentiate between cost-based and demand-based methods of pricing
- be able to calculate price elasticity and use it to evaluate pricing decisions
- know circumstances where elasticity is consistently larger or smaller
- understand why temporary price cuts (price promotions) are potentially damaging.

CHAPTER OUTLINE

///

KEY TERMS

direct cost pricing

fixed costs (or overheads)

full (total or absorption) cost pricing

functional (or realistic) range
     of prices

marginal cost pricing

market-based pricing

optimisation

price elasticity

temporary price promotion

value-based pricing

variable costs

SETTING PRICES IN AN IMPERFECT WORLD

◢ **LEARNING OBJECTIVE**
Understand the role of
price in the marketing mix

The price placed on a good or service has a direct effect on sales revenue (revenue = volume × price), and therefore the profit or loss of a firm (profit = revenue – costs). Price is the only element of the marketing mix that has such immediate effect on the bottom line. There are many pressures and temptations to change price, which seems easy to do—after all, it is only a number on a price tag. Usually the pressure is to reduce prices in order to help raise sales volumes. In line with standard economic theory, lowering prices generally does increase sales, but it is also likely to reduce profits, as we demonstrate below in the section 'Marketing knowledge of price elasticity'. Let's start by looking at how we arrive at prices.

In a modern competitive market economy where people have discretionary spending power and can choose between an ever-widening range of goods from competing producers, variables such as price are of great importance. These days, sophisticated markets and imperfect competition are the norm. That is, most categories have large numbers of both buyers and sellers of various sorts, and consumers have incomplete knowledge of the alternatives. Some of these sellers are very large and have diverse product lines, high market share, numerous brands and a great deal of market power, especially over price, which means they are able to withstand pressure to reduce prices.

With all products and services there is an upper and a lower price level, bounded by what customers are willing to pay at the upper end, and by the costs of supplying the product at the lower end. Outside this range, the company would simply not be viable, and so the goal is to determine the **functional (or realistic) range of prices**. Highly competitive firms tend to offer products and brands that are very much like each other and also competitively priced.

◢ **functional (or realistic) range of prices:** The highest and the lowest prices for a category of closely substitutable goods, found in the normal course of trade.

This is because for any company it is generally less risky to offer what the market can be seen to be buying—in the form of competitors' offerings—than it is to offer something very different, or even innovative. So, to be competitive firms tend to copy each other, and this applies to pricing as well.

This is why in many categories there are not just similar products on offer, but those products have similar prices as well. For instance, a visit to an electronics shop reveals dozens of very similar televisions at a price of $399, and other clusters of sets at $499 or $999. This is because manufacturers seek to be competitive with each other at as many product or price levels as possible; many markets have price bands or price tiers.

As a result, price setting for many organisations, especially smaller ones, is relatively straightforward. They map out the range of prices in a particular category, and then see if they can produce profitably within that range. Leading firms or those that intend to offer new products face a more complex task in which they must:

1　set an initial price structure for new products

2　consider how to react to competitive prices

3　consider distribution channel margins, stock turnover and inter-channel competition

4　forecast the sensitivity of resellers and retailers to prices and margins

5　estimate the relative sensitivity to price of similar offerings in different segments or related categories

6　organise prices for products with interrelated production costs

7　arrange prices for products differing in cost and profitability

8　determine the appropriate timing, frequency and amount of price changes, including promotion, using temporary price-related changes (cutting price, 'buy one get one free' and so on).

In practice, pricing for large organisations tends not to be handled by upper management but by lower-level and middle managers because they have a more intimate knowledge of market conditions. However, price-setting must also consider priorities laid out by top management, such as:

1　profit targets

2　whether the company intends to communicate a corporate image that is closely identified with price levels, such as a reputation for high quality

3　the company's short-term and long-term objectives for profitability and how these are to be applied to products or product groups, and whether the same policies are to be applied to home markets as overseas

4　the strategic vision for different products—penetration, market share maintenance or cash generation? And to what extent short-term profit can be traded off against strategic or long-term goals

5　the company's views on responding to competitive price pressures such as discounters or price-related promotions.

 CRITICAL REFLECTION

1　Why do you think there are upper and lower limits to what a consumer is willing to pay for a product?

2　What do you think determines the levels at which price tiers emerge? Why might a firm offer a very highly priced product variant even though it will sell few of them?

3　With which aspects of price management are middle managers more concerned compared to senior managers? Why is that?

STARTING AT THE FLOOR: THE COST BASE

All companies have to produce revenue that recovers their costs, otherwise they are trading illegally and risk going bankrupt. Hence, a common way of working out a price consists of estimating the cost of producing a product and adding a mark-up on that cost to cover other costs that have not been included (such as costs that are difficult to allocate directly to production, such as the Managing Director's salary), plus a profit. In practice, this method can be complex.

Costs can be classified as fixed or variable.

Fixed costs (or overheads) are fees and expenses that a company incurs to be in business. They do not vary with the level of sales. These costs include the cost for the business to house itself (such as rents), wages for staff, factory or 'plant' and facility maintenance. Fixed costs can be regarded as fixed in the short term (a year, perhaps), but over longer periods an organisation can change accommodation and hire or fire people, and therefore change its underlying cost structure.

Variable costs are entirely incurred in the product or service being provided. For example, a company making mobile phone handsets will have costs of making or acquiring the components that go into a phone, and the direct labour cost of assembling the bits (see Table 9.1). Variable costs are also known as direct costs. For profit and loss calculations, they are usually given as a cost per unit. The same is true of services, where the costs directly attributable to providing each unit of service will be mostly made up of the labour required to provide the service.

fixed costs (or overheads): Costs that are not dependent on the level of goods and services produced by the business. They are generally tied to time periods, such as salaries paid per month, or rents paid quarterly or yearly.

variable costs: Costs that change in proportion to the activity level of the business.

●●● **TABLE 9.1** VARIABLE COSTS FOR A MOBILE PHONE

ITEM	$
Direct labour cost	1.00
Plastic casing	2.00
LED screen	1.50
Handset buttons	0.50
Electronic components	3.50
SIM card	1.50
Total	**10.00**

In theory, the variable costs per phone will be the same whether 10 are produced or 100. Of course, in real situations this may not be true if a company produces much larger numbers of items so that it acquires enough bargaining power with suppliers to drive down component costs.

Information about fixed and variable costs should be known inside the company. That is, the accounting department will track fixed costs, and gather information from the production or service department on variable costs. This is one reason that a great many organisations practise cost-based pricing—all the information is on hand and accessible.

While both fixed and variable costs are simple in concept, they still involve managerial decisions. For example, suppose the mobile phone manufacturer has fixed costs of $500. If it then produces 100 phones, it would allocate 1/100th of the total overhead costs to each phone:

$$\$500/100 = \$5 \text{ per phone}$$

As a result, the cost of production for each phone for this company will be the variable cost of $10 (from Table 9.1) plus $5 of fixed costs = $15 per unit.

Suppose the company decides to produce 200 phones instead. In this case, the variable costs per phone do not change, but the fixed costs are now spread across twice as many units, so each unit now receives only 1/200th of the fixed costs:

$$\$500/200 = \$2.50 \text{ per phone}$$

Therefore the total cost for each phone is now $10 plus $2.50 = $12.50.

Two things should be clear from this example. First, when fixed costs are allocated over a larger number of units, the cost per unit is driven down. This is core to achieving economies of scale and explains why companies pursue volume increases. It also provides an explanation for the relentless pursuit of cost reductions.

Second, it should also be obvious that one of the main problems with cost-based pricing is that the end price per unit varies with the number of units produced. In practice, this may not matter very much for very high volumes of production in which fixed costs are a very small portion of total costs, but for organisations with a high proportion of fixed costs, the total number of units produced will be critical to cost calculations.

Another problem arises when a company has to decide how to allocate fixed costs across quite different products. For example, suppose the phone manufacturer makes 100 mid-level phones with a variable cost of $10, and 100 more basic models with a variable cost of $6 per unit. If the firm has fixed costs of $500, then it may decide to allocate costs evenly per unit:

$$\$500/200 = \$2.50 \text{ per unit}$$

The effect on total costs is shown in Table 9.2.

●●● **TABLE 9.2** COSTS FOR MID-LEVEL VERSUS BASIC MOBILE PHONES

	MID-LEVEL PHONE	BASIC PHONE
Variable cost	$10.00	$6.00
Fixed cost allocation	$2.50	$2.50
Total cost	**$12.50**	**$8.50**

Alternatively, the company might decide to allocate fixed cost in proportion to the variable costs, so the more expensive model carries about 65 per cent or $350/100 = $3.50 per phone, and the less expensive model takes 35 per cent or $150/100 = $1.50 per phone. In this case, the final total cost for the mid-range phone would be $10 plus $3.50 = $13.50, while the basic model would be $6 plus $1.50 = $7.50. The phone maker might decide on proportional allocation because it allows it to put a slightly lower price on the basic model. In any case, the decision results in quite different costs per phone. If the company uses a standard mark-up, this will have a big effect on the end price.

COST-BASED PRICING

If a company only produces one product, then all costs, fixed or variable, have to be covered by the revenue from that product. But the more usual case is that a company produces more than one product or variant of a product, so costs have to be allocated to individual products to produce a cost base. Three main techniques are used:

1   full (total or absorption) cost pricing
2   direct cost pricing
3   marginal cost pricing.

Full cost pricing

Full (total or absorption) cost pricing attempts to apportion all company expenses, whether they can be traced directly to a product or not. Apportionment of fixed costs generally follows some 'reasonable' method, but is in essence arbitrary—a managerial decision. If all the overheads are not allocated to a product, there is a danger that revenue will fall short of costs in total, which would be unacceptable. While this approach appears to avoid the danger of incomplete recovery of overheads, it does not take account of market conditions, nor of the fact that some products will be more price sensitive than others. As a result, use of full cost pricing tends to overprice some products and underprice others. In the oil industry, for example, the production of one good is inextricably linked with others—petrol, kerosene, propane gas and heavy fuel oil are all distilled from crude oil, and oil distillates and by-products go into ink, crayons, bubble gum, dishwashing liquid, plastics, DVDs and many other goods. So, there are major difficulties in allocating joint costs to particular products (this also goes some way to explain why changes in the price of oil affect all manner of goods).

That said, this method, or something quite close to it, is very widely used—especially by smaller organisations that do not have the time and resources to devote to more complicated pricing approaches. Instead, every product or every quote for service is priced according to the same equation. The equation is essentially direct costs (of the product or project) plus a proportion of fixed costs (an additional percentage mark-up for profit might also be added at this point). For example, a market research company might calculate a price for carrying out a survey by costing the hours worked on the project by staff designing the questionnaire, contacting the respondents, collecting the information and processing it, then adding a proportion of the cost of running the office, developing new business, advertising and so on (costs that are necessary for the business, but not directly related to the project). Companies offering professional services (such as law firms, architects, advertising or research agencies) typically use this approach, and rarely offer discounts or other sorts of pricing flexibility. The result is that they have very similar prices when they offer to provide similar services.

This is worth remembering when as a marketer you are buying a marketing service. If an advertising agency or market research agency quotes a very different price from others, it is almost invariably because they are going to provide a different service, so a cheap price means they are missing out on something (perhaps by accident or perhaps the firm interpreted your brief differently). So check before you grab that bargain!

◢ **LEARNING OBJECTIVE**
Be able to differentiate between cost-based and demand-based methods of pricing

◢ **full (total or absorption) cost pricing:** A method of accounting for costs that includes the full or total cost of manufacturing a product or providing a service. Costs of materials and labour and all manufacturing overheads (fixed and variable) are also included.

Direct cost pricing

direct cost pricing:
A method of accounting for costs that identifies all costs that can be associated with a product or service.

The **direct cost pricing** approach attempts to include only those costs that are directly incurred and that could be avoided in the medium or long term if the particular product were discontinued. Such costs may include factory costs, selling or marketing costs and expenses such as research and development (R&D), or distribution costs that are specific to a product or product range. Both fixed and variable costs are included. This method seems similar to full cost pricing, but the difference is that no allocation of fixed costs that are shared with other products is made. For example, if a product has a dedicated production line, those costs will be included in the direct costing. But the costs of warehousing that are shared across products will not be allocated.

One of the disadvantages of this method is that it ignores the distinction between fixed and variable costs. This makes it much harder to know how changes in volume will affect costs and therefore profit.

Marginal cost pricing

marginal cost pricing:
A method of accounting that focuses on determining the change in cost (marginal cost) of producing one extra unit. This can be useful in arriving at a cost for a tiny change in quantity at a given level of production—that is, the cost per unit.

Marginal cost pricing is known as variable cost pricing in some countries. In this method, emphasis is placed on separating costs into two main classes: fixed and variable. The marginal cost is then the cost of producing one extra unit of the product; that is, the variable cost at that level of production. If a price higher than this marginal cost is achieved, the revenue from the volume becomes a 'contribution' towards recovery of fixed costs, overheads and profit.

This method has advantages in its ability to allow different prices to be set for different slices of business. Rather than attempt to recover fixed and variable costs in proportion with every unit sold, marginal cost pricing enables fixed costs to be recovered over a portion of the volume. Additional volumes can be given lower prices, with any revenue above the variable costs going towards profit without needing to contribute to fixed costs. Profit/volume sensitivity is particularly important where the level of fixed costs is high. High fixed costs indicate a marginal level of price above which a sales order is preferable to leaving plant idle. But selling a bit less will quickly lead to overall losses, because revenue will soon fail to cover the fixed costs.

▼ CRITICAL REFLECTION

1   What is the difference between fixed and variable costs, and why is it useful to distinguish between them in making pricing decisions?

2   What are the advantages and disadvantages of the different kinds of cost pricing?

The two main drawbacks of marginal costing are that there are often practical difficulties in segregating fixed and variable expenses, and that such a segregation is only valid for specified levels of output and time. There is also a danger that if every price decision is taken on the basis of marginal cost, fixed expenses and profit will not be adequately recovered. That is, once fixed costs are covered, any revenue above marginal costs is profitable, but the danger is that volume achieved at a price based on marginal costs may be at the expense of volume at full cost, and then total costs will not be covered.

Elders Rural Services: Developing a unique method for price setting

Elders is Australia's leading rural and regional company. Elders has grown significantly over the last 170 years and now operates in three core business areas (rural services, forestry and automotive) and offers a large range of associated products and services within those areas. Rural Services (which includes financial and real estate services) is the largest and most important part of the company, employing almost 2500 people and operating both in Australia and overseas. Years of experience have made Elders one of the most trusted brands in providing products and services to Australian farmers.

The marketing team for Elders Rural Services was asked to develop a new pricing system for selling farm supplies, with the aim of increased annual profits for the firm. The pricing system needed to make sure that the Elders products maintained a competitive market position (not significantly more expensive or cheaper than competitor prices) and also that the profit margin was maximised.

Deciding on a pricing strategy is difficult for a large firm like Elders. All commonly used price-setting methods have advantages but are not suitable for all products; a method that might work perfectly for one product could be completely unsuitable for another product. It's particularly problematic for big firms such as Elders that offer a large range of products that vary significantly on important factors such as consumer demand, level of competition and power of suppliers. Of course, it is possible to use different pricing methods for different products, but it makes pricing reviews and performance comparisons much more difficult.

To avoid the problems related to selecting just one of the common methods, or trying to use several at once, the Elders team came up with a unique pricing system. For each product, an analysis is conducted focusing on the potential value of the product for clients and the product pricing sensitivity (elasticity of demand). The system also gathers ongoing feedback from different sales branches about competitor prices to make sure that Elders prices are in line with the alternatives available on the market (this stage is particularly important because they change continuously). Then a price is set based on all the information that is gathered. The same system works for every product and it also has the benefit of flexibility—prices can be reviewed and revised regularly as market conditions change.

Since the implementation of the new pricing system, Elders' profit margin has increased by 2 per cent without any added cost to the firm. Because farm supplies have relatively low profit margins, the 2 per cent improvement was a great result for Elders that has led to a significant uplift in earnings.

REVENUE AND PROFIT

At its simplest, revenue can be calculated as price per unit × the number of units sold. Suppose the phone maker we've been discussing sells its mid-range model for $18 (using a standard mark-up of 30 per cent, with rounding) and the basic model for $12. If the company sells all that it produces (100 of each), then revenue will be $3000, as shown in Table 9.3.

●●● **TABLE 9.3** REVENUE IF ALL MOBILE PHONES ARE SOLD

Mid-range model	100 × $18 = $1800
Basic model	100 × $12 = $1200
Total sales revenue	**$3000**

We can work out the profit figure for the company by subtracting costs from the total revenue figure of $3000. The costs are shown in Table 9.4.

●●● **TABLE 9.4** COST OF PRODUCING 100 MID-RANGE PHONES AND 100 BASIC PHONES

COSTS	$
Mid-range model	100 × $10 = $1000
Basic model	100 × $6 = $600
Subtotal: variable costs	*$1600*
Fixed costs	*$500*
Total costs	**$2100**

Thus the profit can be worked out as:

Total sales revenue – Total costs = Profit

$$\$3000 - \$2100 = \$900$$

One of the ways companies evaluate their performance is by looking at the total amount of profit, which in this case is $900 for the year. This figure might be compared to previous years to give an indication of whether the firm is improving its results.

Profit margin

Another way of comparing the performance of the business is to look at profit margins, or the percentage of revenue made up of profits. For the mobile phone company, we would calculate the profit margin as follows

$$\text{(Total profit/revenue)} \times 100 = \text{Profit margin}$$
$$(\$900/\$3000) \times 100 = 30 \text{ per cent}$$

We can't tell whether this 30 per cent figure is good or bad by itself. But we can compare this to the previous year's performance to gauge whether the company is improving not just in terms of total profits but also in profitability; that is, the level of profit produced relative to the level of sales. This can be useful to monitor because it is possible for sales and total profits to increase but at the same time for the profit margin to decrease. In such a case, it might be that costs have grown too quickly, or that there are market pressures on prices, or that the company is simply not pricing its products appropriately. Margins may also be compared to those of other products and, if the information is available, to those of other companies as well.

The analysis of profit can be taken further and broken down by products. For example, the mid-range phone generated revenue of $1800, had direct costs of $1000, fixed costs of $350 and therefore generated profits of $1800 − ($1000 + $350) = $450. The same type of calculation for the basic model is: $1200 − ($600 + $150) = $450. In this case, both phones produce 50 per cent of the total company profits.

However, when we look at profit margin, the calculation separates out the profit and revenue for each model, and for the mid-range model, $450 profit divided by $1800 revenue = 25 per cent, while for the basic model it is $450/$1200 = 38 per cent. On this basis, the cheaper model seems to be more productive of profits and the company might decide to concentrate on its production rather than on the mid-level phone.

Remember, however, that the allocation of fixed costs was made in proportion to the variable costs. If, on the other hand, the fixed cost allocation was simply based on numbers produced (so $2.50 per phone), the calculation for profit margin would be $550/1800 × 100 = 31 per cent for the mid-range phone and $350/1200 × 100 = 29 per cent for the basic phone. In which case, the company might decide to concentrate on the mid-level model. This illustrates the real dilemmas that arise with cost allocation.

Despite the often arbitrary nature of cost allocations, cost pricing is popular with many organisations, across many industries. Partly this is because it relies on easily gathered and accessed internal information, as opposed to fuzzy external information, and partly because it gives an air of financial probity. In other words, it is a technique that looks to cover all the bases, and therefore financial managers like it. Marketers and salespeople, on the other hand, often feel that it inhibits their ability to either set competitive prices in the first place, or to negotiate later.

Case study
Santa Lucia Wholefoods: Product development decisions
By Elizabeth Gunner

Santa Lucia Wholefoods has been making dried pasta for fifteen years. They have always just produced and sold one product line: a standard dried pasta brand distributed at supermarkets in a range of shapes. Now, the company directors have decided to invest in producing a second product line so that they can increase company profits. The product development team are considering two options for the new line: luxury pastas or gluten-free pastas.

Currently, Santa Lucia Wholefoods sells 900,000 units of

standard pasta annually at $2.10 per pack. It is predicted that if they produced a luxury brand they would sell 500,000 units of it each year (at $4.60 per pack); if they produced a gluten-free brand they would sell 750,000 units (at $3.75 per pack). The variable costs per unit are $0.70 for standard pasta, $1.70 for luxury pasta and $1.50 for gluten-free pasta. The annual fixed costs for the company are $1,500,000.

	SCENARIO A		SCENARIO B	
	STANDARD	LUXURY	STANDARD	GLUTEN-FREE
Estimated sales (units)	900,000	500,000	900,000	750,000
Price per 500g pack	$2.10	$4.60	$2.10	$3.75
Variable cost per pack	$0.70	$1.70	$0.70	$1.50

Questions

1   Divide the list below into fixed and variable costs:

   a   flour for making the pasta

   b   rent of the factory

   c   wages for employees

   d   eggs for making the pasta

   e   machinery within the factory

   f   packaging for the products

   g   maintenance on machinery

   h   advertising expenses

2   Assuming that Santa Lucia Wholefoods achieves the predicted sales targets, what would the fixed cost allocation per unit be if they produced standard pasta and luxury pasta (scenario A)? What would the fixed cost allocation per unit be if they chose the gluten-free pasta instead of the luxury pasta (scenario B)? (Note: Fixed costs should be allocated evenly for all pasta units sold.)

3   Calculate the sales revenue for both products in both scenarios.

4   Which scenario would give a greater total profit for the firm?

5   For both scenarios calculate the profit margin for each product.

MARKET-BASED PRICING

Up until this point, the phone company we've been discussing has been inwardly focused on the information it has on hand. It produces phones and assumes that it can sell the phones it produces. It can also work out how well it is performing in terms of profits and margins.

However, if this company is to live in the real world, it must also pay attention to the competitive offers available on the market and the customers who buy them. The ability to sell a phone for $18 or $12 is not a given, but reflects the interaction of suppliers and customers in the marketplace. The prices the company is able to charge successfully reflect all the other products on offer.

Market-based pricing means different things in different contexts. Here it means pricing based on the prices being offered by the competition. For the phone company, which is a small player in relation to Nokia or Samsung (clear market leaders), pricing might simply be a process of following what the leaders do—pricing similar products at the same or slightly lower prices to their competitors.

In many commodity markets, such as crude oil, bulk chemicals, basic foodstuffs and so on, market-based pricing is the norm. The reason is that the products these firms sell are often identical and there is rapid and complete communication of transaction prices. Firms in these categories don't make pricing decisions per se; rather, they take the price as given and adjust their outputs accordingly. For commodities, there is no alternative to market-based pricing.

Smaller companies, new entrants and low-cost competitors might also adopt market-based pricing. In essence, they set their prices with reference to the market leaders, generally at just under the leader's price. The pricing policy for this type of strategy is simply to price at a particular differential to the leader's price; for example, a new budget airline might always have a price of $10 less than the market leader, or the daily rate for a rental car company might always be set at $1 less than the bigger firms.

In practice, a great many companies use some form of market-based pricing. This is especially the case for smaller companies and those in categories dominated by large competitors; this can be a good way to grow and drive market share. However, following the leader too slavishly means letting competitors set the company's price, and does not allow a company to capitalise on changes in value perceptions, nor to build on any differences that customers may perceive between one company and its competitors. If a company wants to maximise profits, it needs to pay attention to what its competitors are doing, maintaining a realistic differential, and adjusting its own relative position to reflect current market conditions and customer perceptions of its offering—not forgetting to take account of how its own costs are changing.

> **market-based pricing:**
> A pricing method in which an organisation evaluates the prices of similar products on the market and sets its own price so that it is competitive. This can also be called competition-based pricing.

Case study
Game makers give it away—and increase their profits
By Dag Bennett

It used to be that downloading games onto a laptop or smartphone generally cost 99 cents or $1.00. At that price, thousands of people bought games, generating a modest revenue stream for the game designers. These days, there are many free games and millions of people download them.

You might think that this is a silly, or at least a risky, strategy. However, many game and application designers have found that when they charge up front for a product, sales stay small, but if they give the game away as a free download, millions of people will download it without thinking twice about it. Once they start playing, the games get sticky, or even addictive, and people will then become willing to pay for extra features to 'up' their game; for example, new characters, extra lives, power-ups or special boosters. Even if only a small percentage of the millions of players buy extra features, the games makers find they can increase their revenues.

One company that has been particularly successful at this pricing strategy is Zynga, which capitalised on FarmVille and its other Facebook games with an initial public offering that raised US$1 billion. FarmVille is free to play, but players can purchase 'farm cash' that can be used to make crops immediately ready for market.

This strategy of giving something away, sometimes called 'freemium' pricing, presents customers with what they may perceive to be a great deal by allowing them to use a product as much as they like, and then decide to give a couple of dollars to the game developer. Once they pay, they also tend to play more. In addition, customers can then be exposed to new game features and other, again initially free, games.

The buying process can be made simple by including a virtual store inside a game. Flurry, a mobile software analytics firm, estimates that about 65 per cent of all revenue generated in the iPhone app store—about US$2 billion—comes from free games that charge for extra goods or features. Apple makes it very easy for people to make purchases within apps by keeping credit cards on file. Google's app store, Android Market, on the other hand, has generated little revenue so far because making payments is more difficult with it. The bottom line seems to be that free games can hook buyers, but to deliver revenues buying has to be easy.

VALUE-BASED PRICING

value-based pricing:
A method of pricing in which an organisation estimates the value of its product or service to the customer and uses that as its basis for setting price.

In its broadest sense, **value-based pricing** means that pricing ought to relate to customer perceptions of value. In other words, customer perceptions ought to be the key driver of price. The question, of course, is how to arrive at a realistic view of those customer perceptions; historically, the answer has been 'market research'. Customer surveys, focus groups and elaborate choice models (such as conjoint analysis to estimate how customers value a product relative to its alternatives) have long been used to set prices, especially in consumer goods markets, and when new products are being introduced.

In practice, however, there are difficulties with this method. For example, it is very difficult to discern individual customer perceptions at the point of sale (unless there is an extremely astute salesperson on hand), so models rarely include the important influence of the sales environment. There is generally a difference between the 'value' that a potential buyer might place on a product and what they would actually pay in the marketplace. As always, what customers say and what they do are different. Also, the inability to control the competitive environment means that a product never really faces the same set of competitors in the marketplace as it does in a research study. This apparent inconsistency is easy to understand because the real-world marketplace is flexible, with the number and type of offerings in constant flux, and therefore the situation that confronts the buyer at any given purchase occasion is likely to be unique. These methods ask people to think about product features and benefits much more than they normally would. Therefore, in research survey settings people will place higher value on product features than they do in real life. In short, this means that companies almost always have to price lower than they would like.

Case study
Kindle Fire: $199 looks like a bargain

By Dag Bennett

In December 2011, Amazon introduced the Kindle Fire at a price of US$199. The Fire had a seven-inch full colour touch screen, WiFi and a cloud-accelerated web browser and gave access to movies, games, apps, music and books. The Fire looked to be competitive with Apple's iPad2, although the iPad2 had more functions, and sold at the time for US$499. How is it that Amazon could set a price that seemed so low?

According to @CNNMoneyTech, the answer lay in what was included in the machine and what was left out. Comparing the Fire with the iPad2 you can see that the cost (based on industry-standard parts) of the core components for the Fire was substantially lower:

	COST FOR KINDLE FIRE ($)	COST FOR APPLE IPAD2 ($)
TI processor	18	25
Hard drive	8	20
Battery	12	20
Glass touch screen	60	80
Shell, components	45	80
Cameras, microphones	–	45
Total	143	270

Across the board, lower componentry costs were achieved by installing a smaller hard drive and shifting memory functions to the cloud, and leaving out certain accessories altogether, such as cameras (the iPad2 has two of them). Even so, it is clear that the $56 difference between cost and list price does not leave much to cover costs of assembly or other expenses, or for profits, compared to the iPad's $230.

Apple routinely reports its sales figures, claiming sales of around 11 million iPads in the last quarter of 2011. Amazon, on the other hand, is reticent about releasing its sales figures, but industry analysts estimate that 2 to 3 million Kindle Fires were bought in the holiday quarter, making it the bestselling competitor to the iPad.

One key difference between the Amazon and Apple strategies is that Amazon uses its e-book reader as a platform to sell other Amazon products, such as Amazon Prime and Kindle Books. In other words, the Kindle

Fire can be sold at a lower price than its functionality might indicate because it gives Amazon a built-in means of capturing additional revenue from customers.

Questions

1   When a person buys a Kindle Fire, what are they really buying?

2   Can you think of other examples of 'captive pricing' where the ownership of a product leads to sales of supporting products or services?

3   How low do you think the price of the Kindle Fire can go?

4   Can you conceive of competitive strategies that Apple might adopt in response to the Kindle Fire?

CRITICAL REFLECTION

1   What are the main differences between cost-based, market based and value based pricing?

2   What are some of the pitfalls you might encounter in establishing what customers are willing to pay for something? What steps can you take to overcome these difficulties?

THE REALITY OF SETTING PRICES

Cost-based pricing, market-based pricing and value based pricing are all popular means of arriving at prices. Each method has its advocates and many companies do very well using one or other of these systems.

In practice, however, most companies are not purists when it comes to setting prices. Managers might start by using cost-based pricing, but they will also modify their approach when circumstances demand it. For example, during the recession of 2008–09, many industries faced contractions in demand and pressure to lower prices, and many companies were forced to adopt survival strategies in which they were only able to cover some of their costs. Even in more normal times, companies will react to the actions of their competitors by changing their prices.

Pricing is also subject to the current strategy in use by the company at the time—such as harvesting profits or growing market share—and the occasional vogue in management such as 'focusing on the customer'. In short, most companies are not strictly devoted to any one pricing approach. This is actually a survival instinct—any company that rigidly tried to stick to any of the three approaches above would probably very quickly find itself in trouble. What is most often seen is a hybrid approach, using aspects of all three methods, complemented by improvisation. In summary, pricing is an area with lots of imprecision, even confusion, and rarely a consistent justification or approach applied across all pricing decisions.

Research insight

Mckinsey & Company, a consultancy, in studies of the Global 1200 companies, finds that operating profits average about 9 per cent, variable costs average 66 per cent and fixed costs 25 per cent. The actual figures for individual industries vary greatly; declining industries, for example, tend to have lower operating profits.

From a pricing standpoint, we can make some interesting deductions from these numbers. For example, with a 9 per cent profit margin, a 1 per cent increase in price will result in an 11 per cent increase in operating profit (1% / 9% = 11%). Similarly, a 1 per cent increase in sales will result in a 3.8 per cent profit increase, and a 1 per cent decrease in variable costs will increase profit by 7.2 per cent. Thus, while it is clear that reducing costs can increase profit, it is also apparent that the biggest impact on profit can be had from changes in price.

The obvious question from these numbers is: why don't companies raise their prices? The answer is that it is vital to understand how the marketplace—consumers and competitors—will react to such changes. No company is insulated from the reactions of both customers and competitors. In other words, price can be regarded as a dynamic variable. When price is changed, it has effects on the marketplace, which will affect sales levels and therefore profits. In short, marketers must have a notion of *elasticity*.

Price changes

LEARNING OBJECTIVE
Be able to calculate price elasticity and use it to evaluate pricing decisions

Perhaps the majority of pricing decisions are not about setting a price, but about changing an existing price. When a company changes the price it charges for a product, it will want to know what is likely to happen as a result. Generally, if the price of something goes up, then demand for it will go down, while if the price is lowered demand will increase. This is the law of supply and demand.

The key question in changing a price is: how much will demand change as a result? If the price goes up by 10 per cent, will demand go down by 10 per cent, or 20 per cent? The answer depends on how consumers respond. Will they cut back purchases a little or a lot? This question of consumer responsiveness to price changes is measured by **price elasticity** (sometimes formally called price elasticity of demand).

Elasticity is a measure of responsiveness to price. Ultimately, we want to know how many fewer units we will sell if we increase the price by a certain amount. By expressing the change in price and volume as percentages, we can compare the measured change in price to the resulting measure of decrease in demand. Suppose the response to a price rise of 10 per cent is a decrease in demand of 20 per cent; the decrease in demand is twice the increase in price, which hints that consumers are sensitive or responsive to changes in price. Knowing how responsive consumers are to changes in price is important for any manager considering price changes. Using elasticity as a metric also allows easy comparison of effects across different price levels and changes, and across brands and categories.

price elasticity:
A measure of responsiveness to price, calculated as the percentage change in quantity divided by the percentage change in price.

Elasticity can be calculated in several ways. The most simple is to divide the percentage change in quantity by the percentage change in price.

$$\text{Elasticity} = \text{Percentage change in quantity} \div \text{Percentage change in price}$$

If price increases by 10 per cent and consumers respond by decreasing purchases by 20 per cent, the elasticity coefficient is $-20 \div 10 = -2$. Elasticity results are always negative because changes in price lead to changes in the opposite direction in demand. In practice, since elasticity numbers are always negative, the minus sign is often dropped and we refer to an elasticity of 2. Dropping the minus sign is particularly relevant when referring to the magnitude of elasticity as being larger or higher when the coefficient is bigger (strictly, of course, -1 is a higher number than -3, but we call an elasticity of -3 a larger elasticity.)

The higher the elasticity number, the more elastic is the demand.

Economists refer to a product as *inelastic* if its price elasticity is less than 1, and *elastic* if its elasticity is greater than 1. An elasticity coefficient of 2 indicates that consumers respond quite a lot to a change in price. If, on the other hand, a 10 per cent change in price causes only a 5 per cent decrease in sales, the elasticity coefficient will be only 0.5, less than 1. When elasticity is 1, revenue remains the same whether price is raised or lowered. If elasticity is greater than 1, a company wishing to increase revenue (price × quantity) would be better off lowering its price, whereas if elasticity is less than 1, it could earn more revenue by raising the price. Whether price changes results in more *profit* is another story, which we will touch on later.

Highly addictive products such as cigarettes or cocaine, and products with few good substitutes such as petrol (as a category, not brands of petrol), generally have a lower elasticity of demand than products with many substitutes. So more broadly defined products have a lower elasticity than narrowly defined products. The price elasticity of demand for pasta will be lower than the price elasticity of vermicelli, and MP3 players will be less price elastic than Apple iPods. Indeed, the price elasticity of brands in a category is always bigger, often much more so, than the category in total. For example, the Wikipedia entry on Price elasticity (accessed 30/9/2010) quotes price elasticity for both Mountain Dew and Coca-Cola as 4, whereas the elasticity for the overall category of soft drinks is less than 1.

Time also plays a role in both consumer and producer responsiveness—the longer the time to adjust, the more adjustments will be made. When the price of petrol rose rapidly in 2007, the only adjustment consumers could initially make was to drive less. With time, they could also find jobs closer to home, or switch to more fuel-efficient cars or hybrids, and as petrol prices climb even higher, the fall in demand is accelerating.

◢ LEARNING OBJECTIVE

Know circumstances where elasticity is consistently larger or smaller

Marketing knowledge of price elasticity

This general knowledge about price changes is fairly well understood in business, but it is not particularly helpful because it is not specific enough for the situations under which most marketers operate. Nor does it have any underlying market-based principles to help guide a brand manager confronted with a pricing decision. Are there, for example, consistent factors that marketers should know about that either raise or lower customer responses to changes in price?

It turns out there are. Scriven and Ehrenberg (2004) did a series of tests in which consumers were confronted with changes in price. They were able to identify five factors that consistently raised elasticity. These were:

1 passing an explicit reference price—changing a brand's price so that it becomes either more or less expensive than other brands, especially the brand leader

2 raising the price, rather than decreasing it—customers are more resistant to upward moves

3 starting at a price close to the average category price—implying that the middle of the price range is most competitive and brands that are located at extremes (either high or low) are less affected by changes in price

4 being a small share brand—customers of small share brands have many options to choose between and small brands are punished for getting out of line, but also gain relatively more when price is cut

5 signalling the price change—it helps to be noticed, which is why sales and price related promotions are heavily publicised, and conversely why legislation is designed to stop manufacturers from trying to disguise price increases or to claim cuts that are not genuine.

In practical terms, although larger cuts may produce bigger sales increases, marketers may find that small price cuts, to fractionally below the major competitors, are likely to be more profitable. Small price rises to just below the major competitors might increase profits even more. On the other hand, big brands and expensive ones seem to generate less response from lowering their prices and therefore would theoretically have little incentive to do so.

One explanation for these findings is that people often do not have an exact knowledge of the price of things they buy, even things they buy regularly and often. However, they may have a reasonably accurate impression of where the brands they buy are ranked vis-à-vis other brands in the category. It is often the relative, rather than the imperfectly remembered absolute, price that matters, which is why signalling is important. This is why some companies display price comparisons, or include a recommended retail price (RRP) on their price tags—it gives a basis for comparison or relative price position.

 CRITICAL REFLECTION

1 Thinking about the five circumstances above that result in higher elasticity of price, do you think they are intuitively what you would expect? Why do you think that?

2 What are some of the strategic implications of the findings on elasticity? Do you think that small companies should adopt different pricing strategies than market leaders?

3 Does market positioning play a role in pricing strategy?

Promoting with temporary price cuts

◢ **LEARNING OBJECTIVE**
Understand why
temporary price cuts
(price promotions) are
potentially damaging

◢ **temporary price
promotion:** Setting a
price lower than the usual
price or offering a special
deal, such as two for the
price of one (effectively
a 50 per cent price cut),
for a limited time. After
the promotion period,
the price goes back to the
previous level.

Brands do sometimes change their regular price, usually when underlying costs increase or decrease, or when there is a major shift in competitive prices. But the most common form of price change is a **temporary price promotion**, where the brand reduces its price for a fixed short period. Why do brand managers do this? The obvious answers are to increase volume, increase profit and attract new customers. It turns out that only one of these is generally the outcome.

Temporary price cuts do increase volume, often dramatically, for the duration of the promotion. But as Ehrenberg, Hammond and Goodhardt (1994) found in their analysis of over 100 price promotions in consumer packaged goods categories, volume quickly returns to the 'normal' pre-promotion levels after the promotion ends. There is no carry-over from any new customers. Almost everybody who buys in a price promotion has bought the brand previously, so there are virtually no new customers. And buying in a promotion does not alter future propensity to buy (either up or down).

What about increasing profit? Even if the sale price is more than the marginal cost of production, there may not be extra profit, because of the margin given away on sales that would have been at full price if the promotion had not happened. Table 9.5 shows the level of sales uplift that would be required, for a brand with a contribution margin of 50 per cent at normal price, to break even at various combinations of price cut and contribution margin. It is easy to see that big price cuts require a massive increase in volume to avoid losing money.

●●● **TABLE 9.5** SALES UPLIFT REQUIRED TO MATCH CONTRIBUTION WHEN PRICE REDUCED

PRICE REDUCTION (%)	INCREASE IN SALES NEEDED TO MATCH CURRENT CONTRIBUTION (%)	PRICE ELASTICITY NEEDED
1	2	2.0
5	11	2.2
10	25	2.5
15	44	2.9
20	66	3.3
30	150	5.0

So the general conclusion is that price promotions do not stimulate long-term volume and often lose money generating the short-term 'spike' in additional sales. At best, temporary promotions might be seen as a defensive mechanism to help retain volume against competitors.

However, there is another issue, in that this activity will cause competitors to also offer regular price cuts. There is evidence that in product categories where frequent price promotions are the norm, customers become used to buying 'on deal' and can usually find an acceptable brand available at a cut price. In these categories, as much as half the total category volume can be sold at cut-price, and nearly everybody buys 'on deal' at some time (see Table 9.6).

●●● **TABLE 9.6** THE MAJORITY OF CONSUMERS BUY 'ON DEAL' AT SOME TIME

CATEGORIES	PERCENTAGE VOLUME ON PROMOTION	PERCENTAGE BUYING 'ON DEAL'
Chilled and frozen pizzas	51	83
Toilet tissues	35	82
Yoghurt drinks	35	67
Cakes and biscuits	32	98
Fromage frais	29	62
Total fabrics	29	72
Nappies	28	69
Baked beans	17	60
Air fresheners	16	42
Razor blades	9	16
Condiments and spices	7	28
Average	26	62

Source: Ehrenberg-Bass analysis of Kantar Worldpanel data, June 2007

Other reasons to cut prices may be to reach volume targets, to clear surplus stock or to satisfy trade requirements for promotional items. Clearing surplus stock should only be occasionally necessary (if not, you should look at your production planning or demand forecasting processes!). The requirement to reach volume targets, especially those that require growth, is too complex a subject to address here. However, there must be a question as to whether there is any real value in short-term volume blips achieved at the cost of reduced profitability, compared with using marketing spend to attempt to develop long-term propensity, with the profitability that can follow.

The issue of satisfying the trade is also complex. Supermarkets and other large chains believe that they need some special offers in order to continue to entice customers into their stores in what is a highly competitive business. Brand owners need to evaluate objectively how much they have to participate in (and indeed fund) this activity, versus the alternative of using the money in other ways that would benefit the brand.

Finally, we will briefly mention **optimisation**. Is it possible to establish an optimum price? That depends on whether we are trying to optimise for volume, revenue or profit. It is impossible to find a solution that satisfies all three, and in practice the ideal price will involve a compromise of volume, revenue and profit objectives. Lower prices increase volume, but higher prices may deliver higher revenue, and higher prices still deliver maximum profit (but lower revenue and volume).

optimisation: Setting the best price to achieve an organisation's objective, such as maximum profit, sales or profit margin,

Application to business-to-business marketing

As mentioned in prior chapters, there are relatively few customers in most business markets. For example, in Australia there are just three companies producing a total of about two million tonnes of aluminium annually, in six smelting facilities (Australian Aluminium Council, 2010). Therefore, the Australian markets for highly specialised production equipment and related technical services used by these smelting operations comprise just three customers—although collectively their annual purchases of smelting production equipment and related technical services would amount to many millions of dollars.

As this example indicates, for a business-to-business marketer, each of its largest customers could purchase a high proportion of its annual output. Consequently, such customers would have a relatively strong negotiating position with the supplier, since the loss of one of these large customers could result in a major loss of business and profits for the supplier. Clearly, in such situations, a marketer must consider each individual customer when developing pricing strategies.

Similarly, some organisational purchases relate to extremely large projects. For example, the Australian national broadband network has a forecast capital expenditure of more than $35 billion (National Broadband Network Company, 2011). For a major supplier to this project, pricing would have been an extremely important issue, due to the scale of operation, potentially becoming a strategic issue at the corporate level.

Therefore, one major difference between pricing within business-to-consumer and business-to-business marketing situations is the influence of individual (major) customers or projects on pricing strategy within the latter situation. Some business-to-business marketing firms estimate the lifetime value of major prospects or customers, even applying discounted cash flow techniques to those calculations.

Another difference relates to negotiations. On the one hand, substantial negotiations between buyer and supplier organisations often occur within business-to-business marketing situations. For very large projects, such negotiations could involve employees from various functional areas within buyer and supplier organisations, extending over many months or even several years. Such lengthy negotiations almost never occur within business-to-consumer marketing. Conversely, some organisational customers, such as governments, require potential suppliers to submit pricing and related supply proposals via formal tenders (or bids), in which little or no negotiation is possible after the tender submission. Such tendering processes are virtually unknown within business-to-consumer marketing.

Since quantities purchased by large firms are so much greater than those purchased by households, prices paid by those organisations are much lower than those paid for similar products by individual consumers, even if there is a significant degree of customisation of products for particular organisational customers.

From the viewpoint of the organisational customer, price is often of secondary importance to total cost, or to other factors such as product quality or supply reliability. For example, a manufacturer needing to replace production equipment might consider a high-quality but expensive brand of equipment to constitute a lower total cost of ownership (and production) than a low-quality but inexpensive brand, if the former is believed to have a much longer productive life and much lower maintenance costs. Similarly, a manufacturer of a high-quality, high-priced brand might prefer a supplier with a reputation for high-quality components, even if that supplier is more expensive than other suppliers lacking that reputation. Finally, if supply interruptions are extremely serious (perhaps involving a complete cessation of operations combined with high costs of restarting those operations), the organisation probably would prefer a supplier able to ensure supply continuity and reliability even at a higher price.

Such considerations are relevant to services as well as physical goods. For example, many large organisations (including governments) appear willing to pay high prices for advice from prestigious consulting firms rather than risk accepting advice from less expensive but unknown, smaller firms. Quite simply, the risk of implementing poor advice is far greater than the potential cost savings through lower consulting fees.

CONCLUSION

Pricing is complicated. Companies have to price their products to recover their overall costs and to try to generate a surplus (profit) to pay tax and a return to shareholders. But costs vary with volume, which in turn will vary with price. They also have to consider the competitive frame in which they operate, and the value they offer to the consumer relative to that frame and the consumers' wants.

While cost based accounting and margins can set simple formulae for producing a price, these are subject to discretion in cost allocation, and do not consider the competition. There is no simple formula for producing an optimum price. In many companies, the price of products may have evolved without much strategic thought, through a combination of costs and response to competitive and intermediary pressure. This can be regarded as the natural result of market forces; however, smart companies will study their own and market pricing continuously in order to understand the effects of their actions, and to improve if not necessarily optimise their price strategy.

09

SUMMARY

- There are many approaches to setting prices, from basic cost-based pricing to more sophisticated market-based pricing.

- While many companies use cost-based pricing quite successfully, they cannot be sure that they are maximising profits, because the method is inwardly focused on company information and does not take account of what customers are willing to pay.

- Market-based pricing assesses what customers are willing to pay and from there the company can work out whether it can operate profitably.

- Changes in input costs, competitive pressure, or the desire to increase sales or market share may drive a company to change its price level. To do so sensibly, it is vital that the company understands price elasticity—the effect that a change in price has on sales. The most important consideration in elasticity is whether a price change takes a price past that of the price leader or reference price, in which case a large change in sales can be expected.

- Price-based promotions are an addiction for many marketers, and yet they generally do not add new customers, have only temporary sales effects and tend to have a large negative effect on profits.

REVISION QUESTIONS

1   Outline the basic approaches to cost-based pricing. Explain the limitations of these methods.

2   What is price elasticity, and what is known about it in competitive market situations?

3   How do the pricing strategies followed by large firms and small firms differ?

4   Explain the different pressures exerted by sales, marketing, finance and production departments on pricing.

5   Explain why the cheapest brand is generally not the largest brand in its category.

6   Explain why pricing is a compromise between organisational goals such as profit maximisation, sales volume and market share.

7   Give an example of how managerial decisions on cost allocation can affect market prices.

FURTHER READING

Baker, W, Marn, M & Zawada, C (2010) *The Price Advantage*, 2nd edn, Wiley Finance, John Wiley & Sons, Hoboken, NJ.

Ehrenberg, A S C, Hammond, K & Goodhardt, G J (1994) 'The after effects of price-related consumer promotions', *Journal of Advertising Research*, vol. 34, no. 4, pp. 11–21.

Nagle, T, Hogan, J & Zale, J (2011) *The Strategy and Tactics of Pricing: A Guide to Growing More Profitably*, 5th edn, Pearson, Upper Saddle River, NJ.

Phillips, R L (2005) *Pricing and Revenue Optimization*, Stanford University Press, Stanford, California.

Scriven, J A & Ehrenberg, A S C (2004) 'Consistent Consumer Responses to Price Changes', *Australasian Marketing Journal*, vol. 12, no. 3, pp. 6–25.

WEBLINKS

Amazon's Kindle, was it just a flash in the pan?:
> http://tech.fortune.cnn.com/2012/05/04/was-amazons-kindle-fire-just-a-flash-in-the-pan

Amazon's Kindle, what it really costs:
> http://money.cnn.com/video/technology/2011/11/30/t-ts-fire-teardown.cnnmoney/

Australian Aluminium:
> http://aluminium.org.au/australian-aluminium/australian-aluminium

Broadbanding Australia, National Broadband Network Information Pack:
> www.nbnco.com.au/assets/documents/nbn-co-information-pack.pdf

Free:
> www.free.fr

Google Play:
> https://play.google.com/store

iPhone:
> www.apple.com/uk/iphone/from-the-app-store

McKinsey Quarterly:
> www.mckinseyquarterly.com

Zynga:
> http://company.zynga.com

◢ Major case study

The tyre case: Analysing your situation to make good pricing decisions

By Elizabeth Gunner

Four different companies decide to enter the tyre market. Each company decides to produce a different product and although their raw materials are exactly the same, the competition and demand for each market is quite different:

- Company A produces standard car tyres; demand is high but there are lots of established competitor brands including a few large-scale producers that control prices.
- Company B produces special tyres for army tanks; they are contracted by the government, and so they have only one customer and no competitors but the contract will be reviewed annually.
- Company C produces tyres for four-wheel-drive vehicles; demand is lower than for standard car tyres, but there is less competition.
- Company D produces tyres for fixed-gear bicycles; a growing market with few established competitors but with a growing number of new producers entering the market to meet growing consumer demand.

Questions

1   What are the different price setting techniques that the companies could use to set their prices?
2   Select one pricing method for each firm and give a reason(s) why you think this would be the most appropriate method?
3   Think about the differences in the customer base for each product, which types of tyres would be more price elastic and why?
4   The cost of Carbon Black (one of the key raw materials used to make tyres) has increased significantly, causing an increase in the production costs for all four tyre companies.
    a   Would this be an increase in fixed costs or variable costs?
    b   If all four companies raised their prices in response to the increased production cost, whose sales do you think would be most affected and why?
5   Company D is considering a temporary price promotion—list some scenarios where this could be a benefit for the company.

Each company decides to produce a different product and although their raw materials are exactly the same, the competition and demand for each market is quite different

Practitioner profile

Mark Geraghty, General Manager (Sales and Marketing), Elders Rural Services (Adelaide), annual turnover $2 billion in 2011

My first degree was a Bachelor of Science, majoring in chemistry. In fact, it wasn't until I'd finished studying and landed my first graduate job in a large consumer goods company that I became interested in marketing.

I was working as a scientist for Reckitt & Colman's product development department at the time, in a role that required close collaboration with the marketing team. I quickly found myself very interested in the work that the marketers were doing, and became more and more curious about their role within an organisation. Ultimately, it was this experience that inspired me to change career paths and enrol in a Masters of Commerce, majoring in marketing. My decision paid off quickly and, while still studying, I was promoted to the role of Assistant Brand Manager for Deodorants. It was my first hands-on experience: I learnt to analyse markets, identify opportunities for growth and execute marketing plans.

After that, I worked in a variety of marketing roles, gaining experience and developing the knowledge and skills that eventually led to my current role at Elders. Of course qualifications are vital, but the key skills for a senior managerial role are those that develop with experience: a combination of strategic and analytical thinking, relationship management skills and the commercial understanding to make sound business decisions.

Being a marketer does mean hard work—you may face a limited budget and often strong internal pressure to perform, but you'll never be bored. That's probably the thing I like best about my role at Elders: no two days are ever the same. Of course, the core of the responsibility is always to develop and execute the marketing plan, but this breaks down into so many areas: pricing decisions, identifying opportunities for product development, monitoring sales, managing the communication of key

branding messages (using different media) and so much more. Elders, like most big firms, has a huge range of products, so one of the most important aspects of my job is always keeping the 'big picture' in mind— each decision needs to fit with the long-term strategic plan for that product, the product category and the organisation as a whole. It's a lot to be on top of, but it is also incredibly satisfying when you see the results of all your hard work.

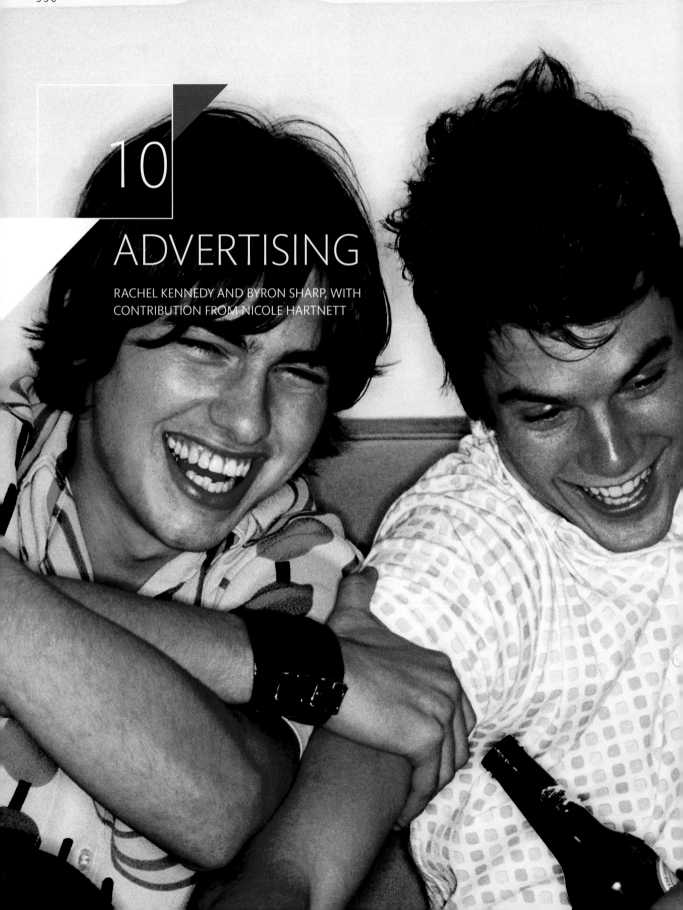

10
ADVERTISING

RACHEL KENNEDY AND BYRON SHARP, WITH
CONTRIBUTION FROM NICOLE HARTNETT

◢ Introduction case

The 'Legend' campaign

By Elizabeth Gunner

In October 2011, the New Zealand Transport Agency (NZTA) launched their 'Legend' campaign, with a comic television advertisement encouraging young boys to tell their mates not to drink-drive (you can watch the ad at: www.youtube.com/watch?v=dIYvD9DI1ZA). Less than three months later, the YouTube link for the ad had 1.5 million views. That is, 1.5 million people chose to watch a government advertisement about driver safety.

Advertising isn't always loved—the industry has been criticised for making people buy things they don't need and for interrupting and cluttering up our lives with sales pitches. But not in the NZTA case—the 'Legend' campaign isn't selling anything, and those YouTube hits represent people who chose to 'waste time' or 'interrupt' their day by watching an ad. But how typical is the 'Legend' ad?

Let's think about a normal week. How many specific ads can you remember seeing last week? And how many times do you remember feeling annoyed by advertising, or conscious of it intruding on your personal time? Do you actually concentrate during an ad break on television or radio? And how much time do you spend looking at the ads when flicking through a magazine or newspaper? The reality is that sometimes we do hate ads and sometimes we love them (and even share them with friends via YouTube), but often we barely notice them. We switch off (mentally) or flick right past them. We are very good at ignoring advertising—at screening out ads and getting on with the rest of our lives.

So what is the point of advertising if most people barely notice it? What can advertising actually achieve for a cause or a brand? And how do some advertisement campaigns, such as 'Legend', break through the clutter?

> But advertising isn't always loved—the industry has been criticised for making people buy things they don't need and for interrupting and cluttering up our lives with sales pitches.

INTRODUCTION

To help you understand what advertising can do in the marketplace, this chapter draws on a broad range of evidence—including how buyers buy, what advertisements look like and how viewers watch advertising—to discuss how advertising works to maintain and build brands and drive sales. This chapter will give you a framework for thinking about advertising and introduce key concepts to help you understand how advertising works and how you can produce great campaigns.

This framework represents a modern view of advertising (Table 10.1 outlines key terms, along with corresponding dated ideas that you need to be cautious of). This chapter draws on recent advances in knowledge from neuroscience and psychology, about how our brains and memories work. These discoveries have important implications for advertising, because advertising works through laying down and refreshing memories. Much thinking (for example during shopping) is now known to be non-conscious and emotional. Yet some theories of advertising are still based on a view that we are usually rational (and occasionally emotional) decision makers, with near perfect memories.

LEARNING OBJECTIVES

After reading this chapter you should:

- have a clear understanding of the role of advertising in brand management and specifically what it is realistic to expect advertising to do
- understand how advertising works on memory to affect buyer behaviour
- be able to brief an advertising agency for an effective campaign and set realistic objectives for a brand in a communications plan
- be able to recognise good advertising
- understand the value of pre-testing and advertising tracking, and begin to appreciate some of the difficulties of conducting research on advertising effectiveness.

CHAPTER OUTLINE

Introduction

Please consider our brand!

The advertising business

What can advertising do?

Briefing to get great advertising

What great ads look like

Advertising research

Conclusion

KEY TERMS

advertising

advertising avoidance

advertising budget

advertising copy

advertising tracking

banner advertising

brand recall

brand recognition

comparative advertising

creatives

interactive advertising

mandatory brand requirements
(mandatories)

pre-testing

product positioning

public relations (PR)

search engine advertising

single-source data

traditional media

Warc

wearout

●●● **TABLE 10.1** A NEW FRAMEWORK FOR ADVERTISING THEORY

PAST WORLD VIEW	Rational or emotional	Message comprehension	Unique selling propositions	Persuasion	Teaching	Positioning
NEW WORLD VIEW	Emotional and rational	Getting noticed	Relevant associations	Refreshing and building memory structures	Reaching	Salience

Source: Sharp, 2010

PLEASE CONSIDER OUR BRAND!

Advertising is a weak force in the sense that it doesn't have the ability to change our minds the way that recommendations from family and friends (and even authority figures) can. We are exposed to a great deal of advertising, almost all of which we pay very little attention to, but this doesn't mean that advertising doesn't affect us. Advertising helps us navigate our world and keeps us up to date. Advertisers invest huge amounts of money in advertising, which pays for the development of television programs and free services (such as Google, YouTube and Facebook). They expect a return; they would not spend money on advertising if it did not generate sales—which it does. The weak force of advertising helps maintain our loyalties, helping to prevent us forgetting about brands that we occasionally buy. And it helps us learn about new features and new brands. The gentle nudges of advertising are an important part of a competitive marketplace. Advertising works for marketers because it is cheap on a per person basis (typically a few cents per person), making it a cost-effective way of communicating with many buyers.

advertising: Most advertising is paid for, marketer controlled (written and produced) one-way communication with potential buyers. However, in recent years we are seeing more examples of advertising that is interactive, less tightly controlled or more akin to unpaid public relations.

Warc: A useful resource (www.warc.com) for those interested in advertising. It provides access to industry data, articles and case studies concerning a wide range of advertising, marketing, media and research subjects.

THE ADVERTISING BUSINESS

In 2011, **Warc** forecast a global advertising spend of US$443,000,000,000. Each year about 2 per cent of world GDP is spent on advertising (Nayaradou, 2006), similar to worldwide military expenditure. It is a very big industry (as a point of comparison, this is higher than the spend on agriculture in developed countries, and education takes up only 5 per cent of world GDP). Advertising takes up a very large part of many marketers' budgets. Many marketing graduates work in advertising agencies that develop advertising or media agencies that plan and buy the media space where the advertising goes. Advertising is something you need to know about.

Once upon a time, the world was more straightforward, and marketing textbooks would use the term 'advertising' to mean only paid, marketer-controlled (written and produced), one-way communication with potential buyers. 'Public relations' (PR) referred to unpaid communication that wasn't completely within marketers' control (but could be encouraged and influenced). And 'selling' referred to communication that was interactive and so allowed orders to be taken from customers. However, in today's media environment the distinction between paid advertising (also called marketing communications) and unpaid public relations is blurring—it's certainly very possible to end up producing a lot of content and spending a great deal of money on both. Similarly, advertising is less able to be so tightly controlled as in the past—an advertisement posted on YouTube can not only be seen by people that the marketer did not intend, but it can also be imitated and parodied. For an example, see the Volkswagen Super Bowl ad, <http://youtu.be/R55e-uHQna0>, and this Toyota parody: <http://youtu.be/1jtH4beRWAo>. Technology is also allowing advertising to be increasingly interactive. The terms, advertising, public relations and selling are still useful, but it is more difficult to make absolute distinctions between them. In this chapter's discussion of advertising, we continue the textbook convention of largely discussing paid, marketer-controlled, communication, but you should keep in mind that not all advertising fits neatly into this box.

The advertising world is changing with the emergence of new media, new ways of advertising and new ways of measuring the buying and viewing of advertising. Advertisers are still working out how they can utilise these new opportunities. In 2009, the Wharton School (University of Pennsylvania) and the Ehrenberg-Bass Institute (University of South Australia) jointly hosted a conference that invited some of the world's leaders in advertising thinking to present research that would give insight on the future of advertising. One of the surprising conclusions was that **traditional media** such as television are proving astonishingly resilient and adaptable (see Table 10.2). So marketers still need to understand (and continue to research) television, print, radio and outdoor media, as well as the new media.

●●● **TABLE 10.2** DISTRIBUTION OF WORLD ADVERTISING EXPENDITURE BY MEDIUM (%), 2010

MEDIA	% OF WORLD ADVERTISING SPEND
Television	38%
Newspapers	23%
Internet	15%
Magazines	10%
Radio	7%
Outdoor	6%
Cinema	0.5%

Source: www.warc.com/NotesOnAdspendData

public relations (PR):
Unpaid communication that is not completely in the control of the marketer, but which can be encouraged and influenced by them. In modern marketing, the line is becoming blurred between unpaid PR and paid advertising.

traditional media:
Traditional platforms for communicating messages, pre-dating the internet—television, press (newspapers, magazines), radio, outdoor and cinema.

Another important conclusion from this conference was that there are law-like patterns that govern advertising consumption and effect. These well-validated discoveries, particularly those that have lasted over decades of social change, can help us navigate the future of advertising. In this chapter we build on this knowledge.

Industry insight

●●● **FIGURE 10.1** SCENES FROM OLD SPICE TELEVISION COMMERCIAL

Source: Wieden + Kennedy

Old Spice's campaign 'The Man Your Man Could Smell Like' campaign, staring Isaiah Mustafa, is an example of great television advertising. This Super Bowl advertisement by Craig Allen and Eric Kallman of the advertising agency Wieden Kennedy gained a lot of attention. For instance, it was featured on *The Oprah Winfrey Show* (2 April 2010) and *The Gruen Transfer* (July 2010), and it was awarded a prestigious Cannes Lions International Advertising Festival award.

The Old Spice campaign

If you haven't already seen the ad—which went 'viral', being shared on many social network sites and spawning myriad parodies—you can view it on YouTube at <www.youtube.com/watch?v=owGykVbfgUE>. As Old Spice summarises: 'We're not saying this body wash will make your man turn into a romantic millionaire jet fighter pilot, but we are insinuating it'. This is a fun and creative parody on advertising, in a way that is relevant to the brand.

The commercial starts in a location where people might think about the product category—specifically, in a bathroom. With many quick scene changes that hold attention (on a boat, holding diamonds and on a horse) the ad manages to include relevant *brand memory associations*. These associations are important, because advertising works through memory. In this chapter, we explain how memory works (the more memory links to a brand an ad builds, the greater the propensity of viewers to notice, recognise and recall the brand).

The ad grabs the viewer's attention (and creates willingness to watch again and again) through many different mechanisms, including humour, use of an appealing character with a great voice, beautiful settings and fast-paced set changes. It is a great example of creativity, which is so important in advertising to help get a brand noticed among all the clutter that exists in the modern world.

On a slightly more subtle level, the ad primes the brand with regular pack shots and use of its distinctive assets: the brand's red colour, sailing ships and lots of mentions of its smell: 'Smell like a Man, Man', all important recall and recognition cues for the brand.

Critically, this ad is part of a campaign—that is, a series of related advertising executions. Consistency

●●● **FIGURE 10.2** OLD SPICE'S DISTINCTIVE ASSETS

Source: Wieden + Kennedy

●●● **FIGURE 10.3** SCENES FROM OTHER EXECUTIONS IN THE OLD SPICE CAMPAIGN

Source: Wieden + Kennedy

across executions (and campaigns, pack and other marketing activity) helps the advertising to quickly and easily refresh the associations for the brand in viewers' memories—building mental availability for the brand, making it easier for consumers to notice or think of it in buying situations.

The creative team who developed this campaign said that they aimed for relevance while talking to a broad audience—that is, they aimed to appeal to both men and women.

For some insights on the making of the ad, see an interview with the creatives behind it: <www.fastcompany.com/1670314/old-spice-youtube-videos-wieden>.

Questions

1   Think of (or find) another great advertisement or campaign. What characteristics does it share with the Old Spice campaign? How much new information does it give you about the brand, if any? If it is a television or radio commercial, how long is it? Or how many words does it contain if it is in print or online?

2   What other approaches could Old Spice have used to sell their brand?

WHAT CAN ADVERTISING DO?

◢ **LEARNING OBJECTIVE**
Have a clear understanding of the role of advertising in brand management and specifically what it is realistic to expect advertising to do

It's often thought that the purpose of advertising is to tell consumers about new things: new products, new features for existing products, sales and events. Certainly advertising does this, yet it turns out to be particularly good at reinforcing existing loyalties (and memories) and it does this by reminding people of things they already know. Advertising helps established brands stay in the market, just as much as it helps new products find customers. Both of these effects are important for society: new products need a chance to win customers, and firms who have developed good products and services (and importantly got them into consumers' hands) deserve to enjoy some economic returns for doing so. No firm would invest in the risky business of entering a market or launching a new product if they thought that their success would have absolutely no chance of lasting a while.

Organisations advertise for a variety of reasons. Sometimes they do so just to be seen to be doing something: to appease distributors and motivate the sales force; or to show voters or employees that something is happening. That is, some advertising is mainly concerned with maintaining a good public image (it's really a form of PR). However, the majority of advertising is done to encourage a particular behaviour, such as getting people to quit smoking, drink milk or invest in superannuation. The bulk of advertising that seeks to affect behaviour is brand advertising aimed at encouraging people to buy (or keep buying) a particular brand. Encouraging buying behaviour is our main focus in this chapter, but many of the lessons also apply to advertising that has different aims.

A famous early model of advertising, AIDA (attributed to E St Elmo Lewis in 1898 by Strong, 1925), was initially developed for training salespeople and was (unfortunately) transferred to try to explain how advertising works. This model said that advertising moved viewers through a range of stages: from Attention to Interest to Desire to Action. Advertising is, however, very different from a salesperson's interaction with a customer. A television ad, for example, will typically be 15 or 30 seconds long; in comparison, an interaction with a salesperson can easily be 15 or 30 minutes long; most advertising is a one-to-many communication (that is, not tailored) yet sales staff specialise in reacting to individual customers and tailoring their message (on the fly even) to what is most relevant to help sell to that one person on that day. So a salesperson can be far more persuasive than advertising. But an advertisement can reach thousands if not millions of consumers with a single showing for a very low cost per contact.

Old models such as AIDA reflect the common notion that the purpose of advertising is to drive sales by telling us things we don't know or changing our beliefs, such as convincing us that we should be buying a different brand from the ones we usually do: 'buy toilet paper X—it is softer than [the other brands]'. However, advertising is a weakly persuasive force; people don't tend to pay it as much attention as marketers would like and consumers aren't pushovers—they expect and largely discount persuasive claims (they know advertising is a biased message trying to sell them something—this bias and exaggeration is called *puffery*). Ask yourself: of the probably hundreds of advertisements that you were exposed to yesterday, how many did you pay close attention to, and how many changed your mind about a brand? From a persuasion perspective, the vast majority of advertising looks completely ineffectual. In fact, the majority of advertising barely seems to even *try* to persuade us (Ehrenberg, Mills & Kennedy, 2000; Mills et al., 2000)—for example, the most common political ad doesn't talk about what the candidate stands for or what they will do for us if elected; the most common political ad merely says 'vote for X', usually with a picture of the candidate and the political party's colours and logo.

So how does advertising work then? The answer is that advertising largely works without forcing people to consider and change their opinions. And this is why much advertising can get away with being very 'soft sell', with few or no claims of product superiority (or just standard or vague claims that the brand is merely good, such as 'a bank you can trust' or 'our restaurant features fine wines'). But how can advertising drive sales without persuasion? We will now explain this.

We learnt in Chapter 2 that what brands people buy depends heavily on what brands they notice, recognise and recall. Mental availability matters a great deal, and how mentally available a brand is varies over time and between situations. Advertising plays a crucial role in building and refreshing mental availability.

People have a tendency to see advertising for brands that they already use, and are less likely to notice advertising for brands that they do not use. It's very common for people to report, with some surprise, that after buying a car they notice lots of advertising for the brand they bought that they did not see previously. This is because we have a tendency to pay more attention to things we like, and we have more developed memory structures for brands we use, so it takes less mental effort to process advertising for brands we buy. Consequently, users of a brand are two to three times more likely to recall its advertising than non-users of the brand (Sharp, Beal & Romaniuk, 2001).

This means that advertising is particularly good at refreshing existing memories. It can do this rather quickly and without us giving the advertising much dedicated attention or deep mental processing.

Advertising is comparatively weaker at building new memories, and rather poor at convincing people to form intentions to change their behaviour. So it has a natural advantage in encouraging existing loyalties—encouraging people to continue doing what they already do.

So a very large role of advertising is to help prevent sales erosion; to prevent consumers forgetting about the brand and so buying it less often. An important goal of advertising is that the brand holds its market share. This is why large market share brands are almost always substantial advertisers. It is possible for a small brand to grow without advertising, but it is difficult for a large brand to stay large without advertising. For example, in its early days Starbucks largely avoided advertising, focusing instead on rolling out stores across the United States to capitalise on the growing demand for espresso-based coffee—but today, now that Starbucks is a large brand with many competitors, it advertises.

Does the largely defensive nature of advertising mean that it doesn't generate sales? This is a common misunderstanding. Advertising, even if it just allows a company to hold on to market share, still works by generating sales; preventing a sale from being lost is generating a sale that otherwise would not have happened.

Marketers sometimes talk of 'brand advertising', contrasting it to advertising that aims to generate sales; 'brand advertising' they say is to 'build the brand, not generate sales'. This is confused thinking: the purpose of brand advertising is to affect buying behaviour (to cause sales), and this is how it builds the brand.

It is true that much advertising causes no obvious spike in sales when the advertising is turned on, and no slump when the advertising is turned off. This can be mistakenly seen as advertising failing to drive sales. But there are three important reasons why the sales effects of advertising are hard to see in changes in weekly sales figures.

First, the effect of advertising is spread very thinly over time. It typically takes some while to reach all the consumers in a market, and each of their (small) reactions to the advertising can take a long while to be revealed, because most consumers don't buy from the category very often; for example, commonly bought categories such as deodorant are typically only bought about two to three times a year. So the effect of advertising isn't seen immediately the ads are switched on, nor does it disappear the moment they stop—some of the effects of advertising last a lifetime. For instance, once you have learnt that the golden arches represent McDonald's, that's something you are unlikely to ever forget fully—small effects go on and on.

Second, there is much 'noise' in the market. Noise here refers to the many other factors that affect this week's sales—competitor advertising, sales promotions, price changes, new product launches, even changes in the weather. These make the effect of advertising hard to see and measure, but that doesn't mean the advertising isn't nudging sales.

Finally, advertising is rarely switched on and off neatly. While a television, radio or web campaign might feature for a specific time period, other advertising can stay in the market for some time (for instance, magazines and posters linger) and some advertising (some signage or shelf displays) never stops. And some activity, such as word-of-mouth and publicity, is largely beyond marketers' control—advertising stimulates it but can't control its timing. So again, this means that sales don't move neatly up and down at the start and end of an advertising campaign.

To understand the in-market effect of advertising, we need to draw on what we know about how people buy, to see how advertising affects buying behaviour.

Relationship to buyer behaviour

To understand what we expect of brand advertising, it is useful to recap what we have learnt of buyer behaviour in earlier chapters and discuss the relevance to advertising.

Key patterns in buyer behaviour that have relevance to advertising are that:

- repertoire buying is the norm in most categories
- most buyers are very light buyers of a brand, and light buyers of the category
- brands differ greatly in terms of market share, yet brands show little variation in loyalty levels (Ehrenberg, 1988)
- the user profiles of competing brands seldom differ (that is, users of brand A are mostly very similar to the users of competing brand B in terms of their demographics, psychographics and so on) (Kennedy, Ehrenberg & Long, 2000; Uncles et al., 2010).

Given that most buyers are comfortable buying a range of competing offerings (their repertoire), and have a history of doing so, there is typically very little that advertising can say that will convince them that one competitor is better than the others they buy. Hence, persuasion that one brand is 'better' or 'the best' is rarely an achievable goal for most brand advertising. It is generally not possible (or believable)—given that competing brands vary little in terms of features, quality and so on, and that most ads have little capacity for persuasion due to a range of reasons such as their length (15 or 30 seconds of content) and the nature of the medium (low involvement). Fortunately, it isn't necessary to convince people that the brand is better than they thought it was in order to positively influence their behaviour, to encourage them to keep on buying or nudge them to buy a little bit more often.

Because most buyers are light buyers, and often there are many months or more between purchases, many shoppers need to be reminded to think about the brand in order for them to buy it. Reminding advertising can help encourage shoppers to:

1 purchase a category they rarely consider—for example, if a mother were to consider a treat for her children when shopping, she could easily alternate between chocolate, ice cream, biscuits or a toy, without consciously considering what she was excluding from her evaluation. Advertising can nudge shoppers in certain category directions.

2 think of a brand they might not (on that day) have considered—brands do move position within people's repertoires over time, and some new brands enter their repertoires. A big advertising challenge is just to ensure shoppers even consider a brand on the next purchase situation. For example, there are lots of great chocolate bars that you might buy—while you may be very happy with many of them, you will probably only consider two or three on any particular occasion when you buy chocolate. This is out of something like twenty to sixty alternatives that might be sitting on the shelf in front of you.

While the small nudge you receive towards one category over another, or to one brand over another, may not be noticed by you as a buyer, nudging many shoppers can have a big effect on sales for an advertiser over time. Evidence indicates that advertising for established brands does indeed nudge users (see Jones & Blair, 1996) and hence prevents sales erosion and/or delivers growth.

Given that competing brands usually sell to the same sorts of people, it means brands do not need executions for their special audience. Advertisers must understand who buys their category (for instance, parents with babies are the main audience for nappy ads). But they should take care not to limit their audience unnecessarily (nappy ads can still be appealing for parents while also appealing to grandparents, nannies, future parents and the like). Reaching a broad audience clearly has media implications, but it also has implications for **advertising copy**—executions should not alienate unnecessarily. It's vital to talk to light users of the brand, because there are so many of them, and they are the route to growth. This is more tricky than talking to people who know the brand well and have well-developed mental structures. It's easier for light brand users to mistake which brand the advertisement is for, and it's easier for the advertisement to fail to refresh relevant memory associations because these users have so few memory associations devoted to the brand. This means that advertising will be more effective if it is consistent and uses the brand's most established distinctive assets.

A further implication of the patterns we see in repeat-purchasing is that advertisers should be careful with **comparative advertising**. The norm of repertoire buying tells us that your customers (at least many of them) already buy rival brands (see the duplication of purchase law for further details) as part of their repertoire. So in mentioning a competitor (even showing part of a pack), you could in fact just be advertising for them. Poorly branded ads sometimes fall prey to a similar trap—people can like them but misattribute the brand and take them to be for a competitor (Kennedy, Sharp & Rungie, 2000). This is not a minor problem—on average, only around 40 per cent of viewers register the brand correctly (Franzen, 1994; Rossiter & Bellman, 2005). Hence, care should be taken to avoid colours, images or other elements in your advertising that are commonly associated with your competitors, and to ensure your ads always look like people expect your advertisements to look.

Without memory there is nothing

Apart from a very small amount of direct response advertising (and some online **search engine advertising**) advertising must work through memories. This is an uncontroversial statement, yet it is still common for marketers and academics to forget the essential role of memory and instead think advertising works largely through persuasive arguments or creating strong feelings about the brand.

advertising copy:
Creative text printed or recorded for use in an advertisement.

comparative advertising:
Advertising that aims to influence consumer preference by comparison with competitor brands.

▼ CRITICAL REFLECTION

For companies who have a portfolio of offerings (such as different flavours or formats), should their focus be on brand' advertising or 'product' advertising (that is, focused on selling a specific SKU or offering)?

In considering your answer, look at the Schweppes Spring Valley campaign 'Where spring comes from' in Figure 10.4.

●●● **FIGURE 10.4** EXECUTIONS FOR SPRING VALLEY, PROMOTING DIFFERENT FLAVOURS

Source: Schweppes Australia

LEARNING OBJECTIVE
Understand how
advertising works on
memory to affect buyer
behaviour

**search engine
advertising:**
Paid listings that increase
visibility of a website when
specific search terms are
entered into a search
engine such as Google
or Yahoo!.

interactive advertising:
Planned promotion or
advertising that seeks
to generate an active
response from consumers.

banner advertising:
A paid form of online
advertising where an
image (still or animated)
that links to the advertised
brand's website is
embedded into a relevant
web page.

While there is some **interactive advertising** (see Figure 10.5 for a muesli bar example), most advertising still needs to work entirely through viewers' memories (see Table 10.2 for a list of media that still dominate). And all advertising, even if it is interactive, is interpreted based on our existing memories. Besides, most viewers of interactive ads do not place an order at the time they are exposed to the ad; click-through rates on web advertising average only one tenth of one per cent, so memory is still important if the interactive ad is going to have much of an effect on sales. For example, when Campbell's ran an interactive advertisement featuring a vegetable matching ingredient game, less than 1 per cent of users that saw the ad clicked through—and most probably did so because at the time this sort of advertising was new and the matching ingredients game was novel; few would have done so because they wanted to buy soup then and there. Many of the viewers who did not play the game still would have been reminded that Campbell's makes all sorts of soups with vegetables. Research shows that a very substantial part of the effect of **banner advertising** occurs in offline sales and from people who did not click on the banner advertisement (Fulgoni & Morn, 2009).

Hence, advertisers need to understand how our brains and specifically memories work and the role of emotion in responding to advertising. Then we can create great ads that affect memory.

For an advertisement to affect memory, it must be received and encoded by viewers, readers or listeners. This mental processing of the advertisement itself depends on memories and so will vary from consumer to consumer—heavy buyers of the brand will process it more easily and accurately. The individual execution must be able to be readily processed or it often will not be encoded in a way that helps the advertiser. It is not uncommon to watch a very funny ad, and perhaps remember something of it, with no link at all being made in your memory with the brand being promoted. This is a waste for the advertiser. Having sufficient branding in the advertising is essential to avoid this situation. Research suggests that in television advertisements you should show the brand early and often—and have at least one verbal mention—while there is no indication that simply having the brand present on screen for a long time is effective (Romaniuk, 2009).

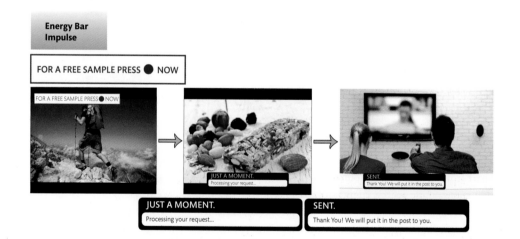

●●● **FIGURE 10.5** AN EXAMPLE OF AN INTERACTIVE ADVERTISEMENT

Source: Adapted from Steven Bellman and Duane Varan, http://audiencelabs.com (2009), 'A comparison of three interactive television ad formats', *Journal of Interactive Advertising*, vol.10, no.1, <http://jiad.org/article122>.

How memories are encoded and stored matters, affecting their chance of being retrieved at a brand relevant opportunity (that is, when the viewer is making a category purchase, giving brand advice to a friend and so on). What is recalled, at any time, is influenced by the network of other associations we have to the item of interest (Bower, 1998; Anderson & Bower, 1973). Our brains store information in nodes, which are connected to other nodes (Anderson & Bower, 1973; Collins & Quillian, 1969). When a node is activated (that is, sparked by a physical need such as hunger or social desire, or by exposure to something in an ad or store), other connected nodes can also be activated (Anderson, 1983). A goal of marketers is to maximise the activation of their brand node in as many relevant situations as possible, so relevant connections are key.

Connections are learnt when two pieces of information are presented together. This has been described as Hebb's law: 'neurons that fire together, wire together'. It is a nice reminder of how brand associations (that is, relevant links to the brand node(s)) are built—our advertisements need to link our brand to cues that might later be triggered in buying situations.

This is the same way that brand distinctive assets are built. If a symbol or colour is repeatedly shown along with the brand name, consumers learn to associate the two. Then the distinctive asset starts to work in the same way as the brand name (so it brands the advertising). McDonald's has not always had the symbols it has today (its brand's distinctive assets), but for decades the burger chain has been consistent in joint use and promotion of its name with its colours and symbols— symbols that are now uniquely and firmly linked with the brand for most users. The arches, for example, have been around since the mid 1950s, being updated into the golden arches we know today in the late 1960s. Ronald McDonald first appeared in a national television commercial in 1966 and his friends in the early 1970s (McDonald's, 2012a). Decades of consistency helps to build these strong brand associations and memories—and clearly for McDonald's these associations help the brand and its outlets be noticed with ease.

●●● **FIGURE 10.6** SYMBOLS OF MCDONALD'S FROM DECADES PAST

●●● **FIGURE 10.7** DÉLIFRANCE ADVERTISEMENT: 'READY TO BAKE AT HOME'

Source: Délifrance

Distinctive assets help the advertising to work for that particular brand. Advertising then needs to build as many links as possible to the cues that signal a relevant category need or want (for example, McDonald's links to hunger, breakfast, lunch, dinner or a snack, as well as somewhere to meet friends or take the kids, a quick coffee stop, healthy meal options, and so on). The more relevant links, the higher the probability a brand will be recalled at a moment that is beneficial to the brand.

Being recalled is also a function of the strength of the links, which is determined by the uniqueness of the node relative to other nodes (Meyers-Levy, 1989); the number of pathways between two nodes (Unnava & Burnkrant, 1991); and repeated use (Anderson, 1983; Fazio & Williams, 1986, Martindale, 1991).

Therefore an important advertising task is to reinforce and deepen associations that are already there, and occasionally build new associations that will increase the propensity of the brand to be thought of in relevant buying situations. For example, see how this McDonald's ad builds the link to McDonald's as a reward for your child: http://youtu.be/5ZdALTZ6aA8. Doing so increases the brand's mental availability (Romaniuk & Sharp, 2004).

Generally, it is a very good rule for advertisers to tap into existing memories. These include the memories for the brand and also more general associations that exist in the population (particularly valuable for new brands that do not have any existing associations). A simple example is shown in Figure 10.7, an ad for Délifrance, with French bread cut into slippers to demonstrate a link to home.

This simple image makes the association between the two concepts (Délifrance and home) and it communicates both rationally and emotionally (like most communication). The unusual image piques our interest. The cleverness of the idea is appealing (it's enjoyable, and makes us smile—on the inside at least). Finally, fresh bread and the notion of home are both things that trigger warm, reassuring feelings.

Stories, fairy tales, mythology, symbols and archetypes are often used in advertising because they work fast to engage the audience's heart and mind. Because we give advertising only fleeting attention, there is a high risk much will be missed and it will have less chance of affecting memory. Archetypes help advertisers communicate very quickly, because they tap into memories that are already well-established. In the John Lewis ad in Figure 10.8, the simple inclusion of the word 'Princess' on a UK road sign with a relevant image conveys to the audience—at a glance and in an appealing, emotive way—that all their beauty needs will be met at this one stop.

●●● **FIGURE 10.8** JOHN LEWIS ADVERTISEMENT

Source: John Lewis UK

We can't help being emotional. Even purely rational information can trigger emotional reactions (for example, how we may react to '24-hour sale on Jimmy Choo shoes today'). Although our emotional reactions are usually so mild they are undetectable to us, sometimes we clearly notice our attention being grabbed.

The Advertising Research Foundation and the American Association of Advertising Agencies, in a study of consumers' emotional responses to television advertising, argued that advertisements that tell a branding story work better than ads that focus on **product positioning**. For storytelling ads to be effective, the plot needs to tie to the brand. As Bill Cook said: 'When the emotional peaks align with the presence of the brand, or the impact of the brand in the story, the emotional connection with the brand is greatest' (quoted in Facenda, 2007).

Our emotions help us determine what in our surroundings we should give attention to (or screen out). Emotions are also necessary for the process of making a decision (Damasio, 1994).

Advertising agencies enjoy making emotional advertising. The **creatives** in good advertising agencies are experts in making us laugh, cry, feel relieved and so on. This is all well and good, unless they lose track of the main purpose of advertising: to reinforce and build mental availability for the brand. The creative content of advertising should never overwhelm or run contrary to highlighting the brand and linking it to relevant cues.

product positioning: Using advertising to try to create a brand identity or develop a specific image for a product or organisation in the minds of consumers.

creatives: The people responsible for developing the creative content of advertisements and other planned promotions.

●●● **FIGURE 10.9** MECCANO AD TAPPING INTO STORIES THAT CHILDREN THE WORLD OVER ACT OUT AND PLAY

Source: Meccano

The role of creativity

Most people are very busy with lots of important things on their minds (a new love, bills to pay, holidays to plan, children to look after and so on). When this is combined with the growing clutter that dominates most media, getting ads noticed is a difficult task for advertisers. Creativity plays a critical role here. There are many creative devices that advertisers use, from unexpected sounds to cute animals, sexy models, famous characters and more.

Good advertising tends to be more engaging that poor advertising, meaning that it is less likely to be screened out and more likely to be watched. That said, another (potentially complementary) route to effectiveness is for the advertising to require very little processing. There is some evidence that emotional (low information content) advertising can be effective with very little active processing by consumers (Heath, Nairn & Bottomley, 2009). Good advertising should be easy to understand. Some advertising tries to be deliberately clever or tricky, and a little hard to understand. This is fine if this creative device leads to greater processing by consumers, but it is clearly very risky: many consumers are unlikely to bother; many will simply not understand the advertisement or ignore it.

Gaining attention isn't the only purpose for creativity. An advertisement can be noticed but still fail to refresh and build appropriate memories, and so fail to affect mental availability and hence sales. Good advertising finds a creative way to throw a spotlight on the brand. While refreshing memories means telling people things they already know, it need not be boring. Fortunately people are very happy to accept such (old) messages—indeed they tend to be more resistant to messages that tell them new things, particularly messages that conflict with existing beliefs. They are happy to pay attention to 'old news' so long as it is presented in an entertaining way. Finding new interesting ways to deliver old news is one of the central creative challenges for advertising.

As mentioned above, the danger is in letting creativity overpower the brand. Many viewers of television advertisements, for instance, do not give their complete attention to the whole ad (viewers head off to get coffee, check what else is on, have the sound muted or hold conversations at the time the ad is playing). Creativity and branding need to work together, ideally in a way that requires little viewer thought or attention.

Sales-effective advertising

To make advertising sales-effective, it is useful to think about what memories are needed. What would assist consumers to think of and buy your brand? Often these are very simple things such as what your brand looks like, where it is sold and in what situations people use it. To neglect communicating these aspects for long can be fatal: the market needs reminding over and over.

One aspect to consider is the relative importance of the need for **brand recall** versus **brand recognition** (Rossiter & Bellman, 2005). For example, many categories are purchased in a supermarket when the shopper finds the item among a group of competitive offerings (for instance frozen peas or tinned tomatoes). In these situations, noticing and then recognising the pack, logo and/or other distinctive assets of the brand (such as colours) is vital, but knowing the brand's name might not be as critical. Shopper studies suggest that about 50 per cent of product and brand decisions are made in stores (Rubinson, 2010)—so think about what memories have to be built and refreshed in order to help the shopper in stores.

Similarly, many products are bought online after a web search. Search advertising—that is, paid weblinks—works better if consumers notices and recognise the brand name. It is important for marketers to understand search engine advertising. The key feature is that your ads go straight to people who have expressed a direct interest in the focus of your brand by their use of keywords in a search engine. To learn more about Google 'Adwords', read up and experiment with the response as you enter different search terms into your browser.

In other circumstances, consumers may need to think of a brand themselves. For instance, they may need to ask for a specific brand of beer in a café, type the name of a book retailer into Google, or the name of a specific book into Amazon. Brand recall is required here. It is typically a harder memory retrieval task than brand recognition.

Where children are likely to be asking parents for the brand, one strategy marketers use to help them verbalise their request is jingles: 'I like Aeroplane jelly, Aeroplane jelly for me, I like it for dinner, I like it for tea, A little each day is a good recipe, I like Aeroplane Jelly, Aeroplane jelly for me!' As any pre-school teacher will attest, songs and rhymes (such as jingles) help children learn words—in this case, brand names.

brand recall: The ability of a customer to retrieve the name of a brand from their memory unprompted or with a category prompt.

brand recognition: The ability of a customer to correctly recognise a brand in a situation where they are prompted with stimuli (such as packaging in a supermarket or brand names on a drinks menu).

New brands, especially in new categories, will typically have more 'new news' they may wish to communicate. But even so, the main message is typically a simple one—specifically that the brand exists, what it is, what it looks like and perhaps where to find it.

Advertising challenges for new brands

New brands lack mental availability and often physical availability too; hence, we have different expectations for what advertising can and should do for them. New brands have the novelty that they are new to the world and this may gain them some attention, but their lack of mental and physical availability is a major disadvantage.

Brands without extensive physical availability face the disadvantage that much of their advertising effort will be wasted because it will reach consumers who have very little opportunity to buy. Also, the advertising will lack impact because it will not be reinforced by people seeing the brand in stores. A solution is to find media that distributes advertising to the same places as where the brand is physically available—if this is possible. Otherwise, much wasted advertising has to be accepted but used to help gain physical availability, as retailers are more inclined to start stocking a brand if they see it is well advertised.

If people don't know the brand, they find it harder to mentally process the brand's advertising. Advertising is particularly good at reinforcing existing memories, but in the case of new brands people know nothing about them. This is why some advertisers try to 'borrow' existing memory structures, to relate the new brand to things that consumers already know. The Werther's Originals campaign featuring grandfathers, and more recently fathers, giving their product to small boys is an example of a brand benefiting from people remembering the treats they were given as a child (and linking those feelings with the brand).

The job of advertising for new brands is to build some usually very simple memory structures that give the brand a chance of being purchased. The most obvious message is to say 'a new brand of [product/service category] is available'. Other important memories that need to be implanted in potential buyers' brains are:

- the brand name, logo and other identifying devices
- what the product/brand looks like (for example on display in stores)
- what branches look like (for a new store, bank or other retail service)
- where it can be found.

Then the advertising has to build and refresh memory links that make the brand likely to come to mind in potential buying situations. This is why advertisements often show people using the brand in consumption situations. It is sensible to show how using the brand will fit into consumers' lives.

New brand advertising also often includes messages telling people why they need the brand. This is because marketers believe they need to sell the brand's benefits and provide buyers with motivating reasons to buy. In situations such as the launch of Wii (see Figure 10.10) this may be appropriate, but if the benefits are largely common to existing brands in the category it is very probable that these other brands will be the ones to benefit from the new brand's advertising.

●●● **FIGURE 10.10** LAUNCH ADVERTISEMENT FOR WII

Source: Nintendo Australia

Many launches are extensions to existing brands that already have established distinctive assets (known logos, looks, colours and so on). This is demonstrated in Figure 10.11, which shows the online launch advertisement for the puppy version of My Dog. Existing memory structures give the new launch a head start; however, it is still difficult to communicate the story of the new brand variation. It is likely that many consumers will simply see the advertising as being for the existing brand.

Occasionally, a launch will be for a brand and product that is truly revolutionary, which might require significant learning and/or changes in consumer behaviour (e.g. the launch of Apple's iPad—a product that presented a significant technological development). In such cases, explanation is required, but the messages that are required are still mostly straightforward. The key points in this type of situation are to show the product, show some key features (for the iPad, that it is very slim and easy to take everywhere), show people buying or using the product, show why it is appealing (some of the cool things it can do) and, most importantly,

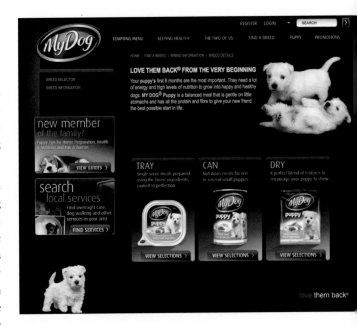

●●● **FIGURE 10.11** ONLINE LAUNCH ADVERTISEMENT FOR MY DOG PUPPY

Source: Mars Petcare Australia

brand it well. Once people know what it is, the branding is the dimension that will support the brand into the future.

CRITICAL REFLECTION

1   Memory structures, existing memories and brand-related memories are all important ingredients in advertising. Without these, the chance that consumers will buy your brand will be practically zero. Imagine that you are launching a new brand. What simple memories must you get into the heads of potential buyers for:

a   a new brand of wine

b   a new dry-cleaning business

c   a new music album from an established artist

d   a politician?

Remember—keep it simple.

2   Why does advertising need to keep telling people things that they already know?

3   What memories help consumers to keep on repeat-buying a brand?

Very soon, 'new news' demonstrated in a launch campaign is not new. But repetition is often required to keep memories fresh (and therefore easier to be retrieved). Clearly branded Apple ads continue to show the iPad in different ways—delightfully so (see examples at www.apple.com/au/ipad).

Mostly, iPad advertisements continue to creatively publicise the product, while demonstrating its features and clearly reinforcing the mother brand. Importantly, Apple ads are appealing, so people want to watch them—this is vital, as ads that bore viewers get fast-forwarded or just ignored.

In terms of response, launch ads can appear to have a large sales impact, something rarely seen for ads for mature brands, especially those with a tradition of advertising. One needs to remember that new brands start with no customers and no sales, so any increase is large in percentage terms. Often new brands are simultaneously rapidly building physical availability and launching with promotions and special offers—factors that help make the impact of a campaign look extra good. We should expect greater percentage sales volume changes at launches than we will ever see for campaigns for established brands.

Case study

Meat & Livestock Australia—We love our lamb

By Elizabeth Gunner

The Meat & Livestock Australia 'We love our lamb' campaign is an example of how advertising can work. Meat & Livestock Australia (MLA) is a producer-owned company that works in partnership with farmers and the government to make sure that the red meat industry is sustainable and profitable. This means conducting marketing on behalf of over 47,000 producers and promoting beef, lamb and other red meat products nationally.

The 'We love our lamb' campaign is part of an ongoing marketing effort by MLA to revamp the image of lamb. This effort began during the 1980s and early 1990s, when lamb meat was widely considered an old-fashioned, fatty meat, and more shoppers were opting for alternatives such as chicken or pork. The aim was to get more lamb on Australian dinner tables and to counteract declining sales by improving consumers' perceptions of lamb.

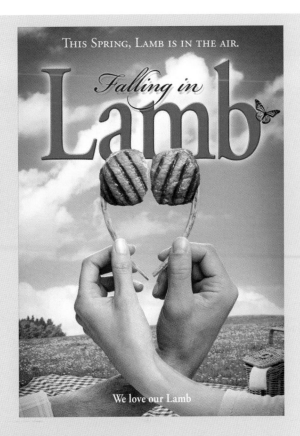

●●● **FIGURE 10.12** MLA ADVERTISEMENTS FROM THE 'CHUCK A SUNDAY' AND 'WE LOVE OUR LAMB' CAMPAIGNS

The 'We love our lamb' campaign has been running since 1999 and has been a great success, resulting in:

- a sustained, strong domestic demand for lamb (despite challenges of rising retail prices and fluctuating supply)
- the development of the 'We love our lamb' brand, which is now well recognised across Australia
- a link between lamb and key calendar events:
  - Australia Day—'Don't be un-Australian, serve lamb on Australia Day'
  - Mother's Day—'She'll love you for it'
  - spring—'This spring, lamb is in the air'.

The success of this ongoing campaign can be attributed to great media planning, strong creative execution and a marketing strategy that applied an understanding of buyer behaviour.

Because sustained demand was one of the key objectives, MLA targeted a wide audience with their campaign. The media schedule focused on mass media (including television) with a year-round presence, for maximum reach with continuity. They particularly wanted to reach light buyers, because of the potential for sales growth with that group.

The 'We love our lamb' branding is now a well-known feature of MLA advertisements. Although each of the advertisements is unique, the style of all of MLA's communications is consistent, using a tongue-in-cheek sense of humour. This makes the ads memorable and likeable (the 2012 Australia Day advertisement gained over 642,000 YouTube views in two months).

Another asset for the brand is the 'Lambassador': media personality, sports commentator and former AFL player Sam Kekovich. Kekovich has featured in MLA lamb commercials since 2005, and is now very much a part of the 'We love our lamb' brand.

This great execution and media planning has contributed to cementing a new image for lamb and building great mental availability. Although the domestic market has faced some difficulties, with high retail prices and shortages, demand in Australia remains strong. Coupled with the success of marketing lamb meat for the international market, it has been a winning combination for MLA and for the producers they work for.

◢ LEARNING OBJECTIVE
Be able to brief an advertising agency for an effective campaign and set realistic objectives for a brand in a communications plan

BRIEFING TO GET GREAT ADVERTISING

Typically, great campaigns are developed and produced by professional creatives from an advertising agency. Some firms have internal creative departments, but again these tend to be staffed by specialist staff. A creative team typically comprises a range of people with different skills and titles such as Creative Director, Art Director or Copywriter. They will use words, pictures, images, stories and so on to bring attention to your brand through an advertisement or campaign.

For a list of some notable agencies, visit http://en.wikipedia.org/wiki/List_of_advertising_agencies. Explore some of their websites to see the sort of advertising they do.

A written brief is an important first step in the process of designing a great ad or campaign. It ensures that all parties are clear on what is required, it helps ensure consistency over time and gives the basis for evaluating the concept once it has been developed—that is, does the ad do what you asked?

Below is a template to help you know what information you should provide in order to brief an agency to produce great advertising. Once you have provided a good brief, you should give the agency the freedom to be creative and to create excitement about your brand within your boundaries. Note that most **mandatory brand requirements** should be consistent for long periods of time (years or decades). Examples might be that all Coke ads must show the bottle, all Huggies ads must include a happy baby wearing Huggies, all McDonald's ads must show the golden arches and so on. The distinctive brand assets listed must come from market research so they reflect what is in the memory of many shoppers, as opposed to what the marketing team think or would like there to be.

◢ mandatory brand requirements (mandatories): Words, images or any other requirements that the creative team must include in the advertising; for example, brand name, logo, a specific font and so on.

Adapt the following template by using the headings and tailoring the necessary detail as required.

Creative agency briefing template

1 Objectives for the advertising job

Create a well-branded, liked campaign that will get noticed by distracted viewers.

- The campaign should remind the marketplace about brand X (creatively publicise it), so as many category users think of it in relation to these [specify] buying situations. It should link the brand to the category and/or reasons people purchase the category. (Provide relevant research in attachment.)
- It must use brand X's distinctive assets (specified colour(s), character(s), and/or tagline) and/or occasionally build a new association.

Occasionally it may provide relevant information or news (launch of new flavour, winner of award or new outlet) but within the framework of helping publicise the brand and refreshing brand associations.

2 Who are we talking to with the campaign?

The default audience is category users (and potential category users), including the many light buyers.

3 Mandatories

The advertising must make it easy for people to notice and recognise the ad as one for brand X. It should typically show the brand early and often—and have at least one verbal brand mention. One to three of the following known brand associations must be central to the execution: colour x; sound, music or tone x; logo; character(s); celebrity(ies); style(s) x; font(s) x; scene(s), etc.

4 Campaign-specific requirements

If there is a specific reason to be advertising at this time, mention it: for instance cues to relevant issues in the marketplace, seasonal images such as Christmas, Halloween and so on, if relevant to the category.

Can the advertising tell viewers anything that makes it easier to purchase our brand now? For instance, 'Available in all Coles stores' or 'Look for the blue box'. Give the telephone number, website address, etc.

Can we tell them anything that will create excitement about our brand, such as new flavours, features or awards? Remember that great ads do not have to contain much information. Relevant news can be of interest, but should be secondary to publicising the brand and its distinctive elements. New news is only new once, so ads promoting new news should always do it within a framework of distinctiveness (that is, still looking like the brand).

5 Requirements

What does the agency need to deliver? For example, a thirty-second television commercial, leaflet, insert, outdoor advertisement, website, media plan, etc.

Timings (allowing time for pre-testing).

6 Budget

Within $X budget.

7 Contact information

Appendix: Background

Attach background information, relevant research on what is known about buying of the brand/category, the brands' established memory structures, product samples—anything that can inspire the creatives to know and have fun with your brand.

Complexities in briefing

The template creative agency briefing template above is simplified to allow you to focus on the fundamentals. In practice, there may be other complexities that need to be considered.

The objectives may be more complex and include dimensions such as the advertising generating further activity, including:

advertising avoidance:
When viewers avoid being exposed to advertisements. Avoidance can be active (switching the channel, turning a page or leaving the room) or passive (talking or concentrating on something else).

- publicity and word-of-mouth—for example, the character from the Old Spice ads made a Twitter fan's marriage proposal online
- online activity (such as YouTube downloads and tweets). Some marketers may have the specific goal of developing content that will 'go viral'; that is, spread online through people's social networks or encourage interactivity and engagement with the brand. Examples include competitions where brands encourage the public to produce ads for their products.

Not only does this offer the potential of cheap media, but it can overcome some of the **advertising avoidance** problems discussed elsewhere.

As discussed earlier, television still dominates the media horizon with few viewers wanting to interact with brands through the likes of Twitter or YouTube.

But other media can play an important role, especially for certain product types. For instance, radio is great for takeaway food as you can hit people while they are out and about, magazines can be wonderful for fashion items that need a high-gloss image but not movement, and newspapers for quick turnaround campaigns such as 'one day sale on tomorrow'. In briefing creatives, you may not want to specify a medium but rather focus on your objective and then see what media (or combinations) achieve your goal most effectively. How the creatives will work across the required media is an important consideration.

●●● **FIGURE 10.13** MILKY WAY PACKAGING FROM DIFFERENT PARTS OF THE WORLD

Many advertisers also require some ability for the creatives to work across countries (with minor adaptations, for example for different languages and legal requirements). The flow of people and content now moves across markets rapidly, so brand differences that were unnoticed in times past can now be an issue that can not easily be solved if established memory structures vary across markets (see Figure 10.13).

▲ **advertising budget:** The sum of money available for communication of a brand through advertising. It incorporates spend on production (non-working media) as well as media placement (working media).

How much to spend

Determining the **advertising budget** for a campaign or brand is a regular issue faced by marketers. Unfortunately, there is no single formula for determining the ideal advertising budget.

However, observation in many stable markets has shown that bigger brands tend to spend less than expected given their market share, so that their share of all advertising spent in the category—known as their share of voice—is less than their share of the market (Jones, 1990), this being a key advantage of scale. In 1990, John Philip Jones formalised this observation across hundreds of markets through his advertising intensiveness (AI) curve, which was later supported by Danenberg (2008) and Hansen and Christensen (2005), who demonstrated that the main characteristics of the AI relationship were remarkably robust.

The implication that stems from this research is that within a category there is a level of spend that any brand must meet in order to maintain its market share. Thus, a small brand will need to spend more than their market share to remain stable, while a big brand can spend less than their market share and still maintain their share. This is an empirically based, practical starting point for start budget setting.

The inputs required for such analysis are simple metrics such as market share and the corresponding levels of advertising for the brands in the market, which the 'reasonable' marketing manager can access quickly, easily and reliably (Danenberg, 2008).

Another useful guideline is provided by Professor Malcolm Wright (2009). In his article 'A new theorem for optimizing the advertising budget', he suggests that managers should set their advertising budget as their gross profit multiplied by the advertising elasticity of their brand. If they don't know their advertising elasticity, a reasonable guide is 0.10 (based on the academic literature), so a firm should spend 10 per cent of their gross profits on advertising. Gross profits are the money a firm

▼ CRITICAL REFLECTION

Figure 10.14 shows an image from an interactive Pedigree campaign on www.puppy.com.au. It allows the viewer to train the virtual puppy to play ball, fetch a Pedigree Dentabone, lick the screen (action shown) or eat their food.

1   If you were the brand manager for Pedigree, what aspects of buyer behaviour would you think were important to consider in your advertising planning? How would this knowledge impact your advertising?

2   Why might you include a puppy in your advertising?

3   What distinctive assets would you list as mandatories (subject to support from research)?

4   What memory structures would you be hoping to refresh or build?

●●● **FIGURE 10.14** AN INTERACTIVE BILLBOARD AD FOR THE PEDIGREE 'TRAIN YOUR PUPPY' WEBSITE

Source: Advertising Agency: Whybin\TBWA\TEQUILA, Australia, retrieved from www.ibelieveinadv.com/2008/11/pedigree-train-your-puppy.

makes on each sale (the contribution to overheads), so if a firm's gross profits are negative then it shouldn't advertise because it loses more money the more sales it makes. Until it increases its prices and/or decreases costs there is no point in advertising.

Marketers are advised to take this knowledge and then consider their tasks and objectives for the planning period. For instance, a brand hoping to grow, with a plan of exciting launches, will be in a different situation from a brand that is being phased out. Budgeting requires considerable effort in number crunching alternative routes to reach an objective; for example, what gives us better reach, a mix of television and social media or television and outdoor, and at what cost? Experimentation over time is also highly recommended, in order to know expected sales response from competing activities.

Case study

Interactive marketing goes high-tech: QR coding

By David Fortin, University of Canterbury, New Zealand

Interactive marketing: What is the next big thing?

The core principles behind the emerging area of interactive marketing (IM) are, surprisingly, not really new but mostly reinvented for an era facilitated by technological innovation. Some have compared IM to a *conversation* or *dialogue* where each participant responds and reacts to stimulus information provided by the other (Deighton, 1996). The richness of such an interaction is arguably more powerful in developing a sense of engagement and/or involvement with that exchange, which in turn might lead to repeat behaviour in the future. Sound familiar? If concepts of consumer involvement and brand loyalty came to mind, you are probably right. Think about the old-fashioned business model of the 'general store' that used to be found in every small town at the turn of the twentieth century. Every transaction event was much more than a purely economic exchange; it involved an interaction and dialogue with the store owner, who probably knew you by name and may have asked about the current situation of your two sons and daughter; the owner could do that because he had access to that information and could retrieve it in memory to engage in an enhanced interaction with his customers. As markets and populations became larger, this eventually became unrealistic, but the need to interact never really disappeared. What we are witnessing today is the ability to re-engage with consumers to mimic a closer relationship, and this is now made possible by innovations in communication technology.

In marketing terms, we are seeing a move away from the traditional model of *push*, or one-way communication through mass media, to a *pull* model that involves two-way communication and where the receiver gets to interact by providing feedback to the original source. This loop is recursive and feeds on the previous exchange to enhance communication. Several examples of successful web-based ventures, such as Amazon, eBay, trademe.co.nz in New Zealand, and even Google now includes advanced features that allow users to interact by providing feedback that becomes integrated into the overall platform. This has led to the widespread use of user-generated content,

which may be found in the form of product reviews, blogs, opinions and more recently as providers of creative content for advertising campaigns that are actually aired on major broadcast networks. With the introduction of smart phones using 4G mobile technology, consumers now have access to new tools to engage with their brands outside the limitations of a computer within a specific location. Perhaps one promising innovation coined as 'the next big thing' in IM is QR coding technology.

QR codes

QR is short for 'quick response', meaning that they can be quickly read to provide extra bits of useful information about a product, brand or anything else really. Think of it as a fancier version of the standard barcode that we are used to finding on most packaged goods. QR codes are actually matrix-type codes that are two-dimensional, and hence can carry a lot more information (see Figure 10.15). The technology itself is not necessarily new and was developed originally by Toyota in the early 1990s to track cars going through the manufacturing stages. The interest in this innovation here for IM is that consumers now have the technology at their fingertips to be able to scan the code pretty much in any form to get access to more details about that product or brand and engage in an interactive process. QR codes typically provide access to hyperlinks that will connect the consumer to a firm's website and/or will provide them with key bits of information needed for them to engage further; for example a secret code to enter a promotion. Their physical capacity at the moment is limited to 4296 alphanumeric characters, but this may evolve in the future. The real attractiveness comes from their ease of use, as everyone owning a smart phone can

●●● **FIGURE 10.15** SAMPLE QR CODE

download an application that will allow the codes to be easily scanned and recognised, which was the major hurdle explaining their limited use for consumer markets in the last twenty years.

●●● **FIGURE 10.16** GODADDY.COM ADVERTISEMENT

Building brands through consumer engagement

As the technology evolves and more consumers get exposed to it, we can expect a wider array of uses and applications through creative innovation in message tactics. Standard applications for QR codes, already in use, include train tickets (in China), business cards and print magazine advertisements. They are now found on outdoor posters and signs, on the back of buses and on several consumer goods. Codes can also be read from electronic media such as a computer or television screen. The controversial campaigns for GoDaddy.com ran for several years in the USA, and they used QR codes in their television ads, aired during the 2012 Super Bowl (www.youtube.com/watch?v=8WjYH8KuOao). This provider of domain names and websites for the greater consumer market used the QR codes on screen to link consumers to their website (see Figure 10.16), where they could view an extended version (or follow-up story) of the advert being screened. The end result is the active engagement of the consumer, as they physically interact with the traditional media (television) to link up using a different technological platform (the smart phone).

In Australia, communication agency Euro RSCG 4D used the QR codes to create an engaging promotional campaign to support the Sony brand in the launch of the James Bond movie *Quantum of Solace*. Participants were required to act as spies in a game that required them to gather codes and bits of information by scanning QR codes appearing on posters. They then connected via their phone's internet to interact with other participants via Facebook. This example took consumer engagement to a whole new level. Results appear to be promising, with a reported $21.3 million in generated sales value, which is claimed to be 33 per cent over their initial target (see Euro RSCG 4D, 2012).

Two cases from New Zealand: Panasonic and Brancott Estate Wines

In New Zealand, Panasonic and Brancott Estate Wines have each used QR codes in different innovative ways. Panasonic included a QR code on the cover of a trade magazine and Brancott Estate Wines used the codes on their wine bottles to tie in with a revamp of their brand. Both cases are reviewed in more detail below.

Panasonic

The agency Publicis Mojo Auckland developed a clever rendition of an enlarged QR code to appear on the December 2011 cover of trade magazine *Wares NZ*, a magazine directed at leading trade appliance retailers in the country. The giant QR code (Figure 10.18) was actually made up of a range of Panasonic products, such as televisions, remote controls, projectors and so on, and was

●●● **FIGURE 10.17** *QUANTUM OF SOLACE* POSTER

captioned with the campaign slogan 'Panasonic: Ideas for Life'. In addition to the increased penetration in consumer markets, this accolade is a clear sign that the QR technology is also making inroads at the trade and intermediary levels, where it can be used as an additional selling tool to provide a better service to customers at point of purchase.

Brancott Estate Wines

Brancott Estate Wines has been better known for its Marlborough region Sauvignon Blanc range, under the brand name 'Montana Wines', for the last few decades. The global owner of the brand, Pernod Ricard, undertook a bold rebranding exercise in 2011 to revitalise an existing brand of the portfolio to make the product more appealing to a global audience. In support of this relaunch, they adopted a 'Stay Curious' advertising theme that appeared on their website and in broadcast television advertisements. The wine range also underwent a packaging design revamp that led to the concept of 'The World's Most Curious Bottle', and a smartphone application was developed to allow consumers to explore information appearing on that bottle in more detail (see Figure 10.19). By using the app, consumers can explore decodable bits of information that appear on the front and back labels, and of course one of those includes a specially designed QR code. This makes the product attractive to consumers, who can explore the wine bottle either at point of purchase or in their home environment. This tool generates consumer engagement and also possibly reduces the degree to which consumers hold conflicting thoughts about the product after purchase. The interesting application here of the QR technology is that it isn't used just as a novelty gimmick: it actually fits in with the creative concept developed for the brand in its IM communication strategy.

●●● **FIGURE 10.18** *WARES* COVER PAGE, FEATURING PANASONIC

Questions

1   From a marketer's perspective, what is the appeal of interactive applications such as the QR code technology? Why?

2   In the three cases of Sony, Panasonic and Brancott Estate, what are the key differences in their use of QR codes to engage their consumer base? Hint: Look at the media platform and the likely different objectives associated with their respective uses.

3   Sony used the technology to promote a movie called *The Quantum Code*. What marketing principles would apply here, in your opinion?

4   Brancott Estate has recently undergone an extensive branding re-alignment, including a packaging revamp and a migration from the historical 'Montana' brand to 'Brancott'. How do you think this fits in with their 'World's Most Curious Bottle' concept?

5   Some critics would argue that this technology could lose its appeal over time. Can you think of other marketing tactics based on technology that have been short-lived in the last decade?

●●● **FIGURE 10.19** BRANCOTT ESTATE SMARTPHONE APPLICATION

WHAT GREAT ADS LOOK LIKE

Great advertisements clearly look like they are for the brand they are advertising. This requires consistency across campaigns, ideally for decades, so it is very easy for passive viewers to pick up who the advertising is for. That does not mean that ads should not be fun, attention grabbing or exciting. All of these things can help effectiveness, as long as it is what viewers are expecting for the brand, and it successfully refreshes (or builds) memories for the brand.

CRITICAL REFLECTION

There is an explosion of screens upon which advertising can be presented to people. The lounge room television is no longer the only screen in people's lives. It is being supplemented by computer screens, mobile phone screens, iPad screens and electronic billboards. Research by Professor Duane Varan and colleagues (Varan, 2012) shows that consumers' reactions to an advertisement are very similar across all these screens. What opportunities do these different screens offer marketers?

As mentioned earlier, direct branding (that is showing and /or saying the brand name) is often critical. This can and should be creatively supported by use of the brand's distinctive assets. Given that a main advertising goal is to nudge mental availability—a brand's propensity to be considered in purchase situations—it often makes sense to show the pack shot, and the brand being bought or used in a range of relevant situations. Cues that get the brand considered in different situations are useful, such as showing people drinking Coke with friends, Coke at the beach, Coke at Christmas and so on.

●●● **FIGURE 10.20** GREAT ADVERTISING IS ALL ABOUT THE BRAND

ADVERTISING RESEARCH

Some advertisements are great; others are lousy. Individual advertising executions for a brand can vary greatly in how sales effective they are (or are not) (Jones & Blair, 1996; Tellis, 2009; Wood, 2009). A difference of four times the level of sales has been shown for different advertising executions for the same brand (Brandt & Biteau, 2000). A large media spend is a very ineffectual and hideously wasteful compensation for a poor advertisement. So it makes sense to research advertising to ensure that an ad will work (or is working).

There are a number of stages where advertising research is conducted. They include: **pre-testing** (also called copy testing in some parts of the world), which is conducted prior to airing, and **advertising tracking,** which tracks finished ads once they are out in the market.

There are many different measurement approaches and quite varied ideas about what should be measured and how. Many approaches have traditionally focused on advertising's intermediate effects—for example, consumer knowledge and attitudes—rather than on its behavioural effects, such as its effects on brand choice (sales).

In evaluating any approach or provider it is useful to understand the theory underpinning how that particular form of advertising works. Different theories of advertising result in very different methodologies and different research questions asked. Those who feel that advertising needs to provide information about the brand and persuade will tend to ask respondents about their comprehension of messages, believability and changes in attitudes to the ad or brand. Those who believe that advertising works mostly through emotion will tend to avoid verbal responses altogether, instead trying other approaches such as getting respondents to select images that represent how they feel when they watch an ad, or measuring physiological responses. For a more detailed appreciation of advertising theory, refer to the works listed in 'Further reading' at the end of this chapter. We will discuss some of the key alternatives below.

Pre-testing

Pre-testing occurs prior to the finished advertisement being aired, played or published. It simply sets out to ask which of a series of executions is likely to be the most effective. (Is copy A better than copy B?)

About 60 per cent of the time for television and 30 per cent for magazines, pre-testing is qualitative (verbal feedback); about 30 per cent of the time for both television and magazines it is quantitative (numeric feedback) (Prue, 1996). Sometimes it is a mix of both. Traditionally much qualitative ad research has been conducted in focus groups, but it can also be conducted in interviews or online approaches. Quantitative research has traditionally been conducted face to face or via the telephone, but much is now conducted online. Quantitative research alternatives include second-by-second evaluations based on adjusting dials (in cinemas or laboratories), biometric measurement or observations of reading/watching behaviour. Quantitative approaches typically include much larger samples of respondents.

LEARNING OBJECTIVE
Understand the value of pre-testing and advertising tracking, and begin to appreciate some of the difficulties of conducting research on advertising effectiveness.

pre-testing: Advertising research conducted before an advertisement has been aired/placed or on a concept before it has been produced.

advertising tracking: Advertising research that measures the effects of an advertisement after it has been aired/placed.

Whether qualitative or quantitative, the ad concept is presented in one of a number of different formats:

- *storyboards*, which are a sequence of images, with text to demonstrate the proposed flow of the ad
- *animatics/videomatics*, which take the images and sequence them with motion, timing and sound to mock up something closer to the final ad
- *finished format*, which is most common if testing an ad taken from another market.

Typically the aim is to get the audience's views on the ad, which can be very important since marketers can get bored with their ads and formats before customers do, or customers may get confused with features more easily due to different levels of attention and knowledge.

Outputs from pre-testing research can include: a prediction of which execution is going to be the best (or a suggested media allocation for a range of executions for a campaign); diagnostics of what is working or what could be improved; warnings of possible areas of confusion or misunderstanding; and feedback on whether the ads fit the overall strategy or not.

Criticisms of pre-testing

While pre-testing has been used for many years and is a big business, there is almost no sound scientific evidence supporting the ability of any pre-testing method to reliably forecast the future (in-market) sales ability of an advertisement. This is not surprising for the use of questionable research practices such as focus groups, but it also applies to professional pre-testing services. The few validation studies that have been published have either been done by the market research agency that owns and sells the special method, or have been subsequently refuted.

Criticisms of pre-testing include that pre-testing can be harsh, unforgiving, black and white, and can give a 'go'—'no go' result, but provide no clear understanding of why or how an idea works (or not) (Davies, Mills & Baxter, 2002). Assumptions are often made that one measure fits all situations; for example, the measuring of persuasion favours 'new launches ... new news ... and the rational' (McDonald, 1993).

Given these criticisms, advertisers and researchers have looked to alternatives. Moves in the right direction include:

- research that more closely emulates a typical viewing situation; for example online research where people are shown a concept in their own home, or research in mock living rooms in family or friendship groups that would normally view together
- showing ads in context or as close to as possible; for example recruiting people to look at mock-ups of whole magazines or websites so their focus is on the overall content rather than directly on the advertising.

Other approaches include expert testing and biometric testing.

Expert tests

Expert tests, or management judgement tests, are a very different approach from consumer pre-testing.

As proposed by Rossiter and Bellman (2005), expert tests include six to twenty brand or marketing managers assessing proposed executions against a checklist for the presence of logos, key brand cues, compliance to a brief and so on. Rossiter and Bellman (2005) suggest that such tests should only be used for new executions of existing campaigns as a brand hygiene check.

Assuming that the checklist is well thought out, such an approach can help avoid disasters (such as an ad not looking like it is for the brand it is supposed to be promoting) and generally improve the advertisement; expert texts can be relatively cheap and quick.

Independent experts (people trained for the task to ensure consistency across time and individuals) can also be used to independently rate ads without detailed brand-specific knowledge. Basic aspects that they can check include that the pack is shown (where relevant), direct branding can be seen and that the brand's colours or other distinctive elements are shown. Such aspects should be systematically checked on all new executions.

Biometric pre-testing

Neuroscientists are discovering a lot about how our brain works and how to measure what captures our attention, generates emotion and is encoded in memory without needing to ask directly. Given that attention, emotion and memory are key tasks of advertising, it is no surprise that the new developments in biometric measurement are making their way into advertising pre-testing.

Advertising research companies offer a range of biometric or physiological approaches, including facial electromyography (EMG), skin conductance, heart rate, respiration, motion, electroencephalography (EEG) or steady-state topography, and functional magnetic resonance imaging (FMRI). Here is a brief introduction to some of the key approaches:

- *facial electromyography (EMG)* measures the tiny electrical impulses that are generated when the muscle fibres in the respondent's face move. Smile or frown and you will feel the muscles—but the technology is much more sensitive. The technique is used to measure the emotional reaction to an ad and track how it varies across time.

- *skin conductance responses (SCR)* is one of the most promising biometric approaches for marketers (Poels & Dewitte, 2006, LaBarbera & Tucciarone, 1995) with many decades of testing (Peterson & Jung, 1907), though not in the advertising area. Skin conductance also measures electrical activity (responses within the autonomic nervous subsystem) and subsequent tiny changes in the respondent's moisture level or sweat glands (LaBarbera & Tucciarone, 1995) via electrodes attached to the respondent's fingers. Skin conductance is used to measure arousal, which is linked to emotional response, attention and cognitive effort (Mangina & Beuzeron-Mangina, 1996; Cahill, 1997; Critchley et al., 2000; Micu & Plummer, 2010).

- an *electroencephalograph (EEG)* records 'electrical potentials' through electrodes placed on the respondent's head in response to brain activity (Ritter & Villringer, 2006). A positive feature of this technique is that the measure is essentially simultaneous with its generation (Astolfi et al., 2009) allowing the marketer to know exactly which part of the ad is being responded to. However additional analysis (such as steady-state topography) is needed for complex stimuli such as television advertising (Silberstein & Nield, 2008).

- *functional magnetic resonance imaging (FMRI)* provides a picture of the brain in action by measuring blood flow. To measure a viewer's response to an ad, the respondent enters an imager where the test ad is projected, and the equipment measures the changes in the electromagnetic field of their blood flow in the brain as the respondent watches the ad. It is normal for a number of regions of the brain to light up in response to an ad. While these are being interpreted as measures of attention, emotion and memory (Quartz & Asp, 2005; Kennedy et al., 2010), more work will be needed before there is complete agreement among the experts on what is being measured. Hence, even though FMRI is exciting, given its expense and infancy it is unlikely to be a tool used by many marketers for the present time.

A common finding is that there are discrepancies between what is measured physiologically compared with self-report (Hazlett & Hazlett, 1999; Quartz & Asp, 2005). This is good in that if self-report metrics have not performed well, in the limited testing of them it's possible that biometrics may do better, since they measure something different. However, it's important to remember that emotional responses and the workings of the brain and nervous system are complex and not yet fully understood, particularly their response to marketing stimuli. While these approaches hold promise, much more testing needs to be done.

To conclude, there is currently little evidence that pre-testing can help you to identify a winning execution. Some approaches look more promising than others, but much serious R&D work is needed to establish which methods should be used, in what way, for what types of ads, and for what type of advertising objective.

Advertising tracking

Advertising tracking is conducted once the advertising is airing in the market. It can therefore be used to assess both the advertising content and the media strategy, and/or the interaction of both.

Advertising tracking usually measures memories and perceptions rather than behaviours, because it can be difficult to isolate the effects of advertising on behaviour from the influences of price promotions and other marketing interventions. When behaviour is measured it is typically simply in the form of changes in overall sales; this has the problem of including the buying of many people who were not exposed to the advertising. So drawing conclusions from sales data can be rather difficult: it is easy to make a mistake. This is the main reason why advertising tracking of memory and perceptions was developed.

Tracking can take a number of forms, such as a continuous panel (weekly tracking), in waves (quarterly) or tracking direct response (monitoring calls or web responses for different ads). Quantitative research is the norm. A range of approaches, are possible, including face-to-face, mail and telephone interviewing, but today online interviewing dominates. Passive measurement holds promise for the future and is discussed later in this chapter.

Sometimes advertising tracking is stand-alone (tracking a particular ad or campaign); sometimes it is part of an ongoing brand health monitor. Sometimes it is just focused on a single brand; at other times it looks at all advertising in an industry. In all cases, the aim is to guide the marketer in decision making about advertising.

Typical purposes of tracking include:

- to evaluate the performance of the ads in the market
- to determine why a campaign is or is not working
- to monitor **wearout** to help adjust total spend and spend across individual spots or campaigns
- to keeping track of competitors' actions.

Verbal measurement

Tracking based on verbal measurement typically includes measures of ad and brand awareness, recognition, correct branding, likeability, the message taken away, media preference, attitude shifts and usage. In considering the measures you want to include, refer to Chapter 2. Remember that attitudes towards a brand reflect behavioural loyalty; intentions reflect past behaviour and brand knowledge is probabilistic. Given this, such measures are not required in your tracking.

It is important to order questions so as to minimise priming: screening questions should come first; then awareness questions (recall prior to recognition), with usage questions last. Often a category prompt is used to see if people have any recall of the brand campaign (for example, 'Can you recall any recent campaigns for shampoo?'). If this is not sufficient to gain a response, a description of the relevant ads, screenshots or edited versions of the ads will be shown. Branding is removed so that a check can then be done on who respondents think the ads were for, thereby checking the levels of correct branding.

The sample will typically be category users, but it is vital to record brand usage, given that we know people respond differently to advertising for brands they buy/use.

It is very important to separate out the effects of the advertising content from the effects of the advertising spend (the media strategy). Obviously a campaign with greater spend should have greater effect, and this should not be used to indicate the quality of the advertisement. One way to do this is to gain tracking data immediately after the advertisement airs, when those who have been exposed to the advertisement will have been exposed a few times. Rather than reporting overall market shifts in metrics such as awareness, a comparison should be made between those who have been exposed and those who have not. Did they notice the advertising? Did they correctly register which brand it was for? So long as these people do not differ in other ways from the unexposed consumers, this will give an indication of the quality of the advertising content. Having made this assessment of ad quality allows for later shifts in overall market metrics to be assessed in light of the quality of the ad in order to evaluate how well the media strategy is doing.

Individual-level single-source measurement

The gold standard for measuring the sales impact of advertising is individual-level **single-source data**. Such data has been used to impressively demonstrate that advertising works to drive sales (Jones, 1995c). It is the necessary data to determine return on advertising investment, and to best equip marketers to make decisions in the complex media-fragmented environments.

This measurement involves gathering data from a large panel of shoppers who agree to have both their buying and their media exposure tracked.

wearout: When advertising that has been in the media for a long time loses its effectiveness.

single-source data: Data gathered by tracking individuals' levels of advertising exposure and their purchases, over a long period of time.

Typically the data recorded includes when a television is on, and on which channel for each home or person (ideally passively). This is then matched to what ads were playing at the time. Potentially, data for other media (radio, online or print) can also be collected, but this is currently costly and complex. Buying behaviour for the same respondents is also tracked; for example from loyalty card data, or by respondents recording their purchases with a scanner at home.

This single-source data is used to extract groups as if an advertising experiment had been done. The groups are made up of purchases, not purchasers (people). Essentially an 'exposed' group (of purchases made after an exposure to the brand's advertising) is compared to an 'unexposed' group and the difference is the effect of ad exposure. To describe it more correctly, the brand's share of category purchases that were not preceded by any exposure to the brand's advertising is compared to its share of the purchases that were preceded by exposure to the advertising. For example, say 10,000 fast-food purchases were made that were not preceded in the prior fortnight by exposure to KFC advertising, and that 20 per cent of these purchases were of KFC. Meanwhile 2000 fast-food purchases were made that *were* preceded by exposure to the new KFC advertisement within the prior fortnight, and KFC's share of these purchases was 30 per cent. So if we compare the 'exposed' metric (30 per cent) to the 'unexposed' (20 per cent) we see that KFC's share among exposed purchases is 50 per cent higher ($30 - 20 \div 20$). Put another way: buying that is preceded by exposure to the new KFC advertisement is 50 per cent more likely to favour buying KFC over other fast-food brands. The ad works, and very well!

Now this sounds like a huge sales increase, but remember it comes only from those category purchases that were preceded by an exposure to the KFC ad; most purchases were not preceded by an exposure. So this sales effect is unlikely to show up in weekly sales figures, especially since they bounce around a fair bit in response to weather, competitor promotions and other marketing. This is why aggregate sales data (for example weekly sales) should not be used to judge advertising effects. It's quite possible to air a sales-effective advertisement and for sales to stay flat or even continue to decline, especially if the media budget is small (or poorly planned), and/or if competitors are active. Marketing mix modelling might help control for some of the other effects, but it is extremely unlikely to be able to correctly quantify the 50 per cent bump in buying propensity that this advertisement delivers. This is why single-source data is so useful to advertisers; in the absence of controlled experiments it is the only way to quantify the selling impact of an advertisement.

It's also quite possible to compare the effect of one exposure compared to two (or three or four and so on) within a particular time period prior to purchase. So single-source data can be used to learn about media effects, not just to evaluate the effectiveness of particular advertisements.

Single-source panels are difficult to set up, and given the huge volume of data that they can generate analysis can be tricky. However, recent advances in technology and more widespread appreciation by marketers of the value of single-source data means that it is becoming increasingly available around the world. This 'gold standard' has an exciting future and we expect it to be the data used by marketers of the future. For now the two most common measures are AdImpact (Wood, 2009) and STAS (Jones, 1995a, 1995b, 1998, 2007). Both are ways to measure whether seeing the ad nudges buying behaviour.

Buying centres involved in major purchase decisions usually comprise members from various functions within the customer organisation, who often have different specific concerns about product or supplier issues. Marketing communication aimed at business markets must take account of the more formal buying process and the range of needs of different functions within organisations. For example, if advertising within trade journals, a firm must consider different categories of publication read by people within different functions (such as accounting, engineering, manufacturing and purchasing). Different features and benefits might need to be emphasised in different publications to cater to the range of priorities across different functions within the organisation.

Organisational customers require detailed information about potential suppliers and their capabilities when considering major purchases of complex, customised products. Often, detailed discussions are required between potential customers and suppliers. Consequently, personal selling is typically the major component of marketing communication within business-to-business marketing. This is especially evident in those business markets with low numbers of potential customers, resulting in advertising being inefficient as a marketing communication medium. For example, there are currently just three car manufacturers in Australia (Ford, Holden and Toyota). There would be little value in a manufacturer of automotive components advertising through mass media to reach buyers and other members of buying centres within just these three firms! Clearly, personal selling would be much more efficient.

In situations involving complex products (or services) and very high purchase values, it is typical for teams, rather than just individual salespeople, to undertake the selling task. The key account salesperson would often be supported by technical specialists from different functions within the supply firm. These specialists would assist the salesperson to identify customer needs and the best product configuration to match those needs, perhaps liaising directly with their counterparts within the customer organisation. They could also assist the salesperson in presenting the final supply proposal to the customer organisation, presenting complex features and benefits in detail.

In some business markets, there are fairly large numbers of potential customers (although still relatively small numbers in comparison to consumer markets). For example, there are 30,000 firms within the financial services sector in Australia (Innovation and Business Skills Australia, 2010). Such markets could be reached effectively and efficiently through a mix of advertising and personal selling. Indeed, there is research evidence that advertising can 'open doors' for business-to-business salespeople, creating company awareness among prospective customer organisations that assists salespeople when they attempt to gain initial appointments (Lichtenthal, Yadav & Donthu, 2004). This is why airports are full of advertisements for management consultants, IT infrastructure providers and other B2B marketers.

Application to business-to-business marketing

CRITICAL REFLECTION

1   What is the difference between advertisement effect and advertisement effectiveness?

2   What measurement approaches are useful for each?

CONCLUSION

Advertising cannot build memory structures if it is not processed, and these memory structures cannot generate sales if they aren't associated with the brand that is being advertised. Most advertising exposures fail these two simple hurdles, so the money spent pours down the drain or, worse, refreshes memories for competitor brands. Less than 20 per cent of television advertising exposures are both noticed and correctly branded; that is, there is more than 80 per cent wastage (see citation in Sharp, 2010: 7). This figure is probably similar, and perhaps worse, for advertising in other media. Part of the reason that advertising is so often ineffective is that the people who commission and design the ads have incorrect assumptions about how advertising works. As we have seen in this chapter, the dominant way that advertising works is by refreshing, and occasionally building, memory structures that improve the chance of the brand being recalled and/or noticed in buying situations, and hence bought. These memory structures include what the brand does, what it looks like, where it is available, when and where it is consumed, by who, with whom and so on. Associations are built with cues that bring the brand to mind.

A simple recipe for sales-effective advertising is:

- Reach and appeal to a broad audience (ideally all category buyers).
- Get noticed and engage; avoid being screened out by consumers.
- Have a clear brand link (ideally many clear links). A brand's distinctive assets indirectly brand the advertising, and verbal and visual brand name mentions are also important, as are pack shots and showing the product in use. Consistency over time is vital for branding to work.
- Refresh and build memory structures that make the brand more likely to come to mind and be easier to notice in potential buying situations.
- Finally, if you have something genuinely persuasive and motivational to say then say it, so long as it does not interfere with achieving the above objectives.

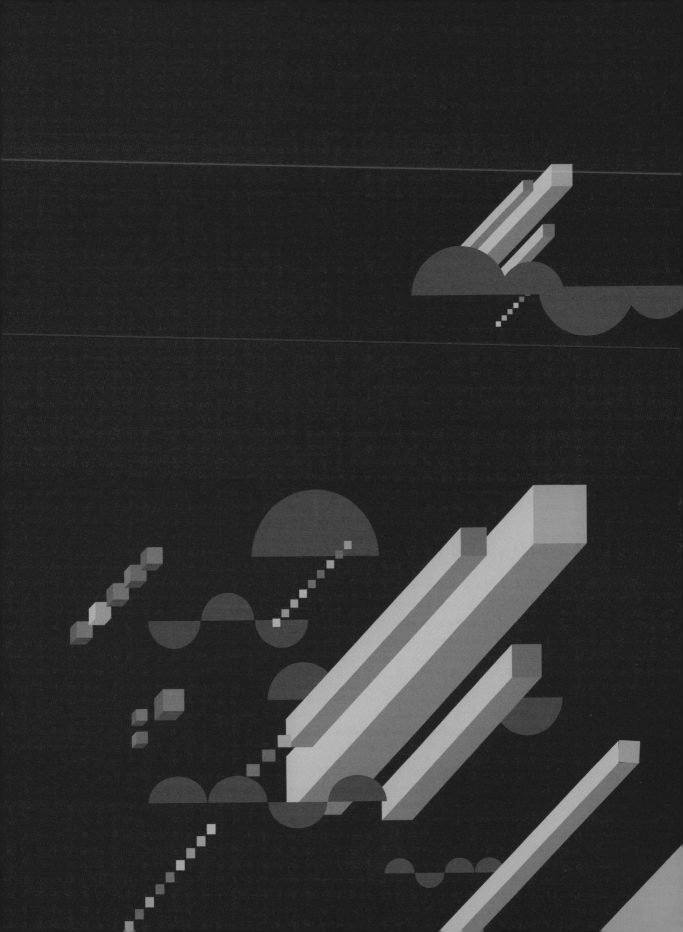

10

SUMMARY

- Most brand advertising is (mainly) brand publicity.

- The core focus of advertising is to get the brand noticed and thought about in buying situations (building and maintaining salience). In most situations advertisements do not have to say anything profound or earth-shattering; they don't even have to say your brand is better than others.

- Advertising should aim to make brands easier to recognise, recall and notice in the purchase situation by creating and refreshing memory associations for your brand (mental availability).

- Creativity and good media buying help the ad to make an impact by reaching as many potential buyers as possible.

- Great ads reach and appeal to a broad audience, capture attention, get the brand noticed, use clear brand associations consistent with what viewers expect from the brand, and build and refresh memory structures.

- Advertising research—pre-testing and advertising tracking—can be valuable when used correctly, but there are several challenges with it, including the high cost.

REVISION QUESTIONS

1 How does a typical television or print ad compare to a salesperson's interaction with a customer? You may like to think about a specific brand, such as a real estate company or clothes retailer.

2 Why is memory important to advertising?

3 Watch the Orcon Broadband 'Together Incredible' advertisement with Iggy Pop: www.youtube.com/watch?v=EmF4v8AoKv0. Discuss whether the demonstration of the product justifies the creativity and lack of branding until the end. What are the risks with this approach?

4 Compare and contrast the likely advertising and selling activities undertaken by a major car dealership when targeting:

   a individual household buyers, each typically purchasing a new car every four to five years, trading in their old car at the same time

   b large business firms buying or leasing cars for company executives and salespeople, with perhaps dozens of cars being traded in or dozens of three-year car leases being renewed each year by each firm.

5 Think about a new brand launch in a category of interest to you. Did the campaign provide lots of information? Why or why not? Was the campaign effective? What would you have done differently?

6   What are three key problems that can plague pre-testing?

7   What sort of data are marketers in the future likely to use to evaluate the sales impact of advertising? Why is it beneficial?

8   Select an advertisement (in any media) and, working backwards from the execution and using the template provided, write what could have been the original brief for the ad or campaign.

FURTHER READING

Ambler, T, Broadbent, S & Feldwick, P (1998) 'Does advertising affect market size? Some evidence from the United Kingdom', *International Journal of Advertising*, vol. 17, no. 3.

Barnard, N & Ehrenberg, A (1997) 'Advertising: Strongly persuasive or nudging?' *Journal of Advertising Research*, vol. 37, pp. 21–8.

Ehrenberg, A S C (1974) 'Repetitive advertising and the consumer', *Journal of Advertising Research*, vol. 14, pp. 25–34.

Ehrenberg, A S C, Barnard, N, Kennedy, R & Bloom, H (2002) 'Brand advertising as creative publicity', *Journal of Advertising Research*, vol. 42, no. 4, pp. 7–18.

Heath, R & Feldwick, P (2008) 'Fifty years using the wrong model of advertising', *International Journal of Market Research*, vol. 50, no. 1, pp. 29–59.

Petty, R E & Cacioppo, J T (1983) 'Central and peripheral routes to persuasion: Application to advertising', in Percy, L & Woodside, A G (eds) *Advertising and Consumer Psychology*, Lexington Books, Massachusetts.

Rossiter, J & Percy, L (1997) *Advertising Communications & Promotion Management*, The McGraw-Hill Companies, Inc., New York.

Rossiter, J R, Percy, L & Donovan, R J (1991) 'A better advertising planning grid', *Journal of Advertising Research*, vol. 31, pp. 11–21.

Taylor, J, Kennedy, R & Sharp, B (2009) 'Making generalizations about advertising's convex sales response function: is once really enough?', *Journal of Advertising Research*, vol. 49, no. 2, pp. 198–200.

Tellis, G J (2009) 'Generalizations about advertising effectiveness in markets.' *Journal of Advertising Research* 49, 2, pp. 240–5.

Vakratsas, D & Ambler, T (1999) 'How advertising works: What do we really know?' *Journal of Marketing*, vol. 63, pp. 26–43.

WEBLINKS

For case studies, data and academic literature:

www.warc.com

For a list of some notable agencies:

http://en.wikipedia.org/wiki/List_of_advertising_agencies

Lamb campaigns:

www.mla.com.au/Marketing-red-meat/Domestic-marketing/Lamb-campaigns

◢ Major case study

Can marketing actually make people's lives better?

By Ekant Veer, University of Canterbury, New Zealand

Marketing tends to have a bad reputation. In his 2011 documentary *The Greatest Movie Ever Sold*, Morgan Spurlock explored the way in which advertisers and marketers covertly place products in television shows and movies to encourage viewers to purchase them. In the documentary, Spurlock interviewed some leading consumer advocates, advertisers and marketing academics to explore how marketers are perceived in the twenty-first century. Some common concerns included:

- marketing causes consumers to feel worthless unless they purchase products
- marketing exploits consumers' insecurities and fears
- marketers purposely lie
- marketing, as an industry, is driven by profits above other concerns.

However, what the documentary failed to examine in any real depth is how marketing techniques and concepts can be used to improve consumers' lives and society as a whole.

How did you learn to recycle? If you were born in the 1990s, it is likely that it has always been a part of your life. But in the 1980s, someone would have had to teach you to recycle. That person could have been a parent or guardian, a teacher at school or even a city council official. This is an example of social marketing. Safe-sex education, healthy living, anti-smoking, good citizenship, anti-bullying, responsible drinking and many, many other campaigns are the domain of social marketers.

Some see social marketers as people working hard to better society; others see them as the thought police, purposely looking to ruin your fun. In this case study, we look at what social marketing really is, how it is used and why it should be a key part of your future studies in marketing.

Alan Andreasen (2003) defines social marketing as 'the application of commercial marketing technologies to the analysis, planning, execution, and evaluation of programs designed to influence the voluntary behaviour of target audiences in order to improve their personal welfare and that of the society of which they are a part.' First and foremost, social marketers are not doing anything new. Social marketers do not create new theories, concepts or technologies, but rather use existing practices that have been established by commercial marketers. Much of social marketing is founded on the concept of exchange, which was introduced to marketing by Richard Bagozzi (1975). Exchange theory suggests that we give up something we have for something we want. Marketing aids that exchange by explaining the benefits of products available and making them desirable. Social

Another key aspect of social marketing is that the goal is to encourage the target audience to change their behaviour *voluntarily*.

marketing tries to do the same by explaining the benefits of a behaviour and making it desirable to adopt it. Social marketers also use traditional practices to do this, such as education programs, advertising, personal selling (coaching) and celebrity endorsements.

Another key aspect of social marketing is that the goal is to encourage the target audience to change their behaviour *voluntarily*. Forcing people to change their behaviour by banning a product is not social marketing. If your city council banned all alcohol sale and consumption, similar to prohibition in the United States during the 1920s and 1930s, there would likely be a marked change in drinking behaviour. However, people would still want to drink and they would find ways to get alcohol. If you want to change drinking behaviour, you need to make people *want* to change their behaviour. In one study, I was able to encourage a significant change in university students' likelihood of binge drinking by explaining the benefits of responsible drinking in a manner that mattered to them (Veer & Kilian, 2010). Most anti-binge-drinking advertisements focus on the health benefits of responsible drinking, which we found to be of little interest to university students. Drinking is a social activity and, for many, a key part in forming social relationships while at university. So, rather than focus on students' physical health, we showed how binge drinking can damage social health. We showed students ads that described how binge drinking can damage their relationship with their friends. The ads had tag lines such as 'No one wants to carry your drunk ass around town all night', 'Next time, they won't even ask you to come out with them' and 'Don't ruin their night because you've drunk too much'. We found that messages like this were far more effective in discouraging binge-drinking behaviour, especially among first-year university students, who were desperate to form social relationships.

Social marketing has a long history of trying to scare people into changing their behaviour through campaigns that show the gory results of a car crash or the impact of smoking on a person's lungs. However, more and more, marketers are finding that while such ads have an initial shock value that catches our attention, they have little impact on future behavioural change (Donovan, 2003). As a result, social marketers are becoming more creative in their approaches, with humour being used more often to convey a message—such as in the NZTA's 'Legend' campaign, discussed at the start of this chapter.

By understanding a target audience better and understanding what will and won't encourage them to change their behaviour, social marketers can steer away from the obvious 'this will kill you' type of advertising towards more effective messages. My very first social marketing campaign was launched when I was an undergraduate business

> At the end of the day, social marketing can be fun and, when effective, can make a significant improvement to people's lives and the world we live in.

student. I wanted to encourage recycling on campus, especially because it seemed that every corner of campus had a student from some random club handing out flyers, which would inevitably end up not being recycled or simply thrown around campus and end up as litter. I took the basic concept of handing out flyers and adapted it to encourage recycling. I borrowed a loudspeaker, had a couple of thousand flyers printed off and stood with some friends on campus during lunchtimes yelling, 'All flyers are rubbish, but at least you can recycle them.' We would hand out flyers that just said 'throw me away, but do it responsibly' and had a map showing where recycling bins were. I didn't have a debate on the benefits of recycling, I didn't hug a tree and I didn't get in people's face about how evil it is to hand out flyers. Most people saw the irony in the stunt (handing out flyers to encourage recycling) and it curbed a lot of junk mail on campus, as students began recycling it straight away.

Social marketing doesn't have to be boring. It doesn't have to rely on fear or shock. It doesn't even have to 'make sense' sometimes. As long as people voluntarily change their behaviour for the better in response to the campaign, you have a social marketing campaign.

However, being a social marketer is not without its drawbacks. Social marketers tend to have far fewer resources with which to get their message across compared with commercial giants, who can encourage unhealthy behaviour. Social marketers are also stigmatised as being 'boring' or simply out to ruin a fun time. Volkswagen's <www.TheFunTheory.com> is a classic example of social marketing that takes a counter-fear approach to behavioural change. By making laborious activities more fun and novel, Volkswagen were able to see a marked change in behaviour. Their most famous example, the piano stairs (<http://youtu.be/2lXh2n0aPyw>), made walking up the stairs, rather than taking the escalator, more enjoyable and increased stair use during the experiment by 66 per cent. Similarly, The speed camera lottery (<http://youtu.be/iynzHWwJXaA>) reduced average speeds on a busy road by 22 per cent simply by rewarding people adhering to the speed limit with an entry into a lottery with a cash prize, rather than only punishing speeders.

At the end of the day, social marketing can be fun and, when effective, can make a significant improvement to people's lives and the world we live in. It isn't always easy and it isn't always as glamorous as marketing high-end products, but knowing people are living longer, living happier lives and maintaining our planet's resources in a more efficient way can be immeasurably rewarding.

Questions

1   Explain the difference between social and commercial marketing.

2   Why do you think advertising based on fear and shock is ineffective?

3   If you were charged with reducing binge drinking among people of your age group, what sort of messages do you think would work? Would a message that focuses on the potential for social exclusion (as described in this case study) work?

4   It has often been said that social marketers should give up. Competing with huge corporations with an almost infinite marketing budget as well as trying to market to a group of people who may not want to change can often seem just too hard. Do you think social marketing has a place in our lives? Why or why not?

Practitioner profile

Sylvia Mason, Joint Managing Partner/Strategy Director, KWP! Advertising (Adelaide)

I didn't set out in life with a dream of a career in an advertising agency. In fact, I fell into advertising by default. I started my career in the publishing industry, working in Singapore. I had a job with a publishing company that produced high-quality photographic travel guides and I was General Manager for their stock photo library. It was a small unit, and part of my role was to promote our services to travel photographers, other publishers, advertisers and anyone else in the market for stock imagery.

I continued working in publishing in Singapore for some years, until I moved to Adelaide, a one-paper town. There was very little opportunity to find work in publishing and so I fell back on my social communications media background and moved into the advertising field.

The best thing about a career in advertising is that there are so many options. This is particularly true working for KWP!—an organisation that really encourages people to take risks and find their own destiny. I have been Account Executive, Account Director, Group Head and Head of Strategy, and each of these roles were very different (see below). The variety has meant that I've kept learning, developing new skills and applying knowledge across different areas. More importantly, it has kept me passionate about my work.

However, while experience is important, I really believe that my strongest asset is an attitude more than a skill: a willingness to take on new challenges, to be open to constant learning, to collaborate with others and to be interested in people.

Here are the key skills and attitudes I needed in each of my roles.

Account Executive

- Understand the client's needs.
- Manage timelines and budgets—and delivery of them.
- Make sure communication is smooth and well reported.
- Have ideas, know what's going on in the advertising industry and keep abreast of the competitive environment.
- Be a details freak.

Account Director

- Manage relationships and people.
- Have excellent knowledge of the industry and the client.
- Be strategically minded and focused.

Group Head

- Be able to manage several key client accounts at a senior level.
- Have great staff management skills.

Strategy Director

- Have an in-depth knowledge of (or a background in) market research.
- Know consumers—understand their needs, motivations and habits.
- Understand market dynamics.
- Be a good storyteller and an engaging presenter.
- Unearth interesting ways to take messages to the market that will engage and activate.

11

MEDIA DECISIONS: REACHING BUYERS WITH ADVERTISING

BYRON SHARP, ERICA RIEBE AND KAREN NELSON-FIELD

◢ **Introduction case**

'Holiday at home': Managing a media campaign

Because of the strong Australian dollar and the growing number of low-cost airlines, more and more Australians are flying to Asia for their holidays. To encourage Australians to 'holiday at home', a large advertising budget was given to the Department of Tourism. The marketing manager, wanting get the campaign running quickly, split the department into teams—one team for television, another for radio, a third for print media (newspapers and magazines), a fourth for online advertisements and a final group for outdoor (events, billboards and bus shelters). At the end of two weeks, the groups were asked to present their proposals. Each team had come up with fantastic ideas, but none fitted within the allocated budget.

> To help encourage Australians to 'holiday at home', a large advertising budget was given to the Department of Tourism.

The teams also had different ideas about who the advertising should target and how often. The manager looked over the plans and had no idea what to do—each media option had advantages and disadvantages, but they were so different that it was impossible to fairly compare one against another—and integrating the campaigns into a whole looked impossible. The Marketing Manager had no choice but to set the proposals aside and start again, looking at the campaign as a whole. Media planning for the campaign was much more complex than it had originally appeared. Trying to rush things and failure to take an integrated approach had ended up delaying the progress instead of making it easier.

INTRODUCTION

During your marketing career, you will often be involved in spending large amounts of money on media space, to place your advertising in front of buyers. Few textbooks cover these decisions in detail, leaving many marketers underequipped to make sound decisions. Yet media decisions are very important, because media is such a costly item, and because advertising can not be sales-effective unless it reaches buyers and does so at an appropriate time and place.

LEARNING OBJECTIVES

After reading this chapter you should be able to:

- describe the general media environment and the major media-centric challenges facing marketers
- understand the overall media planning process
- recognise and set realistic media objectives
- discuss the characteristics of a range of different media vehicles
- recognise key terminology (including data and tools) used in media planning
- describe the concept of effective scheduling and a range of scheduling patterns
- discuss appropriate techniques for evaluating media campaigns
- discuss and critique key factors in media decision making.

CHAPTER OUTLINE

Introduction

Commercial media

The media industry

The media planning process

Media characteristics

Putting a mix together: Integrated marketing communications

Developing the media schedule

Media data, tools and campaign evaluation

Conclusion

///

KEY TERMS

above the line media

advertising clutter

audience accumulation

audience targeting

below the line media

circulation

commercial media

concurrent media usage

cost per thousand (CPM)

direct mail (DM)

duplication of viewing/
    listening law

frequency of exposure

full-service agencies

gross rating points (GRPs)

integrated marketing
    communications (IMC)

long tail

make-goods

mass media

media agencies

media auditing

media buying

media planning

media vehicle

optimisation software

opportunity to see/hear (OTS)

out of home media

paid search advertising

product placement

program rating

ratings data

reach

selective vehicles

selectivity

syndicated data

target audience measurement
    (TAM)

target audience rating points
    (TARPs)

touch points

wastage

COMMERCIAL MEDIA

Media deliver entertainment, information and advertising to vast audiences and they play an important role in contemporary society. Media that carries advertising is often called **commercial media**. Compared with other forms of advertising delivery (such as personal selling or telemarketing), commercial media provide a convenient and relatively inexpensive method for delivering a message to vast numbers of people.

The twentieth century and the recent digital revolution saw an amazing increase in the amount of commercial media available to advertisers. Today, advertisers have more choices than ever for where they can place their advertising. This makes the job of choosing media for advertising more complicated.

History of commercial media

Inscriptions on rock walls of commercial and political messages have been found in the ruins of Pompeii. Today we refer to this as outdoor or **out of home media** (which includes posters and signs). In the Middle Ages, with a largely illiterate population, branding came to the fore as cobblers, tailors, blacksmiths and so on would display their name, trade and/or 'logo' (or associated image) on signage hanging outside and above the door of their place of business.

The advent of the Gutenberg printing press in the 1400s allowed large-scale commercial and public announcements to be printed. Regarded as one of the world's most influential inventions, the printing press with its movable type was the catalyst for the world's first **mass media**: newspapers and magazines. The rise of print, however, was slow by modern standards, as it depended on literacy levels, which initially were low. In 1836, the French newspaper *La Presse* was the first to include advertisements. This, along with its other innovation of selling by street vendors, allowed

LEARNING OBJECTIVE
Describe the general media environment and the major media-centric challenges facing marketers

commercial media:
Media that carries paid advertising.

out of home media:
Media that is consumed outside the home; for example, on a billboard or shop window.

mass media: Media that reaches vast numbers of people quickly; for example, television.

it to have a lower price, lift its readership and earn more profits. This business model was quickly copied, and by the twentieth century, print (largely newspapers and magazines) was the first mass advertising media.

Radio, the first wireless technology, was introduced in the early 1900s and became the first broadcast media. By the mid 1920s, hundreds of radio stations (whose content included advertising messages) were transmitting across most countries. It was the first time that advertisers could quickly reach national audiences.

Television was introduced in the 1940s and it transformed the commercial media landscape. For the first time, the delivery of verbal and visual messages to vast audiences was possible. In recent years, there has been much talk about a decline in television viewing but this has not happened— viewing levels have not declined, and the number of new screens continues to grow. In 2011, Nielsen Media reported that most (56 per cent) of US households have three or more television sets. Only 18 per cent of households feature a single television set, yet about 30 per cent of US households consist of a single person. In developed countries, television sets outnumber people and the television population continues to grow fast. In developing countries, television is also a rapidly growing medium. So television remains the dominant medium in terms of both time spent watching it and the amount marketers spend advertising on it. Understanding how television advertising works is therefore of vital importance to many marketers, especially those with global consumer brands.

The digital revolution has delivered a host of new and emerging media that advertisers can use. Online advertising has grown extremely quickly, with 15 per cent of global advertising expenditure today going to online. This growth has been fuelled by increases in the numbers of people online and how long they each spend online. This is now rather steady in most developed markets, so the explosive growth in online advertising is now slowing. Online advertising continues to deliver most of the growth in global advertising spend, but these new advertising dollars are skewed towards developing countries.

Today the internet can be considered a 'mature' media, in that the online audience in developing countries is no longer growing, but as with other mature media much change is still occurring. For example, television is increasingly being viewed online, and more online time is from mobile devices rather than desktop computers. The distinction between online and other media such as print and television is fading. There are 'print media' newspapers and magazines that are never actually printed on paper, and many television and radio channels broadcast on the internet; indeed some only broadcast online.

It is an exciting but also challenging time to be involved in advertising and media. Increasingly, jobs in these areas are being taken by well-qualified professionals who must work to maintain an extensive knowledge of the media landscape.

The current media landscape

Increasingly, we live in a wireless, always connected world, and have great flexibility in terms of how we consume media. We can subscribe to magazines and newspapers from around the world online, and we can view 'live', 'catch up' and 'on demand' television content. Smartphones in effect put television, computers, newspapers and magazines in our pockets. The result of this increased availability is that people consume more media than ever before.

The big change for advertisers is the bewildering array of choices for where to spend advertising dollars. There are many more television channels, radio stations, outdoor advertising opportunities (with flexible digital delivery) and online advertising opportunities. For the first time, there are platforms that can potentially reach a global audience, and in a few cases can do so quite quickly. On top of this, consumers are also creating their own media content, and using social media to interact with one another (including talking about brands). So, for marketers there are more opportunities to reach consumers, in different ways, at different times and in different situations. This sounds very promising—and it is—but it also brings risks. There are more ways to waste money now than ever before, and unfortunately very little is known about the effectiveness of many of these options.

Wherever there is a lack of knowledge, myths and rumours will abound. For example, there is already a large volume of industry opinion pieces and case studies on how marketers should use social media—self-declared 'experts' are everywhere. There is much hype and advocacy masquerading as disinterested advice. The reality is that there is little credible (and rarely any generalisable) research on social media (yet). This is not overly surprising, given we have had fifty years to research and understand what television has to offer our advertising dollar—and yet our knowledge about it is still rather limited. There is a serious need for marketers to do small-scale experiments with media in order to learn, rather than rushing headlong into uncertainty.

Case study

Pepsi's 'Refresh Project': A social media pioneer

In 2009, Pepsi announced that it was going to revolutionise their marketing by taking much of their television budget and moving it into social media related activities. The Pepsi 'Refresh Project' included offering US$20 million in grants to individuals and organisations to promote new ideas to positively affect their community, state or the nation. Ideas were accepted on a special website and people could vote online.

The Refresh Project saw market share decline in a shrinking soft drink category. Diet Coke replaced Pepsi as the number two ranked brand for market share in the United States. One commentator summed it up (Ad Contrarian, 2011):

> The Refresh Project accomplished everything a social media program is expected to do: over 80 million votes were registered; almost 3.5 million 'likes' on the Pepsi Facebook page; almost 60,000 Twitter followers. The only thing it did failed to do was sell Pepsi.

In 2011, Pepsi announced their first new television campaign in three years, and the departure of their Chief Marketing Officer.

THE MEDIA INDUSTRY

The media industry comprises the audience, media providers (owners), advertisers and media agencies.

Audience

The audience is the people that use the media as a source of information and/or entertainment. Audiences can be measured in different ways; for example, the amount of people who read a particular magazine will be different (usually larger) from the amount of people who paid and bought the magazine. Obviously advertisers are interested in how many people saw and/or heard their advertisement. As a marketer, you therefore need to carefully understand what the audience measurement metrics really refer to. For example, not everyone who reads the front pages will read other sections of the newspaper. Similarly, television ratings generally refer to the average audience for a program, but this varies over the program—more people are watching at the start of a movie than at the end, and viewing always drops a little during commercial breaks (which, of course, is the real audience that advertisers care about).

For each medium there tends to be one, or a few, research agencies, such as Nielsen Media, that provide audience measurement figures. Typically audiences are measured by **ratings data** for television and radio, and readership and **circulation** figures for press. The size of the audience is the currency by which the media is then sold to advertisers. Other audience measurement metrics are used, particularly for online vehicles, such as page views, 'unique visitors', 'click throughs' and downloads.

ratings data: Audience measurement tool to determine the size of the audience, which is used by media sellers and buyers (the higher the ratings, the more audience: thus the higher the price for the spot).

circulation: Usually refers to how many copies of a print medium (e.g. a magazine) are sold. Readership is therefore always a higher figure.

Media providers (owners)

A media provider (owner) is an organisation that makes media content (such as television programming or magazine articles) available to audiences. Many large providers span a range of media classes; for example, Network Ten in Australia operates three television channels, websites and, until recently, an outdoor arm (Eye Corp); Time Warner operates many television channels (including CNN), radio stations and magazines, as well as making and distributing Hollywood movies.

Media providers therefore have two major clients: the audience, who consume the provided content; and the advertisers, who use these media platforms to advertise to potential consumers of their products and services.

The bigger the audience, the greater the value and hence the higher the cost of advertising space within that content. So media providers try to deliver attractive content to generate large audiences. They may also try to appeal to particular types of viewers (for example wealthy people) if they know that there are advertisers who value advertising particularly to these people. Media providers try to sell as much advertising space as they can, for as high a price as possible, but there is a trade-off because too much advertising decreases ratings—which means having to sell the space to advertisers for lower prices. Some media are legally constrained in how much advertising space they can offer; for example, commercial television channels in Australia are limited to an average of thirteen minutes of space per hour during the evening.

Advertisers

Advertisers include both private and public sector organisations: government departments, fast-food chains, retailers, consumer goods companies, car manufacturers and not-for-profit organisations such as charities. The key benefits for advertisers in buying space in media to advertise their products or services (as compared to running PR campaigns) are the cost efficiency with which they can reach many consumers quickly and the control they can have over the message and timing.

Media agencies

When you advertise, you need to buy some media space, and this can be complicated—bookings have to be made, and prices and conditions negotiated. **Media agencies** provide this service to advertisers. Because they act on behalf of many advertisers, they buy media space in bulk and so can negotiate lower prices. So while advertisers may negotiate media placement purchases with the media provider directly, much advertising space (especially for larger multimedia campaigns) is booked by media agencies.

media agencies: Agencies that consult and liaise between media buyers and media providers.

Another reason that marketers use media agencies is to access their specialist knowledge; media agencies will advise on when to advertise, which media to use and even how much to spend. It's not uncommon for advertisers themselves to have very little knowledge about media strategy (few university courses teach it) so they rely heavily on the advice of their media agency. This is dangerous: media budgets are large, so it is irresponsible of marketers not to develop their own in-depth knowledge; all large advertisers should be conducting ongoing research into media strategies. Another reason not to depend solely on the advice of a media agency is that there can be fundamental conflicts of interest between media agencies and their clients. Media agencies want their clients to spend as much as possible on advertising, not as much as is sensible. They also want to buy whatever media packages are easiest and cheapest for them to organise. They'll tend to buy what they know how to buy, not what is necessarily best for the brand. And finally, because media agencies buy media in bulk—for example, they make commitments to television channels (and other media) to buy a certain amount of space each year—they are under pressure to on-sell this 'inventory' to their clients. If they don't sell their inventory of advertising space, they will lose a good deal of money on it—this pressure will sometimes lead them to recommend using certain media, or advertising at a certain time, not because it is the best strategy for the brand but because it is best for the media agency. This isn't to say that media agencies can't provide a lot of value, but advertisers need to be *well-educated* clients or they are very unlikely to gain full value from their media agencies.

Industry insight

The future of OzTAM's television audience measurement service

OzTAM is an audience measurement service that has long been acknowledged as providing the most robust and accountable consumer behaviour data in Australia. Every single day OzTAM, calculates minute-by-minute viewing data for both free-to-air and subscription television channels (covering around 100 television channels). They know how many people are watching, and what they are watching, for every minute of every day. This unique and comprehensive data resource is used widely throughout the Australian advertising and marketing industries, as well as by program producers and media analysts, as a research and analysis tool.

One of the big advantages for OzTAM clients is that the total viewing audience can be broken down into dozens of viewer demographics. For example, a

marketer for a woman's magazine who has placed an ad on Network Ten during a break at 7.43 on Thursday night will know the next morning how many women living in the Adelaide metropolitan area, aged between thirty and forty, were watching Channel Ten at that time. A week later, they can also see the number of women in the target demographic that recorded the relevant program and played it back within seven days of the original broadcast. Marketers and advertisers use such data to make all sorts of decisions (such as at what time and on what channel to place an ad) and also as a tool for measuring the results of their ad campaigns.

OzTAM's rating service provider, Nielsen TAM, uses people meters to collect the ratings data. Specifically, they use a sophisticated metering system called UNITAM that uses audio matching technology to measure and report both live and time-shifted viewing. They recruit Australian households to join panels, measure the real viewing behaviour within those households and aggregate the data to form ratings estimates. There are six household panels—one in each of the five major metropolitan areas (Brisbane, Sydney, Melbourne, Adelaide and Perth) to measure the free-to-air and subscription television audience—and a national panel that measures and reports on viewing behaviour in subscription television homes nationally. The households within each panel are carefully selected and screened for a variety of demographics so that as a whole they are an accurate representation of the overall viewing population.

Each day, the minute-by-minute viewing behaviour of each household within the panel is measured. Every television set in the house is fitted with equipment that records the times the television is on and off, and also which channel it is tuned to. To track who is watching, the members of the household (as well as guests) use a remote control to register that they're in the room and watching television. Each day the data is sent electronically to Nielsen TAM where it is collated and analysed. The result is a complete picture of the minute-by-minute viewing behaviour for both free-to-air and subscription television networks, which can be accessed by OzTAM's clients the following day.

Until recently, measuring the television viewing audience was relatively easy. Television programs were broadcast at specific times and if the audience wanted to watch something they would generally switch on and watch at that time. Although VCRs have been around for a generation, it has only been in the past few years that technological developments have led to a significant shift in the options for television viewers. The choice of free-to-air digital channels in Australia has trebled in the past two years, and approximately 90 per cent of Australian homes now have at least one digitally enabled television set. Meanwhile, more people are using digital recorders and watching programs at a time of their choosing after they are broadcast. A small but growing number of households are supplementing their viewing via new services such as catch-up television, IPTV (internet protocol television) and other new technologies such as online video, smartphone applications and video downloads to handheld devices.

The use of these technologies is still relatively low (in most markets around the world about 98 per cent of viewing is still via the television set in homes), but there is no doubt that the landscape is changing. For the marketing and media industries, understanding these changes and measuring and reporting on them will become increasingly important. OzTAM is taking a leadership role in investigating how to incorporate these new usage behaviours into their measurement system. It is a huge challenge that will require extensive industry cooperation and collaboration, but it is essential in order to enable the company to adapt its service to meet evolving consumer behaviour and client needs.

THE MEDIA PLANNING PROCESS

Up until the late 1950s, the role of media role in the marketing communications process was viewed from an operations or tactical viewpoint. Media was considered the 'mailroom of advertising' by practitioners, with the creative and account planning functions of the **full-service agencies** attracting the talent and applause (Ephron in Sissors & Baron, 2002). However, as media became more complex with media proliferation, audience fragmentation, changing media usage habits and an

media planning: The
strategic scheduling of
media expenditure and
measurement.

media buying: The
process of purchasing
media, typically
undertaken by an agent
or a brand (for example,
Coca-Cola is a media
buyer).

▲ **LEARNING OBJECTIVE**
Discuss and critique key
factors in media decision
making

▲ **LEARNING OBJECTIVE**
Recognise and set realistic
media objectives

media vehicle: A specific
media source employed in
an advertising campaign.

reach: The proportion of
the total population that
is exposed at least once
to an advertisement.

audience accumulation:
Total net audience
reached by a media
vehicle.

**target audience rating
points (TARPs):** An
audience measurement
tool that measures the
proportion of a target
audience among the
total audience. It is
measured within a specific
media vehicle, such as
a television channel or
program.

**gross rating points
(GRPs):** The total number
of rating points for a
particular period of time.
It can be calculated
from reach multiplied by
frequency.

increase in availability of data and selection tools, **media planning** and **media buying** started to evolve into specialised disciplines and became more important in the marketing communications process (Surmanek, 1996; Turk & Katz, 1992; Wicken & Spittler, 1998; Bogart, 2000; Veldre, 2005).

In turn, there has been increasing advertiser interest in media strategy with it even preceding the creative strategy in terms of the decision making process (Jacobs, 1991; King, 1997; Summerfield, 2003; Veldre, 2003; Bainbridge, 2004). The primary reason is the large investment in media placement: advertisers typically invest between 70 and 90 per cent of the marketing communications budget in media alone (Jacobs, 1991; Rossiter, 2005; Paech, 2005; Boivin & Coderre, 2000), with the remaining portion of the budget being that which is spent on the creation of advertising (this expense is sometimes called 'non-working media spend'). So more knowledgeable advertisers are demanding that agencies and media providers display more knowledge about how media planning and buying decisions influence campaign effectiveness.

Decision factors

Media planning involves a media agency or advertiser selecting particular media to achieve marketing communication objectives. In simple terms, the role of the media planner involves working with the advertiser to set media objectives, then prescribing specific tactics for attaining those objectives (Rossiter & Danaher, 1998). Once objectives are determined, the media buyer then directly negotiates with the media owners on the price, positioning and timing of the media space (Katz, 2003).

One of the most important decisions within the media planning process is the selection of individual **media vehicles** (rather than overall type of media). In addition to the intrinsic qualities of a media type, there are particular criteria or factors, under the control of the media provider, that are most commonly used to determine which vehicle best meets the advertiser's objectives (Gensch, 1970; Boivin & Gagné, 1996; Surmanek, 1996; Sissors & Baron, 2002; McLuhan, 2003; Belch & Belch, 2004). These factors are: reach; frequency; budget; selectivity and wastage; clutter; advertising avoidance; engagement, context and consumer relevance; and other qualitative considerations. We will now look at each of these in turn.

Reach

Expressed as a percentage of the total potential population, **reach** is a measure of the number of people that are exposed at least once to a media fragment (for example a television program, an advertisement, a publication or a fifteen-minute block of radio transmission) in any given time. It captures **audience accumulation** and is the primary measure used to assess an advertiser's access to the audience of a media vehicle (Sissors & Baron, 2002). The way in which reach is measured and used by media companies and advertisers varies across media platforms, but in most media, and together with the frequency of exposure among the audience, it forms the currency by which advertising space is sold to advertisers. For instance, **target audience rating points (TARPs)** and **gross rating points (GRPs)** are calculated by multiplying reach by frequency (frequency is discussed in more detail below).

Reach in broadcast terms (for television or radio) is generally expressed as a **program rating**. For example, achieving one rating point for a television program means that 1 per cent of all television households in a particular geographic area tuned in to that specific program. So, advertising space with better ratings demands a higher price. This explains the attention media companies place on creating and finding popular programs and in promoting their programs to drum up viewers.

program rating: The number of viewers or listeners of a program.

For advertisers, reach is a fundamental consideration in their media decision making. As well it should be—it is the measure that captures the size of the audience and should therefore be the key factor in discriminating between media options. In research conducted with single source data, the sales response from advertising has been shown to be convex—rather than sigmoidal (s-shaped) or linear—in shape. (A range of potential advertising response functions is shown in Figure 11.1.) This means that the returns diminish from advertising to an audience more than once within a particular space of time, so reaching an extra potential buyer with advertising will have more effect on sales than reaching the same person a second time. Not surprisingly, being exposed a second, third or tenth time to an advertisement on a particular evening has less effect on learning and memory than the first exposure. Repeated exposure to the same advertising is boring and may encourage advertising avoidance. The implications of the convex response function for media scheduling are discussed in more detail in the section on 'Scheduling for reach' later in this chapter.

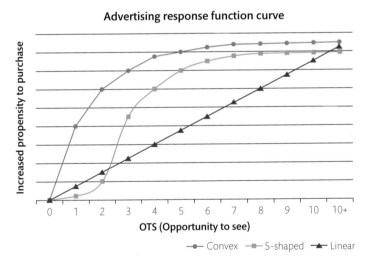

●●● FIGURE 11.1 THEORETICALLY POSSIBLE ADVERTISING RESPONSE FUNCTIONS

While reach is usually the key focus for most advertisers, they often trade off the reach they could achieve in favour of other considerations. Given our knowledge of how brands grow and how advertising works (see Chapter 10) there are good reasons to worry about this; advertisers should be very careful and wary of losing reach.

A growing challenge to achieving reach is the fragmentation of the media audience. Fragmentation is the splitting up of a previously united audience. Additional media vehicles divide the available audience; for example, more and more radio channels mean that it is rare for an individual

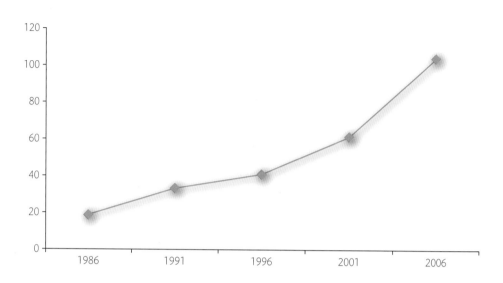

●●● **FIGURE 11.2** NUMBER OF TELEVISION CHANNELS AVAILABLE IN THE AVERAGE US HOME

Source: Data from Nielsen (2008) 'Average US home now receives a record 118.6 TV channels, according to Nielsen', 6 June, The Nielsen Company, retrieved 29 May from <www.nielsen.com/us/en/insights/press-room/2008/average_u_s__home.html>

radio network to command a large audience. In recent years, there has been much fragmentation in magazines, television and radio, and online is already a very fragmented medium. However, newspapers have tended to show a reverse trend, with most cities served by fewer newspapers than before.

Audience fragmentation has affected how people consume media, how advertisers buy space for their messages and how media owners sell that space to advertisers. It is said to be an inevitable consequence of the increasing supply of media options in a 'fixed pie' of viewers (Montanus, 1998; Picard, 1999). Franz (2000) sums up this predicament:

> This is the situation media research has to face in the near future: an unimaginable number of media for a more or less constant number of media users with limited time, money and (most important) attention capacities.

For consumers, this change has predominantly been positive. Never before have we had so much choice. Choice in terms of the devices by which we consume media content (laptops, tablet computers, mobile phones and so on), but also choice in terms of which vehicle we will choose to use to access content. As a result, the way in which we consume media has changed. We spread our time across many more vehicles, but we still only have twenty-four hours in a day and actual time spent consuming media has remained relatively stable over time (an average of just over eight hours in 1999, 2005 and 2009) (Papper et al., 2005; Hess, 2009). Subsequently, and not surprisingly, the degree of **concurrent media usage** is increasing (Papper et al., 2005; Hess, 2009; Block et al., 2009). The time spent concurrently using different media, however, is not spread equally across platforms. The time spent and frequency of use for new media such as mobile phones varies significantly from that of traditional forms of media (television, radio or cinema) (Papper et al., 2004; Block et al., 2009; Hess, 2009).

Figure 11.3 shows the media that are most likely to be concurrently used, and the media with which they are most likely to share audience time.

> **concurrent media usage:**
> Using more than one form of media at the same time; for example, posting updates to Facebook while watching television.

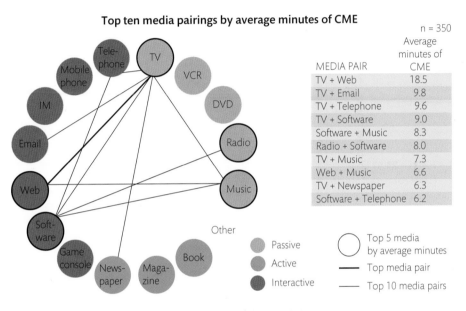

Top ten media pairings by average minutes of CME

n = 350

MEDIA PAIR	Average minutes of CME
TV + Web	18.5
TV + Email	9.8
TV + Telephone	9.6
TV + Software	9.0
Software + Music	8.3
Radio + Software	8.0
TV + Music	7.3
Web + Music	6.6
TV + Newspaper	6.3
Software + Telephone	6.2

- Passive
- Active
- Interactive

- Top 5 media by average minutes
- Top media pair
- Top 10 media pairs

Note: Computer-only pairings (for example, web and email) are excluded.

●●● **FIGURE 11.3** CONCURRENT MEDIA USE

Source: Adapted from Holmes et al., 2005, p. 19

For advertisers, media proliferation (the growth of media options) and audience fragmentation bring both opportunities and complexity. There are opportunities in terms of choice of media and vehicles to use, in terms of audience to reach and in relation to how much is spent (as more competition leads to price competition in this market). On the other hand, this complexity makes it easier to make the wrong media decision. For example, fragmentation makes it increasingly difficult to reach mass numbers of target consumers through a single top-rating program or station.

Fragmentation means that each advertising spot reaches fewer people. There are more spots available so prices are lower, but advertisers have to buy more to obtain the same reach. Because each additional spot will reach some people already hit by previous spots, an advertiser will find that buying double the number of spots does not double the reach.

In the United States, prime-time ratings on free-to-air television networks fell by over 40 per cent from 1977 to 2003 (Bianco, Lowry et al., 2004), not because people were watching less television but simply because much of their viewing went to new cable channels. In the 1950s, the top-rating show, *I Love Lucy*, generated a household rating of around 40, whereas in the 2001–02 season even the top-ranking comedy *Friends* only managed a rating of 15 (Green, 2002). Today very few shows rate higher than 5: even the top-rating finales—*Sex in The City* (February 2004), *Sopranos* (June 2007) and *Lost* (May 2010)—reached only a rating of 4. Despite a decline in ratings as a result of the growth in supply of media, advertising revenue generated from the industry continues to grow. Advertisers are now spending more across many more vehicles to reach the vast numbers that in the past could be bought on just a few stations, with just a few media buys and with a lot less money.

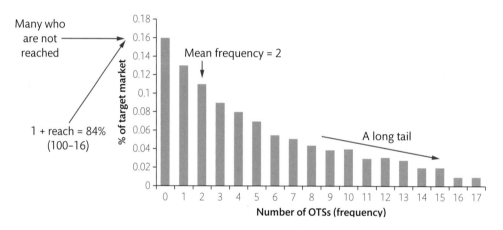

●●● **FIGURE 11.4** FREQUENCY DISTRIBUTION WITHIN TARGET AUDIENCE

Frequency

frequency of exposure: The number of times a consumer is exposed to an advertisement.

The other measurable element that forms the basis of media costs for most advertising space is the average **frequency of exposure**: the number of times potential consumers are exposed to an advertisement within a particular period. Together with reach, frequency of exposure reveals the total number of exposures that have occurred.

While the average frequency of exposure provides some indication of how many spots in a campaign the audience sees or hears, the reporting of an average frequency can be quite misleading. Frequency of exposure among the population is a skewed distribution; that is, most people see or hear very few of the advertisements in a campaign (as shown in Figure 11.4).

long tail: The skew of customers who are exposed to a large number of advertisement spots.

Regardless of budget and how well advertisements are placed, it's likely that many potential consumers of a product or service that is being promoted will not get any exposure to the campaign, with a few being exposed to a very large number of advertisement spots (this is known as the **long tail**). Given this skew in the distribution of exposure rates, the average frequency disguises the fact that many potential buyers must be exposed to a very large number of advertisements in order for the average frequency of exposure across a population to be much greater than 1. The implications of this for media planning strategy are addressed in the 'Reach don't teach' section later in this chapter.

Budget

The size of an advertiser's budget affects the type of media they might use and the amount of space they will buy. For example, a local doctor's surgery may have an annual advertising budget of $5000, and so could not afford to make a decent television commercial, nor could they afford to buy even one advertising spot in a high-rating television show (which may cost around $20,000). Even though this one spot might deliver cost-effective reach, it has the disadvantage that a single spot gives little coverage over time, and people are getting sick every day of the year. The doctor's surgery needs to look for media that provides cost-effective reach and coverage over time.

For many small businesses, the geographical location of potential consumers might be a very important consideration. If they only serve a limited catchment area, they do not want to pay for media that reaches outside of this area.

While the overall marketing communications budget limits the platforms that can be used and the total amount of advertising that can be purchased by an advertiser, there is still the potential for advertisers to get very different media purchases for their budget. Within a media type (such as television), there is still significant choice in what to spend one's money on and this is where comparative cost measures such as CPM are useful tools for advertisers.

Cost per thousand (CPM) is the cost of a media spot (for example the price of a single advertisement within a magazine) divided by the number of people reached by that spot. CPM can be calculated for any medium that provides an individual advertisement unit cost and the size of the audience that is reached by that unit of advertising. It is an indicator of the efficiency of media spend when compared within a single platform: for example, it is useful for comparing the cost of one television channel's advertising with that of another television channel. Akin to comparing apples with oranges, it is not possible, however, to make such cost comparisons across media platforms—to compare a television station to a radio station, for instance—as the intrinsic qualities of different media types are expected to deliver very different types of exposure for different types of media.

cost per thousand (CPM): The cost of a single advertisement divided by the number of people who can be reached by that one spot.

For many marketers, comparing CPM within a media platform is an effective way of evaluating their individual return on investment. However, such comparisons should also be made with the absolute reach potential of a vehicle in mind. Small media can look very cost-effective on a cost per reach basis; however, if they do not offer the ability to reach many potential buyers in total, they still may not constitute an effective media purchase. For instance, if Media X has a CPM of $1.90 and reaches a total audience of 120,000, but Media Y has a CPM of $2.20 and reaches a total audience of one million, it may still be worth buying space on Media Y in order to ensure that such large reach can be achieved quickly with a single advertisement purchase, despite its higher CPM.

Selectivity and wastage

Another factor that advertisers and media buyers take into consideration when choosing a media vehicle is the extent to which it is able to provide a specific type of audience. CPMs can be calculated for the particular target audience so that different media options can be compared. An option might reach many people who are highly unlikely to buy the advertised product or service, but this does not mean that it is necessarily unsuitable—it might still have a reasonable CPM for reaching the people that matter. It's important that marketers do these calculations and not make the mistake of rejecting some media because they don't look targeted enough.

Selectivity refers to the extent to which a media vehicle delivers a specific type of audience (based on the audience's demographic, psychographic or product usage characteristics). For example, *Vogue Bridal* magazine may be selective in delivering an audience made up primarily of women who are about to get married; this may be the target audience for a wedding photographer.

Conversely, **wastage** is the proportion of the audience delivered by a media that falls *outside* of the advertiser's target audience. For example, if the advertiser's core target is women, and they buy an advertisement in a medium that delivers an audience of which 40 per cent are male and 60 per cent are female; the wastage would be 40 per cent. For advertisers, a key advantage of choosing a media vehicle that is selective in reaching a desirable target market is that wastage will be reduced. If there are no (or limited) cost implications associated with making such a targeted media choice, then this would represent a significant efficiency for the advertiser. However, this is rarely the case, so accepting some wastage is usually the most cost-effective option.

The desire to limit wastage presents a rationale for advertisers to choose a more selective vehicle that provides an audience that is more closely aligned with their own target market. A foundational concept from the 1960s, **audience targeting** is the practice of placing advertising where it is most likely to be seen by members of the target market for the purpose of having the greatest impact while eliminating costly wastage (Walker, 1998; Sissors & Baron, 2002; Kemplay & Davis, 2008; van der Wurff, Barker & Picard, 2008).

Media vehicles offer advertisers vehicles that they claim reach these desirable segments more effectively than competing offerings. They use this positioning to attract advertisers and even may charge a premium above and beyond the reach they obtain to benefit from the advertiser's desire to reduce wastage. For advertisers, however, there are some problems with this approach.

First, advertisers may mistakenly assume that their brand appeals more strongly to particular (usually demographic) segments than their competitors (Cannon & Rashid, 1991). The demographic variables that are usually used include age, gender, income, occupation and education (Walker, 1998; Sissors & Baron, 2002). While targeting on the basis of demographic variables is most common, other variables can also be used as a basis for matching a target market with a target audience of a medium (Winter, 1980; Cannon, 1984; Assael & Poltrack, 1991; Cannon & Rashid, 1991, Fennel & Allenby, 2002), such as psychographics, media or product category usage. This assumption that a brand's customer base is dramatically different from the customer base of its competitors has been shown to be incorrect (Kennedy & Ehrenberg, 2000), suggesting that rather than choosing a targeted, selective media vehicle, advertisers may be better positioned if they bought space in more mass vehicles.

selectivity: The extent to which a media vehicle delivers a specific type of audience; for example, a golfing magazine may largely deliver golfers and may be geared towards men.

wastage: The proportion of an audience that is not within the advertiser's target audience but who see the advertisement anyway.

audience targeting: Choosing media that specifically target a particular customer type; for example, advertising in a horse magazine to reach horse riders.

Direct and indirect matching

Regardless of the variables used, matching a target market with a target audience of a medium may be done either by direct matching or indirect matching. Direct matching involves (often syndicated) single source data where, for a group of individuals, both media use product use and demographic (or other) characteristics of the individual are recorded. This allows advertisers to know what kinds of media their customers use. While it is the gold standard for many forms of media research, single source data is very expensive to collect and is generally difficult for most marketing managers to access. As a result, many advertisers use indirect matching of two sets of data to guide their targeting efforts. This involves the use of fused data, where media use is captured for a group of individuals along with their demographic information, and product usage and demographic information is recorded for a separate group of individuals. The demographic (or other personal characteristic data) is then matched from one data set to another. For example, if in data set A fifteen- to nineteen-year-olds are more likely to listen to Rock FM, and in data set B fifteen- to nineteen-year-olds are more likely to be buyers of Product X, then it is assumed that all fifteen- to nineteen-year-old buyers of Product X are also listeners of Rock FM. Product X may then choose to spend more of its budget advertising on this station in order to reach its target market.

Second, advertisers may mistakenly assume that competing media have different audience profiles. Media providers often make these claims to make up for low or declining reach, and to benefit from advertisers' desires to target (Nowak, Cameron & Krugman, 1993; Picard, 1999; Dimmick, 2003; Nelson-Field, Lees, et al., 2005). Their claims can be found in their promotional material, which is readily available in press releases and on media websites. Here are a couple of examples:

> We are the most broadly appealing station targeting an audience of 25–54 year olds.
>
> Mix 94.5 Perth Station Profile <www.austereo.com.au>,
> cited in Nelson-Field et al., 2007

> Fox FM is an energetic listener driven radio station primarily targeting 18–39 year old females.
>
> Fox 101.9 Melbourne Station Profile < www.austereo.com.au>,
> cited in Nelson-Field et al., 2007

Despite such claims, it has been shown that, overall, media audiences are surprisingly homogenous. For example, even children's television channels (such as Nickelodeon) have a mostly adult audience—they have three to four times the proportion of children viewers than other networks, but adults still account for more than 50 per cent of their viewers. Similarly, despite the fact we may think it would appeal more to men, the US Super Bowl skews only slightly to male viewers (54 per cent) (Sports Business Daily, 2012). Furthermore, the differences in audience between two similar media vehicles (for example two news networks) are very slight. Thus, the differences in the audiences delivered by competing media vehicles are far less dramatic than the audience selectivity claims media providers typically make (Nelson-Field & Riebe, 2010). On average, half of a vehicle's audience falls outside of its claimed target market and the more targeted a vehicle claims to be the less well their claim actually describes their real audience. In many cases, where a media vehicle claims to appeal to a specific segment, several of its competitors actually reach far more of that specific segment than the claimant. For advertisers, this means that those who choose targeted media actually get less reach within the chosen segment than they would if they had simply bought a less targeted media, despite the so-called 'wastage' that may come with that decision.

Given that media skews are normally reported as the percentage of an audience that can be described by the chosen desirable demographic (or other characteristic), it is perhaps unsurprising that advertisers are sometimes confused about the effectiveness of buying apparently selective media. The evidence suggests that mass media often do a better job of providing access to these segments than the supposed **selective vehicles**, and often also with less wastage. Consider the example of two media vehicles, one mass media vehicle that makes no claim about reaching a specific audience, and the other a selective vehicle that claims to reach more females aged eighteen to thirty years of age (as shown in Figure 11.5).

selective vehicles: Media platforms that claim to reach a select group of potential consumers with little wastage.

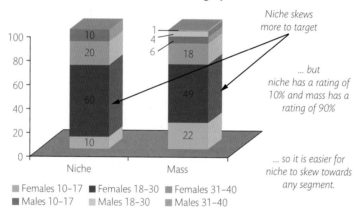

% of audience in chosen demographic

Niche skews more to target

... but niche has a rating of 10% and mass has a rating of 90%

... so it is easier for niche to skew towards any segment.

■ Females 10–17 ■ Females 18–30 ■ Females 31–40
■ Males 10–17 ■ Males 18–30 ■ Males 31–40

●●● **FIGURE 11.5** SELECTIVITY CLAIMS

The selective media is not being entirely untruthful in its claim. Its audience is proportionally made up of more females aged eighteen to thirty than that of its competitor, even though both vehicles attract many viewers in this segment. However, if the ratings of the two vehicles are also considered, the picture is very different. A far larger vehicle, with a smaller skew towards a particular segment, may actually allow an advertiser to reach more (in absolute numbers) of the desired audience. In this case, if the ratings of the two media were 90 per cent and 10 per cent respectively (that is, these vehicles alone made up the entire market), then the mass brand would allow the advertiser to contact 88 per cent of all the women aged eighteen to thirty in the market, while the selective vehicle (despite its audience skew) would only deliver 12 per cent of this segment to the advertiser (as shown in Figure 11.6).

So, while it is important to consider whether potential buyers of your product are likely to be using the media in which you are advertising, do not consider only the skew of an audience proportionally towards your desired target market, but also the overall reach ability of the vehicle in which you choose to advertise.

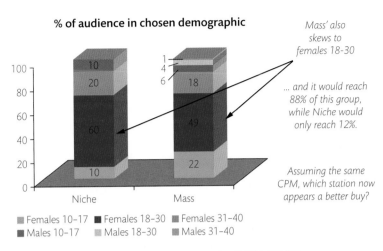

% of audience in chosen demographic

Mass' also skews to females 18-30

... and it would reach 88% of this group, while Niche would only reach 12%.

Assuming the same CPM, which station now appears a better buy?

■ Females 10–17 ■ Females 18–30 ■ Females 31–40
■ Males 10–17 ■ Males 18–30 ■ Males 31–40

●●● **FIGURE 11.6** SELECTIVITY CLAIMS AND ACTUAL REACH

Clutter

In comparing different media options, advertisers may also consider a range of more qualitative factors. One of these considerations is **advertising clutter**: the level of advertising and other non-programming material (such as community service announcements, station promotions or news bulletins) that appears in a medium (Speck & Elliott, 1998). It is reported that advertising clutter in all media is increasing (Green, 2003) and it is suspected that this clutter reduces the effectiveness of advertising by limiting the ability of the audience to notice and/or effectively process advertising (Brown & Rothschild, 1993; Webb & Ray, 1979).

Certainly, increases in the sheer amount of advertising make it more difficult for all advertisements to be remembered (Riebe & Dawes, 2006; Hammer, Riebe & Kennedy, 2009) and may lead to increased advertising avoidance. In addition, the first and last positions in an advertisement break have been shown to be more effective (Webb & Ray, 1979; Brown & Rothschild, 1993; Riebe & Dawes, 2006). Therefore less advertising (less clutter) in a vehicle is more likely to result in any one advertiser's material being in a favourable position.

Given this, clutter is an important consideration in choosing media vehicles. As with comparing media on a CPM basis, making comparisons between different types of media in relation to the level of clutter they contain can be ineffective. However, when comparing one radio station that has a lot of advertising with another radio station that contains far less advertising, for example, it follows that it is sensible to consider the clutter. Unfortunately for advertisers, media that do offer significantly less cluttered advertising environments realise that these environments are preferable and also need to recoup the losses associated with having less advertising inventory to sell. As a result, low clutter advertising space tends to cost more. Smaller (or newer) media often make claims about intentionally having less advertising clutter (for which they charge accordingly), but sooner or later, once they have the ratings to support selling more advertising space, they reduce their reliance on this strategy and instead try to charge more for having equally as cluttered advertising environments as their competitors (this occurred recently with the Nova radio station in Australia).

◣ **advertising clutter:**
The amount of other advertising and other non-program material that appears within a medium.

When it comes to clutter, the question for advertisers therefore needs to be whether the price premiums are really worth the additional effectiveness gained from advertising in low clutter environments. In a study of three different types of clutter in television, radio and print, Hammer, Riebe and Kennedy (2009) showed that only clutter caused by the sheer volume of advertising, rather than its arrangement or the presence of competitors' advertising, had a significant effect on audience memories of advertising. Furthermore, reducing the amount of advertising would not produce sufficient improvement in advertising recall and recognition to justify the price increases for that advertising space. This was later found to also be true in the context of social media: Nelson-Field, Sharp and Riebe (2012) replicated the study in a large-scale Facebook experiment and found that in the highly cluttered Facebook environment, where respondents were exposed to less clutter, they were more likely to recall an advertising exposure, but that halving clutter did not double an advertisement's chance of being recalled.

Advertising avoidance

opportunity to see/ hear (OTS): A measure of how many people had the chance to see or hear an advertisement. Note that this is distinguished from actual exposure, which is the number of people who *did* see an advertisement.

Related to the issue of advertising clutter is that of advertising avoidance. In selecting a media vehicle, advertisers may consider the extent to which **OTS (opportunity to see/hear)** directly translates into actual exposure. OTS is most commonly discussed in relation to television audiences, although it does not necessarily have to be restricted to this platform. OTS determines the likely audience of an advertisement, as measured by the people meter device. The people meter records how many people are in the room during a particular program. Program ratings are not truly reflective of the true size of the audience for advertising. Around one third of the television audience for a program actively avoids advertising when it is aired (they leave the room, switch the station and so on). Such active avoidance is captured by considering the OTS of a particular thirty-second advertising position (reflected in the people meter data), rather than the overall ratings for a program.

What is not captured in the OTS measure, however, is the third of the audience who passively avoids advertising by muting the ads, talking with friends or using the internet while having the television on, and so on. This avoidance behaviour is not captured by the people meter and is a significant consideration. In choosing a vehicle in which to promote their products, advertisers therefore need to consider the likelihood that a particular position is more or less likely to result in advertising avoidance behaviour from the audience.

Engagement, context and consumer relevance

Another factor that advertisers and media buyers take into consideration when choosing media vehicles is the extent to which the context of the placement affects the effectiveness of the advertising.

Much of the impetus for work in this area arose in the 1980s with the concept of involvement. Clearly, we are more interested in some media content than others. Potentially we are also more likely to be affected by advertising when it is placed in certain positions, based on our level of interest in the context for that advertising. And similarly, the congruence between the advertising and the media content could ensure that we are more accepting of advertising content when it is aired within related content. How advertising effectiveness is altered by the audience's involvement or engagement with the media content in which advertising is placed, however, has not yet thoroughly been answered. So far the answer appears to be, 'It's complicated'—sometimes more involvement is good for the advertising and sometimes it is not. Nonetheless, there has been renewed vigour in this area of research, thanks largely to smaller media (of which there are more, due to proliferation and fragmentation) and social media.

As advertisers scramble for a rationale to justify their advertising and media choices, engagement is a useful crutch (Ephron, 2005). But the question still remains—are environments where the audience is more interested, involved or engaged environments where audiences are more likely to notice, effectively process and then act upon the advertising? The empirical evidence that does exist in this area is conflicting, thanks largely to the different conceptualisations used for the engagement construct (Plummer, 2006; Andrews, Durvasula & Akhter, 1990; Calder et al., 2009).

Potentially, advertising that is more congruent with its context—that is, the product is related (an ad for soccer equipment placed during the telecast of the World Cup) or the creative is tied to the context (such as a car ad that involves references to tennis and is placed during a tennis telecast)—may be more effective than advertising that is unrelated to its context. Certainly there is a targeting effect, in that tennis programs reach people who are somewhat more interested in tennis than the average person, but whether this related context helps advertising attention and processing is not well known. It's certainly not a simple effect, nor very strong.

Other qualitative considerations

In addition to all of these different considerations that media buyers need to make, there are myriad other situation-specific factors that come into play. For example, the availability of existing creative executions, inherent characteristics of the particular category or brand being promoted (such as seasonal sales effects), discounts available for particular sectional positions, sponsorship deals, and the timing and number of spots that are made available by the provider may all influence the final media decisions that are made by the planner or buyer (Spittler, 1998).

While the onus is on the media planner to determine the relevance and importance of each factor relative to the particular campaign or product (Gensch, 1970), Abatt and Cowan (1999) suggest that more importance is placed on certain selection factors over others when considering media choice. After surveying the top 100 South African advertisers (by advertising volume) and their media agencies, Abatt and Cowan found that the medium's ability to reach a specific demographic audience was considered over all other media decision factors to be the most important and to have the most potential to influence their media decisions. This finding was also noted in a similar earlier study of small advertisers by Nowak and colleagues (1971). There has particularly been heated debate in industry publications about how these priorities might affect scheduling practices, such as how a focus on maximising reach or effective frequency might lead to different scheduling approaches (Ephron, 1995b, 1997, 2000b; Broadbent, 1998). Scheduling decisions are discussed later in this chapter.

◢ LEARNING OBJECTIVE
Discuss the characteristics
of a range of different
media vehicles

MEDIA CHARACTERISTICS

Media choice and media vehicle selection are among the important media planning decisions an advertiser needs to make. Choices are usually made early in the media planning process and the procedure for doing so is based partly on quantitative data (on reach and cost), and partly on the intrinsic qualities of these media types and the advertising message.

The media plan can be driven by many factors, such as existing creative material, availability of advertising space or whether management has a desire to be advertising on a particular medium. However, this is not good practice. There should be three key considerations that affect the choice of media type:

1   the sales effect of advertising exposures in that media
2   the overall size of the audience that the media vehicle can deliver and when
3   the cost of the media.

With these factors in mind, the intrinsic qualities (and disadvantages) of different types of media are now described in more detail.

Television

Television tends to take the largest single slice of advertising dollars in developed countries. This is because almost everyone watches television, on average for several hours a day. So it can reach a lot of consumers, and it can do so rather quickly compared to other media.

There are other media that are cheaper to create ads for, and in other media it costs less to buy a single spot, but often these media deliver far smaller audiences, which means that in order for the advertiser to reach the consumers they want to within a certain time (this week or month), they have to buy an awful lot of space. For example, if you wanted to reach everyone in Sydney using newspaper advertising, it would be difficult—there are groups of people (especially teenagers) who seldom if ever read a newspaper—and it would require paying for a lot of newspaper space over a long time. So, while television might appear more expensive, it can work out to be the cheapest way to meet the advertiser's reach objective. This is why many large consumer brands spend 80 per cent or more of their entire advertising budget on television. Retailers, who often have objectives to reach a lot of consumers *this week*, also tend to use a lot of television advertising—they need the quick reach of television because they often need to tell consumers about something that is happening in-store this week, and next week they will run a different ad. For similar reasons, politicians use a great deal of television advertising during elections.

Because of its fast and vast reach, and because television delivers video and sound, television campaigns create buzz and get spoken about far more than campaigns in other media. This additional publicity and word-of-mouth benefit adds to the effectiveness of television. Advertisers often dream of their advertisement 'going viral', meaning people pass on copies of the ad or links to it on Facebook, YouTube, Twitter and so on. Similarly, they hope that journalists will start talking about their advertisement or brand, especially journalists that write for high-rating television shows.

Television is often considered the premium advertising medium because of its high-quality colour, video and sound. Marketers can create advertisements that look good and that consumers want to watch, and they can show their brand in all its glory—or at least associate it with relevant beautiful scenes and people. Television advertising can be very entertaining, as evidenced by programs that feature nothing but top advertisements, and by the amount of people who post television advertisements to YouTube for others to watch.

It's true that people do not watch every advertisement during the programs they watch—they fast-forward, switch channels, mute the sound, do some other activity or leave the room—but television viewers do still watch a lot of television advertisements and are generally willing to do so. People like the model of receiving free (or heavily subsidised) programs in exchange for watching (some) advertising. Research shows that on average people watch about one third of television commercials; another third of the time they passively avoid them (they give something else—such as surfing the web or talking to someone else in the room—their attention) and for the final third of the time they completely avoid the ads by switching the channel or leaving the room (Paech, Riebe & Sharp, 2003). There is evidence that this has not changed much over the years in spite of new technology and channels (Sharp, Beal & Collins, 2009; du Plessis, 2009). Today digital video recorders provide different ways of avoiding ads (such as fast-forwarding) but these avoidance methods largely replace older ones: the total amount of television advertising avoidance has not increased. Also, television viewing is quite a passive, relaxed and relaxing activity, so consumers are willing to let ads 'wash over them'. This is in complete contrast to environments where people are goal-directed or concentrating on a task (such as shopping in a supermarket or writing to friends on Facebook)—in such active environments consumers are extremely good at screening out advertising, which means that they just don't see it. Radio also shares this advantage with television, as does print advertising in magazines: as with television advertising, we sometimes enjoy reading print ads, which in some magazines are extremely similar to the actual content (look at the fashion ads in *Vogue*, for instance).

While television may reach large numbers of potential consumers, in some countries there is a lot of fragmentation (that is, lots of channels splitting the audience up), so no individual channel can deliver a large audience. Fortunately for advertisers, in most countries a few large channels still dominate—they have the highest ratings, which allows them to fund the best shows, which in turn deliver large audiences.

It's important to note that while television can, potentially, deliver fast and vast reach, many individual low-rating channels are not able to deliver this promise. Low-rating specialist channels often claim that in compensation they deliver a specialist audience (for example the business news channel might claim to deliver wealthy viewers). These claims should be treated with scepticism and checked out carefully. Research shows that small specialist channels largely deliver the same sort of audience as larger reach channels—they just deliver far fewer viewers (Sharp, Beal & Collins, 2009). Once an advertiser has bought some space on a large television channel, there is usually little value in also buying space on a very low rating channel: it doesn't deliver any additional reach.

The strengths of television advertising are that it:

- is both *audio and visual:* Advertisers are able to demonstrate how the product or service that they are promoting is used. This provides more creative flexibility: a great deal can be done with video, sight and sound. Television can strengthen an advertiser's distinctive assets (whether these be verbal or visual cues).

- *delivers mass reach quickly:* This is important for new brands and any brand that needs to reach a lot of people quickly; for example supermarkets who want to reach most shoppers every week.

- *delivers mass reach cheaply:* Television advertising is quite cheap on a per person basis: even in expensive developed countries it only costs a few cents to play an ad to one person (that is, only $20 or so to reach 1000 people). Television is also often the cheapest way for an advertiser to achieve a particular reach objective, particularly if the requirement is to reach a lot of people in a fairly short space of time.

Television advertising, particularly on top-rating shows, signals that the product is successful and selling well (psychologists refer to the phenomenon of 'social proof': if many other people are buying a brand, we infer it must be good and should not be socially embarrassing for us to also buy). This is why the slogan 'as seen on TV' is sometimes used on packaging and point-of-sale material. Economists point out that large visible advertising expenditures are a signal of the firm's faith in its brand and a signal of its commitment to the market. So, television advertising can make sense for risky products, or for ones that consumers find hard to assess the quality of before purchase (such as insurance or cars): the sheer dollars of expenditure signals quality.

The weaknesses of television advertising are:

- *production costs:* Television can be expensive in terms of both creative development and production (filming) costs; however, this latter cost is declining due to new technology.

- *long lead times:* It takes longer to plan and execute an advertisement on television than it does in other media.

- *limited geographic selectivity:* Television is a mass medium. It allows for state-based and urban/regional selectivity, but it usually isn't possible to target smaller geographic areas, which is why small retailers with very limited catchment areas (for example a small local hardware store) tend to use other media, such as print.

- *wastage:* Being a mass medium, television is more likely than some other platforms to reach people outside the target audience. This isn't necessarily a weakness unless the target market for the brand is particularly narrow (for example, Catapiller selling heavy-moving equipment to councils and large builders). This is one of the main reasons why business-to-business marketers make little use of television.

- *time placement:* Television audiences are strongly skewed towards evening (before midnight). Television doesn't reach people close to when they are shopping.

- *brief exposure:* Television commercials are fleeting (often only 30 seconds) and therefore not well suited to communicating detailed technical information.

Radio

Radio listening generally occurs in conjunction with other activities, such as driving or working at home, and so radio said to be the most versatile medium in that it moves with us. However, as radio is more of a 'background' medium, doubts are raised about the extent to which listeners actually listen to the advertising.

Radio is sometimes recommended as a medium that can be combined with television, as the prime times for these media differ, allowing the advertiser to build cumulative reach by reaching different audiences with each media at different times of the day. While television viewing hits a peak at night-time (between 6 and 10 pm), radio prime time is morning (6 to 9 am) and afternoon (4 to 6 pm) drive time.

The strengths of radio advertising are:

- *the opportunity for audience selectivity:* Radio is a medium that is predominantly bought at a local level, making it more suitable than television for products and services with geographically specific availability. This is why many of the ads on radio are for local brands (such as a specific retail store).

- *the low absolute cost:* Both in terms of creative production and individual spot cost, radio is less expensive than some other media. It is worth noting, however, that cheap spots are nearly always cheap because they reach only a very small audience.

- *short lead times:* A radio campaign can be planned and executed very quickly.

- *being closer to the point of purchase:* Radio has the potential to reach an audience as they approach a potential purchase occasion; for instance in the car on the way to the grocery store.

- *frequency medium:* Radio is considered a frequency medium, which means advertisers can afford (due to the low absolute cost) to buy many spots and hit listeners with many exposures. However, research has shown that additional exposures within a short time frame delivers declining sales effects (see the section on 'Reach' above).

The weaknesses of radio advertising are:

- *limited reach:* Radio is a highly fragmented medium, with the listening audience divided among many stations, so no single station can deliver much reach.

- *brief exposure:* Unlike print, radio commercials are fleeting (sometimes only a few seconds long). There is a substantial risk of the advertisement not being correctly heard or understood.

- *audio only:* The absence of a visual component to radio limits the ability of advertisers to use the medium to strengthen their visual brand cues.

- *clutter:* Radio is a cluttered medium, particularly as a result of the low spot costs that make radio an option for many small businesses that cannot afford even a single low-rating television or magazine spot. For advertisers, this means the creative quality of radio advertising is particularly important in order for radio ads to stand out and be noticed. This may be even more difficult with an audio-only platform.

Print (magazines and newspapers)

Magazines and newspapers are generally viewed as a higher involvement media because reading requires more cognitive effort from the audience than, say, watching television or listening to the radio. This is an advantage for advertising that wants consumers to do a degree of thinking, which is why financial services make a lot of use of print advertising. Conversely, if you have a very simple (possibly visual) message (such as a picture of a perfume bottle or the statement 'home loans at 4.1 per cent') then print is often a cost-effective medium.

Magazines are a highly fragmented media, with most magazines delivering extremely small audiences, and with low cumulative reach over issues; that is, each new issue is largely read by the same people who read the previous issue. However, they do deliver specialist targeted audiences—because people pay to read specialist magazines, an advertiser can be confident that the readers are interested in that topic. For example, home renovation magazines are often read by people who are currently or soon to be renovating their house, wine magazines by people interested in buying expensive wine, and so on.

Newspapers are traditionally known for providing current news. As a result, they are commonly thought of as a 'morning medium'—a medium that is consumed by its audience early on the day of publication. This can be very useful for advertisers who wish to pay only for reaching consumers on a particular day (there is little value in telling people on Monday about the sale that was held on the prior weekend). In comparison, magazines are read over a period of weeks, and sometimes re-read.

Classified advertising in newspapers has largely disappeared, migrating to the internet; however, newspapers still carry a lot of advertising—and the distinction between newspapers and magazines has blurred, as many newspapers have added non-news content, such as fashion, health and home renovation supplements.

Regional newspapers can deliver targeted geographical audiences, right down to individual suburbs in the case of suburban newspapers. For regionally based advertisers this can be very attractive; for national advertisers this is no advantage.

The strengths of print media are:

- *opportunity for targeting:* Many print publications, such as newspapers, offer local audiences (from specific geographic regions), and magazines offer audiences interested in specific topics (for instance motorcycles).
- *potential for high quality creativity:* In comparison to other media, print offers flexibility in relation to the creative aspects of advertising (both in terms of allowing for a prestigious look and also in terms of tactical elements such as providing for a call to action, coupons or trialling).
- *long shelf life:* Magazines (though not newspapers) are typically read and re-read, as they linger around for a while before finally being recycled.
- *high reach:* Print media generally (not including small 'niche' magazines) have the ability to reach large audience numbers.

The weaknesses of print media are:

- *long lead times:* Due to the nature of print, it takes longer to plan and execute an advertisement in this medium than in many others. This is more of a problem for magazines than newspapers given the regularity of the publications and the quality of the printing typically used for both types of print (that is, colour printing can take longer to arrange).
- *clutter:* Print (in particular for magazines) is perhaps the most cluttered of all media.
- *total absolute cost:* Print can be expensive both in terms of creative development and the cost associated with individual advertising spots. However, as for television, on a cost for reach basis this medium isn't particularly expensive relative to some other forms of media.
- *visual only:* The absence of an audio component to print media limits the ability for advertisers to strengthen their auditory brand cues when using it to advertise.

Outdoor

Outdoor or out of home (OOH) advertising encompasses all forms of promotional material that are experienced out of the home: in cinemas, in shopping malls, on billboards and even advertising on transport vehicles. While it accounts for only 4 per cent of all media spend, it is a growing medium that is around us constantly, and people are often unaware of just how much advertising they are exposed to in this mode.

Even in outdoor advertising, digital technology is having an effect. Increasingly, digital, moving outdoor displays are available as advertising devices.

The strengths of outdoor advertising are:

- *high visibility:* Outdoor ads can be physically large and located in high traffic areas. This means that they have the ability to stand out and be noticed.

●●● **FIGURE 11.7** OUTDOOR ADVERTISING

- *closer to point of purchase:* Outdoor has the ability to reach consumers as they approach potential purchase occasions; for example in the mall on the way to buy shoes.
- *wide coverage (locally):* Outdoor has the ability to be cost-effective, have a wide reach and result in strong word-of-mouth among local communities.
- *new technologies:* Some outdoor is now digital, which brings flexibility in terms of content.
- *media supplement:* Outdoor is commonly considered to be a great extension of television advertising. With most of the content for the advertisement being conveyed via the television version of the commercial, an outdoor execution can be far less detailed and yet act as a reminder of any previous exposure to the television commercial.

The weaknesses of outdoor/transient advertising are:

- *wastage:* Being a mass medium, outdoor is likely to reach people outside the target audience.
- *limited message and brief exposure:* Unlike for print, the message needs to provide limited information.
- *visual only:* The absence of an audio component means outdoor advertising does not provide the ability for advertisers to strengthen their auditory brand cues.
- *difficult to measure:* Metrics for outdoor advertising are generally limited to traffic reports (information on the number of cars that drive past an outdoor billboard location within a week).
- *clutter:* Outdoor media competes with everything else in a person's line of sight. Thus, there is clutter for outdoor advertising beyond simply competing advertising.

Case study

FarmFoods Direct: Planning for reach

Philip runs a business in a small rural town in Queensland, selling boxes of locally sourced organic fruit and vegetables. He's been selling the boxes for a few years now at a local level—selling just under one hundred boxes per week to members of the local branch of the Association of Organic Farmers and to neighbours and some people in nearby towns. Recently, due to the growing popularity of healthy eating and demand for locally produced organic food, Philip decided to invest in a big expansion for the business. His aim is to develop a recognised brand (FarmFoods Direct) with distribution networks across the region as well as in the closest capital cities, Brisbane and Sydney.

Philip knows that the most important step in successfully growing his business will be to tell people about the brand: 'If they don't know about it, they can't buy it.' So he sets aside a significant portion of the money that he's borrowed from the bank for advertising. His target market is very broad—everyone who eats—so he wants to use the budget in the most cost-efficient way so that he can tell as many people as possible about

FarmFoods Direct. The problem is that he has no idea how to spend the budget: he has very little experience with advertising and marketing, and his research has presented him with conflicting ideas.

Question

Consider and discuss the following ideas to help Philip build his campaign. Which of these strategies would be best?

1 The best way to reach a lot of people would be to run a television ad during the last episode of a popular reality TV cooking show on the big free-to-air television station (although just one ad would use up 80 per cent of the budget for the first half of the year).

2 A good idea would be to focus the spend on ads in women's food magazines because women do most of the shopping and those that are interested in cooking are more likely to be interested in FarmFoods Direct.

3 Dedicating the whole spend on weekly ads in the Association of Organic Farmers' newsletter and banner ads on the Association's website would be the best way to reach people interested in organic food. There is no point running radio ads to complement a television commercial because it would just reach the same people. Also, radio listeners are not very engaged and it is not a good medium for this campaign because the quality of the produce can't be shown without a visual.

Product placement

In comparison to outdoor, radio and print media, **product placement** is a relatively new (albeit increasingly popular) consideration for the media budget. Product placement is simply the insertion of the advertiser's product in the production of movie and/or television content, whereby the audience sees the product used (by an actor) in a natural setting. Perhaps one of the most famous early product placements in movies is Reese's Pieces (American chocolates) in the 1982 movie *ET*, and most of us will have seen James Bond (see Figure 11.8) driving an Aston Martin, drinking Dom Pérignon champagne and wearing a Rolex.

product placement:
The presence of a branded product or service within an entertainment program; for example, a Starbucks cup in the television show *Friends*.

The strengths of product placement are that it:

- *curbs advertising avoidance:* As the product appears within the context of the programming and may even be written into the script for the media content, there is less chance of the advertising being avoided by channel switching, muting or leaving the room during the break. The product placement may not even be viewed by the audience as advertising, which in itself has advantages for the commissioning organisation.

- *is demonstrative:* The product placement typically involves the product being consumed by an actor. This allows for demonstration of the product's real use and also implies endorsement from the actor.

- *builds mass reach and awareness quickly:* Similar to television campaigns, product placement (given it appears within programming content) gains reach fast.

●●● **FIGURE 11.8** PRODUCT PLACEMENT: JAMES BOND 007

The weaknesses of product placement are:

- *wastage:* Being a mass medium product placement it is likely to reach people outside the target audience.
- *limited message and brief exposure:* Product placement is usually fleeting and incidental to the story, which is quite different from a (good) advertisement.
- *clutter:* With the increase in popularity of this alternative approach to traditional advertising, product placement is becoming overly cluttered in many instances and somewhat cliché for audiences.
- *high absolute cost:* Given its popularity, product placement has a certain level of exclusivity attached to it. So for many advertisers, product placement can be cost-prohibitive.
- *lack of control:* An advertiser has less creative control than they might do when advertising in other media. The placement of products can be at the director's discretion.

Direct mail

direct mail (DM):
Advertisements that are delivered to homes directly.

above the line media:
Typically traditional media that is usually booked through a media or advertising agency (TV, radio, print).

below the line media:
Typically non-traditional media expenditure such as DM or CRM. The term is sometimes also used to encompass in-store activity and even price promotions.

Direct mail (DM) is the delivery of advertising material to recipients of postal mail. Its popularity has been propelled by the fascination with customer relationship management (CRM) and loyalty marketing among practitioners in recent years, and it is a huge and growing industry. Parts of marketing budgets have moved from **above the line** media into **below the line media,** such as DM and CRM.

The strengths of direct mail are that it is:

- *personal:* An advertiser using DM can target the message to the right people, ensuring that those who they reach are qualified leads.

- *flexible*, both in terms of creative execution and timing.
- *measurable:* With CEOs being increasingly concerned with the return on investment from advertising expenditure, DM is one medium that can provide measurability.
- *information rich:* DM allows the advertiser to provide detail about product specifics and to provide much more information about the offer than could be provided using another medium.
- *good for trialling:* DM is a good medium through which to provide new trial packs of products (such as sachets of hand cream).

The weaknesses of direct mail are:

- *limited reach:* Cost (and often a lack of available and accurate customer data) typically prohibits mass reach from being achieved using DM.
- *high cost:* The cost of creative and delivery means a very high cost per reach point. Continuous scheduling of advertising using this vehicle is therefore impossible for most advertisers.
- *limited response rates:* As DM is often evaluated on the basis of the direct response achieved as a result of a mailout, it is important to note that DM has a notoriously low response rate.
- *difficult to maintain:* The success (or otherwise) of DM campaigns is driven by the quality of the database used for mail-outs. This data needs to be kept accurate and up to date, and this is expensive and time-consuming.
- *negative perceptions:* DM is often considered as junk mail and as an invasion of privacy.
- *clutter:* DM is prolific and hence it is often avoided by the potential audience (thus the typical low response rates).
- *visual only:* The absence of an audio component means advertisers cannot strengthen their auditory brand cues using DM.

Sponsorship

Sponsorship is not new; in the Ancient Olympic Games, athletes required the support of 'patrons' in order to cover their training and expenses. Types of sponsorships today include:

- sport—athletes, sporting events, sporting clubs, and grounds and stadiums
- arts—events, festivals, artists, galleries, art competitions and prizes
- cause-related—charities, research foundations, prizes and scholarships
- programs—news spots and program series.

A common criticism of sponsorship has been the lack of attention paid to quantifying the returns and why this expenditure is appropriate, but this is changing. Sponsorship managers are under increasing pressure to justify their spending, especially because sponsorship pricing varies considerably and because there are many competing options. Also, the number of large national and international events with several sponsors has increased. So sponsors have to work harder to attract consumers' attention. Previously regarded as a donation from the sponsor (company) for altruism or goodwill, sponsorship is now usually considered a commercial decision, and compared to other media options.

The strengths of sponsorship are:

- it provides a *talking point* for the brand, which may bring it attention: This is particularly important for brands in categories that are difficult to interest consumers in, such as electricity or insurance.
- it drives *good will:* Seen by many as more than just advertising, sponsorship can be viewed more positively by the audience since a commercial entity is supporting a worthy cause.
- *wide coverage (locally):* It has the ability to deliver cost-effective, wide reach and word-of-mouth among local communities.
- *long shelf life:* Sponsorship can have a long-term return for the advertiser. For instance, an athlete may wear a sponsor's clothing across an entire year of events at which they perform.

The weaknesses of sponsorship are:

- *wastage:* Sponsorships are likely to reach people outside the target audience.
- *limited message:* The message delivered via a sponsorship provides limited (or no) information to the audience.
- *clutter:* With the increase in popularity of this type of advertising, sponsorship (like product placement) is becoming overly cluttered and somewhat cliché.
- *high absolute cost:* Sponsorship for many advertisers can be cost prohibitive depending upon the requirements of the sporting star, program directors, causes and so on.
- *difficult to measure:* Understanding the exact value of sponsorship, particularly in terms of reach and particularly when it involves less measured vehicles (such as television program sponsorships), is difficult.

The internet

Many of the media we have already discussed are now online. Print media (newspapers and magazines) will increasingly be read on tablets such as iPads. Television and radio are also being consumed via the internet. However, we don't include them as part of this discussion of online advertising, although they are, of course, online.

Most companies have their own websites for the provision of information for their prospective customers or to allow customers to place orders. Maintaining these websites has become a significant activity for most marketing departments. The cost of this effort isn't counted in any estimates of the global expenditure on online advertising.

Somewhat surprisingly, online advertising is dominated by just a few types of advertising. **Paid search advertising** still represents more than half of all the advertising dollars spent online. This advertising revenue is taken by the search engines: mainly by Google, but also Baidu, the dominant search engine in China, and Microsoft's Bing, which powers Yahoo! Search.

paid search advertising: Paying for links to appear alongside the top search results in a search engine.

When a consumer types search terms such as 'cheap flight to Phuket' into a search engine, the search engine not only brings up relevant web pages but also relevant links that have been paid for by advertisers (see Figure 11.9). ZenithOptimedia (a media agency) estimated that advertisers globally would spend US$40 billion on such paid links in 2012—about 8 per cent of total advertising

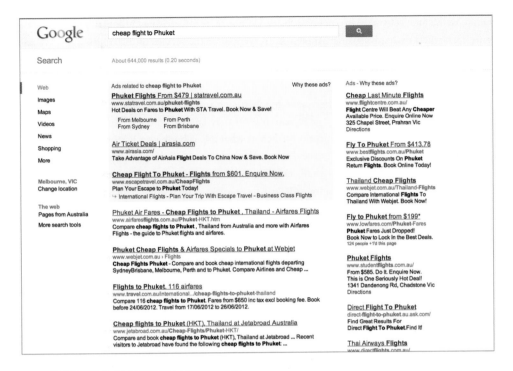

●●● **FIGURE 11.9** PAID SEARCH ADVERTISING

expenditure, which means that slightly more advertising dollars are spent on paid search than radio, almost as much as is spent on magazine advertising.

Paid search advertising has largely replaced classified advertising in newspapers and Yellow Pages advertising. Previously, such advertising generated substantial revenues for newspapers and the owners of directory services. Today much of that revenue now goes to one company, Google, which has allowed it to rapidly climb to be one of the top fifty most profitable public companies in the world, even though it is barely ten years old.

Newspaper classified ads and printed 'Yellow Pages' weren't just replaced by search advertising; they also replaced themselves by moving online. So, today advertising on specialist classified websites (such as drive.com.au and tradingpost.com.au) makes up about 15 per cent of online advertising.

The rest of online advertising (less than half) mainly goes to display advertisements on web pages. Given that there are easily more than 100 million unique websites and more than a trillion web pages, buying space online looks astonishingly complicated. First, there is the decision of where to buy space, and then there is the issue of how—given that these websites have many different owners. Things are made more simple by the fact that most websites attract very little traffic, with only very few generating sizeable audiences. Those that do generate large audiences include YouTube, ninemsn and Yahoo!7. ComScore (2011b) reports that the top ten web 'properties' (groups of websites with the same owner) account for half of all Australian web browsing (these properties have owners such as Microsoft, Google, Apple, Facebook, Yahoo!, eBay, Wikimedia,

Glam Media and Telstra). Also, many websites do not carry advertising (Wikipedia or iTunes) or only carry their own advertising (Apple). Ad servers offer the service of distributing display ads across many different websites: Google is a major ad server.

The strengths of internet advertising are:

- *highly targeted/reduced wastage:* Search advertising reaches those who are interested in the product category—indicated by the search term they entered. Other online advertising can be targeted based on other indications (such as what a Facebook user has indicated they like). However, a casual inspection of the display ads that feature on the web pages we visit quickly reveals that little targeting is actually employed.
- *low production costs:* Much online advertising consists of little more than a few words, and is thus very cheap to produce.
- *wide coverage:* Internet advertising has the ability to deliver very cost-effective, wide reach to a global audience.
- *long shelf life:* The platform can be maintained and available for as long as it is deemed necessary.
- *message delivery:* Internet campaigns allow for the provision of detailed messages.
- *direct response:* Internet campaigns are particularly good for getting and recording the direct response of the audience. Sales can be processed via the medium.
- *measurement:* Very detailed information can be easily and quickly gathered about the audience for internet campaigns (click-through rates, time spent on site, direct response/sales and so on).
- *audio and visual:* Advertisers are able to demonstrate how the product or service that they are promoting is used, and both auditory and visual brand cues can be strengthened.

The weaknesses of internet advertising are:

- *fragmentation and clutter:* The web is a highly fragmented medium, making it extremely difficult for a particular campaign to reach a large audience—let alone stand out among the clutter.
- *goal-directed behaviour*: In many instances of online viewing the audience have a clear goal (such as talking to friends on Facebook) that conflicts with them viewing advertising. Viewers are extremely good at screening out (not seeing) advertisements in such situations.
- *reach is restricted to heavy users:* By far the biggest disadvantage of some internet campaigns is that they reach the very heaviest of a brand's users. To search for a brand online or join as a Facebook fan of a brand requires some effort, which you are most likely to exert if there is something in it for you (for instance the chance to win competitions for a brand or product you already buy). Increasingly, internet campaigns are becoming more likely to be mass campaigns (and so are reaching more light brand users), but for the most part such campaigns allow the advertiser to spend money advertising to those who would have bought the product or brand anyway.
- *under-researched:* The internet is by far the most under-researched advertising medium (largely due to its rate of growth). This poses issues for advertisers when considering moving media money from one (tried and tested) medium to one that is relatively new.

Case study
Heathman Lodge learns to use online advertising effectively

Heathman Lodge (CL) is an upmarket hotel in the US state of Washington that caters for people who seek an outdoor holiday but comfortable, well-catered accommodation. It began what was judged a not very successful online advertising campaign where it placed advertisements on the Google search results pages for people who had searched for certain key words such as 'hotel in rural Oregon'. In this advertising method, an advertiser only pays Google when someone clicks on the advert (a click through) and this is called a 'pay-per-click' (PPC) advertising campaign. CL's management had had a website for several years but had not used PPC advertising previously and devised its approach based on advice it had read in business magazines. CL subsequently realised it had suffered from using overly broad keywords and no testing of its PPC advertisement text. Further, those who clicked on its adverts were led to the hotel's home page instead of to a customised landing page tied to the advertisement.

To improve the initial results, the company learnt from this first foray into online advertising that it needed to improve its entire approach based on a complete rebuild of its website, new landing pages tied to the PPC campaign and close attention to three strategic search areas: keyword management, uncovering top-assisting keywords and buying high-performing natural search keywords, including branded keywords. All of the decisions about its new approach were to be driven by using online data metrics.

The new PPC effort was exclusively tied to one search engine (Google), response data was tracked via the new landing pages and the initial expenditure was kept low, as the main purpose was to learn about how to manage this form of marketing communications and its effectiveness.

The results from the revised approach campaign were very impressive. The Hotel Director stated: 'In January, we had 105 total conversions and we did $16,040 in revenue, whereas in the previous October, before the new PPC campaign, we only had 41 conversions and made just $6093 in revenue through PPC ads.'

What were the steps the management went through?

1 Selection of the keywords to use

It was important to keep track of keywords that had a very high cost-to-click number and weren't converting to sales. In this case, the keywords that underperformed were general, odd-matched keywords such as 'Portland', a well-known city in the state, 'Oregon' and 'Washington'.

Identifying the top performing keywords in the campaign was important because these words and phrases were used to guide the content of the landing pages tied to the campaign, as well as the entire hotel website.

The Hotel Director explained that the PPC project team built their campaign landing pages based on the ad keywords and tied the online hotel room booking system to the landing pages to make the entire buying process very easy for prospective guests.

Top keywords were uncovered by looking at click-through rate (CTR) data, conversions in the form of a booked hotel room, clicks, cost-per-click and any keywords that weren't contributing to the bottom line. In PPC campaigns, results can be tracked in real time, so keywords that aren't performing can be removed.

2 Learning from previous campaigns

The original PPC effort had a number of problems:

- It did not use or test all keyword match types, such as broad match, phrase match, exact match and negative match, for best performance.
- The keywords used in the original campaign tended to be very general and competitive terms.
- Some of the PPC campaigns were targeting the entire United States rather than staying focused on the north-west region. This meant it was creating web visits from less targeted and less ready-to-convert visitors.
- It wasn't a branded campaign. It didn't include landing pages specific to the ads, so clicks were simply going to the hotel's home page, and the actual ad text was not being tested.

The new PPC effort addressed all these problem areas by:

- very specifically geotargeting of the north-west region of the United States
- testing multiple variations of ad text to uncover best performing ads
- utilising all keyword match types
- sending clicks to landing pages that were specifically created for the advertisements.

One early problem even in the new campaign was a lack of measurement of all key variables, and without this it was very difficult to learn. For the first two months of the new effort, the CL online booking system wasn't able to track results from the PPC campaign. Once this was solved, hotel management was able to see exactly how the results of the campaign were, compared to the advertising expenditure.

What were the results?

The most important metric was that even a small monthly PPC advertising spend of around $500 created significant revenue for the company. The Hotel Director stated, 'What we are generating in revenue is just amazing to me.' He added that as the PPC campaign is further refined through collecting all the relevant metrics, both advertising impressions served to attract potential clients, and conversions of those who click through to the hotel landing page will continue to rise.

The more specific results were:

- an 81 per cent increase in return-on-ad-spend over four months
- a 75 per cent increase in hotel reservations over four months
- a 74 per cent decrease in cost-per-click over four months
- a 2464 per cent return on ad spend.

Over the four-month period of the new, 'learning' PPC campaign, the total media spend was $1909 and revenue generated was $41,420.

Source: Adapted from Kirkpatrick, D (2011) 'PPC Campaign: Marketer learns from unsuccessful campaign to deliver 75% increase in sales', *Marketing Sherpa*, 7 April, retrieved 2 August from <www.marketingsherpa.com/article.php?ident=31882>

Social media

While social media is the new kid on the block, its growth is unparalleled. It is estimated that by 2015 social media will become a mainstream mass media platform, with one third of the world's population being users of social media. This offers advertisers access to 80 per cent of global consumer expenditure (Nuttney, 2010).

However, to put this in perspective, currently Australians in total spend about 60 million hours using social media each month. But they spend about 2200 million hours watching television each month. Half of this huge (almost forty-fold) difference is because in any month only about half the population uses social media, while practically everyone watches television. This lack of reach has significant marketing implications for social media, even though it is growing.

Social media can be defined as 'the online tools that people use to share content, ideas, thoughts, opinions, experiences, and media itself' (Campbell, Conare & Hernandez, 2010). But for most people (and marketers) social media today means Facebook, YouTube and a little bit of Twitter and LinkedIn.

Facebook is the second most visited website in Australia (after Google) and the average user spends more than five hours a month on Facebook. Yet Facebook currently captures only a few per cent of online advertising revenue. How much will this change in the future?

The conversation prism (Figure 11.10) by Solis and Thomas (2009) perhaps offers a view of the social media universe, categorised and also organised by how people use each network.

As social media usage grows generally, it is the Facebook platform that continues to dominate on all metrics (time spent consuming, reach, advertising revenue and sharing). In 2010, three out of ten internet sessions included a visit to the site (comScore, 2011a). Subsequently, it now boasts more than 750 million active users (Facebook_Press_Room, 2011). The unrivalled scale of Facebook, in terms of its available reach, combined with its advertising model that targets on the

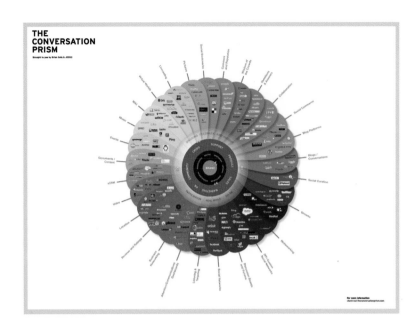

●●● **FIGURE 11.10** THE CONVERSATION PRISM

basis of demographic matching, locality and relevancy, makes it an obvious choice for marketers wanting to invest in social media space. Its success is shown in the incredible growth in advertising revenue in only a few short years. In 2009, Facebook advertising revenue was reportedly around US$800 million, where conservative estimates for 2012 are closer to $6 billion (Frederickson, 2011).

●●● **TABLE 11.1** FACEBOOK STATISTICS, AUSTRALIA

Total users	almost 11 million
Penetration of population (%)	51
Penetration of online population (%)	64
Average CPC ($)	0.60
Average CPM ($)	0.26
Largest age group user (years)	25–34
Male users (%)	46
Female users (%)	54

These metrics are for the past six months as at 19 March 2012.

Source: Social Baker (2012) 'Australia Facebook Statistics', retrieved 19 March 2012 from <www.socialbakers.com/facebook-statistics/australia>

The strengths of social media are:

- capacity message sharing
- low cost to advertisers
- flexibility

- global reach
- the fact that you can build networks.

The weaknesses of social media are:

- that it is monopolised by a few social giants
- that brand networks (fans, followers) are typically heavy buyers of the brand
- that technology changes near daily—it costs to keep up
- it has high fragmentation, making it hard to reach vast numbers easily
- there is little credible research, so many advertisers are flying blind.

Social Baker is a statistics pool covering a range of social media sites such as Facebook, Twitter, Google+, LinkedIn and YouTube. Its purpose is to provide data to brands on their 'engagement' metrics. Table 11.2 details the metrics offered by Social Baker.

●●● **TABLE 11.2** SOCIAL MEDIA METRICS REPORTED BY SOCIAL BAKER

MEDIA	METRICS REPORTED	
Facebook	Number of fans	Engagement rate
	Demography by country	Average response rate
	Population penetration	Change in fans (growth/decline)
	People talking about metric	
Twitter	Followers	Change in followers and following
	Following	Measured by country, brand and category
Google+	Followers	Change in followers and following
	Following	Measured by country, brand and category
YouTube	Channel views	Change in channel views
	Subscribers	Change in video views
	Uploaded video views	

PUTTING A MIX TOGETHER: INTEGRATED MARKETING COMMUNICATIONS

◢ LEARNING OBJECTIVE
Recognise key terminology (including data and tools) used in media planning

◢ **integrated marketing communications (IMC):** Advertising placed across media in a complementary and harmonious manner.

While all media types have there own intrinsic advantages and disadvantages, there is no rule to say that media plans have to focus on one single medium. It is widely believed that a combination of media types can be more successful then those that only use a single media and certainly different media have different features that may complement one another. However, there is little in the way of solid research findings that support this belief, and even less that can give guidance on how to assemble a good multimedia campaign.

Multimedia platform synergy

The media world is complex and fragmented, making returns from media budgets harder to maximise. Media synergy creates value over and above that delivered by each individual media platform. So how can different media be pieced together to create effective synergy?

●●● **FIGURE 11.11** WHAT IS SYNERGY?

A decade of change

The media sector around the world has profoundly changed. New ways for consumers to interact are offered via social media and tablets. These changes offer exciting possibilities for advertisers. However, more options make decision making complex and increase the risk of wasting media dollars. Spreading budgets over more media does not necessarily lead to great effectiveness, so smart planning and synergy matter!

The power of television

Despite the explosion of new media, studies continue to endorse television's importance for advertisers, and campaigns that include television in the multi-platform media mix outperform those that omit television. Where possible, television should be the foundation (not the limit) for any multi-platform campaign.

Four keys to synergy

- Build cumulative reach more effectively.
- Broaden the timing and context of consumer **touch points**.
- Provide enhanced repetition.
- Build a neuro-rich campaign environment.

1 Build cumulative reach more effectively

touch points: Media sources that potential consumers might see or hear throughout the day.

Advertising can only impact the people it reaches. Cumulative reach, where you reach as many people as possible at least once, is an important campaign consideration. Consumers need to be reached!

Evidence to date shows that advertising's greatest sales effect occurs when an individual moves from zero to one exposure (Wind & Sharp, 2009). Additional close-by exposures also increase the chance of a consumer purchasing the brand, but the effect of each following exposure is each not as much as the preceding exposure (see Figure 11.12).

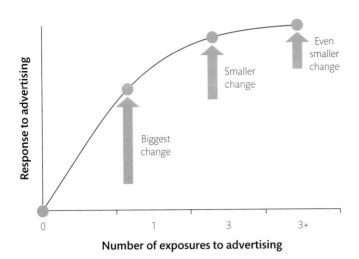

●●● **FIGURE 11.12** SALES RESPONSE TO ADVERTISING EXPOSURE

So an effective multi-platform media mix needs to reach more people without wasting advertising dollars by hitting the same consumers multiple times with the same stimuli within a short window.

The aim of multi-platform media planning is to pull fragmented audiences together to achieve a reach reflective of the brand's audience. When this has been achieved, then there is the potential for other multi-platform media synergies to emerge.

CNBC's recent EV Series sponsored by Credit Suisse is a good example of an effective multi-platform campaign in action. The campaign was extended from television into outdoor, online and print and mobile. Research demonstrates a gradual build in ad awareness across multiple platforms when using more than just television alone (see Figure 11.13).

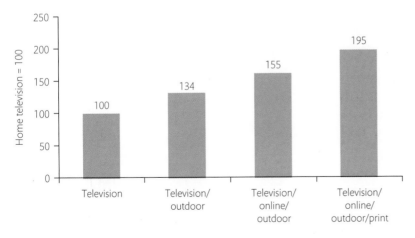

●●● **FIGURE 11.13** BUILD IN AD AWARENESS ACROSS MULTIPLE PLATFORMS

2 Broaden the timing and context of consumer touch points

Think about where and when you use media:

- in the morning (newspapers)
- on the bus (radio and mobile)
- at work (computers and social media)
- at home (television and tablets).

By placing advertising in a multi-platform mix, you can insert the advertising into people's lives, enhancing receptivity around varied purchase consideration points.

3 Provide enhanced repetition (rather than just frequency)

Enhance the impact of repetition rather than achieving the lower impact of ordinary frequency. Excess frequency is close repetition of similar stimuli in the same media. Two ways to help turn frequency into enhanced repetition are to vary the context and to space out the exposures.

Vary the context

Varying the context stimulates forward encoding: where an ad in one medium improves the performance of the ad in a second medium because:

- the second exposure gains more attention and the brain is tricked into thinking the stimuli is more novel than familiar
- the varied contexts are seen as two separate (rather than repetitive) exposures and are processed as such.

●●● AN ADVERTISEMENT FOR A FILM, SEEN IN AN OUTDOOR CONTEXT

Space out exposures

Allowing time in between exposures means the stimuli is processed more deeply; that is, longer intervals between exposures result in better learning and up to 20 per cent improvement in memory than shorter intervals. Heavy bursts of stimuli close together are not always an efficient way to gain reach. Use multiple media to space out advertising.

4 Build a neuro-rich campaign environment

A 'neuro-rich' campaign heightens the long-term processing of the campaign in memory. The art of the media mix is drawing on the strengths of each medium and choosing media that mesh together to provide a wide scope for stimulating consumers' senses (see Figure 11.14).

Different media types provide opportunities to expand the possible ways consumers can process the campaign exposure.

●●● ANOTHER ADVERTISEMENT FOR THE FILM, WHICH MIGHT BE SEEN IN OTHER CONTEXTS

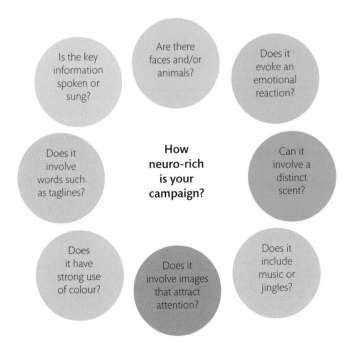

●●● **FIGURE 11.14** QUESTIONS TO ASK WHEN EVALUATING A CAMPAIGN TO INCREASE NEURO-RICHNESS

There are two key patterns that demonstrate how different types of media compete for their audience. The implications of these patterns are that certain combinations of media being used in a plan might be more effective than others.

Double jeopardy law in media

In Chapter 3 we discussed the double jeopardy law as it applies to the buying of brands. We see this same pattern in the way that audiences use media (Redford, 2005), in that less popular (that is smaller reaching) media draw both a smaller audience and an audience who spend less time with the media that they use. Figure 11.15 shows this pattern. While there are some media that break the general rule by being used for less time than their reach would suggest, generally the more popular a media is, the more time its users will spend using it.

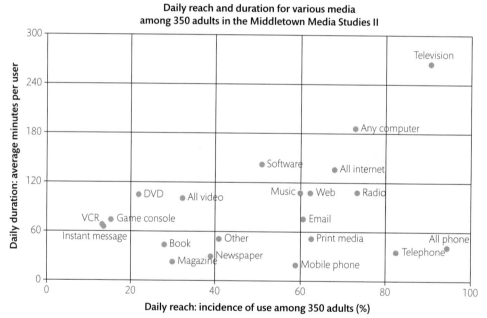

●●● **FIGURE 11.15** RELATIONSHIP BETWEEN REACH OF A MEDIUM AND TIME SPENT USING IT

Source: Song, Y-B (no date) 'Finding the missing piece in online frequency', *Atlas Institute Digital Marketing Insights,* Atlas DMT, LLC, p. 2

Further research (Goodhardt, Ehrenberg & Collins, 1975; Barwise & Ehrenberg, 1988; Collins, Beal & Barwise, 2003; McDowell & Dick, 2005; Nelson-Field, Lees, Riebe & Sharp, 2010), has also shown that this pattern applies to vehicles within a medium for both television and radio content, and across a range of markets and changes in the structure of these markets. Therefore, the more popular a particular program is, the more often viewers will tune in, and the longer they will spend watching or listening to that program.

For advertisers, this means that competing media largely deliver an audience that differs mainly in relation to its size or reach, not in relation to how much their audience uses them. Small media that reach very dedicated users appear to be more the exception than the rule.

Duplication of viewing/listening law

Another pattern that we discussed earlier (Chapter 6) in relation to how brands share consumers is the duplication of purchase law. A similar pattern has been shown to apply to the way in which competing media share their audience: the **duplication of viewing/listening law**. Competing media share their audiences with one another in line with their size or reach. This pattern has been observed at many levels of media competition. For example, radio shares more of its audience with television and less of its audience with magazines. Within a media class, magazines, an individual publication will share most of its audience with a very wide-reaching magazine (such as *Australian Women's Weekly*), but far less of its audience with a smaller publication (such as *Vogue*) (Redford, 2005; Goodhardt, Ehrenberg & Collins, 1975; Barwise & Ehrenberg, 1988; Collins, Beal & Barwise, 2003). This pattern is demonstrated in Table 11.3, with UK television station data.

duplication of viewing/ listening law: The pattern observed in the sharing of audiences across media platforms. Media share viewers and listeners in line with market share: the smaller media platforms (such as magazines) share more customers with bigger media platforms (such as television).

●●● **TABLE 11.3** DUPLICATION OF VIEWING IN UK TELEVISION

UK INDV. 4+ M/C HMS 2001	PERCENTAGE WHO ALSO VIEWED:						
VIEWERS OF	BBC1	ITV1	BBC2	CH 4	CH 5	SKY 1	UK GOLD
BBC1	–	83	71	67	52	35	29
ITV1	92	–	71	68	54	33	28
BBC2	95	85	–	73	56	33	29
Ch 4	94	86	77	–	58	36	30
Ch 5	87	94	76	75	–	38	33
Sky 1	89	76	70	66	54	–	43
UK Gold	92	81	71	70	58	54	–
Average	92	83	73	70	55	38	32

For advertisers, this means that adding smaller media to a campaign that already involves a wide-reaching medium will likely mean you do little to broaden your reach and instead build additional frequency, as the audience of the small medium is probably already reached by advertising with the larger counterpart.

Searching for the small but consistent exceptions to these patterns is a useful part of building a successful media mix. For example, outdoor advertising may be useful in reaching light television viewers (people who watch less television) because they are out and about and therefore see more billboards.

▲ **LEARNING OBJECTIVE**
Describe the concept of
effective scheduling and
a range of scheduling
patterns

DEVELOPING THE MEDIA SCHEDULE

One of the key aspects of media planning is deciding upon the scheduling strategy that will be applied to each annual campaign's media plan. Many advertisers determine media budgets and develop approximate scheduling plans on an annual basis (leaving some scope for flexibility to respond to market changes). From there, the annual media plan is commonly divided into weekly blocks (the standard industry unit for media scheduling) and key campaign statistics such as reach and frequency are reported at a weekly level. Given this industry orientation, in this book we also discuss media scheduling on the basis of weekly purchasing for annual campaigns.

There are a few overall strategies that are used in developing a media schedule. Here we discuss the two main approaches used, although these can vary dramatically between practitioners.

Scheduling for reach

As suggested earlier, maximising the cumulative reach among category buyers should be every advertiser's and every media planner's main objective. Media planning strategies that focus on achieving continuous reach are most likely to lead to brand growth. The relationship between frequency of advertising exposure and sales response has been shown to produce a convex distribution (see Figure 11.12). Thus, the impact of increased advertising exposure (frequency) on sales is considerably less than that resulting from expanding the reach of the campaign (Taylor, 2010; Jones, 2007; Jones, 1992; Ephron, 2001; Taylor, Kennedy & Sharp, 2009). The scheduling implication of this is that maximising cumulative reach across a campaign should produce the best sales effect, therefore seeking maximum reach should be the focus in scheduling media.

'Reach don't teach'

Advertisers need to reach as many category buyers as possible. They also want coverage over time so that when any consumer goes to buy from the category they have seen an advertisement recently.

The cheapest way of achieving these two objectives is usually to space out advertising over time, to use a variety of media, and to advertise at different times of the week, month or day in order to reach different people with different media habits.

Media must always be evaluated in terms of its reach, and whether it reaches *new* potential customers. For example, a thirty-second advertisement during the US Super Bowl is very expensive: *Forbes* magazine reports an average cost of US$3 million (Smith, 2012). But when this is put into context, it appears that this can be exceedingly good value, because 111 million Americans watched the Super Bowl, and viewers look out for the advertising during the game (there is minimal advertising avoidance), plus the advertising is often later shared on the internet and discussed on other media. So even if the Super Bowl spot only reached those who viewed the game, that would represent a CPM of only $27 (that's 2.7 cents to reach a viewer).

For an advertiser who had a media budget of exactly $3 million, it would be very difficult for them to spend it any other way and gain similar reach for thirty seconds of video exposure—it would certainly be difficult to do it so quickly. So, for an advertiser that needed to reach a lot of people around the time of the Super Bowl (for example a movie release) this would seem like the perfect media buy. However, for other advertisers, even if they wanted this much reach, it suffers from the fact that it reaches people on one single day of the year, leaving all other days silent. So unless the ad's memory effects could be guaranteed not to erode (which is most unlikely) it would be better for an advertiser with a $3 million budget to spend it gradually over the year—aiming to gradually, but as efficiently as possible, cumulate reach.

For an advertiser with a budget of more than $3 million, they would look seriously at a Super Bowl spot to gain some pure cost-effective reach, but would spend their remaining budget on advertising over the rest of the year—again aiming to cumulate reach as efficiently as possible.

If it were possible to know which potential consumers were to buy our category on a particular day, based on this evidence we would ensure that we advertise to them the day (or even hour) that they are to make that brand choice. However, as marketers we do not have that knowledge and so, as purchases of most categories occur relatively equally across the year, this means that a continuity schedule is most likely to deliver maximum reach. Across time, a continuous advertising schedule would involve advertising weight being equally spread across all weeks of the year. This is shown in Figure 11.16, which applies such an approach to an annual media budget of 2600 TARPs for television. The x-axis represents each of the fifty-two weeks of the year. The y-axis shows the TARPs that have been allocated to each week of the year. While this figure shows the case of a television schedule, the same approach could be applied regardless of the media platform chosen.

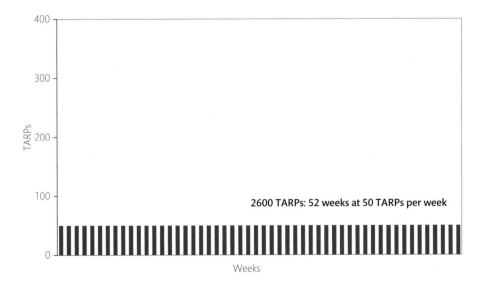

● ● ● **FIGURE 11.16** CONTINUITY SCHEDULE

Given some buying in most categories occurs every day of the year, more potential targets should be reached if advertising is spread out across that year (ensuring a continuous advertising presence for the advertiser).

One of the common criticisms of this scheduling approach is that advertisers do not believe they have the budget to advertise so continuously. While it is indeed impossible, even for those with enormous media budgets, to reach every category buyer just before every purchase opportunity (100 per cent reach within the target audience every day, with an average frequency of just 1), this does not mean that they should not aspire to that ideal, and there are many ways of implementing a broad reach-based approach to scheduling media.

Regardless of budget, this approach can (at least broadly) be applied to any campaign schedule. For example, if you can afford only twelve ads per year, then buy one per month, rather than twelve within a single month. It may simply be a case of adjusting the type of media used (for instance choose print instead of television) in order to maximise the reach achieved for the assigned budget. Similarly, the length of each individual planning unit can be adjusted to accommodate smaller budgets (advertising each month instead of each week). The key to applying a reach-based scheduling approach is having reach maximisation as the ultimate objective.

Media researchers Herb Krugman and Erwin Ephron simplified the continuous reach strategy by likening media planning to physical distribution. They suggest advertising must 'rent the shelf' so that the brand is 'always there' when a buyer needs to access it from their memory (Ephron, 1995a: 2–4).

> … Visualise a window of advertising opportunity in front of each purchase. Advertising's job is to influence the purchase. The planner's job is to place the message in that window … Purchases are made each week, and planners don't know who will make them, so the goal is to reach as many different consumers as possible in as many different weeks as possible. It is a continuous reach strategy, which results in more weeks at lower weight than a traditional plan.

Another common criticism of continuous schedules is that they require low advertising weights for any single week in which the campaign is 'on air'. This criticism assumes that a threshold weight of advertising is required in order for advertising to work. There is no reliable empirical evidence to show that such a threshold exists. Rather, practitioners have learnt that a given level of advertising weight is required in order for advertising's effect to be captured in typical advertising tracking instruments. This demonstrates a lack of sensitivity in these measures, rather than a threshold requirement to produce an advertising effect. Single source data is a more sensitive measurement instrument, and all research that has been conducted using this data shows no such threshold. The gold standard for scheduling practice should therefore involve aiming to maximise reach in media scheduling.

Despite this approach (on face value) being potentially easy to implement, bursts of advertising (followed by long silences) are very common. Many marketing departments are structured around producing campaigns that are followed by periods of planning for the next campaign. However, leading-edge companies are moving away from this practice.

Case study

The Turkey Farmers Association: Complexities of communication and the media

The Australian Turkey Farmers Association has decided to pool the advertising spend of each member farm and develop a national 'eat turkey' marketing campaign. The aim of the campaign is to get Australians to eat turkey more often by reminding people that turkey is not just a meal for Christmas day, but a healthy alternative to red meat or chicken that is inexpensive and versatile. After voting for the idea of a joint campaign, and deciding on thea financial contribution per farm (the ad budget), the board gave each of the farmers a month to discuss the idea with their marketing departments and to come up with suggestions for the campaign plan and media schedule. Most of the smaller producers had no marketing team and were happy to go along with the status quo, but the four biggest producers came back with proposals from their marketing managers.

- *Company 1*: There is so much advertising these days, if we really want people to put turkey on the table they need to see/hear our ads several times so that the message sinks in.
- *Company 2*: Most people do shopping on Thursdays or Saturdays so we should use the budget to run radio ads just on those two days so people hear it on the way to the supermarket.
- *Company 3*: The goal should be to try get as many people as possible to see our ad at least once. We should compare the CPM across television, radio, newspapers and magazines, pick the option that gives us the biggest bang for our buck and then schedule ads evenly across all days of the week.
- *Company 4*: A combination of direct marketing, in-store samples and a Facebook group would help us develop an ongoing dialogue with our customers. Also using those media would make it easier for us to track the success of the campaign.

Questions

1   Define reach and frequency and identify the companies which are making media decisions based on those aspects.

2   The committee decides that they want to maximise reach. Which of the following suggestions would be the most appropriate way to divide the ad spend each week (and why?):

   a   Company 2's suggestion—all ads on shopping days Thursday and Sunday

   b   Company 3's suggestion—steady advertising across the week.

3   Compare the ideas of Company 1 and Company 3. Identify and discuss any problems with that you find.

4   What would be the advantages and disadvantages of using Company 4's ideas (direct marketing, in-store samples and Facebook) in this instance?

◢ **LEARNING OBJECTIVE**
Discuss appropriate techniques for evaluating media campaigns

MEDIA DATA, TOOLS AND CAMPAIGN EVALUATION

Available media data

Any manager who is involved in buying or selling media space for advertising needs to use data in order to make media buying decisions and then to evaluate and justify the decisions made. This data is largely collected by commercial market research companies, who sell it to numerous media agencies and advertisers on a subscription basis. Such data is known as **syndicated data**, as it is provided in the same format across media and advertisers. It often comes with its own user-friendly software for analysis and interpretation. Other data that can also be helpful to advertisers in making decisions are provided by both market research companies (in ad hoc research studies) and by the media themselves (for instance, circulation figures for print are often provided by the publications rather than by a separate independent company).

◢ **syndicated data:** Data collected by commercial market research firms, such as OzTAM, who then sell that data to media agencies and advertisers.

Regardless of the media platform, providers sell their ability to reach an audience—they sell eyeballs and/or ears. Thus, data that captures the number of exposures delivered is necessary for any media buyer or seller. The exact format of this data differs by country, but for each media such data often acts as the currency upon which advertising space is bought and sold. For example, for television such data (**target audience measurement** data or ratings) is collected by way of people meter technology in most countries. For print, it is circulation or readership information, and for the internet it is either impressions, clicks or page landings.

As the process of selecting a media and advertising spot is complicated, and as buying directly from the media company can be expensive, many advertisers hire media agencies to recommend and actually make purchases on their behalf. Both media agencies and media companies typically possess **optimisation software**, although these tools are largely used only for guiding television purchasing and so are often not as extensive as one might expect. They are designed to output a recommended media mix, based upon some prescribed inputs. For most optimisers these inputs include (but are not limited to) the overall budget, the target market and the objectives for the campaign. The particular algorithm used to determine the media suggestions that are eventually made is often proprietary and based on specific assumptions the media company or agency makes about how advertising and media work. The outputs of such optimisation tools are particular reach and frequency recommendations. Optimisers are typically only used to aid a recommendation largely driven by the planner's experience and understanding of vehicles (and their audiences), or they are used by the planner as a post-hoc rationalisation for their (pre-determined) media recommendations (Paech, 2005).

target audience measurement (TAM): Data collected to capture the number of audience members (reach) delivered via television.

optimisation software: Systems typically owned by media agencies, based on specific assumptions about how marketing works, and used to recommend a media mix, reach and frequency to media buyers.

Evaluating the media buy

There is a growing demand for media to demonstrate their contribution to the overall success of advertising campaigns (Wicken & Spittler, 1998; White, 2000; Coen, 2002).

From a tactical point of view, media companies can conduct post-campaign analysis for their advertiser clients. This involves using ratings or readership data to compare the media purchases that have been made (for instance TARPs ordered) with what was actually delivered by the media. It may seem irrational that what is actually delivered may not be an exact match for what was originally bought. It is, however, not possible to know with certainty a week earlier how many people will watch a particular episode of *Desperate Housewives*—and yet the advertising space has to be sold before the screening of the program. So it is necessary to assess the reach and frequency that is promised by the media with what they were actually able to provide. For television companies, advertising prices are estimated ahead of time based on historical data (the ratings that were achieved for the same time slot last week, or last year) and other knowledge of likely spot performance. For example, for advertising spots being sold in a new program, this may be the ratings that were achieved for the same program when it ran in a different country or how the program genre usually rates.

Where the reach purchased is less than what was actually achieved, the advertisers happily accept their good fortune and the media companies adjust their charges for future spots. Where media companies accept that they have not delivered what was bought, they may give the advertisers

make-goods: Free spots provided to an advertiser to match original audience-size goals (TARPs or spots) that were not initially achieved.

media auditing: Post-campaign analysis that includes analysing return on investment: whether an advertiser really received the advertising spots they paid for.

'make-goods'. **Make-goods** are free spots that are given to the advertiser to match the TARPs, spots and so on that were not achieved with the original placement.

Once the campaign is completed, it is in the advertiser's interest to check that these estimates were correct, and that they received what they ordered. Post-campaign analysis is not always undertaken for all campaigns. Many advertisers move on quickly after a campaign is completed and fail to determine whether their purchase decisions were justified. Post-campaign evaluation should be more common than it is. Some advertisers (rightfully) go further than relying on a post-campaign analysis from the media provider: they get their purchases audited. **Media auditing** companies provide post-campaign analysis similar to that provided by the media companies. However, they also provide an indication of value for money. As most media advertising spots are bought through a media agency, who negotiates large bulk buys of advertising positions annually and then on-sells space, different agencies can provide similar spots at very different rates. Media auditing companies are able to determine whether the rate received by the advertiser is reasonable given what they know about the negotiated deals made by the agencies, the prices charged to other advertisers, and the total amount being spent by the advertiser.

Marketers may also try to evaluate the impact of media on consumers by measuring behavioural or attitudinal change, such as increases in sales, changes in brand awareness and/or recall of the advertisements. Such output metrics are generally collected by the advertiser via their own internal data collection mechanisms (such as sales data) or through ad hoc research that they commission with their market research consultant. Teasing out the contribution of the media strategy from the effects of the advertising content, and the many other things occuring in the marketplace, can be very tricky.

Cross-media measurement

Despite the accelerated use of IMC, both practitioners and academics agree that there are severe difficulties in terms of measuring its effect (Ephron, 2000a; Paech, 2005). It's usually not even possible to generate traditional media metrics such as reach and frequency for a cross-media campaign. Most data systems used for media planning cannot fully account for an individual's cross-media flow, duplication and interrelationships (McConochie & Uyenco, 2003). Thus, the quantitative benefits of IMC, in particular gaining additional reach of 'different' consumers, are generally based more on the assumption that the audiences of different media are largely different (audience segmentation), than on a quantifiable cross-media measure. Consequently, not a great deal is known about synergy effects and how integrated cross-media campaigns perform.

CONCLUSION

There is much to be gained by managing (the often very large) media expenditure wisely, in line with clear objectives and understanding rather than fashion fads. Unfortunately few university marketing degrees teach much about media, so many practising managers are underqualified in this important area.

The key point to remember is that advertising needs to reach all category buyers, and quite regularly, so that their brand memories are fresh at the moment of potential purchase. Media strategy should be fundamentally guided by this principle. Then the characteristics of different media should be exploited to best deliver messages that will build and refresh the memories that the brand needs.

While this does not sound too difficult, many complex trade-offs have to be made due to availability, costs (media prices vary and change) and other practical considerations. Astute managers use these changes to undertake carefully controlled media experiments, because there is enormous opportunity to boost profits from more efficient and effective media strategies, by both lowering media costs and increasing the sales effects of advertising.

11

SUMMARY

- Marketers use media to place their advertising where it will be seen or heard by potential category buyers.

- Media that can reach more category buyers are more valuable, as are media that can reach buyers that are difficult to reach with other media.

- Media that can deliver advertising in a way that is more likely to be noticed are more valuable.

- Media that can deliver a more memorable exposure are more valuable.

- Marketers should plan their media so that they expose as many buyers to their advertising as possible. In practice, this means spreading out advertising placement over time, and across different timeslots, channels and media.

REVISION QUESTIONS

1 Imagine you worked for Stratco or Bunnings—and your boss wanted to invest most of the media budget into print advertising focused on home care magazines and television programs such as *Better Homes and Gardens*. What is your opinion of this decision?

2 Imagine you started a job for a beer brand such as Carlton Draught. Currently the majority of the media budget is spent in a few campaign bursts, particularly one at the start of summer. Drawing on your knowledge of consumer behaviour, as well as media planning concepts, what changes would you recommend to the marketing manager and why?

3 Is 'engagement' a worthy element for media buyers to consider when placing media spots? For example, if you are the brand manager for Pedigree, is it more beneficial for you to put your ads on *Animal Hospital* or the nightly news? Why?

4 List and discuss the kinds of avoidance behaviour.

5 Explain the difference between reach and frequency. Discuss the relationship between them.

6 Discuss the impact of fragmentation of television for media buyers, media sellers and audiences.

7 If the cost per spot for TV Show 1 is $5000 and the audience reached is 300,000, and the cost for TV Show 2 is $20,000 and audience reached is 350,000, calculate the CPM for each. Discuss which television show you would choose and why.

8 What is effective frequency and how might this impact on media purchasing?

9 Discuss methods of evaluating media purchases.

10 What is the role of media planning in modern day marketing activities?

11 Explain what above the line and below the line media activities are.

FURTHER READING

Creamer, M (2012) 'Only 1% of Facebook 'fans' engage with brands', *AdAge*, 27 January, retrieved 6 August 2012 from <http://adage.com/article/digital/study-1-facebook-fans-engage-brands/232351>.

Ehrenberg, A S C (1974) 'Repetitive advertising and the consumer', *Journal of Advertising Research*, vol. 14, pp. 25–34.

Gardner, J (2012) '6 habits of highly effective mobile marketers', *Mashable Business*, 26 July, retrieved 6 August from <http://mashable.com/2012/07/26/mobile-marketing-tips-2>.

Rosen, M (2012) 'The fast-changing media landscape', 1 April, *Radio: The Radio Technology Reader*, retrieved 6 August 2012 from <http://radiomagonline.com/features/fast-changing_media_landscape_0412//index.html>.

Pan, J (2012) 'How augmented reality is shaping the future of retail', *Mashable Digital*, 20 June, retrieved 6 August 2012 from <http://mashable.com/2012/06/20/augmented-reality-retail>.

WEBLINKS

Pepsi Refresh:
http://en.wikipedia.org/wiki/Pepsi_Refresh_Project

Warc:
www.warc.com

Media Federation of Australia:
www.mediafederation.org.au

Mashable:
www.mashable.com

Nielsen:
www.nielsen.com

Mumbrella:
www.mumbrella.com.au

Ephron on Media:
www.ephrononmedia.com

◢ MAJOR CASE STUDY

Kondoot: A new social network site

By Steffen Zorn

Companies have several possibilities to grow. As described in the Ansoff matrix (Watts, Cope & Hulme, 1998), companies can remain in the same market with an existing product and try to get a higher market share through different market penetration strategies, such as promoting or repositioning their product. Another option is to develop a new product for an existing market. For example, blu-ray DVD players and high-definition television sets both offer movie lovers a new high-definition watching experience. Alternatively, companies can focus on a new market for their existing products, such as selling them in a foreign country in addition to the domestic market. The highest risk strategy is product diversification—establishing a new product in a new market.

The first social networking site, SixDegrees.com, launched in 1997, is a good example of a risky venture offering a new product in a new market. Although most features of SixDegrees—such as the abilities to create a profile, list friends and surf other users' friends lists—already existed in some form, SixDegrees was the first social networking site to combine all these elements. SixDegrees attracted millions of users but failed to become sustainable. Its founder believes the site was ahead of its time. Early internet users had only a few friends who were also online that they could connect to, and there was little interest in connecting to strangers. Another early social network, Friendster, launched in 2002 and quickly grew to 300,000 users through word of mouth, but frustrated its users in the United States because of technical difficulties and problems in handling its rapid growth (Boyd & Ellison, 2008). The site proclaimed itself dead in 2011 and asked users to move on (Steinberg, 2011).

In the meantime, hundreds of other social networking sites, such as Facebook, Twitter and LinkedIn, have attracted millions of users. Building on the same features as SixDegrees, these sites support the maintenance of existing social networks or connection with strangers based on shared interests or other characteristics, such as a common language. Users can connect to other users in a bi-directional relationship and become 'friends'. On a one-directional basis, social networking site users can also 'follow' or 'like' someone or something; for instance a brand or a celebrity. Most social network sites offer additional features such as photo sharing or different communication opportunities, such as leaving a public message on the profile of a friend, and private or instant messaging (Boyd & Ellison, 2008). It is important for social networking sites to manage their audience and decide between exclusivity or mass distribution. While Facebook only offered its service to Harvard students in the beginning, it opened to everyone later (Feeney, 2012).

In 2011, 65 per cent of all online adults use a social networking site and new users were still flocking to sites such as Facebook, Twitter, LinkedIn or Google+ (Madden & Zickuhr, 2011). Facebook doubled its members within less than two years from 400 million in February 2010

> Companies can focus on a new market for their existing products, such as selling them in a foreign country in addition to the domestic market. The highest risk strategy is product diversification—establishing a new product in a new market.

to more than 800 million users in August 2011, with 50 per cent logging on every day (Ostrow, 2011). Twitter announced it had grown by 100 million users in 2010, and reached 200 million users by 2011 (McCafferty, 2011; Twitter, 2010). Consequently, Twitter's ad revenue rose by 210 per cent in 2011 (eMarketer, 2011). Another success story could be Google+. Although new Google+ users needed an invitation to join the social networking site in the earliest stage, it attracted 10 million users within a few months, and invitations to Google's new social networking site were even sold on eBay (Schroeder, 2011; Wortham, 2011).

Given that so many social networking sites already exist, it might seem challenging to launch another social networking site. Yet Mark Cracknell, 21, and Nathan Hoad, 25, both from Brisbane, started Kondoot, a social live video network. The founders investigated the social networking sphere and found none of the major players offered video broadcasting. Since its launch in late 2011, subscribers from 133 countries use it as a live or recorded broadcast option, or as an instant messaging service (Tan, 2012). Free mobile apps give its users the possibility to broadcast from almost anywhere. Similar to SixDegrees, Kondoot's features are not new, as existing services such as Facebook, Skype and YouTube cover these areas already. Yet, using Kondoot allows users to select on one platform who they want to connect with—friends, strangers or the world—and then, for example, share their video messages in real time from fixed lines or mobiles (Feeney, 2012).

One business model for Kondoot is to generate fees from musicians or bands selling online tickets for virtual attendance of a live concert. Launched in the United States and attracting US$3.2 million in funding, Mark and Nathan plan to tap the Australian market in partnering with a recognisable festival in summer 2011–12. The European market is next and Kondoot's founders already have ideas to diversify into other areas such as sports broadcasting. While the pair compare themselves with Facebook founders Mark Zuckerberg and Eduardo Saverin, they are aware of the challenges the company faces (Tan, 2012). Perhaps the greatest of these challenges is acquiring enough users. The motivation for a user to join a social networking site is being able to connect to their pre-existing social network in real life. Finding only few real-life friends there makes joining a a new social networking site pointless. Furthermore, it is important to have a large enough user base to justify advertising efforts (BBC News, 2008).

Questions

1   Why do you think social networks are so successful? Which consumer needs do social networking sites address?

2   What might have been the reasons for Facebook starting in a market niche—Harvard students—and then opening its service to the public, and Google+ starting by invitation only? Could a similar approach be successful for Kondoot?

3   How could Kondoot segment its market?

4   Explain the marketing mix element 'price' for users of social network sites such as Kondoot.

5   How could Kondoot acquire customers? What limitations in terms of promotion are there for new social network sites such as Kondoot?

Practitioner profile
Doug Peiffer, CEO, OzTAM (Australian television audience measurement service), Sydney

Technically I am not a marketer by trade. In fact, although I've always been interested in consumer behaviour, I have never worked in a traditional marketing role. But during the twenty-five years that I've spent in television audience measurement and research, I've worked with marketers almost every single day. Understanding the role and needs of marketers (my clients) has been essential throughout my career.

I am the CEO of OzTAM, an organisation that measures and reports on Australia's interaction with television—who is watching, how much they are watching and what they are watching. This is what determines the value of television to advertisers: its ability to deliver audiences for their advertisements.

OzTAM ratings give our clients access to a minute-by-minute picture of the Australian television audience, for both free-to-air and subscription television. But ratings are only the surface; there is so much more that we can learn about consumer and viewer behaviour through deeper analysis of the data, and this knowledge has real practical application within the industry.

One of the most important aspects of my job is meeting with clients (media buyers and planners, strategists and marketers) and helping them to understand how they can use our data for forecasting and planning their advertising campaigns. It is essential that I have a good understanding of the roles and responsibilities of my clients, so that I can provide useful information about how they can apply our services to help their decision making.

To be good at my job, I need up-to-date information about how audiences consume and engage with media. This means being aware of changes in the media landscape and understanding or predicting what effect those changes will have. Lately I have spent a lot of time updating clients on the recent changes in television viewing behaviour, particularly the effect of the new digital free-to-air channels and digital devices in Australian households. Our clients need to know the extent to which these new devices are changing viewing behaviour and what that means for their advertising campaign planning.

Over my career, I have spent decades developing extensive relationships within the advertising and marketing community, building research skills and knowledge of audience measurement techniques, as well as leadership and business development experience. It took me a long time to get to where I am now, but it was the combination of skills I accumulated during that period that has helped me to get there. Now I am CEO of an organisation that is at the forefront of audience measurement research at a time when the television and media landscape is changing significantly. We can work towards understanding what those changes mean, but we can't predict everything—it's incredibly exciting.

12
STRATEGIC MARKETING AND PLANNING

ADRIAN PALMER, ADAPTED BY LARRY LOCKSHIN

◢ Introduction case

Virgin Australia

By Margaret Faulkner

When we start a new venture, we base it on hard research and analysis. Typically, we review the industry and put ourselves in the customer's shoes to see what could make it better. We ask fundamental questions: is this an opportunity for restructuring a market and creating competitive advantage? What are the competitors doing? Is the customer confused or badly served? Is this an opportunity for building the Virgin brand? Can we add value? Will it interact with our other businesses? Is there an appropriate trade-off between risk and reward.? (Virgin, 2012)

Imagine opening your own store, creating a brand that signals your lack of experience and within forty years the technology underlying your product transforms (twice), making it no longer necessary to physically visit a store.

Without strategic planning, the story of Virgin Records would be similar to that of Cobb & Co. coaches. Cobb & Co. carried passengers and mail for seventy years in Australia and overseas in New Zealand, South Africa and Japan. Over time, the company replaced horses with motor vehicles, but structural changes and the rise of personal automobiles led to Cobb & Co. becoming obsolete.

Virgin took another path, continually exploring ways to grow by extending their brand into new markets. The brand and its co-founder, Sir Richard Branson, are still associated with having fun, challenging established brands and being the white knight in shining armour for customers. Decisions for the brand are strategic and informed by market research.

This included expansion into Australia, and while Virgin is no longer selling music in this country, it offers air travel, mobile phone and financial services. Its air travel services have succeeded where others, such as Ansett, Compass and Air Australia, failed. It has changed the market: Qantas launched Jetstar to compete with the threat of Virgin Blue entering as a low-priced carrier in the wake of Ansett's departure.

In 2011, a re-launch as Virgin Australia signalled Virgin's transition to becoming a full-service carrier, creating greater competition with Qantas for the business class market, in addition to their well-established economy market.

> We ask fundamental questions: is this an opportunity for restructuring a market and creating competitive advantage? What are the competitors doing? Is the customer confused or badly served?

INTRODUCTION

This chapter provides a guide to marketing planning based on the knowledge of the previous chapters. Too many marketing plans fail to be implemented effectively, and this chapter explores the bases for effective marketing management. Marketing management involves a continual process of analysis, planning, implementation, and control. Timely and relevant information, acted upon by appropriately structured and motivated management, is crucial to success.

LEARNING OBJECTIVES

After reading this chapter you should:

- understand the five key stages of the marketing management process
- understand the differences and importance of strategic, tactical and contingency periodic planning
- understand the interfunctional integrator nature of planning
- be able to identify and understand the basic elements of a marketing plan
- understand methods of organising the marketing management function and where each may be applicable
- understand why the integration of marketing management with other management functions is important for the organisation
- understand the importance of information management in marketing management and know some useful metrics to collect.

CHAPTER OUTLINE

Introduction

Managing the marketing effort

The marketing management process

Strategic, tactical and contingency planning

Organising the marketing management function

Integrating marketing management with other management functions

Marketing management and smaller businesses

Are entrepreneurs born or bred?

Managing information

Conclusion

MANAGING THE MARKETING EFFORT

Most people will have had experience of companies that do not appear to have the management capabilities necessary for success. At the operational level, inadequate investment in staff training and a distribution system that results in the wrong products being delivered late to the wrong place can be signs of bad management. At a strategic level, poor management can be seen as a preoccupation with declining products at the expense of new opportunities and a lack of information about current market conditions.

There is an ongoing debate about whether management should be more like an art or more like engineering (that is, based on science). Those who advocate a more scientific approach set great value in structured procedures; for example in the way information is routinely collected and analysed. Rationality and reassurance underlie the scientific approach. Most large companies have systematic procedures for management that make them a relatively safe bet for investors, even if they lack the occasional sparkle of smaller and more volatile companies.

Advocates of a creative, artistic approach would argue that the business environment is changing rapidly and therefore well-developed procedures may no longer be valid in the future. Furthermore, rigorous analysis slows decision making, which may be a disadvantage in a fast-moving market.

This textbook provides a strong empirical grounding for marketing decision making, which should help managers make faster decisions. The recommended approaches are based on long-term patterns of behaviour. Many companies use approaches that are called scientific management but are really just systematic procedures. Being systematic is useful if the strategies being implemented are developed to increase mental and physical availability. Creative approaches can work, but only if they too build mental and physical availability. Later in this chapter we will explore how different management structures and processes can either help or hinder the process of developing a good **marketing plan**.

marketing plan:
A systematic approach to the achievement of strategies and goals. It will usually include at least a SWOT analysis, target markets, objectives, a marketing strategy including action programs, implementation, control and review, and evaluation.

Information is a key element of the marketing management process. We saw in Chapter 4 how, in large organisations, information is a medium for keeping in touch with customers, employees, suppliers and intermediaries. Getting the right information to the right people at the right time is crucial if the management of a company is to be able to develop and implement a strategy. Without appropriate information, strategy formulation can become guesswork and the implementation of that strategy may be half-hearted. Inadequate monitoring may not warn of problems until it is too late to do anything about them.

◢ **LEARNING OBJECTIVE**

Understand the five key
stages of the marketing
management process

THE MARKETING MANAGEMENT PROCESS

Marketing management can be seen as a continual process. In this section, we identify the key elements of the process, although just who should be responsible for each element is a subject to which we will return later when we explore how marketing management is organised.

There are four key stages in the marketing management process (Figure 12.1).

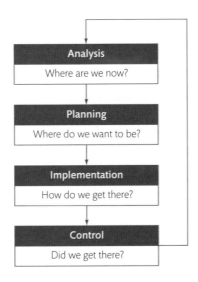

●●● **FIGURE 12.1** THE MARKETING MANAGEMENT PROCESS

Analysis of the current market position

A vital starting point for marketing planning is an analysis of a company's current marketing environment, often undertaken by means of a SWOT analysis or a marketing audit. A marketing audit is part of the larger management audit and is concerned with the marketing environment and marketing operations (McDonald, 2002).

◢ **marketing audit:**

A systematic evaluation
of a company's
existing marketing
environment, objectives,
strategies, programs
and organisation, with
a view to determining
effectiveness and areas
for improvement.

A **marketing audit** typically includes analysis of the organisation's markets and its current market share, sales, profits, penetration and other metrics that were described in Chapter 3. The internal strengths and weaknesses of the organisation, in terms of production, personnel and financial resources, are also evaluated. A marketing audit uses both quantitative and qualitative data where appropriate. Audits are performed infrequently, but constant monitoring of any changes to the current position as established in an audit or SWOT analysis is recommended.

How much analysis of the current situation should a company undertake? While it is nearly always true that a sound analysis of the current situation is an essential prerequisite to developing a marketing plan for the future, excessive preoccupation with the current situation can have its costs.

Analysis on its own will not provide the management decisions that are necessary for defining the future marketing plan. 'Paralysis by analysis' can occur in organisations that avoid making hard decisions about the future because they are continually seeking more information about the present. A plateau is usually reached at which little additional information is available that will improve the quality of marketing plan decisions. Worse still, in markets that are fast changing, excessive analysis of the current position can put a company at a competitive disadvantage to firms that are more willing to take a risk and exploit a market opportunity ahead of their competitors.

However, research shows that firms that undertake formal strategic planning outperform those that do not (Armstrong, 1985, 1991; Armstrong & Reibstein, 1982).

Setting market objectives

Without clearly specified **market objectives**, marketing management can drift aimlessly. Writing down a firm's objectives serves a number of purposes:

- It checks if management share the same objectives, and helps bring everyone into alignment.
- It adds to the sense of purpose within the organisation, without which there would be little focus for managers' efforts.
- It helps to achieve consistency between decisions made at different points within the organisation; for example, it would be inconsistent if a production manager used a production objective that was unrelated to the marketing manager's sales objective.
- Objectives are used as motivational devices and can be used in a variety of formal and informal ways to stimulate increased performance by managers.
- Objectives allow for more effective control within an organisation. Unless clear objectives have been defined at the outset, it is very difficult to know whether the organisation has achieved what it set out to achieve, or what corrective action to take if its efforts seem to be going adrift during the plan period.

To be effective, objectives must be capable of realistic achievement and must be accepted as such by the people responsible for acting on them. The objectives must also not be based on mistaken assumptions about how consumers behave or how brands compete (Sharp, 2010). If objectives are set unattainably high, the whole process of planning can be brought into disrepute by the company's employees. Wherever possible, objectives should be quantified and should clearly specify the time period to which they relate. Inconsistency between objectives should be avoided. This sometimes occurs, for example, where sales objectives can be achieved only by reducing selling prices, thereby making it impossible to achieve a profitability objective.

Developing a marketing strategy

There are usually many ways in which marketing objectives can be achieved. For example, a financial return objective could be satisfied by different portfolios of products and even categories. Identifying the strategic alternatives open to an organisation relies on interpreting data and evaluating a number of possible future scenarios. Within this evaluation, factors such as the likelihood of success, the level

market objectives:
Marketing goals for an organisation, or part of an organisation. They should be specific, measurable, achievable, reasonable and time-based (SMART).

of downside risk, and the amount of resources required to implement a strategy should be taken into consideration. What may be an appropriate strategy for one company may be quite inappropriate (or impossible) for another, on account of differences in financial resources, past history and personnel strengths, among other things.

Implementing the strategy

Having chosen a strategy, the next step is to implement it. This is usually done through a twelve-month marketing plan, although the length of the plan period can depend on the amount of turbulence in a company's marketing environment. The marketing plan sets out programs for, among other things, the timing and costing of promotions, pricing plans and the recruitment and payment of distributors. The plan should clearly show who is responsible for implementing each aspect of the plan. The detailed marketing plan should flow directly from the marketing strategy, which itself starts from marketing objectives. The plan may go through a series of iterative stages of consultation before it is finally accepted. Too many companies develop a strategy that sounds fine, but they fail to think through fully the detail of implementation. For example, the success of a new brand will depend enormously on its ability to quickly gain a certain degree of physical and mental availability. So both sales and advertising plans are needed that give the new brand a realistic chance of achieving these levels of both physical and mental availability among enough people to hit the brand's sales targets.

Monitoring and controlling the marketing program

Marketing plans are of little value if they are implemented only half-heartedly. So marketers need to check whether the implementation is going to plan. Even if the implementation is going to plan it is extremely unlikely that results were just as forecast—control systems allow a company to adapt, making changes to the plan as events unfold.

Effective control systems monitor the implementation and results of the plan and allow managers to seek an explanation of any deviation from it. They require timely, accurate and relevant information about an organisation's operations and environment. Control systems require three underlying components to be in place:

1   setting of targets or standards of expected performance (these are the objectives)
2   measurement and evaluation of actual performance
3   corrective action taken where necessary.

Many control systems fail because employees within an organisation have been given inappropriate or unrealistic targets. Even where targets are set and appropriate data are collected, control systems may fail if management does not act on the information that flows in. Control information should identify variances from targets and should be able to indicate whether the variance is within or beyond the control of the person responsible for meeting the target. If it is beyond that person's control, the issue should become one of revising the target so that it becomes achievable. If the variance is the result of factors that are subject to a manager's control, a number of measures can be taken to try to revise their behaviour, including incentive schemes, training and disciplinary action.

STRATEGIC, TACTICAL AND CONTINGENCY PLANNING

LEARNING OBJECTIVE
Understand the differences and importance of strategic, tactical and contingency periodic planning

From the above description, we can see that marketing planning is best viewed as a continuous process. However, it is necessary to produce periodic statements of a plan, so that all individuals in an organisation can read it and ensure they are working towards it. Three types of periodic plan can be identified:

1   The *strategic* element of a marketing plan focuses on the overriding direction that an organisation's efforts will take in order to meet its objectives.

2   The *tactical* element is more concerned with plans for implementing the detail of the strategic plan. The division between the strategic and tactical elements of a marketing plan can sometimes be difficult to define. Typically, a strategic marketing plan is concerned with mapping out direction over a five-year planning period, whereas a tactical marketing plan is concerned with implementation during the next twelve months. Many business sectors view their strategic planning periods very differently, and in the case of large-scale infrastructure projects such as airports or railways, the strategic planning period may be very long indeed. On the other hand, many small-scale, low-technology businesses may find little need for a strategic plan beyond the immediate operational period.

3   A **contingency plan** seeks to identify scenarios where the assumptions of the analysis on which strategic decisions were based turn out to be false. For example, a food manufacturer might have assumed that there would be no significant change in consumers' attitudes towards a particular category of food. However, the possibility of a food scare, such as that associated with salmonella in chickens, could seriously affect the implementation of a marketing plan. A contingency plan would allow a firm to react quickly to such a scenario; for example by increasing its promotional expenditure and cutting back on production capacity.

contingency plan: A plan to be implemented only upon the occurrence of future events other than those in the accepted plan.

Marketing planning and corporate planning

Marketing management is just one of the specialist management functions that can be identified within most commercial organisations. What is the relationship between marketing management and corporate management?

At one extreme, the two can be seen as synonymous. If an organisation stands or falls primarily on its ability to produce revenue from customers, then it can be argued that marketing planning is so central to the organisation's activities that it becomes **corporate planning**.

The alternative view is that marketing is just one of the functions of an organisation that affects its performance. Marketing takes its goals from corporate plans just as the personnel or production functions of the organisation do. In business sectors where customers have relatively little choice and production capacity is limited, the significance of the marketing plan to the corporate plan will be less than for a company facing fierce competition. Many public sector service organisations operating in relatively uncompetitive markets claim to go through the

corporate planning: Corporate planning is distinct from corporate strategy in that strategy involves the decisions about what to do next in the marketplace, while planning is the methods to go about implementing the strategy.

marketing planning process, when in fact, although the term 'marketing planning' may be used, it is given much less significance than the development of production plans or personnel plans to serve a stable market.

The relationship between the processes of marketing and corporate planning can be two-way, again reflecting the importance of marketing to the total planning process. Marketing information is fed into the corporate planning process for analysis and formulation of the corporate plan in a process sometimes referred to as *bottom-up planning*. In a top-down process, the corporate plan is developed and functional objectives are specified for marketing.

◢ LEARNING OBJECTIVE
Understand the interfunctional integrator nature of planning

Planning as an interfunctional integrator

The marketing planning process helps to integrate the efforts of a diverse range of people throughout an organisation. The plan allows everybody to 'sing from the same hymn sheet'. Without the plan, individuals may end up doing things that are in direct conflict with their colleagues.

Corporate and marketing planning processes act as integrators in horizontal and vertical dimensions (see Figure 12.2).

In the horizontal dimension, the planning process brings together the plans of the specialised functions that are necessary to make the organisation work. Marketing is just one function of an organisation, each of which generates its own planning process. Other functional plans found in

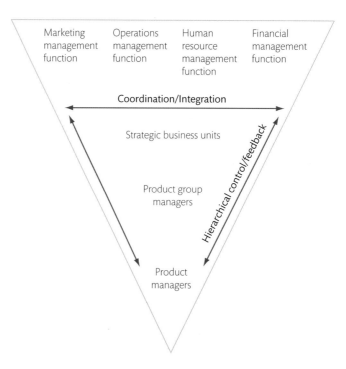

●●● **FIGURE 12.2** THE PLANNING PROCESS AS A VERTICAL AND HORIZONTAL INTEGRATOR WITHIN ORGANISATIONS

most organisations are financial plans, personnel plans and production plans. The components of these functional plans must recognise their interdependencies if they are to be effective. For example, a car manufacturer's marketing strategic plan that anticipates a 20 per cent growth in sales of its cars over a five-year planning period should be reflected in a strategic production plan that allows for output to increase by a similar amount, as well as a financial plan that identifies strategies for raising the required level of finance for new investment and work in progress, and a personnel plan for recruiting additional staff. Within the marketing department, a plan helps to ensure that the activities of the market research or market insights staff are mutually supportive of the activities of sales and advertising staff, for example.

In the vertical dimension, the planning process provides a framework for decisions to be made at different levels of the corporate hierarchy. Objectives can be specified in progressively more detail, from the global objectives of the corporate plan to the information required to operationalise these objectives at the level of individual operational units (or **strategic business units**) and, in turn, for individual products or product lines often implemented in each country separately.

> **strategic business unit (SBU):** A smaller part of a business but large enough to require its own marketing plan and specific campaigns. SBUs can be part of larger SBUs. For instance, a company might have an SBU for 'dental care' and then smaller SBUs for specific brands.

The mission statement

A corporate **mission statement** provides a focal point for the marketing planning process. It can be likened to a hidden hand that guides all employees in an organisation in developing and implementing marketing plans. Drucker (1973) identified a number of basic questions that management needs to ask in drawing up a mission statement:

- What is our business?
- Who is the customer?
- What is value to the customer?
- What will our business be?
- What should our business be?

> **mission statement:** A brief statement, no longer than a few sentences, that describes the company's raison d'être—the reason it exists.

By forcing management to focus on the essential nature of the business it is in and the nature of customer needs it seeks to satisfy, the problem of 'marketing myopia' identified by Levitt (1960) can be avoided. Levitt argued that in order to avoid a narrow, shortsighted view of their business, managers should define their business in terms of the needs that they fulfill rather than the products they produce. In his classic example, railway operators lost their way because they defined their output in terms of the technology of tracked vehicles, rather than in terms of the core benefit of movement that they provided. They lost out to the development of cars and buses, which provided similar benefits using different technologies.

But companies also have to be aware of their capabilities; changing with the market may require completely different capabilities, so a company may instead be better to think of new uses for its existing capabilities. For example, a horse and buggy company may be better to become a manufacturer of leather suitcases than try to transform itself into a car manufacturer.

The nature of an organisation's mission statement is a reflection of a number of factors, including the organisation's ownership (public sector versus private sector), the previous history

CRITICAL REFLECTION

Revisit the case study about Virgin at the start of this chapter. Think about start of the Virgin empire when it just had a single record store. What would the mission statement have been?

In a mission statement, how important is it to be realistic, with a view of keeping everyone on track, compared to being forward thinking and having a view of the future?

of the organisation, the resources available to it, and major opportunities and threats faced by the organisation.

In service organisations, where the interface between consumers and production personnel is often critical, communication of the values contained within the mission statement can be very important. The statement is frequently repeated by organisations in staff newsletters and in notices at the place of work. Some examples of mission statements that are widely communicated to the workforce as well as to customers are shown in Figure 12.3.

'To give ordinary folk the chance to buy the same things as rich people'
—Wal Mart

'To organize the world's information and make it universally accessible and useful'
—Google

'To make people happy'
—Walt Disney

'To provide our customers with safe, good value, point-to-point air services. To effect and to offer a consistent and reliable product and fares appealing to leisure and business markets on a rangeof European routes. To achieve this we will develop our people and establish lasting relationships with our suppliers'
—easyjet

'To be the consumer's first choice for food, delivering products of outstanding quality and great service at a competitive cost through working faster, simpler and together'
—Sainsbury's

●●● **FIGURE 12.3** SOME EXAMPLES OF CORPORATE MISSION STATEMENTS

Basic elements of a marketing plan

Executive summary

The purpose of the executive summary is to give the reader a quick overview of the contents and outcomes of the plan. It should outline the major objectives, findings and recommendations of the plan, without going into the detail that is included in the body.

Introduction

▲ **LEARNING OBJECTIVE**
Be able to identify and understand the basic elements of a marketing plan

This section introduces the company and describes the current market position. This would include a brief background of the company, a description of the products and services on offer, the current financial standing of the company, as well as key marketing metrics (market share, penetration and other metrics from Chapter 3).

In this section you can also outline the accomplishments and successes of the company to date. This section should only be an introduction, as the in-depth analysis will be included in the SWOT analysis section of the marketing plan.

Vision, mission statement and objectives

Vision—a statement about where a company wants to be in the future: the ultimate goal, even if it is something far-reaching or very unlikely to be achieved.

For example, Adelaide Fringe Festival's vision statement is: *To be the leading open-access fringe festival in the world* (Adelaide Fringe, 2012).

Mission statement—a few sentences that outline why a company exists and what it aims to achieve. This can also include a statement about its values or work ethics.

For example, PeoplesChoice Credit Union's mission statement is: 'Providing good financial products and member service to ensure lifelong financial relationships' (PeoplesChoice Credit Union, 2012).

Objectives—company objectives are more specific than the mission statement and are often action-oriented. Objectives should be measurable and often include a time frame for completion.

For example, the objectives of the RSPCA Australia (2012) are:

- To prevent cruelty to animals by ensuring the enforcement of existing laws at federal and state level.
- To procure the passage of such amending or new legislation as is necessary for the protection of animals.
- To develop and promote policies for the humane treatment of animals that reflect contemporary values and scientific knowledge.
- To educate the community with regard to the humane treatment of animals.
- To engage with relevant stakeholders to improve animal welfare.
- To sustain an intelligent public opinion regarding animal welfare.
- To operate facilities for the care and protection of animals.

Team description

This section should give insights into the organisational structure, specifically that of the team that will work to deliver the objectives of the plan. Here you can also give details of the skills and capabilities within the team, as well as any other relevant resources within the organisation.

Macro-environment and dynamics

There are several macro-economic trends and forces (as outlined in Chapter 5) that possibly will affect the plan. This section should cover an analysis of any relevant factors, especially those likely to change during the plan, and their potential impact; for example a rise in unemployment, a reduction in interest rates, government regulation, changes in import duties and so on.

Target market description

A description of the customers that the product or organisation aims to target, including:

- a description of the target market and any segments identified
- the size of the target market

- any relevant characteristics, habits or patterns in behaviour
- a description of wants, needs and desires in relation to the product category
- a description of buying habits.

Competitive analysis and issues analysis

A competitive analysis is a comprehensive description and analysis of competitor companies, both current and potential. An issues analysis should list any key external issues (new legislation or technological advancements) that would lead to potential challenges or opportunities for the business. These are more specific and shorter term than the trends covered in the macro-environmental analysis.

SWOT analysis

This section provides a detailed analysis of the current situation—focusing on the strengths, weaknesses, opportunities and threats (SWOT). This is an important section because the knowledge and information generated from the SWOT analysis will be used as a reference point and guide for the rest of the plan.

- Strengths and weaknesses are generally determined by the internal elements. Strengths are any available company resources that can be used to improve market share or financial performance.
- Weaknesses are any company resources that may cause a loss in competitive advantage, position or financial state.

A strengths and weaknesses analysis should consider:

- philosophy or mission
- product features, benefits or quality
- competitive advantage (is there one?)
- key market metrics, such as market share and penetration, and trends of these
- distribution methods
- pricing structure (and comparison with competitors)
- customer awareness and knowledge
- the personnel in marketing and those that affect marketing, such as production and customer service.

An opportunities and threats analysis can vary depending on the type of organisation. A practical method of analysing the opportunities is to focus on questions such as:

- What problems do customers have with the product that could be addressed by improving it?
- What steps do the customers go through to purchase, use and dispose of the product? (This may lead to insights about packaging.)

Threats can include:

- activities of competitors (new product launches, promotoions and so on)
- specific market trends (shifts in needs, behaviours and so on)
- predicted changes in the macro-environment, such as new legislation or economic turmoil.

The following template can be used to assist with the SWOT analysis. Also see Chapter 5 for further information about conducting a SWOT analysis.

SWOT template

	STRENGTHS	WEAKNESSES	OPPORTUNITIES	THREATS
1 Company/product reputation				
2 Market share				
3 Product's ability to meet market needs				
4 Product's ability to meet market trends				
5 Value product brings to market				
6 Product quality				
7 Customer service and support quality				
8 Quality/effectiveness of past marketing				
9 Pricing				
10 Distribution				
11 Geographic location				
12 Operational leadership				
13 Financial strength				
14 Manufacturing capabilities				
15 Responsiveness of workforce				
16 Other				

Marketing objectives

This section lists the specific objectives that the plan aims to achieve. Marketing objectives should be clear, measurable and have a time frame; for example 'increase sales by 30 per cent in one year' or 'gain 5 per cent market share within 18 months'. The rest of the plan will outline the marketing strategy and tactics that will be used to meet these goals.

Marketing strategy (the marketing mix)

This section details the actual strategy for each element of the marketing mix (product, price, promotion and place) that will be used to meet the marketing objectives. Strategic decisions should be steered by the knowledge and information from the SWOT analysis, as well as the customer and competitor analysis.

Product (or service): Any strategies based on product or service features should be outlined and discussed in this section. One of the major factors in setting the product or service plan is determining what customers value. Things that are of particular value can be focused on in the product positioning strategy. Where the product or service (or bundle) offers something that competitors do not (a point of differentiation) there could be an opportunity. However, true differentiation is rare and is usually quickly copied by competitors. Particular attention should be paid to developing and maintaining distinctiveness for the product or service in all its marketing activities. This section should also include decisions about the manufacturing process and detail new product development where applicable.

Price: Pricing decisions are an essential part of marketing planning and strategy. You must select a price that the target market is willing to pay and that will also generate a profit for the company. There are several approaches to setting prices that can be considered (see Chapter 9), though competition usually defines the range of acceptable prices. This section of the marketing plan should also include any decision about plans for temporary price discounts or price promotions.

Promotions (or marketing communications): This section details the activities that will be used to promote or build mental availability for the product or service and to achieve the objectives. This includes decisions about advertising, direct marketing, personal selling, public relations, events and so on. Typically, this section is where most of the marketing budget is allocated (due to the high cost of advertising). The promotions plan should include:

- a description of the promotional program and tactics
- projected costs of the promotional programs for the year (or the period of the plan)
- explanation of how your promotional tactics will support the marketing objectives
- measures of success for promotional programs.

Place (physical availability): This section of the plan determines how and where the product or service is available to the buyers. This will outline whether the product will be sold directly or indirectly, and detail any decisions about channels of distribution. Customers' perception of your product may be considered when selecting the distribution as well as what competitors are doing.

Budget

The budget for achieving the plan should be outlined in this section. The budget forms an important part of the monitoring and control activities, as well as providing management with a projection of overall costs to be agreed.

Controls/monitoring

This section should outlines the controls and measures that will be used to monitor the success of the plan based on the objectives and the budget.

Source: Adapted from Doyle, 2011

Marketing planning may look simple, with each step clearly set out, but the practice of marketing planning requires a good deal of work. For a plan to work, it requires the cooperation of many people, so the development of the plan will require much consultation. Afterwards, the plan will need to be internally marketed to staff. It should go without saying that the plan must be well written, and easy for many people to read and understand. In practice, many marketing plans are poorly written. As discussed in Chapter 1, marketing managers need to be good at both written and verbal communication.

ORGANISING THE MARKETING MANAGEMENT FUNCTION

LEARNING OBJECTIVE
Understand methods of organising the marketing management function and where each may be applicable

A marketing plan depends on having the right people, organised into appropriate teams to implement the process and make it a success. There have been too many cases of marketing planners developing a plan for which the operational implications have not been fully thought through and that therefore fails to deliver value to customers and profits to the company.

A frequent problem occurs where the marketing planning function becomes cut off from other functional departments. The whole issue of organising a company so that it has a company-wide focus on marketing is considered in a later section. Here we look inwardly at the marketing department and ask how it can best be organised in order to meet marketing objectives.

Responsibilities given to the marketing department vary from one organisation to another, reflecting the competitive nature of a company and also its traditions and organisational inertia. Within marketing departments, four basic approaches to allocating these responsibilities are identified here (shown in Figure 12.4 using the example of an airline), although, in practice, most

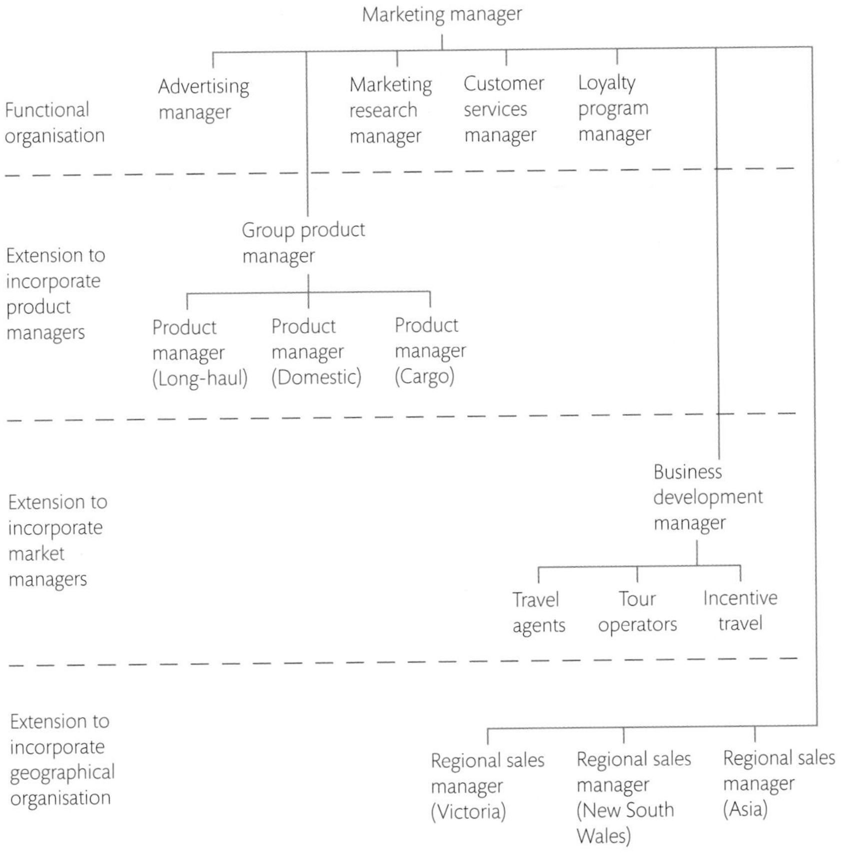

FIGURE 12.4 ALTERNATIVE FORMS OF MARKETING DEPARTMENT ORGANISATION STRUCTURE, SHOWING TYPICAL APPLICATIONS TO AN AIRLINE OPERATOR

marketing departments show more than one approach. The four approaches allocate marketing responsibilities by functions performed, geographical area covered, products or groups of products managed, and market segments managed.

The great diversity of organisational structures highlights the fact that there is no one unique structure that is appropriate to all firms, even within the same business sector. Overall, the organisation of a marketing department must allow for a flexible and adaptable response to customers' needs within a changing environment, while aiming to reduce the level of confusion, ambiguity and cost inherent in some structures.

Management by functional responsibility

A common basis for organising a marketing department is to divide responsibilities into identifiable marketing functions. Typically, these functions may be advertising, product or brand management, sales, marketing research or customer insights, and customer services. The precise division of the functional responsibilities will depend upon the nature of the organisation. Buying and merchandising are likely to be important features in a retailing organisation, while research and development will be important for an electronics company.

The main advantage of a functional organisation lies in its administrative simplicity. Against this, there can be a tendency for policy responsibility on specific products or markets to become lost between numerous functional specialists. There is also the possibility of destructive rivalry between functional specialists for their share of marketing budgets; for example rivalry between an advertising manager and a sales manager for a larger share of the promotional budget.

Management by geographical responsibility

Companies selling a product nationally or internationally usually organise some of their marketing functions, especially the sales function, on a geographical basis. For companies operating internationally, there is usually some geographical basis to the organisation in the way the marketing activities are organised in individual national markets. Often more than one person oversees activities, such as a global market research or market insights manager working with a local manager in each region or country.

Management by product type

Where a company produces a variety of products, it is quite common to appoint a product or brand manager to manage a particular product or product line. This form of organisation does not replace the functional organisation, but provides an additional layer of management, which coordinates the functional activities. The product manager's role includes a number of key tasks:

- developing a long-range strategy and short-term annual plan for a product, brand or group of products

- working with internal and external functional specialists to develop and implement marketing programs; for example in relation to advertising and sales promotion
- monitoring the performance of the product or brand and noting changes in the marketing environment that may pose opportunities or threats.

In theory, a product manager can react more quickly to changes in the product's marketing environment than would be possible if no one had specific responsibility for the product. Although product management structures can allow for a focused strategy to be developed in respect of individual products, there are nevertheless some shortcomings. The most serious one arises when a product manager is given a lot of responsibility for ensuring that objectives for the product are met, but relatively little control over the resource inputs she has at her disposal. Product managers typically must rely on persuasion for the cooperation of advertising, sales and other functional specialist departments. Confusion can arise in the minds of staff within an organisation as to whom they are accountable to for their day-to-day actions: the product manager or a functional specialist such as a sales manager? Product management structures can lead to larger numbers of people being employed, resulting in a higher cost structure, which may put the organisation at a competitive disadvantage in price-sensitive markets.

Management by market segment

Many companies sell basically similar products to different types of customers who vary significantly in their needs. For example, an airline provides services targeted at leisure travellers, business travellers, tour operators and freight forwarders, among others; each of these groups has differing requirements in terms of speed, reliability, price and so on, and a market segment manager can become expert in understanding these needs and developing an appropriate product offer for each group. Instead of being given financial targets for a specific product, market managers are usually given growth or market share targets.

The main advantage of this form of organisation is that it allows marketing activity to be focused on meeting the needs of distinct and identified groups of customers, something that should be at the heart of any truly marketing-oriented organisation. Also, new products are more likely to emerge within this structure than where an organisation's response is confined to traditional product management boundaries. Market management structures are also arguably more conducive to the important task of developing relationships with customers, especially in business-to-business markets. Where an organisation has a number of very important customers, it is common to find the appointment of key account managers to handle relationships with those clients in order to develop marketing opportunities that are of mutual benefit to both.

Many of the disadvantages of the product management organisation are also shared by market-based structures. There can again be a conflict between responsibility and authority, and this form of structure can also become expensive to operate.

Case study
Marketing the unmanageable?

Adapted by Kellie Newstead

In any organisation, the aspirations of marketing managers can be quite different from those of the employees who have to deliver the promises that marketers make. It can be naïve to imagine that marketers simply concentrate on identifying customers' needs, then operations people develop products that will satisfy those needs. In reality, front-line employees may have cherished ways of working that they may feel are threatened by new ideas from the marketing department. This is especially true in services, and the problem can be acute where the front-line employees have considerable knowledge and power.

For example, consider some challenges that the public health system may face. More and more managers in the public health system have no clinical background. As marketing managers are appointed outside of the medical profession, the public health system is becoming increasingly aware that the sector is market-driven. As 'patients' become 'consumers' to managers, understanding and responding to patients' needs becomes increasingly important. Although a CEO may have ultimate authority over all employees, many people would recognise that it could be the medical consultants who have the real power in a hospital. If they do not like a change that is proposed by the chief executive, they can point to their professional codes of conduct and years of training that have given them knowledge-based power. Consultants may argue that they have patients' long-term interests at heart, because they have invested heavily in their specialised training and will be around for many years to deal with the consequences of their actions. By contrast, a marketing manager may be perceived as having relatively simple training, and will soon move on to another job with no professional responsibility to see through the consequences of his or her actions. Marketing managers with non-clinical backgrounds may become too focused on relatively superficial quality-of-service issues such as car parking and food, while consultants could argue that only they can judge the true quality of the core service of a hospital, namely the outcome of medical and surgical procedures. They may point out that a typical patient is incapable of assessing clinical performance, owing to their limited knowledge and the fact that the outcome of many clinical procedures will not fully present themselves for many months or even years into the future. In short, only consultants, with their professional training and codes of conduct, can manage the nature of interaction between a health system and its patients.

For a marketing manager, the professional, knowledge-based power of consultants may be seen as a source of frustration. For example, marketing managers may wish to utilise operating theatres as often as possible. For a marketing manager, one method of increasing the number of patient admissions would be to use these very expensive facilities on Friday afternoons, rather than to leave them idle. Consultants may argue that it is bad professional practice to commence operations just before the weekend, when there is only limited cover available in a hospital to rectify any clinical complications. Cynics may claim that consultants are using professional arguments as a smokescreen for giving themselves a long weekend and a chance to get away early to play golf. However, some have pointed out that consultants may use Friday afternoons to undertake profitable private surgery elsewhere.

Questions

1   How can a chief executive or marketing manager with a non-clinical background argue with the knowledge and professional responsibilities of a consultant?

2   What does marketing management mean in the context of an environment of highly skilled professionals?

3   Many would argue that management is not about command and control, but more about facilitating others to achieve their goals. Which model of management is right?

4   Who should decide whether consultants are right in their goals of keeping Friday afternoons free for professional reasons, or whether they are doing it because they know a good personal opportunity when they see one?

INTEGRATING MARKETING MANAGEMENT WITH OTHER MANAGEMENT FUNCTIONS

◢ LEARNING OBJECTIVE
Understand why the integration of marketing management with other management functions is important for the organisation

Should an organisation actually have a marketing department? The idea that the existence of a separate marketing department may in fact hinder the development of true customer-centred marketing orientation is becoming increasingly popular. By placing all marketing activity in a marketing department, non-marketing staff may consider that responsibility for winning sales has nothing to do with them, but should be left to the marketing department. So it is becoming fashionable to talk about everybody becoming a 'part-time marketer' (see Gummesson, 2008). However, a marketing department is usually required in order to coordinate and implement those functions that cannot sensibly be delegated to operational personnel. Advertising, sales management and pricing decisions, for example, usually need some central coordination by a marketing department. The importance that a marketing department assumes within any organisation is a reflection on the nature of its operating environment. A large organisation would typically attach great importance to its marketing department as a means of producing a focused marketing mix strategy by which it could gain some advantage over its competitors. On the other hand, a small service company may delegate most of its marketing to customer contact staff. It is our belief that marketing strategy and plans for implementation should be centred within a marketing department or—in a smaller company—with a marketing manager.

Case study
Should companies build Chinese walls?

The idea of an integrated internal work environment may be fine in theory, and may reassure customers that 'the left hand really does know what the right hand is doing', but in practice there are many instances where professional codes of conduct require that staff within an organisation do not talk to each other.

This is often the case for financial services institutions, where one group of employees may have 'inside information' about the shares, activities or financial condition of a company, which, if made public, would be likely to have an effect on the price of that company's shares. For example, information about a proposed takeover bid for a company may be price-sensitive in relation to other companies in the same sector.

This reality leads many institutions to create 'Chinese walls', which are barriers to the passing of information. They are designed to manage confidential information and prevent inadvertent spread and misuse of information. Many banks have set up global Chinese walls policies. Those areas that routinely have access to inside information (such as corporate finance), and which are considered 'inside areas', must be physically separated from those areas that deal in or advise on financial instruments (such as bonds and shares), which are considered 'public areas'.

The problem has become particularly acute in the accounting sector, where a firm of accountants may sell both auditing services and management consultancy services to a company. There have been many allegations that accountants have been too ready to accept compromises in their auditing function in order to pick up lucrative management consultancy business. The investigation of the US accounting firm Arthur Andersen's involvement with the failed energy company Enron in 2002 revealed evidence of unethical practice in the way that the firm had mixed accountancy and consultancy activities, and fed renewed debate about the ethics of 'one-stop' accountancy/consultancy businesses. The consultancy arm of the firm split from the accountancy side in 2000 and continues to operate, now known as Accenture.

Chinese walls are also used by solicitors in cases where they are dealing with clients in dispute with each other. Other service industries can be identified where similar ethical problems can be lessened by the adoption of a product management structure.

Questions

1   How do large diversified services firms convince their customers that information given in confidence to one section of the organisation will not be used against them in another section?

2   In 2011, *The Australian* covered a story about Chinese walls in the Department of Defence (Foo, 2011). The article reported that the Defence was unable to account for $300 million of its $1.2 billion technology budget in the 2011 financial year as a result of 'limited visibility'. In a situation such as this, do you think it is appropriate to use Chinese walls? What about if it was $500? Or the whole $1.2 billion?

In a marketing-oriented organisation, customers are at the centre of all of the organisation's activities. Customers are the concern not simply of the marketing department, but of all the production and administrative personnel whose actions may directly or indirectly impinge upon the customers' service. In the words of Drucker (1973):

> Marketing is so basic that it cannot be considered to be a separate function. It is the whole business seen from the point of view of its final result, that is, from the customer's point of view.

The activities of a number of functional departments can impinge on customers' perceptions of the value they get from a company:

- Personnel plans can have a crucial bearing on marketing plans. The selection, training, motivation and control of staff cannot be considered in isolation from marketing objectives and strategies. Possible conflict between personnel and marketing functions may arise where, for example, marketing demands highly trained and motivated staff, but the personnel function pursues a policy that emphasises cost reduction and uniform pay structures.

- Marketing managers may try to respond to competitor activities, but encounter opposition from production managers, who argue that a product of the required standard cannot be achieved. A marketing manager may want large numbers of product variants in order to satisfy variety-seeking buyers, whereas a production manager may seek large production runs of standardised products.

- Ultimately, finance managers assume responsibility for the allocation of the funds that are needed to implement a marketing plan. At a more operational level, finance managers' actions in respect of the level of credit offered to customers, or towards stockholdings, can also significantly affect the quality of service and the number of customers that the organisation is able to serve.

The problem of how to bring people together in an organisation to act collectively while also being able to place responsibility on an individual is one that continues to generate considerable discussion. Organisations that produce many different products for many different markets may experience difficulties if they adopt a purely product-based or market-based structure. If a product management structure is adopted, product managers would require detailed knowledge of very diverse markets. Likewise, in a market management structure, market managers would require detailed knowledge of possibly very diverse product ranges. To avoid the problem of functional managers acting and thinking with a 'silo' mentality, there has been a tendency for organisations to develop clusters of individuals who focus on creating value for targeted groups of consumers and profits for their company. Within such a cluster, product managers can concentrate on excellence in production, while market managers focus on meeting consumer needs without any preference for a particular product. An example of a 'matrix structure' (as this is sometimes known) can be found in many airlines where market managers can be appointed to identify and formulate a market strategy in respect of the distinct needs of private leisure customers, corporate clients, travel agents and so on. Market managers work alongside product managers who can develop and manage specific products and processes, such as business and first-class cabin service (see Figure 12.5).

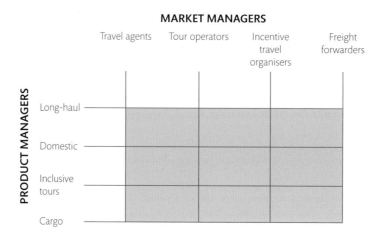

MARKET MANAGERS

Travel agents   Tour operators   Incentive travel organisers   Freight forwarders

●●● **FIGURE 12.5** MATRIX ORGANISATION STRUCTURE APPLIED TO AN AIRLINE

The most important advantages of such clusters are that in principle they can allow organisations to respond rapidly to environmental change. Short-term project teams can be assembled and disbanded at short notice to meet changed needs. Project teams can bring together a wide variety of disciplines and can be used to evaluate new products before full-scale development is undertaken. A bank exploring the possibility of developing a mobile-phone-based payment system might establish a team drawn from staff involved in marketing to individual customers and staff responsible for technology-based research and development. The former may include market researchers and the latter software developers.

The flexibility of such structures can be increased by bringing temporary workers into the structure on a contract basis as and when needed. During the past two decades, there has been a trend for many service organisations to lay off significant numbers of workers, including management, and to buy these back as short-term contractors when needed. As well as cutting fixed costs, such organisations have the potential to respond very rapidly to environmental change.

Where interfunctional clusters exist, great motivation can be present in effectively managed teams. Against this, matrix-type structures can have their problems. Most serious is that confused lines of authority may result. Staff members may not be clear about which superior they are responsible to for a particular aspect of their duties, resulting in possible stress and demotivation. Where a matrix-type structure is introduced into an organisation with a history and culture of functional specialisation, it can be very difficult to implement effectively. Staff may be reluctant to act outside a role that they have traditionally defined narrowly and guarded jealously. Finally, such structures invariably result in more managers being employed within an organisation. At best, this can result in a costly addition to the salary bill. At worst, the existence of additional managers can also slow down decision-making processes where the managers show a reluctance to act outside a narrow functional role.

Having multi-functional clusters of individuals may represent a desirable structure for an organisation, but getting there can be a slow and painful process. Most management change within organisations occurs incrementally. The result of this is often a compromised organisation structure, which is unduly influenced by historic factors and vested interests that may be of no continuing relevance. Some organisations have been more radical and started with a clean sheet of paper and asked: 'How would we design our structures and processes if we were starting out today?'

The underlying principle of business process re-engineering is to design an organisation around key value-adding activities. Essentially, re-engineering is about radically redesigning the processes by which an organisation does business in order that it can achieve major savings in cost, improvements in service levels, or both. Seen as a model, the organisation that is most effective is the one which adds most value (as defined by customers) for the least cost. To be effective, re-engineering needs to be led by strong individuals who have authority to oversee implementation from beginning to end. They will need a lot of clout because fear, resistance and cynicism will inevitably slow down the task.

Application to business-to-business marketing

All strategic marketing planning issues discussed already are relevant to business-to-business marketing situations. However, some issues have different relative importance between consumer and industrial marketing organisations.

The relationship between marketing planning and corporate planning can become closer when a large proportion of an organisation's sales revenue is derived from a small number of very large customers. For example, car components manufacturers in Australia have just five potential customers (car manufacturers) in the national market. Therefore, the loss of one customer can have dire consequences for such suppliers. Not surprisingly, senior management becomes closely involved in the marketing (and sales) planning in such situations. In addition, it becomes necessary for various functional areas of the company—especially production, logistics and, perhaps, research and development—to work closely with marketing and sales to ensure consistency in forecasting and other planning processes.

Of course, most manufacturers selling their consumer products through supermarkets have to deal with a small number of very large supermarket chains. In Australia, for example, Coles and Woolworths have upwards of 80 per cent of the supermarket business (Stuart Alexander, 2012). Again, given the leverage of those two chains, senior management in supplier organisations would be involved in the planning (and possibly implementation) of sales strategies and tactics relating to Coles and Woolworths.

With respect to target market description, business-to-business marketers need to recognise that identification and analysis of buying habits and customer needs are more complex due to the existence of multiple buying influences within organisations. Indeed, some customer organisations comprise national or even international operations, requiring consideration of national or global supply opportunities.

There can be very large differences in the size of organisational customers, and some organisations have very different needs from others due to different business strategies. Therefore, market segmentation tends to be more important within business-to-business marketing operations than within consumer marketing.

Finally, due to the larger size of organisational customers, the role of the sales force tends to be much more important in relation to the marketing function within business-to-business marketing organisations.

MARKETING MANAGEMENT AND SMALLER BUSINESSES

Much of what has been written so far in this chapter about marketing management processes and structures might sound fine for larger organisations, but what about smaller businesses, where the very idea of a 'management structure' and a formalised marketing planning system may seem quite alien?

The importance of small businesses should not be underestimated. In Australia, statistics from the Department of Industry, Innovation, Science, Research and Tertiary Education for 2009–10 highlight the importance and diversity of the small business sector: 96 per cent of the more than two million businesses actively trading in Australia were small businesses (1,961,337). In 2009–10, small businesses provided almost half of total industry employment and around a third of industry added value, thus showing that small business are an integral part of the Australian economy.

In terms of marketing management, **SMEs** have a number of important characteristics:

▲ **SMEs:** Small-to-medium enterprises, sometimes known as SMBs (small-to-medium businesses). SMEs far outnumber larger businesses and are often faster to innovate. Definitions vary, but SMEs usually have between ten and 250 employees.

■ They generally offer much greater adaptability than larger firms. With less bureaucracy and fewer channels of communications, decisions can be taken rapidly. A larger organisation may be burdened with constraints, which tend to slow the decision-making process, such as the need to negotiate new working practices with trade union representatives, or the need to obtain the board of directors' approval for major decisions. As organisations grow, there is an inherent tendency for them to become more risk-averse by building in systems of control that can make them slower to adapt to changes in their business environment.

■ Small businesses tend to be good innovators. This comes about through their greater adaptability, especially where large amounts of capital are not required. Small firms can also be good innovators where they operate in markets dominated by a small number of larger companies and the only way in which they can gain entry to the market is by developing innovative products aimed at a small group of buyers. The breakfast cereal market in Australia is dominated by a small number of large producers, yet it was a relatively small company that identified a niche for allergen-free and organic snack foods back in 1990 in Melbourne. Norganic has successfully introduced a range of new products to the Australian market since that time.

It is not only small entrepreneurs who create new small businesses. Many larger organisations have also recognised their value and have tried to replicate them at a distance from their own structure. Many large manufacturing organisations operating in mature markets have created autonomous new small-business units to serve rapidly developing or specialist niche markets, free of the bureaucratic culture of the parent organisation. In the education sector, many universities have established small research companies at arm's length from the universities' organisational structures.

While small businesses have certainly seen a resurgence in recent years, it should also be recognised that they have a very high failure rate. Conclusive evidence of the failure rate of small businesses is difficult to obtain, especially in view of the problem of identifying new businesses that do not need to register in the first place.

ARE ENTREPRENEURS BORN OR BRED?

Is there such a thing as an 'entrepreneurship gene'? Further developments in the science of genetics may one day add some evidence to the debate about whether entrepreneurs are born or bred. But what about students leaving university today? There is some anecdotal evidence that some students have 'entrepreneurship genes'. An example is the founder of Nudie Juice, Tim Pethick, who set up the company in 2003 in the front room of his house in Balmain, Sydney. Tim began producing juice made of 'nothing but fruit', with only one stockist, a team of three people (including Tim) and 256 pieces of fruit, making forty bottles of product in the first week. The operation has now grown to a team of over 70 people around Australia with over 5000 stockists (including Coles, Woolworths, Gloria Jeans, McDonald's and 7-Eleven), over three million pieces of fruit per week and a state of the art fruit-squeezing facility in south-east Sydney. Tim built Nudie from the ground up and after two years in business Nudie had turned over $18 million and was recognised as one of the top ten most influential brands in the Asia–Pacific Region.

Of course, for every entrepreneurial success story there are scores of failures, and it is commonly estimated that at least a third of new entrants to self-employment leave within three years— even more during periods of economic recession. Very often, an entrepreneur can be good at creating a business but much weaker at handling the procedures that are necessary to keep a larger organisation on track. Typical of this tendency is Michelle Mone, inventor of the cleavage-enhancing Ultimo bra. She launched her business, MJM International, in 1996 and enjoyed an annual turnover of more than £1 million within just a few years. Her products went on to achieve global fame when Julia Roberts wore an Ultimo bra for her role in the Oscar-winning film *Erin Brockovich*. In 2001, turnover reached £3 million, and Mone announced plans to float her company. But when the planned float failed to take off, her fortunes seemed to unwind. The bank called in the company's overdraft, she began experiencing problems with designers, and a department store cancelled its order, leaving her business with 15,000 unsold bras. It seemed that designing stylish bras for the rich and famous was one thing, but handling relationships with large retail buyers was quite another. Mone pulled her products out of department stores in 2001 to sell direct to the public via a website. This strategy helped Ultimo remain solvent and it re-entered the department store market a few years later. The bras are still sold direct, but are also available in a range of department stores in the United Kingdom and the United States.

So what are the characteristics of an entrepreneur? Most experts tend to agree that a willingness to take risks is crucial—it really does seem to be necessary to speculate in order to accumulate. Of course, taking risks implies that while some entrepreneurs will succeed beyond their wildest dreams, many will fail. Good entrepreneurs are able to pick themselves up quickly following a failure. Being optimistic and spotting opportunities is important, as is the ability to work long hours, and to have a belief in yourself and your ideas (Northouse, 2006).

CRITICAL REFLECTION

It would seem that many would-be entrepreneurs do not set out on the road to entrepreneurship because they have a fear of failure. Some cultures condemn individuals who have failed, but in other countries, such as the United States, there is an environment in which failure is recognised as a sign of a well-intentioned individual who hit a bit of bad luck, and success is about more than having a bit of undeserved good luck. Can this difference in cultural values explain why some countries seem to have a larger number of entrepreneurial companies?

MANAGING INFORMATION

We saw in Chapter 5 how information represents a bridge between an organisation and its environment. It is the means by which a picture of the changing environment is built up within the organisation. Marketing management is responsible for turning information into specific marketing plans. The marketing management function of any organisation requires a constant flow of information for two principal purposes:

1   to provide information as an input to the planning of marketing activities
2   to monitor the implementation of marketing programs and allow corrective action to be taken if performance diverges from target.

A timely supply of appropriate information provides feedback on an organisation's performance, allowing actual performance to be compared with target performance. On the basis of this information, control measures can be applied that seek, where necessary, to put the organisation back on its original targets. Organisations also learn from the past in order to understand the future better. For making longer-term planning decisions, historical information is supplemented by a variety of continuous and ad hoc studies, all designed to allow better-informed decisions to be made.

Marketing information cannot in itself produce decisions: it merely provides data, which must be interpreted by marketing managers. As an interfunctional integrator, marketing information draws data from all functional areas of an organisation, which in turn use data to focus on meeting marketing objectives more effectively.

You will recall from Chapter 5 that to be useful to management, information should be collected from a variety of sources in a systematic manner and turned into knowledge that can be shared throughout the organisation and acted upon. An important task of marketing management is to plan the collection, analysis and dissemination of information in a way that balances the costs of collecting the information against the costs of a poor decision based on inadequate information. A number of factors will determine the efficiency and effectiveness of these activities:

- the accuracy with which the information requirements have been defined. It can be very difficult to identify what information should be of relevance in a company's information-gathering activities and to separate relevance from irrelevance. This is a particular problem for large multi-output firms expanding into new markets or products. The mission statement of an organisation may give some indication of the boundaries for its information search.
- the extensiveness of the search for information. A balance has to be struck between the need for information and the cost of collecting it. The most critical elements of the marketing environment must be identified and the cost of collecting relevant information weighed against the cost that would result from a poorly informed management decision.
- the appropriateness of the sources of information. Information for decision making can usually be obtained from numerous sources; for example, customers' perceptions regarding a product can be measured using a variety of quantitative and qualitative techniques.

- the speed of communication. A marketing manager must facilitate rapid communication of information to the people capable of acting on it. Deciding what information to withhold from an individual and the concise reporting of relevant information can be as important as deciding what information to include if information overload is to be avoided.

Of course, information itself will not produce decisions, and as was noted earlier a preoccupation with data collection and analysis may lead to 'paralysis by analysis'. A crucial skill of management is to interpret information, and a variety of quantitative and qualitative techniques are used to support management decisions. We have seen in previous chapters how rules-based systems have been used to help decisions in relation to such issues as retail location and the allocation of advertisements between different media. Rules-based techniques may need to be supplemented with the intuition and experience of the marketing manager. Rules-based systems for decision support may be fine in stable and predictable environments, where historically collected data may be a good guide to the future. However, they may be of much less value where the environment is changing and the old 'rules' are no longer appropriate. Many successful entrepreneurs have spotted such changes and, using a combination of intuition, experience and analysis, have exploited new opportunities.

Useful metrics to collect

Previous chapters have discussed the importance of market share and related measures in determining benchmarks for actions. Many companies also track brand attitudes, although—as was discussed in Chapter 5—this is far less valuable than is commonly believed. However, mental availability, the propensity for a brand to be thought of in a purchase situation, does relate to behaviour and is becoming popular as a measure for tracking marketing performance, such as advertising. Below are lists of recommended market information to aid in decision making for both broad-scale measures and brand- and product-based measures.

◢ **LEARNING OBJECTIVE**
Understand the importance of information management in marketing management and know some useful metrics to collect

Broad scale measures

- Competitor activity, such as advertising, new product launches, new or extended channels for purchase and/or delivery
- Changes in other key environmental areas
- Technology—new ways of obtaining the product
- Legal/political—changes to laws or reporting requirements
- Social and cultural—changes to how people behave
- Demographic—immigration or other rapid changes to demographics
- Ecological—changing expectations for corporate behaviour in relation to the environment

Brand- and product-based measures

- Market share and changes in market share
- Penetration and changes to penetration
- Average price
- Promotion by week, and subsequent sales
- Average purchase rate
- Repeat buying rate
- Share of category requirements
- Defection rate
- Distribution intensity or coverage by channel
- Brand noticing, recall and recognition
- Advertising
- Effectiveness of ads
- Reach
- Mix by media

Using information for control

So far, we have looked at information primarily as a means of improving planning for the future. But it must not be forgotten that marketing managers have a control function as well as a planning function. Indeed, many people have criticised the marketing profession for being good at planning and sometimes lacking in implementation skills, but much worse at monitoring and evaluating their efforts. Control is an important and often overlooked function of marketing, and the key to effective control is to give the right information to the right people at the right time. Providing too much information can be costly in terms of the effort required to assemble and disseminate it, and can also reduce effective control where the valuable information is hidden among information of secondary importance. A control system will show variances between budgeted performance and actual performance, and will highlight those differences that are beyond a specified zone of tolerance. An analysis of variance from target should also indicate whether the variance is within or beyond the control of the person responsible for meeting the target. If it is beyond his or her control, the issue should become one of revising the target so that it becomes once more achievable. If the variance is the result of factors that are subject to an individual's control, a number of measures can be taken to try to revise behaviour.

Where performance is below target, the reasons may not be immediately obvious. A comprehensive marketing information system can allow an organisation to analyse variance. A uniform fall in sales performance across the organisation, combined with intelligence gained about the state of the market, would suggest that remedial action aimed at improving the performance of individual sales personnel may not be as effective as a reassessment of targets or strategies in the light of the changed sales environment.

Successful control mechanisms require three underlying components to be in place:

1   the setting of targets or standards of expected performance

2   the measurement and evaluation of actual performance

3   the means to take corrective action where necessary.

There is a great deal of evidence of marketers' unwillingness or inability to measure marketing performance (O'Sullivan & Abela, 2007; Seggie, Cavusgil & Phelan, 2007). Some specific reasons were identified by Ambler (2000):

- The board is not marketing or customer oriented, and has no senior marketing representation on it. Little board agenda time is made available to discuss marketing issues.

- Determination and effort may be considered more important than objectivity. To use an analogy, the First World War would never have been won if the soldiers had known the 'score'—it was won by sheer determination.

- Some company boards believe that accountants should be solely responsible for accounting for all that matters. Internal measures may be interpreted as navel gazing, and are no substitute for measuring sales and market share.

- Marketers may argue against having their effectiveness measured too closely by pointing out that marketing is the business of the whole company, and so they cannot be held specifically accountable.

- Marketers are often too busy fighting the next battle and feel that this should take priority over worrying about the last one.

- Marketing effectiveness may be perceived as something essentially unmeasurable, which should be assessed by more subjective 'feel good' or 'good news' aspects.

- The environment changes too fast, so results need to be judged by the new realities, not those in place or forecast when the plan was drawn up.

- Creating new measurement systems takes too long—the current marketing team will have moved on by the time the report comes out.

It is important to note that measuring overall marketing performance is not the same as measuring marketing expenditure effectiveness (for example measuring the sales outcome of specific advertisements, or the sales volumes of individual sales personnel). More importantly, the effectiveness of the marketing expenditure budget cannot be assessed without measuring the change in the asset of brand equity. Brand equity is fundamental to assessment of this broader measure of marketing effectiveness, and the results of marketers' actions should live on after the current financial period. You will recall from Chapter 3 that this corresponds to the mental and physical availability of the brand. There is plenty of evidence of organisations whose marketing is ineffective and who have seen their brand equity diminish. Qantas's decision in 2011 to stop services during a dispute between management and unions caused many commentators to suggest that Qantas's brand equity was in decline. However, there was almost no effect on sales in the months following the dispute. On the other hand, Coles' supermarkets lost market share to competitor Woolworths during the 2000s until their takeover by Wesfarmers. Once Coles began communicating their store refurbishments, lower prices and new ranges, their market share rose against Woolworths. Woolworths, which had been the market leader for more than a decade, did not respond quickly with any new marketing strategies, or even new communications, so it lost share of voice, share of mind, and market share.

Industry insight

Viva España! Marketing Spain as a tourism destination

Many experts in destination marketing agree that Spain has overseen the most successful implementation of a destination marketing program. Key to this success was a tourism marketing campaign launched in 1982 for the football World Cup held in Spain. The campaign used Joan Miró's sun design to symbolise the modernisation of Spain. This logo has since become Spain's tourism logo.

Overseeing the brand is the Instituto de Turismo de España (TURESPAÑA), an administrative unit of the Spanish central government. Its main responsibilities are promoting Spain as a tourism destination in international markets, and support of the marketing of Spanish tourism services abroad in cooperation with regional and local authorities and the private sector.

Key to TURESPAÑA's strategy has been the development of a brand communication strategy that highlights the unique and differentiating elements that a visit to Spain would provide, compared with other competing destinations. The brand values of Spain have particularly focused on the way of living and the general lifestyle existing in Spain; the cultural traditions of Spain; and the size and diversity of the country.

TURESPAÑA was particularly keen to broaden the brand appeal beyond its association with sun and sea vacations. Like many tourist destinations, Spain experiences seasonality and over-concentration of tourism in a few key areas. A key part of TURESPAÑA's marketing strategy has therefore been to encourage visitors to come out of the peak summer season and to explore the diversity of tourism attractions beyond the coastal resorts.

With a country as big and diverse as Spain, TURESPAÑA recognises that it must leverage as much as possible out of its budget by working with others. It has therefore worked with regional and local authorities on a variety of regional brand destination campaigns.

Many commentators agree that Spain has developed and executed one of the most successful examples of national tourism destination branding. The advertising guru Wally Olins noted how until just a few decades ago, Spain was seen as an isolated, backward, poor country on the fringes of Europe. The reality of Spain has changed, and today it is a modern, vibrant and democratic country. The branding campaign reflected the reality of Spain's new position in Europe. The Barcelona Olympic Games of 1992 and the Seville International Exhibition also helped to put the country on the map in many people's minds. The restoration of Spain's major cities, including Barcelona, Valencia and Bilbao, soon inspired confidence among visitors that this was no longer a backward country.

The marketing of Spain as a tourism destination has succeeded where many other countries have failed. Other countries have tried to promote an image that does not reflect reality, or identified particularly indistinctive aspects of a brand. Many new countries have emerged during the past two decades in central and eastern Europe, but the brand development in many of these has made little impact because of the lack of truly distinctive positioning that has value in the minds of potential tourists. Many attempts at destination branding have failed because of the often conflicting demands of tourism marketers to position their brand on the basis of a country's history, while those responsible for inward investment want to drop these images as quickly as possible and portray their country as thoroughly modern. A great achievement of the Spanish tourism branding campaign has been to incorporate many modern icons, such as the Guggenheim museum in Bilbao (pictured), into the brand image without having to rely exclusively on outdated images such as flamenco dancing.

Source: based on Instituto de Turismo de España (TURESPAÑA) website (www.tourspain.es/TourSpan/ Home?Language = en); Olins, 1999

CONCLUSION

This chapter has provided an overview of marketing management. There are now many books about how marketing management can be improved, and this chapter has only been able to provide a summary of the main issues involved. Planning and control is central to marketing management. However, marketing plans do not develop by accident, so it is essential that an organisation has a structure that facilitates the development of a strategy and its implementation. Marketing management cannot be separated from other business functions, especially finance, production management and human resource management. Numerous approaches to improving the effectiveness of an organisation's marketing implementation have been discussed, and the importance of focusing on key processes that create customer value has been stressed.

12

SUMMARY

- The marketing management process is a continual process made up of a marketing audit to assess the current situation, setting marketing objectives, developing marketing strategy, implementation and monitoring of controls.

- Strategic planning outlines the overriding direction of the organisation and tactical planning involves the detailed planning of operations, whereas contingency planning is concerned with outlining potential scenarios and the subsequent response of the organisation should an event arise.

- Planning must incorporate diverse people and functions within an organisation: both horizontally (across marketing, financial and personnel functions) and vertically (individuals and strategic business units within a department).

- A marketing plan is made up of many elements including the executive summary, introduction, vision, mission, SWOT analysis, marketing objectives, strategy, budget and controls.

- The marketing management function can be organised by geographic borders, functional responsibility, product type or market segment. The method or methods chosen will depend upon the organisational structure and business sector.

- Without effective integration of personnel, financial and production, the marketing function and the organisation as a whole will struggle to collaborate and achieve organisational goals.

- Timely and accurate information is power; it not only provides input into marketing activities, but also allows for the control and corrective action to be taken. Useful metrics such as marketing share, penetration, repeat buying rate, competitor activity, mental and physical availability, and defection rate are important metrics to collect.

REVISION QUESTIONS

1   What is the difference between marketing planning and corporate planning? Should they be considered synonymous?

2   Do you agree with the notion that a marketing department can actually be a barrier to the successful development of a marketing orientation? Give examples.

3   What is the value of contingency planning? Identify one sector where the production of contingency plans is likely to have significant marketing benefits, and the factors that need to be taken into account.

4   How does marketing control help marketing planning?

FURTHER READING

Baker, M J (2007), *Marketing Strategy and Management*, 6th edn, Palgrave Macmillan, Basingstoke.

Doyle, P & Stern, P (2006), *Marketing Management and Strategy*, 4th edn, FT Prentice Hall, London.

Kotler, P & Keller, K L (2012), *Marketing Management*, 14th edn, Prentice-Hall, Englewood Cliffs, NJ.

Sargeant, A (2009) *Marketing Management for Nonprofit Organizations*, 3rd edn, Oxford University Press, Oxford.

Please see Chapter 3 for more on metrics.

WEBLINKS

Competition between Coles and Woolworths and its effect on consumers:
www.youtube.com/watch?v=M1et_HBmLYw&feature=youtu.be

Instituto de Turismo de España (TURESPAÑA) website:
www.tourspain.es/TourSpan/ Home?Language = en

Introduction to scenario thinking and planning:
www.gbn.com/about/scenario_planning.php

Planning the marketing mix:
www.cim.co.uk/marketingplanningtool/tech/tech4.asp

Pricing:
www.themanager.org/Knowledgebase/Marketing/Pricing.htm

Super brands in Australia:
www.superbrands-brands.com

Word-of-mouth marketing association:
http://womma.org/main/

◢ Major case study

Marketing a contemporary art museum: The White Rabbit Gallery

By Kim Lehman, University of Tasmania

Source: Courtesy White Rabbit Gallery, Sydney

Introduction

There has been considerable change in the arts and cultural sectors since the 1970s. Increasing pressures on funding and the subsequent need for greater accountability has driven a more professional approach to business processes. Simultaneously consumers have become better educated, have increased disposable income—though less time—and are offered a multitude of competing activities. Museums have had to take account of these social and economic changes, and have had to transition from being just a source

> Increasing pressures on funding and the subsequent need for greater accountability has driven a more professional approach to business processes.

of information and learning towards providing an appealing and satisfying experience in a distinctive environment. In other words, they needed to modify their product offering and the strategies they used to communicate with their consumer. Consequently, there is now a strong emphasis on marketing in the arts and cultural sectors.

The White Rabbit Gallery is an example of a private art museum that has developed a niche within the highly competitive Sydney cultural experience market, and has become significant on a national and international scale (Wilson, 2009). To understand how they have achieved this, we can analyse the philosophy and approach of the Gallery, the nature of their product and their consumers, and the marketing strategies that they have used to connect to them.

Contemporary art as a product

The White Rabbit Gallery is dedicated to Chinese contemporary art produced after 2000. While it is the case that products in the marketing sense can fall anywhere on a continuum between a pure good and a pure service—usually some mix of the two—whether contemporary art (or any cultural item) can be viewed as a product is the subject of some debate (O'Reilly & Kerrigan, 2010). Certainly artists do not view their work as a product driven by consumer needs (Lehman, 2009). However, once the work has been sold, either to a private or institutional buyer, it is another matter. It can then be sold again, auctioned, loaned to a museum or exhibited at will. Furthermore, the work as originally produced forms part of the artist's creative output and therefore part of their brand. And this is partly what determines whether the work sells or not, what price it might fetch, and how collectible it will be. Importantly, when owned by a museum an artwork becomes part of their marketing mix; part of their product offering to visitors.

However, that does not mean that an artwork necessarily has the same attributes as, say, a box of breakfast cereal. Cereal, when viewed through a marketing lens, possesses attributes that can be accentuated (positives) or diminished (negatives), both of which may form part of a marketing campaign theme. For example, at the centre of the marketing for Kellogg's Nutri-Grain is the product claim that it is a healthy food for children. Links to this claim can then be seen in their television commercials, with proud mothers and growing sons interacting, and in Kellogg's choosing to sponsor Iron Man events. Can such marketing communication strategies be effective for artwork? This is a particularly difficult question when the artwork is challenging or is not readily understood by the viewer, as could be said to be the case for Chinese contemporary art. As it happens, these two issues are actually positives for the White Rabbit Gallery brand. The key to understanding why this is so can be found in the make-up of their target market, the cultural consumer.

Are cultural consumers different?

The consumption of cultural products is based not on the utilitarian, functional needs and wants of human behaviour, but on the hedonistic and affective ones—the drive for pleasure and self-gratification (Colbert, 2007). For cultural organisations such as the White Rabbit Gallery this means that their offering needs to be shaped in such a way as to connect to the needs and wants of a consumer whose desire is for a product that goes beyond simply solving a basic consumer 'problem'.

●●● WORK BY CHEN WENLING

Source: Courtesy White Rabbit Gallery, Sydney

Certainly the cultural consumer may have a rational reason for visiting the gallery; for instance to view a work by a favourite artist, or as a 'must see' excursion while on holiday. However, viewing cultural consumers as rational decision makers focused on the functional features and benefits of products ignores a significant motivation: the search for a cultural experience that gives them pleasure, however that might be defined. Cultural consumers are individuals who seek an emotional involvement in an enriching experience. Further, they are not discouraged if the experience challenges them, providing it is authentic (Foo & Rossetto, 1998).

●●● WORKS BY SHI JINDIAN (BIKE) AND WANG LUYAN (WATCH)

Source: Courtesy White Rabbit Gallery, Sydney

Understanding cultural consumer behaviour is important given the significance of cultural tourism to Australia's economy, and to the arts and cultural sectors particularly. Nearly 60 per cent of Australia's 2.6 million international cultural and heritage visitors in 2009 visited a museum or art gallery during their stay. These tourists are also prepared to spend to obtain their cultural experience—the average amount spent per trip (which is also longer than that of other tourists) was $6280, compared with other international visitors who spent on average $3830 (Australian Bureau of Statistics, 2011a).

How White Rabbit communicates its message

As has happened in many product categories, there has been a move away from a mass media approach to marketing in the arts and cultural sectors. For a start, the budgets in these sectors are smaller. This is also true for private art museums such as the White Rabbit Gallery. Significantly, though, cutting through the advertising clutter is perhaps more of an issue than budget. The need to get maximum value from marketing dollars is uppermost in the minds of managers. What are the ways to effectively use small marketing budgets to connect to cultural consumers? White Rabbit Gallery goes about it in three ways.

The collection as a branding device

The individuality of any museum's collection is a vital part of its brand strategies. Although the relative place of the collection within public museums has shifted—collecting for the sake of collecting has been replaced with a focus on the customer—collections and exhibits are still the core product offerings for museums, and represent the point of differentiation with competitors (Kotler, Kotler & Kotler, 2008). This is certainly true for the White Rabbit Gallery, which was established by Kerr and Judith Neilson in a converted knitting factory in the inner city suburb of Chippendale in 2009. Exhibiting a selection of the Neilson collection of contemporary Chinese art, which was personally chosen by Judith Neilson in consultation with Chinese artist Wang Zhiyuan, the gallery is managed by the Neilsons' daughter Paris. Consequently, the White Rabbit Gallery has a very personal approach to the concept of an art museum, with the collection the focal point for the brand.

Creating an experience

This personal approach is reflected in the feel of the museum. While there are professional staff, reception areas, shiny elevators and the various safety items you would expect from a large building open to the public, there is also a sense that you are viewing the private collection of an individual. Indeed, Judith Neilson stresses this aspect: being able to decide which art to exhibit, what to buy or not to buy, all without reference to committees or government funding bodies is one of the major benefits for a private museum (Neilson, 2010).

Cultural consumers also require authenticity of experience. That is, there still needs to be a focus on interpretation and education, which reinforces the credibility of the collection and gives White Rabbit the status of a 'real' art museum. White Rabbit has a significant library open to the public, and has a number of education programs that encourage school and adult learners. For cultural consumers, a privately owned collection is okay, but they would not be attracted to the offering if they felt it was just wealthy people 'playing with' a museum.

The evangelist visitor

This is not the case, and visitors come away from the White Rabbit Gallery satisfied that they have had an authentic experience. Part of that satisfaction relates to the marketing communication interactions between the gallery and the consumer. Attracting visitors tends to done more through public relations than advertising—opening nights, invited speakers, media releases, publishing books and catalogues ... all such devices are used to gain editorial coverage. White Rabbit has a strong social media presence, a comprehensive website (www. whiterabbitcollection.org) and an email newsletter that engages readers. There is a free film club, showing Chinese classics, kung-fu and gangster movies, as well as documentaries and propaganda movies. White Rabbit also runs various events, such as book and poetry readings.

Evident throughout these activities is engagement with the core theme behind the White Rabbit Gallery: genuine enthusiasm for Chinese art and culture and for communicating with the visitor. Consumers recognise the authenticity of the experience, and potentially become 'brand evangelists', meaning they will visit again and encourage others to visit.

●●● INTERIOR AT WHITE RABBIT GALLERY

Source: Courtesy White Rabbit Gallery, Sydney

Conclusion

The White Rabbit Gallery is one of four recently completed privately funded art museums in Australia. Along with the TarraWarra Museum of Art in outer Melbourne, the Lyon Housemuseum in suburban Melbourne and the Museum of Old and New Art (MONA) in Hobart, the White Rabbit Gallery challenges the notion of what an art museum can be in Australia, and provides a alternative experience to the established government-funded public state museums and art galleries.

With the development of the cultural consumer, and the increasing significance of cultural tourism, these art museums are filling a need in Australia's cultural landscape. However, the strategies that art museums such as the White Rabbit Gallery need to use to communicate with cultural consumers have to be carefully considered. By concentrating on what is different about their collection (the core product of a museum) through education and interpretation, seeking to involve visitors in the museum experience, and then developing relationships with them, White Rabbit can provide a memorable and distinctive cultural experience.

Questions

1   Select a cultural institution or event with which you are familiar. Provide a profile of the sort of consumer that would visit it. What characteristics do they have that makes them different from non-visitors? Why is it useful to profile non-visitors?

2   The consumer is said to pass though five stages in the buying process. How does that process relate to visiting an art gallery, and would visitors go through all stages?

3   Will an art museum such as the White Rabbit Gallery have a finite life? What would they need to do to keep appealing to changing consumer tastes?

4   Define the concept of a cultural experience product. What competitors does the White Rabbit Gallery have in this category? Do they have competition from other sectors as well?

5   Consider the profile of the visitor to the White Rabbit Gallery from question 1, as well as the gallery's current marketing strategies. Suggest alternative marketing communication tools that the gallery could use to connect with cultural consumers.

Practitioner profile

Chami Gunasinghe, Marketing Manager, HeartKids Australia

I first knew I wanted a career in advertising or marketing in Year 10 Commerce, when we learnt about the four 'Ps' of marketing. After high school, I completed the advanced certificate in advertising and marketing at University of Technology, Sydney, while working as an advertising executive in a direct marketing firm in North Sydney. This role continued to increase my love for marketing, as I was lucky enough to work with some major clients such as BHP, AFR and King Gee. While in this role, I also completed the Australian direct marketing certificate, which taught me a lot more of the practical side of direct marketing. I then moved on to different agencies and roles, working for other blue-chip clients, such as Telstra, Nokia and Australian Rugby Union.

After over ten years in the industry, I took a break to have my two beautiful children. I wanted to take on a different role and use my previous marketing experience to give back to the community. My role at HeartKids Australia, a charity, has a very personal meaning, as my son got very sick with Kawasaki Disease, an acquired heart condition, when he was a baby. I love my role as marketing manager here: being able to do everything I can to raise awareness as well as organise fundraising campaigns to raise funds and the profile of this charity, for these very special children. Every day six babies are born with heart disease in Australia, so it's a great feeling to be doing my part to help this organisation.

Coming from working in large companies, working at a charity with small budgets has been challenging for me, but very interesting. It has really taught me to look for the best returns for our marketing dollar. I have also really seen the power of social media while working at HeartKids and how it can be one of your best assets when you have limited budgets but need to reach a large audience.

My love for marketing has only grown over the years and I still get a thrill seeing my work in print or on television, and I look forward to learning more about this industry each day.

13

GLOBAL MARKETING

MAXWELL WINCHESTER AND TIFFANY WINCHESTER

◢ Introduction case

Foster's Lager: The taste of Australia that Australians don't drink!

In the 1960s, Foster's Lager was a beer produced by Carlton and United Breweries and sold in its home market in Victoria, Australia. Through licensing agreements and a successful marketing program, by the 1980s it became one of the best-known Australian products in the United Kingdom, Canada and the United States. In 1983, Carlton and United Breweries was bought out by Elders IXL, who changed its name to Foster's Group to reflect its best-known brand in 1990. Although Foster's almost went bankrupt in the late 1980s and early 1990s, it has survived.

Now Foster's Lager is one of the largest beer brands in the world and has become synonymous with Australia, being one of Australia's best-known brands.

Now Foster's Lager is a large beer brand and has become synonymous with Australia, being one of Australia's best-known brands. It is a truly global brand, being brewed under licence in markets as far from Melbourne as Russia and India. In the United Kingdom in 2011, it was Britain's second largest selling beer.

Although Foster's Lager may be seen as the epitome of Aussie iconography for much of the world, paradoxically, in Australia it is not widely available and is not bought by many beer drinkers.

INTRODUCTION

Over the last few decades, businesses have been operating in an increasingly global environment. World trade continues to grow at a healthy pace, which has meant that many marketing careers involve having to market a product or service in a number of countries. Understanding marketing at a global level is therefore crucial for marketers. This chapter provides an overview of the major issues a global marketer needs to consider.

LEARNING OBJECTIVES

After reading this chapter you will be able to:

- compare and contrast the ways companies pursue international markets
- critically evaluate the relevance of different approaches to marketing in a global environment, including standardisation and localisation
- examine how socio-cultural, technological, economic and political forces may affect the marketing mix.

CHAPTER OUTLINE

Introduction

Growth of global marketing

Differences from domestic marketing

Standardisation or localisation?

Global marketing environment

Conclusion

KEY TERMS

country of origin (COO)

electronic data interchange (EDI)

glocalisation

grey market

import quotas

localisation

radio frequency identification (RFID)

regionalisation

socio-cultural environment

standardisation

GROWTH OF GLOBAL MARKETING

Global marketing has been around for many years. Indeed, one of the major incentives for explorers to discover new countries or new, faster ways of reaching foreign countries was to trade.

Growth in world trade has grown twenty-seven-fold since 1950, which is three times higher than world output growth (WTO, 2007). This means that many companies are moving from selling in a domestic market to selling in one or more international markets. International markets provide growth opportunities not just because of their size, but also because they have different needs. Growth can allow a company to gain economies of scale, which makes it more competitive in its original market. Also, by learning to compete with overseas rivals in overseas markets, a company lowers the risk that it will be knocked out of its home market by the entry of better overseas competitors. Staying at home may sound like the safe option but it often turns out to be dangerous, or at least naïve.

 CRITICAL REFLECTION

As a student of marketing you may wonder whether global marketing is that important. However, globally marketed products are everywhere. Consider what actions you took before leaving the house this morning. What products did you use? For example, what products did you use in the shower, what did you have for breakfast? How many of these are globally marketed?

DIFFERENCES FROM DOMESTIC MARKETING

Domestic marketing is marketing aimed at a single market. Generally, this market faces a limit of competitive, economic and market issues, and deals with only one country's customers, though not necessarily one country's competitors.

When companies go global, however, things get more complicated. At the simplest level, the company makes one or more of its marketing mix decisions across national boundaries. The four 'P's of marketing still have to be managed—they just apply differently. Table 13.1 demonstrates a few of the issues that should be considered in a global marketing environment, many of which are covered in greater depth further in this chapter. The key issue to consider is the multi-dimensionality and complexity of foreign markets.

●●● **TABLE 13.1** ISSUES THAT NEED TO BE CONSIDERED IN A GLOBAL MARKETING ENVIRONMENT

MARKETS	These are widespread and sometimes fragmented, and may even be defined differently across countries.
DATA	Primary data may be difficult to obtain and often expensive, and there may be trust factors involved with some secondary data.
POLITICAL SYSTEM	Regimes vary in stability, and political risk an important variable as changes in regulation may affect the freedom for firms to operate, as does the government's attitude towards foreign business.

(Continued)

●●● **TABLE 13.1** ISSUES THAT NEED TO BE CONSIDERED IN A GLOBAL MARKETING ENVIRONMENT (*CONTINUED*)

ECONOMIES	The degree of economic freedom, GDP, population growth and varying exchange rates must all be factored in.
SOCIO-CULTURAL ENVIRONMENT	Buyer behaviour and consumer needs are largely driven by cultural norms, which may be internalised in the individuals, or embodied in institutions. Yet our perception of the needs of the overseas market may be blocked by our own cultural experience.
TECHNOLOGY	Though technology has had a major impact on the global marketplace, many models are not equally applied globally.
LEGAL ISSUES	International companies have to conform to more than one legal system, and laws against competitive behaviour and certain practices may be dramatically different.
ENVIRONMENT	Though some argue the increasing importance of social and environmental issues, each country's definition of what constitutes 'environmentally friendly practices' still varies, as do the commitments towards legally binding agreements.

STANDARDISATION OR LOCALISATION?

▲ **LEARNING OBJECTIVE**
Compare and contrast the ways companies pursue international markets

▲ **standardisation:** Offering the same products everywhere with global marketing campaigns. By standardising products and promotions, the global company forces costs and prices down, and pushes quality and reliability up.

Increasingly companies trade, and even operate across multiple countries. So how should a company globalise? Some argue that the world is becoming a homogenous global village, so a company can use a similar marketing strategy everywhere, and they argue for **standardisation** (for example, see Levitt, 1983). This means that companies would offer the same products everywhere and run global marketing campaigns. By standardising products and promotions, the global company forces costs and prices down, and pushes quality and reliability up. People who subscribe to this point of view would argue that customers prefer world-standardised products. According to Levitt (1983: 191), this theory holds 'regardless of what conventional market research and even common sense may suggest about different national and regional tastes, preferences, needs and institutions'. This has worked for some companies (such as Coca-Cola, BMW and Rolex) who offer largely the same products worldwide. It has been argued that standardisation applies particularly well to upscale markets and certain groups, such as young people, business executives and wealthy individuals who themselves are more like 'global citizens'. Take, for example, the British BMW 530d pictured in Figure 13.1. This same vehicle is offered across Europe (with the exception that it is left-hand drive), but also as far away as Asia, Australia and South Africa. You will also find the web pages for each of these countries for BMW very standardised, and often standardised to the extent that the web page will be in English even for countries where English is not the first language.

Other global marketers argue for **localisation**, and are sceptical of the global village idea. They maintain that consumers differ from country to country, and therefore products and advertising must be tailored to different cultures. Sometimes advertisers fail to understand and adapt to foreign cultures. Certainly, even mass appeal brands such as Coca-Cola, Levis, Nike and Apple practise some localisation (such as testing ads to see which ones might work in which countries).

●●● **FIGURE 13.1** BMW OFTEN STANDARDISES ITS PRODUCTS ACROSS MARKETS

●●● **FIGURE 13.2** DIET COKE BOTTLE LOCALISED FOR KUWAIT

LEARNING OBJECTIVE
Critically evaluate the relevance of different approaches to marketing in a global environment, including standardisation and localisation

localisation: The process by which globally launched campaigns, products and services can be customised and made relevant to the local market; or marketing exclusively to local markets with in-depth knowledge of their needs, wants, tastes and so on.

regionalisation: The process by which marketing concentrates on a population in a particular area that has characteristics that are distinguishable from other areas. A region can be a nation state or a group of nation states, such as Western Europe or South-East Asia.

glocalisation: Global marketing that incorporates considerable local adaptations.

Rugman (2001: 11) argues 'globalisation is a myth and does not exist in terms of a single world market with free trade', citing issues such as cultural differences and government regulations among the external constraints to standardisation. Other constraints include trade restrictions, differences in marketing infrastructure, the character of resource markets, differences in the availability and costs of resources, and differences in competition from one country to another. Rugman recognises **regionalisation**, rather than globalisation.

For example, in the United States the most popular vehicles on the road were built in the US or Canada, for the North American market; North Americans tend to drive large cars on straight wide roads with low speed limits (Pinchin, 2008; Henry, 2008). On the other hand, the top-selling vehicles in Europe are built in Europe, as Europeans tend to like vehicles that are smaller and can handle the twisting and turning roads with higher speed limits (Cato, 2010).

Realistically, neither extreme of the above ideas would work in the real world. Standardisation, while being more efficient, would ignore important cultural differences, and localisation would cost far too much. So is globalised localisation (also known as '**glocalisation**') the answer? This is also called thinking global and acting local. In this ideal world, companies balance the efficiencies of standardising operations with the need for localising. For example, many Pepsi or Coca-Cola products are similar in different countries as products, yet are advertised and packaged differently; Diet Coke, for instance, is largely standardised as a product, but the cans are localised for different countries (see Figure 13.2).

Another example of glocalisation can be found in car companies. For Ford's 'world' car, the Focus, the North American version is distinctly different from what is on offer elsewhere, as it has softer suspension, for example. As pointed out earlier, BMW sells largely the same 5 Series models in different countries and therefore they are largely standardised, but BMW is able to localise to the tastes of local markets by offering different engine combinations. For example, in Europe, where economy is important, among a range of engines the 520d is a popular choice; it offers a four-cylinder turbo diesel motor that can achieve around 1200 kilometres per tank. In Canada, where fuel costs are half as much, only the large six and eight cylinder petrol engines (528i and 535i) are available, and these only achieve around 700 kilometres per tank.

Case study

SABMiller: Glocalisation

In 1895, The South African Breweries Limited (SAB) was incorporated in London. It was listed on the London stock exchange in 1999. The group purchased the Miller Brewing Company in North America in 2002 and changed its name to SABMiller. Its history of overseas expansion, including importing brands Pilsner Urquell and Miller Genuine Draft, has led it to become the world's second largest brewer in terms of volume, trailing only Anheuser-Busch Companies, Inc. It owns the Foster's beer brand in India.

But with fewer opportunities to expand by acquisition, international brewers must find ways to boost their brands, especially in developing countries. 'The key to growth is going to be growing organically, unless people start drinking more, which they probably aren't,' said Harry Schumacher, publisher of *Beer Business Daily*. 'That means taking share from each other, or from wine and spirits' (quoted in Schultz, 2010). To do so, SABMiller is asking managers in its seventy-five countries to focus more on marketing and less on back-office tasks.

Nick Fell, the brewer's marketing director, describes this approach as 'local intimacy'. Examples include (Schultz, 2010: 1):

- Peru, where bottles of its Cusqueña brand feature replica stones of an Incan wall that, Fell said, 'pay tribute to the elite standard of Inca craftsmanship that continues to this day in every bottle'. Bottles of the Arequipeña brand show fighting bulls, a tribute to the bull-on-bull sport fighting popular in a region of the country.

- Romania, where a TV ad shows an empty barrel of Timiș, oreana beer being rolled out of a bar then back in time through quaint villages, scenic landscapes and finally filled at the original 18th-century brewer that created the beer.

- Ecuador, where the brewer plays off the nation's tradition of holding many festivals by offering limited-edition packaging for Pilsner and giving away gifts and prizes to the community.

- Poland, where the Tyskie campaign includes a group of Czechs raising their glasses to the Polish brew.

SABMiller still spends a lot on its standardised international brands—Miller Genuine Draft was introduced in Colombia and Peru in 2010—but when doing so, the brewer looks to access 'a quick cultural reference that will help people understand what the brand stands for,' Mr Fell said (Schultz, 2010). For example, in Columbia, Miller Genuine Draft was positioned as 'an icon of cosmopolitan cool' to appeal in urban areas.

In 2012, the company reported revenues of US$31 billion (up 11 per cent) and profits of US$5.6 billion. Lager volume sales were up 5 per cent on 2011. Much of this sales growth came from Africa and South America.

Questions

1. To what extent do you think that SABMiller follows a standardised or customised approach?

2. 'The best promotional strategy for a global company is a standardised one.' Discuss this statement, giving examples from a global company of your choice.

GLOBAL MARKETING ENVIRONMENT

▲ **LEARNING OBJECTIVE**
Examine how socio-cultural, technological, economic and political forces may affect the marketing mix.

As we can see, most companies do have to localise but also like to globalise efficiently. There are a number of factors that marketers have to consider in determining the extent to which they localise a product or service. These fall into four categories: the socio-cultural environment, the technological environment, the political and legal environment, and the economic environment.

Socio-cultural environment

The differences in **socio-cultural environments** between markets is the most important consideration for global marketers. The global marketer must study and understand the culture(s) of the countries in which they will be doing business and incorporate this understanding into the marketing planning process. Buyer behaviour and consumer needs are largely driven by cultural norms, so knowledge of the cultural environment matters for two main reasons:

▲ **socio-cultural environment:** The various institutions and forces that affect society's values, perceptions and behaviours, and determine its culture.

1   It is a major factor in shaping marketing mix.

2   It can pinpoint market opportunities.

So what is culture? These are some of the ways it has been defined:

■   'The sum total of the beliefs, rules, techniques, institutions, and artifacts that characterise human populations.' (Brady & Isaac, 1975)

■   'That complex whole which includes knowledge, belief, art, morals, law, custom, and other capabilities acquired by man as a member of society.' (Tylor, 1920)

■   'The collective programming of the mind which distinguishes the members of one human group from another ... Culture, in this sense, includes systems of values; and values are among the building blocks of culture.' (Hofstede, 1984)

In essence, culture has three factors:

1   It can be learnt—you are born into a culture and acquire its norms.

2   It is dynamic—it dictates acceptable behaviour, which can change.

3   It is subjective—we attribute meaning to events or practices based on our experience.

The easiest way to understand culture is to look at the elements that can make up a culture, including language, religion, customs and manners.

Language

Language is critical to culture because it is the primary means used to transmit information and ideas. Knowledge of a local language can permit a clearer understanding of a situation, provide access to local people, and allow the person to pick up nuances, implied meanings and other information that is not stated outright. Thus, countries with more than one spoken language have more than one culture. For example, Canada has two official languages and there is an English-speaking culture and a French-speaking culture. For a Canadian marketer, this means that all promotional campaigns must be in both French and English, and a balance must be struck in order to appeal to both sets of cultures, and not alienate or even annoy the other.

Unspoken language also has culture relevance, most importantly in non-verbal cues and/or gestures. Gestures are culture-specific and can convey very different meanings in different social or cultural settings. Although some gestures, such as pointing, differ little from one place to another (though in some cultures it can be considered rude), most gestures do not have invariable or universal meanings but connote specific meanings in particular cultures. For example, the 'okay' gesture, made by connecting the thumb and forefinger and holding the other fingers mainly straight, may symbolise the word *okay* to us, but in some parts of the Middle East and South America the gesture is considered vulgar (Armstrong & Wagner, 2003).

But surely English is, well, English? Anyone that has travelled between Australia, the United States, Canada and the United Kingdom will be familiar with regional variations. Often the same word can have different meanings in two different countries and different words are used to mean the same thing. For example, are they french fries, potato chips or crisps? In the evening, is your main meal dinner, tea or supper? Are they pants or trousers; flip-flops or thongs?

Religion

Religions also affect culture, as they influence lifestyles, beliefs, values and attitudes. Religion can have a dramatic effect on the way people in a society act towards each other and towards those in other societies. Religion also influences the work habits of people, and the work and social customs (from the days of the week on which people work to their dietary habits), as well as politics and business. Many global companies have struggled to not cause offence to different religions as they have expanded. For example, any food company wishing to expand to the Middle East has to ensure there are no pork products in food production and that the food is halal compliant.

Customs and manners

Customs are common or established practices, and manners are behaviours regarded as appropriate in a particular society. For example, how do you greet a business colleague from the United States? France? China? Brazil? What about something as simple as a business lunch: do you talk business or talk about your family? Again, the customs and manners of the country you are in, or the culture of the people with you, can determine what types of behaviours you display.

CRITICAL REFLECTION

Can you think of any company that has successfully standardised service? What are the risks in standardising service?

Impact on product

Certain products are more culture-bound than other products. For example, food needs to be adapted to suit different markets, while computer chips are a standardised global product. Cultural values can also determine consumers' buying motivations, so where Americans tend to be more concerned about features when buying a car, Europeans tend to be more concerned about build quality, such as panel fit and paint finish, or the vehicle's design.

Cultural norms can present market opportunities and threats. One could assume that since Italians do not tend to have a lot of canned food, this could present a business opportunity. But according to Italian culture, food does not come in a can!

Looking back at the standardisation or localisation discussion, a company should try to standardise as much as feasible, without losing the uniqueness of localisation for that particular culture.

There are three levels of product attributes that should be considered in determining the level of standardisation:

1   Physical attributes (size, weight, colour and so on) offer the greatest potential for economies of scale. Physical attributes are obviously the easiest to standardise, especially as there is a trend for international standardisation (accredited by schemes such as CEN, CENELEC, ETSI and ISO). But some differences—such as climate, usual sizes and packaging, technical standards, hygiene regulations and basic differences in consumer taste—still need to be recognised. For example, people's taste preferences differ in different countries, so colas in Asia tend to be sweeter and less bubbly, while colas in the United States tend to be more bubbly and sweeter. If you went into a pub in Britain and asked for an ale, you would likely come up with a large glass of lukewarm, dark beer. In most other countries you'd end up with a bottle of ice-cold, light-coloured beer. Thus, just as different countries have different languages, cultural differences are reflected in the physical attributes of the product. As well, different countries have different laws and regulations for nutrition and ingredients. In some countries such as Australia and New Zealand, fast food must have nutrition information printed on burger wrappings, while in others this is not necessary.

2   Service attributes, on the other hand, are more difficult to standardise as they are more heavily dependent on culture. Therefore there are limited potential for pure economies of scale. However, there is some potential for economies related to learning, so international transfer of knowledge is a key issue. Delivery processes vary cross-culturally, as do customer interactions. One simply has to dine in restaurants around the world to see the different attitudes towards service. For example, in a typical dining experience in a pub in Britain, you would choose your own table, order at the bar and pay at the bar (every cost is included in the bill), then your food would be brought out to you. In a typical Canadian pub restaurant, you must be seated by the host or hostess, your menus are brought to you, you give your order to the waiter or waitress, your food is brought out to you, you are then checked on by your waiter or waitress at least once to make sure 'everything is awesome', then your bill is brought to you, which you pay. In addition to the cost of the food prices on the menu, you are expected to pay provincial and federal taxes and a tip.

3   Categories of symbolic attributes include symbolic associations related to physical attributes, such as colour, shape or meanings related to brand name. Colour is important to consider, as different colours have different meanings in different cultures. Black is not universally the colour of mourning, as in Western cultures. In Asia, the colour of mourning is often white, in Brazil purple, and in Mexico yellow. The colour red symbolises good fortune in China, while in Turkey it symbolises death. Pink is seen as a feminine colour in the United States, while it can be yellow that is considered feminine in other parts of the world. And it doesn't end there! Mints in the United States or the United Kingdom are usually wrapped in blue or green, but in Africa they would be wrapped in red. While we may be very used to a lemon scent suggesting freshness,

it is associated with illness in the Philippines. And numbers? In the West, we view thirteen as unlucky, whereas the unlucky number is four in Japan and seven in Ghana, Kenya and Singapore (Copeland & Griggs, 1985).

There are also connotative meanings of product design and aesthetics. For example, is it functional? Easy to use? Modern? Luxurious? Symbolic attributes also include consumer perceptions of product origin, such as manufacturing origin ('made in'), country of design and/or country suggested by the brand name. With **country of origin** (COO), it includes the ethnic image of generic products, such as leather from Italy, perfume from France or jeans from the United States. It also reflects the national image of the manufacturing company. However, this image can be diffused by the brand name. Having a 'made in' label, stating the manufacturing origin, legally appended to the product is mostly mandatory in international trade. There is ample evidence that shows that for many products the 'made in' label matters a great deal to consumers. But COO effects are not stable; perceptions change over time. In general, consumers prefer domestic products over imports. The critical factor appears to be the place of manufacture rather than the location of the company's headquarters, though consumer demographics can make a difference. For example, working class Americans will proudly drive domestically built cars, while middle and upper class Americans prefer to overlook domestic cars for European or Japanese models. Also, the significance of COO depends on the product category. Over the last twenty years, there has been a big push by Australian companies and government for consumers to 'buy Australian'. This culture is especially strong with food products. And it isn't limited just to Australia: similar government programs have been implemented in New Zealand, Canada and the United Kingdom, to name a few. To deal with cultural pride and to overcome negative connotations for American companies entering Canada, many add a Canadian maple leaf to their packaging to emphasise the 'Canadian-ness' of the company! McDonald's Canada and Rona, a hardware chain from the United States, both have made a point of having the maple leaf prominent in the logo of their Canadian subsidiaries.

▲ **country of origin (COO):**
The country where the products are made; COO can influence consumers' perceptions regarding the product.

Case study

Starbucks and McDonald's: Two different strategies for coffee drinkers in Australia

McDonald's launched its first McCafé in the Swanston Street store in Melbourne, Australia, in 1993. Sales of coffee at McDonald's stores in Australia were not strong, and as a result the concept of a more sophisticated style of café was developed: the McCafé. Unlike a regular McDonald's store, McCafés sell items such as lattes and cappuccinos in real cups; meanwhile, cakes you'd more likely see in a patisserie are lined up in display cases. The sophisticated culture of coffee drinkers in Australia responded to this so well that the decision was made to take the concept globally. In 2001, it brought the concept to the United States and McDonald's is now in the process of installing McCafés in 14,000 stores across the United States. This has since resulted in the biggest revamp to its global menu in thirty years.

Starbucks is famous for bringing café culture to the United States. They have done particularly well in countries where there was not already an established coffee culture. Starbucks entered the Australian market by opening a store in Sydney in 2000. Their strategy was to bring the famous Starbucks culture of coffee to Australia. However, in Australia there was already a thriving and sophisticated European-style café culture, due to the large numbers of Greek and Italian immigrants, particularly in Melbourne, which is famous for its pavement cafés.

In Melbourne, cafés tend to be small and boutique. Starbucks, with its American style of café culture, did not fare so well (Patterson, Scott & Uncles, 2010). When Starbucks opened its store in the centre of Melbourne's famous Italian café district, Lygon Street, local traders lobbied Melbourne City Council to have the chain store closed down (Fonesca, 2001). Starbucks were not fazed by this reaction and continued training their baristas for the Lygon Street store, in preparation for opening.

However, by 2008, there was a cull of Starbucks stores around Australia, with three quarters of all Australian outlets closed, including the one on Lygon Street (Delany, 2008; Mescall, 2008; Wilson & Petrie, 2008). Starbucks CEO Howard Schultz acknowledged that Australia had presented them with unique challenges to their business. According to the BBC, the answer was much simpler: Starbucks just didn't know how to make good coffee in a country full of people who are passionately snobby about coffee (Mercer, 2008).

Questions

1 In comparing McDonald's and Starbucks, which company standardised their coffee offering and which localised it?
2 Does the long-term outcome for both companies support a strategy of standardisation or localisation?

Impact of the socio-cultural environment on price

Pricing is a complex aspect of international marketing, and most companies have different prices for the same product in different markets. One question that remains to be seen is will the internet change this?

The degree of willingness to pay for a certain product varies across cultures. Take food, for example: its relative importance varies between cultures. In the United States, Canada and the United Kingdom, people like 'cheap' food, therefore only around 10 per cent of disposable income is spent on food. This trend is changing in the United Kingdom. However, for cultures in Australia, France, Germany and Italy, food is more important: hence people spend more—closer to 15 per cent of disposable income.

Case study
What are they willing to pay? Exploiting locals until the grey market opens

Marketers work hard to keep brands exclusively distributed in markets, which sometimes enables them to charge a price premium in wealthier markets. With the introduction of internet shopping and multinational retail chains, **grey market** imports have become more problematic.

One famous example was the time Tesco, one of the world's largest retail companies, began importing Levis jeans directly from the United States, then selling them in its stores at significantly lower prices than the authorised retailers. Levi Strauss & Co. took legal action trying to stop Tesco importing their products from other countries without buying them from the authorised distributors in the United Kingdom (Antia, Bergen & Dutta, 2004).

◢ **grey market:** A market where an agent imports a brand without using the brand owner's distribution network. This can mean the brand owner can lose control of the pricing and distribution of its brand in a particular market.

Impact on promotion

There is a number of key decisions that a global company must think about when working with promotion, but the largest is whether to use global (standardised) or local communication policies, and how these transfer into standardisation versus localisation of advertising campaigns. Which strategies and executions should be adapted to local markets? And is a basic ad strategy more standardisable than execution?

The company must question how to account for cultural cues to avoid blunders in multi-local campaigns. We've already discussed issues such as the symbolic attributes of the product, but how can these be communicated? In high-context cultures (such as parts of Asia), communication is more indirect and subtle, so there should be less copy and more symbols. In low-context cultures (such as Western Europe or Australia), the trend is for more copy and factual communication.

Local cultural taboos and norms also influence advertising style. For example, it can be more risky to use sexual innuendos in much of the world, compared with in Europe or Australia. Advertising laws can also influence to what extent sex is represented in advertising. For example, Guidere (2012) describes two advertisements for Tuscany Perfume, one for Europe and one for the Arab market. The ad campaign was adapted slightly to reduce the sexual nature of the ad for the Arab market, although social mores are relaxing in some parts of the Arab world. For example, while in most Arabian countries very little exposed skin would be acceptable, the Dove ad shown in the United Arab Emirates shows a woman's shoulders and most of her legs (see www.youtube.com/watch?v=xE5VIS1O7KA). By comparison, Singapore's version of the Dove campaign shows much more of the woman's body (see www.youtube.com/watch?v=yS3cyxOdgjo).

Another cultural issue to be aware of in promotion is the representation of gender roles. For example, in Saudi Arabia, women may appear only in those commercials that relate to family affairs, and their appearance must be in a manner deemed 'decent' and that ensures 'feminine dignity'. Women must wear long dresses that fully cover their bodies except for their face and palms.

Another issue is with the family model: what individual roles are taken on by each person in the family? In the United Kingdom, for example, laundry powder is often advertised by having a woman discuss dirty clothes. However, in recent years there has been a shift to showing men and women sharing domestic responsibilities.

Another interesting culturally relevant aspect of advertising is the use of humour. Humour is extremely culturally specific, and ads that choose to use humour often need a less standardised campaign, as what may be funny in one culture may be seen as odd, dull or even rude and offensive in others. An example of this was the 'Where the bloody hell are you?' campaign for Tourism Australia. The campaign was banned in Canada for using the word 'hell' and banned in the United Kingdom for using the word 'bloody'. Similarly, while in the United Kingdom use of the word 'bloody' is considered unacceptable, road safety campaigns in the state of Victoria, Australia, have been using the 'If you drink then drive, you're a bloody idiot' campaign for many years without significant uproar.

Case study

Range Rover is a posh brand and practical for farmers ... or is it?

Land Rover released the Range Rover in 1970. It was an upmarket, more luxurious four-wheel drive vehicle aimed at wealthier farmers in the United Kingdom's 'country set'. To this day, a Range Rover in the UK is seen as a status symbol for those who are farmers or who live in the countryside.

Range Rover has seen growth in other market segments, too. It is now known as being popular with city familes (for the 'school run') and with middle-aged executives.

Question

Do you think Range Rover could viably target any of the segments discussed above in China? Why or why not?

Impact on place

In the marketing mix, place is defined as the location where a product can be purchased. It is often referred to as the distribution channel. It can include any physical stores as well as virtual stores on the internet. There are a number of place variables for consideration, such as channels of distribution, outlet locations, sales territories and warehousing system. Transport infrastructure is also very important, as products will be hard to distribute if transportation infrastructure is insufficient. Another aspect that varies globally is available shelf space, which is also affected by the size of stores carrying the product. Globally, retail outlets may be very different: consider a US superstore versus a European boutique.

The cultural implications of place may not be as obvious as those of product or promotion, but they are still important to consider. Take shopping behaviour, for example. Culture may affect what people consider time wasted. And what about the standard for return of goods? In the United States, most retailers pride themselves on a 'no questions asked' policy for return of goods for up to twenty-eight days. In other countries, you may buy something from a retailer and never be able to return it.

Other place variables may be the opening hours. We've already mentioned that religion can impact what days people work on, but what about what hours they can work? These may vary between different cultures.

Another global trend is the spread of hypermarkets. However, these types of super-discount stores will not and do not work everywhere. Australia, for example, is a vast country but is heavily urbanised. So major retail companies are concentrated in those urbanised areas. Portugal is small but the people are spread out—so hypermarkets don't work so well there.

Key distribution channels worldwide are summarised in Table 13.2.

●●● **TABLE 13.2** KEY DISTRIBUTION CHANNELS GLOBALLY

RETAIL OUTLETS	WHOLESALE AND MAJOR DISTRIBUTORS
Type and size of retail outlets	Short versus long distribution channels
Degree of concentration of major retail companies	Relationship of manufacturers to wholesalers and retailers
Product range carried in particular type of stores	
Services and interaction with shoppers in the store environment	Degree of conflict within the distribution system

CRITICAL REFLECTION

Do these changes affect culture? Is culture affected by the increase in hypermarkets?

The reverse relationship can also be explored: what impact do elements of place have on culture? Multinational retailers prefer retail parks as they cost less per square metre of retail space, have lower council taxes and allow retailers to offer more car parking. However, an increase in retail parks affects town planning.

Technological environment

Technology has transformed the global marketplace in terms of logistics and transportation, as well as communication. Improvements to fax, phone, mobile phone and email technologies have greatly influenced the way marketers can communicate. Previously, one of the greatest developments was said to be the advances in e-commerce, although we would argue that more recently social networking sites (such as MySpace, Facebook and Twitter) have had a greater influence on marketing.

Impact on the marketing mix

The impact of technology on the marketing mix has therefore been considerable. Products and services can be made more cheaply and to a higher standard. Distribution has been changed by new technologies and advancements in logistics and transportation (such as **EDI** or **RFID**). One can now read books via the internet and book air tickets without going to a travel agent. Communication with consumers has also changed. Banner advertising is much more common, and customer relationship management (CRM) has been considerably affected by advances in technology. Again, similar to the standardising services discussion earlier, the culture's uptake of technology 'enhanced' service may be reflective of their attitude towards service in general.

But with all these technological advances, come many considerations for international marketing. For instance, three questions that may need to be asked are:

1   Do copyright, intellectual property laws or patents protect technology in other countries?
2   Does your technology conform to local laws? For example, the plug types and voltages are different in different countries (see Figure 13.3). Pity the poor person who plugs their North American (110V) PlayStation into a UK plug (220V) without a converter … unless they enjoy the smell of burnt plastic!
3   Are technologies at different stages in the product life cycle in various countries? For example, there are different DVD region codes around the world, allowing more control over movie release dates (and price changes).

EDI (electronic data interchange): The structured transmission of data between organisations by electronic means. It is used to exchange information automatically between organisations, leading to far-reaching efficiencies.

RFID (radio frequency identification): A device, usually in the form of a tag, attached to a product that allows tracking of its movement. It is commonly used in a supply chain operation or in retailing for security purposes.

●●● **FIGURE 13.3** ELECTRICAL ITEMS HAVE DIFFERENT VOLTAGES AND PLUGS IN DIFFERENT PARTS OF THE WORLD

With regards to copyright and intellectual property laws, consider China, Europe's fastest growing export market. Exports from the European Union to China grew by 75 per cent between 2003 and 2007, yet it is still not the biggest export market for the EU. The EU still exported more to the 7.5 million people who live in Switzerland than the 1.3 billion people who live in China. Why? Barriers to trade in China are estimated to cost EU businesses €21 billion in lost trade opportunities every year, and this figure changes dramatically depending on how one defines 'business costs'. Intellectual property rights theft remains a huge problem for European businesses in China. Almost 60 per cent of all counterfeit goods seized at European borders in 2006 came from China.

But think back to how cultures are different in values and attitudes. While the WTO has sent China many warnings regarding its black market, and the United States has lodged eight complaints against China with the WTO—more than any other government—China still continues to generate revenue from its black market. Why? Because Chinese culture does not see the black market as an issue (Bennett, 2009).

Social networking—the global marketing potential ... and the reality

A social network is an online community of people who share interests or activities, or who are interested in exploring the interests and activities of others. The potential for social networking is vast, and its success thus far marks a dynamic shift in how people are using the internet. It has changed how people search for information, and how we create and participate in social spaces with other individuals.

For a marketer, social networks can be efficient platforms for spreading the marketing message, as they often have large volumes of visitors and thousands of page views. Positive comments include:

- 'The social networking strategy is *not* optional. It's imperative.' (Kringdon, 2006: 1)
- 'Popular social networking sites, including MySpace and Facebook, are changing the human fabric of the Internet and have the potential to pay off big for investors.' (Knowledge@ Wharton, 2006: 1)

From these glowing reviews, one could assume that globally marketing via a social network is the next big development.

The reality of marketing via social networks, however, entails some complications. For example, a study of liking a brand on Facebook suggested that under 1 per cent of those who like a brand on Facebook actually engage with the brand regularly (Nelson-Field & Taylor, 2012). Network access and internet usage varies around the world, as does the culture of e-commerce. Globally speaking, the United States makes up less than 20 per cent of the world's connected population but accounts for over 80 per cent of e-commerce transactions, so the e-commerce model is more viable in some places than others. E-commerce provides the potential for shifting consumers to more efficient distribution channels, but unless consumers are willing to take it up, social networking sites become little more than just another communication tool, rather than driving customers to websites for purchases. This issue has been highlighted in Europe, where the penetration of credit cards is a fraction of what it is in the United States: as a result, in many European countries debit cards now come with a number like a credit card, so that consumers can use their savings accounts to buy products online.

Companies themselves aren't social by design, and are generally confused by how to incorporate social strategies into what they do (Slutsky, 2011). Because social networking is still relatively new, most companies have no structure in place, and limited or no knowledge in the marketing teams of how to use social networking for global marketing. And just because it is there, doesn't mean you can use it! Social networking sites have been blocked intermittently in several countries, including Syria, China and Iran. Iran unblocked Facebook in 2009, but it is still blocked in some other countries such as China. Many workplaces also restrict access to it.

Case study
Facebook aims to double its global user base

Mark Zuckerberg, founder of Facebook, predicts that the mobile web will have a key role in the future of social media, particularly in India and other localities, where PC penetration levels are comparatively low. 'We are getting our first crop of countries now that have more mobile usage than web usage,' he said. 'I think most people think it's only a matter of time before that starts happening more universally' (Bradshaw & Gelles, 2010: 1). Mobile ad spend is set to rise from US$2.3 billion in 2009 to around $24.1 billion by 2015, with much of that growth coming from China and India (Smith, 2010). Combined with fast-moving consumer goods (FMCG) brands in India upping their spending on online advertising, most likely tripling their online spending, India's online market looks like a fantastic option for online campaigns.

However, in reality, there are other issues.

From a company perspective, senior management are mainly from a generation that did not spend their time on the internet. Also, the availability of technology may be an issue: for online-video advertising to take off in the country, there is a need to increase broadband penetration, as it is not yet fast enough to handle the videos and other media that FMCG companies use for internet marketing.

On the other hand, Saurabh Bhatia, co-founder and chief business officer of video ad network Vdopia, said, 'FMCG brands in India are increasingly spending online, and this is a growing trend. Nevertheless there is still a long way to go, because FMCG brands are still experimenting with the medium, whereas by now it should have already been a part of their media plan' (Thomas, 2009: 1).

Questions

1   If you were working for a company that wanted to expand into India, what would you recommend?

2   What external issues do international marketers need to consider before investing heavily in social media?

Political and legal environment

Marketers looking to operate in foreign countries must understand that it is not possible to transfer principles and practices from domestic to foreign markets in a straightforward manner, since political and legal systems of different countries vary.

The political environment can be defined as 'any national or international political factor that can affect the organisation's operations or its decision making' (Doole & Lowe, 2008: 15).

The basics of political influence include the current government's attitude towards business, the freedom for firms to operate and the stability of political regimes, and therefore possible changes in regulations. These can be influenced by political parties and interest groups, as well as local governments. Political influence can therefore define the political risk and stability of the environment in which the global marketer must operate.

The political system can be broken down into three main components:

1   political system stability

2   form of government

3   parties and interest groups.

Political system stability is probably the most important political factor, as it can have a major impact on the economic development of a country. If the political regime is unstable, it makes the environment itself less predictable. This is key, because stability influences the perceived risk of investors, as predictability can be one of the factors for success.

Different forms of government vary in the extent to which they permit political participation by the general population. The word 'democracy' is derived from the Ancient Greek *demos* meaning 'people' or 'citizens' and *kratos* meaning 'rule' or 'strength'—thus the implication is that people are politically and legally equal. In a true democratic government, citizens are entitled to freedom of thought, opinion, belief, speech and association. They hold elections where voters decide who will represent them, and there is a limited term for elected officials. Countries which are on the more democratic end of the spectrum include Canada, Australia, New Zealand, the United States, the

United Kingdom and Denmark. In a totalitarian government, a single agent (individual, group or party) monopolises all political power. Forms of totalitarianism include:

- authoritarianism—where one group has power over all others
- fascism—where the goal is to control people's minds and souls
- secular totalitarianism—where control is enforced through military power
- theocratic totalitarianism—where religious leaders are the political leaders.

Examples of countries more on the totalitarian end of the spectrum include Cuba, Iran and North Korea.

Why does this matter? From a Western democratic perspective, political stability is judged by what kind of government a country has. However, a democratic form of government does not always equate to political stability. Imagine moving from tightly controlled (communist dictatorship) regimes to dealing with democratic politics, and the confusion and chaos this could cause. While stable political environments may allow fast economic progress (for example in China) how far can this go without changes in the political system? A number of authors over the years have observed with interest the preference for global companies to invest in China, while overlooking the more democratic India (Aitra, 2003).

Parties and interest groups are concerned with political parties. Which parties exist? How powerful are they? The role of foreign business can be influenced by the philosophies of those parties. For example, if the Green party gains seats in Germany, how could business there be affected? They could defeat businesses activities that have adverse effects on the environment. Other interest groups could include the influence of unions (for example, one only has to look to France in 2010 to see the influence of unions on their transit system), special interest groups (for example, the pressure that Greenpeace is able to exert on Esso, Shell and governments) and lobbyists. Lobbyists are very important in the United States, Western Europe, Australia and New Zealand, but their ability to influence government depends on a variety of factors, such as the lobbyists' professionalism, the quality of their arguments, their knowledge about who to contact, and the number and importance of supporters they can mobilise.

Depending on who is in power and their view of the world, governments have many different objectives. However, common general themes are maintenance of political sovereignty, enhancement of national prestige and prosperity, national security and protection of cultural identity. The impact of these themes on the marketing mix is explored below.

Impact on product

One of the objectives of governments is to further or maintain their country's international prestige. However, this can lead them to protect or subsidise national industries, creating distorted competition. Global marketers hoping to introduce a new product may have to contend with government views on how competitive their product might be and whether it has the possibility to drive out local businesses. This is why governments support exports with tax incentives, subsidies and governmental assistance, but often discourage imports through tariffs, import controls and non-tariff barriers such as quotas, discriminatory procurement policies, restrictive customs procedures, arbitrary monetary policies and restrictive regulations. All these import regulations have an impact not only on what products you can export to the country, but also how many you can import and what you may have to pay to do so.

All countries want to be competitive, but local labour costs vary considerably. While some trade agreements stipulate minimum social standards in global competition, such as no child labour or forced prisoner labour, and others have a guarantee of minimum wages and freedom of association, not all countries subscribe to these sets of rules, allowing for drastically different products (and prices) to be made.

Another governmental goal is the protection of cultural identity. Each society has specific rules of conduct, which are passed on from one generation to the next. However, rules change over time and can lead to more or less conflict between generations. But when members of society perceive that changes come from outside, resistance is the strongest; for example, the resistance against fast food by some religious groups in India is very strong.

Impact on price

Government action can be a real threat to subsidiary operation, because rules on transferring funds out of the country can impact where and how much money is transferred. Subsidies need to make use of sourcing to remain competitive. For example, agricultural subsidies make it difficult for foreign marketers of processed food to compete on price.

Case study

Anti-competitive practices: Can marketers get away with them?

Most countries a global marketer will enter have some form of law against anti-competitive behaviour. However, putting such laws into action is very difficult for many of the competition watchdogs. The Australian Competition and Consumer Commission (ACCC) has conducted many investigations in industries such as airlines and fuel companies, often with little legal action taking place at the end of such investigations. This type of scenario is not uncommon in other countries or regions.

The European Union is a recent exception, with very large fines handed out to companies such as Microsoft (US$1.4 billion in 2008) and Intel (US$1.45 billion) for anti-competitive behaviour. Is this an indication of what is to come? Do you believe we will see more legal action taken against anti-competitive behaviour globally? Why/why not?

Impact on promotion

Often, promotional material must be adapted because of legal reasons, such as laws governing comparative advertising, what products can be advertised when, product placement in movies or television shows, and deceptive advertising.

Comparative advertising aims to directly compare a product with a competitor's product, but such direct comparison is illegal in many countries. Comparative advertising is very common in the United States (consider the many Coke versus Pepsi or Microsoft versus Apple campaigns). It is restricted in the United Kingdom and Australia, but the use of comparative advertising claims is completely prohibited in Saudi Arabia. In China, trademark owners need to be careful with advertising, as aggressive campaigns, which might work in other countries, can be punishable by law. In China, advertising laws are more about consumer protection than freedom of speech.

Impact on physical availability

In order for a company to get its products or services to another country, it must be able to move them from A to B. However, the political environment may limit market access, causing issues with global logistics and channel decisions. These may occur because of local content laws (such as those in the EU) or balance of payments problems. Governments may impose **import quotas,** or raise the share of local equity in joint ventures. For example, China has a policy to allow foreign company direct investment only if investors would manufacture (to a certain extent) in China. In Australia, international airlines cannot fly domestic flights, yet Australian airline companies can be 100 per cent foreign owned.

◢ **import quotas:** Trade restrictions limiting the amount of commodities allowed to be imported during a specific time period and often by specific countries.

In addition to political environments, global companies have to conform to more than one legal system. In addition to marketing specific laws, they also need to be aware of laws against bribery and corrupt practices, laws regulating competitive behaviour (such as antitrust laws), product liability, bankruptcy, and patents, trademarks and copyrights. All these have an impact on the marketing mix.

Economic environment

When selecting foreign markets for export or investment, global marketers need to consider the economic situation of the country being entered. Currency fluctuations largely determine which markets are attractive. For example, is a strong UK pound good for exporters in the United Kingdom? Is a strong Australian dollar good for Australian universities? While a strong currency may be great if you are heading overseas for a holiday, a strong currency is not good for local exporters.

In the last few years, the British pound and US dollar have both seen a dramatic fall against other major currencies. Such changes have a profound impact on global marketing; for example, the US dollar is of particular concern for Canadian exporters, as their largest export market by far is the United States. Prior to the US dollar fall, a Canadian dollar may have bought 80 cents US. By 2011, the Canadian dollar became stronger than the US currency, with each Canadian dollar fetching about USD$1.05. Add to this the weakening economy in the United States and the effect on Canadian exporters was dramatic, as not only have the price of Canadian imports in relative terms increased by over 20 per cent, but because of the weakening US economy, it is also harder to sell the imports.

Application to business-to-business marketing

Global marketing within the business-to-business context has been influenced by some additional factors not directly relevant to global marketing within the business-to-consumer context. In particular, the move by many large multinational firms towards a global approach to their purchasing has resulted in fundamental changes to business-to-business marketing by their worldwide suppliers.

In recent decades, many multinational firms have introduced global purchasing programs aimed at providing negotiating leverage through pooling worldwide corporate requirements, as well as obtaining worldwide product compatibility and consistent levels of customer service (Capon & Senn, 2010; Quintens, Pauwels & Matthyssens, 2006). In response, many multinational supplier firms have introduced global marketing strategies, increasing the coordination of their business-to-business marketing operations across different countries and introducing global account management for those global customers.

Some large supplier firms have appointed global account managers to coordinate customer-related operations across the different countries in which the supplier and customer organisations operate, and to develop effective relationships between the supplier firm and the global business units of the customer (Harvey et al., 2003). However, those firms often face challenges when first establishing global account management, since their underlying organisational structures still comprise separate country-level subsidiaries, with those subsidiaries traditionally being responsible for customer management (Hastings & Saperstein, 2010).

For firms that don't yet have global operations, entry into foreign markets can provide challenges relating to business-to-business sales strategy. For example, a firm that commences exporting must consider whether to use resellers or its own sales force in foreign markets. If it decides to use its own sales force, the firm must decide whether to recruit salespeople in those markets or to utilise salespeople from its home office (and whether the latter option should involve salespeople being transferred to new overseas sales offices or remaining in the home country but making regular visits to the foreign markets.) Each option has advantages and disadvantages, influenced by the capabilities of the firm and the specific nature of its environment.

CONCLUSION

This chapter has given an introduction to what is a very complex area of marketing. Moving from understanding a domestic market to even a single international market requires an exponential increase in knowledge about a different country's culture, politics and society. A marketer needs to understand the political system of the country they wish to enter. The marketer will need to understand what makes an acceptable advertisement there, and where consumers like to buy the product being marketed. Being a global marketer means operating at another level all together, with far more complexity, as knowledge of so many more countries is required. While many global companies are successful, there are countless examples of such companies that have made mistakes in their global marketing efforts, demonstrating the importance of understanding each new market entered.

13

SUMMARY

- Companies expand globally for two main reasons. First, there may be a limited market in the home country that is already saturated, limiting growth opportunities. Second, it allows for increased levels of production and the efficiencies that can be gained from this, making the company more competitive internationally.

- Marketers have to decide how standardised and localised their marketing mix will be in each market. While standardisation reduces costs, it may lead to market failure.

- In deciding how to adapt or localise a marketing mix for any particular market, a marketer must consider the ways in which the socio-cultural, technological, economic and political forces are different from other markets they operate in.

REVISION QUESTIONS

1. Assess the impact of the political and legal environment on the marketing mix, providing examples of your choice.

2. 'Social networking will revolutionise marketing practices for international marketers.' Assess the relevance of this statement, using examples where appropriate.

3. 'Adapting promotions to a new market is a waste of money—keeping promotions standardised across markets is much more sensible'. Discuss this statement.

4. Outline the four elements of culture and illustrate how these aspects may affect the promotion of products in different countries.

5. Within the socio-cultural environmental forces, there are some global demographic changes marketers have to prepare for. Some of these currently include:

   a an ageing population

   b a decrease in the proportion of traditional nuclear families

   c changing gender roles in the household

   d changes in attitudes towards the environment.

   Take one of these sociocultural changes and choose a product or service you are familiar with. Imagine yourself as an international marketing consultant. What changes do you recommend to your chosen product or service given the demographic change you have focused on?

6   Visit the websites of General Motors and Mercedes-Benz across a number of markets. Although the argument presented in this chapter is that BMW is more standardised than Ford, you will find in this case that the German company is not necessarily more standardised than the American one. Review the websites and consider the communications tactics and products available. Which one is more standardised and more localised to each market? Support your findings with evidence. You will need to know that General Motors uses brands that include Opel in Europe, Vauxhall in the United Kingdom, Holden in Australia and New Zealand, and Chevrolet, Buick, Cadillac and GMC in the rest of the world. Mercedes-Benz have the Mercedes-Benz, Maybach and Smart brands.

FURTHER READING

Brookes, R & Palmer, R A (2004) The *New Global Marketing Reality*, Palgrave Macmillan, New York.

Budden, M (2009) 'Popular everywhere else, why don't Aussies rate Fosters lager?', *Connect*, January–March, p. 84.

Czinkota, M R & Ronkainen, I A (2006) *International Marketing*, 8th edn, Dryden Press, Fort Worth.

Dick, H & Merret, D (2007) *The internationalisation strategies of small-country firms: The Australian experience of globalisation*, Edward Elgar Publishing, Cheltenham.

Funding Universe (2010) 'SABMiller plc history', retrieved 16 June 2012 from <www.fundinguniverse.com/company-histories/SABMiller-plc-Company-History.html>.

Keegan, W J & Hollensen, S (2010) *Global Marketing Management: International Version*, 8th edn, Pearson Education, London.

Main, A (2011) 'The world reaches for a Foster's', *The Australian*, 22 June.

Schultz, E J (2010) 'SABMiller Thinks Globally, but Gets "Intimate" Locally', *AdAge*, 4 October, retrieved 16 May 2012 from <http://adage.com/article?article_id=146256>.

White, L (2009) 'Foster's Lager: From local beer to global icon', *Marketing Intelligence & Planning*, vol. 27, no. 2, pp. 177–90.

WEBLINKS

Advertising Age:
    www.adage.com

Austrade:
    www.austrade.gov.au

EUbusiness:
    www.eubusiness.com

Forbes magazine:
www.forbes.com

Fortune magazine:
http://money.cnn.com/magazines/fortune

Fosters:
www.fosters.com

KnowThis.com:
www.knowthis.com

Mother Jones:
www.motherjones.com

Organisation for Economic Cooperation and Development (OECD):
www.oecd.org

World Trade Organization (WTO):
www.wto.org

◢ **Major case study**

Dilmah Ceylon Tea: Market development in Australia

By Rodney Arambewela, Deakin University

Background

Dilmah Pure Ceylon Tea is a popular brand in the quality end of the Australian tea market. The brand was first introduced in 1984, at a time when the Australian market was dominated by multinational and major national brands such as Lipton, Bushells, Lanchoo, Tetleys, Harris and Twinings, and the barriers to new entry were very high. Sri Lanka was formerly called 'Ceylon'—the country's name was changed to Sri Lanka in 1972, when it became a republic and tea from Sri Lanka has continued to be called 'Ceylon tea' to leverage on the high consumer awareness of the quality of the tea. The launch of Dilmah Ceylon tea was a logical undertaking, but it was challenging to revitalise the Ceylon tea market position in Australia. Ceylon tea exports from Sri Lanka to Australia were at their highest peak in the 1960s and 1970s, accounting for nearly 70 per cent of all teas imported to the country. However, the Ceylon tea market share started to decline in the early 1980s, both in terms of volume and value, and an overhaul of the Ceylon tea marketing strategy was therefore considered necessary to arrest this decline.

Following extensive marketing research and market analysis, a new strategy was developed to consolidate all marketing and promotional efforts on pre-packed pure Ceylon teas imported directly from Sri Lanka. This was to ensure a clear identity for Ceylon tea as single country origin tea compared to other products, which were of mixed origins. The outcome was the launch of Dilmah Pure Ceylon Tea in Australia.

Australian tea market

Australia is among the largest tea-consuming countries in the world, with a per capita consumption of around 0.55 kilograms per year. Tea consumption was much higher in the 1960s, 1970s and 1980s: demographic and lifestyle changes over the years have had a major impact on tea consumption habits and consumer preferences continue to change. The greatest threat to tea came from coffee and carbonated beverages, as consumers looked for variety and convenience. The advent of teabags, green tea and herbal tea products was a direct result of the trends towards convenience and healthy lifestyles, which have had a major impact on the marketing of tea in Australia.

As Table 13.3 indicates, the Australian tea market is currently dominated by two large multinational companies—Unilever and AB Food and Beverage (a subsidiary of Europe's largest food marketing companies)—with a combined share of 56 per cent of the market, followed by numerous products and labels competing with each other for the balance 44 per cent share, indicating a fragmented market. In 2010, the grocery value of tea was estimated at $294.5 million, while the total volume stood at 11,184 tons. The value of the market increased by 2.3 per cent, while the volume decreased by 2.1 per cent. Despite the resourceful competition from multinational companies, Dilmah was able to carve out nearly a 14 per cent share of the market in terms of value and 12 per cent in terms of volume, demonstrating a higher value for its products than most of its competitors.

The brand was first introduced in 1984, at a time when the Australian market was dominated by multinational and major national brands such as Lipton, Bushells, Lanchoo, Tetleys, Harris and Twinings, and the barriers to new entry were very high.

●●● **TABLE 13.3** AUSTRALIAN TEA MARKET

COMPANY/BRAND	VALUE (%)	VOLUME (%)
Unilever	34.9	35.5
AB Food & Beverage	20.8	21.0
Dilmah	13.9	11.7
Tata global	11.5	11.5
Nerada	5.7	7.1
Madura	4.5	3.5
Private labels	2.3	3.5
Others	6.4	6.1

Source: Retail World (2010) 'Grocery market sales and shares', *Annual Report*, December, pp. 46–7

Market development strategy of Dilmah tea

Until the late 1990s, most of the teas consumed in Australia were packed locally by major packers such as Lipton and Bushells, although a small quantity of pre-packed teas were still imported from Sri Lanka, India and other tea producing countries. The packers imported tea in bulk from different sources for blending and packing under their own brand names. Some of these brands were identified with the country of origin, such as Sri Lanka (Ceylon). Although Ceylon tea had a major share of the Australian market in the 1960s and 1970s, with packers using more Ceylon tea in their blends, price competition from new sources of origin such as Indonesia, Papua New Guinea and East Africa drastically affected the pre-eminent position held by Ceylon tea in the market. Moreover, the growing teabag market called for a quick infusion tea, which could be produced through a different process of manufacture called the 'cut, tear and curl (CTC)' method. At this stage all Sri Lankan tea manufacturing was based on the 'orthodox' or traditional method, which focused on the flavour and aroma of tea, while the new sources of origin specialised in CTC teas destined mainly for teabag production. As the Ceylon tea content in the blends and products of major packers declined, the share of Ceylon origin tea in the market dropped to the very low percentage of 8 per cent in 1983, compared to its 70 per cent share in the 1960s and 1970s. This was a major blow to Sri Lankan tea market in Australia and a complete overhaul of the tea marketing strategy for the Ceylon tea brand was therefore necessary.

Successful marketing strategies begin with identification of an attractive market opportunity. It is also about matching market opportunities to the organisation's resources and its objectives. Ceylon tea products were not new to the Australian market, but the challenge was to identify and develop new markets for Ceylon tea given the changes in the marketing environment. Another key challenge to the Ceylon tea concept was repositioning its image as a quality product, but this was hampered by the absence of any distinctive brand name that could be directly identified with the country of origin. The marketing research indicated that the country of origin effects on Ceylon tea products (typically communicated by the phrase 'Pure Ceylon tea packed in Sri Lanka'), has had a significant influence on the quality perception of the product among Australian consumers. Sri Lanka was considered one of the major tea-producing countries in the world, with

Successful marketing strategies begin with identification of an attractive market opportunity. It is also about matching market opportunities to the organisation's resources and its objectives.

a long history and expertise in tea production. While the consumer perception of the quality of Ceylon tea was widespread, the market research also indicated that Australian consumers had little or no access to pure Ceylon tea products, due to the declining Ceylon tea content in products marketed by major packers. This was a major opportunity for Sri Lanka to capitalise on in its future strategic planning to develop brands of its own. So it was not only a case of a pure market development exercise but also of developing a credible identity for Ceylon tea to support market development strategies. There were a number of motivating factors that favoured the entry of a Ceylon tea brand packed in Sri Lanka to be marketed in Australia:

1   the cost advantages that Sri Lanka could achieve due to its low cost of production and packaging at the source

2   sharing the benefits of the profit margins available in the distribution chain

3   the absence of any import duties or taxes for tea in Australia. All tea imports to Australia from any country of origin were exempt from import duties or taxes.

The Sri Lanka Tea Promotion Bureau (a Sri Lankan government entity) in Melbourne, Australia, initiated the new market development efforts with the support of the Sri Lanka Export Development Board (an export promotion agency funded by the government of Sri Lanka) and one of the major Ceylon tea exporters, Merrill J Fernando & Co., to introduce a Sri Lankan owned brand of tea packed in Sri Lanka. The Sri Lanka Tea Promotion Bureau commissioned a number of marketing research studies supported by consumer focus groups, surveys and product sampling to evaluate the market potential for a new Sri Lankan brand of tea followed by rigorous business analysis. This resulted in the development of marketing and communication mix strategies including branding, packaging, advertising and promotion. Freshness and quality were the key attributes that were promoted to differentiate Dilmah from other tea products in the market. The price positioning was between the mainstream retail brands such as Lipton and the imported high-priced speciality teas such as Twinings to reflect its value proposition.

Dilmah was launched as a teabag product initially, but the product range was expanded on a progressive basis to cater to different segments of the market. Dilmah currently markets a wide range of tea products, ranging from gourmet black tea, original gardens teas, green tea, decaffeinated tea, real white tea, organic tea and real chai to a variety of herbal infusions (Dilmah Australia, 2011). It has been responsible for rejuvenating the image of Ceylon tea, as well as rebuilding the trust and confidence of consumers and the tea trade that the 'pure Ceylon tea' concept is marketable.

Questions

1   Based on information provided in the case study, briefly describe the tea marketing environment in Australia in the early 1980s.

2   What are the key factors that prompted Sri Lanka to introduce a Sri Lankan owned tea brand to the Australian market?

3   Describe the process followed by Sri Lanka to introduce Dilmah Ceylon Tea to Australia.

4   Do you think the country of origin has had an impact on the success of Dilmah Ceylon tea in Australia?

5   Visit the Dilmah Ceylon tea website (www.dilmah.com.au) and comment on what future strategies the company should consider in order to sustain its market position in Australia.

Practitioner profile

Elaine Mitchel-Hill, Managing Partner, Ethical Comms, PR Consultancy

I worked in a communications consultancy after graduating, where I found that I really loved PR. It can communicate such complex messages. I left to set up my own business, which I merged four years later with an advertising agency to form a substantial communications consultancy. After six years working on large consumer brands, it seemed obvious to me that sustainability and ethics would become increasingly important, so in 2002 I started up my own PR company, Ethical Comms, to help clients focus specifically on issues of sustainability, ethics and social responsibility.

At the time, this was a move away from mainstream marketing, but I was motivated by my personal values. I never wanted to use my skills just to encourage consumers to consume more things they didn't need. I always wanted to communicate socially important issues effectively through PR.

The main difficulty is still a lack of understanding on the part of potential clients regarding sustainability. They may not consider at first that the issues relate to their own business at all, although there have always been some smaller organisations that grasped the potential market advantage of providing ethical products and they were happy to work in this area. It was less difficult to get clients to focus on corporate social responsibility (CSR), although in some instances this was initially just box ticking. I think, though, that CSR can be harnessed as a business differentiator and driver. Specialist knowledge in this area really helps, and clients work with us because they need guidance and information, so I feel that I am using my time to make a social contribution while engaging with a very wide range of issues that really matter.

I see rising consumer resistance and declining confidence in large corporations and in once-trusted brands. Consumers have become much more demanding and use the internet to research and share concerns. Businesses, brands and the public and third sectors must find ways to be transparent and honest, and to show effectiveness and efficiency in response. CSR is no longer a box-ticking exercise that can be dealt with in isolation—it pervades every area of a company's operations. In order to act, many will have to take a hard look in the mirror and set about making big changes in the way they see the world and the way they do business.

14

SOCIAL RESPONSIBILITY AND ETHICS

ANITA PELEG AND CHARLES GRAHAM

◢ Introduction case

Marketing encouraging recycling in a 'throw away' society

The problem of municipal waste has reached epic proportions in the United Arab Emirates. According to government statistics, the average inhabitant of Abu Dhabi bins 4.2 kilograms of domestic rubbish daily, far in excess of the 1.5 kilogram average for Western countries. Between 2007 and 2008, the Emirates produced nearly 6 million tonnes of waste, most of it simply disposed of in desert landfill and dump sites, where the biodegradable content generates methane, a powerful greenhouse gas that contributes to global warming.

Even if consumer awareness and behaviour changes overnight, recycling has not actually been possible until very recently. The necessary infrastructure has not been in place: there are no domestic collections or public recycling bins, no facilities to handle such a large volume of waste, and no processing plants in the region to convert or recycle items such as paper, plastics and metals. What's more, exporting large quantities of waste for recycling elsewhere defeats the purpose since it would generate further damaging emissions.

A number of private companies have seen the potential to make money from recycling and are now working with the Emirates Environmental Group (EEG), a government agency, both to improve the infrastructure and to change the culture. Recycling in the Emirates is growing, but is still in its very early days.

One such company, Zenath, has invested across the Gulf, including in Abu Dhabi, to collect and recycle papers, plastics and metals, and is building a 1.5 million square foot recycling park in neighbouring Dubai. Another company,

Envirofone, is collecting around a thousand unwanted mobiles a day from workplaces, and from dump bins in schools and universities. They now have plans to collect other forms of e-waste, including laptops, all of which can be locally recycled for profit.

In order to meet targets for reductions in landfill disposal and resource recovery, the biggest stumbling block is now to change the societal habits of the residents of Abu Dhabi. The message to consumers is 'reduce, recycle and reuse', and a major new initiative has recently been launched to encourage these behaviours. In 2011, Majid Al Mansouri (UAE Interact, 2009), who heads the Centre of Waste Management in Abu Dhabi, said:

> We are launching an eco-friendly recycling scheme, the first of its kind in the region, to help make our city a greener place. Its success depends upon the participation of each member of the public and our aim is to create awareness and ensure maximum cooperation.

People are being encouraged to think about what they buy in order to minimise wastage, and to segregate materials at source as part of their daily routine. Colour-coded bins for waste and recyclables are now provided, and an army of volunteers recently went door to door distributing leaflets and offering advice. Incentives will be offered to residents who join the scheme, while penalties are being considered for those who don't.

The necessary infrastructure has not been in place: there are no domestic collections or public recycling bins, no facilities to handle such a large volume of waste, and no processing plants in the region to convert or recycle items such as paper, plastics and metals.

INTRODUCTION

Marketing plays a large part in our lives. How the marketing industry behaves has the potential to both harm and improve society now and in the future.

Every marketing activity involves a relationship between the brand, the consumer and a wide range of other stakeholder groups, each often demanding conflicting returns. Shareholders want profit; consumers like cheaper, better products; and society would like to see precious resources conserved for future generations. Ethical concerns are often created from these differences in outlook. And brands, particularly famous ones, can be very publicly held to account for the way they are manufactured and how they are marketed.

How do marketers decide about what is right and wrong when faced with these conflicting demands? In this chapter, we show you how to identify and avoid questionable marketing practices and improve ethical marketing decision making for societal well-being.

We continue the discussion from Chapter 1 by demonstrating the current and potential contribution of marketing to society, and the way in which sustainability is now shaping the marketing concept.

LEARNING OBJECTIVES

After reading this chapter you will:

- understand the complexities of serving diverse stakeholder groups
- understand the relationship between marketing and ethics
- be familiar with some philosophical definitions of ethics
- understand the ethical challenges faced by marketers in practice
- be familiar with the emerging concept of sustainable marketing
- be able to discuss and analyse questions of ethical and sustainable marketing.

CHAPTER OUTLINE

Introduction

Who needs ethics?

A delicate balance of responsibilities and benefits

Theories of ethics

Ethical marketing in practice

Sustainable marketing

Conclusion

///

KEY TERMS

cause-related
    marketing (CRM)

corporate citizenship

corporate social
    responsibility (CSR)

Ethicability®

ethics

personal selling

triple bottom line (TBL or 3BL)

WHO NEEDS ETHICS?

Ethics has an influence on marketing decision making. There is a clear duty for individuals, organisations and governments to behave ethically in order for society to function to the benefit of all. If the behaviour of any organisation is perceived to be unethical by any of its stakeholder groups, it undermines trust developed sometimes over many years. Marketing plays an important role, but all stakeholders need to behave responsibly within these relationships or risk damaging them.

> **ethics:** The principles of morality (that is, concepts of right and wrong) that influence attitudes and behaviour.

Organisations

According to Mallen Baker (2009) the long-term health and reputation of an organisation and its brands are dependent on the relationships developed with their numerous stakeholders:

> Marketers have a huge responsibility. They define what brands mean to a company's customers. They set the tone for how the company interacts with those customers and other important stakeholders. They create the reasons for it becoming famous or, sometimes, notorious.

> **LEARNING OBJECTIVE**
> Understand the complexities of serving diverse stakeholder groups

Long-term relationships have three requirements that are a significant part of the marketing function. First and foremost, there is a requirement of honesty and transparency. Consumers and all other stakeholders must be able to trust the word of the organisation and see that its commitments are matched by its behaviour. Second, products and services offered must satisfy the needs of the consumer and comply with all relevant legal standards. Third, the organisation is required to create healthy profits so that its existence is a benefit to society, creating employment, wealth and trade with other nations.

How can the operations of any organisation—and in particular its marketing department—benefit society? Twenty years ago, Archie Carroll identified these components of business relationships as **corporate social responsibility (CSR)**, describing them as a pyramid (see Figure 14.1), and adding a philanthropic duty at the apex. Carroll suggested that for a long time it was enough for firms simply to 'do no harm'. Now there is an expectation that firms can and will contribute by doing good. As we will see, marketing does this efficiently to the benefit of the organisation itself, as well as to wider society.

> **corporate social responsibility (CSR):** A commitment by business to behave ethically, to contribute to economic development and to improve the quality of life of the workforce, their families, the local community and society at large.

Responsibilities
Be a good corporate citizen.
Contribute resources to the community.
Improve quality of life.

PHILANTHROPIC

Responsibilities
Be ethical.
Avoid harm.
Obligation to do what is right, just and fair.

ETHICAL

Responsibilities
Obey the law.
Play by the rules of the game.
Law is society's codification of right and wrong.

LEGAL

Responsibilities
Be profitable.
The foundation upon which all others rest.

ECONOMIC

●●● **FIGURE 14.1** THE PYRAMID OF CORPORATE SOCIAL RESPONSIBILITY
Source: Carroll, 1991, p. 42

Cause-related marketing

One way in which marketers now fulfil their corporate social responsibility to the community is by aligning their organisation or brand with a cause that can be supported over time, in collaboration with consumers. In her book *Who Cares Wins*, Sue Adkins reveals how, increasingly, organisations understand the value of engaging with society through such **cause-related marketing (CRM)** because it can help build trust, enhance reputation and ensure consumers understand the values and the principles of the organisation's CSR. By making these programs visible, the marketing department 'helps the organisation translate words and promises into action, offering a win-win-win for business, charities and good causes, and consumers' (Adkins, 2004).

cause-related marketing (CRM): An alliance between a brand and a charity or cause in order to benefit each.

▼ CRITICAL REFLECTION

Melbourne-based Cavill + Co, an experience cause-related marketing (CRM) consultancy, offer the following advice on their website (Cavill + Co., 2012): 'We're committed to long-term partnerships where a CRM campaign reflects a company's commitment to the community as well as one that is an expression of their brand values. CRM is about marketing, and the achievement of marketing outcomes. It is at the commercial end of community engagement and investment and is therefore quite different from pure philanthropy.'

Is it ethical for a marketing manager to regard CRM as a source of competitive advantage? What might cause such thinking to lead to failure or success? How would you measure success or failure?

CRM works best when the cause and the brand share some common purpose, so consumers more easily understand the partnership. It also matters that the cause means something to the customers of the brand. Take the long-running partnership between Pampers and UNICEF, through which vaccines against maternal and neonatal tetanus are delivered to the most vulnerable women and their children around the world. This disease is completely preventable through vaccination, and parents can get involved just by purchasing the brand. A single vaccination is donated for every pack of Pampers bought, and over 45 million have been donated so far. Awareness has been raised through this CRM initiative, which aims to eradicate tetanus completely. The Pampers philanthropic contribution builds trust and reputation for the brand, the connection with UNICEF adds authority, and the program actively engages and involves consumers by playing on the common experience of motherhood.

Long-term sustainable marketing

While consumers have grown to expect organisations to have a social conscience, many have grown cynical of marketing departments whose only motive appears to be profit and who seem to have no obvious link to the charity or community they are promoting. With more and more companies now involved in CRM and touting their commitment to being good corporate citizens, consumers and governments are becoming suspicious of 'green washing'. Groups such as Greenpeace are starting to play a more prominent role in judging the claims made by companies. Another example is Two Tomorrows, a UK-based 'corporate responsibility agency', which releases ratings of how well they consider companies are managing their most pressing environmental and social issues. In 2011, they gave Nestlé, Intel, Nike, Unilever and six other corporations their top AAA rating. Executives take such independent ratings seriously, and benchmark their company's score against others in their industry.

As a result, while CRM initiatives continue to grow, businesses are beginning to understand that their involvement with charitable and societal causes cannot simply be a means of gaining competitive advantage. Stakeholders now expect long-term commitments that assist in reducing the harmful effects of human activity and promote sustainable processes of production.

Shell, for example, must, among other things, balance the profit requirements of its shareholders, which involve oil exploration and extraction in areas of the world where biodiversity is already threatened, with its corporate social responsibilities. Shell invests large sums in researching alternative and sustainable energy sources, including bio-fuel and wind power, and must also constantly clean up the current extraction, production and distribution effects of its carbon fuels. These activities have long-term implications, and the sensitive balancing act is a matter for corporate strategists. However, the company's decisions and actions must be communicated widely and convincingly to the public, who may want to hold the company to account, and this is a marketing function usually handled in partnership with public relations and advertising agencies and other media specialists. Shell, in common with many other major companies, now publish an annual sustainability report that details their impact on the environment and the steps they are taking to mitigate that impact, in as transparent a form as possible.

Increasing societal pressures and new legislation are both challenging marketers to identify and meet emerging long-term needs with more creative solutions. Examples of such solutions include:

- communicating and encouraging environmental responsibility in consumers through cause-related or long-term marketing initiatives, such as the 'Generation Green' package offered by Bendigo Bank
- developing and bringing more sustainable product to market, such as recyclables and products manufactured with natural raw materials or from fair trade or organic sources
- social marketing, as explored in case studies on pages 513 and 525
- social enterprise, which is a new business model that puts long-term societal benefit first, reducing overconsumption and encouraging sustainable practices. For example, as described by Talbot, Tregilgas and Harrison (2002), Tumby Bay was a declining township badly affected by economic change. Through social enterprise initiatives, the locals formed an action group to revitalise the town, creating streetscaping projects, a new information technology hub and a marina. As a result, retirees were attracted to the town and have now boosted the population again.

New socially responsible roles in marketing

As a result of the new emphasis on cause-related marketing, corporate social responsibility and social marketing, new management roles and responsibilities are developing within marketing departments. These marketing roles are attracting people with special interests and experience in sustainability, the environment or specific charitable and humanitarian projects. For example, at the Melbourne Football Club a large department works closely with the local community, developing family days, after-school clubs and other activities. They also support several charitable projects that match the concerns of the board of directors or the players or complement the club's mission, such as Berry Street Foster Care Camp, the Lord Mayor's Charitable Fund and the Prostate Cancer Foundation of Australia.

There is mutual gain in this new type of work; individual managers drive initiatives that they may well feel passionate about, while the club clearly benefits from the positive relationships developed with a wide variety of other stakeholders.

Application to business-to-business marketing

Ethical behaviour is also important within business-to-business marketing environments, since researchers have found that trust appears to be linked to cooperation, commitment and customer satisfaction (Wood et al., 2008). As explained in the case study on page 528, a firm risks loss of business if an organisational customer with high ethical standards (such as Billabong) discovers the supplier is operating unethically. This is particularly true if the customer organisation believes it could have been disadvantaged by the unethical practice, as illustrated earlier in reference to an oil company that discovered bribery of members of its staff by a steel supplier.

Many business-to-business marketing organisations recognise the appropriateness of adopting relationship marketing practices. However, cooperative relationships cannot be maintained without ethical integrity, since many customer organisations seek supply partners that demonstrate a commitment to a long-term relationship based on reliability and trustworthiness (Murphy, Laczniak & Wood, 2007). This is especially true in situations in which confidential information needs to be shared between suppliers and customer organisations as part of cooperative development programs, such as the introduction of a new car model that requires the simultaneous development of new components.

In some situations, a reputation for strong compliance to ethical standards provides clear marketing benefits. The market research industry provides an interesting example. Many research firms demonstrate awareness and enforcement of ethical codes of behaviour to develop a perception of high-quality, reliable research within their organisational markets (Ferrell, Hartline & McDaniel, 1998). No doubt, such standards would reassure many marketing organisations purchasing and using market research services.

Salespeople often face an ethical tension due to the conflicting pressures of achieving immediate sales results and long-term customer satisfaction (Abratt & Penman, 2002). Since business-to-business salespeople often work away from their office, with little supervision, and are often under pressure to achieve results, they are susceptible to potential ethical dilemmas (Mulki, Jaramillo & Locander, 2009). Salespeople and their managers often have close contact with various members of buying centres within their major customer organisations. Not surprisingly, such close relationships occasionally lead to unethical behaviour between individuals involved in purchase negotiations with large revenues (and rewards) at stake.

It seems appropriate for business-to-business marketing organisations to include ethics-related content within salesforce training programs, and to ensure that sales management clearly identifies what is considered to be appropriate (and inappropriate) salesperson behaviour. Sales managers also should emphasise that unethical behaviour is likely to undermine attempts at customer relationship development and, therefore, to adversely affect long-term sales performance (Ferrell, Hartline & McDaniel, 1998).

For those companies marketing to governments and not-for profit organisations, there is a need to recognise that such organisations typically have stakeholder pressures to demonstrate the highest of ethical standards in all of the operations, including those related to purchasing. Besides the need for compliance with demanding ethical standards, there is often also a requirement to comply with inflexible bidding or tender procedures for all major supply arrangements.

Internal ethics

Successful marketing focuses not only on external stakeholders but also on internal relationships. Any organisation has a responsibility to treat employees with respect and fairness, ensuring confidentiality, anti-discrimination policies, and procedures to encourage professional and self-development of the individual. For the organisation, the employee is the first customer. Employees that are well informed, satisfied and motivated will be good ambassadors, work more productively and help their organisation achieve its wider goals. Good employers attract the best employees.

An active **corporate citizenship** program creates opportunities for employee development and satisfaction. For example, Procter & Gamble integrate all of their global corporate citizenship initiatives under the 'Live, Learn and Thrive' banner, which focuses social investments into improving life for disadvantaged children and youth, and extends to over one hundred projects in sixty countries. Thousands of employees are taking an active part in these projects, often applying their management skills to new challenges in difficult situations, volunteering work and time, sometimes over several months. Corporate citizenship is thus woven throughout the business, and management encourages these activities because they recognise the self-actualising benefits for the people involved.

corporate citizenship:
The concept that corporations, like people, have both rights and obligations to the societies within which they exist.

Organisational versus individual ethics

What happens when there is a conflict between the ethics of the organisation and the ethics of the employee? Peter Drucker (1981), considered the father of management theory, suggested that there should be no difference: that the corporation should not be allowed a different standard of ethics from the individuals within it. Nevertheless, managers may sometimes face complex decisions as to whether to uphold the core values of the organisation or their own values. If they follow the corporate objectives, they might argue that they are following rules and carrying out their duty. Is this ethical, or should they abide by their own standards and refuse to carry out the work? To avoid such conflicts, many organisations establish ethical guidelines that are acceptable to both the company and its employees. One example of such transparency is the Johnson & Johnson ethical statement 'Our Credo', first written in 1943, which is still used to manage and evaluate ethical behaviours throughout the business and to match individual and company standards.

Individuals

Does the consumer base purchase decisions on their own personal ethical values? The claim is that because consumers are becoming more aware and more concerned about corporate social irresponsibility generally, they may be rewarding socially responsible behaviour with brand loyalty.

According to Carrigan and Attalla (2001), 'there may be very little commercial reward in terms of consumer purchasing to be gained by behaving as an ethical marketer'. They reveal mixed evidence of consumers punishing unethical behaviour or even rewarding ethical behaviour, indicating that there are still gaps between attitude, purchase intention and behaviour. Some authors suggest that this might be because of a lack of information to help distinguish between those companies behaving ethically and those not. Others such as Auger and Devinney (2007) and Boulstridge and Carrigan (2000) identify convenience, price, value, quality and brand familiarity as still being the most important purchase criteria and conclude that while there are groups of ethical consumers, most customers buy for other than societal reasons. The evidence in the cases of Nike, The Gap and, in Europe, the discount fashion retailer Primark, is revealing. All three companies have been criticised for child labour practices at their suppliers' factories, yet consumers continue to patronise the brands and the brands continue to grow.

Brinkmann and Peattie (2008) have suggested that ethical consumption will only occur where the marketer and consumer work together. If there is an understanding of how a sense of responsibility can be developed and divided within the market, there can be an integrated and shared sense of social co-responsibility between marketers and consumers.

▼ CRITICAL REFLECTION

In July 2002, a group of overweight Americans filed a lawsuit in New York against several fast-food restaurant companies. The claim? That firms had misled consumers by enticing them with greasy, salty and sugary food. Six months later, a group of obese teenagers filed a suit in a Manhattan federal court claiming that McDonald's was responsible for making them fat. One of the teenagers had eaten at McDonald's every day for three years. In the United States, about 54 million people are believed to be obese, half the population is overweight, and hundreds of thousands of deaths annually are attributed to obesity (BBC News, 2002).

How should this affect McDonald's marketing?

What does this indicate to the marketer? Evidence suggests that many consumers do not care enough to make ethical considerations a priority, but most regard organisations that demonstrate ethical behaviour more positively, and this may enhance corporate image and reputation. While this might not translate into purchase behaviour today, it is possible that as the movement towards socially responsible behaviour and sustainability becomes more established, firms without a clear CSR positioning will be at a disadvantage. Belk, Devinney and Eckhardt (2004) suggest that consumers are looking for leadership in this area, wanting businesses to take the first step, so that they can follow.

People who live in a free society have freedom of choice, but of course this comes with responsibilities; while ethical purchasing may mean choosing to support socially responsible firms, it also means making responsible choices between other competing marketing claims.

Government and society

In a democracy, the government chosen by its citizens is expected to be the champion of justice, social and economic development and social order. Government must ensure that business (including the marketing function) acts within the law, abides by societal norms and does not abuse its economic power by disadvantaging vulnerable consumers or selling products and services that are harmful to the individual or to society. In particular, government must be forward looking and try to anticipate the future needs of its society.

Through legislation and taxation, governments are able to change behaviour for the good of society; for example through differential duties on fuels, or by road charging. As in Australia, the July 2007 ban on smoking in enclosed public spaces in England is said to have led to a rapid acceleration in the number of smokers quitting the habit. Cancer Research UK (2008) estimate that at least 400,000 people quit as a result, helping to prevent at least 40,000 deaths over the following ten years.

A DELICATE BALANCE OF RESPONSIBILITIES AND BENEFITS

◢ LEARNING OBJECTIVE
Understand the relationship between marketing and ethics

The primary role of an organisation is to provide a product or service to its target public at a profit. Profit is not just a motive; it is also an obligation. Without a profit, the organisation cannot survive. It cannot invest in developing the company, nor can it provide employment to its staff; it cannot buy raw materials from its suppliers, nor can it depend on future finance from its investors or provide them with returns. The firm must also uphold the rules and laws of the societies in which it operates and serve the interests of the industry in which it competes. As a result, all organisations must weigh up the needs of different stakeholders to ensure that all parties are satisfied. This can be a complex balancing act. Freeman (1991) defines stakeholders as 'any group or individual who can affect, or is affected by the activities of the organisation'. This generally includes: customers, employees, suppliers, shareholders, local communities, local and national government, industry bodies, regulatory bodies and the media.

Customers

The customer is the focus of the marketing-oriented business. The role of the marketer is to create products or services to satisfy the needs of the customer. In return, the customer buys the company's product, endorsing the reputation of the company through use and by communicating its benefits to others: thus the customer benefits through satisfaction and the company benefits through revenues and reputation.

Employees

The employee is the lifeblood of the organisation. The organisation has a responsibility to create a positive environment where the employee can be most productive and derive satisfaction from their work. Satisfied employees in the front line of the company project a positive brand image to the consumer, but the organisation has a responsibility of care to each of their employees. In return, the employee has a responsibility of loyalty and hard work to assist the organisation to achieve its goals.

Suppliers

Suppliers provide the organisation with the materials and services it requires to develop product for market. The organisation relies on the supplier to provide quality products at an affordable price. The supplier is dependent on the organisation for its custom and the two will therefore work hard to achieve a positive relationship and satisfy each other's needs.

Shareholders

Shareholders provide the finance for the company to develop and grow. Investor finance might be necessary for the company to innovate and expand. In order to attract shareholders, the company must be able to deliver a return on investment; otherwise there is little incentive to invest.

Local communities

The communities in which an organisation operates are vital to its success. An organisation that is not welcome in a community will find it difficult to manage and develop its operations. Consequently, as well as providing jobs and local taxes, firms often contribute in many other ways to the local community to gain acceptance and recognition.

Local and national government

Local and national governments act in the interest of the citizens who elect them, to promote crime-free streets, employment and thriving businesses and productivity. Government activities are funded by local and national taxes from individuals and the businesses that employ them. Organisations must comply with regulations, but develop relationships in order to influence legislation.

Case study

Going green? The Conservative Party in the United Kingdom

By Peter Reeves, Salford Business School, University of Salford, United Kingdom

The green agenda is often claimed to be a fundamental force in contemporary consumer behaviour. Consumers are increasingly encouraged to make environmentally friendly choices, whether this be in terms of lower fuel consumption, locally grown foods to reduce food miles or recycling of household waste. The green agenda has also become a factor in politics around the world, with voters increasingly being influenced by the environmental records and promises of political parties. Green issues became important in the run up to the 2010 British general election for the main opposition party, the Conservative Party. The Conservative Party had lost three consecutive elections in 1997, 2001 and 2005 and had recognised that it needed to change in order to be able to win government in future elections.

In 2005, a major development occurred in this quest for change, with the election of the new Conservative Party leader, David Cameron. Cameron led a major reappraisal of the Conservative Party's approach. It was often claimed that the Conservative Party were perceived as being too far to the right of majority public opinion, with an overemphasis on free markets, low taxation and smaller government. Whether or not this was true is a matter of individual political opinion, but nonetheless the Conservative Party needed to demonstrate that it had learnt lessons from its electoral defeats and that it had changed. One way this was achieved was through stressing that the Conservative Party was environmentally responsible.

The party undertook a number of significant changes to stress its environmental credentials. First, the logo of the party was changed from the 'torch of freedom' to that of an 'oak tree'. Second, the party campaigned under the slogan 'vote blue, go green' (blue being the traditional Conservative campaigning colours). Third, Cameron was often seen riding his bicycle through the streets of London, and even on one occasion visiting the Arctic and riding a sleigh propelled by huskies. These events and activities attempted to symbolise that the party had changed, but created a debate among some commentators as to whether the change was a genuine shift in Conservative Party policy to embrace the green agenda. An alternative interpretation was that it was a means to reposition the brand in the broader sense that the party had become more socially progressive and caring, and thereby act as a means to effectively challenge the left-of-centre Labour Party.

While the Conservative Party won the 2010 general election, the electorate did not seem to be fully convinced that the party had changed, since the party did not win by enough to form a parliamentary majority. Also, the first ever Green Party Member of Parliament was elected. In order for the Conservative Party to form a government, and for David Cameron to become Prime Minister, they had to enter into a coalition with the third largest party, the Liberal Democrats.

Questions

1   To what extent do you believe that the green agenda has become an important consideration in political decision making?

2   How effective do you believe the Conservative Party in the United Kingdom has been between 2005 and 2010 at changing its image to one of a more caring, environmentally sustainable party?

Industry bodies

Industry bodies serve to promote professionalism and act to represent their members' interests. An organisation requires the endorsement of its industry body and can benefit from the research and representation that it offers. A member organisation therefore has an obligation to uphold the professional reputation of the industry as a whole and to participate in industry-wide activities.

Regulatory bodies

While regulatory bodies are not directly affected by the organisation's achievement, the organisation is affected by regulation enacted by them, and therefore must develop a positive working relationship so that their interests are understood.

The media

The media is not normally affected by the activities and objectives of an organisation, but plays a significant role in influencing its reputation. It is essential that the media is provided with timely information and a positive relationship is developed to ensure accurate reporting.

Case study

Diageo plc: Stakeholder analysis

Diageo plc is one of the largest alcoholic drink and beverage companies in the world, with some of the most recognised brands in its portfolio, such as Johnnie Walker, Smirnoff, Guinness, J&B and Baileys. Trading in 180 markets and employing 23,000 people around the world they achieved an income of £9,936 million in 2011. (Diageo plc, 2011a)

In their 2011 Corporate Social Responsibility Report (Diageo plc, 2011c) they state:

We believe that financial success is only achievable in the long term if the way we achieve that success—the way we do business—is sustainable. This includes how we treat our people; the culture we promote internally; how we live our values in all our business relationships; how we use the natural resources that we rely on; and the effects we have on the communities in which we operate.

We structure our Sustainability & Responsibility Strategy around our 'impacts'. By impacts we mean who or what our business affects, and in what way. Ensuring we focus on our most material impacts involves engaging our stakeholders to understand their interests and concerns.

Here is how Diageo (2011b) summarise their impacts in various areas:

- Alcohol in society—Working to create a positive role for alcohol in society through responsible marketing, consumer information, programs that address alcohol misuse, alcohol policies and stakeholder dialogue.
- Water—Addressing the water challenge in the communities in which we operate through our operations, community investment and collective action.
- Environment—Contributing to broader environmental sustainability through programmes to reduce carbon dioxide, and waste reduction, to promote sustainable packaging and more.
- Community—Supporting local social and economic development in the communities in which we operate.
- Our people—Creating a great place to work for our employees.
- Governance and ethics—Holding ourselves to the highest ethical standards.
- Our suppliers—Partnering with suppliers to maximize the positive impact of our supply chain.
- Our customers and consumers—Working with our customers to promote our sustainability and responsibility agenda to consumers.

Questions

1   Who are the different stakeholders that Diageo must take into consideration when working to fulfil its priorities?

2   What strategies would you suggest to Diageo's marketers to meet the needs of all these stakeholders?

◢ LEARNING OBJECTIVE
Be familiar with some
philosophical definitions
of ethics

THEORIES OF ETHICS

Marketers are faced with ethical decisions, both large and small, every day. In order to understand and apply the moral principles that guide decision making through ethical reasoning, it is helpful to be acquainted with the underlying philosophy of ethics. Here we look at three main philosophical approaches.

Teleology and utilitarianism

Teleology (from the Greek *teos*, meaning 'an end or purpose') is the most widely understood of the various ethical theories. Explored first by Plato and Aristotle, it proposes that a moral choice or activity must be judged by its outcome. Utiliarianism, which was developed from this approach in the eighteenth and nineneenth century, suggests that a moral choice should maximise happiness. Both theories suggest that where a decision or activity produces the greatest good (utility) for the greatest number of people then it is considered an appropriate moral decision. In marketing, the teleological process would therefore consider the benefits of different activities to different stakeholder groups.

This approach has been at the forefront of business decision making. A board of directors might conclude, for example, that maximising profitability produces the greatest good for the greatest number of stakeholders because it guarantees the future health of the organisation, it contributes to the well-being of the nation's economy, it provides continuous employment to the local community, it produces desirable products and services for its customers and it pays national and local taxes to fund important civic projects. However, profit maximisation may well mean putting shareholder needs for corporate profitability before the needs of other groups, such as employees and local communities.

A branded clothing retailer may well reason that it has considered the benefits provided to a large number of consumers by marketing lowest-cost products at market-beating prices. The company contracts its production to manufacturers wherever labour is cheapest (and this may include child labour), thereby making the products affordable to the greatest number of people, and thus be judged to be achieving the greatest good. Such a strategy often provides much needed employment in the manufacturing country and also in the markets where the clothing is retailed. It generates strong revenues and the profits to keep shareholders satisfied.

But does this teleological reasoning really imply a fair approach? There are four main problems.

First and foremost, who decides what the 'greatest good' is? Do the benefits the customer and shareholder receive really outweigh that of the factory employee who may be subject to poor work practices? The brand owner may see the greater good in terms of the customer and the shareholder, whereas labour organisations in local communities may well prioritise the employees and their working conditions.

Second, does the end justify the means? Where the outcome is considered the most important, does this mean that the process of achieving that outcome is not important? Are the means by which the clothing is produced less important than the satisfaction of the consumer and shareholder?

Third, while the greatest number of people may receive some benefit from a particular good or service, a minority may suffer as a result. How are minority needs taken into consideration by this approach, or have they been marginalised by the process?

Finally, is the greater good a short-term or long-term goal? When applied to business ethics, one must also be cautious of a decision that offers material benefit to many in the present but is not beneficial to the environment in the future. In this example, the potential long-term cost of carbon emissions involved in the shipping of the garments is not being recovered.

Commentators such as Nantel and Weeks (1996) have suggested that if marketing decisions must satisfy a moral outcome we must question the process used and the outcome itself.

Deontology

Deontology (from the Greek *dei*, meaning 'it is right') suggests that the outcome of an action is not the primary focus but rather that there are universal actions and behaviours that must be performed as part of one's duty to society. These duties suggest that the process of achieving an outcome is therefore of utmost importance.

For business, this might mean not simply choosing the most profitable outcome but instead following a process that is considered right and just. For example, lying, stealing and murder are universally forbidden; therefore, no matter what the outcome, they are unethical. It is clearly wrong to steal the intellectual property of another brand owner in order to pass off your goods as theirs. For marketing, meeting the needs and wants of better informed and socially concerned consumers will not just involve the process of delivering the end product or service but will also involve the process by which those goods are produced.

What problems do marketers face in adopting a deontological approach? Is a universal moral code possible? In reality, different philosophers, different cultures and different societies have produced different standards, and some duties require a trade-off between one and another. Certainly, in today's complex multicultural environment, universal rules are very difficult to agree on, leading Macintyre (2003) to suggest that different rules are needed in different cultural situations.

For the clothing brand that contracts manufacturing in India, whose rules are followed? Australian law clearly outlaws the employment of minors and Australian society is unanimous in its condemnation of child labour. However, in India many communities welcome and indeed depend upon it, as it brings in money to families that might otherwise not have enough food. In many cases among the poor in India, large families are considered fortunate, as the children can go out and earn a living, ensuring that the youngest children and elders of the family are provided for.

Murphy and Laczniak (2006) have suggested that deontology does not take into account the potential conflict of certain moral duties that might require trade-offs between one and another. For business and marketing, ethical decision making is best achieved by strict compliance to established rules and norms of behaviour. At a basic level, these might be laws established by national or local government. They could also be voluntary ethical codes established by national or global bodies; for example the Social Accountability International (SAI) SA8000 benchmarks that define acceptable working practices, and the Australian Association of National Advertisers (AANA) code of ethics are both standards for self-regulation. Accreditation with or adherence to such codes offers significant reassurance to both marketers and consumers.

Industry insight

Billabong: Managing a global supply chain

Billabong International has a direct global workforce in excess of 3500 people, the majority located in Australia's Gold Coast, southern California and south-west France. Billabong also has an extensive network of manufacturers within its global supply chain. The company is acting to influence working practices and employment conditions at these third-party contractors, ensuring that they move towards compliance with internationally accepted standards.

It is a challenging task to oversee, given the complexity and diversity of statutory requirements and cultural attitudes that exist across the range of countries within the group's global supply chain. This has prompted Billabong to adopt Social Accountability 8000 (SA8000) as the global standard by which to measure the performance of its supply chain.

The company has established a department of trained auditors and quality control specialists to monitor the global supply chain. It is based in Hong Kong, with a second office in mainland China, positioned close to the majority of the group's manufacturers. The auditors undertake initial SA8000 compliance visits to the supply chain factories, and after a first audit any corrective action plans are implemented. Further audits are then undertaken to ensure continuing compliance.

This is no small undertaking. In the year 2010–11, the group was monitoring 339 factories. It conducted 231 full factory audits, putting in place 142 corrective action plans, while 26 factories gained full SA8000 certification.

Working towards the SA8000 standard gives the company the ability to measure the performance of suppliers, but does not guarantee that they will consistently follow accepted work practices. Between audits, Billabong may become aware of a breach, and in these instances a remedial process is implemented.

Members of the operations team are notified of the alleged breach and all compliance records from prior audits are retrieved. An audit team is then assembled within twenty-four hours in the Asian region, or as soon as practicable in other regions, and dispatched to the supplier's factory. They prepare a report for immediate action by management who consider options, including, in the case of underage workers:

- cancellation of the purchase order
- implementing a plan to provide education or training courses until the child reaches the minimum working age
- committing to providing the child with living expenses and, once at the minimum working age, a job opportunity, in accordance with the SA8000 guidelines.

The costs of such remedial actions are at the supplier's expense.

Source: Adapted from Billabong (2010), 'Why adopt a standard', retrieved 25 May 2012 from <www.billabongbiz.com/phoenix. zhtml?c=154279&p=social>

Virtue ethics

A third moral philosophy, virtue ethics, was first proposed by Aristotle (c. 325 BCE). He suggested that the individual must establish personal characteristics to lead a just and virtuous life. Virtue ethics is not about a single decision or a rule to be followed; it calls for the individual to develop characteristics that lead to virtuous behaviour, so that ethical decision making becomes a natural action. A moral virtue might be fairness, truthfulness or justice. According to Aristotle, we learn virtuous behaviour by practising it and by following the behaviour of moral role models (Aristotle, 2008):

> [E]thical virtues do not come about by nature ... we are naturally constituted so as to acquire them, but it is by habit that they are fully developed ... by doing just things we become just.

While deontology and teleology concern the decisions and actions we take, virtue ethics concerns our individual character and our motivations. Important questions to ask in virtue ethics systems therefore include:

- What sort of person do I want to be?
- What virtues are characteristic of the person I want to be?
- What actions will cultivate the virtues I want to possess?
- What actions will be characteristic of the sort of person I want to be?

To apply this philosophy in business and marketing, the organisation will normally establish the virtuous principles of behaviour it expects of its people, and encourage that behaviour among its management. Managers then act as role models for their colleagues who develop their own virtuous behaviour until it becomes automatic in any situation.

There are three difficulties with the application of virtue ethics:

- defining the virtues to be followed—there are many celebrated in our society
- how to deal with conflicting virtues
- how to translate those virtues into individual and corporate behaviour, because:
  - virtues are often written in broad terms and can be open to interpretation
  - virtuous behaviour very often requires great courage or even sacrifice. Managers must feel supported by the virtuous corporation in the decisions they take.

Nevertheless, there are many examples of companies that adopt this approach through their corporate culture, and who use an expression of their moral virtues to characterise their distinctiveness. Like Johnson & Johnson, Coca-Cola publish their values, along with a call to everyone in the company to live them when going about their business.

Which theory?

How can these different theories guide behaviour and decision making in business? Consideration of different ethical viewpoints and alternative courses of action can facilitate better decision making. It is certainly a useful approach when considering the conflicting views of different stakeholders.

Some academics have contributed to the discussion of marketing ethics with their own moral decision-making frameworks, often combining the approaches of the three philosophies described above.

In his Ethicability® framework, Roger Steare (2009) suggests that the sum of all these virtues is integrity: 'those shared values, attitudes and behaviours that help us act correctly in our lives at home at work and in society'. We have integrity if we act according to our virtues or principles. He suggests that each of the three moral philosophies can contribute to ethical decision making in a process that involves preparation for the decision, asking the RIGHT questions (where RIGHT is an acronym), and then testing the alternatives before taking a final decision. The sequence is set out in Figure 14.2.

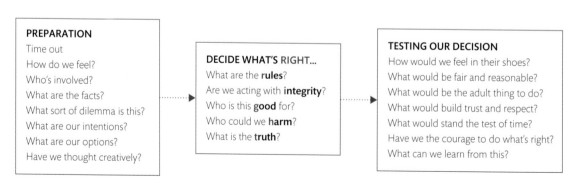

PREPARATION
Time out
How do we feel?
Who's involved?
What are the facts?
What sort of dilemma is this?
What are our intentions?
What are our options?
Have we thought creatively?

DECIDE WHAT'S RIGHT...
What are the **rules**?
Are we acting with **integrity**?
Who is this **good** for?
Who could we **harm**?
What is the **truth**?

TESTING OUR DECISION
How would we feel in their shoes?
What would be fair and reasonable?
What would be the adult thing to do?
What would build trust and respect?
What would stand the test of time?
Have we the courage to do what's right?
What can we learn from this?

●●● **FIGURE 14.2** THE ETHICABILITY® FRAMEWORK

Source: adapted from Steare, 2009, p. 116

Case study

A little local difficulty with ethical sourcing

Woolworths and Coles between them have around 80 per cent share of the Australian grocery market. Both retailers have well-developed ethical sourcing policies, designed to ensure the rights of workers in all their suppliers' businesses. Both retailers source fresh produce, fruit and vegetables from domestic and overseas businesses in order to maintain year-round supply and an exciting variety of available choices. The retailers' market power and the number of their suppliers makes it possible to negotiate lower prices, but it also brings challenges in maintaining consistent quality and in managing supplier relationships.

Both retailers have recently introduced new and more onerous ethical sourcing policies, which they now apply to all suppliers wherever they are. These policies have caused Australian growers to cry foul.

AUSVEG, the national industry body representing the interests of around 9000 Australian vegetable and potato growers, remains seriously concerned. According to their CEO (AUSVEG, 2010):

> All this policy does is place further regulations on Australian growers who already comply with state and federal laws, while growers overseas are exporting produce into Australia.

He added:

> [W]hy do they continue to import vegetables from overseas when Australian consumers consistently say they would prefer to buy locally grown produce?

A supplier in China may comply with their local law, but still may not be treating their workforce in the same manner as Australian growers already do. Workers in such countries do not have the same rights to freedom of association as the Australian workforce.

Australian growers are already inundated with audits and paperwork from state and federal government departments. Further cost simply makes it harder to compete with imports.

Questions

1   Using any one of the three ethical philosophies, construct an argument to put to the Woolworths board on behalf of AUSVEG, which makes the case for fairer treatment.

2   Do the same on behalf of a Chinese grower.

3   How would your argument differ if you applied a different ethical philosophy? Could you make a more persuasive case?

4   Applying the Steare Ethicability® framework, how would you come to a conclusion?

▲ **LEARNING OBJECTIVE**

Understand the ethical
challenges faced by
marketers in practice

ETHICAL MARKETING IN PRACTICE

For marketers, ethical decision making is essential for the health of the brand, but moral decisions are complex and affect stakeholders in a variety of ways. It is important, though, to remember that the major challenge facing any marketer is the intensity of the competition in a crowded marketplace and the need to win and build business from rivals. It is always in the marketer's interest to make ethical decisions in order to maintain consumer trust, but from time to time the balance between a competitive and an ethical choice can be difficult. Some areas of the marketing mix that may be difficult to manage ethically are shown in Figure 14.3 and we will now look at some examples of marketing practice that have been challenged.

One further pressure on many marketers is to keep their category as free from regulation as possible. The sale of some products—for example tobacco or alcohol—is restricted by laws in many countries for the well-being of society. Such products are also often highly taxed in order to constrain consumption. Marketing tools are also controlled. For example, it is illegal to advertise cigarettes in Australia (since 1976), or to target television advertising at children in Sweden (since 1991). It is not so hard to imagine further laws being introduced that cover categories such as fast-food or other communications such as advertising if public opinion moves firmly enough in that direction. While legal restrictions apply to all brands, most marketers would prefer to regulate

●●● **FIGURE 14.3** PRESSURES ON ETHICAL MARKETING DECISION MAKING

Adapted from Baker, M (2009) *Marketing Responsibly—Addressing the Ethical Challenges*, Institute of Business Ethics, London, p. 10

themselves through such means as the Advertising Standards Bureau, which governs advertising in Australia. Consumers, however, may tend to trust the government more than marketers and feel their interests better protected by the certainty of legislation.

Product management

The product that is offered to market is the heart of the marketing mix. In terms of product management decisions, several areas attract criticism, such as planned obsolescence, product safety, and packaging and labelling choices. An important new avenue for competitive advantage is sustainability in product design, which we discuss in the final section of this chapter.

Harmful versus healthful products

The sale and marketing of potentially harmful products attracts critical attention and is often regulated. For example, the alcohol content of beers, wines and spirits is standardised in many countries, and there are pressures on the fast food industry to reduce salt, fat and sugar content. Marketers will often improve their product to match evolving needs and wants, and also avoid regulation. For example, Food Standards Australia New Zealand (2010) found that intakes of trans fatty acids from manufactured foods had fallen by between 25 and 45 per cent in two years by 2009 as a result of voluntary changes to industry practice. Arnott's (2012) claim that you would now need to eat forty Tim Tam biscuits to reach the maximum daily intake of TFAs recommended by the World Health Organization.

But where do ethical marketers draw the line in creating products to meet consumers' needs and wants? Padded bras for seven-year-old girls, 'lad mags' for twelve-year-olds that discuss sex, booze and hooning, and some drastic dieting products are all marketed without controls. Is regulation the responsibility of parents, individuals or the government? Is it ever right in a free society to restrict choice?

Planned obsolescence

Products created with a deliberately limited life span benefit firms through early replacement. Software is frequently updated, for example, while razors have moved from twin blades to those with four and more cutting edges with this goal in mind. While many like to own the latest fad, for others the previous model is still good enough. Critics of marketing see this technique as wasteful, but others see it as progress.

Product safety

The consumer has a right to safety, but any new product carries a degree of risk no matter how well tested. For some breakthrough technologies, such as genetically modified crops, the risk to safety has been considered too great in many jurisdictions, but marketers will always face pressure to bring product to market quickly, partly to beat the competition and partly to start to recoup development costs. At best, a faulty product will not satisfy consumers and will fail. At worst it may do serious harm. Marketers are responsible, too, for taking the expensive decision to withdraw or recall products; some have been criticised for doing this too slowly, often a bad choice in the long run with possible repercussions for brand image.

Misleading packaging and labelling

Nowhere is competition more intense than on the supermarket shelf, where brands jostle to attract consumer attention and choice. Marketers and their agencies therefore agonise at length over pack style, size and design. For example, where a product appears in oversized packaging to create the impression of value for money, consumers may be disappointed and will not buy the product a second time. Marketers must also take care not to make misleading claims. For example, 'low fat' or 'no added sugar' might suggest that a product is healthy. In fact, many low fat products have a high sugar content, while the statement 'no added sugar' ignores the addition of sweeteners or the natural sugar content of other ingredients. The use of such claims may be confusing for consumers and can result in increased regulation. Environmental claims are now becoming common, but if they are not supported by evidence this is termed 'greenwashing'.

Case study
Greenwashing

In 2004, complaints were levelled at an Australian tampon manufacturer who used Swedish organic certification on the packaging of its organic cotton tampons without permission. The brand was on sale at a 30 per cent premium to the market. KRAV, an organic certifier authorised by the Swedish National Board of Agriculture, was concerned about misuse of its logo, which is meant to guarantee that a product had been 'inspected and certified from farming until consuming'. The cotton was grown organically in Texas and was certified by the Texas Department of Agriculture and by KRAV, but later processing into tampons in Australia did not fulfil KRAV's conditions. Organic by Nature has responded by agreeing to stop using KRAV's name on future packaging.

Source: Needham (2004)

Setting prices

Price is often the factor that is of most importance to consumers; it is the only element of the marketing mix to generate revenues and profits, and it is also a communication tool. Pricing often includes distribution decisions that have ethical and legal implications. Marketers are challenged on many issues of pricing, since price is directly related to the concept of fair value for money.

Transparency

For a simple product it is easy to understand the real price demanded. It is therefore straightforward to compare prices to judge if a price represents value for money. For complex technological products or financial services, comparison becomes very difficult. Comparison websites often come to the consumer's aid, but there have been cases where such sites have taken commission from providers for business steered their way.

Product labelling and sizing regulations help make comparison easy and guidelines for transparency in pricing have been developed, although they are hard to implement.

Predatory pricing

Questionable pricing strategies may not only harm the consumer; they can also be focused on a company's main rivals. Predatory pricing temporarily reduces prices with the aim of eliminating competitors so that the price can be raised again. Large corporations are often able to set low prices, but for small companies remaining competitive and meeting that price for any length of time may mean that they will go out of business. Microsoft has often been accused of a version of this practice. By offering free software such as Internet Explorer bundled in with its operating system, it has eliminated several competitors who could not compete with a 'better than free' offer (France & Hamm, 1999).

Price fixing

Price fixing requires agreement between two or more sellers or buyers; coordinating pricing can result in high prices and high profits for all involved. It is illegal since it acts against the interests of consumers. For example, in New Zealand the Commerce Commission initiated proceedings against thirteen airlines, including British Airways and Qantas, for extensive and long-term price fixing activity in the air cargo market (Commerce Commission, 2008).

Social impact of everyday low price

Every consumer wants to pay the lowest possible price, and low pricing allows more people from all income backgrounds to be able to buy; it can therefore have a desirable social impact where all members of the population can afford more than just the basic necessities of life. However, there can also be negative impacts, including overconsumption. Governments worldwide are grappling with the problem of binge drinking and obesity, and are extremely critical of some supermarkets' low pricing strategies for alcohol and high sucrose high fat (HSHF) foods.

Low pricing may also cause problems for those working in the supply chain. Big retailers are often criticised for using their buying power to force farmers into situations where they are supplying produce at extremely low margins.

Accessibility and exclusivity

The power of the biggest brands can result in anti-competitive actions in the supply chain; for example where a powerful brand insists on the retailer or wholesaler only stocking one brand in exchange for lower prices. In 2005, Coca-Cola was forced to change its exclusivity deals with retailers by the European Union (Baker, 2009).

Supply chain management

Issues of ethics in distribution are closely connected to the pricing issues discussed above. They can occur when companies collude over production quotas, and when companies abuse their monopoly status or exploit their supply chain partners.

Collusion

Collusion can occur where companies collaborate to squeeze out other competition or to protect their own market. The OPEC oil cartel and the UK Net Book Agreement are examples of collusion that generate price and distribution benefits to those involved but can result in unfair consumer prices as well as anti-competitive practices.

Abuse of monopoly status

In March 2004, the European Union levied a half-billion euro fine against Microsoft for abusing its near monopoly status. The EU anti-competition authority called for Microsoft to offer a version of Windows that did not contain its digital media player within three months and to release a complete and accurate interface code to other software companies in the server market within four months to ensure interoperability between different competitor companies' products (BBC News, 2007b).

Supply chain exploitation

In a competitive environment, large retailers and wholesalers squeeze suppliers for more favourable prices and better payment and service terms. This behaviour is occasionally reported in the media as exploitation by large companies of smaller ones. An alternative view is that terms of trade are negotiated competitively and simply reflect the cost of access to large groups of consumers.

Accessibility and exclusivity

Consumer access to certain products can be restricted through distribution arrangements that create a monopoly. For example, Sky inhibited access to Premier League football in the UK through its exclusive deals, but has been forced to sell matches to competitors by the regulator.

Communications and promotion

personal selling: Any persuasive communication conducted directly between sellers and potential consumers face to face or orally, with the intention of making a sale.

The high visibility of marketing communication makes it a common area for ethical criticism. As new communications tools, techniques and media emerge, it is becoming an area that is increasingly difficult to regulate. There are examples of ethical breaches and of strong consumer reaction in every element of communications, from advertising to **personal selling**. Some common problems are again of misleading claims, questions of taste and decency, messages directed towards vulnerable groups (particularly children) and the use of buzz, viral and 'stealth' marketing.

Misleading claims

Apart from any moral consideration, it is bad business to mislead the consumer when your goal is repeat purchase. But of course it is also unethical: the AANA ethical code states: 'Advertisements shall not be misleading or deceptive or be likely to mislead or deceive.' Misleading claims in advertising can include partial truth and exaggeration. The advertising industry in Australia, as elsewhere, is self-regulated. While self-regulation does not create a national law, an industry that regulates itself well understands the benefits of ethical practice to the reputation of the industry and all the players in it. For most industry members this is preferable, as government intervention means a loss of control. For example, misleading claims by internet providers as to the speed of their service have been investigated in both Australia and the United Kingdom, but with different outcomes. In 2009, the Australian Competition & Consumer Commission (ACCC) advised the industry to adhere to the *Trade Practices Act 1974*, making it illegal to publicise 'up to' speeds where only a proportion of people could achieve those speeds. It suggested that service providers should give far more detailed information, or face the consequences of the law. UK internet users were receiving similarly misleading messages, but Ofcom (the regulator) ruled that service providers should generate their own guidelines to ensure an end to such claims (Ofcom, 2010).

Shock and sexual appeals

In order to create advertising that grabs attention and stays with us, agencies quite frequently use shock and sexual appeals. Sex sells, and shocking adverts achieve significantly higher attention, recall and influence (Dahl, Frankenberger & Machanda, 2003).

An important outcome of an advertising campaign is for the advertising to be memorable and to generate word of mouth. Controversy is not always unwelcome. A startling, edgy, sexy or shocking ad can achieve publicity, especially if it has to be discontinued. The shock technique is designed to cause moral outrage, but when does it cross the line to become irresponsible? The question is answered democratically in Australia: if complaints are received by the Advertising Standards Bureau (ASB), the advertisement is investigated, defended by its sponsor and a public judgment given, which could involve the advertisement being amended or even pulled if the complaint is upheld. The ASB publicises its deliberations on its website, which is always interesting to visit. In one case, a witty television advertisement showed how Red Bull helped a boy to visit a strip club. Complaints to the ASB focused on the overt sexualisation of children, the depiction of women as sex objects for men or boys, the fact that it demeaned women, and that it undermined the authority of parents. Complainants felt it was not appropriate to depict a boy at a strip club at any time on television. The company defended the advertisement, referring to its obvious humour, the energising claim and the timing of the media schedule. The ASB, following the guidelines set up by the industry, dismissed most of the complaints, understanding that the ad was not targeted at children and was intended to be funny. However, it upheld the complaint with particular reference to the depiction of an underage child at a strip club, and Red Bull were forced to discontinue the ad (ASB, 2010).

Stealth marketing

Stealth marketing is defined by Baker (2009) as the 'use of surreptitious marketing practices that fail to disclose or reveal the true relationship with the company that produces or sponsors the marketing message'. In the age of social networking, consumers trust the opinion of other consumers rather more than the advertiser's message and search out product and company reviews online. Some companies disguise their presence on social networking sites by getting independent bloggers or tweeters to discuss and promote their products. The ethical challenge for marketers is in the openness or stealth with which this is handled.

Buzz marketing

Buzz marketing is an organised word-of-mouth (WOM) campaign, but the technique has been criticised wherever the buzz was orchestrated by the company and not by consumers. When Witchery wanted to create awareness for its new range of menswear, they staged a YouTube video with a hired actress, claiming to be looking for a man she had met in a café. The Cinderella-style search for the young man who had left his jacket with the Witchery label spread quickly. When it was exposed as a marketing ploy, it was denied, by showing that the woman existed. The continued deception resulted in much debate and bad publicity for Witchery and a significant drop in traffic to the YouTube Video (Netregistry, 2009).

Advertising to children

Concern is frequently expressed that children are unable to differentiate between advertisements and other television content, and do not understand the purpose of advertising. This distorts the balance of power between the consumer and the advertiser, and undermines the principle of fair play. It is therefore considered that children are unfairly influenced by advertising, and it has been suggested by Young Media Australia (2009) that television advertising is responsible for negative body image and eating disorders among young adolescent girls. Advertising targeting children is banned in Sweden, Québec and Norway and there are legal restrictions in place in the United Kingdom, Greenland, Denmark and Belgium. Elsewhere, advertisers conform to the International Chamber of Commerce rules on advertising and on self-regulation.

Case study
Advertising to children in Sweden

Sweden was one of the first countries to ban advertising to children. This radio and television law, originally passed in 1996, bans advertising messages that are targeted towards children under twelve and any advertising before or after programs that are specifically for children under twelve.

While these rules are now generally accepted, it is interesting to consider the reality of consumer behaviour. Young Swedes are well connected: they surf the internet as much as they watch television. A quarter of twelve- to fifteen-year-olds spend at least three hours a day online, while half of all five-year-olds and one in five three-year-olds have used the internet. The teenagers prefer social networking, but under-elevens are more interested in playing computer games (The Swedish Institute, quoted in Sweden.se, 2009).

In researching children's internet use in Sweden, Plogell and Wardman (2009) found that more than half of the home pages children visited contained advertising targeted at under-twelves. Products such as sweets, crisps, carbonates, ice cream and biscuits were overwhelmingly represented, and some brands were embedded into games.

The rise of social networking and the practices of stealth and buzz marketing online have the potential to side-step Sweden's advertising restrictions. Compared to other media, the internet is cheap, easy and efficient at delivering relevant content (social communication, news, research, music, pictures and movies) and able to target relevant groups easily. Children are able to find exactly what they are searching for. So, despite stringent television advertising restrictions and a general ethos of consumer protection, Plogell and Wardman conclude that in Sweden 'the internet is still a grey area and not regulated more than with guidelines'.

SUSTAINABLE MARKETING

LEARNING OBJECTIVE
Be familiar with the emerging concept of sustainable marketing

The concept of green marketing is evolving, and according to Peattie (2001) shows three distinct stages leading to the emergence of the concept of sustainable marketing. For businesses and consumers to adopt the principles of sustainable marketing, many changes to current practice will be necessary.

Development of sustainable marketing

During the 1960s, attention focused on the depletion of natural resources resulting from continuous business expansion and consumption. The movement focused attention on symptoms such as air pollution and oil spills, and the ecological impact of pesticides such as DDT. Over the course of the next decade, issues were debated with a limited number of businesses, oil companies and agri-chemical producers, with a view to clean up the effects of this expansion rather than enact fundamental changes in practice. This led to some environmental legislation and the creation of some pioneering, values-driven green businesses such as The Body Shop and Ben & Jerry's.

The tragic events at Bhopal in 1984, the discovery of the damage to the ozone layer in 1985, the Chernobyl nuclear disaster in 1986 and the Exxon Valdez oil spill in 1989 all served to turn the media spotlight onto the effects of business and consumer activities on the environment. Consumers reacted. There was a global boycott of products using CFCs, 'green' political parties gained voter acceptance, and marketers began to look for the 'green consumer' buyers willing to pay a premium for eco-friendly goods and services.

Importantly, the concept of sustainability was defined in 1987 with the publication of the United Nations' Brundtland report, 'Our Common Future' (United Nations, 1987).

According to this report, sustainable development:

- meets the needs of the present without compromising the ability of future generations to meet their own needs. It contains within it two key concepts:
  - the concept of 'needs', in particular the essential needs of the world's poor, to which overriding priority should be given; and
  - the idea of limitations imposed by the state of technology and social organization on the environment's ability to meet present and future needs.

The importance of this definition for marketers lies in its identification of the needs of future generations, and the current and essential needs of the world's poor. The concept of 'wants' is noticeably absent.

Environmental marketers moved from 'end-of-pipe' clean-up solutions to clean technology: designing new products with less waste and pollution. In doing so, they targeted green consumers, who were identified mainly by the products they said they would avoid. Polonsky (1994) reports an Australian study that found that nearly three quarters of respondents had changed their purchasing behaviour in response to environmental concerns, and so marketers came to believe that technical innovation improved socio-environmental performance, which in turn created competitive advantage. This was summarised by Porter and van der Linde's (1995) 'win–win' scenario—that competitive eco-performance will drive greater and greater benefits for both companies and the environment. New goods and services were introduced to compete on the basis of green performance, and recyclable packaging became normal. Some companies realised that they could go further than compliance with new legislation, and sought partnerships with environmental critics to improve performance. Even so, progress was slow and eventually hit the 'green wall' (see Figure 14.4).

Porter and van der Linde's 'win–win' scenario was difficult to achieve for a number of reasons, amounting to a barrier that came to be termed the 'green wall'. Green products are vulnerable to price competition, and complex green claims can be easily challenged. This became particularly common in the media, where brand claims were often investigated. It is also hard for consumers to decide which of several alternatives is the 'greenest' when information is complicated, confusing and biased.

For companies, the easiest green decisions provide a financial return because they eliminate waste, but once these have been taken, the rewards are less tangible. At that point, the sustainability agenda has been shifted by many managers into the corporate social responsibility arena, where real further progress becomes slow.

Finally, where is the green consumer? The levels of consumer concern being voiced indicate a strong desire to make a change, but in reality this is not being matched in buying behaviour.

1970s ⟶	1980s and 1990s ⟶	Twenty-first century
Ecological marketing	*Environmental marketing*	*Sustainable marketing*

- Narrow focus on pollution and depletion
- Individual companies or industries targeted
- Narrow 'front line'
- Minority interest
- Increasing legislation

- Broader front line: from oil to paper
- Focus on physical system
- Global implications for new products and markets
- Eco-compliance and innovation

- Full environmental costs covered
- High price / low cost
- Supply loops
- Benefits in use not purchase
- Local production
- Diffusion of ideas

> *The green wall*
> - No sustainable competitive advantage
> - Easy media target
> - Corporate culture clash
> - Where are the green consumers?

●●● **FIGURE 14.4** THE EVOLUTION OF SUSTAINABLE MARKETING

Model adapted from Peattie, K (2001) 'Towards Sustainability: The Third Age of Green Marketing', *The Marketing Review*, vol. 2, pp. 129–46

Around the turn of the millennium, marketers began to consider combining the environmental aspects of green marketing with the concept of sustainable development outlined in 'Our Common Future' (United Nations, 1987). Fuller (1999) defines this concept of sustainable marketing as:

> the process of planning, implementing and controlling the development, pricing, promotion and distribution of products in a manner that satisfies the following three criteria: (1) customer needs are met, (2) organizational goals are attained, and (3) the process is compatible with eco-systems.

For marketers, the idea contains some real challenges. First, classical marketing considers the needs of the current generation as more important than those of any future generation. Second, sustainability explicitly calls for a fairer social distribution of costs and benefits. And third, marketing is mostly directed towards meeting consumers' *wants* in the developed economies, while sustainable development means meeting peoples' most basic *needs* around the world.

According to Peattie (2001), sustainable marketing will involve changes to some important aspects of production and consumption. For example:

- *Product costs.* Some product costs are currently being ignored in price calculations. New car buyers do not pay for air pollution, oil depletion, or road deaths and injuries. The price of fish in a supermarket does not reflect the cost of overfishing. The environment is often subsidising prices. While governments may make up some of the shortfall through taxes, most 'green' products currently look expensive as they carry a full environmental cost.

- *Cost not price.* For marketers, value is usually seen as a function of price. Many times though, an eco-friendly product calls for a larger initial investment but a lower cost in use. Low-energy light bulbs or energy-efficient buildings are examples.

- *Industry structure.* Marketers talk of supply chains, from extraction of raw materials to consumption and disposal. Sustainable marketing uses supply loops where consumers become suppliers of materials for recycling and reclaiming; for example returning empty printer cartridges.

- *Purchasing vs consuming.* Consumers benefit more from the use of the product than the ownership of it. In a more sustainable economy, ownership will be replaced with opportunities for renting and leasing, replacing products with services.

- *Distribution.* The environmental impact of a product is strongly influenced by the length of the supply chain, and the quantities of fossil fuels consumed in distribution. Local sourcing rather than global supply chains will become normal. This may involve micro-manufacture through networks of small factories benefiting from shared resources.

- *Beyond niche.* There are some green consumers prepared to pay a premium for sustainably marketed products. However, reductions in environmental impacts from sustainable marketing will only happen if practices change throughout entire industries. In some cases, competitors are sharing know-how (for example in the reduction of CFCs in refrigerants). Elsewhere, advances may only come about as competitors imitate each others' initiatives. While social pressure for environmental change and fairness is increasing, changes in consumer behaviour are lagging. This may be because buyers do not understand the issues, cannot see that their individual actions can directly make a difference, and are sometimes not convinced by sustainable product offers when compared with choices at lower prices.

Case study
Sprout Design and the Reee Chair

The overall emphasis in sustainable product design is dematerialisation—less material in a product, less use of materials by a product, and fewer products manufactured and therefore used through multi-functionality. Pli Design and Sprout Design have designed a revolutionary chair that uses recycled plastic from discarded Playstation consoles, diverting 2.3 kilograms of virgin plastic per chair away from landfill sites. The benefit for the designer is that this plastic comes from only one source, which means that its properties are known, are uniform and can therefore be developed into another high-value product: an ergonomic stacking chair. Designed and manufactured in the United Kingdom, it competes with virgin plastic chairs on both price and quality and was awarded 'Best Interior Lighting or Furniture Product' at the 2009 Hidden Art Awards in the United Kingdom.

Evaluating sustainable marketing

How do we measure the success of sustainable marketing against profit? John Elkington (1999) suggested that rather than evaluating success by measuring profit, the **triple bottom line** (TBL) means that 'People, Planet, Profit should be equally held to account in any organisation'.

This is easier said than done. Norman and MacDonald (2004) claim that it is impossible to measure certain ecological and social issues in monetary terms. They also suggest that the TBL approach encourages image washing or greenwashing: too main green claims rather than any positive action.

Some environmentalists and eco-socialist philosophers such as Pepper (1993) and Kovel (2002) also take issue with the TBL, claiming that business, marketing and sustainability are natural opposites, and that environmental and social concerns should take priority over economic concerns.

Despite the difficulties, companies are gradually turning their attention to defining measures to assess TBL performance.

LEARNING OBJECTIVE
Be able to discuss and analyse questions of ethical and sustainable marketing

triple bottom line (TBL or 3BL): A set of summary business performance measures that report the social and environmental impacts for the period along with the financial results.

Industry insight

Marshalls Fairstone,® sustainable marketing and the triple bottom line

Accusations of the widespread use of child labour and poor working conditions go beyond the clothing and footwear industries. Save the Children UK (2012) reported 218 million child labourers worldwide, with over half being employed in mining, quarrying and other hard and hazardous labour. An estimated fifteen million children were found to be working to pay off a relative's debt: the illegal practice of bonded labour.

Marshalls is a leading UK provider of paving and patio stone. The company became aware that their suppliers of Indian sandstone were using child labour and bonded labour, and that there were few health and safety regulations in place. Low wages, excessive working hours and exploitation of migrant workers were also in evidence, while the quarrying techniques were causing environmental damage. Marshalls quickly responded under the leadership of the Group Marketing Director, Chris Harrop, and took responsibility for the following initiatives in India:

- environmental and social research to understand the wishes and needs of the community, followed by improved working conditions in Marshalls' sandstone quarries

- consolidating supply through one sole agent in order to control working conditions

- adherence to health and safety rules

- health benefits and education for workers and their children through new health and education facilities

- investment in quarrying techniques and equipment to reduce carbon footprint by 80 per cent by 2050.

In the United Kingdom, Marshalls is now committed to consumer education regarding the sourcing of Indian sandstone and to sector education with industry peers and industrial associations. It is a company mission to improve conditions across the industry. In India, they lobby hard for the implementation of existing laws. Through this work they have been able to introduce Marshalls Fairstone,® a range of natural Indian sandstone products quarried and produced in line with ethical and sustainable values and commitments, underwritten by the Ethical Trading Initiative (ETI) and the United Nations Global Compact (UNGC).

When measured against a triple bottom line (see Figure 14.5) the results have been extremely positive against economic, social and environmental objectives (Marshalls, 2010).

- economic progress—Marshalls has received accreditations and awards for its work in India, which have raised its industry profile and consumer reputation. Improved market share, sales and cost efficiencies have been achieved in manufacture and production.

- environmental progress—sales of Fairstone® have grown significantly. Progress is being made in the reduction of carbon emissions and in efficient quarrying techniques. This has led to large new national and international commercial contracts.

- social progress—a measurable positive impact on the quarrying communities in India, establishing schools and communities of care for workers and their children. Societal results in India are monitored by a Social Auditor who reports on conditions, and on the operation of the education and health camps. UK colleagues are encouraged to visit the schools and communities they have established.

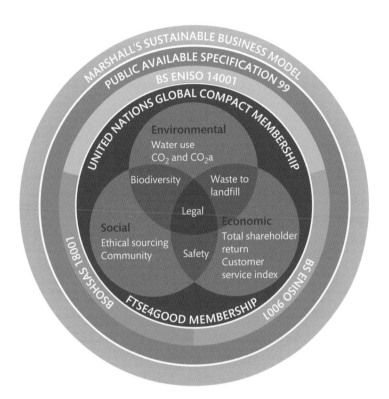

●●● **FIGURE 14.5** MARSHALLS' SUSTAINABLE BUSINESS MODEL (TRIPLE BOTTOM LINE APPROACH)

Source: Marshalls (2010) Marshalls Communication on Progress Report 2009, retrieved 2 August 2012 from <www.marshalls.co.uk/sustainability>, p. 4

Grant's green marketing grid

The concept of sustainable marketing is challenging for both consumers and companies. One wants less consumption, the other more; one rejects consumerism, the other drives it. John Grant argues in *The Green Marketing Manifesto* (2007) that environmental and ethical objectives can develop economic prosperity, and that what is right for the environment is also good for business. For example, sustainable marketers can demonstrate a long-term vision to their bankers and investors, which satisfies future consumers and stakeholders.

Grant believes that firms should use the tools of marketing to engage and educate consumers to change the habits and culture of consumption, He suggests the process must be 'making green stuff seem normal and not about normal stuff seeming green'.

The green marketing grid (Table 14.1) demonstrates how companies can engage at different levels in an innovative, collaborative approach to achieve this. The grid challenges the marketing profession to move from setting and communicating new standards, to using its power to take responsibility and to collaborate with consumers in supporting and fuelling innovation that changes the way products are used.

●●● **TABLE 14.1** THE GREEN MARKETING GRID

	A (GREEN)	B (GREENER)	C (GREENEST)
1 Public company and markets	Set an example to demonstrate activity	Develop the market with innovative sustainable ideas	New business concepts—develop new social enterprise ideas
2 Social brands and belonging	Credible partners Partner with not-for-profit social or environmental concerns	Tribal brands Create enthusiasm for products and brands across a broader range of people	Trojan horse ideas Develop innovative and inclusive marketing tools
3 Personal products and habits	Marketing a benefit Show the benefits of a sustainable activity	Change usage Motivate consumers to change usage habits	Challenge consuming by challenging the way and the amount that consumers use
	Set new standards Communicate	Share responsibility Collaborate	Support innovation Culture reshaped

Source: adapted from Grant, J (2007) *The Green Marketing Manifesto*, John Wiley & Sons, Chichester, UK p. 61

To date, smaller companies such as Sprout Design have been the innovators in this process, pushing the boundaries, developing sustainable products and championing the triple bottom line approach. These innovators have moved furthest along the grid, with some entering the greenest phase through social enterprise, sustainable design and innovation. Larger companies (such as Coles, Woolworths and Billabong) traditionally have been slower to react, but now appear to be taking on the challenge set by these innovators, working hard to demonstrate their position in the green phase, through genuine corporate social responsibility programs and initiatives to reduce their carbon footprint. Most notably, however, there are some national and international concerns, like Marshalls and Marks & Spencer that have gone one step further, challenging their industry sector in providing leadership, setting targets and collaborating with consumers. These companies are entering the greener phase, with their sights now set on the greenest phase.

Case study
Plan A at Marks & Spencer

UK retailer Marks & Spencer (M&S) has set a challenge to other businesses by integrating sustainability into its core strategy. Through their 'Plan A' campaign, launched in 2007, they made 100 commitments to the five Plan A Pillars: climate change; waste; natural resources; fair partnership; and health and well-being. In the 2010 Plan A report (Marks & Spencer, 2010), they claimed the following progress:

- We've motivated one million M&S customers to raise over £2.2m for Oxfam and saved 4 million items of unwanted clothes from going to landfill.

- We've improved energy efficiency by over 10% in our stores.

- We've reduced packaging on our foods by 16%, without compromising freshness, quality or shelf life—and cut costs in the process.

- We've improved fuel efficiency by over 20% and introduced our instantly recognizable 'tear drop' aerodynamic lorry trailers.

- We've made clothes hanger recycling 'mainstream'—with 120 million re-used or recycled each year.

- We've reduced the number of food carrier bags we give out by 400 million each year.

- We've purchased Green Palm Certificates to cover all of the palm oil used in our M&S products. By doing this we are rewarding palm oil producers for working in a sustainable and responsible way.

In the 2010 report, M&S announced that they intend to become the world's most sustainable retailer by 2015, extending the number of commitments across business, suppliers and customers from 100 to 180. The most important new commitments are (Marks & Spencer, 2010):

Involving our customers

We plan to bring Plan A into the core of what we do, helping customers to live more sustainably. We will:

- Make sure that all of the 2.7 billion individual M&S products we sell each year have at least one Plan A quality by 2020.
- Help 1 million customers to create their own personal Plan A by 2015 and 3 million by 2020.
- Run a continuous programme of Plan A marketing communications, to encourage customers to take action.

Making Plan A how we do business

We want to accelerate moves to make Plan A how we do business—part of the Marks & Spencer DNA. To support this aim, we're going to:

- Launch a 5-year, £50 million Plan A innovation fund to support new ideas in our business.
- Help our suppliers create 200 Plan A factories and 10,000 farmers join our Sustainable Agriculture Programme.

People

Our people are key to making Plan A how we do business. We want to involve all of our employees in Plan A and help them share information about doing this with family, friends and M&S customers. That's why we're going to:

- Offer all our eligible employees free home insulation and a home energy monitor.
- Give all our employees one paid day's leave every year to do volunteer work in the communities where they and our customers live.

Since 2010, Marks & Spencer have expanded their Plan A commitments and continue to work towards their targets, as reported in the 'How We Do Business Report 2011', accessible at: <http://plana.marksandspencer.com/media/pdf/how_we-do_business_report_2011.pdf>.

Questions

1 How could Plan A be seen as a catalyst for industry-wide innovation in sustainability and social progress?
2 How is Plan A helping Marks & Spencer engage with its customers?
3 How do the Marks & Spencer Plan A activities fit into the green marketing grid?
4 Is it the responsibility of Marks & Spencer to lead society in setting social and sustainable goals, or should they concentrate on selling products that meet consumer needs?

CONCLUSION

The prevailing view of marketing among consumers is often one of cynicism. There is growing unease with the global scale and power of today's business, and the role and scope of marketing is not well understood. The marketer is responsible for the relationship that every business has with its consumers, through the brands that contribute to the efficiency of modern life. Since brands are so completely integrated into our lives, brand marketing activities are held responsible for a variety of public concerns. Marketing stands accused of causing (among other things) obesity, global warming, consumer debt, anorexia, pollution, waste, greed, family break-up, free-floating dissatisfaction, erosion of biodiversity, brainwashing and binge drinking. In this chapter, we have argued that while there may sometimes be no smoke without fire, generally marketers behave ethically and marketing can be a force for good. Nowhere is this more obvious than in the emergence of sustainable marketing, and the diffusion of its principles to larger and larger businesses.

Most marketing decisions have an ethical dimension since their repercussions affect a wide assortment of stakeholders with different (and sometimes conflicting) needs, but the central efficiency of marketing is prolonging brand loyalty. Marketers can hardly do anything but act ethically if they want repeat purchase, since loyalty depends on trust. One way marketing now develops trust and aligns stakeholder and brand is through philanthropic cause-related marketing, and in delivering and communicating the firm's corporate social responsibility programs. These activities bring many internal as well as external stakeholder benefits.

To arrive at the most ethical decision, managers apply three different philosophies. Teleology or utilitarianism advocates an outcome that offers the greatest good to the greatest number of people. Deontology describes the universal duties and obligations to society in the process of achieving any outcome. A third, virtue ethics, promotes a personal moral code that can be learnt through practice and by following moral role models. All three philosophies might give a different moral complexion to a decision, and a number of management models exist that combine elements of each.

Marketing managers prefer to self-regulate their behaviour where possible, being conscious that laws are often introduced in response to decisions that go against consumer interests. Nevertheless, competitive pressure on marketing to deliver results means that managers sometimes make ethical mistakes. These are normally highly visible, and so as well attracting the attention of the legislature they can seriously damage brand image.

As consumers become more connected, better informed, more cynical and more marketing savvy, they are demanding that companies take more responsibility for their activities. Firms are responding: there is some financial reward in sustainable marketing, and until recently it was a differentiator for small brands. Now the biggest brands are signing up too. This is good news for the planet, as some of the biggest brands are now communicating the benefits of sustainability to consumers and increasing the pace of change.

14

SUMMARY

- It is a common belief that marketing is unethical by nature because it *makes* people do things they would prefer not to. Even a limited knowledge of marketing shows that this cannot be the case.

- Marketing is, generally speaking, a force for good. Driven by competition, it enhances the lives of people in developed and developing economies through large-scale technological change and continuous product improvements.

- Since all firms want repeat purchase, brands must foster trust with their consumers. For this reason alone, marketers must behave ethically or risk breaking hard-earned loyalty.

- Marketing is at the forefront of the new sustainability agenda, bringing benefits by safeguarding the needs of future generations through cause-related marketing initiatives or complex corporate social responsibility programs.

- Most marketing decisions have an ethical dimension because they affect the firm's stakeholder groups, who often have conflicting interests. This can be resolved by viewing the decision through an ethical prism, and various management frameworks describe this.

- Another important driver of corporate ethical behaviour in many markets is the desire to remain self-regulating, thus avoiding restrictive legislation by choosing to act more in the interests of consumers.

- Sustainable marketing theory suggests that products should carry their full environmental cost. There have been a number of solutions to the obvious pricing problem this implies, and creative marketers will doubtless find many more over the coming decades.

REVISION QUESTIONS

1   Marketers are accused of creating desires that lead to overconsumption. Do you agree?

2   Compare and contrast the differing needs of three groups of stakeholders of a company you know well. Explain how the marketing department might help to resolve any conflicts responsibly.

3   Describe the differences between deontology, teleology and virtue ethics. Identify an example of a questionable ethical decision in the following areas:

    a   pricing

    b   communication

    c   distribution

    d   product management

4   For your examples of questionable ethical decisions in question 3, explain why you think they are questionable and how you might have handled them differently.

5   Define sustainable marketing. Describe the main challenges in implementing a sustainable marketing strategy.

6   Are you an ethical consumer? Would you consider yourself to be a green consumer? What do you consider when faced with a fair trade brand that costs more?

7   To what extent do you think that marketing can be a responsible force for good?

FURTHER READING

Abela, A V (2006) 'Marketing and consumerism. A response to O'Shaughnessy and O'Shaughnessy', *European Journal of Marketing*, vol. 40, nos 1/2, pp. 5–16.

O'Shaughnessy, J & O'Shaughnessy, N J (2002) 'Marketing, the consumer society and hedonism', *European Journal of Marketing*, vol. 36, nos 5/6, pp. 524–47.

Wilkie, W & Moore, E (1999) 'Marketing's Contributions to Society', *Journal of Marketing* (Special Issue 1999), pp. 198–218.

WEBLINKS

Australian Competition and Consumer Commission, 'Green Marketing and the Australian Consumer Law':
www.accc.gov.au/content/index.phtml/itemId/815763

The Coca-Cola Company, 'Mission, Vision and Values':
www.thecocacolacompany.com/ourcompany/mission_vision_values.html

Gannon, Z & Lawson, N (2010) 'The advertising effect. How do we get the balance of advertising right?' available at Compass Online:
www.compassonline.org.uk/publications

Generation Green, Bendigo Bank:
http://tasmanianbankingservices.com.au/public/generationgreen/index.asp

Johnson & Johnson, 'Our Credo Values':
www.jnj.com/connect/about-jnj/jnj-credo

Marks & Spencer, How we do business report 2011:
http://plana.marksandspencer.com/media/pdf/how_we_do_business_report_2011.pdf

Marks & Spencer, Plan A:
http://plana.marksandspencer.com/about

Melbourne Football Club Community Partners:
www.melbournefc.com.au/community%20partners/tabid/15909/default.aspx

Procter & Gamble, Pampers and UNICEF working together for healthy babies:
www.pg.com/en_US/sustainability/social_responsibility/pampers_vaccinations.shtml

Procter & Gamble, social responsibility, 'Live, Learn and Thrive':
www.pg.com/en_US/sustainability/social_responsibility/live_learn_thrive_overview.shtml

Shell Sustainability Reports:
www.shell.com/home/content/environment_society/reporting/s_reports/

Social enterprise in Australia:
www.socialtraders.com.au/sites/www.socialtraders.com.au/files/SocialEntPart1_2.pdf

Sprout Design (UK):
www.sproutdesign.co.uk

World Business Council for Sustainable Development (WBCSD):
www.wbcsd.org

◢ **Major case study**

Asbestos: A toxic trade

By Nicholas McClaren, Deakin University

The manufacture and use of asbestos products and the importation of asbestos into India is booming. With government concessions, asbestos cement roofing is steadily displacing safer options such as thatch, tiles and steel. Asbestos products are even referred to as 'poor man's roofing', and despite concerns that the manufacture and use of the product carries health risks, it is still being used as a low-cost roofing material. Asbestos products have been banned in many developed countries, including Australia, for some years.

Nearly half of India's mineral wealth is found in the Jharkhand state. Home to some of India's poorest people, it has made some Indians very rich. In the Roro Hills, the waste from a mine abandoned in 1983 by one of India's biggest corporations has left a lunar-like landscape with a toxic mix of 0.6 million tons of asbestos waste and chromite-bearing host rock (chromite is a cancer-causing mineral) that extends several metres into the paddy fields, poisoning the local residents. In twenty years, no study had been done to assess the fate of this hazardous waste dump, despite the United Mine Workers Union issuing a press release in 1981 stating that thirty workers from Roro mines had died of asbestosis, and despite children still using it as a playground (Black Smith Institute, 2012).

The Chamanpura slum in Ahmedabad, India, has no toilets, no clean water, and huts roofed with scraps of tin and tarpaulins. Replacing these rooves with corrugated cement was seen by Indian companies as a commercial bonanza. This corrugated cement contains asbestos sourced from Canada, and at least as early as 2009 reports of Canadian involvement in the asbestos trade with India appeared in the press. In 2009, the Canadian Broadcasting Corporation filmed inside the Eagle Asbestos factory near Ahmedabad, a place where Canadian asbestos was used until recently, and where employees worked in a fog of carcinogenic dust, scooping up armfuls of raw asbestos fibre.

Superficially, the properties of asbestos cement sheeting are attractive compared to thatched, tarpaulin or tin rooves. It is less noisy in the monsoon rains, it's easily secured against high winds, it's fireproof, it won't corrode and it's virtually indestructible. Cement sheeting is also nearly three times cheaper than polypropylene alternatives. '[I]t is a magic mineral and no other substitute can match its properties,' says the Visaka Industries website (Visaka Industries Limited, 2012).

Not only are some employees being exposed to the asbestos used as insulation in buildings, but they have also been bringing the potentially harmful material into their homes from their workplace. Seventy-one-year-old Naran Mehra is sick after years of exposure to asbestos. His wife, Sevita Devi, having spent years shaking dust from his work clothes, now also has the disease. Little safety equipment is provided for asbestos workers in India, and few workers are likely to receive compensation if they develop respiratory illnesses such as asbestosis or a cancer such as mesothelioma, and are unlikely to be able to pay for proper medical treatment. As Peacock (2011) states, 'Asbestos illness in India is under-diagnosed and mostly unrecognised as a health problem.'

For thirty-one years, Muthuswami Munion and employees like him worked at Gujarat Composite, an asbestos cement manufacturing factory, covered in asbestos dust. He now has asbestosis in his lungs, is breathless, and lives in extreme pain. Muthuswami still works at the factory that's slowly killing him. It's most likely he'll

Not only are some employees being exposed to the asbestos used as insulation in buildings, but they have also been bringing the potentially harmful material into their homes from their workplace.

be dead in two years. Raghunath Munawar is a campaigner for sick asbestos workers, like Muthuswami, who, with little or no medical support, die unrecorded deaths in their villages. But being an activist has its problems—he has had death threats from union officials at Gujarat Composite, who accuse him of jeopardising workers' jobs. The Personnel Manager of Gujarat Composite believes that no worker there has become sick or diseased from asbestos, despite current workers being diagnosed with asbestosis.

In 1981, Gaddam Vivekanand founded Visaka Industries Ltd with the purpose of manufacturing asbestos cement sheets to replace thatched roofing in rural areas. Asbestos cement sheet was seen as the best alternative in terms of price, usage and market potential. Now Gaddam is an industrialist and a member of the ruling Congress Party. He owns and is vice-chairman of at least seven factories, and will be commissioning an eighth in the massively impoverished state of Orissa. He was elected to the Lok Sabha, one of India's houses of parliament, in 2008.

The use of asbestos cement sheeting has increased in India. Demand has increased more than 10 per cent yearly for Visaka Industries. In the 1980s India produced approximately half a million tonnes of asbestos cement roofing annually. This figure has grown to four million tonnes annually with Visaka Industries becoming India's third-largest producer. Although Visaka Industries sources asbestos from countries including Brazil, Russia, and Zimbabwe, Canada has historically been an important supplier. India is the largest importer of Canadian asbestos. Everest Industries Ltd is a competitor to Visaka Industries and is aware that five new fibre cement production lines, with a capacity of about 35,000 tonnes a month, are planned for the future.

There is debate about the safety and use of asbestos. Asbestos comes as three main types—blue or crocidolite, brown or amosite, and the most common white or chrysolite type. The blue form potentially causes cancer that only becomes apparent thirty or more years after exposure. All types of asbestos could cause the disease 'asbestosis', which is a scarring and shrinking of the lungs as they fill with asbestos fibres.

Not only is India using products that have been banned in other countries around the world, but asbestos is also being sourced, in part, from countries such as Canada, where its use is not permitted in their own domestic markets. As Professor Amir Attaran says, 'It amounts to Canada being a purveyor of death around the world. Our country is an exporter of a deadly substance, and we enjoy it ... at least our federal government does' (quoted in Peacock, 2011). Professor Attaran also says that 'The argument that chrysotile asbestos is safer than other kinds of asbestos is the most scientifically ridiculous nonsense I've ever heard. It's like saying light cigarettes are safer than regular cigarettes' (quoted in Peacock, 2011).

Arguments about the safety and use of asbestos range from the belief that it does not cause harm to 'relative risk'. Gaddam Vivekanand believes that the mineral does not cause cancer, but also argues on the basis of relative risk: 'Which product in the world is safe? Even a toothpick can be a dangerous thing' (quoted in Peacock, 2011). The asbestos industry is pouring millions of dollars into a campaign to assure India and to convince any other developing nation that may be in the market that white asbestos, or chrysotile, is safe.

In 2007, the National Institute of Occupational Health in Ahmedabad announced the launch of research into the health effects of exposure to asbestos in the workplace. But many people had doubts about the integrity of the study, given that it was to be funded by the industry itself and that a draft form of the report would be vetted by the industry. Visaka Industries funded about one-sixth of the estimated cost of the research, or $23,500. To date, the report has not been released.

Arguments about the safety and use of asbestos range from the belief that it does not cause harm to 'relative risk'.

The Chrysotile Institute advocates the safe use of certain forms of asbestos (Chysotile Institute, 2012a). The Chrysotile Institute, comprising industry, labour and government representatives, was established with the objective to promote the adoption and application of appropriate prevention and control measures, regulations, standards, work practices and techniques for the safe use of chrysotile. The Institute states that it relies on the cooperation of a large network of medical, scientific, legal and technical experts and advisors, who provide services upon request.

The Chrysotile Institute suggests that the banning of chrysotile is inconsistent with all current scientific evidence (Chrysotile Institute, 2012b). They note that the vast majority of scientists who attended a workshop co-sponsored by the International Commission on Occupational Safety and the International Programme on Chemical Safety recognised that the risk associated with exposure to chrysotile at today's standards is very low. They believe it is important to use solid science to guide decisions in matters such as this, and that the chrysotile industry has a responsibility to promote its safe use. The Chrysotile Institute claims asbestos can be used safely and that Canada supports the safe-use principle, which entails risk assessment and risk management not only for chrysotile, but for all minerals and metals. The institute believes products such as chrysotile cement, when used safely, do not pose any discernible risk to human health. The fact that countries banning chrysotile do not proceed to the removal of in place chrysotile-cement roof tiles, pipes and building plates, they say, supports this statement.

The Chrysotile Institute also suggests that the assertion that Canada is exporting chrysotile to developing countries and is not using the product itself is erroneously based on the quantity consumed in Canada compared to its shipments or the quantities consumed in other countries. They assert that on a per capita basis, Canada's consumption is 20 per cent greater than most consuming developed countries. They suggest that the use of chrysotile in developing countries—as a part of a material used for the distribution of potable water for irrigation purposes and for housing projects—do not pose a health threat to the public. Alternative products are more expensive to use and do not permit the development of a local industry. They claim that some of the substitute products are not safer than chrysotile. The Chrysotile Institute also asserts that claims that asbestos will kill 100,000 people a year around the world is far from reality and that the calculation does not establish the differences between all asbestos fibres. People, they say, should know that amphiboles are far more dangerous for health than chrysotile and that the data used by those wanting to ban asbestos

are extrapolated from exposure to asbestos fibres, mainly amphiboles.

Others doubt the credibility of the Chrysotile Institute, claiming that the Canadian government has poured millions of dollars into a lobby group that peddles the message that asbestos can be used safely in the developing world, even though it clearly hasn't been in Canada. As Professor Amir Attaran says, 'There is absolutely no disease that affects workers more in Quebec than asbestos disease, mesothelioma, so it has killed hundreds, if not thousands of people in Canada, particularly the miners, but in other industries too' (quoted in Peacock, 2011). There is also argument about whether the mining of asbestos has ceased in Canada. Following the closure of the Jeffrey Mine in Asbestos (Quebec) for financial and environmental reasons, and the announcement early in 2011 that production was halted at the Lac d'amiante du Canada mine (also in Quebec), commentators claimed that Canada's asbestos mines were quiet. But the owner of the Jeffrey Mine says his mine isn't closed and both companies continue selling asbestos from their reserve stock. A Montreal asbestos trader is working to reopen the Jeffrey Mine and to resume production in 2012 (Ban Asbestos Now, 2011).

Thetford Mines produces asbestos and Luc Berthold, its Town Mayor, is convinced that the product offers many advantages and is acceptable if used safely. Canada's Prime Minister, Stephen Harper, says in India asbestos is legal, so Canada is entitled to export it. But how can India be expected to exceed safety standards the rest of the world has never met? In June 2011, the Canadian Medical Association wrote an open letter to Stephen Harper expressing their association's concern with his support of the Canadian asbestos industry, referring to significant scientific evidence that exposure to asbestos through mining, processing and use is harmful to human health. Asbestos, they wrote, including the chrysotile variety, causes cancer, including lung cancer and mesothelioma. They noted that the World Health Organization estimates that globally at least 90,000 people die each year of asbestos-related lung cancer, mesothelioma and asbestosis resulting from occupational exposure. They urged him to end his support for an industry that exports asbestos to nations that do not have the health and safety infrastructure or regulations to ensure conditions of controlled use (Canadian Medical Association, 2011).

Hyderabad Industries Limited's asbestos cement sheets are produced in eight factories around India and it is Canada's biggest customer of asbestos. The Managing Director, Abhaya Shanker, is also the head of the industry lobby that promotes asbestos. 'This particular asbestos has not been known to give cancer so far,' he says, and people '... are wrong about chrysotile asbestos because they have banned asbestos when the blue asbestos, which is the dangerous kind, was being used and that was giving them health problems because the Western world were using it irresponsibly' (Black Smith Institute, 2012). But he seems to be ignoring the warning that this asbestos can cause fatal diseases like cancer that are printed on the bags of Canadian asbestos in his own factory. Hyderabad Industries was the same company that owned the mine at Roro.

Questions

1 Evaluate the first three levels of corporate social responsibility in the case using the pyramid of corporate social responsibility (Carroll, 1991).

2 Based on the information provided in the case, explain the decision making of Gaddam Vivekanand, founder of Visaka Industries Ltd, in terms of deontological and teleological ethical approaches.

3 Using your responses to the preceding question, what action would you take if you were head of the government department responsible for the health and safety in India?

4 What other information would you want to obtain to inform your decision about the action you would take if you were head of the government department responsible for the health and safety in India?

5 What actions would you take if you were the marketing manager of an Indian company that planned to continue to manufacture and sell asbestos cement sheeting? Assume that this is a legal but potentially harmful product and that the public pressure against its use will increase.

6 Assume you are the marketing manager for an Indian company that sells asbestos cement sheeting to building and construction as well as individual users, and that you have positioned it as a safe but potentially harmful product. Provide an outline of your target market strategy including only the details of the distribution and promotion decisions that address corporate social responsibility concerns for these two targets.

GLOSSARY

100% loyals

Consumers of a brand who bought only that brand and no other brand during a period of analysis.

above the line media

Typically traditional media that is usually booked through a media or advertising agency (television, radio, print).

advertising

Most advertising is paid for, marketer controlled (written and produced) one-way communication with potential buyers. However, in recent years we are seeing more examples of advertising that is interactive, less tightly controlled or more akin to unpaid public relations.

advertising agencies

Providers that are contracted by an organisation to develop campaign concepts, as well as to produce and find placements for finished ads.

advertising avoidance

When viewers avoid being exposed to advertisements. Avoidance can be active (switching the channel, turning a page or leaving the room) or passive (talking or concentrating on something else).

advertising budget

The sum of money available for communication of a brand through advertising. It incorporates spend on production (non-working media) as well as media placement (working media).

advertising clutter

The amount of other advertising and other non-program material that appears within a medium.

advertising copy

Creative text printed or recorded for use in an advertisement.

advertising tracking

Advertising research that measures the effects of an advertisement after it has been aired/placed.

agent

An individual or organisation employed to provide a specific service.

Ansoff matrix

A simple planning framework indicating that there are four ways for a company to expand its sales: grow its market share, introduce a new product, move into a new market or diversify its activities (Ansoff, 1965).

(brand) attributes (in memory)

Small pieces of information that a buyer links to a particular brand—these may be conscious or subconscious associations. For example, Coca-Cola may be linked with the attributes 'red', 'white', 'refreshing', 'summer', 'beach' and 'pizza'.

audience accumulation

Total net audience reached by a media vehicle.

audience targeting

Choosing media that specifically target a particular customer type; for example, advertising in a horse magazine to reach horse riders.

banner advertising

A paid form of online advertising where an image (still or animated) that links to the advertised brand's website is embedded into a relevant web page.

below the line media

Typically non-traditional media expenditure such as DM or CRM. The term is sometimes also used to encompass in-store activity and even price promotions.

birth rate

The number of live births per 1000 people per year.

'black box'

How the metric is measured or calculated is kept hidden. Research consultancies claim it is secret because the measure is so special and valuable, yet they all offer very similar services, and staff move between the market research agencies, so it is unlikely that there really is anything special or unique inside any of the black boxes. Keeping them secret, however, prevents marketers from evaluating the metric and really finding out what they are buying.

brand

A distinctive and individual name or logo that is given to a product (or group of products) that distinguishes the products of one company from the products sold by their competitors.

brand equity

The financial value of a brand's market-based assets (mental and physical availability). Also sometimes used to refer to a consumer's subjective assessment of how much better or preferred the brand is. Under this latter (not very useful) definition, higher quality, higher priced brands have higher equity.

brand image

The perception of the brand in the minds of consumers.

brand performance metrics

The different statistics that marketers measure and use to track the performance of their brand. These include market share, penetration, repeat-buying rate and other metrics (described in Chapter 3).

brand recall

The ability of a customer to retrieve the name of a brand from their memory unprompted or with a category prompt.

brand recognition

The ability of a customer to correctly recognise a brand in a situation where they are prompted with stimuli (such as packaging in a supermarket or brand names on a drinks menu).

business cycle

The periodic fluctuation in levels of economic activity, influencing profitability, output, productivity and employment. The cycle consists of periods of boom, downturn, recession and upturn.

business model

The way a business competes and makes money; for example, Google's business model is to provide free search services to consumers and then sell search advertising to businesses.

business-to-business (B2B) marketing

Marketing products or services to other businesses rather than to consumers.

campaign

A planned series of advertisements that appear in one or more media over a specific time period. The advertisements often share an idea or theme.

capital investment

Investment in fixed assets for business or industrial use, such as machinery, equipment and so on.

category

A grouping of all brands that are selling the same product or providing the same service; for example, Fanta belongs to the soft drink product category.

causal research

Research that looks at the relationship between variables and the direction of the relationship between them; for example, 'What is the impact of an increase in store opening hours on store traffic?'

cause-related marketing (CRM)

An alliance between a brand and a charity or cause in order to benefit each.

centrally planned economy

An economy that is controlled by the government. Instead of fluctuating with demand, prices are set by the government, which also determines what will be produced, who will produce it and how much they will be paid. Shown to be disastrous for economic growth. North Korea may be the last centrally planned economy in the world, although market economies of countries vary in the degree of government intervention.

chains

Multiple outlets that are commonly owned and controlled, have centralised buying and merchandising, and sell similar line of merchandising; for example, supermarket chains.

choice situation

The moment when and place where a consumer makes a purchase decision. Examples include selecting a type and brand of milk in the supermarket aisle, deciding on a charity to donate money to, or ordering a drink at a bar.

circulation

Usually refers to how many copies of a print medium (e.g. a magazine) are sold. Readership is therefore always a higher figure.

cognitive effort

Mental effort, using reasoning, intuition or perception.

commercial media

Media that carries paid advertising.

comparative advertising

Advertising that aims to influence consumer preference by comparison with competitor brands.

competitors

Organisations that compete for the same consumer spending, with a directly or indirectly substitutable product.

concurrent media usage

Using more than one form of media at the same time; for example, posting updates to Facebook while watching television.

confidence interval

The margin or numerical range of sampling error around a research result.

confidence level

The level of certainty that the true population result lies within the stated confidence interval.

conglomerates

Large corporations that are made up of diverse companies operating in different fields.

consumer products

Products bought by private people for their personal use or consumption, or for the personal use of other people such as their family members or friends.

consumers

The people or companies who use the service or product.

contingency plan

A plan to be implemented only upon the occurrence of future events other than those in the accepted plan.

continuous innovations

Products with a minor innovation to other existing products; for example, a toothpaste product introducing a new ingredient.

corporate citizenship

The concept that corporations, like people, have both rights and obligations to the societies within which they exist. Philanthropic behaviour such as support for a charity, cause or artistic enterprise might be regarded as good corporate citizenship.

corporate planning

Corporate planning is distinct from corporate strategy in that strategy involves the decisions about what to do next in the marketplace, while planning is the methods to go about implementing the strategy.

corporate social responsibility (CSR)

A commitment by business to behave ethically, to contribute to economic development and to improve the quality of life of the workforce, their families, the local community and society at large.

cost per thousand (CPM)

The cost of a single advertisement divided by the number of people who can be reached by that one spot.

country of origin (COO)

The country where the products are made; COO can influence consumers' perceptions regarding the product.

creatives

The people responsible for developing the creative content of advertisements and other planned promotions.

customer-based metrics

Metrics that measure things such as customer satisfaction, awareness and perceptions of the brand. They can be quantitative and/or qualitative.

customer lifetime value (CLV)

An estimate of the profitability of a customer to a firm over their lifetime as a customer.

customer relationship management (CRM) systems

Information systems for gathering and analysing information on existing clients with a view to deepening knowledge, improving relationships and growing sales to those customers.

customer satisfaction

The measurement of how many consumers are satisfied with the company's product/service, thought to capture how well an organisation meets or exceeds customer expectation.

customer value

The profits a firm earns by having a particular customer during a particular time period (such as last year).

demographic groups

Groups used by marketers as a way of dividing the population into useful segments; for example, based on gender, race, income and/or location.

demography

The study of human populations in terms of size, density, location, age, sex, occupation, education and other characteristics.

descriptive research

Research that establishes the incidence of an issue or behaviour, such as how many people buy a product, when they buy or what they buy; for example, many people regularly 'tweet'.

differentiation

Being perceived by most or many buyers as meaningfully different from other rival brands in the category.

direct cost pricing

A method of accounting for costs that identifies all costs that can be associated with a product or service.

direct mail (DM)

Advertisements that are delivered to homes directly.

discontinuous innovations

Products with a completely new set of attributes to other existing products and that require users to change or learn new behaviour; for example, digital music downloads.

disintermediation

Removing the middleman, bringing consumers directly in contact with the manufacturer. It was thought that the internet would remove all middlemen, but many have simply changed form, becoming places to research products before trying them in store.

distinctive assets

Non-brand-name elements that are unique to the brand and can evoke the brand in the memory of many consumers (for example, characters such as Louie the Fly for Mortein).

distribution

Making goods and services physically available to buyers use. This can involve selecting retailers to sell the product and supplying them with the goods.

double jeopardy law

A marketing law that states the relationship between size and loyalty metrics: brands with less market share have far fewer buyers, and these buyers are slightly less loyal (i.e. small brands suffer twice).

duplication of viewing/listening law

The pattern observed in the sharing of audiences across media platforms. Media share viewers and listeners in line with market share: the smaller media platforms (such as magazines) share more customers with bigger media platforms (such as television).

dynamic continuous innovations

Products that utilise a new technology in an existing product but do not require the user to change or learn new behaviour; for example, LED lights for car headlights.

ecological environment

Commonly referred to as 'the environment'—anything from the natural world that will have an effect on the business, be it climate change, the need to avoid polluting, or a flock of birds interfering with power transmission lines.

economic growth

An increase in the output of an entire economy—that is, the amount of goods or services produced—in real terms.

EDI (electronic data interchange)

The structured transmission of data between organisations by electronic means. It is used to exchange information automatically between organisations, leading to far-reaching efficiencies.

empirical

Based on direct observation and data gathered from the real world, rather than theories, logic or preconceived models.

ethics

The principles of morality (that is, concepts of right and wrong) that influence attitudes and behaviour.

evidence-based marketing

Marketing in which decisions are based on reliable, generalised knowledge about how the world works, how buyers buy and how market interventions work.

exploratory research

Research in order to gain an understanding of what the issues are; for example, how the presence of children under five years of age affects a parent's supermarket shopping trip.

eye-tracking studies

A research methodology that determines which part of an advertisement or packaging consumers look at, by tracking the pattern of their eye movements.

fertility rate

The number of babies a woman would have in her lifetime were she to have the exact current average number of babies for women her age.

fixed costs (or overheads)

Costs that are not dependent on the level of goods and services produced by the business. They are generally tied to time periods, such as salaries paid per month, or rents paid quarterly or yearly.

frequency of exposure

The number of times a consumer is exposed to an advertisement.

full (total or absorption) cost pricing

A method of accounting for costs that includes the full or total cost of manufacturing a product or providing a service. Costs of materials and labour and all manufacturing overheads (fixed and variable) are also included.

full-service agencies

Marketing agencies that can provide a full range of services, from market research and analysis to implementation.

functional (or realistic) range of prices

The highest and the lowest prices for a category of closely substitutable goods, found in the normal course of trade.

glocalisation

Global marketing that incorporates considerable local adaptations.

grey market

A market where an agent imports a brand without using the brand owner's distribution network. This can mean the brand owner can lose control of the pricing and distribution of its brand in a particular market.

gross domestic product (GDP)

The total value of all goods and services produced by an economy (usually a country) in a single year.

gross rating points (GRPs)

The total number of rating points for a particular period of time. It can be calculated from reach multiplied by frequency.

heavy buyer

Someone who buys the category or brand more frequently than the average.

heuristics

Experience-based mental tools that people use to simplify decision making. Examples include rules of thumb, hunches, common sense, trial and error approaches, and so on.

import quotas

Trade restrictions limiting the amount of commodities allowed to be imported during a specific time period and often by specific countries.

industrial products

Products bought for further processing and sale or for use in conducting a business.

infrastructure

The basic physical and organisational structures and facilities (such as buildings, roads and power supplies) needed for the operation of a society or enterprise.

integrated marketing communications (IMC)

Advertising placed across media in a complementary and harmonious manner.

interactive advertising

Planned promotion or advertising that seeks to generate an active response from consumers.

intermediaries

Middlemen, such as wholesalers, resellers or transport agencies. They help large companies to deal with smaller companies, who then deal with consumers individually.

internal environment

Components of an organisation, such as the employees, physical tools and communication methods, which affect corporate culture. The internal environment is the most important determiner of how well an organisation responds to change.

light buyer

Someone who buys the category or brand less frequently than the average.

line extension

Further versions of a product in the same category put into the market using the same brand name as the original; for example, the many versions of powdered coffee bearing the Nescafé brand name.

localisation

The process by which globally launched campaigns, products and services can be customised and made relevant to the local market; or marketing exclusively to local markets with in-depth knowledge of their needs, wants, tastes and so on.

long tail

The skew of customers who are exposed to a large number of advertisement spots.

loyalty (in a behavioural sense)

Restricting buying to a personal repertoire of brands, which is relatively stable over time. This means buying some brands much more often than others.

macro-environment

The larger, wider forces that have influence over companies and economies, including political, social and economic forces.

make-goods

Free spots provided to an advertiser to match original audience-size goals (TARPs or spots) that were not initially achieved.

mandatory brand requirements (mandatories)

Words, images or any other requirements that the creative team must include in the advertising; for example, brand name, logo, a specific font and so on.

manufacturing

Producing or making some thing on a large scale with the help of machinery and equipment.

many sets of data (MSoD) approach

Identifying commonalities and repeated patterns across multiple sets of data.

marginal cost pricing

A method of accounting that focuses on determining the change in cost (marginal cost) of producing one extra unit. This can be useful in arriving at a cost for a tiny change in quantity at a given level of production—that is, the cost per unit.

market

The total number of potential buyers for a product or service.

market-based assets

The mental and physical availability that makes a brand easier to buy for more people, in more situations.

market-based pricing

A pricing method in which an organisation evaluates the prices of similar products on the market and sets its own price so that it is competitive. This can also be called competition-based pricing.

market economy

An economy in which consumer demand guides production and prices, and there is competition between privately owned businesses.

market objectives

Marketing goals for an organisation, or part of an organisation. They should be specific, measurable, achievable, reasonable and time-based (SMART).

market partitions

Closely competing products within an overall market; for example, children's cereal products among all cereal products.

market penetration

The extent to which a product is recognised and bought by customers in a particular market.

market research

The gathering of factual information (often through observations and surveys) about the market—including what buyers think and do, particularly their watching (of advertising), buying and consuming.

market segmentation

Analysing the differences and commonalities in buyer behaviour in order to identify target segments.

market share

The total category sales that are devoted to a particular brand. It can be measured in terms of units sold, volume or dollars.

marketing audit

A systematic evaluation of a company's existing marketing environment, objectives, strategies, programs and organisation, with a view to determining effectiveness and areas for improvement.

marketing environment

The individuals, organisations and forces external to the marketing management function of an organisation that impinge on the marketing management's ability to develop and maintain successful exchanges with customers.

marketing interventions

The different actions that marketers carry out in order to meet strategic goals and grow their brand; for example, advertising campaigns.

marketing metrics

Measures used to evaluate marketing actions and brand performance, and to inform marketing decisions.

marketing mix

Set of manageable elements in a brand's marketing plan, adjusted to implement the marketing strategy: product, price, promotion and place.

marketing plan

A systematic approach to the achievement of strategies and goals. It will usually include at least a SWOT analysis, target markets, objectives, a marketing strategy including action programs, implementation, control and review, and evaluation.

marketing science

The study of marketing, which seeks to develop scientific laws and patterns that repeat under known conditions.

marketing strategy

The way marketing activities are put together to achieve the organisation's aims for the brand. Marketing strategy is usually developed by the marketing leaders in consultation with key stakeholders.

mass marketing

A strategy where the marketer focuses on the entire market rather than a specific segment of consumers.

mass media

Media that reaches vast numbers of people quickly; for example, television.

media agencies

Agencies that consult and liaise between media buyers and media providers.

media auditing

Post-campaign analysis that includes analysing return on investment: whether an advertiser really received the advertising spots they paid for.

media buying

The process of purchasing media, typically undertaken by an agent or a brand (for example, Coca-Cola is a media buyer).

media planning

The strategic scheduling of media expenditure and measurement.

media vehicle

A specific media source employed in an advertising campaign.

memory structures

Categories and interrelations within memory that help information recall.

mental availability

The likelihood of a brand being noticed and/or thought of in buying situations.

merchandise

Goods bought and sold.

micro-environment

All those other organisations and individuals that, directly or indirectly, affect the activities of the organisation.

mission statement

A brief statement, no longer than a few sentences, that describes the company's raison d'être—the reason it exists. It should embody its values and work ethic, and be re-evaluated every few years to reflect changes in the organisation.

multivariate analysis

Analysis that involves looking at multiple variables simultaneously and establishing the statistical relationships between them in that set of data.

negative inflation

Falling prices, resulting in growth in sales not occurring.

net promoter score

A measure of customers' claimed willingness to recommend a company's product or services to others.

new media

New platforms for communicating with consumers that are typically digital and often linked to the internet; for example, social media sites, podcasts and e-books.

non-probability sampling

Method of sampling where a set of respondents are selected by a researcher or when respondents elect themselves to be involved.

non-profit organisations

Businesses (such as charities) that do not operate with the key purpose of making a profit.

non-response rate

The proportion (percentage) of the sample initially selected to take part in the survey that was either not contactable or refused to participate.

offerings

The different products (and associated benefits) that a company sells. A product offering includes many other features than just the physical product (for example, packaging, service, customer support, design, special features and so on).

open-ended questions

Questions in a qualitative survey that have a text field for the response, allowing consumers to type in their own answers of any length.

opportunity to see/hear (OTS)

A measure of how many people had the chance to see or hear an advertisement. Note that this is distinguished from actual exposure, which is the number of people who *did* see an advertisement. OTS is particularly useful for out of home advertising, as it is nearly impossible to count actual impressions but much easier to count how many had the opportunity (for instance, one can calculate how many people could have seen a billboard through traffic videoing).

optimisation

Setting the best price to achieve an organisation's objective, such as maximum profit, sales or profit margin.

optimisation software

Systems typically owned by media agencies, based on specific assumptions about how marketing works, and used to recommend a media mix, reach and frequency to media buyers.

out of home media

Media that is consumed outside the home; for example, on a billboard or shop window.

paid search advertising

Paying for links to appear alongside the top search results in a search engine.

panel data

Repeat-purchasing (or repeat-viewing) data collected over time from a panel of respondents so patterns of buying over time can be seen at the individual or household level.

panel scanner data

Data captured at the point of sale by scanning the barcodes of products.

personal selling

Any persuasive communication conducted directly between sellers and potential consumers face to face or orally, with the intention of making a sale.

physical availability

How often the product or service is literally available in a buying situation.

polygamous (or divided) loyalty

The propensity for buyers to be loyal to several brands within a category (to shop within a repertoire).

positioning

Developing a brand image to appeal to a particular target segment.

pressure groups

Groups that stand for a cause, sometimes known as lobby or advocacy groups. For example, the RSPCA advocates for the ethical treatment of animals, and Mothers Against Drink Driving oppose, of course, drink driving.

pre-testing

Advertising research conducted before an advertisement has been aired/placed or on a concept before it has been produced. Pre-testing aims to determine if the ad or concept will be an effective use of media spend and/or if improvements need to be made.

price elasticity

A measure of responsiveness to price, calculated as the percentage change in quantity divided by the percentage change in price.

probability sampling

Method of sampling where a set of respondents are selected from the population or database at random.

probability theory

The theory that if a sample is sufficiently large and well chosen, it will likely provide results that are accurate and similar to the results for the true population. Probability theory provides estimates of how close the sample's score should be to the true population score. See *confidence interval*, and *random sampling variation*.

product category life cycle (PLC)

The pattern of a product category's sales and profits over time from introduction. It is suggested that there are four stages that are passed through, after product development: introduction, growth, maturity and decline.

product placement

The presence of a branded product or service within an entertainment program; for example, a Starbucks cup in the television show *Friends*.

product positioning

Using advertising to try to create a brand identity or develop a specific image for a product or organisation in the minds of consumers.

product variation

When one company offers more choice to the consumer by selling different variations of the same product; for example, Coca-Cola, Diet Coke, Coke Zero, Vanilla Coke, and so on—or even different brands (Fanta, Sprite).

production department

The area of a business concerned with manufacturing the product.

profit contribution

The piece of your sales that contributes to your profit; the sales price received minus the expenses or variable costs.

profit margin

The amount by which revenue from sales exceeds costs for a business.

program rating

The number of viewers or listeners of a program.

public relations (PR)

Unpaid communication that is not completely in the control of the marketer, but which can be encouraged and influenced by them. In modern marketing, the line is becoming blurred between unpaid PR and paid advertising.

purchase frequency

How *often* the customers who bought the brand during the period (its penetration) bought it (on average) during that same period.

random sampling variation

The error in survey results because a random sample can only ever be approximately representative of a larger population. With repeated samples a score can vary (bounce around) even if the true value in the population is stable. For example, if 37 per cent of Australians have wi-fi in their house, one survey of a random sample of Australians might report that 33 per cent do, while another might report that 41 per cent do.

ratings data

Audience measurement tool to determine the size of the audience, which is used by media sellers and buyers (the higher the ratings, the more audience: thus the higher the price for the spot).

reach

The proportion of the total population that is exposed at least once to an advertisement.

regionalisation

The process by which marketing concentrates on a population in a particular area that has characteristics that are distinguishable from other areas. A region can be a nation state or a group of nation states, such as Western Europe or South-East Asia.

relational market-based assets (rMBAs)

Assets that arise from the co-mingling of the firm and its product with entities in its external environment, including distributors, retailers, end-customers, other strategic partners, community groups and even governmental agencies. The bonds constituting these relationships and the sources of them may vary from one stakeholder type to another. For example, brand and channel equity reflect bonds between the firm and its channels and customers. Brand equity may be the result of extensive advertising and superior product functionality. Channel equity may be in part a result of long-standing and successful business relationships between the firm and key channel members (Srivastava, Shervani & Fahey, 1998).

repeat-purchasing (or repeat-buying)

When a consumer purchases the same category, or the same brand twice in a row (two consecutive purchase occasions). A brand's repeat-purchasing rate is a metric that measures the proportion of a brand's customers that are repeat purchasers.

repertoire

The different brands that a customer buys within a product category. Consumers are rarely 100 per cent loyal, but instead purchase from their own particular repertoire of brands.

research brief

Written by the research client, this document outlines the management problem behind the research, what the research objectives are, and the resources the company has for the project in terms of existing knowledge, budget, time and staff.

research objectives

What the research project is broadly about; for example, to identify usage of and attitudes towards a brand, to identify key drivers of customer satisfaction, or to identify how customers navigate a store.

research population

The group of people who meet the criteria to be included in the research. Sample results from research are generalised back to this research 'parent' population.

research proposal

Written by the research provider, this document sets out how the market research agency proposes to meet the client's research objectives. It is written in response to the research brief and is a selling document for the research provider, outlining why they are well sited to conduct the research and how they will go about it.

response rate

The proportion (percentage) of the sample initially selected to take part in the survey that actually participates in the research.

retail

Selling goods or services directly to the final consumer for their personal, non-business use.

retail partner

A retailer that has an agreement to stock a company's products.

retailer advertising

Advertising by retailers about their products, offers and specials.

retailers

The physical and online stores where the consumer can buy the end product; for example, supermarkets. Retailers buy goods in large quantities from the manufacturer and sell them to many buyers.

RFID (radio frequency identification)

A device, usually in the form of a tag, attached to a product that allows tracking of its movement. It is commonly used in a supply chain operation or in retailing for security purposes.

sales

Total revenue or number of products sold during a given time frame.

sample size

The total number of people from whom data is collected.

satisfice

To satisfy and suffice: a term coined by Nobel Prize–winning economist Herbert A Simon (1957).

search engine advertising

Paid listings that increase visibility of a website when specific search terms are entered into a search engine such as Google or Yahoo!.

secondary data

Data that exists for purposes other than the project at hand. It can be past research projects, company records, industry reports or any other information that can be used to assist with the current research problem.

selective vehicles

Media platforms that claim to reach a select group of potential consumers with little wastage.

selectivity

The extent to which a media vehicle delivers a specific type of audience; for example, a golfing magazine may largely deliver golfers and may be geared towards men.

shareholders

In effect, the owners of a company. Ownership is split into many parts, each for sale on the share market. Shareholders have a range of rights, from a share of profits (that is, a dividend) to control over the company.

share of category requirements (SCR)

The proportion of category purchases that go to a particular brand in a given period of time. It is always a percentage ranging from 0 to 100 per cent.

share of mind

The quantity and quality of memory links that connect information to a particular brand in the consumer's mind.

share of voice (SoV)

A measure of the total number of mentions that a company gets in its target media relative to its main competitor. It is a measure of awareness and image in the media rather than in the minds of the target audience.

significance level

Also known as the p-value, the chance that this result has arisen by chance due to random sampling variation. It does not mean that the result is important or useful; nor that the result will occur again under different conditions.

single-source data

Data gathered by tracking individuals' levels of advertising exposure and their purchases, over a long period of time.

SMEs

Small-to-medium enterprises, sometimes known as SMBs (small-to-medium businesses). SMEs far outnumber larger businesses and are often faster to innovate. Definitions vary, but SMEs usually have between ten and 250 employees.

socio-cultural environment

The various institutions and forces that affect society's values, perceptions and behaviours, and determine its culture.

stakeholders

Everyone who will be affected by the actions of the organisation, or who will be charged with carrying out these actions. This may include suppliers, customers, employees, people who live nearby, and so on.

standardisation

Offering the same products everywhere with global marketing campaigns. By standardising products and promotions, the global company forces costs and prices down, and pushes quality and reliability up.

statistically significant

Unlikely to have occurred by chance.

stock-keeping units (SKUs)

Each product stocked by a store; for example, different pack sizes or flavours of a particular brand.

strategic business unit (SBU)

A smaller part of a business but large enough to require its own marketing plan and specific campaigns. SBUs can be part of larger SBUs. For instance, a company might have an SBU for 'dental care' and then smaller SBUs for specific brands.

supply chain

The sequence of processes that moves a product or service from its production point to the point of availability to the consumer.

sustainable

Able to be maintained perpetually.

sustainable marketing

Marketing that involves an ongoing analysis of long-term risks in order to ensue that the business model and customer demand is sustainable.

SWOT analysis

An important part of a marketing plan, outlining the internal strengths and weaknesses, and external opportunities and threats. Threats can sometimes be viewed as opportunities, and weaknesses can sometimes be viewed as strengths.

syndicated data

Data collected by commercial market research firms, such as OzTAM, who then sell that data to media agencies and advertisers.

target audience measurement (TAM)

Data collected to capture the number of audience members (reach) delivered via television.

target audience rating points (TARPs)

An audience measurement tool that measures the proportion of a target audience among the total audience. It is measured within a specific media vehicle, such as a television channel or program.

targeting

Adjusting the marketing mix to cater for different target segments or choosing not to serve some segments.

target marketing

A strategy that identifies a target segment and focuses marketing communications on speaking directly to this group.

target segment (or target group)

A group of potential buyers within a market that share some common attributes and that are seen as desirable and valuable as customers.

technology boom

When one technology or capability is added to an unrelated product or service and creates an added benefit through the synergy that occurs. For example, adding cameras to mobile phones has made taking photographs and the pleasure from this much more widespread than when people had to carry around both a phone and a separate camera; it has also made mobile phones more desirable and they now carry higher prices.

temporary price promotion

Setting a price lower than the usual price or offering a special deal, such as two for the price of one (effectively a 50 per cent price cut), for a limited time. After the promotion period, the price goes back to the previous level.

touch points

Media sources that potential consumers might see or hear throughout a day.

trade

Exchanging one thing for another; buying and selling goods and services.

traditional media

Traditional platforms for communicating messages, pre-dating the internet—television, press (newspapers, magazines), radio, outdoor and cinemas.

triple bottom line (TBL or 3BL)

A set of summary business performance measures that report the social and environmental impacts for the period along with the financial results.

univariate analysis

Analysis that involves looking at each variable's relationship with another in turn.

value-based pricing

A method of pricing in which an organisation estimates the value of its product or service to the customer and uses that as its basis for setting price.

variable costs

Costs that change in proportion to the activity level of the business.

Warc

A useful resource (www.warc.com) for those interested in advertising. It provides access to industry data, articles and case studies concerning a wide range of advertising, marketing, media and research subjects.

wastage

The proportion of an audience that is not within the advertiser's target audience but who see the advertisement anyway.

wearout

When advertising that has been in the media for a long time loses its effectiveness.

word-of-mouth (WOM)

Unpaid, uncontrolled oral or written communication about a brand or business circulated by the public; it can be positive or (more rarely) negative.

BIBLIOGRAPHY

AAP (2012) 'Oroton profit gains but shares slump', *The Sydney Morning Herald*, 21 March, retrieved 10 May 2012 from <www.smh.com.au/business/oroton-profit-gains-but-shares-slump-20120321-1vj01.html>.

Abatt, R & Cowan, D (1999) 'Client-agency perspectives of information needs for media planning', *Journal of Advertising Research*, vol. 39, pp. 37–52.

ABC News (2011) 'Supermarkets ordered to keep price war records', *ABC*, 20 October, retrieved 10 May 2012 from <www.abc.net.au/news/2011-10-20/accc-keeping-27close-eye27-on-coles2c-woolworths/3580358>.

Abratt, R & Penman, N (2002) 'Understanding factors affecting salespeople's perceptions of ethical behavior in South Africa', *Journal of Business Ethics*, vol. 35, no. 4, pp. 269–80.

Ad Contrarian (2011) 'Social Media's Massive Failure', *The Ad Contrarian*, 21 March, retrieved 6 August 2012 from <http://adcontrarian.blogspot.com.au/2011/03/social-medias-massive-failure.html>.

Adelaide Fringe (2012) 'About', retrieved 15 May 2012 from <www.adelaidefringe.com.au/about>.

Adkins, S (2004) *Who Cares Wins*, Business in the Community, London.

Advertising Standards Bureau (2010) 'Advertisements modified/discontinued', Red Bull (Food and Beverages), March, retrieved 3 May 2010 from <www.adstandards.com.au/pages/casestudy_c.asp>.

Ahmed, P K & Rafiq, M (2002), *Internal Marketing: Tools and Concepts for Customer Focused Management*, Butterworth Heinemann, Oxford.

Aitra, R (2003) 'Why India's economy lags behind China's', *Asia Times*, 27 June, retrieved 16 May 2012 from <www.atimes.com/atimes/South_Asia/EF27Df04.html>.

Ambler, T (2000) 'Marketing metrics', *Business Strategy Review*, vol. 11, no. 2.

——, Broadbent, S & Feldwick, P (1998) 'Does advertising affect market size? Some evidence from the United Kingdom', *International Journal of Advertising*, vol. 17, no. 3.

Anderson, J R (1983) 'A spreading activation theory of memory', *Journal of Verbal Learning and Verbal Behavior*, vol. 22, pp. 261–95.

——& Bower, G H (1973) *Human Associative Memory*, Washington, Winston & Sons.

Andreasen, A R (2003) 'The life trajectory of social marketing', *Marketing Theory*, vol. 3, no. 3, pp. 293–303.

Andrews, J C, Durvasula, S & Akhter, S H (1990) 'A framework for conceptualizing and measuring the involvement construct in advertising research', *Journal of Advertising*, vol. 19, pp. 27–40.

Anschuetz, N (1997) 'Point of view: Building brand popularity: The myth of segmenting to brand success', *Journal of Advertising Research*, January/February.

Ansoff, I (1965) *Corporate Strategy*, McGraw-Hill.

Antia, K, Bergen, M & Dutta, S (2004) 'Competing with gray markets', *MIT Sloan Management Review*, vol. 46, no. 1, pp. 63–9.

Apple (2012) 'Supplier responsibility at Apple', retrieved 30 April 2012 from <www.apple.com/supplierresponsibility>.

Aristotle (2008) 'Nicomachean Ethics' in J Cottingham, *Western Philosophy: An Anthology*, 2nd edn, Blackwell Publishing, Oxford.

Armstrong, J S (1985) 'Evidence on the value of strategic planning in marketing: How much planning should a marketing planner plan?' in H Thomas & D Gardner (eds) *Strategic Marketing and Management*, John Wiley & Sons, pp. 73–87.

——(1991) 'Strategic planning improves manufacturing performance', *Long Range Planning*, vol. 24, no. 4, pp. 127–9.

——& Reibstein, D J (1982) 'The value of formal planning for strategic decisions: Review of empirical research', *Strategic Management Journal*, vol. 3, pp. 197–211.

Armstrong, N & Wagner, M (2003) *Field Guide to Gestures: How to Identify and Interpret Virtually Every Gesture Known to Man*, Quirk Books, Philadelphia.

Arnott's Biscuits Limited (2012) 'FAQ', retrieved 3 June 2012 from <www.arnotts.com/faq.aspx>.

Assael, H (1970) 'Segmenting markets by group purchasing behaviour: An application of the AID technique', *Journal of Marketing Research*, vol. 7, pp. 153–8.

Assael, H & Cannon, H (1979) 'Do demographics help in media selection', *Journal of Advertising Research*, vol. 19, pp. 7–11.

Assael, H & Poltrack, D F (1991) 'Using single source data to select TV programs based on purchasing behavior', *Journal of Advertising Research*, vol. 31, pp. 9–17.

Astolfi, L, Fallani, F D V, Cincotti, F, Mattia, D, Bianchi, L, Marciani, M G, Salinari, S, Gaudiano, I, Scarano, G, Soranzo, R & Babiloni, F (2009) 'Brain activity during the memorization of visual scenes from TV commercials: An application of high resolution EEG and steady state somatosensory evoked potentials technologies', *Journal of Physiology-Paris*, vol. 103, pp. 333–41.

Auger, P & Devinney, T M (2007) 'Do what consumers say matter? The misalignment of preferences with unconstrained ethical intentions', *Journal of Business Ethics*, vol. 76, pp. 361–83.

Australian Aluminium Council (2010) Australian Aluminium, Australian Aluminium Council Ltd, retrieved 12 March 2012 from <http://aluminium. org.au/australian-aluminium/australian-aluminium>.

Australian Bureau of Statistics (2006a) 'Family formation: Older mothers', *Australian Social Trends, 2001*, ABS 4102.0, retrieved 9 May 2012 from <www.abs.gov.au/AUSSTATS/abs@.nsf/2f762f95845417aeca25706c00834efa/b130815d4b2de356ca2570ec000c1c60! OpenDocument>.

——(2006b) 'Trends in childlessness', *Australian Social Trends, 2002*, ABS 4102.0, retrieved 9 May 2012 from <www.abs.gov.au/AUSSTATS/abs@. nsf/2f762f95845417aeca25706c00834efa/1e8c8e4887c33955ca2570ec000a9fe5!OpenDocument>.

——(2008) 'Migration: Permanent additions to Australia's population', *Australian Social Trends, 2007*, ABS 4102.0, retrieved 9 May 2012 from <www.abs.gov.au/AUSSTATS/abs@.nsf/7d12b0f6763c78caca257061001cc588/928af7a0cb6f969fca25732c00207852!OpenDocument>.

——(2009a) 'Case study 1: Retail trade following the December 2008 government stimulus package', *Australian Economic Indicators, August*, ABS 1350.0, retrieved 15 May 2012 from <www.abs.gov.au/AUSSTATS/abs@.nsf/Lookup/1350.0Feature+Article1Aug+2009>.

——(2009b) *Household use of information technology, Australia, 2008–09*, Australian Bureau of Statistics, Canberra.

——(2009c) 'Labour force participation across Australia', *Australian Social Trends, 2008*, ABS 4102.0, retrieved 9 May 2012 from <http://abs.gov.au/ AUSSTATS/abs@.nsf/Lookup/4102.0Chapter7002008>.

——(2011a) *Arts and Culture in Australia: A Statistical Overview*, 4172.0, 19 December, Canberra.

——(2011b) 'Australian households: The future', *Australian Social Trends, 2010*, ABS 4102.0, retrieved 9 May 2012 from <www.abs.gov.au/AUSSTATS/ abs@.nsf/Lookup/4102.0Main+Features20Dec+2010>.

——(2012a) 'Changing role of women', *Australian Social Trends, December 2012*, ABS 4102.0, retrieved 9 May 2012 from <www.abs.gov.au/AUSSTATS/abs@.nsf/Lookup/4102.0Main+Features30Dec+2011#changing>.

——(2012b) *Gender Indicators*, Australia, Jan 2012, ABS 4125.0, retrieved 15 May 2012 from <www.abs.gov.au/AUSSTATS/abs@.nsf/DetailsPage/4125.0Jan%202012?OpenDocument>.

——(2012c) 'Household income, expenditure and wealth', *Year Book Australia, 2012*, ABS 1301.0, retrieved 2 June from <www.abs.gov.au/ausstats/abs@.nsf/Lookup/by%20Subject/1301.0~2012~Main%20Features~Household%20income,%20expenditure%20and%20wealth~193>.

Australian Communications and Media Authority (2010) *Report 1—Australia in the digital economy: The shift to the online environment*, communications report 2009–10 series, Australian Communications and Media Authority.

AUSVEG (2010) 'Woolworths and Coles ethical sourcing policies seem flawed', AUSVEG, 2 January, retrieved 29 May 2012 from <http://ausveg.com.au/media-release/woolworths-and-coles-ethical-sourcing-policies-seem-flawed?A=SearchResult&SearchID=4950381&ObjectID=473702&ObjectType=35>.

Babinec, T (1990) 'CHAID response modeling and segmentation', *Quirk's Marketing Research Review*, June/July, pp. 12–15.

Bagozzi, R P (1975), 'Marketing as exchange', *Journal of Marketing*, vol. 39, no. 4, pp. 32–9.

Bailey, M (2011) 'Best place to work revealed', *BRW*, 22 June, retrieved 9 May 2012 from <www.brw.com.au/p/sections/opinion/best_place_to_work_revealed_ztn2hNdbkLEzy1haPTD0KM>.

Baim, J, Galin, M, Frankel, M R, Becker, R & Agresti, J (2009) 'Sample surveys based on internet panels: 8 years of learning', *Worldwide Readership Research Symposium*, Valencia, pp. 1–14.

Bainbridge, J (2004) 'Creative media agencies are the future of planning', *B&T Weekly*, 16 June, retrieved 2 August 2012 from <www.bandt.com.au/news/archive/creative-media-agencies-are-the-future-of-planning>.

Baker, M J (2007) *Marketing Strategy and Management*, 6th edn, Palgrave Macmillan, Basingstoke.

——(2009) *Marketing Responsibly—Addressing the Ethical Challenges*, Institute of Business Ethics, London.

Baker, W, Marn, M & Zawada, C (2010) *The Price Advantage*, 2nd edn, Wiley Finance, John Wiley & Sons, Hoboken, NJ.

Ban Asbestos Now (2011), 'Is This Really the Death of Canada's Asbestos Mine Empire?', 12 August, retrieved 3 January 2012 from <www.banasbestosnow.com/blog/2011/12/08/canada-asbestos-mine-closes>.

Barbaro, M (2008) 'Wal-Mart savings ads assailed', *New York Times*, 31 March, retrieved 10 May 2012 from <www.nytimes.com/2008/03/31/business/media/31walmart.html>.

Barnard, N & Ehrenberg, A (1997) 'Advertising: Strongly persuasive or nudging?', *Journal of Advertising Research*, vol. 37, pp. 21–8.

Bartels, R (1951) 'Can marketing be a science?', *Journal of Marketing*, vol. 15, pp. 319–28.

Barwise, P T & Ehrenberg, A S C (1987) 'The liking and viewing of regular TV series', *Journal of Consumer Research*, vol. 14, pp. 63–70.

——& Ehrenberg, A S C (1988) *Television and its audience*, Sage Publications, London.

——& Meehan, S (2004) *Simply Better: Winning and Keeping Customers by Delivering What Matters Most*, Harvard Business School Press, Boston.

Bass, F M (1974) 'The theory of stochastic preference and brand switching', *Journal of Marketing Research*, vol. 11, pp. 1–20.

BBC News (2002) 'McDonald's targeted in obesity lawsuit', BBC, 22 November, retrieved 3 May 2010 from <http://news.bbc.co.uk/1/hi/world/americas/2502431.stm>.

——(2007a) 'Firms withdraw BNP Facebook ads', BBC, 3 August, retrieved 13 June 2012 from <http://news.bbc.co.uk/2/hi/6929161.stm>.

——(2007b) 'Microsoft loses antitrust appeal', BBC, 17 September, retrieved 3 May 2010 from <http://news.bbc.co.uk/1/hi/6998272.stm>.

——(2008) 'Mobile web reaches critical mass', BBC, 10 July, retrieved 27 May 2012 from <http://news.bbc.co.uk/2/hi/7499340.stm>.

——(2012) 'John Carter flop to cost Walt Disney $200m', 20 March, retrieved 13 June 2012 from <www.bbc.co.uk/news/business-17442200>.

Bednall, D, Cavenett, P-M & Shaw, M (2000) *Response Rates in Australian Market Research*, paper presented at the 2000 conference, Market Research Society of Australia—inquiry/knowledge/insight, 15–18 October, Sydney.

Belch, G & Belch, M (2004) *Advertising and Promotion: An Integrated marketing Communications Perspective*, 6th edn, McGraw Hill, New York.

Belk, R, Devinney, T & Eckhart, G (2004) 'Consumer ethics across cultures', *Consumption Markets and Culture*, vol. 8, pp. 275–89.

Bennett, D (2009) 'The black market in China lightens up', *Proceedings of the 2009 Australian & New Zealand Marketing Academy Conference*, Melbourne.

Bentham, J (1961/1789) *An Introduction to the Principles of Morals and Legislation*, Doubleday, Garden City.

Bianco, A, Lowry, T, Berner, R, Arndt, M & Grover, R (2004) 'The vanishing mass market', *Business Week*, vol. 3891, pp. 60–8.

Bird, M & Ehrenberg, A S C (1966) 'Intentions-to-buy and claimed brand usage', *Operational Research Quarterly*, vol. 17, pp. 27–46.

—& Ehrenberg, A S C (1970) 'Consumer attitudes and brand usage', *Journal of the Market Research Society*, vol. 12, pp. 233–47.

Black Smith Institute (2012) 'Roro Hills: Legacy asbestos mines', retrieved 15 June 2012 from <www.blacksmithinstitute.org/projects/display/94>.

Blanchard, O & Sheen, J (2009), *Macroeconomics Australian edition*, 3rd edn, Pearson Education, Harlow.

Blight, D (2012) 'Marketer shortage "extreme" but there's hope yet: recruiters', *AdNews*, 6 September, retrieved 12 September 2012 from <www.adnews.com.au/adnews/marketer-shortage-extreme-but-there-s-hope-yet-recruiters>.

Bock, D & Treiber, B (2004) 'Studying new product performance in virtually created retail environments', ESOMAR Techovate Conference, Barcelona.

Bogart, L (2000) 'Buying services and the media marketplace', *Journal of Advertising Research*, vol. 40, no. 5, pp. 37–41.

Bogomolova, S (2009) 'The effect of sole versus multiple service provider usage on service quality perceptions', European Marketing Academy Conference 2009, France.

Boivin, Y & Coderre, F (2000) 'Fewer is better', *Journal of Advertising Research*, vol. 40, pp. 45–53.

Boivin, Y & Gagné, M (1996) 'Intermedia comparisons through the structure of media rates', *Journal of Current Issues and Research in Advertising*, vol. 18, pp. 45–53.

Bologlu, S, Weaver, P & McCleary, K (1998) 'Overlapping product-benefit segments in the lodging industry: A canonical correlation approach', *International Journal of Contemporary Hospitality Management*, vol. 10, no. 4, pp. 159–66.

Boulstridge, E & Carrigan, M (2000) 'Do consumers really care about corporate responsibility? Highlighting attitude-behaviour gap?', *Journal of Communication Management*, vol. 4, no. 4, pp. 355–68.

Bound, J A & Ehrenberg, A S C (1989) 'Significant sameness', *Journal of the Royal Statistical Society*, vol. 152 (Part 2), pp. 241–7.

Bourque, C, Hobbs, R & Hilaire, D (2011) 'Apples and oranges: Does a web survey produce similar results to social media tracking?', *Marketing Research*, Fall, American Marketing Association, pp. 9–13.

Bower, G H (1998) 'An associative theory of implicit and explicit memory' in M A Conway, S E Gathercole & C Cornoldi (eds) *Theories of Memory*, Psychological Press, Hove, England.

Bown, S (2005) *A Most Damnable Invention: Dynamite, Nitrates, and the Making of the Modern World*, Thomas Dunne Books, New York.

Boyd, D M & Ellison, N B (eds) (2008) 'Social network sites: Definition, history, and scholarship', *Journal of Computer-Mediated Communication*, vol. 13, no. 1, pp. 210–30.

Bradshaw, T & Gelles, D (2010) 'Facebook targets China and Russia', *Financial Times*, retrieved 12 June 2012 from <www.ft.com/intl/cms/s/2/35b709ae-7ec4-11df-ac9b-00144feabdc0.html#axzz1xZXUNlNS>.

Brady, I A & Isaac, B L (1975) *A Reader in Cultural Change*, vol. 1, Schenkman Pub. Co, Cambridge, Massachusetts.

Brandt, D & Biteau, B (2000) 'Pre-testing and sales validation', *Admap*, vol. 35, no. 2, pp. 23–6.

Breen Burns, J (2011a) 'Shoppers thrill to embrace of Zara', *The Age*, 16 June, retrieved 26 April 2012 from <www.theage.com.au/lifestyle/fashion/shoppers-thrill-to-embrace-of-zara-20110615-1g3tv.html>.

——(2011b) 'Spain's Zara the model of the successful retailer', *The Age*, 8 June, retrieved 26 April 2012 from <www.theage.com.au/victoria/spains-zara-the-model-of-the-successful-retailer-20110607-1fr28.html>.

Brennan, M (2004) 'The Juster purchase probability scale: A bibliography', *Marketing Bulletin*, vol. 15.

——& Esslemont, D (1994) 'The accuracy of the Juster Scale for predicting purchase rates of branded, fast-moving consumer goods', *Marketing Bulletin*, vol. 5, pp. 47–53.

Brinkmann, J & Peattie, K (2008) 'Consumer ethics research: reframing the debate about consumption for good', *Electronic Journal of Business Ethics and Organisation Studies*, vol. 13, no. 1, pp. 22–31.

Broadbent, S (1998) 'Campaign evaluation through modelling' in J P Jones (ed.) *How Advertising Works—The role of research*, Sage Publications, Thousand Oaks.

Brock, T & Sergeant, B (2002) 'Small sample market research', *International Journal of Market Research*, vol. 44 (quarter 2), pp. 1–10.

Brookes, R & Palmer, R A (2004) *The New Global Marketing Reality*, Palgrave Macmillan, New York.

Brown, T J & Rothschild, M L (1993) 'Reassessing the impact of television advertising clutter', *Journal of Consumer Research*, vol. 20, pp. 138–46.

Bruell, A (2010) 'Burger King, Edelman set to part ways', 25 July, *AdAge*, retrieved 26 April 2012 from <http://adage.com/article/agency-news/burger-king-edelman-set-part-ways-pr-review/228920>.

Bryson, E (2010) 'Burger King to launch kids' breakfast meal', *Los Angeles Times*, 22 July, retrieved 26 April 2012 from <http://articles.latimes.com/2010/jul/22/business/la-fi-burger-king-20100722>.

Bryson-York, E (2009) 'Hershey Reports Reese's, Kisses Regaining Share', *Advertising Age*, retrieved 6 August 2012 from <http://adage.com/article/news/hershey-reports-reese-s-kisses-regaining-share/136235>.

Budden, M (2009) 'Popular everywhere else, why don't Aussies rate Fosters lager?', *Connect*, January–March, p. 84.

Burda, M & Wyplosz, C (2009), *Macroeconomics: A European Text*, 5th edn, Oxford University Press, Oxford.

Butler, S (2011) 'Specsavers founder sees plenty of challenges ahead', *The Guardian*, 27 October, retrieved 29 May 2012 from <www.guardian.co.uk/business/2011/oct/27/specsavers-founder-mary-perkins-interview>.

Buysight (2010) 'What are people really buying online?', *Infographics*, 27 February, retrieved 10 May 2012 from <www.permuto.com/blog/2010/02/27/what-are-people-really-buying-online/>.

Cadbury, D (2010) *Chocolate Wars: From Cadbury to Kraft: 200 Years of Sweet Success and Bitter Rivalry*, Harper Press, London.

Cahill, D J (1997) 'Target marketing and segmentation: Valid and useful tools for marketing', *Management Decision*, vol. 35, pp. 10–13.

Campbell, S (1998) 'Customer segmentation in the post-modern era', *Admap*, vol. 33, pp. 31–4.

Canadian Medical Association (2011) 'Letter to the Prime Minister of Canada', retrieved 15 June 2012 from <www.cfpc.ca/uploadedFiles/Publications/News_Releases/News_Items/oldNews/Asbestos%20Letter%20to%20the%20Prime%20Minister.pdf>.

Cancer Research UK (2008) 'Smoking ban triggered the biggest fall in smoking ever seen in England', press release, 30 June, retrieved 25 May 2012 from <http://info.cancerresearchuk.org/news/archive/pressrelease/2008-06-30-smoking-ban-triggered-the-biggest-fall-in-smoking-ever-seen-in-england>.

Cannon, H (1984) 'The "naïve" approach to demographic media selection', *Journal of Advertising Research*, vol. 24, pp. 21–25.

——(1987) 'Can national product media indices be used to improve media selection efficiency in local market areas?' *Journal of Advertising*, vol. 16, pp. 34–42.

——& Rashid, A (1991) 'When do demographics help in media planning?' *Journal of Advertising Research*, vol. 30, pp. 20–26.

Capon, N, & Senn, C (2010) 'Global customer management programs: How to make them really work', *California Management Review*, vol. 52, no. 2, pp. 32–55.

Carmone Jr, F J, Kara, A & Maxwell, S (1999) 'HINoV: A new model to improve market segment definition by identifying noisy variables', *Journal of Marketing Research*, vol. 36, no. 4, pp. 501–9.

Carrigan, M & Attalla, A (2001) 'The myth of the ethical consumer—do ethics matter in purchase behaviour?', *Journal of Consumer Marketing*, vol. 18, no. 7, pp 560–77.

Carroll, A B (1991) 'The pyramid of corporate social responsibility: Toward the moral management of organizational stakeholder', *Business Horizons*, vol. 34, pp. 39–48.

Cato, J (2010) 'European cars coming to Canada in a big way', *CTV News*, 25 October, retrieved 16 May 2012 from <http://autos.ctv.ca/CTVNews/Autos/20101022/europe-cars-canada-101025>.

Cavill + Co. (2012) 'How to use the tree: Background', retrieved 25 May 2012 from <www.cavill.com.au/csrtree/csrtree01.html>

Charles, CV, Dewey, CE, Daniell, WE & Summerlee, AJS (2011) 'Iron-deficiency anaemia in rural Cambodia: Community trial of a novel iron supplementation technique', *The European Journal of Public Health*, vol. 21, no. 1, pp. 43–8.

Charlton, P & Ehrenberg, A S C (1973) 'McConnell's experimental brand choice data', *Journal of Marketing Research*, vol. 10, pp. 302–7.

Christensen, C M, Anthony, S D, Berstell, G & Nitterhouse, D (2007) 'Finding the right job for your product', *MIT Sloan Management Review*, vol. 48, no. 3, Spring, pp. 38–47.

Chrysotile Institute (2012a) 'About Institute', retrieved 3 January 2012 from <www.chrysotile.com/en/about.aspx>.

——(2012b) 'Frequently asked questions', retrieved 3 January 2012 from <www.chrysotile.com/en/faq.aspx#1>.

Clark, G (2009) 'Time Out looks at the UAE's plans to tackle waste and recycling', *Time Out Abu Dhabi*, retrieved 23 May 2012 from <www.timeoutabudhabi.com/community/features/5223-recycling>.

Coen, B (2002) *Bob Coen's Insider's Report*, McCann-Erickson WorldGroup, retrieved 26 June 2002 from <www.mccann.com>.

Colbert, F (2007) *Marketing Culture and the Arts*, 3rd edn, HEC Montreal, Montreal.

Collins, A M & Quillian, M R (1969) 'Retrieval time from semantic memory', *Journal of verbal learning and verbal behavior*, vol. 8, no. 2, pp. 240–47.

Collins, M, Beal, V & Barwise, P (2003) 'Channel use among multi-channel viewers: Patterns in TV viewing behavior', Report 15 for Corporate Members, Ehrenberg-Bass Institute for Marketing Science, Adelaide.

Commerce Commission (2008) 'International cargo cartel to be prosecuted', Commerce Commission, retrieved 3 May 2010 from <www. comcom.govt.nz/mediareleases/detail/2008/internationalaircargocarteltobepro>.

ComScore (2011a) *The Power of Like. How Brands Reach and Influence Fans Through Social Media Marketing*, comScore white paper, comScore Inc, retrieved 6 August 2012 from <www.comScore.com/Press-Events/Presentations-Whitepapers/2011/The-Power-of-Like-How-Brands-Reach-and-Influence-Fans-Through-Social-Media-Marketing>.

ComScore (2011b) *State of the Internet—Australia*, comScore Inc., retrieved 6 August 2012 from <http://www.comscore.com/Press_Events/Presentations_Whitepapers/2011/State_of_the_Internet_in_Australia>.

Copeland, L & Griggs, L (1985) *Going International: How to Make Friends and Deal Effectively in the Global Marketplace*, Random House, New York.

Crassweller, A, Rogers, J & Williams, D (2008) 'Between random samples and online panels—where is the next lily pad?', paper presented at the Panel Research, Dublin.

Critchley, H D, Elliot, R, Mathias, C J & Dolan, R J (2000) 'Neural activity relating to generation and representation of galvanic skin conductance responses: a functional magnetic resonance imaging study', *The Journal of Neuroscience*, vol. 20, pp. 3033–40.

Dahl, D W, Frankenberger, K D & Machanda, R V (2003) 'Does it pay to shock? Reactions to shocking and non shocking advertising content amongst university students', *Journal of Advertising Research*, September, vol. 43, no. 3, pp. 268–80.

Dall'Olmo Riley, F, Ehrenberg, A S C, Castleberry, S B, Barwise, T P & Barnard, N R (1997) 'The variability of attitudinal repeat-rates', *International Journal of Research in Marketing*, vol. 14, pp. 437–50.

Damasio, A R (1994) *Descartes' Error: Emotion, Reason, and the Human Brain*, Putnam, New York.

Danenberg, N (2008) 'Testing the advertising intensiveness law in budgeting', unpublished PhD thesis, University of South Australia.

'DaveKing' (2012) comment posted in response to T Ryan 'Older Shoppers Irritated by Supermarket Layout Changes', *RetailWire*, 12 March, discussion article, retrieved 13 June 2012 from <www.retailwire.com/discussion/15870/older-shoppers-irritated-by-supermarket-layout-changes>.

Davies, A, Mills, D & Baxter, M (2002) 'Pre-testing radical advertising', *Admap*, vol. 37, no. 3, March, pp. 38–40.

Davies, C (2012) 'Tesco sales slump part of consumer revolution changing the way we shop', *The Guardian*, 12 January, retrieved 10 May 2012 from <www.guardian.co.uk/business/2012/jan/12/tesco-consumer-revolution-internet-shopping>.

Dawes, J G (2009) 'The effect of service price increases on customer retention: the moderating role of customer tenure and relationship breadth', *Journal of Service Research*, vol. 11, pp. 232–45.

——& Sharp, B (2000) 'The reliability and validity of objective measures of customer service: "Mystery shopping"', *Australasian Journal of Market Research*, vol. 8, pp. 29–46.

——, Mundt, K & Sharp, B (2009) 'Consideration sets for financial services brands', *Journal of Financial Services Marketing*, vol. 14, pp. 190–202.

Deighton, J A (1996) 'The future of interactive marketing', *Harvard Business Review*, vol. 74, no. 6, November–December, pp. 151–60.

Delany, B (2008) 'Starbucks to go', *The Guardian*, 30 July, retrieved 13 June 2012 from <www.guardian.co.uk/commentisfree/2008/jul/30/australia.starbuck>.

Demicheli, V, Rivetti, A, Debalini, M G & Di Pietrantonj, C (2012) 'Vaccines for measles, mumps and rubella in children', *Cochrane Database of Systematic Reviews*, vol. 2, retrieved 16 February 2012 from <www.mrw.interscience.wiley.com/cochrane/clsysrev/articles/CD004407/frame.html>.

Diageo plc (2011a) 'About our business', *Sustainability and Responsibility Report 2011*, Diageo plc, retrieved 3 June 2012 from <http://srreport2011.diageoreports.com/overview/about-our-business.aspx>.

——(2011b) 'Our impacts', *Sustainability and Responsibility Report 2011*, Diageo plc, retrieved 3 June 2012 from <http://srreport2011.diageoreports.com/our-impacts.aspx>.

——(2011c) 'Overview', *Sustainability and Responsibility Report 2011*, Diageo plc, retrieved 3 June 2012 from <http://srreport2011.diageoreports.com/overview.aspx>.

Dibbs, S & Simkin, L (1996) *The Market Segmentation Work Book: Target Marketing for Marketing Managers*, Routledge, London.

Dick, H & Merret, D (2007) *The Internationalisation Strategies of Small-Country Firms: The Australian Experience of Globalisation*, Edward Elgar Publishing, Cheltenham.

Dickson, P R & Ginter, J L (1987) 'Market segmentation, product differentiation, and marketing strategy', *Journal of Marketing*, vol. 51, pp. 1–10.

Dillman, D (1978) *Mail and Telephone Surveys*, John Wiley, New York.

Dillman, D A (2000) *Mail and Internet Surveys: The Tailored Design Method*, 2nd edn, John Wiley, New York.

Dilmah Australia (2011) 'The world of Dilmah', retrieved 2011 from <www.dilmah.com.au>.

Dimmick, J W (2003) *Media Competition and Coexistence: The Theory of the Niche*, Lawrence Erlbaum Associates, New Jersey/London.

Donaldson, B & O'Toole, T (2007), *Strategic Market Relationships: From Strategy to Implementation*, 2nd edn, John Wiley, London.

Donkers, B, Verhoef, P C & De Jong, M G (2007) 'Modeling CLV: A test of competing models in the insurance industry', *Quantitative Marketing and Economics*, vol. 5, pp. 163–90.

Donovan, R J (2003) 'Scare tactics do work ... sometimes' in *Social Marketing for Social Profit Conference*, Local Government New Zealand, Wellington.

——(2011) 'Social marketing's mythunderstandings', *Journal of Social Marketing*, vol. 1, no. 1, pp. 8–16.

Doole, I & Lowe, R (2008) *International Marketing Strategy*, 5th edn, Thomson Learning, London.

Doughty, S (2007) 'Women to be the major breadwinners in a quarter of families by 2030', *Daily Mail*, 3 August, p. 17.

Doyle, C (2011) *Oxford Dictionary of Marketing*, Oxford University Press, New York.

Doyle, P & Stern, P (2006), *Marketing Management and Strategy*, 4th edn, FT Prentice Hall, London.

Drill, S (2012) 'Ford workers to be locked out with CMI Industrial on brink of administration', *Herald Sun*, April 26, retrieved 12 May 2012 from <www.news.com.au/business/worklife/ford-workers-to-be-locked-out-with-cmi-industrial-on-brink-of-administration/story-e6fr-fm9r-1226338749404>.

Drucker, P (1973) *Management Tasks, Responsibilities and Practices*, Harper & Row, New York.

——(1981) 'What is business ethics?', *The Public Interest*, no. 63, pp. 18–36.

Du Plessis, E (2009) 'Digital video recorders and inadvertent advertising exposure', *Journal of Advertising Research*, vol. 49, no. 2, pp. 236–9.

East, R (1997) *Consumer Behaviour*, Pearson Education Limited, Essex, United Kingdom.

——(2008) *Measurement Deficiencies in the Net Promoter Score*, ANZMAC, Sydney.

——& Uncles, M (2008) 'In praise of retrospective surveys', *Journal of Marketing Management*, vol. 24, nos 9–10, pp. 929–44.

——, Harris, P, Willson, G & Lomax, W (1995) 'Loyalty to supermarkets', *The International Review of Retail, Distribution and Consumer Research*, vol. 5, no. 1, pp. 99–109.

——, Romaniuk, J & Lomax, W (2011) 'The NPS and the ACSI: a critique and an alternative metric', *International Journal of Market Research*, vol. 53, p. 15.

——, Wright, M, & Vanhuele, M (2008) *Consumer Behaviour: Application in Marketing*, Sage, London.

The Economist (2011) '1100100 and counting', *The Economist*, vol. 399, no. 8737, June, pp. 67–9.

——(2012a) 'Disney's "John Carter": The biggest flop ever?', *The Economist*, 23 May, retrieved 13 June 2012 from <www.economist.com/blogs/prospero/2012/03/disneys-john-carter>.

——(2012b) 'The third industrial revolution', *The Economist*, 21 April, retrieved 3 June 2012 from <www.economist.com/node/21553017>.

Ehrenberg, A S C (1974) 'Repetitive advertising and the consumer', *Journal of Advertising Research*, vol. 14, pp. 25–34.

——(1988) *Repeat-Buying: Facts, Theory and Applications*, Oxford University Press, London.

——(1992) 'Report writing—Six simple rules for better business documents', *Admap*, June, pp. 39–42.

——(1994) *A Primer in Data Reduction*, John Wiley & Sons, New York.

——& Bound, J (1999) 'Customer retention and switching in the car market', *Report 6 for Corporate Members*, Ehrenberg-Bass Institute for Marketing Science, Adelaide.

——& Goodhardt, G (2002) 'Double jeopardy revisited, again', *Marketing Insights*, *Marketing Research*, Spring, pp. 40–2.

——, Hammond, K & Goodhardt, G J (1994) 'The after effects of price-related consumer promotions', *Journal of Advertising Research*, vol. 34, no. 4, pp. 11–21.

——, Mills, P & Kennedy, R (2000) 'The form that ads take (FAT)—A snapshot of UK magazine ads as seen by the public', 29th European Marketing Academy Conference, vol. cd proceedings, Erasmus University, Rotterdam.

——, Uncles, M D & Goodhardt, G G (2004) 'Understanding brand performance measures: Using Dirichlet benchmarks', *Journal of Business Research*, vol. 57, no. 12, pp. 1307–25.

——, Barnard, N, Kennedy, R & Bloom, H (2002) 'Brand advertising as creative publicity', *Journal of Advertising Research*, vol. 42, no. 4, pp. 7–18.

Elefteriou-Smith, L-M (2012) 'P&G marketing chief admits it needs to fundamentally change how it operates', *Marketing Magazine*, 14 March, retrieved 25 April 2012 from <www.marketingmagazine.co.uk/news/1122108/P-G-marketing-chief-admits-needs-fundamentally-shift-operates>.

Elkington, J (1999) *Cannibals with Forks—The Triple Bottom Line of 21st Century Business*, Capstone, Chichester.

Ellis, N (2011) *Business-to-Business Marketing: Relationships, Networks & Strategies*, Oxford University Press, Oxford.

eMarketer (2011) 'Twitter ad revenues to grow 210% to $139.5 million in 2011', press release, retrieved 27 May 2012 from <www.emarketer.com/PressRelease.aspx?R=1008617>.

Ephron, E (1993) 'The ghost of network past: TV fragmentation doesn't mean tighter targeting,' *Ephron on Media*, retrieved 29 May 2012 from <www.ephrononmedia.com> (note: log-in required).

——(1995a) *The Shelf Space Model of Advertising*, retrieved 15 October 2004 from <www.ephrononmedia.com>.

——(1995b) *What is Recency?*, retrieved 24 November 2003 from <www.ephrononmedia.com>.

——(1997) 'Media planning: Recency planning', *Journal of Advertising Research*, vol. 37, pp. 61–5.

——(2000a) *Media-Mix. The New Media Plannning is About Picking Combinations of Media*, retrieved 14 October 2004 from <www.ephrononmedia.com>.

——(2000b) 'A Scheduler's Hymnal', *Admap*, vol. 35, pp. 21–3.

——(2005) 'Engagement explained: The confusion is engagement is many different things', *The Ephron Letter*, December, pp. 1–5.

——& Heath, M (2001) *Teaching Tap to the Elephant. Media Planners Have Fewer Scheduling Options Than They Think*, retrieved 7 April 2003 from <www.ephrononmedia.com/article_archive/articleViewerPublic.asp?articleID=94>.

Euro RSCG 4D (2012) 'Work—Australia', retrieved 18 June 2012 from <www.eurorscg4d.com/work-australia.html>.

European Society for Opinion and Marketing Research (2011), *Global Market Research 2011*, ESOMAR, retrieved on 26 April 2012 from <http://www.esomar.org/web/research_papers/book.php?id=2253 2124>.

Evans, F B (1959) 'Psychological and objective factors in the prediction of brand choice Ford versus Chevrolet', *The Journal of Business*, vol. 32, pp. 340–69.

Facebook Press Room (2011) 'Statistics', retrieved from <www.facebook.com/press/info.php?statistics>.

Facenda, V L (2007) 'New ARF study says storytellers succeed: The results of a three-year study say throw old marketing ideas away', *Adweek*, 29 October, retrieved 29 November 2007 from <www.brandweek.com/bw/magazine/current/article_display.jsp?vnu_content_id=1003664386>.

Farey-Jones, D (2012) 'P&G Chief Lays Out $1bn Marketing Efficiency Vision', *Marketing Magazine*, 24 February, retrieved 25 April 2012 from <www.marketingmagazine.co.uk/news/1119124/P-G-chief-lays-1bn-marketing-efficiency-vision/>.

Fazio, R H & Williams, C J (1986) 'Attitude accessibility as moderator of the attitude-perception and attitude-behavior relations: An investigation of the 1984 presidential election', *Journal of Personality and Social Psychology*, vol. 51, pp. 505–14.

Feeney, K (2012) 'US boost for Brisbane social network', *Brisbane Times*, 19 January, retrieved 27 May 2012 from <www.brisbanetimes.com.au/digital-life/us-boost-for-brisbane-social-network-20120118-1q6jn.html>.

Fennell, G & Allenby, G M (2002) 'No brand level segmentation? Let's not rush to judgement', *Marketing Research*, vol. 14, pp. 14–18.

Ferrari (2012) 'The factory', Ferrari, retrieved 15 February 2012 from <www.ferrari.com/English/about_ferrari/Ferrari_today/The_Factory/Pages/The_Factory.aspx>.

Ferrell, O C, Hartline, M D & McDaniel, S D (1998) 'Codes of ethics among corporate research departments, marketing research firms, and data subcontractors: An examination of a three-communities metaphor,' *Journal of Business Ethics*, vol. 17, no. 5, pp. 503–16.

Financial Times (2010) 'SABMiller', *Financial Times*, 19 November, London, p. 1.

Fonseca, M (2001) 'Starbucks invades Lygon Street' *ABC News*, retrieved 13 June 2012 from <www.abc.net.au/pm/stories/s322266.htm>.

Foo, F (2011) 'Chinese walls hamper Defence IT', *The Australian*, 23 December, retrieved 15 May 2012 from <www.theaustralian.com.au/australian-it/government/chinese-walls-hamper-defence-it/story-fn4htb9o-1226229003896>.

Foo, L M & Rossetto, A (1998) *BTR Occasional Paper Number 27, Cultural Tourism in Australia—Characteristics and Motivations*, Bureau of Tourism Research, Canberra.

Food Standards Australia New Zealand (2010) 'Trans fatty acids', December, FSANZ, retrieved 3 June 2012 from <www.foodstandards.gov.au/consumerinformation/transfattyacids.cfm>.

Foxall, G (1997) 'Affective Responses to Consumer Situations', *The International Review of Retail, Distribution and Consumer Research*, vol. 7, pp. 191–225.

——(2002) 'Marketing's attitude problem—and how to solve it', *Journal of Customer Behaviour*, vol. 1, pp. 19–48.

France, M & Hamm, S (1998) 'Does predatory pricing make Microsoft a predator?' *Business Week*, November. retrieved 16 May 2012 from <www.businessweek.com/1998/47/b3605129.htm>.

Franz, G (2000) 'The future of multimedia research', *International Journal of Market Research*, vol. 42, pp. 459–72.

Franzen, G (1994) *Advertising Effectiveness: Findings from Empirical Research*, NTC Publications, Henley-on-Thames, Oxfordshire, United Kingdom.

Fredrickson, C (2011) 'Facebook revenues to reach $4.27 billion in 2011', *eMarketer*. retrieved 22 June 2012 from <www.emarketer.com/PressRelease.aspx?R=1008601>.

Freeman, E R (1991) 'Strategic Management: A Stakeholder Approach' in Murphy, P E & Fuller, D A (2000) *Sustainable Marketing: Managerial-Ecological Issues*, Sage, Thousand Oaks, California.

Frey, C & Cook, J (2004) 'How Amazon.com survived, thrived and turned a profit', 28 January, *Seattle Post-Intelligencer*.

Fulgoni, G & Morn, M P (2009) 'Whither the click: How online advertising works', *Journal of Advertising Research*, vol. 49, no. 2, pp. 134–42.

Fuller, D (1999) *Sustainable Marketing. Managerial-Ecological Issues*, Sage Publications, Thousand Oaks, CA.

Funding Universe (2010) 'SABMiller plc history', retrieved 13 June 2012 from <www.fundinguniverse.com/company-histories/SABMiller-plc-Company-History.html>.

Galbraith, J (2001) 'Building organizations around the global customer', *Ivey Business Journal*, vol. 66, no. 1, pp. 17–24.

Gendall, P (1998) 'A framework for questionnaire design: Lablaw revisited', *Marketing Bulletin*, vol. 9, pp. 28–39.

——(2000) 'Responding to the problem of nonresponse', *Australasian Journal of Market Research*, vol. 8, no. 1, January, pp. 3–17.

——& Esselmont, D (1992) 'Market research: What it can and can't do', *Marketing Bulletin*, vol. 3, pp. 63–6.

General Motors (2012) '2011 CY Highlights', retrieved 15 February 2012 from <http://media.gm.com/content/dam/Media/gmcom/investor/2012/Q4_2011_Chart%20Set.pdf>.

Gensch, D (1970) 'Media factors: A review article', *Journal of Marketing Research*, vol. 7, pp. 216–25.

Gigerenzer, G & Todd, P T (1999) *Simple Heuristics That Make Us Smart*, Oxford University Press, New York.

Gilmore, P (2005) 'Grocery stores and supermarkets', *Encyclopedia of Chicago*, retrieved 10 May 2012 from <http://encyclopedia.chicagohistory.org/pages/554.html>.

Goldman, A (2000) 'Supermarkets in China: the case of Shanghai', *International Review of Retail, Distribution and Consumer Research*, vol. 10, pp. 1–21.

Goodhardt, G J, Ehrenberg, A S C & Collins, M A (1975) *The television audience—Patterns of viewing*, Gower Publishing Company Limited, Hants, England.

Google (2012) 'Google announces fourth quarter and fiscal year 2011 results', retrieved 6 April 2012 from <http://investor.google.com/earnings/2011/Q4_google_earnings.html>.

Graeff, T & Harmon, S (2002) 'Collecting and using personal data: Consumers' awareness and concerns', *Journal of Consumer Marketing*, vol. 19, no. 4, pp. 302–18.

Grant, J (2007) *The Green Marketing Manifesto*, John Wiley & Sons, Chichester, UK.

Green, A (2002) 'Family values', *Admap*, pp. 28–9.

Green, A (2003) 'Coping with clutter', *Admap*, vol. 38, pp. 16–17.

Green, K & Armstrong, J S (2005) 'Competitor-oriented objectives: The myth of market share', *International Journal of Business*, vol. 12, pp. 151–3.

Green, P E & Krieger, A M (1991) 'Segmenting markets with conjoint analysis', *Journal of Marketing*, 55, pp. 20–31.

Grier, S & Bryant, C A (2005) 'Social marketing in public health', *Annual Review of Public Health*, vol. 26, pp. 319–39.

Griffiths, A & Wall, S (eds) (2011), *Applied Economics: An Introductory Course*, 12th edn, Pearson Education, London.

Guidere, M (2012) 'The translation of advertisements: From adaptation to localization', TranslationDirectory.com, retrieved 23 May 2012 from <www.translationdirectory.com/article60.htm>.

Gummesson, E (2008) *Total Relationship Marketing: Marketing Management, Relationship Strategy and CRM Approaches for the Network Economy*, Butterworth-Heinemann, Oxford.

Gutierrez, C (2007) 'Hershey Mired In Chocolate Mess', *Forbes*, retrieved 26 July 2012 from <www.forbes.com/2007/05/10/hershey-decrease-outlook-markets-equity-cx_cg_0510markets11.html>.

Haley, R I (1968) 'Benefit segmentation: A decision-oriented research tool', *The Journal of Marketing*, vol. 32, pp. 30–5.

——(1984) 'Benefit segments: Backwards and forwards', *Journal of Advertising Research*, vol. 24, pp. 19–25.

——& Baldinger, A L (1991) 'The ARF copy research validity project', *Journal of Advertising Research*, vol. 31, pp. 11–32.

Hamermesh, D S & Parker, A (2005) 'Beauty in the classroom: Instructors' pulchritude and putative pedagogical productivity', *Economics of Education Review*, August, vol. 24, no. 4, pp. 369–76.

Hammer, P, Riebe, E & Kennedy, R (2009) 'How clutter affects advertising effectiveness', *Journal of Advertising Research*, vol. 49, pp. 159–63.

Hammond, K, Ehrenberg, A S C & Goodhardt, G J (1996) 'Market segmentation for competitive brands', *European Journal of Marketing*, vol. 30, pp. 39–49.

Hansen, F & Christensen, L B (2005) 'Share of voice/share of market and long-term advertising effects', *International Journal of Advertising*, vol. 24, no. 3, pp. 297–320.

Harvey, M G, Novicevic, M M, Hench, T & Myers, M (2003) 'Global account management: A supply-side managerial view', *Industrial Marketing Management*, vol. 32, no. 7, pp. 563–71.

Hastings, H & Saperstein, J (2010) 'How Cisco creates new value via global customer service', *Thunderbird International Business Review*, vol. 52, no. 5, pp. 419–30.

Hazlett, R L & Hazlett, S Y (1999) 'Emotional response to television commercials: Facial EMIG vs. self-report', *Journal of Advertising Research*, vol. 39, pp. 7–23.

Heath, R & Feldwick, P (2008) 'Fifty years using the wrong model of advertising.' *International Journal of Market Research*, vol. 50, no. 1, pp. 29–59.

Heath, R, Nairn, A & Bottomley, P (2009) 'How effective is creativity? Emotive content in TV advertising does not increase attention', *Journal of Advertising Research*, vol. 49, no. 4, pp. 450–63.

Henry, J (2008) 'The best selling cars and trucks in the US', *Bloomberg Businessweek*, retrieved 8 June 2012 from <http://images.businessweek.com/ss/08/05/0519_top_sellers/source/1.htm>.

Hess, M (2009) *Social media and research*, American Marketing Association, Chicago.

Hilti Corporation (2012) 'Hilti fleet management', retrieved 12 May 2012 from <http://www.hilti.com.au/holau/page/module/home/browse_main.jsf?lang=en&nodeId=-463984>.

Hoek, J, Gendall, P & Kearns, Z (1994) 'What we say or what we do?', New Zealand Marketing Educators Conference, pp. 273–9.

Hofstede, G (1984) *Culture's Consequences: International Differences in Work-related values*, Sage, Beverley Hills, California.

——, Hofstede, G J & Minkov, M (2010), *Cultures and Organisations: Software for the Mind*, 3rd edn, McGraw-Hill, Maidenhead.

Holmes, M, Papper, R, Popovich, M & Bloxham, M (2005) 'Observing consumers and their interactions with media', *Concurrent Media Exposure*, Middletown Media Studies, Indiana, United States.

Hope, J (2001) 'Why Japan banned MMR vaccine', *Daily Mail*, 24 January, retrieved 9 May 2012 from <www.dailymail.co.uk/health/article-17509/Why-Japan-banned-MMR-vaccine.html>.

Hubbard, R & Armstrong, J S (1994) 'Replications and extensions in marketing: Rarely published but quite contrary', *International Journal of Research in Marketing*, vol. 11, pp. 233–48.

IDC (2011) 'Nearly 18 million media tablets shipped in 2010 with Apple capturing 83% share; eReader shipments quadrupled to more than 12 Million', press release, 10 March, retrieved 31 May 2012 from <www.idc.com/about/viewpressrelease.jsp?containerId=prUS22737611&sectionId=null&elementId=null&pageType=SYNOPSIS'>.

INDITEX Group (2012), 'Zara', retrieved 26 April 2012 from <www.inditex.com/en/who_we_are/concepts/zara>.

Innovation and Business Skills Australia (2010) *Environment Scan 2010: Financial Services Industry*, retrieved 6 March 2012 from <www.ibsa.org.au/Portals/ibsa.org.au/docs/Research%20&%20Discussion%20Papers/Sectoral%20report%20-%20Financial%20Services%20Industry%2026%20Feb%2010.pdf>.

Jacobs, B (1991) 'Trends in media buying and selling in Europe and the effect on the advertising agency business', *International Journal of Advertising*, 10, pp. 283–91.

Jargon, J (2010) 'As sales drop, Burger King draws critics for courting "super fans"', *The Wall Street Journal*, 1 February, retrieved 2 May 2012 from <http://finance.yahoo.com/news/pf_article_108728.html>.

Jeffreys, D (2004) *Aspirin*, Bloomsbury, New York.

Jensen, K L, Jakus, P M, English, B C & Wenard, R J (2004) 'Consumers' willingness to pay for eco-certified wood products', *Journal of Agricultural and Applied Economics*, vol. 36, no. 3, pp. 617–26.

Johnson, E J, Moe, W W, Fader, P S, Bellman, S & Lohse, G L (2004) 'On the depth and dynamics of online search behavior', *Management Science*, vol. 50, pp. 299–308.

Jones, J P (1990) 'Advertising: Strong force or weak force? Two views an ocean apart', *International Journal of Advertising*, vol. 9, pp. 233–46.

——(1992) *How Much is Enough? Getting the Most from your Advertising Dollar*, New York, Lexington Books.

——(1995a) 'Single-source research begins to fulfill its promise', *Journal of Advertising Research*, vol. 35, pp. 9–16.

——(1995b) 'We have a breakthrough: single-source data is the key to proving advertising's short term effects', *Admap*, June, pp. 33–5.

——(1995c) *When ads work—New proof that advertising triggers sales*, Lexington Books, New York.

——(2007) *When Ads Work: New Proof That Advertising Triggers Sales*, M.E. Sharpe, Inc, New York.

——& Blair, M H (1996) 'Examining "conventional wisdoms" about advertising effects with evidence from independent sources', *Journal of Advertising Research*, vol. 36, pp. 37–53.

——(ed.) (1998) *How Advertising Works*, Sage Publications, Thousand Oaks.

Kahneman, D (2011) *Thinking Fast and Slow*, Farrar, Straus and Giroux, New York.

Katz, H (2003) *The Media Handbook: A Complete Guide to Advertising Media Selection, Planning, Research, and Buying*, Lawrence Erlbaum, Mahwah, NJ.

Keegan, W J & Hollensen, S (2010) *Global Marketing Management: International Version*, 8th edn, Pearson Education, London.

Keiningham, T L, Cooil, B, Andreassen, T W & Aksoy, L (2007) 'A longitudinal examination of net promoter and firm revenue growth', *Journal of Marketing*, vol. 71, pp. 39–51.

Keller, E (2011) 'Social Brands: A Tale of Two Worlds', 23 February, MediaBizBloggers.com, retrieved 25 May 2012 from <www.mediabizbloggers. com/media-biz-bloggers/Social-Brands-A-Tale-of-Two-Worlds---Ed-Keller.html>.

Keller, E & Libai, B (2009) 'A holistic approach to the measurement of WOM: its impact on consumer's decisions', ESOMAR World Research Conference: Worldwide Multimedia Measurement (WM3), Stockholm, pp. 169–80.

Kemplay, G & Davis, R (2008) 'Making market segmentations work', *Admap*, September, pp. 53–5.

Keng, K A & Ehrenberg, A S C (1984) 'Patterns of store choice', *Journal of Marketing Research*, vol. 21, November, pp. 399–409.

Kennedy, R & Ehrenberg, A S C (2000) 'The customer profiles of competing brands', 29th European Marketing Academy Conference, 23–26 May, EMAC papers session 1.5.3, Erasmus University, Rotterdam.

——& Ehrenberg, A S C (2000) *Brand User Profiles Seldom Differ, Report 7 for Corporate Members*, Ehrenberg-Bass Institute for Marketing Science, Adelaide.

——& Ehrenberg, A S C (2001) 'Competing retailers generally have the same sorts of shoppers', *Journal of Marketing Communications*, vol. 7, pp. 19–26.

——, Ehrenberg, A & Long, S (2000) 'Competitive brands' user-profiles hardly differ', Market Research Society Conference (UK), Brighton, England.

——, Sharp, B & Rungie C (2000) 'How ad liking (LA) relates to branding & the implications for advertising testing', *Australasian Journal of Market Research*, vol. 8, no. 2, July, pp. 9–19.

——, Northover, H, Leighton, J, Lion, S & Bird, G (2010), 'Pre-test advertising—Proposing A New Validity Project', in 39th EMAC Conference, Copenhagen.

King, S (1997) 'Media planning: Counters and creators', *Admap*, vol. 32, pp. 25–7.

Knowledge@Wharton (2006) 'MySpace, Facebook and other social networking sites: Hot today, gone tomorrow?', *Knowledge@Wharton*, retrieved 8 June 2012 from <http://knowledge.wharton.upenn.edu/articlepdf/1463.pdf?CFID=77267930&CFTOKEN=36437478& jsessionid=a8302b8815021536eddf2f74425c1362b243>.

Kotler, N, Kotler, P & Kotler, W (2008) *Museum Strategy and Marketing: Designing Missions, Building Audiences, Generating Revenues and Resources*, 2nd edn, Jossey-Bass Publishers, San Francisco.

Kotler, P & Keller, K L (2012), *Marketing Management*, 14th edn, Prentice-Hall, Englewood Cliffs, NJ.

Kotler, P, Brown, L, Adam, S, Burton, S & Armstrong, G (2007) *Marketing*, Frenchs Forest, Pearson Education Australia.

Kovel, J (2002) *The Enemy of Nature*, Zed Books, London.

Kraus, S J (1995) 'Attitudes and the prediction of behavior: A meta-analysis of the empirical literature', *Personality and Social Psychology Bulletin*, vol. 21, pp. 58–75.

Kringdon, M (2006) 'Social networking is your friend', *ClickZ*, retrieved 8 June 2012 from <www.clickz.com/clickz/column/1704794/social-networking-is-your-friend>.

LaBarbera, P & Tucciarone, J (1995) 'GSR reconsidered: A behavior-based approach to evaluating and improving the sales potency of advertising', *Journal of Advertising Research*, vol. 35, pp. 33–53.

Lages, L F, Lancastre, A & Lages, C (2008) 'The B2B-RELPERF scale and scorecard: Bringing relationship marketing theory into business-to-business practice', *Industrial Marketing Management*, vol. 37, no. 6, pp. 686–97.

Lambert-Pandraud, R, Laurent, G & Lapersonne, E (2005) 'Repeat purchasing of new automobiles by older consumers: Empirical evidence and interpretations', *Journal of Marketing*, vol. 69, pp. 97–113.

Lapersonne, E, Laurent, G & Le Goff, J-J (1995) 'Consideration sets of size one: An empirical investigation of automobile purchases', *International Journal of Research in Marketing*, vol. 12, pp. 55–66.

Lee, J (2009) 'iSnack 2.0 fury prompts re-naming rethink', *The Sydney Morning Herald*, 30 September, retrieved 29 March 2012 from <www.smh.com.au/business/isnack20-fury-prompts-naming-rethink-20090930-gbwt.html>.

Lehman, K (2009) 'Self-marketing and the visual artist', *Conference Proceedings of the 10th International Conference on Arts & Cultural Management*, June/July, Dallas, United States.

Levinson, M (2011a) *The Great A&P and the Struggle for Small Business in America*, Hill & Wang, New York.

——(2011b) 'A history of chain stores, and their enemies: Echoes', *Bloomberg*, 26 November, retrieved 10 May 2012 from <www.bloomberg.com/news/2011-11-25/a-history-of-chain-stores-and-their-enemies-echoes.html>.

Levitt, T (1960), 'Marketing myopia', *Harvard Business Review*, vol. 38, no. 4, pp. 45–56.

——(1983) 'The globalization of markets', *Harvard Business Review*, May–June, pp. 92–102.

Levy, P S & Lemeshow, S (2011) *Sampling of Populations: Methods and Applications*, 4th edition, John Wiley & Sons, Hoboken, New Jersey.

Lichtenthal, J D, Yadav, V & Donthu, N (2004) *Outdoor Advertising for Business Markets*, ISBM Report 3–2004, Institute for the Study of Business Markets, University Park, PA, retrieved 6 March 2012 from <http://isbm.smeal.psu.edu/library/working-paper-articles/2004-working-papers/03-2004-outdoor-advertising.pdf>.

Lindstrom, M (2008) *Buyology: Truth and Lies about Why We Buy*, Doubleday, New York.

Liu, X, Mengqiao, H, Gao, F & Xie, P (2008) 'An empirical study of online shopping customer satisfaction in China: A holistic perspective', *International Journal of Retail & Distribution Management*, vol. 36, no. 11, pp. 919–40.

Lury, A (1990) 'Demographics tell me nothing I want to know', *Admap*, downloaded from Warc.com, pp. 1–5.

Macintyre, A (2003) 'After virtue: A study in moral theory' in N Noddings & M Slote, *Changing Notions of Moral Education*, The Blackwell Guide to the Philosophy of Education, Blackwell Publishing.

Madden, M & Zickuhr, K (2011) '65% of online adults use social networking sites', PewInternet, 26 August, retrieved 27 May 2012 from <www.pewinternet.org/Reports/2011/Social-Networking-Sites.aspx>.

Mahmoud, O (2003) 'Why smart managers don't think straight', *Admap*, February, issue 436.

Main, A (2011) 'The world reaches for a Foster's', *The Australian*, 22 June.

Mangina, C & Beuzeron-Mangina, J (1996) 'Direct electrical stimulation of specific human brain structures and bilateral electrodermal activity', *International Journal of Psychophysiology*, vol. 22, p. 8.

Mangold, WG, Miller, F & Brockway, GR (1999) 'Word-of-mouth communication in the service marketplace', *Journal of Services Marketing*, vol. 13, no. 1, pp. 73–89.

Marks & Spencer (2010) 'Plan A', Marks & Spencer, retrieved 5 May 2010 from <http://plana.marksandspencer.com/about>.

Marshalls plc (2010) *United Nations Global Compact Communication on Progress, 2009*, Marshalls plc, Huddersfield, UK, retrieved 3 June 2012 from <www.marshalls.co.uk/sustainability/publications/pdfs/FINAL%20COP%20Report%20April%2010.pdf>.

Martindale, C (1991) *Cognitive Psychology: A Neural-Network Approach*, Brooks-Cole, Pacific Grove, CA.

Martineau, P (1958) 'Social classes and spending behaviour', *Journal of Marketing*, vol. 23, no. 2, pp. 121–30.

Maslow, A (1954) *Motivation and Personality*, Harper & Row, New York.

Mattsson, L-G & Johanson, J (2006) 'Discovering market networks', *European Journal of Marketing*, vol. 40, nos 3–4, pp. 259–74.

McCafferty, D (2011) 'Brave, new social world', *Communications of the ACM*, vol. 54, no. 7, p. 19.

McConnell, J D (1968) 'The development of brand loyalty: An experimental study', *Journal of Market Research*, vol. 5, pp. 13–19.

Mcconochie, R & Uyenco, B (2003) 'Real cross media intelligence for real cross media planning: The PPM contribution', ESOMAR/ARF Week of Audience Measurement, ESOMAR and ARF, Los Angeles.

McDonald, C (1993) 'Point of view: The key is to understand consumer response', *Journal of Advertising Research*, vol. 33, pp. 63–9.

McDonald, H & Alpert, F (2001) 'Using the Juster scale to predict adoption of an innovative product', Australian and New Zealand Marketing Academy Conference, Auckland, New Zealand.

McDonald, M (2002), *Marketing Plans: How to Prepare Them; How to Use Them*, 5th edn, Butterworth-Heinemann, Oxford.

McDonald's (2012a), 'McDonald's History', retrieved 11 May 2012 from <www.aboutmcdonalds.com/mcd/our_company/mcd_history. html?DCSext.destination=http://www.aboutmcdonalds.com/mcd/our_company/mcd_history.html>.

——(2012b) 'Our Company', retrieved 6 June 2012 from <www.aboutmcdonalds.com/mcd/our_company.html>.

Mcdowell, W S & Dick S J (2005) 'Revealing a double jeopardy effect in radio station audience behavior', *Journal of Media Economics*, vol. 18, pp. 271–84.

McLuhan, M (2003) 'Best practice. How to choose the right medium', *Admap*, November, pp. 11–12.

Mercer, C (2005) 'Tesco Asda price cuts pressure consumers', *William Reed Business Media SAS*, 11 April, retrieved 10 May 2012 from <www.bakeryandsnacks.com/Markets/Tesco-Asda-price-cuts-pressure-producers>.

Mercer, P (2008) 'Shunned Starbucks in Aussie exit', *BBC News*, retrieved <http://news.bbc.co.uk/2/hi/7540480.stm>.

Mescall, J (2008) 'Where did Starbucks go wrong?' *ABC News*, retrieved 13 June 2012 from <www.abc.net.au/unleashed/32188.html>.

Meyers-Levy, J (1989) 'The influence of a brand name's association set size and word frequency on brand memory', *Journal of Consumer Research*, vol. 16, pp. 197–207.

Micu, A & Plummer, J (2010) 'Measurable emotions: How television ads really work', *Journal of Advertising Research*, vol. 50, pp. 137–53.

Mill, J S (1859/1991) *On Liberty and Other Essays*, edited by J Gray, Oxford University Press.

Miller, C C & Bosman, J (2011) 'E-books outsell print books at Amazon', *The New York Times*, 19 May, retrieved 31 May 2012 from <www.nytimes. com/2011/05/20/technology/20amazon.html?_r=1&partner=rss&emc=rss>.

Miller, J & Lundy, S (2002) 'Test marketing plugs into the internet', *Consumer Insight* (Spring), pp. 20–23.

Mills, P, Kennedy, R, Ehrenberg, A & Schlaeppi, T (2000) 'The forms that TV ads take' in D Fellows (ed.) *ARF/ESOMAR Worldwide Electronic and Broadcast Audience Research Conference*, vol. 238, Advertising Research Foundation/ESOMAR, Bal Harbour, Florida.

Mitchell, V W & Haggett, S (1997) 'Sun-sign astrology in market segmentation: An empirical investigation', *Journal of Consumer Marketing*, vol. 14, no. 2, pp. 113–31.

Montanus, G G (1998) '1998 media outlook: Audience fragmentation', *ANA Magazine*, March, pp. 2–5.

Morgan, N A & Rego, L L (2006) 'The value of different customer satisfaction and loyalty metrics in predicting business performance', *Marketing Science*, vol. 25, no. 5, pp. 426–39.

Morwitz, V (1997) 'Why consumers don't always accurately predict their own future behaviour', *Marketing Letters*, vol. 8, no. 1, pp. 57–70.

Mulki, J, Jaramillo, J & Locander, W (2009) 'Critical role of leadership on ethical climate and salesperson behaviors,' *Journal of Business Ethics*, vol. 86, no. 2, pp. 125–41.

Murphy, P E & Laczniak, G R (2006) *Marketing Ethics Cases and Readings*, Pearson, Upper Saddle River, New Jersey.

Murphy, P E, Laczniak, G R & Wood, G (2007) 'An ethical basis for relationship marketing: A virtue ethics perspective,' *European Journal of Marketing*, vol. 41, nos 1–2, pp. 37–57.

Nagle, T, Hogan, J & Zale, J (2011) *The Strategy and Tactics of Pricing: A Guide to Growing More Profitably*, 5th edn, Pearson, Upper Saddle River, NJ.

Nantel, J & Weeks W A (1996) 'Marketing ethics: Is there more to it than the utilitarian approach?', *European Journal of Marketing*, vol. 30, no. 5, pp 9–19.

National Broadband Network Company (2011) 'Broadbanding Australia', retrieved 12 March 2012 from <www.nbnco.com.au/assets/documents/ nbn-co-information-pack.pdf>.

Nayaradou, M (2006) *Advertising and Economic Growth*, University of Paris.

Needham (2004) 'Complaints over tampon labelling', *Sydney Morning Herald*, 20 October, retrieved 23 May 2012 from <www.smh.com.au/ articles/2004/10/19/1097951700655.html?from=storylhs>.

Neilson, J (2010) Personal communication, September.

Neff, J (2012) 'P&G to slash $10 billion in costs over five years', 23 February, *AdAge*, retrieved 25 April 2012 from <http://adage.com/article/ cmo-strategy/p-g-slash-10-billion-costs-years/232914/?utm_source=daily_email&utm_medium=newsletter&utm_campaign=adage>.

Nelson-Field, K & Riebe, E (2010) 'The impact of media fragmentation on audience targeting: An empirical generalisation approach', *Journal of Marketing Communications*, vol. 17, no. 1, pp. 51–67.

Nelson-Field, K & Taylor, J (2012), 'Facebook fans: A fan for life?', *Admap*, May, retrieved 25 May 2012 from <www.warc.com/Content/PrintViewer. aspx?MasterContentRef=b44fad20-c6f7-4d44-aac2-da9ea7cf8383>.

Nelson-Field, K, Sharp, B & Riebe, E (forthcoming) More Mutter About Clutter: Extending Clutter Empirical Generalizations to Facebook.

Nelson-Field, K, Lees, G, Riebe, E & Sharp, B (2001) 'How successful are media differentiation attempts?', *Marketing Bulletin*, vol. 21, pp. 1–8.

Nelson-Field, K, Lees, G, Riebe, E & Sharp, B (2005) 'How well do radio network marketers portray their own audiences? A study of the differences in radio audience demographics with implications for targeting strategy', ANZMAC Conference Proceedings, Perth, WA.

Nelson-Field, K, Lees, G, Riebe, E & Sharp, B (2007) 'A multi-year study of how well radio propositions describe their actual listener base with implications for targeting strategy', ANZMAC conference, Ehrenberg-Bass Institute for Marketing Science, University of South Australia.

Nielsen (2008) 'Average US home now receives a record 118.6 TV channels, according to Nielsen', 6 June, The Nielsen Company, retrieved 29 May from <www.nielsen.com/us/en/insights/press-room/2008/average_u_s__home.html>.

Nielsen (2011) *Television Audience 2010 & 2011*, Nielsen.

Netregistry (2009) 'Marketing the Lie. How Witchery Missed the Point', retrieved 30 March 2010 from <www.netregistry.com.au/blog/?p=97>.

Newstead, K & Romaniuk, J (2010) 'Cost per second: the relative effectiveness of 15- and 30-second television advertisements', *Journal of Advertising Research*, vol. 50, pp. 68–76.

Norman, W & MacDonald, C (2004) 'Getting to bottom of "triple bottom line"', *Business Ethics Quarterly*, vol. 14, no. 2, pp. 243–62.

Northouse, P G (2006) *Leadership: Theory and Practice*, Sage, London.

Nowak, G J, Cameron, G T & Krugman, D M (1993) 'How local advertisers choose and use advertising media', *Journal of Advertising Research*, vol. 33, pp. 39–49.

Nozik, R (1974) *Anarchy, State and Utopia*, Basic Books, New York.

Nuttney, A (2010) 'The social networking opportunity'; quantifying market reach, scale and monetization across the value chain, 2010–15', Business Insights, Birmingham.

O'Dell, J (2011) 'Who's winning: Walmart or Amazon?', 21 June, *Mashable Business*, retrieved 31 May 2012 from <http://mashable.com/2011/06/21/amazon-walmart-infographic/>.

Ofcom (2010) 'Delivering consumer benefits in pay TV', retrieved 3 May 2010 from <www.ofcom.org.uk/media/news/2010/03/nr_20100331>.

Offit, P (2011) *Deadly Choices: How the Anti-Vaccine Movement Threatens Us All*, Basic Books, New York.

Okazaki, S (2009) 'Mobile finds girls' taste: Knorr's new product development', *Journal of Interactive Advertising*, vol. 9, no. 2, pp. 48–59.

Olins, W (1999) *Trading Identities: Why Countries and Companies are Taking on Each Other's Roles*, The Foreign Policy Centre, London.

Ooi, T (2010) 'Eyewear entrant Specsavers shakes up tradition-bound industry', *The Australian*, 9 October, retrieved 6 August 2012 from <www.theaustralian.com.au/.../eyewear-entrant-specsavers-shakes-up-tradition-bound-industry/story-e6frg8zx-1225936176078>.

O'Reilly, D & Kerrigan, F (eds) (2010) *Marketing the Arts: A Fresh Approach*, Routledge, London.

Ostrow, A (2011) 'Facebook now has 800 million users', *Mashable Social Media*, 23 September, retrieved 27 May 2012 from <http://mashable.com/2011/09/22/facebook-800-million-users/>.

O'Sullivan, D & Abela, A V (2007) 'Marketing performance measurement ability and firm performance', *Journal of Marketing*, vol. 71, no. 2, pp. 79–93.

Paech, S (2005) 'Media planning, theory vs practice', unpublished Masters thesis, University of South Australia.

Paech, S, Riebe, E & Sharp, B (2003) *What Do People Do in Advertisement Breaks?* ANZMAC, Adelaide.

Palmer, A & Hartley, B (2011), *The Business Environment*, 7th edn, McGraw-Hill, Maidenhead.

Papper, R A, Holmes, M E & Popovich, M N (2004) 'Middletown media studies: Media multitasking … and how much people really use the *media*', *The International Digital & Media Arts Association Journal*, vol. 1, pp. 9–50.

Parasuraman, A, Zeithaml, V & Berry, L (1988) 'SERVQUAL: A multiple-item scale for measuring consumer perceptions of service quality', *Journal of Retailing*, vol. 64, pp. 12–40.

Patel, K (2011a) 'Apple, Campbell's say iAds twice as effective as TV: A Nielsen study shows iPhone users are paying attention, while TV viewers not so much', *AdAge*, 3 February, retrieved 18 June 2012 from <http://adage.com/digital/article?article_id=148630>.

——(2011b) 'Survey: Consumers Don't Trust Google or Apple with Mobile Payments', *AdAge*, 9 August, retrieved 30 May 2012 from <http://adage.com/article/digital/consumers-trust-google-apple-mobile-payments/229163/>.

Patterson, P G, Scott, J & Uncles, M D (2010) 'How the Local Competition Defeated a Global Brand: The Case of Starbucks', *Australasian Marketing Journal*, vol. 18, no. 1, pp. 41–7.

Peacock, M (2011) 'Toxic Trade', *ABC News*, 8 November, retrieved 3 January 2012 from <www.abc.net.au/foreign/content/2011/s3359246.htm>.

Peattie, K (2001) 'Towards Sustainability: The Third Age of Green Marketing', *The Marketing Review*, vol. 2, pp. 129–46.

Peattie, S & Peattie, K (2003) 'Ready to fly solo? Reducing social marketing's dependence on commercial marketing theory', *Marketing Theory*, vol. 3, no. 3, pp. 365–85.

PeoplesChoice Credit Union (2012), 'About us', retrieved 25 May 2012 from <www.peopleschoicecreditunion.org>.

Pepper, D (1993) *Ecosocialism: From Deep Ecology to Social Justice*, Routledge, Abingdon.

Peterson, F & Jung, C G (1907) 'Psycho-physical investigations with the galvanometer and pneumograph in normal and insane individuals', *Brain*, vol. 30, pp. 153–218.

Petty, R E & Cacioppo, J T (1983) 'Central and peripheral routes to persuasion: Application to advertising' in L Percy & A G Woodside (eds) *Advertising and Consumer Psychology*, Lexington Books, Massachusetts.

Phillips, R L (2005) *Pricing and Revenue Optimization*, Stanford University Press, Stanford, California.

Picard, R G (1999) 'Audience Fragmentation And Structural Limits On Media Innovation And Diversity', Second Expert Meeting on Media in Open Societies, University of Amsterdam.

Pilgrim, D (2008) *Real Life Guides: Retail*, 2nd edn, Trotman, United Kingdom.

Pinchin, K (2008) 'Big like America', *Newsweek*, 16 February, retrieved 8 June 2012 from <www.thedailybeast.com/newsweek/2008/02/16/big-like-america.html>.

Pine, B J & Gilmore, J H (1998) 'Welcome to the experience economy', *Harvard Business Review*, vol. 76, no. 4, July/August, pp. 97–105.

Pinker, S (1994) *The Language Instinct: The New Science of Language and Mind*, Penguin Books.

Plogell, M & Wardman, J (2009) 'Advertising to children in Sweden, legal briefing', *Young Consumers*, vol. 10, no. 4.

Plummer, J (2006) 'Engagement: Definitions and anatomy', Advertising Research Foundation, New York.

Poels, K & Dewitte, S (2006) 'How to capture the heart? Reviewing 20 years of emotion measurement in advertising', *Journal of Advertising Research*, vol. 46.

Polonsky, M (1994) 'An introduction to green marketing', *Electronic Green Journal*, vol. 1, no. 2, UCLA Library, UC Los Angeles, retrieved 25 May 2012 from <http://escholarship.org/uc/item/49n325b7#page-3>.

Porter, M E & van der Linde, C (1995) 'Green and competitive: Ending the stalemate', *Harvard Business Review*, vol. 73, no. 5, pp. 120–33.

Poupee, K (2010) 'Japanese firm rolls out handmade cars', *Sydney Morning Herald*, 7 March, retrieved 3 May 2012 from <http://news.smh.com.au/breaking-news-business/japanese-firm-rolls-out-handmade-cars-20100307-pq0n.html>.

Prenkert, F & Hallén, L (2006), 'Conceptualising, Delineating and Analysing Business Networks', *European Journal of Marketing*, vol. 40, nos 3–4, pp. 384–407.

Prue, T (1996) 'The pre-testing of magazine ads', *PPA Research Report*, HPI Research Group, London.

Quartz, S & Asp, A (2005) 'Brain branding—brands on the brain', *Annual Congress*. California Institute of Technology, Cannes.

Quintens, L, Pauwels, P & Matthyssens, P (2006) 'Global purchasing: State of the art and research directions', *Journal of Purchasing and Supply Management*, vol. 12, no. 4, pp. 170–81.

Rawls, J (1971) *A Theory of Justice*, Harvard University Press, Cambridge, MA.

Redford, N (2005) *Regularities in Media Consumption*, Masters thesis, University of South Australia.

Redmayne, P & Weeks, H (1931) *Market Research*, Butterworth & Co, Bell Yard, Temple Bar, London.

Reichheld, F F & Sasser, W E J (1990) 'Zero defections: Quality comes to services', *Harvard Business Review*, vol. 68, pp. 105–11.

Riebe, E & Dawes, J (2006) 'Recall of radio advertising in low and high advertising clutter formats', *International Journal of Advertising*, vol. 25, pp. 71–86.

Riebe, E, Wright, M, Stern, P & Sharp, B (forthcoming) 'How to grow a brand: Retain or acquire customers?' *Journal of Business Research*.

Ritter, P & Villringer, A (2006) 'Simultaneous EEG-fMRI', *Neuroscience & Biobehavioral Reviews*, vol. 30, pp. 824–38.

Roberts, J & Nedungadi, P (1995) 'Studying consideration in the consumer decision process: Progress and challenges', *International Journal of Research in Marketing*, vol. 12, pp. 3–7.

Romaniuk, J (2000) 'Competitor Salience and Customer Switching' in AD O'Cass (ed.) *Australian New Zealand Marketing Academy Conference*, 28 November–1 December, Gold Coast, Queensland, Griffith University, pp. 1068–72.

–– (2007) *Dimensions of Branding Quality in Television Advertisements*, University of South Australia, Adelaide.

––(2009) 'The efficacy of brand-execution tactics in TV advertising, brand placements and internet advertising', *Journal of Advertising Research*, vol. 49, pp. 143–50.

––& Gaillard, E (2007) 'The relationship between unique brand associations, brand usage and brand performance: Analysis across eight categories', *Journal of Marketing Management*, vol. 23, pp. 267–84.

––& Sharp, B (2000) 'Using Known Patterns in Image Data to Determine Brand Positioning', *International Journal of Market Research*, vol. 42, no. 2, pp. 219–30.

––& Sharp, B (2003) 'Measuring brand perceptions: Testing quantity and quality', *Journal of Targeting, Measurement and Analysis for Marketing*, vol. 11, pp. 218–29.

––& Sharp, B (2004) 'Conceptualizing and measuring brand salience', *Marketing Theory*, vol. 4, pp. 327–42.

– –, Bogomolova, S & Dall'Olmo Riley, F (2012) 'Brand Image and Brand Usage: is a 40-year-old generalization still useful?', *Journal of Advertising Research*, vol. 52, no. 2, p. 599.

Rossiter, J R (2005) 'Reminder: A horse is a horse', *International Journal of Research in Marketing*, vol. 22, pp. 23–5.

——& Bellman, S (2005) *Marketing Communications: Theory and Applications*, Pearson Education, Frenchs Forest.

——& Danaher, P J (1998) *Advanced Media Planning*, Kluwer Academic Publishers, Boston.

——& Percy, L (1997) *Advertising Communications & Promotion Management*, The McGraw-Hill Companies, Inc., New York.

——, Percy, L & Donovan, R J (1991) 'A better advertising planning grid', *Journal of Advertising Research*, vol. 31, pp. 11–21.

RSPCA Australia (2012) 'Mission, vision and objectives', retrieved 15 May 2012 from <www.rspca.org.au/what-we-do/about-us/mission.html>.

Rubinson, J (2010) 'Ten reasons you should care about the shopper', 21 July, retrieved 27 July 2010 from <http://blog.joelrubinson.net/2009/07/ten-reasons-you-should-care-about-the-shopper/>.

Rugman, A M (2001) 'Viewpoint: The myth of global strategy', *International Marketing Review*, vol. 18, no. 6, pp. 11–14.

Rust, R & Oliver, R (1994) 'The death of advertising', *Journal of Advertising*, vol. 23, pp. 71–7.

Salt, B (2006) *The Big Picture*, Hardie Grant Books, Melbourne.

Sargeant, A (2009) *Marketing Management for Nonprofit Organizations*, 3rd edn, Oxford University Press, Oxford.

Save the Children (2012) 'Protecting children from exploitation', retrieved 27 May 2012 from <www.savethechildren.org/site/c.8rKLIXMGIpI4E/b.6192517/k.9ECD/Protecting_Children_from_Exploitation.htm>.

Schell, O (2011) 'How Walmart is changing China', *Atlantic Magazine*, December, retrieved 10 May 2012 from < www.theatlantic.com/magazine/archive/2011/12/how-walmart-is-changing-china/8709/>.

Schroeder, S (2011) 'Google+ about to hit 10 million users', *Mashable Social Media*, 12 July, retrieved from <http://mashable.com/2011/07/12/google-10-million/>.

Schultz, E J (2010) 'SABMiller thinks globally, but gets "intimate" locally', *AdAge*, 4 October, retrieved 16 May 2012 from <http://adage.com/article?article_id=146256>.

Schwarz, N (1999) 'Sel-reports: How the questions shape the answers', *American Psychologist*, vol. 54, no. 2, pp. 93–105.

Scriven, J A & Ehrenberg, A S C (2004) 'Consistent Consumer Responses to Price Changes', *Australasian Marketing Journal*, vol. 12, no. 3, pp. 6–25.

Seddon, G (1970) *Swan River Landscapes*, University of Western Australia Press, Perth.

Seggie, S H, Cavusgil, E & Phelan, S E (2007) 'Measurement of return on marketing investment: A conceptual framework and the future of marketing metrics'. *Industrial Marketing Management*, vol. 36, no. 6, pp. 834–41.

Sharp, B (2008) 'Net promoter score fails the test: market research buyers beware', *Marketing Research*, Winter, pp. 28–30.

——(2010) *How Brands Grow*, Oxford University Press, South Melbourne.

——& Sharp, A (1996) 'Positioning and partitioning' in A M Martin & S R G Starr, Jr (eds) Australia New Zealand Marketing Conference, Department of Marketing, University of Auckland, p. 723.

——& Wind, J (2009) 'Today's advertising laws: will they survive the digital revolution?' *Journal of Advertising Research*, vol. 49, pp. 120–6.

——, Beal, V & Collins, M (2009) 'Television: back to the future', *Journal of Advertising Research*, vol. 49, pp. 211–19.

——, Beal, V & Romaniuk, J (2001) 'First steps towards a marketing empirical generalisation: brand usage and subsequent advertising recall' in S C B Collins (ed.) *Australia & New Zealand Academy of Marketing Conference 2001*, Massey University, Albany, New Zealand.

——, Tolo, M & Giannopoulos, A (2001) 'A differentiatied brand should appeal to a special segment of the market ... but it doesn't!' in S Chetty & B Collins (eds) *Bridging Marketing Theory & Practice*, Australia and New Zealand Marketing Academy, Massey University, New Zealand.

——, Riebe, E, Dawes, J F & Danenberg, N (2002) 'A marketing economy of scale—Big brands lose less of their customer base than small brands', *Marketing Bulletin*, vol. 13, pp. 1–8.

Sharp, B, Wright, M & Goodhardt, G (2002) 'Purchase loyalty is polarised into either repertoire or subscription patterns', *Australasian Marketing Journal*, vol. 10, no. 3, pp. 7–20.

Shaw, B (1998) *Improving Marketing Effectiveness*, Profile Books, London.

Silberstein, R B & Nield, G E (2008) 'Brain activity correlates of consumer brand choice shift associated with television advertising', *International Journal of Advertising*, vol. 27, pp. 359–80.

Sinclair, L (2004) 'Bulla and Herron hit the mark in popularity contest', *B&T*, 12 March 2004, p. 13.

Sissors, J Z & Baron, R B (2002) *Advertising Media Planning*, McGraw-Hill.

Slutsky, I (2011) 'Kids flock to social nets, but few advertisers dare to follow', *AdAge*, retrieved 16 May 2012 from <http://adage.com/article/digital/togetherville-moshi-monsters-hot-advertisers-follow/228289>.

Smith, C (2012) 'Super Bowl ad rates can double within ten years', *Forbes*, retrieved 21 June from <www.forbes.com/sites/chrissmith/2012/02/01/super-bowl-ad-rates can-double-within-ten-years/>.

Smith, N (2010) 'Mobile advertising to grow tenfold by 2015, Informa says', *Bloomberg News*, retrieved 12 June 2012 from <www.bloomberg.com/news/2010-11-23/mobile-advertising-sales-to-grow-tenfold-by-2015-informa-says.html>.

Solis, B & Thomas, J (2009) 'The conversation prism v2.0', Brian Solis, retrieved 10 June 2012 from <www.briansolis.com/2009/03/conversation-prism-v20/>.

Song, Y-B (no date) 'Finding the missing piece in online frequency', *Atlas Institute Digital Marketing Insights*, Atlas DMT, LLC, p. 2.

Sorensen, H (2009) *Inside the Mind of the Shopper*, Pearson Education Inc, Upper Saddle River, New Jersey.

Spaeth, J & Hess, M (1989) 'Single-source data ... the missing pieces', Proceedings of ARF Single-Source Data Workshop, 22 June.

Speck, P & Elliott, M (1998) 'Consumer perceptions of advertising clutter and its impact across various media', *Journal of Advertising Research*, vol. 38, no. 1, pp. 29–4.

Spittler, J Z (1998) 'TV optimisers: Fad or trend?' *Admap*, vol. 33, pp. 25–7.

Sports Business Daily (2012) 'Gap between number of male, female Super Bowl viewers is shrinking', *Sports Business Daily*, retrieved 21 June 2012 from <www.sportsbusinessdaily.com/Daily/Issues/2012/02/01/Research-and-Ratings/SB-demos.aspx>.

Srivastava, R K, Shervani, T A & Fahey, L (1998) 'Market-based assets and shareholder value: A framework for analysis', *Journal of Marketing*, vol. 62, p. 1.

Steare, R (2009) *Ethicability: How to decide what's right and find the courage to do it*, 3rd edn, Roger Steare Consulting Ltd, UK.

Steinberg, S (2011) 'Friendster Is Dead: Encourages U.S. Users to Move On', *Rolling Stone*, 11 May, retrieved 27 May 2012 from <www.rollingstone.com/culture/blogs/gear-up/friendster-is-dead-encourages-u-s-users-to-move-on-20110511>.

Stockdill, R (2012) 'Oroton builds on Asian success', *InsideRetail.Asia*, 21 March, retrieved 13 June from <www.insideretail.asia/InsideRetailAsia/InsideRetailAsianews/Oroton-builds-on-Asian-success-4493.aspx>.

Strong, E K (1925) *The Psychology of Selling*, McGraw-Hill, New York.

Stuart Alexander (2012) 'Australian Market: market overview', retrieved 11 September 2012 from <www.stuartalexander.com.au/aust_grocery_market_woolworths_coles_wholesale.php>.

Summerfield, P (2003) 'What do marketers really think about media?' *Strategy*, 10 February, retrieved 7 April 2003 from <http://strategyonline.ca/2003/02/10/realitycheck-20030210/2012>.

Surmanek, J (1996) *Media Planning: A Practical Guide*, NTC Business Books Illinois.

Sweden.se (2012) 'Children in Sweden: Growing up in Sweden', retrieved 3 June 2012 from <www.sweden.se/eng/Home/Society/Child-care/Facts/Children-in-Sweden>.

Talbot, C, Tregilgas, P & Harrison, K (2002) *Social Enterprise in Australia: An Introductory Handbook*, Adelaide Central Mission Inc., Adelaide.

Tan, G (2012) 'Uni pals' project a Kondoot for success', *The Australian*, 4 January, p. 21.

Tapscott, D & Williams, A D (2010) *Macrowikinomics: Rebooting business and the world*, Portfolio, Penguin Books, Canada.

Taylor, J, Kennedy, R & Sharp, B (2009) 'Making generalizations about advertising's convex sales response function: is once really enough?', *Journal of Advertising Research*, vol. 49, no. 2, pp. 198–200.

Tellis, G J (2009) 'Generalizations about advertising effectiveness in markets', *Journal of Advertising Research*, vol. 49, pp. 240–5.

Theil, H & Kosobud, R F (1968) 'How informative are consumer buying intentions surveys?', *The Review of Economics and Statistics*, vol. 50, pp. 50–9.

Thomas, R (2009) 'Consumer-goods brands likely to triple online spending in india next year', *AdAge*, 1 September, retrieved 16 May 2012 from <http://adage.com/globalnews/article?article_id=138737>.

Thompson, S (2006) 'Hershey defends its marketing strategy', *Advertising Age*, retrieved 6 August 2007 from <http://adage.com/article/news/hershey-defends-marketing-strategy/112585>.

Tucker, W T (1964) 'The development of brand loyalty', *Journal of Marketing Research*, vol. 1, pp. 32–5.

Tulving, E & Thomson, D (1973) 'Encoding specificity and retrieval processes in episodic memory', *Psychological Review*, vol. 80, pp. 352–73.

Turk, P & Katz, H (1992) 'Making headlines: An overview of key happenings in media planning, buying and research from 1985 to 1991', *Journal of Current Issues and Research in Advertising*, vol. 14.

Twitter (2010) 'Who's new on twitter', #Hindsight2010, twitter blog2, retrieved 27 May 2012 from <http://blog.twitter.com/2010/12/whos-new-on-twitter-hindsight2010.html>.

Taylor, J (2010) *Is once really enough? Measuring the advertising response function*, PhD thesis, University of South Australia.

Taylor, J, Kennedy, R & Sharp, B (2009) 'Making generalizations about advertising's convex sales response function: Is once really enough?', *Journal of Advertising Research*, vol. 49, pp. 198–200.

Tylor, E (1920) *Primitive Culture*, J P Putnam's Sons, New York.

UAE Interact (2009) 'Major recycling scheme launched in Abu Dhabi', 4 November, retrieved 23 May 2012 from <www.uaeinteract.com/docs/Major_recycling_scheme_launched_in_Abu_Dhabi/38290.htm>.

Uncles, M (2010) 'Retail change in China: Retrospect and prospect', *International Review of Retail, Distribution and Consumer Research*, vol. 20, no. 1, pp. 69–84.

——(2011) 'Understanding brand performance measures' in M Uncles (ed.) *Perspectives on Brand Management*, Tilde University Press, Melbourne, Australia.

——& Hammond, K (1995) 'Grocery store patronage', *The International Review of Retail, Distribution & Consumer Research*, vol. 5, no. 3, pp. 287–302.

——& Kwok, S (2009) 'Patterns of store patronage in urban China', *Journal of Business Research*, vol. 62, no. I, pp. 68–81.

——, Kennedy, R, Nenycz-Thiel, M, Singh, J & Kwok, S (2012) 'In 25 Years, Across 50 Categories, User Profiles for Directly Competing Brands Seldom Differ: Affirming Andrew Ehrenberg's Principles', *Journal of Advertising Research*, vol. 52, no. 2, pp. 25–61.

United Nations (1987) *Our Common Future. The Report of the World Commission on Environment and Development*, UN Documents, retrieved 16 May 2012 from <www.un-documents.net/ocf-02.htm#I>.

Unnava, H R & Burnkrant, R E (1991) 'Effects of repeating varied ad executions on brand name memory', *Journal of Marketing Research*, vol. 28, pp. 406–16.

Vakratsas, D & Ambler, T (1999) 'How advertising works: What do we really know?', *Journal of Marketing*, vol. 63, pp. 26–43.

van der Wurff, R, Bakker, P & Picard, R (2008) 'Economic growth and advertising expenditures in different media in different countries', *Journal of Media Economics*, vol. 21, pp. 28–52.

Varan, D, Murphy, J, Hofacker, C, Robinson, J, Potter, R & Bellman, S (2012) *Cross-Device Synergy Versus Cross-Media Synergy*, conference paper for EGII: What Works in the New Age of Advertising & Marketing, hosted by the Wharton Future of Advertising Program in cooperation with the Ehrenbass Institute and the Advertising Research Foundation, Philadelphia, May 31–June 1.

Veer, E & Kilian, M (2010), 'I drink, therefore I am: Fear of social disapproval and its impact on attitudes towards anti-binge drinking advertising', European Association for Consumer Research Conference, Royal Holloway University of London: Association for Consumer Research.

Veldre, D (2003) 'Media buyers trading up', *B&T Weekly*, 13 October.

Virgin (2012) 'About Virgin', retrieved 9 May 2012 from <www.virgin.com/about-us>.

Visaka Industries Limited (2012) 'Facts', retrieved 3 January 2012 from <www.visaka.biz/reports/facts.pdf>.

Voltaire, F (1909–14) Part 2, 'Letter XI: On inoculation' in *Letters on the English*, vol. XXXIV, The Harvard Classics, P.F. Collier & Son, New York, retrieved 9 May 2012 from <www.bartleby.com/34/2/11.html>.

Walker, P (1998) 'Minimise waste by targeting more efficiently', *Admap*.

Wallace, A (2009) 'An epidemic of fear: How panicked parents skipping shots endangers us all', *Wired*, 19 October, retrieved 9 May 2012 from <www.wired.com/magazine/2009/10/ff_waronscience/all/1>.

Warc (2010) 'FAQs on data', retrieved March 2012 from <www.warc.com/Pages/ForecastsAndData/NotesOnAdspendData.info%5D>.

Washington, S (2011) 'Coles and Woolworths bullying us, say suppliers', *The Sydney Morning Herald*, 26 November, retrieved 10 May from <www.smh.com.au/business/coles-and-woolworths-bullying-us-say-suppliers-20111125-1nz77.html>.

Watts, G, Cope, J & Hulme, M (1998) 'Ansoff's matrix, pain and gain growth strategies and adaptive learning among small food producers', *International Journal of Entrepreneurial Behaviour & Research*, vol. 4, no. 20, pp. 101–11.

Webb, P H & Ray, M (1979) 'Effects of television clutter', *Journal of Advertising Research*, vol. 19, pp. 7–12.

Weinstein, A (1993) *Market Segmentation*, revised edn, Irwin, Chicago, IL.

Westfall, R (1962) 'Psychological factors in predicting product choice', *Journal of Marketing*, vol. 26, pp. 34–40.

White, A D (1896) 'Theological opposition to inoculation, vaccination, and the use of anæsthetics', *A History of the Warfare of Science with Theology in Christendom*, Appleton, New York.

White, L (2009) 'Foster's Lager: From local beer to global icon', *Marketing Intelligence & Planning*, vol. 27, no. 2, pp. 177–90.

White, R (2000) 'Single-source data', *Warc Best Practice*, April, pp. 1–4.

Wicken, G & Spittler, J Z (1998) 'Account planning? Media planning? Communications planning?', Advertising Research Foundation Workshop.

Wilson, A (2009) 'Dreams of modern China', *The Australian*, 31 July, News Features, p. 10.

Wilson, I & Petrie, D (2008) 'Starbucks shuts stores, backing away from Australia', *Bloomberg News*, retrieved 13 June 2012 from <www.bloomberg.com/apps/news?pid=newsarchive&sid=al6pKGtkBVGs>.

Wind, Y (1978) 'Issues and advances in segmentation research', *Journal of Marketing Research*, vol. 15 (August), pp. 317–37.

Wind, J & Sharp, B (2009) 'Advertising empirical generalizations: Implications for research and action', *Journal of Advertising Research*, vol. 49, pp. 246–52.

Winter, F (1980) 'Matching target markets to media audiences', *Journal of Advertising Research*, vol. 20, pp. 61–6.

Wood, J A, Boles, J S, Johnston, W & Bellenger, D (2008), 'Buyer's trust of the salesperson: An item-level meta-analysis,' *Journal of Personal Selling & Sales Management*, vol. 28, no. 3, pp. 263–83.

Wood, L (2009) 'Short-term effects of advertising: Some well established law-like patterns', *Journal of Advertising Research*, vol. 49, pp. 186–92.

Wong, G (2006) 'Burger King IPO set to fire up', CNN Money.com, 12 May, retrieved 26 April from <http://money.cnn.com/2006/05/12/markets/ipo/burger_king/index.htm>.

World Health Organization (2012) 'Smallpox', retrieved 9 May 2012 from <www.who.int/mediacentre/factsheets/smallpox/en/>.

World Trade Organization (2007) 'The GATT/WTO at 60: WTO World Trade Report examines six decades of multilateralism in trade', *World Trade Report*, 4 December, retrieved 16 May 2012 from <www.wto.org/english/news_e/pres07_e/pr502_e.htm>.

Wortham, J (2011) 'To pique interest, start-ups try a digital velvet rope', *The New York Times*, 17 July 2011, retrieved 27 May 2012 from <www.nytimes.com/2011/07/18/technology/start-ups-try-to-beckon-users-by-invitation-only.html>.

Wright, M (2009) 'A new theorem for optimizing the advertising budget', *Journal of Advertising Research*, vol. 49, no. 2, pp. 164–9.

——& Esslemont, D (1994) 'The logical limitations of target marketing', *Marketing Bulletin*, vol. 5, pp. 13–20.

——,Sharp, A & Sharp, B (2002) 'Market statistics for the Dirichlet model: Using the Juster scale to replace panel data', *International Journal of Research in Marketing*, vol. 19, pp. 81–90.

Yarrow, J (2010) '9 charts that show why Amazon investors have nothing to worry about', *Business Insider*, 17 February, retrieved 31 May 2012 from <www.businessinsider.com/amazon-is-about-to-lose-its-death-grip-on-e-books-but-its-not-a-big-deal-2010-2#sizing-up-amazons-influence-on-the-physical-book-market-it-has-19-share-bigger-than-an-other-single-retailer-4>.

Young Media Australia (2009) 'Effects of advertising on children's body image', retrieved 3 May 2010 from <www.youngmedia.org.au/mediachildren/03_02_ads_body_image.htm>.

INDEX